T0329329

Strategies of Banks and Other Financial Institutions

Strategies of Banks and Other Financial Institutions
Theories and Cases

Rajesh Kumar

AMSTERDAM • BOSTON • HEIDELBERG • LONDON
NEW YORK • OXFORD • PARIS • SAN DIEGO
SAN FRANCISCO • SINGAPORE • SYDNEY • TOKYO
Academic Press is an imprint of Elsevier

Academic Press is an imprint of Elsevier
525 B Street, Suite 1800, San Diego, CA 92101, USA
225 Wyman Street, Waltham, MA 02451, USA
The Boulevard, Langford Lane, Kidlington, Oxford, OX5 1GB, UK

Notice
No responsibility is assumed by the publisher for any injury and/or damage to persons or property as a
matter of products liability, negligence or otherwise, or from any use or operation of any methods, products,
instructions or ideas contained in the material herein. Because of rapid advances in the medical sciences, in
particular, independent verification of diagnoses and drug dosages should be made.

British Library Cataloguing in Publication Data
A catalogue record for this book is available from the British Library

Library of Congress Cataloging-in-Publication Data
A catalog record for this book is available from the Library of Congress

978-0-12-416997-5

For information on all Academic Press publications
visit our website at books.elsevier.com

Printed and bound in the United States
14 15 16 17   10 9 8 7 6 5 4 3 2 1

Contents

PART A

PART B

Instructor website for this book: http://textbooks.elsevier.com/web/Manuals.aspx?isbn=9780124169975

Preface

STRATEGIES OF BANKS AND OTHER FINANCIAL INSTITUTIONS: THEORIES AND CASES

Rapid changes in the technological, economic, social, demographic, and regulatory environments have led financial institutions to evolve their strategies for gaining competitive advantage. The growth of the financial sector around the world depends on critical factors such as globalization, regulatory compliance, risk management, technological innovation, and demographics. The changing landscape of financial institutions in the context of competition, diversification, new products, and new geographic markets has dramatically changed the risk profile of financial institutions. Increasing regulation due to Basel III stipulations has become a critical driver of post-crisis bank profitability in developed countries. Banks in emerging markets are becoming the major growth drivers of the global banking industry.

In the context of technological advances banks face new challenges with shifting digital consumer behavior. Global technology trends indicate increased focus on next-generation remote banking solutions, business intelligence, and analytics in transaction monitoring. This changing demographic profile has compelled banks to develop specialized products and services for serving older generations. The concept of universal banking has also become an established trend. Investment banking, private banking, and bancassurance are among the most profitable and fastest growing segments of the financial service industry. Mergers, acquisitions, and alliances are also key strategies adopted by financial institutions. Consolidation is happening due to disintermediation in the banking sector. A new wave of regulations in banking is being shaped following global financial crises such as Basel III changes, legislation such as Dodd–Frank in the United States, and more concrete actions by G-20.

Strategies of Banks and Other Financial Institutions: Theories and Cases consists of two parts. The first part proposes a useful theoretical framework on strategic perspectives concerning risk, regulation, markets, and challenges driving the financial sectors. The second part presents case studies about the world's largest commercial banks, mortgage institutions, investment banks, investment companies, insurance company pension funds, Islamic banks, hedge funds, private equity firms, and sovereign wealth funds.

The introductory chapter analyzes the strategic trends in the banking industry and the impact of the financial crisis on the global banking system. The chapter highlights the key strategic reform policy and technological trends shaping financial institutions. This chapter also discusses the different types of financial institutions and the concept of the shadow banking system. Chapter 2 focuses on the regulatory environment of financial institutions. This chapter deals with the functions of regulatory agencies, the history of regulatory reforms, and the regulation of banking and nonbanking financial institutions. The major emphasis is on Basel reforms. Chapter 3 explores the risk inherent in financial institutions. The chapter highlights the different types of risk in financial institutions. The major focus is on the risk management framework in banks and the risk mitigation strategies adopted by financial institutions.

The following two chapters highlight the different types of financial markets and financial institutions. Chapter 4 focuses on the money markets, bond markets, and mortgage markets. The chapter covers different types of money market and capital market instruments. Chapter 5 focuses on stock markets, derivatives markets, and foreign exchange markets. Chapter 6 explains the strategies of depository institutions such as commercial banks and thrift institutions comprising mutual savings banks, savings and loan associations, and credit unions. Chapter 7 discusses the strategies of nondepository institutions such as investment banks and finance companies. Chapter 8 covers the strategies of other nondepository institutions such as mutual funds and insurance and pension funds. Chapter 9 deals with the strategic aspects of private equity and hedge funds. Chapter 10 introduces the principles of Islamic finance and various instruments of Islamic finance. The final chapter highlights the trends of consolidation in financial markets and institutions.

Cases are discussed along a framework consisting of structure, strategy, regulatory environment, and risk management of financial institutions. In universal banking, the cases of Bank of America, JPMorgan Chase, Citigroup, Barclays, BNP Paribas, Credit Agricole Group, HSBC, Industrial and Commercial Bank of China, and Deutsche Bank are discussed. The Mortgage institution-related cases discussed include Fannie Mae, Freddie Mac, and Ginnie Mae. Cases on credit unions such as the Navy Federal Credit Union, State Employees' Credit Union, and Pentagon Federal Credit Union are discussed under the category of thrift institutions. Major investment bank cases such as Credit Suisse, Goldman Sachs Group, Morgan Stanley, and UBS Group are also included. The investment management companies highlighted include Vanguard, American Funds, Fidelity Funds, T. Rowe Price, PIMCO, Franklin Templeton, and BlackRock.

The insurance sector chapter covers case studies on insurance companies such as Japan Post Insurance Co., Berkshire Hathaway, AXA Group, Allianz, Generali Group, Nippon Life Insurance, Munich Reinsurance, AIG, and MetLife. The case studies on pension funds consist of sovereign and corporate pension funds. The private equity firms in the chapter include Kohlberg Kravis and Robert (KKR), Blackstone Group, Bain Capital, Carlyle Group, and TPG Capital. The hedge fund cases include Bridgewater Associates, Adage Capital Management, York Capital Management, Graham Capital Management, Brevan Howard Asset Management, etc.

The case studies on Islamic banks include Saudi Al Rajhi Bank, Kuwait Finance House, Dubai Islamic Bank, Abu Dhabi Islamic Bank, Al Baraka Islamic Bank, and Qatar Islamic Bank. The final chapter deals with sovereign wealth funds and includes cases on Norway Sovereign Wealth Fund, SAMA Foreign Holdings, Saudi Arabia, Abu Dhabi Investment Authority, China Investment Corporation, SAFE Investment China, Kuwait Investment Authority, Hong Kong Monetary Authority, Government of Singapore Investment Corporation, Temasek Holding, and Qatar Investment Authority.

Acknowledgments

I would like to thank the production and editorial staff at Elsevier who guided this book through the publishing process. I wish to acknowledge the valuable guidance and support of Scott Bentley, Senior Acquisition Editor at Elsevier. My thanks also to Melissa Murray, Editorial Project Manager, and her team for all the cooperation and support in the publication of this book. I thank Jason Mitchell, Publishing Services Manager, and his team for all the support. I also acknowledge the content of the various websites and sources of information to which I referred. I acknowledge the permissions granted by McKinsey & Company, Investment Company Institute, The Banker Database of Financial Times, World Council of Credit Unions, World Federation of Exchanges, and Insurance Market Research at Conning to use their data in my book. I also thank my family for all their support. Special gratitude to my wife, Sreelatha, for her understanding and support.

Dedication

To my beloved brother, Suresh, and sister, Rajasree

A

STRATEGIES AND STRUCTURES OF FINANCIAL INSTITUTIONS

1.1 INTRODUCTION

Financial institutions basically serve as financial intermediaries between primary saving and borrowing sectors. In the current environment it has become critical for financial institutions to evolve strategies for competitiveness in the context of rapid changes within technological, economic, social, demographic, and regulatory environments. The financial sector encompasses a set of institutions, instruments, and markets as well as the legal and regulatory framework. Globalization, regulatory compliance, risk management, technological innovation, and demographics are the major transformative issues that will determine the growth of the global financial sector. Consolidation and cross-border mergers and acquisitions (M&A) in the context of easing cross-border investment regulations are also visible trends observed in the global financial sector. Technology has transformed products offered by financial institutions into commodities. Technology has transformed the internal operating environment as well as the external market environment. Information technology (IT) is the primary force that keeps the financial industry dynamic.

The biggest banking markets by assets are the United States, the United Kingdom, Japan, China, and France. Of these countries, the United States has the largest number of banking institutions in the world. In 2011, there were 6291 commercial banking institutions with 83,209 branches in the United States. In the 1990s, the number of US banking institutions was approximately 12,000. In 2011, the number of savings institutions was 1067.[1]

US, German, and Japanese banks are dominant both in terms of assets and number of institutions. There are 20 US banks, 16 German banks, and 11 Japanese banks among the top 100 banks.[2]

1.2 BANKING PERFORMANCE TRENDS

A McKinsey Global Institute report indicates that during the next 10 years, the growth rate of the global banking industry will exceed that of the gross domestic product (GDP). Experts estimate that the banking industry is likely to more than double its revenues and profits over this period. The shadow banking system around the world had grown to a $67 trillion market by 2011, according to the Financial Stability Board (FSB) Monitoring Report of 2012.

---

[1] Federal Deposit Insurance Corporation Report.
[2] Eugenio Cerutti, Giovanni Dell'Ariccia, Maria Soledad Martınez Perı´a (2007), How banks go abroad: Branches or subsidiaries. *Journal of Banking and Finance, 31,* 1669-1692.

According to the FSB report, the global banks sector is forecast to have a value of $136,946.8 billion by 2015, which represents an increase of approximately 34% from 2010. Bank credit is the largest segment of global banking, accounting for 59.7% of the total sector value. Europe accounts for 53% of the global banks' sector value. In 2010, the global banks industry group had total assets of $101,880.2 billion, representing a compounded annual growth rate (CAGR) of 7.6% during the period 2006-2010.

The United States accounts for 11.5% of the global banks sector value. By 2015, the US banks sector is forecasted to have a value of $15.617 billion dollars.[3] The Asia Pacific bank sector is forecasted to have a value of $40,669 billion. Currently, China accounts for 47.9% of the Asia Pacific bank sector value,[4] and Japan accounts for a further 31.3% of the Asia Pacific sector. In the year 2011, the biggest banks in terms of market capitalization were the Industrial and Commercial Bank of China, China Construction Bank Corporation, HSBC Holdings, and JPMorgan.

The industry growth rate of assets of the top 1000 banks was 2.7% in the post-crisis period of 2008-2010, as compared to the double-digit growth witnessed by the sector during the period 2006-2007.[5] At the same time, the capital adequacy ratio of the banks registered a growth rate of 3.8% during the period 2007-2010. In the period between 2007 and 2008, the profit before tax of the top 1000 global banks declined by $667 billion.[6]

The highest growth was registered by Latin American banks whose assets grew at a CAGR of 28.1% during 2007-2010. During the same period, the assets of the banking sectors in Asia Pacific and North America grew at rates of 16.3% and 6.9%, respectively, while the assets of European banks declined at a rate of 3.3%.[7]

In the post-crisis period, the cost-to-income ratio showed impressive improvement in North America, Europe, and Latin America. This improvement was primarily because of the reduction of operational costs owing to the adoption of the Basel recommendations.

According to a McKinsey Quarterly report in 2011, "The state of global banking—in search of a sustainable model," despite a strong global profit performance in 2010 and the first half of 2011, the return on equity (ROE) of banks in Europe and the United States has still not recovered, particularly in the context of gaps that arise from the new regulatory requirements. The global banking revenues reached a record $3.8 trillion in 2010 compared to $3.5 trillion in 2009. Global banking profits after tax grew to $712 billion in 2010, up from $400 billion in 2009. But 90% of the profit increase was attributable to a decline in provisions for loan losses. In 2010, US and European banking industries had an ROE of just 7% and 7.9%, respectively. Bank revenues in such developing countries as India, Brazil, and China grew by approximately 19.8%, 17.6%, and 13.7%, respectively, during 2010.[8] In spite of the economic crisis of 2008, total banking assets are predicted to reach an estimated $163,058 billion in 2017 with a CAGR of 8% over the next five years.[9] Table 1.1 highlights the global banking performance trends in terms of profits. Table 1.2 shows the financial position of the global banking industry in terms of loans and deposits, total assets and liabilities during the period 2009-2011.

---

[3]Data monitor (June 2011), Banks in the United States, Reference Code: 0072-2013.
[4]Data monitor (June 2011), Banks in the Asia Pacific, Reference Code: 0200-2013.
[5]Capgemini Report (2011), Trends in the global banking industry.
[6]The Banker Database (September 2011), http://www.thebankerdatabase.com.
[7]The Banker Database (September 2011), http://www.thebankerdatabase.com.
[8]McKinsey Quarterly Report (2011), The state of global banking—in search of a sustainable model.
[9]Lucintel Report (2011), Global banking industry analysis 2012-2017: industry trend, profit, and forecast analysis.

Table 1.1   Global Banking After-Tax Profits (Billions of US Dollars)

Year	Profits
2000	366
2005	681
2006	802
2007	952
2008	852
2009	549
2010	730

Source: McKinsey Global Banking Pools.
The estimated profits realized by banks and nonbanking financial institutions from the provision of banking services to clients. Nonclient driven banking activities such as asset liability management, market making, proprietary trading (the latter two with the exception of Asia Pacific) and banks' nonbanking activities are excluded.

Table 1.2   Global Banking Amounts Outstanding (Billions of US Dollars)

Positions	December 2009	December 2010	September 2011
Total assets	33,841.4	33,989.1	35,878.1
Loans and deposits	21,664.1	22,083.7	23,303.2
Total liabilities	32,338.9	32,801.6	34,878.7

Source: BIS Quarterly Review, March 2012.

1.3 STRATEGIC TRENDS

The gap for bank revenue growth is expected to widen between growing markets in emerging markets and saturated developed markets. Banks from the emerging markets will become the growth drivers of the global banking industry. Geographically the regions of biggest potential are China, India, Brazil, and Russia. The most populous nation in the world, China has one of the largest savings rates at 40% of the GDP. Financial institutions have spent billions to acquire stakes in Chinese banks. Chinese markets are characterized by a large savings rate and a dearth of health care and pension funds.

With the imposition of more stringent capital adequacy and risk management standards, banks face strains on their traditional business models and operating margins. The financial crisis highlighted the differences that exist between the performances of the banking sectors of emerging and developed markets. The banking industry in the emerging markets of Asia Pacific and Latin America remained resilient during the crisis in contrast to the developed markets of Europe and the United States, which registered heavy losses. China, India, and Brazil account for a growing share of the world's economic activity and provide challenges for banking. China, Russia, and India provide an abundance of retail and wholesale customers.

Two thirds of the world's economic growth will come from emerging markets through 2015. It is estimated that the share of global GDPs generated by emerging markets will rise from 31% to 41%. The BRIC countries (Brazil, Russia, India, and China) are established growth markets where banks are expected to continue to invest. But regions such as China, although an ideal target for global banks, provide challenges as Chinese banks have large deposits and the mortgage and deposit rates are set by the government. The next battleground for financial services businesses will be in the markets of Asia and Africa, where it is expected that the urban population will grow by almost 1.8 billion people.

One trend that has been observed is that the increasing regulation stemming from the Basel III requirements have emerged as the single largest driver of post-crisis bank profitability in the United States and Europe. Another trend observed is the squeeze on capital and funding owing to credit demand in the developing world. The sovereign credit crisis followed by the Eurozone capital market crisis has created new challenges for banks.

In spite of global challenges, the banking industry provides immense opportunities through expansion in new markets, technology, and personalization to enhance customer relationships. The process of deregulation has enabled banks to expand through M&A. The 1990s witnessed a wave of consolidation in the United States, whereas the last decade saw many cross-border banking deals in the European market.

With the explosion of digital technology, particularly consumers' use of mobile phones and tablets, banks face new challenges with respect to shifting consumer behavior.

Banks will start focusing on captive operations or a mix of captive and outsourcing functions instead of relying only on traditional outsourcing. Offshoring, which emerged as a competitive necessity over a decade ago, has resulted in cost savings for financial institutions. According to a research study by Deloitte,[10] offshoring services generate a savings of $5 billion a year for financial firms; this amounts to more than 40% of the cost of running the same operations onshore. There will, however, be renewed efforts to reconnect with customers through a combination of state-of-the-art technology and personal service. Customers interact with banks through online sites, branches, ATMs, and call centers. A bank's competitive edge comes from the way customers feel about these interactions. Another underlying fact is that convenience, value, and service are keys to improving customer service rather than product innovation, as products are rarely differentiated and are quickly copied.

The changing demographic profile has made it imperative for banks to develop specialized products and advisory services aimed at an older population. The concept of bancassurance has immense potential to address the needs of older customers. Insurance with its annuity features and tax advantages is well established in European regions and in the Asian markets of Singapore and South Korea. Financial institutions have to pursue policies to enhance retirement products especially in the graying markets of the US, Europe, and Asia where much growth prospect exists. The trend observed is that the responsibility for retirement security is increasingly shifting toward the individual and away from the government and employers.

The commercial banking industry is facing stiff competition from the investment banking sector as marketable instruments compete with loans and demand deposits. Many commercial banks have diversified into the investment banking arena as it has become increasingly difficult to get acceptable margins from traditional banking business. The situation is such that banks have to compete with money-market mutual funds for deposit business, commercial papers (CPs), and medium-term notes (MTNs) for bank loans. On account of squeezed margins, commercial banks in the United States and Europe have undertaken cost-cutting initiatives such as reducing the number of branches. These banks also diversified into pensions, insurance, asset management, and investment banking. Thus, traditional commercial banks are facing an identity crisis owing to the changes in the fundamental structure of their organizations. What is becoming established in the current era is the concept of

---

[10] Deloitte Research Report (2005), Global financial services off shoring: scaling the heights.

universal banking, where "everybody does everything." Investment banking, private banking, and bancassurance are the most profitable and fastest growing segments of the financial services industry. This changing landscape of the banking industry in the context of competition, diversification, new products, and new geographic markets has dramatically changed the risk profile for banks. In short, the deep transformation the sector is witnessing can be attributed to a number of factors, including the technology innovations that facilitated e-banking and e-finance, worldwide consolidation and restructuring, increasing competition in terms of markets and products, deregulation, and changing demographic profiles.

The traditional core business of commercial banks has been retail and corporate banking. As economic markets integrate, banks compete with other financial services companies to provide mutually exclusive products and services to the same customer segments. About two decades back, most Western banks derived 90% of their revenues from interest income, but now this percentage ranges from between 40% and 60%. New income sources such as fee-based income from investment services and derivatives account for an increasing proportion of income for major banks. The risk profile of commercial banks is changing as a consequence of diversification, signifying the importance of market risk management.

Consolidation in the sector is happening owing to disintermediation in the banking sector. In retail banking, the focus is shifting from transaction management toward the sales of financial products. With the aid of powerful technological delivery channels and new aggressive competitors, retail banking has adopted competitive changes. Telephone banking and web-based banking have assumed significant positions in the retail banking sectors.

Private banking is one of the fastest growing sectors in the banking industry. As private banking is basically an asset management service, the importance of effective financial risk management has become a key issue for modern bank management.

Investment banking has emerged as the most globalized segment of the financial services industries. These sectors provide multinational companies with a broad range of financial services products, which include M&A services, market trading, financial lending, and fund management.

Many Western governments are faced with the challenges of the need to cut expenditures for old-age benefits to keep deficits under control. In this context, private pensions, mutual funds, and private banking operations are important.

A key strategy employed by multinational banks is merger and acquisition, the organic expansion and collaboration with local banks. The late 1990s witnessed a wave of consolidation in the banking sector. In 1997, the Swiss banks UBS and SBC merged to create one of the largest banks in the world. In 1998, the world's largest financial group, Citigroup, was created by the merger between Citibank and Travelers. The concept of bancassurance has led to interindustry consolidation whereby insurance companies were able to expand their widespread network of points of sales, such as bank branches. Bancassurance involves insurance companies buying small banks or being bought by large commercial banks to achieve synergy in the distribution process. The acquisition of investment banks by commercial banks was intended to widen the services offered by commercial banks. In the case of international diversification, foreign banks are acquiring domestic banks to circumvent regulatory barriers that exist in domestic banks.

Banks ought to focus more on nonbalance sheet-intensive products and services. These include fee-generating services such as asset management. Banks could also establish a wide range of products and services for the emerging strong middle class and for businesses within the framework of the regulatory changes. Wealth management businesses consisting of fee-generating services have become more relevant for retail banking as offering loans has become less profitable due to lower interest rates. In wholesale banking, the allocation of resources should be balanced between developed and emerging markets. Banks also need to invest heavily in IT. Additionally, banks ought to grow deposit-based operations and have a wide array of retail products and services.

1.4 REFORM POLICY TRENDS

The post-economic crisis period saw attempts by policy-framing bodies like the G-20, Basel Committee for Banking Supervision, US's Financial Stability Oversight Council, UK's Financial Policy Committee, and the European Systemic Risk Board to alter the structure and business models of large multinational banks. The new policy guidelines underline the obligation of financial institutions to carry a new Tier 1 capital common equity ratio of 4.5%, a Basel III capital buffer of 2.5%, and an additional capital surcharge of up to 2.5%. Agreements on global bank capital, liquidity regimes, and FSB standards on effective banking supervisions and resolutions regimes are major reforms.

The new central clearing regulations would make the over-the-counter (OTC) derivative business more challenging in nature. New regulations are designed to encourage more standardization of derivatives and other asset-backed securities (ABS) while driving trading from OTC markets to exchanges. The regulatory changes are bound to affect a bank's institutional and retail customer relationships. Basel III, which was implemented in January 2013, is facing the problem of uneven implementation. National differences also occur in the calculation of asset risk, which determines the capital needs of the bank. Because of Basel III's increased capital requirements, there is an increasing trend toward closure of proprietary trading desks and less capital-intensive operations such as advisory business, private banking, and wealth management.

In the wake of the global financial crisis, the production of private-label mortgage-backed securities (MBS) has been ceased in the market by government-sponsored entities.

1.5 TECHNOLOGY TRENDS
1.5.1 THE GROWING RELEVANCE OF DIGITAL BANKING

The financial crisis has led banks to adopt operational efficiency as a strategic necessity in the real sense. Global technology trends indicate increased focus on next-generation remote banking solutions, business intelligence (BI), and analytics in transaction monitoring. There will also be an increased focus on enterprise payment hubs in payment processing. European regions will witness implementation of customer relationship management (CRM) to enhance channel capabilities. In Asian regions the impetus would be on the enhancement of multichannel technology capabilities. Remote deposits are becoming more prevalent in the US market.

In fact, Internet and mobile applications have made next-generation remote-banking solutions a critical priority for banks. Banks could improve their personalized services for customers through the use of Web 2.0 online banking sites. Other technological innovations such as cloud computing and virtualization could improve the productivity and usability of web-based banking applications. Cloud computing enables a wide variety of technologies and services that are accessible and less expensive.

The advantages of next-generation remote-banking solutions are manifold. For one, banks could generate additional income by charging for web-based value-added services. The service can also be used as a tool to collect data and to facilitate the cross-selling of products and services. Banks would be able to offer more services at lesser costs through online channels. Mobile Internet banking is also growing in relevance in mature markets. Many experts point out that the competitive position of banks could be further enhanced by their adoption of rich Internet application (RIA) technology and Web 2.0. Successful banks need to have a system architecture that enables customers to have a full view of their banking services.

The development of core banking solutions has led to a competitive situation in which it has become necessary for banks to upgrade to core banking systems. Particularly with the increased consolidation in the banking industry, it has become necessary for institutions to replace their core legacy systems with core banking platform migration, which is flexible and customer-centric.

The role of BI and analytics is becoming more relevant in providing customized rewards, products, and investment solutions to customers. Compliance of regulations such as the Sarbanes-Oxley Act, Basel II, Basel III, Solvency II, and Dodd-Frank Act will drive the growth of BI and analytics. BI encompasses a comprehensive suite of dashboards, visualizations, and scorecards. New technologies such as visualization, in-memory analytics, and service-oriented architecture (SOA) are facilitating the development and use of BI applications.

In Europe there has been a greater focus on the implementation of CRM to enhance channel capabilities. European banks have to improve their distribution networks to enhance the specialization of their sales forces and the centralization of back-office operations. The trend could be on identifying and establishing relationships with IT vendors who could deliver modular, multilingual, customer-centric CRM applications. In emerging Asian markets, banks are making huge investments in online and mobile channels. In these markets, the rise of mobile devices has become a key driver for business banking.

Enterprise payment hubs can reduce operational inefficiencies and costs by bringing down the number of payment platforms to a more manageable level. New payment standards and regulatory requirements such as ISO20022 and SEPA are key catalysts for the adoption of such payment systems.

Investment in technology is a key component of any bank's market strategy. It is critical to have technology that is flexible and adaptable. A key trend with respect to technological innovation is that banking technology architectures focus on investment in web-based technology and information. Global integration has become particularly relevant with respect to the integration of foreign exchange and trades into the domestic and international payments platforms. Much of this is done via integration with third-party solutions. These trends reflect the emergence of borderless banking. It is expected that the emergence of new applications built around standards like the SWIFTNet Trade Services Utility, Java Enterprise edition, and SOA will help banks to maximize their return on technology investments. SWIFT operates a global network that allows financial institutions worldwide to send and receive information about trades and transactions.

The improved standardization will benefit bank-to-corporate connectivity. Basel II regulatory compliance has been a factor in banks developing an integrated information systems strategy for IT infrastructure.

Smartphones will become the dominant access point for online banking. As consumers spend more time on their mobile devices than on computers, mobile banking will follow. The mobile platform will act as a catalyst to electronic person-to-person (P2P) payments. Companies are making massive investments in P2P payment networks that enable people to pay each other electronically. The rise of mobile contactless systems based on near field communication (NFC) offers a much faster and secure way to initiate payments with a mobile phone than short message service (SMS). Smartphones equipped with browsers have the multifunctional performance capability of cash, checks, debit and credit cards. Mobile payments are viewed as an effective and secure medium of cashless transactions. In the emerging markets of South Asia, mobile payments transactions have reached 1 billion transactions per year.

The latest technologies do not come from the banks' core system providers but from separate companies, and this creates integration challenges. The core system vendors spend millions each year working on integrating their systems. These challenges have become one of the greatest technology challenges faced by banks. Document imaging has emerged as a strategically important technology that could be integrated into the core system. Well-planned imaging can create a truly paperless new account process. It gives bankers access to all customer data in one place at one time, which benefits the environment by keeping banks green.

Remote deposit capture (RDC) allows businesses to capture and transmit customer payments to their bank as deposits from anywhere in the world. It also allows banks to take deposits and service businesses and their branches from a central set of accounts, regardless of location. Offering RDC can help banks draw in new customers and reduce processing costs. In the United States, RDC is growing in relevance owing to the broad viability of RDC for small businesses and consumers.

Trends have suggested that there is an ongoing shift in payments and other transaction services from banks to nonbanks. The trend could be reversed if banks focus on the emerging payment solutions using mobile devices to transfer money or make point-of-sale purchases. The new payment technologies also provide an opportunity for community banks to offer a wider range of services for making payments.

Social media including Twitter and Facebook are now emerging as leading marketing channels used by banks to announce new products, services, or events and to receive personal feedback. In the era of increased use of technologies, it has become imperative for banks to make adequate investments in analytics and dashboards whereby meaningful analysis or real-time data gives bankers the opportunity to make daily decisions that influence their business.

In the context of increasing bank losses from cybercrime, banks must manage and have strong partners to handle security concerns across channels and devices.

It has become vital for banks to use integrated systems to increase the ease and efficiency of streamlining delivery processes. Efforts ought to be aimed at streamlining channel systems consisting of branch systems (teller, new accounts, loans), ATMs, credit cards, Internet banking, and mobile systems into one cohesive process.

1.5.2 DATA MANAGEMENT AT THE ENTERPRISE LEVEL

Leveraging data as a strategic asset helps banks differentiate markets and strengthen customer relationships as well as realize sustainable growth. Banks are increasingly focusing on ways to become more data-centric for the purpose of a better interactive customer experience across different channels. Data governance and master data management are the two technology best practices that have emerged as the critical success factors for financial institutions to transform their business models.

1.5.3 **NEED FOR SCALABLE ARCHITECTURE FRAMEWORK FOR DIGITAL PAYMENTS**

A critical need of financial institutions is to upgrade their technology architectures to next-generation capabilities. The financial services industry is characterized by high competition, intense regulation, and heavy dependence on technology-based processes and automation for delivering quality services to end users. Financial institutions face the challenge of delivering services with quality assurance in the context of margin compensation. Digital payments have emerged as the key component of any financial institution's digital strategy. In the era of universal banking, when customers prefer one-stop shopping, payments are the gateway for businesses where customers have to deal with automatic bill paying, mortgage payments, and direct deposits.

A scalable architecture is pertinent to support an effective digital payments strategy. With the advent of mobile banking applications, financial institutions face the challenge of cost-effectively integrating consumer and commercial payment functions into an online banking services platform. The scalable architectural framework needs to encompass activities such as consumer payments, peer-to-peer payment, retail payments, bill payments, and commercial/interbank payments. Consumer payments involve payments via credit cards, prepaid cards, debit cards, e-checks, and digital currencies. P2P payment involves intra- and interbank accounts where payments are processed between banks and proprietary service networks via book transfers including Amazon WebPay, PayPal, Automatic Clearing House (ACH), PIN debit, and proprietary card networks. Retail payments involve facilitating the back-office processing of payments through PIN debit networks, proprietary card networks, and the ACH system. Bill payments involving payments for credit card companies, utilities, and mortgage companies are generally processed through the FedACH, the Federal Reserve's network. High-value interbank transfers and Treasury payments for intraday settlements are processed over networks like Fedwire (formerly known as Federal Reserve Wire Network), CHIPS, and SWIFT.

Scalable interaction services will essentially support the function of message entry, disputes, investigation, and other user access services. This commercial portal enables processing between people, processes, and information. A process tier framework would provide a common enterprisewide definition of payment processes. Access services can facilitate the successful integration of trading partners, Treasury services and common payments, gateways and networks. SOA provides the platform for the integration layer enabling orchestration and connectivity. SOA facilitates an improved integration of existing application applications and provides innovation for payment strategies, mega data capabilities, and core banking processes. Security and governance are areas that require attention in the scalable framework.

1.5.4 **INCREASING RELEVANCE OF VIRTUAL CURRENCIES**

Virtual currencies are gaining prominence particularly from online retailers. Banks face competition from established social websites such as Facebook. Banks have to find ways to incorporate virtual currencies and social money transfer services into their bank's service offerings in a legitimate way. In 2011, Facebook introduced virtual currency called Facebook Credits, which failed in the market. In 2013, Amazon introduced a virtual currency program called Amazon Coin, which enables its customers to purchase apps, games, and in-app items on the Kindle Fire.

TECHNOLOGICAL INNOVATIONS AND FINANCIAL INSTITUTIONS

Globally banks are investing heavily in applications for smartphones and digital wallets to support a wide range of banking activities. Interactive tools are also being developed by banks to analyze customer spending habits and strengthen the skills of wealth management. Social networks are also mobilized to build brands. Banks are increasingly facing competition from alternate online payment systems such as PayPal and Google Wallet, which aim to displace banks in daily customer transactions. These emerging trends will transform banks along a structure by channel, product, and geography into an organization based on customer segments. Banks will be able to shrink their physical footprints thereby reducing branches and reducing costs.

Mobile banking has evolved as a regular channel and customer touchpoint in the evolution of the digital ecosystem. Mobile banking solutions have emerged as a top strategic priority for banks to gain a competitive advantage. Consumers prefer real-time access to financial accounts and continuous availability to perform financial transactions across different mobile technology platforms. Studies estimate that within the next five years, approximately 50% of smartphone owners will use phones as a preferred method of payment.[11]

It is estimated that 60 million people in the United States are using banking services on their mobile devices. According to the Bain Report of 2012, mobile usage for US banking transactions has increased to 32% of customers compared to 21% of customers in 2011. According to a Bank Innovation report in 2012, Wells Fargo had 9 million mobile users, JPMorgan Chase had approximately 12.4 million mobile users, while Bank of America had about 12 million mobile users by 2012. It has been reported that Bank of America alone adds 10,000 new mobile users each day.

According to Jupiter Research, worldwide mobile payments were estimated to reach $240 billion in 2013. The average cost of a transaction using an online or mobile device is between 56¢ and 59¢ cents at an ATM, compared to $3.97 when a customer transacts with a bank teller according to a study by the PNC Financial Services Group.[12]

Research shows that consumers have become increasingly interested in transactions involving mobile imaging. During 2012, Bank of America processed 100,000 imaged checks a day through smartphones. Wells Fargo accepted 2.3 million checks and $559 million through mobile RDC.[13] Still, RDC represents only a small percentage of branch and ATM transactions of major banks.

Mobile banking has the advantage of diverting a large volume of high-frequency routine transactions and provides the platform for reduced branch visits, branch redesign, and reduced costs. This is particularly significant in the context that approximately 90% of transactions like cashing checks, making deposits, and checking balances are considered routine bank transactions. According to a Diebold research report, a transaction that costs $4.25 in a branch would cost $2.40 through a call center and only 20¢ online. The same customer transaction through mobile channels would reduce the cost further to 8¢. An example of leveraging online and mobile banking can be found in the case of Coastal Federal Union, which does not employ a single teller and Boeings Employees Credit Union, which has had a teller-less branch for years.[14]

Mobile wallets play an increasing role in the concept of social banking by engaging different users and communities within various segments or groups. There are debit and credit cards where, instead of getting cash back, consumers may donate to their charity of choice.

In the past, banks have had a very high barrier to entry into these types of services. But players such as PayPal, Google Wallet, and Bitcoin have created digital payment strategies without a huge investment. Cheap and powerful cloud solutions replace check-processing equipment worth millions of dollars. Google and Amazon are providing customers compelling offers that banks haven't been able to provide.

New payment technologies include text or email services such as Popmoney, image-scanning credit cards at point of sale like Jumio's Netswipe, paying bills and loading prepaid credit cards online through MoneyGram, and PayPal Mobile e-commerce all offer immense scope in the current banking age.

In the mobile payment segment, many competitive options exist, including NFC-based Google Wallet, a copycat dongle of PayPal, and digital wallets of Visa, MasterCard, and American Express. MasterPass of MasterCard aims to integrate mobile payment for retailers as one multipool option.

---

[11]Mike Panzarella (2012), Banking in the age of mobile technology, http://www.perficient.com/Thought-Leadership/Perficient-Perspectives/2012/Banking-in-the-Age-of-Mobile-Technology.

[12]Michael Hickins (2013), Big banks bet on Mobility and Super Powered ATM, http://mobile.blogs.wsj.com/cio/2013/02/07/big-banks-bet-on-mobility-and-super-powered-atms/.

[13]Greg Mac Sweeney, Mobility's undeniable benefits, http://www.wallstreetandtech.com/it-infrastructure/mobilitys-undeniable-benefits/240149204.

[14]Bain & Company Report (2012), Customer loyalty in retail banking.

The use of tablets and other smart devices by consumers and businesses is changing the way banking is done, which has relevance for banking services strategy. Tablets have become the most efficient means of capturing, processing, storing, and retrieving data. As such, tablets are another "gadget tool" along with smartphones for banking customers. The larger screens of tablets facilitate the integration of personal finance management (PFM) tools, thereby enabling customers to manage their personal finances.

Tablet banking provides the opportunity for financial institutions to strengthen their customer relationships. Bank employees can use the devices to directly interact with customers. Tablets can be used to streamline the processing of opening new customer accounts, and they can incorporate compliance requirements such as signature capture from clients. Financial institutions like Citibank are increasingly focusing on enhancing customer experiences related to desktop tablet and mobile technological applications.

Banks like JPMorgan Chase have introduced innovative ATMs that feature broader screens with video capability, which enables customers to perform more types of transactions and to interact live with a teller. Bank of America is in the process of developing applications that allow commercial customers to manage global transactions like payments and internal fund transfers irrespective of country or time zone.

According to an Infosys and Efma report entitled "Innovations in Retail Banking" online and mobile channels are growing rapidly with the focus on areas of innovation that attract new customers. Digital wallets enable banking services for customers through multiple channels and devices that are cloud based.

American Express launched a Twitter Sync feature that allows customers to get discount deals by tweeting special-offer hashtags and integrating payments into Twitter. The UK-based social money transfer service Azimo is gearing up to offer stiff competition to established players, Western Union and MoneyGram, by rolling out integration with Facebook for users of urban social networks for remittances.

Turkish retail banks, among others, encourage customers to use their smartphones to check their personal loan/credit limits before making a major purchase by sending a secure SMS message to the bank's database. Recognizing the caller's mobile number and PIN, the system automatically confirms the customer's account balance.

Citibank has introduced an ambitious multibillion-dollar IT program called "Project Rainbow" to provide a comprehensive 360-degree view of its customers.

MANAGING BIG DATA

Banking giants like JPMorgan Chase, Bank of America, Citigroup, and Wells Fargo are making use of powerful analytic technology called *big data*, which is designed to quickly process huge volumes of data and generate reports within seconds. This data includes unconventional databases such as social media posts and emails. For example, JPMorgan Chase uses these new capabilities to offer proprietary insights into consumer trends based on huge volumes of transactional data that amounted to more than 1.5 billion pieces of information. Using big data enables banks to reduce interest rates and costs. This emerging trend is advantageous for banks particularly when banks are under enormous margin pressures in a recessionary environment. Its use provides opportunities for cross-selling and for customized marketing.

In the United States, the four big universal banks have spent approximately $10 billion on technology upgrades. Some of this investment is funded by savings achieved through rationalized systems and automated processes. Citi Corp., for one, reduced overall spending in operations and technology by more than $4 billion in a five-year period.

Source: Michael Hickins (2013), Banks using big data to discover "New Silk Roads," http://blogs.wsj.com/cio/2013/02/06/banks-using-big-data-to-discover-new-silk-roads/, *CIO Journal*.

1.6 CHALLENGES OF GLOBAL FINANCIAL INSTITUTIONS

The financial institutions sector operates against a backdrop of rapid development, managed risk, stringent regulation, and fluctuating economic conditions. Financial institutions will face much more complexity in the types of risks they manage. The global banking industry faces varied challenges of regulatory compliances, risk management, customer demands, market consolidation, and M&A activity. As a result of the global financial crisis and the economic and regulatory reforms that followed, banks are facing major challenges in their traditional operating models. The banking industry is facing declining cross-border capital flows, high bank credit default swap spreads, and low market valuations. The traditional banks' market share is being challenged as the proliferation of mobile phones, smartphone and tablets, and social networking is enabling nonbanking firms to provide more banking services.

Rebuilding the asset quality and strengthening capital adequacy are major areas of concern for financial institutions in the aftermath of the economic crisis. They face the challenges of developing their technology architecture to make them scalable and efficient. The financial services sector faces the challenge of managing risk management systems, information management networks, and business analytics tools. The financial services front offices face challenges in terms of delivery channels that focus on real-time business analytics and customer insights.

The low efficiency of existing channels, aging technology, high operating costs, and complex processes are also major challenges faced by financial institutions. Banks face challenges with respect to governance issues, particularly in data collection and reporting.

1.7 **CHANGES IN CONTROL SYSTEM**[15]

The global economic crisis has taught valuable lessons to the banking sector with respect to the need for reviewing risk governance and risk appetite by tightening controls around markets. The agenda of change is focused on governance and risk appetite, the role of the risk function, stress testing, and risk transparency. There is greater emphasis on control measures such as stress testing. There is also the need for improvement of risk return management. Many banks are in the process of adopting risk reporting initiatives to board-level committees. In conventional cases, gap analysis is guided by a top-down approach with significant board and senior management involvement. Banks have also initiated proposals to make risk appetite a more effective tool by including more quantitative measures. The most radical changes are expected to come from those banks that were severely affected by the crisis. The most commonly cited barriers to change are data and systems along with cultural factors. Banks also face the challenge of uncertainty over regulations. In light of the crisis, the regulatory environment is changing fast, making it difficult for banks to plan the right infrastructure for the next decade.

1.8 **BANKING TRENDS IN EMERGING MARKETS**

Regions in Asia enjoys higher rates of economic growth, superior to those of more developed Western markets. A McKinsey report stated that in 2009, Asia accounted for 36% of global corporate banking revenues and 21% of global capital market and investment-banking revenues. The emerging regions of Asia (China, India, and ASEAN countries with the exception of Singapore) will account for 45% of all new growth in global wholesale banking revenues up to 2014. In 2009, Asia accounted for 36% of global corporate banking revenues and 21% of global capital market and investment-banking revenues.[16]

---

[15] E&Y Report (2012), Risk governance – agenda for change, Survey for the implementation of the IIF's best practice recommendations.
[16] Tab Bowers, Emmanuel Pitsilis, JoydeepSengupta, ToshanTamhane (2011), Asian wholesale banking: Winning in the new battleground. *McKinsey Quarterly, March.*

China, India, and the ASEAN countries suffer from underdeveloped infrastructures. It is estimated that in India, for example, electricity generation is 16-20% short of what is needed to meet peak demand. McKinsey Research estimates that there will be more than $1 trillion in infrastructure projects open to foreign investment over the next 10 years, providing ample opportunities for banking institutions.[17] China's wholesale banking is projected to grow more than 10% per annum over the next five years. By 2015, China is expected to overtake Japan as the largest banking market in the Asian region. China has the highest corporate deposit to GDP ratio globally among large economies, with 56% of bank deposits from corporate customers.[18] The biggest banking markets by assets are the United States, the United Kingdom, Japan, China, and France. On a comparative note, the banking assets of developed nations increased by 74% during the 10-year period of 2000-2010, whereas in China the growth rate was 379%.[19]

On account of increased urbanization, fixed-asset investment is projected to remain as the top contributor to GDP over the next five years. Approximately $10 trillion of urbanization-related infrastructure is required during the period 2010-2015.

In India, corporate banking includes lending and fee businesses and accounts for approximately 80% of the total banking revenues, and wholesale banking accounts for the remaining 20%. Wholesale banking is expected to double from roughly $16 billion in 2010 to between $35 and $40 billion by 2015. Corporate banking revenues are expected to reach $30 billion by 2015. Investments in infrastructure totaling $240 billion between 2007 and 2010 have already been made under India's 11th five-year plan.

In the modern era, emerging markets are growing in prominence for both domestic and foreign banks. The strong middle-class segment and sophisticated corporate banking needs are fueling retail, commercial, and investment banking activities. In the emerging markets of China and India, the increased trend of consumerism has increased the demand for mortgages and asset loans. It is interesting to note that the unbanked population of China numbers 597 million, and in India, it is 397 million. Infrastructural development is poised to happen in a big way in the emerging markets as the economy booms, providing scope for project financing. In 2011, four Chinese banks were among the top 10 banks in the world in terms of market capitalization.

There is immense potential for mobile banking in emerging markets. In these regions formal banking reaches only about 37% of the population, compared with a 50% penetration rate for mobile phone users. For every 10,000 people, these countries have one bank branch and one ATM—but 5100 mobile phones. A McKinsey study shows that 1 billion people in emerging markets have a mobile phone but no access to banking services.[20] McKinsey research estimates that 2.5 billion of the world's adults don't use formal banks or semiformal microfinance institutions either to save or borrow money.

By the end of 2010, five of the 10 largest banks in the world by market capitalization were Chinese or Brazilian banks.[21] It has become pertinent for global banks to target markets in Asia, Africa, or Latin America for higher growth rates. It has also been observed that, in emerging markets with high concentrations of state ownership in local banks, local businesses prefer doing business with

[17] Naveen Tahilyani, ToshanTamhane, Jessica Tan (2011), Asia's $1 trillion infrastructure opportunity. *McKinsey Quarterly, March.*

[18] YiWang Jun Hu Anna Yip (2011), China's changing landscape. *McKinsey Quarterly, March.*

[19] KPMG Report (2011), Bruised but not broken: The global banking growth agenda.

[20] Christopher P. Beshouri, Jon Gravråk (2010), Capturing the promise of mobile banking in emerging markets. *McKinsey Quarterly, February.*

[21] KPMG Report (2011), Bruised but not broken: The global banking growth agenda.

local banks. In spite of the large foreign bank presence in China, foreign banks still control only an aggregate 1.8% of the country's banking assets as of 2010. In India, 7.2% of banking assets were held by foreign banks by the end of 2010.

This trend is in sharp contrast to the Western situation where, for example, 46.2% of the United Kingdom's banking assets were controlled by foreign banks. In the United States, 15.4% of total banking assets are controlled by foreign banks.[22] Emerging market banks are in an advantageous position with respect to growth through domestic consolidation as foreign banks face hurdles such as strict foreign ownership rules in the emerging markets. Domestic deals in these markets accounted for 73% of all banking transactions during the period 2005-2010 with only 8% being intercontinental deals.[23]

1.9 THE FINANCIAL CRISIS OF 2008

The roots of the global financial crisis of 2007-2010 can be found in real estate. Housing prices began to show unusual upward movements after the United States emerged from the 2001-2004 economic recession. The immediate trigger was the bursting of the US housing bubble, which peaked in 2005-2006. Many economists had been of the opinion that this housing bubble, characterized by unexpected and temporary inflation in housing prices, was doomed to burst and contract. During the 1980s, the large inflow of foreign funds and steadily decreasing interest rates made easy credit conditions for almost two decades prior to the crisis, which, in turn, led to a boom in housing construction activities and debt financed consumption. Home purchases were promoted by the government as contributors to individual wealth and retirement plans. The Fed Reserve made mortgage interest rates tax deductible, providing further incentive for homeowners to buy houses. Lending institutions began to sell subprime mortgages,[24] which were backed by the government and mortgage security giants Fannie Mae and Freddie Mac. Lending institutions focused on securing high volumes of such mortgages. Major financial institutions such as AIG and Merrill Lynch actively acquired smaller lenders who had reputations for subprime lending. By 2007, it became clear that the risks associated with subprime mortgages were very real. The Fed did not require financial institutions to set aside an adequate amount of money to offset potential losses.

New financial agreements called MBS and collateralized debt obligations (CDOs), which derived their value from mortgage payments and housing prices, enabled financial institutions and investors around the world to invest in the US housing market. From the 1970s, the policy of the US government was to deregulate for the promotion of business, and this resulted in the growing importance of the shadow banking system, which consists of investment banks and hedge funds. These financial institutions were not subject to the same regulations governing commercial banks. But these institutions did not have a financial cushion sufficient to absorb large loan defaults or MBS losses. The value of US subprime mortgages was estimated at $41.3 trillion by March 2007. Major US investment banks and government entities such as Fannie Mae had played an active role in the expansion of higher risk lending.

The overwhelming losses affecting US-based financial institutions sent shockwaves around the world. According to International Monetary Fund (IMF) statistics, during the period from January

---

[22] KPMG Report (2011), Bruised but not broken: The global banking growth agenda.
[23] KPMG Report (2011), Bruised but not broken: The global banking growth agenda.
[24] Subprime mortgages are housing loans that are offered to people with low incomes and/or poor credit.

2007 to September 2009, large US and European banks lost more than $1 trillion on toxic assets and bad loans. Companies that were involved in home construction and mortgage lending were severely affected. Over 100 mortgage lenders went bankrupt during 2007 and 2008. Many financial giants collapsed and were acquired under duress or subject to government takeover. These included Lehman Brothers, Merrill Lynch, Fannie Mae, Freddie Mac, Washington Mutual, Wachovia, and AIG.

The subprime lending industry had been vast and highly integrated into the securitized market. High-risk mortgages were folded into pension, mutual, money market, and other funds to mitigate the risks. Investors from all over the world were made participants in the subprime industry. But when the risks were realized, investors worldwide experienced losses. By November 2008, US S&P 500 was down 45% from its 2007 high. Housing prices dropped 20% from their peak value in 2006. The total losses from savings, pension, and investment assets were estimated to be a staggering $8.3 trillion in the United States alone. This crisis was termed as the worst economic downturn since the Great Depression of the 1930s. The crisis spread fast and developed into a global economic shock characterized by bank failures, declines in various stock indexes, and reductions in the market value of equities and commodities. MBS and credit default obligations purchased by corporate and institutional investors globally along with credit default swap contributed to a greater extent to the crisis. The deleveraging of financial institutions further accelerated the solvency crisis.

The financial crisis resulted in big banking shakeouts. One month after the Lehman Brothers collapse in 2008, the European Central Bank spent approximately €771 billion to provide emergency liquidity to European banks to help these institutions face the growing crisis. The US government executed two stimulus packages totaling nearly $1 trillion during 2008 and 2009. Central banks, like the US Federal Reserve, the European Central Bank, and other central banks, purchased US $2.5 trillion of government debt and troubled private assets from banks. This was determined to be the largest liquidity injection into the credit market ever and the largest monetary policy action in world history.

The financial crisis of 2008 left a hole in the public finance of many countries. In 2010, the IMF estimated the fiscal costs of direct support, net of recovered amounts, at some 2.8% of GDP for the advanced G-20 countries. OECD (Organisation for Economic Co-operation and Development) public debt is now estimated to be 100% of GDP compared with over 70% in 2007.[25] New loans to large borrowers fell by 47% in the last quarter of 2008 compared to the previous quarter. Lending actually declined by 79% compared to the height of the credit boom.[26]

The largest banking collapse suffered by any country in the 2008 crisis was in Iceland, involving all major Icelandic banks. Another glaring and potentially devastating situation during the tail end of this crisis centered in Greece. The 2010 European Sovereign debt crisis was basically one of the long-term worldwide consequences of the economic crisis. The biggest UK banks, such as RBS, were partly nationalized through a €50-billion rescue package by the government. The World Bank Report 2009 observed that the Arab world, on the other hand, was far less severely affected by the credit crunch.

US banks had been putting more emphasis on derivative activity than balance sheet growth. They put increased emphasis on turning depositors into credit card users and mortgage customers and vice versa. Banks also pursued de novo entry into new markets by the organic expansion of existing operations and through cross-border acquisitions. Global banks found it attractive to buy crisis-ridden

---

[25]Sebastian Sdiidi (2011), Banking on a crisis and on its resolution OECD Observer No. 284 Q1.
[26]V. Ivashina, D. Scharfstein (2010), Bank lending the financial crisis of 2008. *Journal of Financial Economics 97*(3), 319-338.

Table 1.3   Banks Affected by Global Crisis in 2008

Bank	Action Taken
Fannie Mae	Nationalized
Freddie Mac	Nationalized
Lehman Brothers	Collapsed
Merrill Lynch	Acquired by Bank of America
AIG	Partly nationalized
HBOS	Taken over
WaMu	Collapsed and sold
Fortis	Nationalized
Bradford & Bingley	Nationalized
Wachovia	Acquired by Wells Fargo
Glitnir	Acquired by Wachovia
Hypo Real Estate	Bailout package
RBS	Partly nationalized
Lloyds TSB	Partly nationalized

nationalized local banks that had loan losses. Domestication of foreign bank operations also resulted because of the decline of unremunerated reserve requirements as part of monetary control.[27] Table 1.3 gives the list of banks affected by the global crisis in 2008 and the actions initiated as a response to the crisis.

Since late 2008, the financial crisis has rapidly weakened the global economy and has demonstrated that no part of the world is isolated from disturbances in the global financial markets. The impact of the crisis can be gauged from the upward revisions to the estimates of the write-downs by banks and other financial institutions from about US $500 billion in March 2008 to about US $3.5 trillion in October 2009. The adverse impact on the real economy was severe. In 2009, the world GDP was estimated by the IMF to have contracted by 0.8% and the world trade volume was estimated to have declined by 12%. It was often argued that while the subprime problem was the trigger, the root cause of the crisis lay in the persistence of the global imbalances since the start of the current decade. Large current account deficits in advanced countries mirrored by the large current account surpluses in emerging market economies (EMEs) implied that excess saving flowed from developing countries to developed countries.

1.10 IMPACT OF FINANCIAL CRISIS ON BANKING SYSTEM

A new wave of regulations in banking are being shaped following the global financial crisis. These include Basel III changes, legislation like Dodd-Frank in the United States, and more concrete actions by the G-20.

---

[27] Robert N. McCauley, Judith S. Ruud, Philip D. Woolridge (2002), Globalizing international banking. *BIS Quarterly Review, March*, 41-52.

The Basel Committee on Banking Supervision adopted the Basel III framework governing capital, leverage, and liquidity of banks. The three-pronged approach governing leverage, liquidity, and capital is a sea change of regulation in banks. The G-20 endorsed the new framework of the Basel committee. In the United States, President Obama signed the Dodd-Frank Act in July 2010, although the lengthy rule-making process of the legislation will not come into full effect for many years.

Other effects of the global financial crisis impacted banks of all sizes. Banks struggle with reduced public confidence, heightened shareholder scrutiny, and increased regulatory oversight. The troubled banks received government assistance, ranging from stimulus packages to full nationalization to modest capital infusions. Other intervention measures included asset purchases and liquidity support as well as guarantee programs. Banks are involved in cleaning their balance sheets and protecting their assets. Many are placing greater emphasis on controlling liquidity risks. Challenges remaining for banks are issues related to nonperforming loans, tax and expense management, and data quality in risk and finance, among others.

The financial crisis has compelled banks to reassess their business fundamentals, including profitability and client relationship management. Banks have to focus on the fundamental assets of customers, staff, and capital for long-term growth. Toward this end, they are increasing risk from transparency to reduce operational risk. Other shifts are a move from a product-centric approach to a client-centric approach with a 360-degree understanding of clients. They are deploying client profitability analytics to enhance performance by analyzing profitability at different levels. Finally, banks are seeking data reporting technology and proactive approaches to better manage clients and portfolios.

Financial conservatism has become the order of the day among small businesses and consumers, particularly in the developed world. With the adoption of Basel III reforms, capital and funding will become more expensive and even scarce. During the two decades leading up to the financial crisis, customers demanded more and more credit, reflecting the appetite for consumption and investment. The extreme demand for credit led to efforts by the banking system to propel the growth of off-balance sheet activities. The upsurge in the junk bonds of the 1980s and the mortgage securities market reflected the trend of loan demand exceeding deposit supply. As banks started to fund their activities through wholesale markets and to distribute credit through off-balance sheet vehicles, their balance sheets ballooned. In the context of relaxing regulatory restrictions, the leverages soared. The median leverage for US banks reached 35 during the financial crisis period. As the crisis appeared, banks slashed assets and built up capital and liquidity buffers beyond the minimum regulatory requirements. Corporate and individual borrowers also reacted to the crisis by cutting expenses. This situation led to supply and demand imbalances where there were too few loans and too much funding of deposits. Fewer companies are borrowing and banks have less capacity to offer credit. Western banks are pursuing more business in the emerging markets of Asia and Australia where economic growth is fueling the demand for credit.

In the changed scenario, balance sheet-intensive activities will become less economically feasible under the new regulatory standards. One of the trends is that banking will become more like an agency business.[28] Banks with a strong presence in less intensive businesses, such as wealth management, asset management, and Treasury services, will have a competitive advantage. Liquidity risk has emerged as a major challenge for global banks. There is an urgent need for a long-term strategic model for risk management, which needs huge resources for implementing changes in liquidity risk management. Table 1.4 lists the major global banks in terms of assets arranged in alphabetic order.

---

[28] The Next Era in Banking (2011), CFO Publishing May.

Table 1.4 Largest World Banks in Terms of Assets[a]	
SL	**Bank Name**
1	Bank of America
2	Barclays PLC
3	BNP Paribas
4	CitiGroup
5	Credit Agricole Group
6	Deutsche Bank
7	Fannie Mae
8	Freddie Mae
9	HSBC Holdings
10	JPMorgan Chase
11	Mitsubishi UFJ Financial Group
12	Royal Bank of Scotland
13	UBS
14	Wells Fargo

[a]*Listed in alphabetic order.*

1.11 STRUCTURES OF FINANCIAL INSTITUTIONS

The financial system facilitates the intermediation of savers and investors. The primary role of any financial sector is to bring together savers and borrowers for the effective allocation of capital for productive purposes and to maximize returns to the savers. Financial institutions basically serve as financial intermediaries between the primary saving and borrowing sectors. This intermediary function transforms one form of security into another. For example, demand deposit can be transformed into long-term mortgage loans. The assets of all types of financial institutions consist of primary securities (claims against individuals and businesses) and liabilities (secondary securities that are claims against financial institutions).

Financial institutions can be segmented based on the types of products offered, customers served, and geographic locations. For example, financial institutions can be categorized into investment banks, commercial banks, and insurance services based on the products they offer. Financial institutions serve different types of customers, including individuals, small businesses, big corporation and government entities. Financial institutions can also be segmented on the basis of regions.

1.11.1 DIFFERENT TYPES OF FINANCIAL INSTITUTIONS

Basically, financial institutions can be classified into depository and nondepository institutions. Deposit-taking institutions consist of commercial banks, savings institutions, and credit unions. Savings institutions, also known as thrift institutions, consist of savings and loan associations (S&Ls) and savings banks. Commercial banks accept deposits and make commercial and other loans. They are profit-seeking institutions that perform many functions in a capitalist economy. Commercial banks are part of the payment system in clearing debts and credits and providing transfer services for their clients. S&Ls accept short-term deposits and make long-term mortgage loans. The primary purpose of a savings bank is to accept savings deposits. Credit unions accept deposits from credit union members and make loans to members. A main advantage of being a depository institution like a commercial bank, a savings bank, or a credit union is access to FDIC deposit insurance.

The nondepository institutions consist of finance companies, insurance institutions, pension funds, investment banks, and investment companies. The sources of funds for finance companies are securities sold to households and businesses, not deposits. These companies acquire funds in the market by issuing their own securities, in the form of notes and bonds. They also offer loans like depository institutions.

Insurance companies engage in the dual services of insurance protection and investment. The insurance offered consists of life insurance and casualty and property insurance. The primary source of funds for insurance companies are policy premiums. Insurance companies compete with deposit-taking institutions by providing loans and with investment companies in providing investment products. The main use of funds for insurance companies are the purchase of long-term government and corporate securities.

Pension funds collect pension contributions from employees and invest the funds in government and corporate securities. Traditionally pension funds aimed for long-term savings in long-term assets.

Investment banks offers a number of services that include underwriting, leveraged buyouts, Treasury funding, venture capital, M&A, merchant banking, and investment management.

Investment companies are those that pool together funds and invest in various types of investments. Investment companies are classified as open-end or closed-end mutual funds. Open-end funds accept new investments and redeem all investments. Close-end funds accept funds only at one time.

Among the financial sector, the banking industry is the most heavily regulated throughout the world. Regulation has emerged as a single critical factor to determine the products and services banks offer, the types of assets and liabilities that banks hold, and the legal structure of banking corporations.

1.11.2 BANKING STRUCTURES BASED ON LEGAL FRAMEWORKS

1.11.2.1 Bank holding companies and financial holding companies

A bank holding company (BHC) is an organization that controls more than 25% of the voting shares in one or more commercial bank. Holding companies are the parent organizations to the banks. Holding companies are further classified into one-bank holding companies and multibank holding companies. In the former structure, the parent holding company will control only one bank, whereas in the multibank structure the parent company owns more than one commercial bank subsidiary. More than 80% of US commercial banks are part of a BHC structure. All large banks with an asset size of more than $10 billion are owned by a BHC. The Bank Holding Company Act of 1956 establishes the term and conditions under which a company can own a bank in the United States. The Federal Reserve supervises all BHCs. Regulation Y deals with the Federal Reserve's primary regulation that implements the BHC Act and governs BHCs. The Federal Reserve has developed a rating system for BHCs, referred to as RFI/C, based on the parameters of risk management, financial condition, and impact.

The Gramm Leach Bliley Act of 1999 amended the BHC Act and permitted a BHC to become a financial holding company (FHC) and to engage in such nonbanking activities as mortgage banking, underwriting, insurance agency, and merchant banking services.

FHCs often have subsidiary structures. For example, BHCs such as Wells Fargo and Bank of America have both a commercial banking subsidiary as well as a finance company subsidiary. Both subsidiaries make loans to both consumers and commercial firms. But finance companies loans are considered to be more risky than commercial bank loans. Finance companies are largely funded with publicly issued debt, whereas banks largely rely on deposits. In 2008, Morgan Stanley and Goldman Sachs became holding companies. Merrill Lynch and Bear Stearns were acquired by BHCs.

1.11.2.2 C corporations and S corporations

Banks are categorized on the basis of tax treatment as C corporations and S corporations. The owners of C corporations are taxed twice, first at the corporate level under the corporation income tax and again at the shareholder level as individuals pay personal income tax on any dividends and capital gains. S corporations avoid this double taxation. With constraints on the number of shareholders, S corporations are generally smaller in terms of asset size than their C corporation counterparts.

1.11.3 DIFFERENT TYPES OF BANKING MODELS

1.11.3.1 Narrow banks and universal banks

In terms of alternative banking structures, banks can be classified as narrow banks and universal banks. The assets of narrow banks are short-term, highly liquid investments that have very low credit risk. Narrow banks provide demand deposits, participate in payment systems, and hold high-grade short-term instruments. Narrow banks are usually prohibited from making commercial, industrial, and mortgage loans. The nondepository institutions or finance companies within the holding structure would make these types of loans. There are also specialized banks such as S&Ls. Narrow banks are designed to reduce fragility and improve stability in the financial system.

Universal banks provide a broad range of financial products and services. They take the role of a "one-stop financial supermarket." Universal banks provide financial services in both financial and investment areas. As both a commercial bank and an investment bank, a universal bank offers services in retail, wholesale, and investment banking. In other words, universal banks offer credit loans, transactions, and financial analysis. The current trend is for these institutions to become big universal banks. Universal banks might own and operate nonfinancial firms or vice versa. They have much riskier assets in their balance sheets, and they engage in more risky activities than narrow banks.

Banking structures in most countries range between the two extremes of narrow and universal banking. Universal banks offer more scope for economies of scale. Research suggests that before the introduction of the Glass-Steagall Act, which forbade commercial banks from underwriting private securities, banks that engaged in a wide range of securities had lower variances in their cash flows, lower default probability, and higher capital ratios.[29] Over the years, the regulatory barriers were removed and many universal banks emerged. In some other countries, the distinction between commercial banks and investment banks is more blurred. In the United States, major universal banks include Citicorp and Bank of America.

1.11.3.2 Retail banks

Retail banks, also known as commercial banks, serve consumers and small business owners. These banking institutions have transactions directly with consumers rather than with corporations or other banks. Their focus is on mass-market products such as current and savings accounts, mortgages, auto loans, other types of loans, and credit cards. Retail banks consist of community and savings banks, community development banks, and postal saving banks.

---

[29] George G. Kaufman, Randall S. Kroszner, How Should Financial Institutions and Markets be Structured? Analysis and Options for Financial System Design, http://idbgroup.org/res/publications/pubfiles/pubWP-338.pdf.

1.11.3.3 Private banks

Private banks normally provide wealth management services to high-net-worth families and individuals. The services of private banks consist of providing protection and growth of assets and offering specialized financing solutions and retirement plans.

1.11.3.4 Offshore banks

Banks located in jurisdictions with low taxation and regulation are called offshore banks. Many offshore banks are private banks.

1.11.3.5 Investment banks

Investment banks are financial institutions that assist individuals and corporations in raising capital by underwriting and/or acting as the client's agent in the issuance of securities. Investment banks provide services related to financial markets, such as M&A and other ancillary services such as market making, trading of derivatives, fixed income instruments, foreign exchange, commodities, and equity securities. The biggest investment banks include JPMorgan, Bank of America, Merrill Lynch, Goldman Sachs, Morgan Stanley, and Credit Suisse. As a result of adoption of the Glass-Steagall Act of 1933, there is a distinction between pure investment banks and commercial banks in the United States.

1.11.3.6 Islamic banks

Islamic banking activities are consistent with the Islamic Principles (Sharias). Sharia, called *fiqh muamalat* (Islamic rules on transactions), prohibits the fixed or floating payment or acceptance of specific interest or fees (known as *riba* or usury) for loans of money. The rules and practices of *fiqh muamalat* came from the Quran and the Sunna, and other secondary sources of Islamic law such as opinions collectively agreed among Sharia scholars (*ijmā'*), analogy (*qiyās*), and personal reasoning (*ijtihad*).

1.11.4 CHANGING FINANCIAL STRUCTURES

The financial system has undergone changes due to the changing nature of the residential mortgage markets and the increased relevance of securitization. Until the 1980s, banks were the dominant holders of home mortgages, but now the sector is dominated by capital market-based institutions like Government Sponsored Enterprise (GSE) mortgage pools, private-label mortgage pools, and GSE holdings.

One of the striking features of the modern financial system is the increasingly close relationship between banking and capital markets. The current financial crisis saw the drying up of the liquidity in the financial system. Traditionally banks were the dominant suppliers of credit, but their role had been usurped by market-based institutions that were involved in the securitization process. Securitization refers to the practice of parceling and selling loans to investors. Securitization was basically intended to transfer credit risk to those better able to absorb losses but, contrary to the objectives, increased the fragility of the entire financial system by allowing banks and intermediaries to leverage up by buying one another's securities. In the recent financial crisis period, it was the market-based supply of credit that witnessed the maximum contraction.

New IT has transformed the landscape of the finance industry with the rapid growth of electronic finance. Electronic finance has blurred the boundaries between different financial institutions enabling new financial products and services. Electronic finance activities include all types of financial activities carried over networks like online banking, electronic trading, delivery of various financial products and services like insurance, mortgage and brokerage, electronic payments, and communication of financial

Assets sizes of major US financial institutions in billions of dollars — year 1990

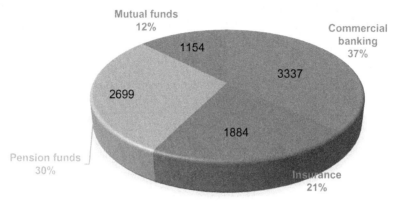

FIGURE 1.1

Changing asset sizes of major US financial institutions.

Data Source: Board of Governors of the Federal Reserve Statistical Release, Z.1 Flow of funds accounts of the US. March 2011.

Assets sizes of major US financial institutions in billions of dollars — year 2010

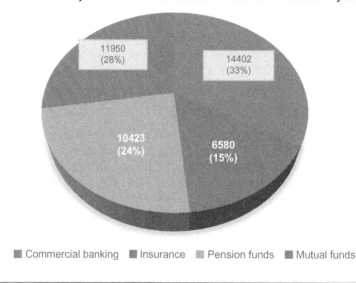

FIGURE 1.2

Assets of major US financial institutions in 2010.

information like SWIFT. Figures 1.1 and 1.2 highlight the asset sizes of US financial institutions in the years 1990 and 2010.

A comparative analysis of the asset sizes of major US financial institutions during the last two decades reveals the growing relative importance of the mutual fund industry. In 1990, mutual funds accounted for 12% of the asset size of major financial institutions in the United States. By 2010, mutual funds accounted for a 28% share. There has been an approximate tenfold increase in the size of the mutual fund industry in 2010 from a decade ago. The relative asset size contribution of other major financial sectors like commercial banking, insurance, and pension funds have shrunk compared to the past two decades. During the period 1990-2010, the assets of the US commercial banking industry and pension funds industry increased approximately four times while assets of the insurance industry increased three and a half times. Figure 1.3 shows the asset sizes of other US major financial institutions during the three-year period of 1990, 2000, and 2010. Table 1.5 lists the top holding banking corporations in the US in terms of assets.

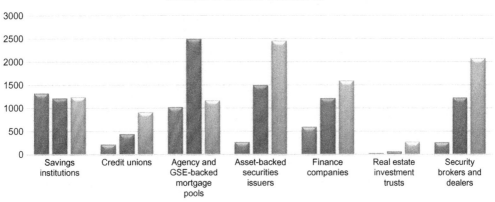

FIGURE 1.3

Asset sizes of other US major financial institutions.

Data Source: Federal Reserve Statistical Release.

Table 1.5 Top US Holding Corporations by Asset Size (December 31, 2012)	
Bank Name	**Consolidated Assets (in Billion Dollars)**
JPMorgan Chase	2359.141
Bank of America	2212.004
Citigroup	1864.66
Wells Fargo	1422.968
Goldman Sachs Group	938.77
Morgan Stanley	780.960
US Bancorp	353.855
Bank of New York Mellon	353.301
HSBC North America Holding	318.801
Capital One Financial	313.040
Source: National Information Center, Federal Reserve System.	

1.12 SHADOW BANKING SYSTEM

After the Great Depression of the 1930s, a series of legislation such as the Banking Act of 1933, the Securities Act of 1933, and the Securities Act of 1934 was introduced to reform the US financial system. The Glass-Steagall Act was designed to prohibit securities activities of commercial banks with the exception of government securities. Thus, the Glass-Steagall Act separated commercial and investment banking activities. The securities activities of commercial banks were perceived to be a major source of speculation and wrong practices that led to the Great Depression. Shadow banks were developed mainly after World War II in the United States.

Since the 1980s, the nature of financial intermediation changed with the rapid growth of the market-based financial system. With competition, regulation, and innovation, the traditional model of banking—which involved borrowing short, lending long, and holding onto loans as investments—had changed dramatically. The 1988 Basel Accord became the catalyst for the growth and development of credit risk transfer instruments. After the banking crisis triggered loan defaults by Latin American governments, the Basel Accord applied minimum capital requirements for banks and more capital protection for riskier assets. Banks responded by reconfiguring their assets using credit transfer instruments such as credit default swaps or CDOs.

The shadow banking system emerged as a network of shadow banks that created credit intermediation through a wide range of securitization and secured funding techniques such as asset-backed commercial paper (ABCP), ABS, CDOs, and repurchase agreements (repos). These funding techniques were disseminated across a wide range of investors with varying risk appetites. These investors include ABCPs, structured investment vehicles (SIVs), commercial banks, broker-dealers, hedge funds, asset managers, and insurance companies.

In the traditional banking system mode, savers transfer their savings to banks in the form of deposits, which are used by banks to provide loans to borrowers. In the shadow banking system, loans, leases, and mortgages are securitized and are converted into tradable instruments. Funding is also in the form of tradable instruments such as CP and repos. Instead of deposits, as is the case with commercial banks, savers hold money-market balances. The activities of investment banks and commercial banks overlap with the shadow banking system. For example, investment banks finance mortgages through off-balance sheet securitizations like ABCP and credit default swaps.

Unlike commercial banking, where credit intermediation occurs in a single step, the process of credit intermediation in shadow banking occurs in a sequential multistep process. These steps include (1) loan origination, (2) loan warehousing, (3) ABS issuance, (4) ABS warehousing, (5) ABS CDO issuance, (6) ABS intermediation, and (7) wholesale funding.

The process of loan origination is conducted by finance companies that are funded through CP and MTNs. The loans include auto loans, leases, and nonconforming mortgages. Loan warehousing is conducted by ABCP conduits. Then the pooling and structuring of loans into term ABS is conducted by broker-dealers' ABS syndicate desks. ABS warehousing is facilitated through trading books and funded through repurchase agreements (repos), total return swaps, or hybrid and repo/total return swap (TRS) conduits. The pooling and structuring of ABS into CDOs is again conducted by broker-dealers' ABS syndicate desks. The process of ABS intermediation is performed by limited-purpose finance companies (LPFCs), SIVs, securities arbitrage conduits, and credit hedge funds, which are funded in a variety of ways including ABCP, MTNs, bonds, and capital notes. The funding of all the above activities is done in the wholesale funding markets by providers such as regulated and unregulated money-market intermediaries like money market mutual funds (MMMFs). These providers fund shadow banks through short-term repo, CP, and ABCP instruments. Pension funds, insurance companies, and fixed income mutual funds also fund shadow banks by investing in long-term MTNs and bonds.

The government-sponsored shadow banking system was created with the establishment of the Federal Home Loan Banks (FHLB) system in the year 1932, Fannie Mae in 1938, and Freddie Mac in 1970.

Initially, CDOs were applied to corporate loans. Banks would pool the corporate loans on the books, which, in fact, are the assets of a CDO, and segregate the pool's underlying cash flows into tranches with varying risk profiles that form the liabilities of a CDO. Payouts from the pool were first paid to the least risky senior tranches, then mezzanine tranches, and finally to the riskiest equity tranches. The accumulation of massive amounts of senior CDO tranches in SIVs and accumulation of enormous securitization through conduits resulted in highly leveraged off-balance sheet vehicles and contributed to the financial collapse of the system during the economic crisis of 2008. SIVs and conduits relied on short-term financing in the ABCP market in long-term assets. In this context, shadow banks were exposed to the classic maturity mismatch that was typical of banks.

Assets in the shadow banking system in developed countries grew rapidly before the crisis, rising from $27 trillion in the year 2002 to $60 trillion in the year 2010. The United States has the largest shadow banking system, with assets of $24 trillion in the year 2010.[30]

1.13 **CONSOLIDATION IN THE FINANCIAL SERVICES INDUSTRY**

Consolidation has considerably changed the landscape of the financial sector. The major drivers encouraging consolidation are advances in IT, financial deregulation, globalization of financial markets, increasing shareholder activism for performance, and financial distress. Over the past two decades, many governments across the world have removed legal and regulatory barriers to financial industry consolidation. During the 1980s and 1990s, ownership linkages and alliances were increasingly formed between insurance companies and investment banks. Consolidation in the financial sector led to the concept of "one-stop shopping." Insurance firms merging with banking companies, often termed *bancassurance*, has become an important trend in Europe.

Over 10,000 financial firms were acquired in industrialized nations during the period 1990-2001.[31] During the past century's quarter period of 1980-2003, the number of US banking institutions decreased from about 16,000 to 8000. During that period, the share of industry assets held by the 10 largest commercial banking organizations ranked by assets rose from 22% to 46%, and the share of industry deposits held by the 10 largest banking organizations in terms of deposits rose from 19% to 41%.[32]

Four megamergers of the US banking industry took place in the year 1998: Citicorp/Travelers, BankAmerica/NationsBank, Bank One/First Chicago, and Northwest/Wells Fargo. The largest European banking groups (BNP Paribas in France, IntesaBsci in Italy, Banco Santander Central Hispano, Banco Bilbao Vizcaya Argentaria in Spain, and NatWest/Royal Bank of Scotland in the United Kingdom) were formed as a result of megamerger deals that happened between 1999 and 2002.

---

[30] Financial Stability Board (October, 2011), Shadow banking: Strengthening oversight and regulation.

[31] Ivan de Souza, Gerald Adolph, Alan Gemes, Roberto Marchi (2009), Perils of financial sector M&A: Seven steps to successful integration, Booz & Co. Report.

[32] Staff Studies Report (2005), Bank merger activity in the United States 1994-2004, Federal Reserve, US.

1.14 IMPORTANCE OF CORPORATE GOVERNANCE IN FINANCIAL INSTITUTIONS

Weak and ineffective governance of systemically important financial institutions (SIFIs) has often been cited as an important contributory factor that led to the massive failure of financial institutions during the global financial crisis.

Boards play a crucial role in corporate governance as they are the main stakeholders involved in the choice of business model, risk profile, and the quality of top management teams. US bank boards are increasingly assuming importance on account of the regulatory reforms enacted in the Gramm-Leach-Bliley Act. Nonexecutive directors (outside board members) can play a greater role in ensuring the transparency of financial institutions. The legislation has placed increased emphasis on governance mechanisms with broad enterprisewide oversight of FHCs. Supervisors and regulators are the major stakeholders who have the responsibility to ensure safety and the soundness and ethical operations of the financial systems. Regulators failed to understand the potential systemic impact of financial products like subprime mortgages during the global crisis. Effective risk governance requires robust and appropriate risk frameworks, systems, and processes. Supervisors have responsibilities related to risk control, fraud control, and conformance to laws and regulations. Values and culture are also a critical aspect of the corporate governance system. In short, governance architecture must be composed of organization structures, processes, people, skills, and values. An effective governance system should empower shareholders to elect an independent board of directors that is competent and has the power to challenge management for nonperformance. Major financial institutions should establish separate risk committees for overseeing the financial institution control networks. The boards need to have sufficient information provided to them to effectively oversee the firm's risks and controls. Financial institutions must also maintain robust risk IT that can create timely, comprehensive cross-product information on exposures in a wide geographic base. Information and disclosures often play an important role in mitigating fundamental market failures and governance failures.

1.15 SUMMARY

A financial sector consists of a set of institutions, instruments, and markets within the legal and regulatory framework. Financial institutions act as an intermediary between primary savings and borrowing sectors. Financial institutions have to face challenges to gain a competitive advantage in the context of rapid changes in technological, economic, social, demographic, and regulatory environments. The deep transformation the financial sector is witnessing can be attributed to a number of factors including technology innovations, deregulation, worldwide consolidation and restructuring, deregulation, and changing demographic profiles. IT is the primary force that keeps the financial industry dynamic.

The post-economic crisis period witnessed a series of policy reforms initiated by regulatory authorities. The global technology trends in the financial industry indicate the relevance of next-generation remote banking solutions, BI, and analytics in transaction monitoring. Financial institutions faces much complexity in the types of risks they have to manage. The trends indicate the growing significance of the emerging Asia market, consisting of China, India, and ASEAN countries, for growth opportunities in the financial services industry.

The global financial crisis had a profound impact on banks of all sizes. A new wave of regulations in banking are being shaped following the global financial crisis: legislation like Basel III changes, Dodd-Frank, and more concrete actions by the G-20.

Basically, financial institutions can be classified into depository and nondepository institutions. Deposit-taking institutions consist of commercial banks, savings institutions, and credit unions. Nondepository institutions consist of finance companies, insurance institutions, pension funds, investment banks, and investment companies. The nature of financial intermediation changed with the rapid growth of market-based financial systems like shadow banking systems. A shadow banking system is a network of shadow banks that create credit intermediation through a wide range of securitization and secured funding techniques. Consolidation has considerably changed the landscape of the financial sector. Corporate governance in financial institutions has become critical in the growth prospects of financial institutions.

QUESTIONS FOR DISCUSSION

1. What are the strategic drivers facilitating the growth of the financial services industry?
2. Explain how technological trends shape the future of financial institutions.
3. Discuss the major challenges faced by financial institutions.
4. Explain the impact of the global financial crisis on the financial system.
5. What are depository and nondepository institutions?
6. Explain the significance of shadow banking systems.

REFERENCES

http://www.thebankerdatabase.com.

www.doughroller.net/banking/largest-banks-in-the-world.

http://www.investopedia.com/terms/p/privatebanking.asp#ixzz1tSRNoB5G.

http://www.gtnews.com/feature/201.cfm, A Strategy for Future Growth: Banking Challenges and Trends.

Ten trends shaping banking, November 2010. Tellervision November 2010, p. 2.

CFO Publishing, May 2011. Moving forward in the wake of crisis, The Next Era in Banking.

Global Banking 2020, Foresights and Insights E&Y Knowledge@Wharton Report.

Roth, Randy, February 2012. 10 tech trends to follow in 2012. Community Banking Report/Focus on Technology, ABA Banking Journal, 32–36.

Global Banking Industry Outlook, Deloitte &Touche USA LLP Report. http://finntrack.co.uk/finance/us_fsi_banking.pdf.

http://media.wiley.com/product_data/excerpt/34/04713931/0471393134.pdf.

Credit crisis – the essentials, July 12, 2010. The New York Times. Retrieved August 30, 2010 from NYTimes.com. http://topics.nytimes.com/top/reference/timestopics/subjects/c/credit_crisis/index.html.

Dickey, R., May 12, 2010. Dissecting the global meltdown. The Philadelphia Inquirer. Retrieved August 13, 2010 from EBSCO Online Database Newspaper Source Plus. http://search.ebscohost.com/login.aspx?direct=true&db=n5h&AN=2W61193250991&site=ehost-live.

Kohn, J., Bryant, S., March 2010. Modeling the US housing bubble: an econometric analysis. Research in Business & Economics Journal 2, 1–14. Retrieved August 13, 2010 from EBSCO Online Database Business Source Complete, http://search.ebscohost.com/login.aspx?direct=te&db=bth&AN=49040213&site=ehost-live.

Auerbach, M.P., 2012. The global financial crisis of 2007-2010. Research Starters, Academic Topic Review.

Industry Profile, Global Banks, Reference Code: 0199-2013.

Vater, D., Cho, Y., Sidebottom, P., 2012. The Digital Challenge to Retail Banks. Bain &Company.

Smalley, A., January 2013. What tablet growth means for your 2013 banking services strategy. http://blogs.perficient.com/financialservices/2013/01/23/what-tablet-growth-means-for-your-2013-banking-services-strategy/.

Bain & Company Report, 2012. Customer loyalty in retail banking.

Will the power of mobile make bank branches disappear. http://jimmarous.blogspot.ae/2013/02/will-power-of-mobile-bank-branches-disappear.html?spref=tw.

Ryan, P., 2013. How many mobile users does Citi bank have? http://bankinnovation.net/2013/02/how-many-mobile-users-does-citibank-have/.

Fisher, J., 2013. Scalable architecture framework for digital payments. http://blogs.perficient.com/financialservices/2013/02/28/scalable-architecture-framework-for-digital-payments/.

http://www.forbes.com/sites/kellyclay/2013/02/05/amazon-announces-new-virtual-currency-for-kindle-fire/.

Beckstead, J.W., 1997. Strategies for Financial Institutions, UVA-F-0855. Darden Business Publishing, University of Virginia.

Kaufman, G.G., Kroszner, R.S. How Should Financial Institutions and Market be Structured? Analysis and Options for Financial System Design. http://idbgroup.org/res/publications/pubfiles/pubWP-338.pdf.

Kahn, C., Winton, A., 2004. Moral hazard and optimal subsidiary, structure for financial institutions. The Journal of Finance LIX (6).

Adrian, T., Pozsar, Z., Ashcraft, A., Boesky, H., July 2010. Shadow banking. Federal Reserve Bank of New York Staff Reports, No. 458.

De Rezende, F.C., 2011. The structure and evolution of the US financial system, 1945-1986. International Journal of Political Economy, Summer 40 (2), 21–44.

Pozsar, Z., Adrian, T., Ashcraft, A., Boesky, H., July 2010. Shadow banking. Federal Reserve Bank of New York Staff Reports, No. 458, Revised 2012.

Pozar, Z., 2008. The rise and fall of the Shadow banking system, Moody's economy.com. Regional Financial Review (July).

Adrian, T., Shin, H.S., July 2009. The shadow banking system: implications for financial regulation. Federal Reserve Bank of New York Staff Reports, No. 382.

Towards Effective Governance of Financial Institutions, Group of Thirty. http://www.ey.com/Publication/vwLUAssets.

REGULATORY ENVIRONMENT OF FINANCIAL INSTITUTIONS

2.1 INTRODUCTION

Financial regulations are the laws and rules that govern financial institutions. These rules are aimed at protecting investors and promoting financial stability. Sustaining confidence in the financial markets is one of the most important objectives of the financial regulatory bodies. A regulatory body is mandated to maintain confidence in the financial system, raise public awareness of the financial system, protect consumers, and prevent and reduce financial crimes.

Regulations have become imperative in the modern financial environment with the growth of multinational companies and the transnational nature of financial markets. Financial crises usually have a catastrophic impact on a global level. Anticipating risks and organizing for their control have become an integral part of risk regulation regimes.

During the economic crisis of 2007, liquidity dried up as financial systems failed to recognize specific shocks that generate contagion and other externalities. Excessive risk takings by organizations had in fact led to the crisis. Large organizations had difficulty detecting risk. In fact, 95% of business units at American International Group (AIG) were profitable when AIG collapsed. Although AIG had 125,000 employees, 80 of them were responsible for tanking the firm.[1]

The regulation of financial organizations primarily focuses on providing stability of the macroeconomic system, fair competition, and consumer protection. Stability is essential; the failure of a financial institution has a contagious effect that can lead to the disruption of the smooth functioning of financial markets. A fair competitive environment implies a level playing field for market entry. On account of the asymmetry of information between firms and consumers, concerns arise owing to the imbalance of power. In this context, consumers may not have the right information to protect themselves while choosing financial products and services.

Usually financial crises give major impetus to new regulations and increased supervision. For example, after the recent crisis, the financial world witnessed a plethora of new regulations.

---

[1]Jeremy Siegel's ideas (2009). Knowledge@Wharton. Lesson one: What really lies behind the financial crisis? January 21.

2.2 **UNIVERSAL FUNCTIONS OF REGULATORY AGENCIES**

The four major areas of focus in regulation and supervision are prudential regulation, systemic regulation and supervision, consumer protection, and competition. The basic functions performed by regulatory agencies are universal in nature and cover the following aspects:

- Prudential[2] regulation for safety and soundness of financial institutions
- Stability and integrity of payment systems
- Prudential supervision of financial institutions and payment systems
- Conduct of business regulations, which deal with rules of how firms conduct business with their customers
- Safety net arrangements such as deposit insurance
- Lender of last resorts performed by central banks
- Crisis resolution, handling of insolvent institutions
- Liquidity issues for systemic stability

Universally central banks are entrusted with the responsibility of maintaining systemic stability, stability of payment, liquidity assistance to markets, and solvent institutions. The emergence of financial conglomerates has challenged traditional demarcations between regulatory agencies. The three broad areas of finance businesses are banking, insurance, and securities trading. Good corporate governance is an important dimension in the regulation and supervision of financial firms. Supervisory agencies have a potentially powerful role in establishing good practice, rules, and requirements with respect to corporate governance in regulated institutions.

2.3 **HISTORY OF REGULATORY REFORMS**

In the early 1970s financial systems were characterized by controls on the prices or quantities of business conducted by financial institutions. These regulations were adopted in line with the social and economic policy objectives of government. In many countries, direct controls were used to allocate finance to preferred industries after the postwar period. One of the reasons for restrictions on market access and competition was the concern for financial stability. The protection of small savers was another important objective of controls on banks.[3] By the mid-1970s there was significant progress toward market-oriented forms of regulations, which led to the partial or complete liberalization of the following elements.

2.3.1 **INTEREST RATE CONTROLS**

During the early 1970s, controls on borrowing and lending rates were prevalent in many countries. These controls typically held both rates below their free market levels. By the 1990s, only a few countries retained these controls.

---

[2]Fundamental capital rule sets the minimum buffer to absorb potential losses.
[3]Edey, Malcolm and Hviding, Ketil (1995). An assessment of financial reform in OECD countries. OECD Economics Department, Working Paper, No. 154.

2.3.2 INVESTMENT RESTRICTIONS ON FINANCIAL INSTITUTIONS

There were quantitative investment restrictions on financial institutions in terms of requirements to hold government securities, credit allocation rules, and preferential lending to favored institutions and control on the total volume of credit expansion. By the 1990s, most of these restrictions were removed in many countries. The statutory holdings of government securities enabled governments to keep security yields artificially low.

2.3.3 LINE OF BUSINESS RESTRICTIONS AND REGULATIONS ON OWNERSHIP LINKAGES AMONG FINANCIAL INSTITUTIONS

Major restrictions, such as the separation of savings and loans and commercial banks, have been largely eliminated in many countries. The legal separation of various types of credit suppliers has also been removed in countries such as Japan. In the United States after the 1929 stock market crash and the nationwide commercial bank failures that caused the Great Depression, the Glass-Steagall Act was adopted (1933), which separated investment and commercial banking activities. Banks were given a year to decide on whether they would specialize in commercial or investment banking. It was stipulated that only 10% of a commercial bank's total income could stem from securities with an exception allowed for commercial banks to underwrite government-issued bonds. In November 1999, Congress repealed the Glass-Steagall Act with the establishment of the Gramm-Leach-Bliley Act, which allowed banking institutions to provide a broader range of services including underwriting and other deal-related activities within a new financial structure of a holding company. Bank branching restrictions were phased out in a number of European countries by the early 1990s.

2.3.4 RESTRICTIONS ON ENTRY OF FOREIGN FINANCIAL INSTITUTIONS

Cross-border access to foreign banks has been significantly liberalized throughout the world. International trade agreements in banking services such as the General Agreement on Trade in Services (GATS) have facilitated this process of liberalization. Other regional agreement forums such as the North American Free Trade Agreement (NAFTA) and the European Commission (EC) have also played a major role in this process. In the European Union (EU), an early condition for banks stipulated that one member state needed to seek approval from other member states on locations at which they intended to establish a branch; that restriction has been revoked. Restrictions on entry of foreign banks still exist in many developing countries, however.

2.3.5 CONTROLS ON INTERNATIONAL CAPITAL MOVEMENTS AND FOREIGN EXCHANGE TRANSACTIONS

Controls on international capital movements have been completely removed in OECD (Organisation for Economic Co-operation and Development) countries and many developing countries as well. Controls with respect to foreign ownership of real estate and foreign direct investment still exist in many countries. Important restrictions are still in place for international portfolio diversification by pension and insurance funds.

2.4 INSTITUTIONAL STRUCTURES OF REGULATIONS

With respect to the practice of supervision and the regulation of financial institutions, three models are used. In the three-pillar models there are separate supervisory frameworks for banking, insurance, and securities sectors. In the twin peak model, the two frameworks for analysis are based on prudential and business conduct. In the integrated model, all types of supervision are placed under one roof. The banking, securities, and insurance markets are becoming increasingly integrated. The financial-sector regulation system is moving toward a greater cross-sector integration of financial supervision.

Regulations of financial institutions differ from one country to another. Basically the financial regulatory bodies control the stock markets, bond markets, foreign exchange markets, and other sections of financial markets. Examples of financial regulatory bodies are the Federal Reserve Bank and the Securities Exchange Commission (SEC) of the United States, and the Financial Services Authority (FSA) in the United Kingdom.

In the United States, the main regulatory governing agencies are the Federal Financial Institutions Examination Council (FFIEC), the National Credit Union Administration (NCUA), the Office of Thrift Supervision, and the Federal Reserve. The US SEC established in 1934 is the enforcing authority of American securities laws. The Financial Industry Regulatory Authority (FINRA) is the US industry association that inspects and regulates broker dealers under the oversight of the SEC. BaFin is the German financial regulator that supervises financial institutions in Germany.

One of the radical changes in the UK institutional structure was the merger of all specialist regulatory and supervisory agencies into a single agency, the FSA, in 1997. Like the United Kingdom, Korea, Iceland, Denmark, and Latvia have also adopted the single-agency approach. The institutional structure is complicated in many countries such as the United States, Australia, and Canada because of the existence of both federal and regional/state agencies.

2.5 DRIVERS OF REGULATORY REFORMS

Financial innovation and rapid technological advancement have become catalysts in the process of reducing the decreasing effectiveness of traditional controls. The development of offshore financial centers, international financial centers, and off-balance sheet methods of financing also contributed to the need for regulatory reform. The competition with nonbanks for many services including consumer credit, business loans, and mortgages also provided the space for regulatory reform. The multilateral agreements liberalizing cross-border banking activities facilitated the regulatory reform process.

2.6 BENEFITS OF REGULATORY REFORM

Regulatory restrictions enabled financial corporations to adopt most efficient practices and develop new products and services. The regulatory reform process increased the role of competition, thereby resulting in improved efficiency by the liquidation or consolidation of relatively inefficient firms and by encouraging innovation.[4] The regulatory reform has led to an increase in efficiency and low costs in the financial services sector. The reform process has contributed to declining relative prices for financial services and considerable improvements in the quality and access to new financial instruments.

The most significant milestone in the modern trend of regulatory activity was the Basel Accord of July 1998, which required the major international banks in a group of 12 countries to attain an 8% ratio between capital and risk-weighted assets from 1992.

The new regulatory environment ought to result in new business models for financial institutions that satisfy the demand of all stakeholders including creditors, customers, and shareholders. The new regulatory environment has to usher in a global liquidity standard that could improve the quality of capital that banks must hold to support risk and strengthen the liquidity of the banking system.

NEED FOR BANKING REGULATION

Banks face the risk of bank runs and moral hazards. It can be stated that all banks have to operate in conditions of fractional liquidity reserves. Banks' liabilities are liquid deposits that are redeemable on demand whereas a majority of assets are illiquid loans. The risk of a bank run occurs if all depositors demand their money back, thereby creating a problem for even the most solvent bank. There is also the risk of excessive risk taking (moral hazard) in banking. In the mid-1990s, several countries in Southeast Asia experienced a severe currency and financial crisis, which resulted in the collapse of domestic asset markets, widespread bank failures, and bankruptcies. In his classic study, Paul Krugman suggests that a key common feature was that the liabilities of financial intermediaries in these countries were perceived as having an implicit government guarantee, but that the financial institutions themselves were essentially unregulated and therefore subject to severe moral hazard problems. In the presence of government guarantees and the complete absence of prudential regulation, banks had an incentive to continue lending, which led to the apparent improved financial position of the financial institutions due to the inflated value of assets. The widespread perceived risk that government would decide to abandon implicit debt guarantees led to the financial crisis, which saw plunging asset prices and the collapse of banks in the region. The provision of deposit insurance also gives rise to a moral hazard problem in banking.

Banking regulations are essential in the context of preventing systemic dangers of bank failures and maintaining stability and security of the payment system. There are basically two mechanisms by which the failure of banks could be distinguished. Consequent failure results when the failure of one bank leads to a decline in the value of assets sufficient to induce the failure of another bank. Contagion failure occurs when the failure of one bank leads to the failure of another fully solvent bank through some contagion mechanism. Many experts point out that in contagion failure there is an important asymmetry between the information available to banks and the information available to depositors and other outside investors. In extreme cases of information asymmetry, depositors cannot distinguish between solvent and insolvent banks. Disruptions in the payment systems carry the risk of creating significant hindrances in the aggregate economic activity. Payment problems are solved to a greater extent by the adoption of a real-time settlement system whereby the intraday buildup of credit exposures are prevented. In real-time trading systems, interbank payments occur at the same time as the exchange of the corresponding assets.

Sources:

1. Biggar, Darryl, Heimler, Alberto (June 2005). An increasing role for competition in the regulation of banks. International Competition Network, Antitrust Enforcement in regulated sectors, SubGroup 1.

2. Krugman, Paul, (1999). Balance Sheet, the Transfer Problem and Financial Crisis. http://web.mit.edu/krugman/www/FLOOD.pdf.

---

[4]OECD (1997). Competition, consumers, and regulatory reform. Chapter 3 in The OECD Report On Regulatory Reform: Thematic Studies; Regulatory Reform In The Financial Services Industry. The OECD Report on Regulatory Reform: Volume I.

ECONOMIC CRISIS: FAILURE OF THE REGULATORY SYSTEM

In fall 2008, the near collapse of the world financial system and the global credit crisis led to widespread calls for changes in the regulatory system. The lax monetary policy, particularly from 2002 to 2005, promoted easy credit and kept interest rates very low for a number of years. Many argue that the root cause of the crisis centered around the financial innovation associated with the securitization of subprime mortgages by banks and investment banks and repo finance of investment banks. Giant institutions including Fannie and Freddie had to commit growing resources to risky subprime loans to maintain government guarantees. In 2008, Fannie and Freddie held $1.6 trillion in exposures to toxic mortgages. Government restrictions on who can hold stocks in banks made effective corporate governance within large banks virtually impossible. The prudential regulation of commercial banks and investment banks proved to be ineffective basically because of risk measurement problems. Regulators used different measures to assess risk depending on the size of the bank. Complex measurement of risk relied on opinions of rating agencies or the internal assessments of banks. The trend was that rate agencies catered to buy-side participants consisting of banks, pension funds, mutual funds, and insurance companies that maintained subprime-related assets. When ratings were used for regulatory purposes, these buy-side participants rewarded agencies for underestimating risk. The "too big to fail" perception of big banks magnified the incentives to take excessive risks based on the expected protection from deposit insurance, Fed lending, and Treasury Fed bailouts. After the rescue of Bear Stearns, Lehman, Merrill Lynch, Morgan Stanley, and Goldman Sachs everyone expected bailout packages from the Fed Reserve or Treasury. After the collapse of Lehman Brothers, other crisis-ridden major investment banks immediately got themselves acquired or transformed themselves into banking holding companies to increase their access to government support.

The crisis highlighted the need for regulatory initiatives and reforms of resolution processes that discouraged too big to fail protection of large complex banks. The crisis also necessitated the need for a new macroprudential regulatory authority to gauge the overall risk in the financial system in the context of dynamic capital and liquidity requirements. There is also the need for new efficient rules governing OTC clearings, disclosure standards for OTC market participants, and market-based measures of risks.

Source: Calorimis, Charles W. Banking Regulatory reform in the wake of crisis. http://siteresources.worldbank.org/INTFR/Resources/Charles_Calomiris.pdf.

2.7 ROLE OF STATE IN REGULATORY SYSTEM

The crucial role of state in regulation and supervision of financial systems is a well-established fact. Globally state governments are responsible for different aspects such as providing strong prudential supervision, ensuring healthy competition, and enhancing financial infrastructure. Strong institutional frameworks are necessary to promote financial stability. Good regulatory practices can improve the efficiency of the financial system.

The failure of one bank can cause a ripple effect on other banks. The depositors and creditors of other banks become panicky and cause stress for healthy financial institutions. This behavioral phenomena is called "contagion," where weakness in one bank can cause stress for other healthy financial institutions, which triggers financial crisis. This is a classic case of bank run. Regulation and supervision by state can limit risk taking by large financial institutions to avoid potential externalities.

During the recent global financial crisis, countries have adopted a number of strategies to revitalize their financial and real sectors. When private banks curtailed their lending activities because of the crisis, state-owned banks stepped up financing to the private sector. Many countries relied on the use of credit guarantee programs. Other countries used a number of unconventional monetary and fiscal measures to prop up credit markets. In Brazil, state-owned banks were authorized to acquire equity stakes from private banks and loan portfolios from financial institutions with liquidity problems. In China, state-owned banks injected credit to specific sectors to promote growth. In Mexico, the state-owned development banks extended credit to large companies. In Germany, state-owned banks increased lending to big companies with short-term liquidity problems. In Finland, the government raised the limits on domestic and export financing for the country's state-owned bank to boost lending to small and medium enterprises.

When the crisis set in, states played a critical role by offering massive rescue packages and monetary measures to avert even worse scenarios. At the global level, the G-20 mandated the Financial Stability Board (FSB) to promote coordinated development and implementation of effective regulatory, supervisory, and financial sector policies. The Basel Committee on Banking Supervision (BCBS) prepared new capital and liquidity requirements for banks under the framework of Basel III.

2.8 FINANCIAL CRISIS: POOR GOVERNANCE OF FINANCIAL REGULATION

The global crisis that led to the collapse of the global financial system can be partially attributed to the systemic failure of financial regulation. In other words, there is a core institutional weakness with the governance of financial regulation.

One classical example is the role of a credit rating agency, which plays a critical role in the financial system. Until the late 1970s, credit rating agencies were not of much significance. In 1975, the US SEC created the Nationally Recognized Statistical Organization (NRSRO). From then on, the SEC relied on NRSRO's credit risk assessment to establish capital requirements on SEC-regulated financial institutions. Worldwide, financial institutions and regulators relied heavily on the ratings provided by NRSRO. Issuers of securities were compelled to purchase these ratings to be successful in selling in the market. The role of credit rating agencies shifted from selling their credit ratings to subscribers to selling their ratings to the issuers of securities. Ratings determine the demand and pricing of securities. Hence issuers attempted to get higher ratings by paying more to rating agencies. The late 1990s witnessed explosive growth of securitized and structured financial products, which led to huge profits for the credit rating business. Credit rating agencies and banks obtained huge fees associated with processing these securities. NRSROs established ancillary consulting services to process securitized instruments. The boom in securitization led credit rating agencies to inflate their ratings for huge profits. The regulatory agencies that relied on these ratings continued to support these rating agencies.

The explosive growth of the credit default swap (CDS) in the derivative market can also be considered as a failure of the governance system of financial regulations. CDSs are financial derivatives that are transacted in unregulated over-the-counter (OTC) markets. Banks use CDSs to reduce credit risk exposure and the amount of capital held against potential losses. By means of purchasing a CDS on a loan, banks can reduce the credit risk if the loan defaults because the counterparty to the CDS will compensate the bank for the loss. With these assumptions the regulator typically allows the bank to reallocate capital to high-risk assets with high expected returns. In 1996, the Federal Reserve allowed banks to use CDSs to reduce capital reserves. Consider the case of a bank that has purchased full CDS protection from insurance giant AIG on collateralized debt obligations (CDOs), which are in fact subprime loans in nature. The problems stem from the fact that these CDOs are treated as AAA securities for capital regulatory purposes because AIG had AAA ratings from a SEC-approved credit rating agency.[5]

---

[5] Tett, G. (2009). Fool's Gold. New York, NY: Free Press International Review of Finance © International Review of Finance Ltd.; Ross Levine (2012). The governance of financial regulation: reform lessons from the recent crisis. *International Review of Finance* 12 (1), 39–56.

Banks used CDSs to reduce capital and invest in riskier assets, which offered higher returns. By 2007, the largest US commercial banks had purchased $7.9 trillion in CDS protection and the overall CDS market had a notional value of $62 trillion.[6] Allowing banks to reduce their capital through CDSs led to the dangerous situation that affected the banking system. Bank counterparties developed huge exposures to CDS risk. In 2007, AIG had a notional exposure of about $500 billion to CDSs with a capital base of just $100 billion to cover all its traditional insurance activities as well as its financial derivative businesses.[7]

2.9 INITIATIVES FOR STABILITY OF THE FINANCIAL SYSTEM

The Financial Stability Forum (FSF) was established in 1999 to promote financial stability through information exchange and international cooperation in financial supervision and surveillance. The FSF consists of finance ministries, central banks, regulators, supervisory authorities from major financial centers, the IMF, the World Bank, the Bank for International Settlements (BIS), the OECD, and the European Central Bank. In 2007, FSF established a senior working group (WG) to examine the causes and weakness of the economic crisis and to set out recommendations. The Work Stream on capital pro-cyclicality is developing jointly with BCBS recommendations to address the pro-cyclicality of the regulatory capital framework. The Work Stream on the pro-cyclicality of bank provisioning practices is examining changes in accounting standards to promote more effective methods through cycle provisioning. The Work Stream on the role of valuation and leverage in pro-cyclicality along with the Committee on the Global Financial System (CGFS) focuses on setting policy options to reduce the buildup of leverage and maturity mismatches in the system. The Work Stream is involved in developing principles for sound compensation practices in large financial institutions.

The G-20 grouping was established in 1999 after the financial crisis in East Asia with the objective of creating a permanent forum to broaden the dialogue on issues of global financial stability between advanced and major emerging economies. The G-20 consists of 19 systemically important countries[8] and the EU, which together account for two thirds of the world population. There are four WGs within G-20. The WGI focuses at mitigating pro-cyclicality; this includes strengthening OTC infrastructure, transparency in valuation and accounting, risk management, and compensation system. The work of WG2 focuses on issues of governance, supervisory standards, crisis management, resolution regimes, issues related to money laundering, tax havens, and offshore centers. WG3 focuses on reforming World Bank and multilateral development banks.

2.10 REGULATION OF THE BANKING SYSTEM

The roots of banking regulation can be traced from the microeconomic concerns of the ability of stakeholders consisting of bank creditors and depositors to monitor the risks as well as the concerns of both

---

[6] Barth, J.R., Li, T., Lu, W., Phumiwasana, T., Yago, G. (2009). The rise and Fall of the US mortgage and credit markets. Hoboken, NJ: Wiley & Sons, Inc.

[7] Ross Levine (2012). The governance of financial regulation: reform lessons from the recent crisis. International Review of Finance 12 (1), 39–56.

[8] Argentina, Australia, Brazil, Canada, China, France, Germany, India, Indonesia, Italy, Japan, Mexico, Russia, Saudi Arabia, South Africa, South Korea, Turkey, the United Kingdom, and the United States of America.

micro- and macroeconomic nature over the stability of the banking system in times of crisis. In addition to statutory and administrative regulatory provisions, a respective government's discretionary powers were also utilized for bailing out sick banks, bank merger decisions, as well as for the consolidation of state ownerships in banks. The most important rationale for regulating the banking sector is to address concerns over the stability of the financial sector, financial institutions, and payment systems.

The banking sector has been subjected to a series of regulatory provisions over the decades, as listed below:

- Restrictions on new entry and branches
- Restrictions on pricing such as interest rate controls and controls on prices or fees
- Line of business restrictions
- Regulation on ownership linkages among financial institutions
- Restrictions on the portfolio of assets that a bank can hold such as requirements to hold certain types of securities, not to hold certain types of securities or requirements, and requirements not to hold the control of nonfinancial companies
- Compulsory deposit insurance/informal deposit insurance for the purpose of bailing out depositors in the event of insolvency
- Capital adequacy requirement
- Reserve requirement
- Directed credit to priority sectors/enterprises
- Financial bailout packages in the form of "lender of last resort" in times of crisis
- Consolidation regulations involving mergers and acquisitions
- Regulations with respect to payment system

Over time, structural regulation has shifted to more market-oriented forms of regulation. As a result, the allocation of credit and the improvement of financial services have become competitive in nature. Typically, micro- and macroprudential goals reinforce each other. Strengthening capital requirements will make individual banks safer and the broader financial system more resilient. The costs of macroprudential policies include higher credit costs, lower credit availability, and slow economic growth. Modern banking crises are often attributed to poorly designed banking system safety nets. In the 1980s, Argentina and Chile invested up to 55% and 42% of their GDP, respectively, in banking system bailouts.

2.10.1 INSTRUMENTS OF BANK REGULATION

2.10.1.1 Deposit insurance

Deposit insurance is a significant aspect of the financial safety net system basically intended to promote financial stability. Deposit insurance is a guarantee that a depositor's debt with a bank will be honored in the event of bankruptcy. The insurance schemes vary with respect to fee structure, degree of coverage, funding provisions, public/private participation, and compulsory versus voluntary participation. Explicit deposit insurance measures are implemented in many countries to protect bank depositors from losses partially or fully due to the inability of a bank to pay its debt. The United States was the first country to officially enact deposit insurance to protect depositors from losses by insolvent banks. In 1933, the Glass-Steagall Act established the Federal Deposit Insurance Corporation (FDIC) to insure deposits at commercial banks. The effect of deposit insurance on the incentives of the bank depends on the nature of the insurance contract. Ironically, financial economists and economic historians regard deposit insurance and safety net policies as the primary reason for the unprecedented financial instability that led to the global recession of 2008.

2.10.1.2 Capital adequacy requirements

The Capital Adequacy requirement stipulates the maintenance of a minimum ratio between capital and an overall balance sheet magnitude such as total assets or liability or some weighted measure of risk assets. The different Basel frameworks have suggested quantitative measures for capital adequacy requirements.

2.10.1.3 Glass-Steagall Act

The Glass-Steagall Act was enacted to prevent a repeat of the mass bank collapses during the Great Depression. Commercial banks were barred from underwriting and distributing the securities of private companies. Commercial banks were not allowed to affiliate with brokerage business and underwriting insurance. Glass-Steagall created the FDIC, providing government protection for depositors whose funds were secured from the activities of the securities businesses. Many conditions were imposed on the banks that received protection. However, gradually, the restrictions were eased and finally the law was repealed by the Gramm-Leach-Biley Act in 1999.

2.11 BASEL REFORMS

One of the key objectives of BIS is to maintain monetary and financial stability. The various standing committees at the BIS-supported central banks and authorities by providing background analysis and policy recommendations with respect to financial stability. The main committees are:

- Basel Committee on Banking Supervision
- Committee on the Global Financial System
- Committee on Payment and Settlement Systems
- Markets Committee
- Central Bank
- Governance Forum
- Irving Fisher Committee on Central Bank Statistics

2.11.1 BASEL COMMITTEE ON BANKING SUPERVISION

The BCBS is a forum for regular cooperation on banking supervisory matters. The focus of the committee is on improving the quality of banking supervision worldwide. The committee prepared international standards on capital adequacy, the core principles for effective banking supervision, and the agreement on cross-border banking supervision. The Basel Committee of Banking Supervision was established in 1974 at the BIS. The initial committee consisted of members of the Group of Ten (G-10) plus Luxembourg and Spain, each represented by their central bank and the authority responsible for domestic banking supervision. Now the committee consists of members from Argentina, Australia, Belgium, Brazil, Canada, China, France, Germany, Hong Kong SAR, India, Indonesia, Italy, Japan, Korea, Luxembourg, Mexico, the Netherlands, Russia, Saudi Arabia, Singapore, South

Africa, Spain, Sweden, Switzerland, Turkey, the United Kingdom, and the United States. The committee circulates to supervisors throughout the world both published and unpublished papers providing guidance on banking supervisory authorities. The Committee's Secretariat is located at the BIS in Basel, Switzerland. The original mandate of the Committee was to deal with the regulatory challenge posed by the increasing internationalization of banking in the 1970s.

The Basel Committee consists of four main subcommittees. The Standards Implementation Group (SIG) focuses on the implementation of the Basel Committee guidance and standards. The SIG group promotes consistency in the implementation of the Basel II framework. The Operational Risk Subgroup advises banks on issues related to implementation of advanced measurement approaches for operational risk. The Task Force on Colleges develops guidelines that enhance the effectiveness in the use and functioning of supervisory colleges and supervisors in implementing such guidance in practice. The Task Force on Remuneration promotes the adoption of sound remuneration practices consistent with the FSB's Principles for Sound Compensation Practices. The Standards Monitoring Procedures Task Force assists the implementation of Basel Committee standards by developing tools and procedures to provide consistency and efficiency in standards monitoring and implementation.

The Policy Development Group (PDG) identifies and reviews emerging supervisory issues and develops policies to promote a sound banking system with high supervisory standards. The seven WGs under the PDG consist of the Risk Management and Modeling Group (RMMG), the Research Task Force (RTF), the WG on Liquidity, the Definition of Capital Subgroup, the Capital Monitoring Group, the Trading Book Group (TBG), and the Cross-border Bank Resolution Group (CBRG). The RMMG assesses industry risk-management practices and develops supervisory guidance to promote enhanced risk-management practices. The RTF serves as a forum to exchange information and engage in research projects on supervisory and financial stability issues. The TBG engages in the review of the trading book capital framework. It also addresses the implementation issues related to the revisions to the Basel II market risks. The WG on Liquidity sets the global standards for liquidity risk management and supervision. The group also promotes steps for liquidity approaches for cross-border banks. The Definition of Capital Subgroup reviews issues related to the quality, consistency, and transparency of capital with a particular focus on Tier 1 capital. The Capital Monitoring Group of the Basel Committee shares national experiences in monitoring capital requirements. The CBRG compares the national policies, legal frameworks, and allocation of responsibilities for the resolution of banks with significant cross-border operations.

The Accounting Task Force (ATF) develops prudent reporting guidelines through international accounting and auditing standards to promote sound risk management at banks. The Audit Subgroup promotes reliable financial information by exploring key audit issues from a banking supervisory perspective. It focuses on responding to international audit standards-setting proposals, other issuances of the International Auditing and Assurance Standards Board and the International Ethics Standards Board for Accountants, and audit quality issues.

The Basel Consultative Group (BCG) is the forum for continuous engagement with supervisors around the world on banking supervisory issues.

2.11.2 COMMITTEE ON GLOBAL FINANCIAL SYSTEM

Formerly this committee was known as the Euro Currency Standing Committee, which focused on the monetary policy implications of offshore deposit and lending markets. The committee focuses on identifying and assessing potential sources of stress in global financial markets and how to maintain the stability of markets. This committee also oversees the collection of the BIS international banking and financial statistics.

2.11.3 COMMITTEE ON PAYMENT AND SETTLEMENTS SYSTEMS

This committee aims to strengthen the financial market infrastructure through promoting sound and efficient payment, clearing and settlement systems. It is the standard-setting body for payment, clearing and securities settlement systems. It also serves as a forum for central banks to monitor and analyze issues in domestic payment, clearing and settlement systems as well as in cross-border and multicurrency settlement schemes. The committee publishes various reports covering securities settlement systems, settlement mechanisms for foreign exchange transactions clearing arrangements for exchange-traded and OTC derivatives, and retail payment instruments.

2.11.4 MARKETS COMMITTEE

The Markets Committee was formerly known as the Committee on Gold and Foreign Exchange. The committee discusses financial market developments as well as longer-term structural trends that have the implications for financial market functioning and central bank operations.

2.11.5 CENTRAL BANK GOVERNANCE FORUM

This forum of BIS aims to foster good governance of central banks as public policy institutions. It compiles, analyzes, and disseminates among central banks a wide variety of information on governance and organizational arrangements.

2.11.6 IRVING FISHER COMMITTEE ON CENTRAL BANK STATISTICS

This is a forum within BIS of central bank economists and statisticians who periodically discuss statistical issues of interest to central banks.

2.11.7 BASEL I CAPITAL ACCORD

The Basel I Capital Accord was formulated in 1988 primarily to strengthen the stability of the international banking system. The objective of the accord was also to set up a fair and consistent international banking system to decrease competitive inequality among international banks. Basel I defined bank capital and the bank capital ratio. Basel I defined capital based on two-tier systems.

2.11.7.1 Tier 1 (core capital)
Tier 1 capital included stock issues (or shareholders' equity) and declared reserves such as loan loss reserves set aside to cushion future losses or for smoothing out income variations.

2.11.7.2 Tier 2 (supplementary capital)
Tier 2 capital included all other capital such as gains on investment assets, long-term debt with maturity greater than five years, and hidden reserves (excess allowance for losses on loans and leases).

Credit risk was defined as the risk weighted asset (RWA) of the bank, which comprises the bank's assets weighted in relation to their relative credit risk levels. According to Basel I, the total capital should represent at least 8% of the bank's credit (RWA). In addition, the Basel agreement stated three types of credit risks:

1. The on-balance sheet risk
2. The trading off-balance sheet risk consisting of derivatives, namely interest rates, currency derivatives, equity derivatives, and commodities
3. The nontrading off-balance sheet risks, including general guarantees such as forward purchase of assets or transaction-related debt assets

Market risk encompasses general market risk and specific risk. There are four types of economic variables that generate market risk. These include interest rates, foreign exchanges, equities, and commodities. The market risk is calculated either with the standardized Basel model or with internal value at risk (VaR) models of banks. These internal models can only be used by large banks that satisfy the qualitative and quantitative standards imposed by the Basel agreement. Table 2.1 gives risk weights of balance sheet assets based on Basel classification.

The Basel I framework was criticized on many grounds. One of the main criticisms was that there was limited differentiation of credit risk. The assumption that a minimum 8% capital ratio is sufficient to protect banks from failure does not take into account the changing nature of default risk. There was also no recognition of the term structure of credit risk. The capital charges were set at the same level regardless of the maturity of a credit exposure. The capital requirements ignored the different levels of risk associated with different currencies and macroeconomic risks. Basel I was becoming increasingly out of line with the more sophisticated measures of capital used by major banks. All of these limitations led to the creation of a new Basel Capital Accord known as Basel II, which added operational risk and defined new calculations of credit risk.

2.11.8 **BASEL II FRAMEWORK**

The Basel II framework was designed to establish minimum levels of capital for internationally active banks. As under the 1988 Accord, national authorities are free to adopt arrangements that set higher levels of minimum capital. The Basel II framework consists of Part 1—the scope of application and three pillars. The first pillar is minimum capital requirements, the second one is supervisory review process, and the third pillar is market discipline. Figure 2.1 provides the framework for Basel II.

Table 2.1   Basel's Classification of Risk Weights of On-Balance Sheet Assets

Risk Weight (%)	Asset Class
0	Cash and gold held in the bank
20	Claims on OECD banks, securities issued by US government agencies, claims on municipalities
50	Residential mortgages
100	All other claims such as corporate bonds, less developed countries' debt, claims on non-OECD banks, equities, real estate, plant, and equipment

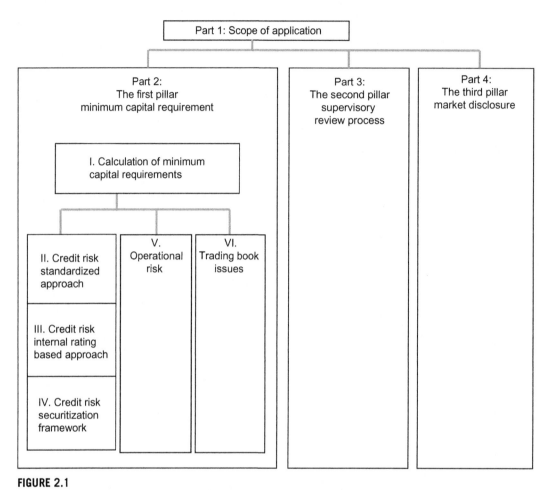

FIGURE 2.1

Basel II framework.

Source: Basel Report, Bank for International Settlements.

2.11.8.1 Part 1—Scope of application

This framework was applied on a consolidated basis to internationally active banks so that the framework captures the risk of the whole banking group. The framework adopted the protection of depositors as one of the principal objectives of supervision. Hence, it is essential to ensure that capital recognized in capital adequacy measures is readily available for depositors. Accordingly, supervisors should test that individual banks are adequately capitalized on a standalone basis.

Significant minority investments in banking, securities, and other financial entities where control does not exist were excluded from the banking group's capital by deduction of the equity and other regulatory investments. The bank that owns an insurance subsidiary bears the full entrepreneurial risks of the subsidiary and should recognize on a groupwide basis the risks included in the whole group. Banks ought to disclose the national regulatory approach used with respect to the insurance entities in determining their reported capital positions. Significant minority and majority investments in commercial entities that exceed certain materiality levels will be deducted from banks' capital.

2.11.8.2 Part 2—First pillar: Minimum capital requirements

Part 2 of the Basel II framework deals with the calculation of the total minimum capital requirements for credit, market, and operational risk. The capital ratio is calculated using the definition of regulatory capital and risk-weighted assets. The total capital ratio must be no lower than 8%. Tier 2 capital is limited to 100% of Tier 1 capital. The total risk-weighted assets are determined by multiplying the capital requirements for market risk and operational risk by 12.5 (i.e., the reciprocal of the minimum capital ratio of 8%) and adding the resulting figures to the sum of the risk-weighted assets for credit risk. The Basel committee recommends the application of a scaling factor to maintain the aggregate level of minimum capital requirements.

2.11.8.2.1 Constituents of capital

The core capital is the basic equity or Tier 1.The main emphasis should be placed on equity capital and disclosed reserves. Equity capital consists of issued and fully paid ordinary shares or common stock and noncumulative perpetual preferred (but excluding cumulative preferred stock). Equity capital is the only element common to all countries' banking systems and is the basis on which most market judgments of capital adequacy are made.

The capital for supervisory purposes has to be defined in two tiers in a way that will have the effect of requiring at least 50% of a bank's capital base to consist of a core element comprised of equity capital and published reserves from post-tax retained earnings (Tier 1). The other elements of capital (supplementary capital) will be admitted into Tier 2, limited to 100% of Tier 1.

The supplementary capital consists of undisclosed reserves, revaluation reserves, general provisions, general loan loss reserves, and hybrid debt capital instruments. The principal form of eligible capital to cover market risks consists of Tier 1 capital (equity and retained earnings) and Tier 2 capital (supplementary capital). At the discretion of the National Authority, banks can employ a third tier of capital (Tier 3) consisting of short-term subordinated debt for supporting market risks. Tier 3 capital will have to be limited to 250% of a bank's Tier 1 capital.

For the purpose of calculating Tier 1 capital, the deductions would be goodwill, increase in equity capital from securitization exposure, investments in subsidiaries engaged in banking, and financial activities that are not consolidated in national systems.

2.11.8.2.2 Capital requirements for credit risk

The two broad methodologies for calculation of capital requirements for credit risk are the standardized approach and internal ratings approach. In the standardized approach, the Basel committee describes the details of risk weights in the standardized approach in terms of (1) risk weights by types of claims, (2) the recognition process for and eligibility criteria of external credit assessment institutions (ECAIs), and (3) implementation considerations. Different risk weights for claims are applied to sovereign, on-central government public-sector entities, multilateral development banks, banks, security firms, and corporate and commercial real estate. The alternative internal ratings-based (IRB) approach introduced by the Basel Committee suggests that subject to certain minimum conditions and disclosure requirements, banks that have received supervisory approval to use the internal ratings approach may rely on their own internal estimates of risk components to determine the capital requirement for a given exposure. The risk components include measures of the probability of default (PD), loss given default (LGD), the exposure at default (EAD), and effective maturity (M).

2.11.8.2.3 Operational risk

The Basel Committee defines operational risk as the risk of loss resulting from inadequate or failed internal processes, people, and systems or from external events. This definition includes legal risk, but excludes strategic and reputational risk. Basel permits the choice of four methodologies for the computation of capital requirement for operational risk.

1. Basic indicator approach
2. Standardized approach
3. Alternative standardized approach
4. Advanced measurement approach

According to the basic indicator approach, banks must hold capital for operational risk equal to the average over the previous three years of a fixed percentage of positive annual gross income. In terms of complexity, the standardized approach falls between the basic indicator and the advancement approaches. In a standardized approach, the capital charge for each business line is calculated by multiplying gross income by a beta factor assigned to that business line. Beta denotes the proxy for the industrywide relationship between operational risk loss experienced for a given business line and aggregate level of gross income for that business line. In the alternative standardized approach, the outstanding loans and advances replace gross income as an indicator for exposure in retail and commercial banking. According to the advanced measurement approach, the banks are allowed to develop their own empirical model to quantify required capital for operational risk.

2.11.8.2.4 Market risk

The final input to the minimum capital requirements under the first pillar is market risk. Market risk refers to risk resulting from movements in the market, in particular, changes in interest rates, foreign exchange rates, and equity and commodity prices. Market risk is often linked to other forms of financial risk such as credit and market liquidity risks. In another perspective, market risk covers various risks run by a bank's trading books. A trading book consists of positions in financial instruments and commodities held either with trading intent or to hedge other elements of the trading book.

The market risk is measured using the standardized approach and internal models.

2.11.8.2.5 Standardized approach

In the standardized approach for market risk involving interest rate, equity positions, and derivatives, the minimum capital requirement is expressed in terms of two separately calculated charges. The capital charge for specific risk is modeled to protect against an adverse movement in the price of an individual security due to factors related to the individual issuer. The capital charge for general market risk is designed to measure the risk of loss arising from the changes in market. In the case of foreign exchange, the methods involved include measuring the exposure in a single currency position and measuring the risks inherent in a bank's mix of long and short positions in different currencies. The methodology for market risks in commodities consists of (1) measuring the directional risk by capturing the exposure from changes in spot prices arising from net open positions, (2) measuring the forward gap and interest rate risk by capturing the exposure to changes in forward prices arising from maturity mismatches, and (3) measuring the basis risk to capture the exposure to changes in the price relationships between two similar commodities.

2.11.8.2.6 Internal models

VaR is the basic internal model used to measure market risk. Banks will follow the minimum standards for the purpose of calculating their capital charge though flexibility exists in devising the exact nature of the models. VaR must be computed on a daily basis. For calculating VaR, a 99th percentile, one tailed confidence interval and instantaneous price shock equivalent to a 10-day movement in prices has to be used. The historical observation period is a minimum length of one year. Banks are required to update their data set once every three months.

2.11.8.3 Part 3—Second pillar: Supervisory review process

This section discusses the key principles of supervisory review, risk management guidance, and supervisory transparency and accountability produced by the committee with respect to banking risks. This includes guidance relating to, among other things, the treatment of interest rate risk in the banking book, credit risk (stress testing, definition of default, residual risk, and credit concentration risk), operational risk, enhanced cross-border communication and cooperation, and securitization.

The supervisory review process of the framework is intended not only to ensure that banks have adequate capital to support all the risks in their business, but also to encourage banks to develop and use better risk-management techniques in monitoring and managing their risks. The supervisory review process recognizes the responsibility of bank management to develop an internal capital assessment process and set capital targets that are commensurate with the bank's risk profile and control environment. Pillar 2 takes into account such factors as interest rate risk in the banking book, business and strategic risk, and factors external to the bank (e.g., business-cycle effects), which are not covered by Pillar Process 1.

The four key principles of the supervisory review are as follows:[9]

Principle 1: Banks should have a process for assessing their overall capital adequacy in relation to their risk profile and a strategy for maintaining their capital levels. Rigorous, forward-looking stress testing that identifies possible events or changes in market conditions that could adversely impact the bank should be performed.

The five main features of a rigorous process are

1. Board and senior management oversight
2. Sound capital assessment
3. Comprehensive assessment of risks
4. Monitoring and reporting
5. Internal control review

Principle 2: Supervisors should review and evaluate banks' internal capital adequacy assessments and strategies, as well as their ability to monitor and ensure their compliance with regulatory capital ratios.

---

[9]BCBS (November 2005). International Convergence of Capital Measurement and Capital Standards: A Revised Framework.

Principle 3: Supervisors should expect banks to operate above the minimum regulatory capital ratios and should have the ability to require banks to hold capital in excess of the minimum.

Principle 4: Supervisors should seek to intervene at an early stage to prevent capital from falling below the minimum levels required to support the risk characteristics of a particular bank and should require rapid remedial action if capital is not maintained or restored.

The committee has also identified specific issues to be addressed under the supervisory review process under the categories of interest rate risk in the banking book, credit risk, and operational market risk. Other aspects of the supervisory process involve supervisory transparency and accountability, as well as enhanced cross-border communication.

2.11.8.4 Part 4—Third pillar: Market disclosure

Market discipline is the term that describes the monitoring and control of a bank's management by outside stakeholders to ensure that the bank acts in their best interests. The committee aims to encourage market discipline by developing a set of disclosure requirements that will allow market participants to assess key pieces of information on the scope of application, capital, risk exposures, risk assessment processes, and hence the capital adequacy of the institution.

For the market discipline mechanism to operate effectively, it is imperative that stakeholders receive frequent, relevant, and meaningful information regarding the risk-taking and operations of banks, and for the disclosure of such information to be mandatory.

The disclosures in Pillar 3 are required on a semiannual basis except for certain general qualitative disclosures that can be disclosed annually. Information on capital adequacy (Tier 1 capital, total capital, and total required capital) is required on a quarterly basis.

The key mechanism through which supervisors can ensure appropriate disclosure is through the inclusion of disclosure in the minimum requirements for advanced methodologies for determining minimum capital requirements.

The general disclosure principle requires that banks have a formal disclosure policy approved by the board of directors that addresses the bank's approach to determining what disclosures it will make and the internal controls over the disclosure.

With respect to risk exposure, Pillar 3 requires information on the key risks that constitute the basis of the Pillar 1 minimum capital requirements: credit risk, operational risk, market risk, and equity risk in the banking book. Disclosure requirements are also required for credit risk mitigation and securitization, which have an impact on Pillar 1 processes. The interest rate risk is included under the Pillar 2 process. There are no quantitative disclosures pertaining to strategic risk, reputational risk, concentration risk, or liquidity risk.

Banks have to disclose their aggregate positions in credit risk and different approaches are used. In disclosing specific information on the approaches applied, the market can differentiate across banks and across jurisdictions. There are three broad categories: general credit risk disclosures across all banks; disclosures for portfolios subject to the standardized approach and supervisory risk weights in the IRB approaches; and disclosures for portfolios subject to IRB approaches. Banks must provide information on key definitions such as past due and impaired loans, and also provide a discussion of their risk management policies. Credit risk exposures should be disclosed, disaggregated by geographic distribution, industry or counterparty type, and residual contractual maturity, together with an analysis of impaired loans similarly categorized.

The main thrust of the accord is to encourage banks to measure and manage risk more effectively and adjust their capital levels accordingly.

Since the financial crisis began in mid-2007, market risk has contributed to huge losses and buildup of leverage that occurred in trading books. The BCBS supplemented the current value-at-risk-based trading book framework with an incremental risk capital charge, which includes default risk as well as migration risk, for unsecuritized credit products. For securitized products, the capital charges of the banking book will apply with a limited exception for certain so-called correlation trading activities, where banks may be allowed by their supervisor to calculate a comprehensive risk capital charge subject to strict qualitative minimum requirements as well as stress-testing requirements. The committee also requires banks to calculate a stressed VaR, taking into account a one-year observation period relating to significant losses. This has to be calculated in addition to the VaR based on the most recent one-year observation period.

2.11.8.5 Basel II failure

Basel II failed to create a more comprehensive approach to risk management with respect to trading book, market risk, and securitization. Banks relied excessively on market risk models to calculate capital requirements for the trading book. VaR models systematically underestimated market risk in the run-up to the subprime mortgage crisis, which incited traders to take excessive risk positions without sufficient capital to cover exposures. As such, Basel II failed to address liquidity and leverage risks. Another failure was that Basel II depended heavily on the banks' own assessment of risk taking. Banks themselves evaluated whether their off-balance sheet vehicles carried any risk to the banks and for what risk they should be accountable. Advocates of the quantitative model approach opine that it is not the model's fault but the bankers' fault who were to implement the model.

Inadequate capital regulation provided by Basel II is often cited as a reason for Basel II's failure. Large international banks were able to systematically manipulate outcomes in Basel II's regulatory process to their advantage. For banks, holding regulatory capital comes at a cost. The tied-up funds could be put into more profitable use, such as lending to prospective borrowers.

Basel II requirements were considered to be too procyclical.[10] In a boom period, the models were perceived to be less risky as banks held lower amounts of regulatory capital for a typical exposure. This situation freed up capital, which facilitated banks to pour more credit into the financial system. This process continued until the economy returned to an upswing mood. When the cycle turned negative and banks started freezing lending, the models suggested that bank should hold higher reserves. Basel II didn't stress LGD and the PDs.

Basel II requirements were not implemented to any great extent before the credit crunch. Basel II regulations were implemented in the EU only in 2007. At almost the same time, a credit crunch began in the summer of 2007. The United States introduced Basel II on a mandatory basis only for the largest banks because the Basel II framework was designed for internationally active banks. Basel II couldn't capture the way risks interact and their systemwide effects. The risks inherent in the derivative positions were not correctly quantified as credit rating agencies failed in performing their real function.

---

[10] Procyclical is a term used to describe how an economic quantity is related to economic fluctuations. It is the opposite of countercyclical. In business cycle theory and finance, any economic quantity that is positively related with the overall state of the economy is said to be procyclical.

Basel II failed to neutralize the systemic threat of undercapitalization, leaving several banks on the brink of insolvency as losses began to emerge in the subprime mortgage crisis. Under the Basel system, banks basically defined their own risk metrics and derivative investments limiting the effectiveness of Basel as a practical assurance tool. In other words, banks could use their own risk models to set minimum capital levels. The internal risk models of many banks greatly underestimated risk exposure, which compelled them to reassess and reprice credit risk. Basel II created perverse incentives to underestimate credit risk. Banks were tempted to be overoptimistic about their risk exposure in order to minimize their risk exposure and maximize profitability in terms of return on equity. During the housing boom, banks were strongly motivated by markets to look at the upward potential but not at the downward movements. During the financial crisis period, bank capital-asset ratios were near historically low levels, typically at about 7% of total assets (on a non-risk-weighted basis).

2.11.9 BASEL III FRAMEWORK

One of the main reasons for the severity of the economic and financial crisis was that the banking sectors of many countries had built up excessive on- and off-balance sheet leverage. The Basel Committee is raising the resilience of the banking sector by strengthening the regulatory capital framework, building on the three pillars of the Basel II framework.

The basic objectives of the Basel III recommendations are to (1) increase quality of capital, (2) increase quantity of capital, (3) reduce leverage through the introduction of backstop leverage ratio, (4) increase short-term liquidity coverage, (5) increase stable long-term balance sheet funding, and (6) strengthen risk capture, particularly counterparty risk.

The first basic regulatory objective of the Basel III recommendations is to increase the quality of capital, which will lead to improved loss-absorption capacity in both going concern and liquidation scenarios. The salient features of the key changes with respect to quality of improvement of capital are:

- Common equity and retained earnings should be the predominant component of Tier I capital instead of debt-like instruments, well above the 50% rule.
- There has to be harmonized and simplified requirements for Tier 2 capital with an explicit target for Tier 2 capital.
- Capital components with little loss absorption capacity such as minority interests, holdings in other financial institutions, and deferred tax assets (DTAs) are fully deductible.
- Gradual phaseout of hybrid Tier 1 components, which includes step-up/innovative/SPV-issued Tier 1 instruments used by banks.

The second regulatory objective is aimed at increasing the level of capital held by institutions as well as providing countercyclical mechanisms.

The key changes proposed include the following:

- The minimum common equity Tier 1 is to be increased from 2% to 4.5% along with a capital conservation buffer of 2.5%. The total common equity requirements to be made are 7%. The changes are to be phased from 2013 to 2019.
- The minimum total capital is to be increased from 8% to 10.5% including a conservation buffer.
- The countercyclical buffer has to be developed on the basis of a capital conservation buffer during the periods of excessive credit growth.

The third regulatory objective is to reduce leverage through the introduction of a backstop leverage ratio. The leverage ratio acts as a non-risk-sensitive backstop measure to reduce the risk of a buildup of excessive leverage in the institution and in the financial system as a whole.

The key changes are as follows:

- The leverage limit is set at 3%. A bank's total assets (including both on- and off-balance sheet assets) should not be more than 33 times bank capital.
- The backstop leverage ratio supplements the risk-based measures of regulatory capital. This ratio is implemented on a gross and unweighted basis.

The fourth regulatory objective aims at increasing short-term liquidity coverage. As a regulatory response to the financial crisis in the context of strengthening liquidity risk management, the Basel Committee proposes three minimum standards for funding liquidity:

- The 30-day liquidity coverage ratio (LCR) is intended to ensure that global banks have sufficient high-quality liquid assets to withstand stressed funding scenarios specified by supervisors.
- For the determination of LCR, the stock of high-quality liquid assets is compared with expected cash outflows over a 30-day stress scenario. The expected cash outflows are to be covered by sufficiently liquid, high-quality assets.
- Assets get a "liquidity"-based weighting varying from 100% for government bonds and cash to weightings of 0-50% for corporate bonds.

The fifth regulatory objective aims to increase stable long-term balance sheet funding. The net stable funding ratio (NSFR) is designed to encourage and incentivize banks to use stable sources to fund their activities to reduce the dependency on short-term wholesale funding. Details include the following.

- The NSFR compares available funding sources with funding needs resulting from the assets on the balance sheet.
- The available stable funding has to be greater than the required stable funding.
- The required and available funding amounts are determined using weighing factors, reflecting the stability of the funding available and the duration of the asset.
- The weighing factors for assets vary from 0% to 5% for cash and government bonds, respectively, to 65% for mortgages, 85% for retail loans, and 100% for other assets.
- For determining stable funding available for liabilities, the weighing factors vary from 100% for Tier 1 capital to 90% for core retail deposits and 50% for unsecured wholesale funding.

The sixth and final regulatory objective aims to strengthen risk capture, primarily counterparty risk. The Basel III proposals primarily modify the treatment of exposures to financial institutions and the counterparty risk on derivative exposures to be effective from January 2013.

The significant changes proposed are as follows:

- Calibration of counterparty credit risk modeling approaches such as internal model methods (IMMs) to stressed periods
- Increased correlation for certain financial institutions in the IRB formula to reflect experiences in the economic crisis, such as new capital charges for credit valuation adjustments
- A "carrot and stick" approach to encourage use of central counterparties (CCPs) for standardized derivatives
- Improved counterparty risk management standards in the areas of collateral management and stress testing

BASEL III Framework Summary	
Proposed Objectives	**Specific Actions**
Improve the quality, transparency, and consistency of the capital base	Tier 1 capital must be mostly common shares and retained earnings. Tier 2 capital instruments will be harmonized. Tier 3 capital will be eliminated
Strengthen risk coverage of capital framework	Focus on integration of market and counterparty credit risk
	Include credit valuation adjustment risk due to deterioration in counterparty's credit rating
	Take actions to strengthen the capital requirements for counterparty credit exposures on account of bank's derivatives, repos, and securities financing transactions
	Reduce pro-cyclicality
	Provide additional incentives to move OTC derivative contracts to CCPs
	Provide incentives to strengthen the risk management of counterparty credit exposures
	Raise counterparty credit risk-management standards by including wrong-way risk
Leverage ratio as a supplementary measure to the Basel II risk-based framework	Put a floor under the buildup of leverage in the banking sector
	Introduce additional safeguards against model risk and measurement error by supplementing risk-based measure with a simpler measure based on gross exposures
Reduce pro-cyclicality and promote countercyclical buffers	Dampen any excess cyclicality of the minimum capital requirement
	Promote more forward-looking provisions
	Conserve capital to build buffers at individual banks
Protect the banking sector from periods of excess credit growth	Require long-term data horizons to estimate probabilities of default
	Make mandatory downturn losses to be given default estimates, as was recommended in Basel II
	Improve calibration of risk functions, which convert loss estimates into regulatory capital requirements
	Require banks to conduct stress tests that include widening credit spreads in recessionary scenarios
Promote stronger provisioning practices	Proposed change in accounting standards toward an expected loss approach
Introduce a global minimum liquidity standard for internationally active banks	Proposed a 30-day LCR requirement underpinned by a longer-term structural liquidity ratio called the NSFR

Source: World Bank 2012. Global Financial Development Report 2013: Rethinking the Role of the State in Finance, Basel Committee on Banking Supervision 2011a.

Through Basel III reforms, global banking regulators tripled the size of the capital reserves that world banks must hold against losses. The new provisions in Basel III establish core capital ratio to 4.5%—double of the current level of 2%—plus a liquidity surplus of 2.5%. The new rules became effective in January 2013 and the process is to be completed by January 2019.

Basel III focuses on microprudentiality, which would increase the resilience of banks in times of stress. With respect to macroprudentiality, Basel III aims to control systemwide risks that are cyclic in nature. The capital requirements under Basel III are meant to create a capital buffer against adverse shocks. Basel III focuses on integrated risk management under a global regulatory framework. It also covers risks generated by capital market transactions. The most important changes adopted by Basel III were with respect to capital, liquidity, and leverage requirements.

The LCRs were lowered and the funding period for long-term lending rate (NSFR) was extended. The leverage ratio was made at 3%. The liquidity reforms advocated by Basel III were basically meant to increase the liquid assets proportion held by banks and to reduce short-term financing. Banks will have to adopt new models of asset management whereby the size of a balance sheet will be determined by liabilities, and then assets have to be matched to liabilities. The increase in Tier 1 capital rate to 7% by 2019 can be considered to be a good measure against potential losses for banks.

2.11.9.1 Impact of Basel III implementation

According to new capital standards, banks are required to deduct most of their assets with less loss-absorbing parameters such as minority interests, goodwill, net DTAs, investment in unconsolidated sub-sidiaries, and mortgage servicing rights (MSRs) from common equity component of capital. The new capital standards will contain only a limited amount of certain intangibles and qualified assets. Hence the market risk capital requirements is bound to increase by an estimated average of three to four times for large internationally active banks. For emerging market banks, this less-absorbing characteristic is low except in Latin America and the Caribbean. Risks and dangers in banking arise primarily from a regulatory framework that is not adapted to the market structure. Large financial institutions turn "too big to fail" because the regulator does not have any means to properly discipline and resolve them.[11]

2.11.9.2 Basel reforms: A critical analysis

Some analysts have highlighted the negative aspects of the Basel frameworks. The rationale for holding regulatory capital consisting of shareholder's equity, reserves, and subordinated debt against bank assets is basically meant to provide a buffer against unexpected losses and create a disincentive to undertake excessive risks. But this process of holding regulatory capital comes at a cost. Banks are compelled to forgo the income that could have been generated from putting the same funds to profitable use by financing new projects or increasing dividends for the shareholders. Bankers found it difficult to fill the gap between the economic capital they have to hold to back loans and the regulatory capital assigned to these loans by the accord. There is no independent standard against which to assess banks' metrics and judgments and the central banks lack the expertise to double-check banks' risk assumptions or assertions.

Banks arbitraged Basel I's capital requirements in two ways.[12] First, they moved toward the riskier assets within a given risk-weight category, which have a higher yield. Second, they shifted assets off the balance sheet, typically securitizing them. These assets were treated as "true sales" for regulatory purposes, even though the bank often retained much of the underlying risk through credit enhancements such as liquidity facilities. The consequence of these activities was that overall capital levels in the banking system, which had risen sharply after Basel I came into effect in the early 1990s, were now beginning to decline.[13]

---

[11] *Economist* (2012). http://www.economist.com/debate/days/view/706.

[12] Jackson, Patricia et al. (1999). Capital Requirements and Bank Behavior: The Impact of the Basel Accord. Basel Committee on Banking Supervision Working Paper no.1 (April). Basel: Bank for International Settlements.

[13] Jackson, Patricia, Nickell, Pamela, and Perraudin, William (1999). Credit risk modeling. Financial Stability Review (Bank of England), Issue 6, 94–121.

The series of quantitative impact studies (QIS) conducted by the Basel Committee forecasted large capital reductions relative to Basel I levels for banks employing the A-IRB approach. Basel II failed to understand the systemic threat of undercapitalization.

2.12 DODD-FRANK ACT

The Dodd-Frank Wall Street Reform and Consumer Protection Act passed by the US Congress in 2010 was aimed at preventing a repeat of the 2008 financial crisis. The Act deals with new rules for banks, hedge funds, and derivatives. The Act also created a new consumer financial protection bureau to protect retail users of banking products. The Financial Stability Oversight Council (FSOC) is a US federal government organization established by Title I of the Dodd-Frank Wall Street Reform and Consumer Protection Act. The broad objectives of the council are to identify and monitor the excessive risks to the US financial system arising from distress or failure of bank holding companies or nonbank financial institutions (NBFIs).

The Dodd-Frank Act introduced several structural changes in the shape of US financial markets. The Dodd-Frank Act aims to increase the power of financial regulatory agencies, reduce regulatory gaps, develop better crisis-management tools, and consolidate the regulation of systemically important institutions.

The Dodd-Frank Act created the FSOC to help identify and mitigate threats to the financial stability of systemically important financial institutions (SIFIs). Addressing the problems of "too-big-to-fail" banks is the central goal of the Dodd-Frank Wall Street Reform and Consumer Protection Act. The act helps financial regulators employ macroprudential approaches to supervision and regulation. The act specifies the types of regulatory standards to be applied in terms of additional capital, leverage, and liquidity requirements. The framework was applicable for bank holding companies with assets over $50 billion.

The modified Volcker rule, named for Federal Reserve chairman Paul Volcker, was introduced in the Dodd-Frank Act. This rule stipulates the separation of proprietary trading from other activities of banks and introduces more stringent rules on the trading of derivatives products. Banks are deterred from using the deposits of customers insured by the FDIC from speculation activities such as trading in derivatives. The derivatives products with trading characteristics and clearing, such as CDS, will be traded in exchanges. The swap dealers will be obliged to register with the Securities and Exchange Commission or the Federal Trade Commission. The OTC derivatives market is the largest market for derivatives and is largely unregulated with respect to disclosure of information between parties.

The salient features of the rule are as follows:

- Requirement of clearing and exchange trading for a number of derivatives
- CA comprehensive framework for registration and regulation of dealers and major nondealer market participants
- Prohibition of proprietary trading in certain derivatives instruments by regulated financial institutions

2.13 SYSTEMICALLY IMPORTANT FINANCIAL INSTITUTIONS

After the economic crisis unfolded, the global community committed to protecting the financial system through the prevention of the failure of SIFIs. The FSB in 2011 published a list of global SIFIs

Table 2.2 The FSB's Systemically Important Financial Institutions			
Bank of China	**Barclays**	**BBVA**	**BNP Paribas**
Bank of America	Bank of New York Mellon	Citigroup	Credit Suisse
Deutsche Bank	Goldman Sachs	Groupe BPCE	Group Credit Agricole
HSBC	ING Bank	JPMorgan Chase	Mitsubishi UFJ FG
Mizuho FG	Morgan Stanley	Nordea	Royal Bank of Scotland
Santander	Société Générale	Standard Chartered	State Street
Sumitomo Mitsui FG	UBS	UniCredit Group	Wells Fargo

(G-SIFIs). The Basel Committee has introduced new regulations to increase bank capital requirements to specifically target SIFIs. These financial institutions act as a holding company that consists of a number of subsidiaries. The Basel Committee views that global systemic importance should be measured in terms of the impact that a failure of a bank can have on the global financial system and wider economy. This viewpoint can be interpreted as a global, systemwide LGD concept. The selected indicators reflect the size of banks, their interconnectedness, the lack of readily available substitutes for the services provided, their global (cross-jurisdictional) activity, and complexity. The methodology gives an equal weight of 20% to each of the five categories of systemic importance—size, cross-jurisdictional activity, interconnectedness, substitutability, and complexity. The score for a particular indicator for each bank is calculated by dividing the individual bank amount by the aggregate amount summed across all banks in the sample for a given indicator. The score is then weighted by the indicator weighting within each category. The weighted scores are then added.[14] Table 2.2 gives the list of FSB's systemically important financial institutions.

2.14 FINANCIAL REFORMS IN EUROPE

Post-crises financial reforms in Europe include the establishment of three regulatory bodies: the European Banking Authority, the European Securities and Markets Authority, and the European Insurance and Occupational Pensions Authority. During 2011, the EC drafted a law proposal called the European Market Infrastructure Regulation (EMIR), which was similar to the Dodd-Frank Act.

2.15 REGULATION IN NONBANKING FINANCIAL SECTORS

Globally the supervision and regulation of insurance lags behind the banking sector. One of the key differences between banks and life insurers is that the maturity of liabilities in banks is generally shorter than those of life insurance companies. The supervisory process in the insurance sector is similar to those that exist in the banking sector with differences mainly in the details of the quantitative prudential standards such as the establishment of adequate technical provisions and underwriting and pricing

---

[14] Global systemically important banks: Assessment methodology and the additional loss absorbency requirement, http://www.bis.org/publ/bcbs201.pdf.

policies. Insurance regulators worldwide depend on the regulatory tools of entry requirements, solvency (capital requirements), balance sheet restrictions, restrictions on associations with other financial institutions, accountability, and governance requirements. In 1994, the International Association of Insurance Supervisors (IAIS) was established to promote international cooperation and standardize insurance regulation.

Another nonbanking financial sector includes provident funds. The bank supervisory process including licensing, prudential standards, and ongoing monitoring and enforcement apply to the supervision of provident funds. One of the important prudential standards with respect to investment regulation aims for diversification and minimization of portfolio risk. Regulations typically restrict holdings by issuer, by type of investment, by risk, by concentration of ownership, and by asset class.

Other nonbanking financial sectors include pension funds and mutual funds. The regulatory framework for pension funds involves licensing requirements, disclosure and governance standards, and minimum capital requirements. Mutual fund regulation relies on a high level of corporate governance. With respect to investment guidelines and restrictions, mutual fund managers have to disclose sufficient information to investors.

2.15.1 REGULATORY MEASURES FOR THE SHADOW BANKING SYSTEM

The shadow banking system and the regular banking systems are highly interconnected. They invest in each others' financial instruments, which leads to exposure to funding interdependencies and common concentrations of risk through asset holdings and derivative positions. Regulatory measures are required to address common risks and to avoid creating cross-border arbitrage opportunities. The task force of the FSB is to prioritize the establishment of regulation for shadow banking, regulatory reform of money market mutual funds, securitization, securities lending, and repos.

2.15.2 REGULATIONS OF NONBANKING FINANCIAL INSTITUTIONS IN THE UNITED STATES

The US prudential standards for registered securities broker-dealers have evolved over time. With the passage of the Securities Amendments Act in 1975, Congress mandated a uniform capital rule for the entire US securities industry. The Securities Investor Protection Act in 1970 established the Securities Investor Protection Corporation to protect customer funds and securities within the specified limits in the event of a securities broker-dealer's insolvency. With respect to government securities, the US Treasury, bank regulatory authorities, and the SEC have regulatory responsibilities. Primary dealers in government securities are selected by the Federal Reserve Bank based on their abilities to perform the function of primary dealer. In the United States, investment companies are regulated by the SEC under the Investment Company Act of 1940. In 1980, the SEC adopted Rule 12 b-1, which directs the manner in which a mutual fund uses the fund's assets to market and sell fund shares to investors, as well as how a broker-dealer can be compensated from the fund for its sales efforts. In 2010, the SEC came out with a new proposal to replace Rule 12-b with the objective of investor protection by limiting fund sales charges and improving the transparency of fees.

Another protection is the Employee Retirement Income Security Act of 1974, which provides basic protection for individual workers for funds invested in private pension funds. Table 2.3 gives the list of principal regulatory agencies in the US along with the institutions and markets in which they operate.

Table 2.3   Principal Regulatory Agencies in the United States

Regulatory Agency	Institutions and Markets
Securities and Exchange Commission (SEC)	Organized exchanges, financial markets, nondepository institutions such as mutual funds and investment companies
Commodities Future Trading Commission (CFTC)	Derivative markets
Office of Comptroller of Currency (OCC)	Federally chartered banks
Federal Reserve System	Banks and bank holding corporation
Federal Deposit Insurance Cooperation (FDIC)	State-chartered commercial and cooperative banks, insured industrial banks
National Credit Union Administration (NCUA)	Federally chartered credit union
Office of Thrift Supervision (OTS)	Savings and loan associations
State banking and insurance commissions	Deposit institutions and insurance companies

2.15.3 REGULATIONS OF NONBANKING FINANCIAL INSTITUTIONS IN EUROPE

2.15.3.1 Regulations of money market funds

In Europe, money market funds fall within the Undertakings for Collective Investment in Transferable Securities (UCITS) framework. On registration in any European country, a UCITS fund can be freely marketed across the EU. The original UCITS was enacted in 1985. The UCITS has been successful both inside and outside of Europe because of the high level of investor protection it offers. UCITS III was introduced in 2001 to include cash funds, index tracker funds, and derivatives. UCITS IV, which became effective in July 2011, was aimed at improving investor information by creating a standardized summary information document.

Private equity, hedge funds, private equity funds, real estate funds, and venture capital funds are generally regulated by the Alternative Investment Fund Managers Directive (AIFMD), which aims to create a comprehensive framework for direct regulation and supervision in the alternative fund industry. The AIFMD aims to equip the national supervisors of the European Securities Markets Agency (ESMA) and the European Systemic Risk Board (ESRB) with the information and tools necessary to monitor and respond to risks facing the stability of the financial systems.

The insurance undertakings are regulated by the solvency framework system whose objective is to provide supervisors with appropriate tools and powers to assess the overall solvency of the institutions based on the risk-oriented approach via the three-pillar structure of:

1. Quantitative capital requirements (solvency capital requirement and minimum capital requirement) to measure and properly manage risks
2. Supervisory review process
3. Disclosure requirements to enhance market discipline

2.16 REGULATIONS IN CAPITAL MARKET

A capital market is a market for securities (equity or debt) where governments and business enterprises can raise funds on a long-term basis. The capital market includes the stock market for equities and bond market for debt. The US SEC oversees the US capital markets whereas the FSA is in charge of capital markets in the United Kingdom. The SEC oversees the key participants in the securities market including securities exchanges, securities brokers and dealers, investment advisors, and mutual funds.

2.16.1 LAWS GOVERNING THE SECURITIES INDUSTRY

2.16.1.1 Securities Act of 1933

This is also known as the Truth in Securities Act. This act requires that investors receive financial and other significant information regarding securities being offered for public sale. The act also prohibits deceit, misrepresentations, and other fraud in the sale of securities. These goals are achieved through the registration of securities.

2.16.1.2 Securities Exchange Act of 1934

Through this act, the Securities and Exchange Commission was created. The act empowers the SEC with powers to register, regulate, and oversee brokerage firms, transfer agents, clearing agencies, and various self-regulatory organizations (SROs). The various SROs include the New York Stock Exchange, the American Stock Exchange, and the FINRA under the NASDAQ system. The act also empowers the SEC to require periodic reporting of information by publicly traded companies. It is mandatory for companies with more than $10 million in assets whose stockholders are more than a specified number to file annual corporate and periodic reports through the SEC's EDGAR database for public information.

2.16.1.3 Trust Indenture Act of 1939

This act applies to debt securities such as bonds, debentures, and notes that are offered for public sale.

2.16.1.4 Investment Act of 1940

This act focuses on the organization of such companies as mutual funds, which primarily are involved in investing, reinvesting, and trading in securities. These companies are required to disclose their financial and investment policies to investors.

2.16.1.5 Investment Advisers Act of 1940

This law stipulates that investment advisers must be registered with the SEC and have to conform to regulations designed to protect investors. In 1996, the act was amended. Advisers with at least $25 million in assets under management are eligible for registration.

2.16.1.6 Sarbanes-Oxley Act of 2002

This act mandated a number of reforms in the areas of corporate responsibility, financial disclosures, and prevention of corporate and accounting fraud. The act created the Public Company Accounting Oversight Board (PCAOB) to oversee activities of the auditing profession.

2.16.1.7 Dodd-Frank Wall Street Reform and Consumer Protection Act of 2010

This act focuses on reshaping the US regulatory system with respect to consumer protection, trading restrictions, credit ratings, regulation of financial products, corporate governance, and disclosures.

2.16.1.8 Jumpstart Our Business Startups (JOBS) Act of 2012

This act requires the SEC to write rules and issue studies on capital formation, disclosure, and registration requirements.

2.17 **SUMMARY**

Financial regulations are laws and rules that govern the workings of financial institutions. Regulations of financial institutions basically focus on providing stability to the financial system, fair competition, consumer protection, and the prevention and reduction of financial crimes. By the mid-1970s, the global financial system witnessed market-oriented reforms that led to liberalization in financial systems such as the reduction of interest rate controls, removal of investment restrictions on financial institutions and line of business restrictions, and control on international capital movements. Financial innovation and rapid technological advancement are the drivers of regulatory reforms. Regulations differ from country to country. The current trend is for financial-sector regulation to move toward a greater cross-sector integration of financial supervision. In 1998, the adoption of the Basel Accord, which required international banks to attain an 8% capital adequacy ratio, was a major significant milestone in banking regulations. The collapse of the global financial system that led to the global crisis can be attributed to the systemic failure of financial regulation. Basel I defined bank capital and bank capital ratio based on a two-tier system. The Basel II framework consisted of Part 1 (the scope of application) and three pillars, the first of which is minimum capital requirements, the second is a supervisory review process, and the third is market discipline. The Basel III framework prepared new capital and liquidity requirements for banks. New initiatives including the FSF and the G-20 grouping have been established to address concerns related to the stability of the worldwide financial system.

QUESTIONS FOR DISCUSSION

1. Discuss the critical role of regulation in the financial environment.
2. Explain the functions of regulatory agencies.
3. List the major regulatory reforms in the financial sector.
4. Why is the failure of the regulatory system often considered a reason for the recent economic crisis?
5. Discuss the major instruments of bank regulation.
6. Discuss the salient features of the Basel reforms.
7. Critically evaluate the Basel frameworks.

REFERENCES

Hutter, B., 2011. Why organizations need to be regulated – Lessons from History, QFinance.

Llewellyn, D.T., June 2006. Institutional structure of financial regulation and supervision: the basic issues. World Bank Seminar, Aligning Supervisory Structures with Country Needs.

IMF Report, 2009. Lessons of the financial crisis for future regulation of financial institutions and markets and for liquidity management. http://www.imf.org/external/np/pp/eng/2009/020409.pdf.

Čihák, M., Podpiera, R., 2008. Integrated financial supervision: which model? North American Journal of Economics and Finance 19, 135–152.

World Bank Global Financial Development Report, 2013. Rethinking the role of the state in finance. Washington, DC: World Bank. http://dx.doi.org/10.1596/978-0-8213-9503-5. License: Creative Commons Attribution CC BY 3.0.

Dedu, V., Niţescu, D.C., 2012. Basel III – between global thinking and local acting. Theoretical and Applied Economics Volume XIX 6 (571), 5–12.

Vedi, V. Basel II – but at what cost? QFINANCE, www.qfinance.com.

Kumăra, A., Chuppe, T.M., Perttunen, P., 1997. The Regulation of Non-Bank Financial Institutions: The United States, the European Union, and Other Countries, Parts 63-362. World Bank Publication.

Van Der Weide, M., 2012. Implementing Dodd–Frank: identifying and mitigating systemic risk. Economic Perspectives, Federal Reserve Bank of Chicago, ISSN 0164-0682.

Tropeano, D., 2011. Financial regulation after the crisis where do we stand? International Journal of Political Economy 40 (2), 45–60.

Biggar, D., Heimler, A., June 2005. An increasing role for competition in the regulation of banks. International Competition Network, Antitrust Enforcement in regulated sectors, SubGroup 1.

http://www.investopedia.com/articles/03/071603.asp#ixzz1wNbI1Uql.

Benston, G., Kaufman, G., 1995. Is the banking and payments system fragile? Journal of Financial Services Research 4, 209–240.

Claessens, S., Laeven, L., January 2005. Financial dependence, banking sector competition and economic growth. World Bank Policy Research Working Paper 3481.

Feldstein, M., 1991. The risk of economic crisis: introduction. In: Feldstein, Martin (Ed.), The Risk of Economic Crisis, Chicago.

Mishkin, F., 1991. Asymmetric information and financial crises. In: Hubbard, R.G. (Ed.), Financial Markets and Financial Crises. pp. 69–108.

Krugman, P., 1999. Balance Sheet, the Transfer Problem and Financial Crisis. http://web.mit.edu/krugman/www/FLOOD.pdf.

Kaufman, G., 1996. Bank failures, systemic risk and bank regulation. Cato Journal 16 (1), 17.

Bank for International Settlements Website.

Basel III, June 2011. A global regulatory framework for more resilient banks and banking systems. Basel Committee on Banking Supervision, Revised.

http://www.kpmg.com/MK/en/IssuesAndInsights/ArticlesPublications/Brochures/Documents/basell-III-issues-implications.pdf.

Lall, R., 2009. Why Basel II failed and why any Basel III is doomed. http://www.globaleconomicgovernance.org/wp-content/uploads/GEG-Working-paper-Ranjit-Lall.pdf, Global economic governance programme.

http://www.nakedcapitalism.com/2008/02/turmoil-reveals-inadequacy-of-basel-ii.html.

Benink, H., Kaufman, G., 2008. Turmoil reveals the inadequacy of Basel II. Financial Times February.

RISKS INHERENT IN FINANCIAL INSTITUTIONS

3.1 INTRODUCTION

Risk management is particularly important for financial institutions because in contrast to firms in other industries the liabilities of financial institutions are a source of wealth creation for their shareholders. For example, financial institutions with derivative business would be out of the market if the credit rating of the investment vehicle was downgraded below acceptable levels. Similarly, insurance companies would collapse if their policies fell to junk ratings.

In practice, financial institutions focus on downward risk. For example, value at risk (VaR) measures downward risk. In other words, it measures the maximum value loss at some confidence level. For example, a firm-wide daily VaR of $500 at the 95% confidence level means that in five days out of a hundred, the bank expects to have a loss that exceeds $100 million. Taking more risks enables a firm to make more profits but also endangers a firm's franchise value.

New initiatives such as more resilient capital adequacy standards, appropriate risk management techniques, central counterparties for over-the-counter (OTC) derivatives, new collateral and margin schemes, and a global identification coding system for market participants are the major hallmarks of the emerging risk system.

3.2 HISTORY OF RISK MEASUREMENT

Until the late 1980s, only interest rate risk was modeled quantitatively at the portfolio level. The measures used were basically simple interest rate-sensitivity measures such as a one-year duration gap. In the context of an explosive growth of interest rate derivatives, the simulation exercises of changes in portfolio values in response to different interest rates were undertaken. Many consider interest rate risk as a form of market risk. Market risk modeling grew in importance after the stock market crashes when financial institutions suffered huge losses. Credit risk modeling by financial institutions came into existence after Basel Committee recommendations. Operational risk is the newest entrant to the taxonomy of risks.

The definition of operational risk in the Basel II accord excludes such risks as strategic risks, reputational risks, and liquidity risks. Unlike market, credit, and operational risks, liquidity risk has not been quantitatively analyzed. Business or strategic risk modeling focuses on cash flow risk (CaR) or earnings at risk (EaR).

3.3 SERVICES PROVIDED BY FINANCIAL INSTITUTIONS

The types of services provided by financial institutions can be characterized as origination, distribution, packaging, servicing, intermediating, and market making.

Origination involves the acts of locating, evaluating, and creating new financial claims issued by the institution's clients. If the originator maintains the ownership of the new asset, it would set its own standards for risk and return for acting as principal. If the originator becomes an agent and sells the product, then it would abide by the underwriting standards of other principals. The origination firms include brokers, investment management companies, and mortgage bankers.

Distribution is the process of raising funds by selling newly originated products to customers who have the resources available to finance them. This process of distribution can be conducted as a brokered transaction or with the institution acting as principal. In brokered transactions, the newly originated assets are placed with investors who directly remit to the issuing firm. In another perspective, the financial institution never owns the asset. When a financial institution acts as a principal, it purchases assets and sells from its own inventory. Most retail sales are carried out on a brokered basis.

Services involve collecting payments due from issuers and paying collected funds to claimants. In this case, assets are originated and held by the same institution. Packaging involves the accumulation of individual financial assets into pools and the decomposition of cash flows from such assets into different categories of financial claim. This repackaging of financial flows increases liquidity for customers. For example, securitizing mortgages in agency-sponsored pools creates a liquid market for residential mortgages.

The process of intermediation involves the simultaneous issuance and purchase of different financial claims by a single financial entity. Intermediation happens when an institution purchases one type of financial instrument for its own account and finances the transaction by issuing a claim against its own balance sheet. The three basic types of financial intermediation activities are insurance, loan, and security underwriting. In insurance underwriting the issuer assumes the policy's contingent liability. In loan underwriting, the intermediary uses its own resources in credit extension to a borrower. Security underwriting involves buying securities to distribute to investors.

Market making is an activity that involves buying and selling identical financial instruments by a dealer. Buyers and sellers take principal risks and the auctioneer gets a commission for acting as an agent by bringing together buyers and sellers as a market maker. Specialist dealers are market makers. Table 3.1 gives the taxonomy of financial services.

Table 3.1 Taxonomy of Financial Services	
Depositories	**Banks, Thrifts, and Credit Unions**
Insurance firms	Life property, casualty, auto, health
Investment companies	Open ended, close ended, REMICS, REITS
Pension funds	Defined benefit, defined contribution

3.4 MAJOR STEPS IN RISK MANAGEMENT OF FINANCIAL INSTITUTIONS

A risk management system should consist primarily of four sequential steps to identify risk, to measure risk, to monitor risk, and to control risk.

Identify Risk

Financial institutions must identify and understand existing risks and any new risks that may arise from new business initiatives. Risks have to be identified in affiliate businesses and subsidiaries of the institutions. Risk also arises from external market forces or regulatory or statutory changes. The consolidation of financial institutions also requires proper risk identification. Risk identification is a continuous process that occurs both at transaction and portfolio levels.

Measure Risk

The measurement of risk in a timely and accurate manner is vital for effective risk management process. In the modern era, sophisticated risk measurement tools have been developed to manage risk because of its increasing complexity. Sound risk measurement tools are used to assess the risk of individual transactions and portfolios, as well as interdependencies, correlations, and aggregate risks across portfolios and lines of business. Banks should periodically test to make sure that measurement tools are within current accuracy limits.

Monitor Risk

Financial institutions monitor risk to ensure a timely review of risk positions. The monitoring reports have to be subjected to appropriate actions. In large companies, monitoring is integral to any management decisions related to products and legal entities.

Control Risks

Financial institutions need to establish and communicate risk limits through policies, standards, and procedures. These limits serve as a means to control exposures to the various risks associated with the bank's activities. The limits are also adjustable according to changes in conditions or risk tolerance.

3.5 GENERIC RISKS IN FINANCIAL INSTITUTIONS

The risks borne by financial institutions can be classified into systematic, credit, counterparty, operational, and legal risks. The systematic risks associated with asset values include interest rate risk, foreign exchange risk, commodity price risk, and industry concentration risk.

Credit risk arises from nonperformance of a debtor. Credit risk can affect the lender who underwrites the contract, other lenders, and shareholders of the debtors. Counterparty risk arises from nonperformance of a trading partner. It is the transient financial risk associated with trading. Operational risk deals with problems of processing, settling, or making deliveries on trades in exchange for cash. Operational risks are associated with processing system failures, recordkeeping, and compliance with various regulations. Legal risks are endemic in financial contracting. New statutes, court opinions, and regulations can challenge well-established transaction processes. For example, bankruptcy laws led to new risks for corporate bondholders. Environmental regulations affect real estate values.

3.6 RISK MITIGATION STRATEGIES

There are three basic generic strategies to mitigate risk. These involve avoidance or elimination of risk by simple business practices, transfer of risk to other participants, and active management of risk at the firm level. Simple risk avoidance initiatives include underwriting, hedges or asset liability matches, diversification, reinsurance, syndication, or appropriate due diligence. For risk transfer techniques, markets exist for the claims issued or assets created by financial institutions. Individual market participants can buy or sell financial claims to diversify or concentrate the risk in their portfolios. Aggressive risk management techniques are used when claims cannot be hedged or traded by the investors. For example, defined pension plan participants cannot trade or hedge claims on an equivalent after-tax basis. This is similar to the case of policies of mutual insurance companies. Index funds that invest in an index or a security dealer engaged in proprietary trading and arbitrage will not be fully hedged.

An active firm-level risk management system involves the establishment of procedures to control risk. The firm adopts a four-step procedure to manage firm-level exposure: standards and reports, position limits or rules, investment guidelines or strategies, and incentive schemes.[1]

Standards and Reports
Risk categorization, underwriting standards, and review standards are considered to be traditional tools of risk control. The standardization of financial reporting is another major integral component. External audit reports and rating agency evaluations are yardsticks to gauge the quality of assets and firm-level risks.

Position Limits and Rules
The establishment of position limits is basically meant to cover exposures to counterparties, credits, and overall position concentrations relative to systematic risks. Summary reports for management aims to highlight counterparty, credit, and capital exposure by business unit on a periodic basis.

Investment Guidelines
Investment guidelines offer firm-level advice for an appropriate level of active management. These guidelines lead to hedging and asset liability matching. Securitization and syndication are techniques for exposure management in investment guidelines.

Incentive Schemes
In these schemes, the incentive contracts and compensation are related to the risks borne by managers. These incentive contracts require proper cost and capital accounting systems.

Passive institutions such as real estate mortgage investment conduits (REMICs) do not engage in active management of their portfolios. These institutions contract out most services offered to investors. The residual claims to the assets of such institutions are sold to investors who are provided with detailed information about the portfolio. Among the active institutions, commercial banks are considered most active.

3.7 RISK MANAGEMENT CRISIS: LESSONS LEARNED

The ability to manage risk is a function of its capital size, bank management quality, and technical expertise. Risks in the banking sector have to be examined on a system-wide basis instead of focusing on individual banks. The focus has to be to establish control over the crowding of speculators from different firms into certain specific types of assets and lead to the creation of market bubbles. These are the lessons to be learned from the collapse of Lehman Brothers and the global credit crisis. In 1998, the

---

[1]George S Oldfield, Anthony M Santomero, (1995) 95-05-B, The Place of Risk Management in Financial Institutions, Wharton Financial Institutions Centre 95-05B, 1-39.

hedge fund Long Term Capital Management collapsed when Russian credit defaults spilled over into Danish mortgage assets.

After the crisis, hedging funds used multiple prime brokerages as sources of funding rather than one single source. The choices are also directed toward trading activities that are less sensitive to financing. There is a greater demand for regulation, particularly for managing risk in the areas of derivatives such as credit default swaps (CDS) ever since the concentration of risk brought insurance giant AIG to the brink of default and required massive government bailout. The standardization of swaps would lead to greater liquidity in the swaps market.

Risk practices can, to some extent, be effective if constraints on compensation for bankers are implemented. Some advocate global standards such as bonus clawbacks if trading strategies cause firms to make losses. Table 3.2 cites the major risk management failures in organizations along with the loss amount, type of products and failures.

Table 3.2   Major Risk Management Failures

Year	Organization	Known Losses	Product Involved	Type of Failure
1988	Hammersmith and Fulham (and other UK authorities)	GBP600 million	Derivatives-swaps	Authority/ documentation and suitability
1994	Metallgesellschaft	US$660 million	Oil hedging	Systems, control, and management failure
1994	Proctor and Gamble	US$157 million	Structured notes	Speculation and control failures
1995	Orange County	US$1.5 billion	Derivatives swaps	Speculation, authority/ documentation, and suitability
1995	Baring Brothers	GBP900 million	Options	Speculation, fraud, systems, control, and management failure
1996	Sumitomo Corp.	US$2.6 billion	Commodity futures	Management oversight failure, speculation, and oversize positions
1998	Long-Term Capital Management (LTCM)	US$4+ billion	Derivatives, debt, and equity options	Speculation, leverage, control, and management failure
2001-2002	Enron	US$50+ billion	Corporate, governance/financial control	Fraud, control, board, and management failure
2002	Allied Irish	US$691 million	Currency options	Unauthorized trading, fraud, control, and management failure
2003	National Australia Bank	US$360 million	Derivatives, currency options	Speculation, systems, fraud, control, and management failure

(Continued)

Table 3.2   Major Risk Management Failures—cont'd

Year	Organization	Known Losses	Product Involved	Type of Failure
2007	Credit Agricole	US$347 million	Credit market indices	Management and control oversight failure, oversize positions
2008	SocieteGenerale	US$7.2 billion	Futures and European equity market indices	Unauthorized trading, fraud, management, and control failure
2007-2008	Systemic Meltdown—Global Impact	US$400+ billion	Structured and securitized product, credit, ABS, funding/liquidity	Speculation, management, regulatory and rating agency failure, leverage, systems, and controls

Source: Independent Risk Consultants P/L; Technical Assistance Consultant's Report Risk and Asset and Liability Management in Banks, Asian Development Bank Report.

With the advent of innovative financial products in equity markets since the 1980s, risk management has become a formidable task. Risk management practices have been revolutionized with new quantitative techniques that allow banks to disaggregate price, package, hedge, and distribute risks. In 1988, the Bank of International Settlements (BIS) introduced the Basel Accord I, which was designed to ensure minimum capital requirements for banks. After the 2008 economic crisis, regulators and policymakers around the world have focused on increasing financial institutions' minimum capital requirements and limiting leverage. The McKinsey report[2] suggests that the ratio of tangible common equity (TCE) to risk-weighted assets outperforms all others as a predictor of future bank distress.

3.8 RISK MANAGEMENT IN BANKS

Banks have always held the dominant position in the financial system. Banks are the main pillars of the payment system and the main conduit of monetary policy. By the very nature of their balance sheet and the huge leverage in which they operate, they are exposed to a variety of risks.

The main objectives of bank management are maximizing profitability, minimizing risk exposure, and observing bank regulations. Risk management in banks is regarded as a problem of unexpected losses in bank assets caused by market, credit, or liquidity risks. The main risks faced by the banking sector can be classified as financial risks, delivery risks, and environmental risks. The main financial risks are credit risk, interest rate risk, liquidity risk, foreign exchange risk, and capital risk. On the basis of banking supervision, risks can be classified into eight categories: credit, interest rate, liquidity, price, operational, compliance, strategic, and reputation.

---

[2]Kevin S. Buehler, Christopher J. Mazingo and Hamid H. Samandari, (Spring 2010) A better way to measure bank risk, *Mckinsey on Finance* Number 35.

The sophistication of a risk management system is directly proportional to the risks and complexity of an institution. Big banks ideally should focus on the overall integrity and effectiveness of the risk management system. It is the fundamental responsibility of banks to identify, monitor, and measure the risk profile of the institution. The risk management system also develops policies and procedures, reviews risks, and identifies new risks.

3.8.1 RISK MANAGEMENT FRAMEWORK IN BANKS: STRUCTURE AND SYSTEM
3.8.1.1 Structure
Different organizations have different risk profiles. It is very important to know the business, analyze, and rank the risks. Then the quantum of risks that can be handled have to be decided. A risk management system must be proportionate to the nature, volume, and complexity of the bank's operations and/or its risk profile. A bank is required to establish a comprehensive and reliable risk management system that has to be integrated in all the business activities in line with the already established propensity to risks. The risk management system will encompass risk management strategy and policies, as well as procedures for risk identification, measurement, and management of risk. An effective and efficient risk management process encompasses mitigation, monitoring, and control of risks that a bank is exposed to and intended to be measured. A bank's internal controls system must ensure provision of timely information to the bank's organizational units and to the people responsible for risk management. It should detect any flaws, and apply the appropriate measure to eliminate such flaws.

With respect to barriers, governance issues pose the most formidable barriers. The vast majority of banks lack an enterprisewide view of risk. Banks face major challenges with respect to organizational structure, decentralization of resources, poor integration of systems, and lack of transparent reporting systems. To tackle these issues under the regulatory Basel framework, many banks have set up a governance structure based on distributed risk function. The structure generally consists of a board of directors and various committees at board and management levels. There is also a centralized risk management function primarily responsible for policy formulation and oversight along with day-to-day oversight of risks.

The board and management have special responsibility for establishing the company's strategic direction and risk tolerances. The board should approve policies that set operational standards and risk limits. In assessing risk management practices, supervisors assess the policies, processes, personnel, and control systems.

The standard risk management function should encompass the organizational structure with a comprehensive risk measurement approach. Banks should have a strong management information system (MIS) for reporting, monitoring, and controlling risks. There ought to be well-laid-out procedures and a comprehensive risk reporting framework with a clear delineation of the levels of responsibility for management of risk. Global banks have been centralizing risk management with integrated Treasury management functions.

The board of directors is primarily responsible for setting risk limits by assessing the bank's risk-bearing capacity. The trend observed is that usually the independent risk management committee reports to the board of directors. The global trend is toward assigning risk limits in terms of portfolio standards or credit at risk and EaR and VaR (market risk).The committee also designs stress scenarios to measure the impact of unusual market conditions and to monitor the variance between actual volatility or portfolio value predicted by risk measures. Within the risk management committee, the asset liability management committee (ALCO) deals with different types of market risk and the credit policy committee (CPC) oversees the credit/counterparty risk and country risk.

3.8.2 RISK MANAGEMENT SYSTEM

3.8.2.1 Stress testing

An effective stress-testing framework covers a banking organization's full set of material exposures, activities, and risks based on effective enterprisewide risk identification and assessment. Credit and market risks are key because they affect banks' profits and solvency. Risks addressed in a bank's stress-testing framework may include credit, market, operational, interest rate, liquidity, country, and strategic risks.

Stress tests for credit risk examine the impact of rising loan defaults, or nonperforming loans, on bank profit and capital. Stress tests for market risk examine how changes in exchange rates, interest rates, and the prices of various financial assets, such as equities and bonds, affect the value of the assets in a bank's portfolio, as well as its profits and capital. This test would assume a drop in the value of various assets in the bank's portfolio. In macro-stress tests, economic assumptions are used to project the quantum by which a bank's nonperforming loans may increase or how much a bank would bear losses from lower asset prices. Changes in default rates and asset prices are often linked to economic scenarios, including a fall in economic growth rates.

Before the Lehman Brothers collapse, liquidity risk was not a matter of concern for supervisors. The liquidity crisis that followed after the economic downturn in 2008 became more widespread and severe than banks and regulators had anticipated. Nonbank financial institutions, such as money market funds and money market participants, stopped lending to banks, which added to the liquidity crisis. Liquidity stress tests focus on the impact of deposit withdrawals or on the inability of a bank to refinance, which could be triggered by a credit downgrade of the institution. The global economic crises have highlighted the importance of expanding the scope of stress tests from individual bank risk management to systemwide risks.

Stress tests have emerged as a critical tool to examine the health of the global financial system particularly after the economic crisis. Sophisticated approaches are needed to examine the impact of economic shocks on financial institutions' asset portfolios, especially in the context of a global scale of bank operations. Prominent among the stress tests are those that are designed to assess the adequacy of capital and liquidity. Capital stress testing can be helpful for a banking organization to assess the quality and composition of capital and its ability to absorb losses. Capital stress testing evaluates the potential for changes in earnings, losses, reserves, and other effects on capital under a variety of stressful circumstances. Liquidity stress testing involves exploring the potential impact of adverse developments that would affect market and asset liquidity, which includes the freezing of credit and funding markets and its impact on banks. These liquidity stress tests also help identify the conditions under which additional funding needs are created.

3.8.2.1.1 Stress-testing approaches

3.8.2.1.1.1 Scenario analysis.
Scenario analysis refers to a type of stress testing in which a banking organization applies historical or hypothetical scenarios to assess the impact of various events and circumstances, including extreme ones. These scenarios involve events such as recessionary conditions, failure of major counterparty, loss of major clients, disasters, interest changes due to inflationary changes, and more. In scenario analysis, the effect of these risk factors is assessed on the bank's capital

and financial results. Stress analysis must be able to identify unique vulnerabilities to factors that affect a bank's exposures, activities, and risks. For instance, if a bank group focuses on business lines such as commercial real estate or residential mortgage lending, then the impact of downturn on those particular market segments should be explored. Bank groups with much lending exposure to oil and gas companies should examine scenarios related to energy sectors. Operational, reputational, and legal risks are also relevant factors for scenario analysis.

3.8.2.1.1.2 Sensitivity analysis. Sensitivity analysis refers to a banking organization's assessment of its exposures, activities, and risks when certain variables, parameters, and inputs are "stressed" or "shocked." For example, through sensitivity analysis, banks can examine the impact on credit losses from a combined increase in default rates and decrease in collateral values. Sensitivity analysis can also be used to examine the impact of declines in net operating income, adverse capitalization rates, and reductions in collateral while evaluating risks from commercial real estate exposures.

3.8.2.1.1.3 Enterprisewide stress testing. Enterprisewide stress testing involves developing scenarios that affect the banking organization as a whole that arise from macroeconomic, market-wide, and/or firm-specific events. Selection of variables is a critical component in enterprisewide stress testing. For example, a set of variables, such as changes in gross domestic product (GDP), unemployment rate, interest rates, and price levels, is essential for capturing the combined impact of recession and financial market downturn.

3.8.2.1.1.4 Reverse stress testing. Reverse stress testing helps a bank evaluate the combined effect of several types of extreme events that threaten the survival of banking organizations. This tool allows a bank to make an assumption related to a known adverse outcome such as a credit loss that breaches regulatory capital ratios or severe liquidity constraints that make it unable to meet its obligations and finally deduce the types of events that could lead to such an outcome.[3]

3.8.2.2 Asset and liability management

Asset and liability management (ALM) is the process of effectively managing a bank portfolio mix of assets, liabilities, and off-balance sheet activities. The process involves the management of two primary financial risks, interest rates risk and foreign exchange risk.

In emerging markets, the Treasury function of banks basically focus on liquidity management and basic foreign exchange activity. In these markets there are constraints for involvement in sophisticated capital market transactions. In developing markets, the Treasury functions range from full balance-sheet management activity involving complex analytics and hedging to marketing and trading of capital market products. In developed markets, the Treasury function has evolved more into a service center for an institutional banking division providing assistance and support for pricing, analytics, and more.

Asset liability mismatch in the balance sheet represents the presence of interest rate and liquidity risk. Various techniques are used to examine the mismatch in a bank's balance sheet. The ALM process undertakes a number of analyses designed to identify any static and dynamic mismatches. The ALM is also used to show sensitivity of net interest income and market value under multiple scenarios, which includes high stress.

Net interest income (NII) is the main measure of performance. More advanced banks are also using market or economic value as a secondary measure. Both of these measures have emerged as important metrics for measuring and managing embedded risks in banks.

---

[3] http://www.federalreserve.gov/bankinforeg/srletters/sr1207a1.pdf

NII has become the industry benchmark tool on account of its simplicity and nonassumption basis. The disadvantage of NII is that it does not consider the whole risks undertaken by banks or reflect fully the economic impact of interest rate movements. Market value simulations offer more complete assessment of risks. But the tool is based on complex assumptions; it is very important to have timely and accurate data for supporting any ALM activity.

3.8.2.2.1 Fund transfer pricing

Fund transfer pricing has emerged as an important ALM tool in banks. It is an internal measurement model designed to assess the financial impact of uses and sources of funds. It is designed to identify interest rate margins and eliminate interest rate and liquidity risk. Fund transfer pricing (FTP) locks in the margin on loans and deposits by assigning a transfer rate that reflects the repricing and cash flow profile of each balance sheet item. It is applied to both assets and liabilities. FTP segregates business performance into discrete portfolios that can be assigned individualized metrics and facilitates the centralization and management of interest rate mismatches. It also effectively allocates responsibilities between organizational business units and the Treasury department. FTP rates are structured to include both the interest rate and funding liquidity risks with the derived transfer yield curve constructed to include appropriate premiums. The curve captures elements linked with banks' funding costs, including holding liquidity reserves, optionality costs, and funding program costs.

Many diversified international banks use internal FTP. Matched funds pricing is the most efficient technique among various FTP frameworks and techniques. In an FTP mechanism, specific assets and liabilities are assigned to profit centers of functional units, such as lending, investment, deposit taking, and funds management. The lending, investment, and deposit-taking profit centers sell liabilities and buy funds for financing their assets from funds management profit centers at appropriate transfer prices. The transfer prices are fixed on the basis of a single curve or a derived cash curve in such a way that asset liability transactions of identical attributes are assigned identical transfer prices. However, transfer prices can vary according to maturity and purpose. The FTP system could be effectively used as a way to centralize the bank's overall market risk and support an effective ALM modeling system.

The FTP provides for allocation of margin franchise and credit spreads to profit centers on original transfer rates and any residual spread (mismatch spread) is credited to the funds management profit center.

Deposit Profit Center
Transfer price (TP) on deposits − cost of deposits − deposit insurance- overheads
Lending Profit Center
Loan yields + TP on deposits − TP on loan financing − cost of deposits − deposit insurance − overheads − loan loss provisions
Investment Profit Center
Security yields + TP on deposits − TP on security financing − cost of deposits − deposit insurance − overheads − provisions for depreciation in investments and loan loss
Funds Management Profit Center
TP on funds lent − TP on funds borrowed − statutory reserves cost − overheads

3.8.3 DIFFERENT TYPES OF RISKS IN BANKS

3.8.3.1 Credit risk

Credit risk is the biggest risk faced by commercial banks. Credit risk or default risk is the inability or unwillingness of a borrower, or counterparty, to meet commitments in relation to lending, trading, hedging, settlement, and other financial transactions. The failure may be the result of bankruptcy, a temporary change in market conditions, or other factors that affect a borrower's ability to pay. The best example is that of a customer failing to repay a loan. Credit events include bankruptcy, failure to pay, loan restructuring, loan moratorium, and accelerated loan payments. Credit risk also arises from exposure to banks' commitments and guarantees, acceptances, trade finance, transactions, and other acitivities. Credit risk also originates from such capital market activities as foreign exchange transactions, derivative activities including futures, swaps, bonds, options, and bullions. In other words, credit risk arises whenever bank funds are extended, committed, invested, or otherwise exposed through actual or implied contractual agreements whether reflected on or off the balance sheet. Credit risk arises from country or sovereign exposure as well as indirectly through guarantor performance. Credit risk is in the form of delivery or settlement risk. This situation arises when a bank enters into a repurchase agreement to buy or sell securities from third parties. The bank faces credit risk when the third party is unable to deliver securities on their due date, thereby constraining the bank to replace the securities at the same price.

The credit risk consists of transaction risk or default risk and portfolio risk. The portfolio risk in turn consists of intrinsic and concentration risk. The simplest credit risk portfolio has only one systematic factor and assumes that all borrowers have the same exposure to the factor. The credit risk of a bank's portfolio depends on external factors such as the state of the economy, wide swings in commodity/equity prices, foreign exchange, interest rates, and economic sanctions. Portfolio risk also depends on internal factors, including an absence of prudential credit limits, deficiencies in loan policies/administration, deficiencies in financial appraisal of borrowers, excessive dependence on collaterals and inadequate risk pricing, or absence of loan review mechanism, and other factors. Credit risk is attributed to the assets in the banking book, including loans and bonds held to maturity. Credit risk is more significant for banks than market risk. The assessment time horizon for credit risk is typically one year.

3.8.3.1.1 Counterparty risk

Another variant of credit risk is counterparty risk. This occurs when the counterparty is unable to perform because of adverse price movements or other external constraints. The counterparty risk is viewed as a transient financial risk associated with trading rather than with standard credit risk. Hence credit risk arises in the trading book as a counterparty credit risk. The most important ingredient to measuring counterparty risk is exposure, which is the net value outstanding for a given counterparty.

3.8.3.1.2 Management of credit risk

Historically a major crisis faced by financial institutions was directly related to credit standards for borrowers and counterparties. A credit risk framework focuses primarily on the measurement of credit risks; credit controls and risk administration and monitoring compliance with credit risk limits and establishment of regulatory/economic capital to support credit risk. The Basel II framework suggests discrete modeling and measurement of credit risk, thus requiring an internal ratings approach both at foundation and advanced levels. Banks can choose a standardized approach for their operations and financial market infrastructure.

The five Cs of creditors are capital, capacity, conditions, collateral, and character. Credit products such as loans and bonds reside in the banks' trading book. The credit quality generally refers to the counterparty's ability to perform on that obligation.

The credit risk management process should be articulated in the bank's loan policy, duly approved by the board. Many banks have a high-level credit policy committee to deal with issues relating to credit policy and procedures and to analyze, manage, and control credit risk on a bankwide basis. The committee should be headed by the chairman/CEO/ED, and should comprise heads of credit, treasury, credit risk management departments, as well as a chief economist.

3.8.3.1.3 Estimating credit losses

The general risk metric often used for estimating credit losses is the adequacy of general and specific loan loss provisions and the size of the general and specific loan loss reserve in relation to the total exposures of the bank. The allowances for loans create a cushion for credit losses in the bank's credit portfolio. This process is basically meant to absorb the bank's expected loan losses. The growing sophistication and automation of lending and the complexity of credit products has led to the emergence of computational approaches to credit assessment and evaluation of individual, retail, and commercial borrowers. The use and accuracy of bankwide credit risk software has also accelerated.

3.8.3.1.4 Measures of estimating credit losses

There is a wide variety of credit risk models that differ in their fundamental assumptions, such as their definition of credit losses. For instance, default models define credit losses as loan defaults, while mark-to-market or multistate models define credit losses as ratings' change of any magnitude. Generally these models forecast the probability distribution function of losses that may arise from a bank's credit portfolio. A credit risk model's loss distribution is based on two components: the multivariate distribution of the credit losses on all the credits in its portfolio and a weighting vector that characterizes its holdings of these credits.[4]

The various measures of estimating credit losses are listed below.

Probability of Default
The probability of default (PD) is the likelihood that the borrower will fail to make full and timely repayment of its financial obligations.

Exposure at Default
The exposure at default (EAD) is the expected value of the loan at the time of default.

Loss Given Default
The loss given default (LGD) is the amount of the loss if there is a default expressed as a percentage of the EAD.

Recovery Rate
The recovery rate (RR) is the proportion of the EAD the bank recovers.

With respect to potential losses, banks are expected to hold reserves against expected credit losses, which are considered a cost of doing business. The simplest basic model considers two outcomes: default and nondefault.

---

[4]Jose A Lopez, Evaluating Credit Risk Models, http://www.frbsf.org/econrsrch/workingp/wp99-06.pdf.

With respect to unexpected losses, statistical approaches are used to estimate the distribution of possible loss values. For individual products in default, loss amounts are not deterministic owing to uncertainty about LGD and collateral value. For a portfolio of credit products with defaults, loss amounts are also uncertain due to a correlation of defaults between products. Credit loss distributions tend to be largely skewed as the likelihood of significant losses is lower than the likelihood of average or no losses. Active loan portfolio management, which involves diversification of exposures across industries and geographic areas, can reduce the variability of losses around the mean.

3.8.3.1.5 Instruments for management of credit risk

3.8.3.1.5.1 Estimating expected loan losses. Risks are quantified through the estimation of the amount of loan losses that banks would experience over a chosen time period. For this purpose, tracking portfolio behavior over a period of five or more years could be utilized. The unexpected loan loss, which is the difference of the amount by which actual losses exceed the expected loss, is determined through standard deviation of losses.

3.8.3.1.5.2 Multitiered credit approving systems. Banks should have multitiered credit approving systems where loan proposals are approved by a committee.

3.8.3.1.5.3 Prudential limits. Prudential limits have to be assigned to manage credit risks. Ratio analysis can be used to stipulate benchmarks for prudential limits. Leverage ratios such as debt equity and profitability ratios such as debt service coverage are particularly valuable instruments for benchmarking prudential limits. Single/group borrower limits can be assigned for the purpose of credit risk management. Industry or sectorwise limits for maximum exposure limits can also be stated. Sensitive sectors that are characterized by a high degree of price volatility and business cycles may be limited. Heavy exposure beyond the limits must be backed by adequate collaterals of strategic nature.

3.8.3.1.5.4 Risk ratings. To account for diverse risk factors, banks should have a comprehensive risk scoring/rating system. The risk rating should reflect the underlying credit risk of the loan book. The risk rating should be based on financial analysis, projections and sensitivity, and industrial and management risks. Banks can consider a separate rating framework for large corporate or small borrowers, traders, and others. For loans to individuals or small business enterprises, credit quality is assessed through a process of credit scoring. Based on the standardized credit score, the lending institution grants credit. For larger institutions a credit analysis is used as the process for assessing the credit of a counterparty.

Many banks and investment and insurance companies hire their own credit analysts who prepare credit ratings. Financial institutions such as Standard & Poor's, Moody's, and Fitch develop credit ratings for use by investors and other third parties.

3.8.3.1.5.5 Risk pricing. Risk return pricing is a fundamental aspect of risk management. Borrowers in a weak financial position who are placed in the high credit risk category have to be priced high. Banks have evolved scientific systems to price credit risk, which is a function of the expected probability of default.

Banks should build a historical database on the portfolio quality and provisioning/chargeoff to help themselves price their risk. Large banks use a risk-adjusted return on capital (RAROC) framework for the pricing of loans. In this framework, lenders charge an interest markup to cover the expected loss based on the default rate of the rating category of the borrower.

3.8.3.1.5.6 Portfolio models. Global banks have adopted various portfolio management techniques for gauging asset quality. Banks also stipulate a quantitative ceiling on aggregate exposure in specified rating categories. Banks have to undertake rapid portfolio reviews, stress tests, and scenario analysis in the context of rapid macroeconomic changes, such as volatility in the foreign exchange (forex) markets, changes in fiscal/monetary policies, and extreme liquidity conditions. Stress tests are meant to detect any gray areas of potential credit risk exposure and links between different categories of risk. Banks also need to evolve a suitable framework for monitoring market risks, especially forex risk exposure of corporations with no natural hedging mechanism.

Global banks use the credit risk model for evaluating credit portfolios. These models offer banks a framework for examining credit risk exposures across geographical locations and product lines. The model analysis involves centralizing data and analyzing marginal and absolute contributions to risk. The models provide estimates of credit risk (unexpected loss) for individual portfolio compositions. The Altman's Z score forecasts the probability of a company entering bankruptcy within a 12-month period. JPMorgan has developed a portfolio model called CreditMetrics for evaluating credit risk. The model focuses on estimating volatility in the value of assets caused by variations in the quality of assets. Credit Suisse has developed a statistical method for measuring and accounting for credit risk known as CreditRisk+.

3.8.3.1.5.7 Loan review mechanism. Because of qualitative improvements in credit administration, the loan review mechanism has become an effective tool for evaluating the quality of loan amounts. The basic objective of the loan review mechanism is to identify loans that develop credit weakness and take corrective actions. The loan review mechanism also provides top management with information on credit administration, including the credit sanction process, risk evaluation, and post-sanction follow-up.

3.8.3.1.6 Managing credit risk in off-balance sheet exposure

Banks are required to evolve an adequate framework for managing their exposure in off-balance sheet products, including forex, forward contracts, and swaps options. Banks classify their risk exposure in off-balance sheet activities in full-, medium-, and low-risk categories. Standby letters of credit, money guarantees, and other forms of credit susbstitutes constitute the full-risk category. Indirect credit substitutes that do not support existing financial obligations, such as bid bonds, letters of credit, indemnities, and warranties, are categorized as medium risk. The low-risk category includes reverse repos, currency swaps, options, and futures.

3.8.3.2 Interest rate risk

Interest rate risk is the risk to current or anticipated earnings or capital arising from movements in interest rates. Interest rate risk has the potential to create adverse effects on the financial results and capital of the bank arising from positions in the banking book. One of the fundamental objectives in banking is to borrow funds at a lower rate and lend them at a higher rate, thereby making profits. Interest rate risk arises due to changes in market interest rates, which have an impact on bank profitability. An interest rate rise puts financial pressure on the client, which may in turn result in default of loan payments. The major factors that lead to increased interest rate risk are the volatility of interest rates and mismatches between the interest reset dates on assets and liabilities.

Interest rate risk is a major component of market risk. The NII or net interest margin (NIM) is dependent on the movements of interest rates. Variations in the NIM of banks occur when there are mismatches in cash flows (fixed assets or liabilities) or repricing dates (floating assets or liabilities). Interest rate risk refers to the potential impact on the NII, the NIM, or the market value of equity (MVE), which is caused by unexpected changes in market interest rates.

3.8.3.2.1 Forms of interest rate risk

3.8.3.2.1.1 Gap or mismatch risk. A gap or mismatch risk arises from holding assets, liabilities, and off-balance sheet items with different principal amounts, maturity dates, or repricing dates, thereby creating exposure to unexpected changes in the level of market interest rates. This risk arises when there is a temporal discrepancy between maturity and new price determination.

3.8.3.2.1.2 Basis risk. The risk that the interest rate of different assets, liabilities, and off-balance sheet items may change in different magnitudes is termed a basis risk. The degree of basis risk is fairly high in banks that create composite assets out of composite liabilities. Basis risk is the result of different reference interest rates in interest-sensitive positions, with similar characteristics regarding maturity or repricing.

3.8.3.2.1.3 Embedded option risk. Embedded option risk results from significant changes in market interest rates that affect banks' profitability by encouraging prepayment of cash credit/demand loans/term loans. Thus, optionality risk arises from contract provisions regarding interest-sensitive positions, such as loans with early repayment options and deposits with early withdrawal options. The exercise of call/put options on bonds/debentures also leads to optionality risk. Banks should estimate embedded options and then adjust the gap statements to estimate risk profiles. Banks also have to periodically carry out stress tests to measure the impact of changes in interest rates.

3.8.3.2.1.4 Yield curve risk. This risk arises from changes in the shape of the yield curve. Banks base their assets and liabilities prices on different benchmarks, including Treasury bill rates, fixed deposits, and call money market rates. When banks use two different instruments that mature at different times for pricing their assets and liabilities, any nonparallel movements in the yield curves will affect the net interest margin. The fluctuations in the yield curve are more frequent when the economy moves through business cycles. Banks should examine the impact of yield curve fluctuations on the portfolio value and operating income. These risks cover adverse effects on a bank's income or underlying economic value resulting from unanticipated shifts in the yield curve.

3.8.3.2.1.5 Price risk. The scenario of price risk arises when assets are sold before their stipulated maturity period. In financial terminology, bond prices and yields are inversely related. Price risk occurs when assets are sold before their stated maturities. Price risk is closely associated with short-term movements in interest rates. Hence, banks that have active trading books have to focus on formulating policies to restrict portfolio size, holding period, duration, stop-loss limits, and marking to market.

3.8.3.2.1.6 Reinvestment risk. Reinvestment risk arises from the uncertainty with regard to the interest rates at which the future cash flows could be reinvested.

3.8.3.2.1.7 Net interest position risk. One of the significant factors contributing to the profitability of banks is the size of nonpaying liabilities. When interest rates are in a downward trend, the interest rate risk is higher for banks that have more earning assets than paying liabilities. In other words, banks with positive net interest positions will experience reductions in net interest income as the market interest rate declines and increases when the interest rate rises.

3.8.3.2.2 Measurement of interest rate risk

There are different techniques for measuring interest rate risk. Banks basically position their balance sheet into trading and investment or banking books. They may use any of the following analysis techniques.

3.8.3.2.2.1 Maturity gap analysis. Maturity gap analysis is one of the simplest analytical techniques for managing interest rate risk exposure. Gap analysis distributes interest rate-sensitive assets, liabilities, and off-balance sheet positions into a certain number of predefined time bands, according to their maturity (fixed rate) or the time remaining for their next repricing, which is based on a floating rate. Assets and liabilities that lack definite repricing intervals, such as bank savings, cash credit, overdraft, loans, and export finance, are assigned time bands according to the bank's judgment and past experience. Time bands are also assigned when actual maturities vary from contractual maturities, such as an embedded option in bonds with put/call options, loans, cash credit/overdraft, time deposits, and the like. Banks with large exposures in the short term should test the sensitivity of their assets and liabilities at very short intervals. To evaluate earnings exposure, interest rate-sensitive assets (RSAs) in each time band are netted with the interest rate-sensitive liabilities (RSLs) to produce a repricing gap for that time band. A positive gap indicates that banks have more RSAs than RSLs. A positive or asset-sensitive gap means that an increase in market interest rates would cause an increase in NII. A negative or liability-sensitive gap implies that the bank's NII would decline as a result of the increase in market interest rates.

The gap is used as a measure of interest rate sensitivity. The positive or negative gap is multiplied by the assumed interest rate changes to derive the EaR. The EaR method estimates how much the earnings might be impacted by an adverse movement in interest rates. Changes in the interest rate can be estimated on the basis of past trends, forecasting of interest rates, or other criteria. The periodic gap analysis indicates the interest rate risk exposure of banks over distinct maturities. It also suggests the magnitude of portfolio changes necessary to change the risk profile of banks.

3.8.3.2.2.2 *Limitations of gap analysis.* The gap analysis quantifies the time difference between repricing dates of assets and liabilities but fails to measure the impact of the basis and embedded option risks. The gap report will not be able to measure the entire impact of a change in interest rates within a stated time band. It has to be noted that all assets and liabilities are matured or repriced simultaneously in gap analysis. Gap analysis also fails to measure the effect of changes in interest rates on the economic or market value of assets, liabilities, and off-balance sheet position. It does not take into account any differences in the timings of payments that might occur as a result of changes in an interest rate environment. In a practical situation, the assumption of a parallel shift in the yield curves is not valid. As such, gap analysis fails to capture the variability in noninterest revenues and expenses.

3.8.3.2.2.3 *Duration gap analysis.* Duration gap analysis is an effective way to protect the economic values of banks from exposure to interest rate risk. In duration gap analysis, the duration of assets and liabilities are matched instead of matching the maturity or repricing dates. The duration gap model considers the change in the market values of assets, liabilities, and off-balance sheet items. In other words, the economic value changes to market interest rates are estimated by calculating the duration of each asset, liability, and off-balance sheet position (OBS), and assigning weights to arrive at the weighted duration of assets, liabilities, and OBS. Based on the weighted duration of assets and liabilities, a duration gap is worked out mathematically. When weighted assets and liabilities are matched, the market interest rate movements have almost the same impact on assets, liabilities, and off-balance sheet items.

Duration is defined as the measure of the percentage change in the economic value of a position given a small deviation in the level of interest rates. The duration gap measure is used to estimate the expected change in the market value of equity (MVE) for a given change in the market interest rate. Banks' net duration is the difference between the duration of assets (DA) and the duration of liabilities (DL). If the net duration is positive (DA>DL), a decrease in market interest rates will increase the market value of equity of the bank. When the duration gap is negative (DL>DA), the MVE increases when the interest increases. Duration analysis provides a comprehensive measure of interest rate risk for the total portfolio. Duration analysis considers the time value of money and is additive in nature, thereby enabling banks to match their total assets and liabilities rather than matching individual accounts. Duration gap analysis fails to identify basis risk because the parallel shifts in the yield curve assumption is made in this case.

3.8.3.2.2.4 Simulation analysis. Many international banks use balance sheet simulation models to gauge the effect of market interest rate variations on reported earnings/economic values over different time zones. Simulation analysis overcomes the limitation of gap and duration analysis. Computer-based simulation techniques model the bank's interest rate sensitivity. Monte Carlo simulation makes assumptions about the future path of interest rates, the shape of a yield curve, pricing, and hedging strategies. In simulation analysis the detailed assessment of potential effects of changes in interest rates on earnings and economic values could be done. The simulation model is an effective tool for understanding the risk exposure in a variety of interest rate/balance sheet scenarios. Simulation models are useful for evaluating the effect of alternative business strategies on risk exposures.

3.8.3.3 Market risk

Market risk is the potential loss owing to changes in market prices or values. In other words, market risk implies the possibility of the occurrence of adverse effects on the bank's financial result and capital from changes in the value of balance sheet positions and off-balance sheet items arising from changes of prices in the market. Market risk describes the sensitivity of the value of positions to changes in market prices and/or rates. In general terms, market risks include foreign exchange risk, price risk on debt instruments, price risk on equities, and commodity risk. The assessment of exposure to market risks must include all bank activities that are sensitive to changes in market conditions. The assessment of market risk should also include open positions arising from bank activities, exposure concentration in the trading book, liquidity of financial markets where banks trade, and also the volatility of market prices and financial instruments traded by the bank. The top management of banks must have clear-cut market risk-management policies, procedures, prudential risk limits, review mechanisms, reporting, and auditing systems. The assessment time horizon for market risk is typically one day. Credit risk drivers are related to market risk drivers, including the impact of market conditions on default probabilities.

Under the Basel II framework, market risk is measured using either a standardized approach or an internal model approach. A standardized approach is a formula-based model while the internal model approach involves extensive data collection, systems, and quantitative expertise.

3.8.3.3.1 Management of market risk

3.8.3.3.1.1 Value at risk models. VaR models have become important standard risk measures at financial institutions. VaR is a single number that statistically measures the maximum likely loss over a specified time horizon at a particular probability level.

VaR models are the primary means by which financial institutions measure the magnitude of their exposure to market risk. The VaR method is employed to assess potential losses that could crystallize on trading position or portfolio due to variations in market interest rates and prices using a given confidence level, usually between 95% and 99%, within a defined period of time. VaR facilitates a number of functions, including generation of management information and oversight, establishment and control of trading limits, evaluation of performances, asset allocation, regulatory reporting, and risk oversight decisions. VaR models estimate for a given portfolio the maximum amount that a bank could lose over a specified time period with a given probability. Thus, VaR models could be used to provide a measure of risk exposure generated by the given portfolio.

Calculation of VaR is based on historical data on market prices and rates, current portfolio positions, and models for pricing these positions. These data inputs are combined in various ways to derive an estimation of a particular percentile of the loss distribution, which is typically the 99th percentile loss. According to Basel Committee norms, the computation of VaR should be based on a set of uniform quantitative inputs, namely a horizon of 10 trading days, or two calendar weeks, a 99% level of confidence, and an observation period based on at least a year of historical data. The securities held in the trading book should ideally be marked to market on a daily basis and the potential market risk should be estimated through internally developed VaR models.

There are basically three methods for VaR estimates: the delta normal approach, historic or back simulation approach, and Monte Carlo simulation approach.

(a) Delta Normal Approach

The delta normal approach is the simplest of the three methods to estimate VaR. In the first step the positions on risk factors, forecasts of volatility, and correlations for each risk factor are estimated. Portfolio risk is then estimated by a combination of linear exposures to numerous factors and by the forecast of the covariance matrix. Risk metrics a specialized form of the delta normal approach that assumes a particular structure for market prices and rates through time. Then it transforms all portfolio positions into their constituent cash flows and performs the VaR computation. This delta normal approach is not appropriate for portfolios that hold options or instruments with embedded options such as mortgage-backed securities, callable bonds, and structure notes.

(b) Historic or Back Simulation Approach

The historical approach is based on a historical record of preceding price changes. It is a simulation approach that assumes that whatever changes in prices and rates that were realized in an earlier period can be extended to the forecast horizon. These actual changes are applied to the current set of rates and then used to revalue the portfolio. The result is a set of portfolio revaluations that corresponds to the set of possible realization of rates. From that distribution, the 99th percentile loss is taken as the VaR. This model requires positions on various securities and valuation models. The method allows for nonnormality and nonlinearity.

The major limitation of this historic approach is that it uses only one sample path, which may not represent future distributions. Moreover, specification of a stochastic process for each risk factor is required.

(c) Monte Carlo Simulation Approach

This approach is the most highly regarded and sophisticated of the VaR methods. In the Monte Carlo method, assumptions are made about the distribution of changes in the market prices and rates. Then it collects data to estimate the parameters of the distribution and uses the assumptions to give successive sets of possible future realizations of changes in those rates. For each set, the portfolio is revalued, outcomes are ranked, and the appropriate VaR is selected. This method is applicable for cases with extreme nonlinearity.

The VaR can be considered as a measure of downside risk as it is the maximum expected loss at a given confidence level over a given period of time. Suppose the senior management of a bank specifies a 99% confidence level. A one-day VaR of $200 million would mean that the firm has 1% chance of making a loss in excess of $200 million based on the correct estimation of VaR. Financial institutions generally report daily VaR measures. VaRs can also be estimated for longer time periods. The daily VaR measure is widely used in financial institutions for assessing the risk of trading activities. Big banks usually disclose the data on VaR measured quarterly and generally report the number of times in a quarter the P&L had a loss that exceeded the daily VaR. VaR is the largest loss the firm expects to incur at a given confidence level, which means that VaR tells us nothing about the distribution of the losses that exceed VaR. In other words, VaR is an estimate of the minimum worst loss expected, as opposed to the expected worst loss.[5]

The RiskMetrics approach proposed by JPMorgan has become a popular method for modeling market risk. This method involves forecasting volatilities and correlations for a number of risk factors with the assumption of normality for returns. The method uses exponential weighting for the forecasts. The risks of the positions are then expressed in terms of exposures to the risk factors. The return of the portfolio is the weighted average of the returns of the risk factors. The volatility of the portfolio is computed using the formula for variance of portfolio. The approach forecasts the risk of the portfolio over the next day with the assumption of expected returns equal to zero.

3.8.3.4 Liquidity risk

Liquidity risk is the risk that occurs when a bank will not be able to meet its cash or payment obligations as they become due. This condition arises because the cash flow on assets and liabilities do not match. Liquidity risk arises when depositors intend to withdraw their funds and the bank may not be in a position to repay except by raising additional deposits at a higher cost or by a forced distress sale of assets. This process results as banks are often made to borrow "short" and lend "long." Depositors can withdraw money either at sight or at the end of fixed terms. The liquidity risk for banks arises on account of funding long-term assets by short-term liabilities thereby making the liabilities subject to rollover or refinancing risk.

In other words, liquidity risk is the possibility of adverse effects on the finances and capital of a bank causing the bank's inability to fulfill its due obligations, which, in turn, is a result of funding liquidity risk or market liquidity risk. Funding liquidity risk arises in situations of withdrawal of existing sources of financing and/or impossibility of securing new sources of financing. Market liquidity risk arises when there are difficulties in converting assets into liquid funds due to market disturbances.

Liquidity risk includes the inability to manage unplanned decreases or changes in funding sources. Liquidity risk also arises from the failure to recognize or address changes in market conditions that affect the ability to liquidate assets quickly and with minimal loss in value. Many banks capture liquidity risks under a broader category—market risk. The nature of liquidity risk has become more complex with increased investment alternatives for retail depositors, sophisticated off-balance sheet products, complicated cash flow implications, and an increase in the credit sensitivity of banking customers. The critical drivers for liquidity are the structure and depth of markets, the volatility of market prices/rates, and the involvement of traders who are market makers ready to invest capital to support trading. The Basel framework provides comprehensive regulatory guidelines with respect to liquidity risk management and supervision.

---

[5]Rene M Stulz, (2008) Risk Management Failures: What are they and when do they happen? Journal of Applied Corporate Finance, 20(4), 58-67.

3.8.3.4.1 Funding liquidity risk

Funding liquidity risk refers to the ability to meet funding obligations either by financing though the sale of assets or by borrowing. Strategically most banks manage funding liquidity risk through the ALM process. During the economic crisis of 2008, access to debt securities markets globally dried up, which compelled many governments to provide massive window facilities to market participants.

3.8.3.4.2 Trading liquidity risk

Trading liquidity, market liquidity, or asset liquidity risk is the ability to continually enter into market transactions. It has been observed that during the recent economic crisis, asset liquidity risks increased substantially when interest rate derivative spreads increased significantly, which resulted in the drying up of the product's availability. The recessionary period was also characterized by a contagion effect, which impacted multiple product groupings.

A bank can be said to have adequate liquidity when sufficient funds can be raised either by increasing liabilities or converting assets. The liquidity risk consists of funding risk, time risk, and call risk. Funding risk arises when there is a need to replace net outflows because of unexpected withdrawal/non-renewal of deposits in both wholesale and retail terms. Time risk arises from the need to compensate for nonreceipt of expected inflows of funds as a result of nonperforming assets. Call risk arises due to the process of crystallization of contingent liabilities and profitable business opportunities.

The symptoms of liquidity risks are as follows:

- Higher rate of interest offered on deposits
- Delayed payment of matured proceeds
- Delayed disbursements to borrowers against committed lines of credit
- Deteriorating asset quality
- Large contingent liabilities
- Net deposit drain

3.8.3.4.3 Principles of liquidity management

The Bank for International Settlements' Basel Committee on Banking Supervision details the key elements for effectively managing liquidity. Banks should formally adopt and implement these principles for use in the overall liquidity management process. Banks must develop a structure for liquidity management. Each bank should have an agreed strategy for day-to-day liquidity management. The bank governing board should approve the strategy and significant policies related to liquidity management. The governing board should approve the strategy and significant policies related to liquidity management. The governing board also must ensure that senior management of banks takes the steps necessary to monitor and control liquidity risks. Banks should also have in place a measurement, monitoring, and control system for its liquidity positions in the major currencies in which it is active. Banks should also undertake separate analysis of its strategy for each currency individually.

3.8.3.4.4 Management of liquidity risk

A bank should use different liquidity risk mitigation techniques such as stress test, sensitivity, and scenario analysis. Use of off-balance sheet activities in the stress tests is required. Banks have to have a contingency plan in place for early detection of possible liquidity problems.

The level of the bank's liquidity is expressed by the liquidity ratio. The liquidity ratio is the ratio between the sum of the bank's liquid first- and second-degree receivables on the one hand and the sum of the bank's sight liabilities or liabilities without determined maturity and the bank's liabilities with maturity. It is the cash held by the bank as a proportion of deposits in the bank.

$$\text{Liquidity ratio} = \text{Highly liquid assets} / \text{Total liabilities not including equity}$$

The general standards imply that banks should maintain a liquidity ratio of at least 15%. The highly liquid assets consist of vault cash, precious metals, deposits with central payments office (CPO), other financial institutions, and marketable securities.

The important liquidity risk measurement ratios are as follows:

(a) Loans to total assets

This ratio measures total loans outstanding as a percentage of total assets. The higher the ratio, the greater the liquidity risk, which denotes higher default rates.

(b) Loans to core deposits

A bank's liquidity can be assessed by the loans to deposits ratio known as the LTD ratio. The LTD is calculated by dividing the bank's total loans by its total deposits. A high value for the ratio indicates that the bank doesn't have enough liquidity to cover any unexpected contingencies. A low ratio indicates a low earning potential status for the bank.

(c) Large liabilities (minus) temporary investments to earning assets (minus) temporary investments ratio

Large liabilities represent wholesale deposits, which are market sensitive. Temporary investments are those investments that can be readily sold in the market.

(d) Purchased funds to total assets

The purchased funds include the entire interbank and other money market borrowings, which include certificates of deposits and institutional deposits.

(e) Loan losses/net loans

This ratio forms part of the asset quality ratios of the bank and determine the quality of loans of a bank.

3.8.3.4.5 Liquidity gap and liquidity management

Liquidity risk management can be studied broadly under three methods: (1) static approach-ratio analysis, (2) dynamic liquidity analysis, and (3) structural liquidity analysis.

(1) Static approach-ratio analysis

This produces the volatile liability dependence ratio (VLDR).

VLDR = Volatile liabilities − temporary investments/net loans + investments due in more than one year

This ratio indicates the extent to which banks rely on volatile funds to support long-term assets.

Static approach-ratio analysis also uses the core deposit growth rate (CDGR).

CDGR = Core deposit growth/asset growth

This ratio shows how much the asset growth was funded by core deposit growth. The higher the ratio the better the liquidity position.

(2) Dynamic liquidity analysis

This cash flow-based analysis tool is used for assessing day-to-day liquidity needs of financial institutions. In this method due importance is given to the seasonal pattern of deposits/loans. In dynamic liquidity analysis, the important factors analyzed include potential liquidity for new loans, unavailed credit limits, loan policy, potential deposit losses, investment obligations, statutory obligations, and more.

(3) Structural liquidity analysis

Structural liquidity analysis involves preparation of a statement of structural liquidity by taking into account the balance sheet on a particular date. The balance sheet items are placed in the maturity ladder according to time periods that are related to expected timings of cash flows. The assets, liabilities, and off-balance sheet items are to be pegged on a particular day and the behavioral pattern and the sensitivity of these items to changes in market interest rates and environment are duly accounted for.

The short-term liquidity ladder takes into account only balance sheet items in eight maturity buckets and does not recognize any future business growth involving additional inflows and outflows.

The negative gaps in the individual time periods are controlled by placing prudential limits on bases of business structure and financial flexibility of individual banks.

The use of the maturity ladder and calculation of cumulative surplus or deficit of funds at selected maturity dates is recommended as a standard tool. Banks have to analyze the behavioral maturity profile of various components of on/off-balance sheet items on the basis of assumptions and trend analysis supported by time series analysis. Banks are also required to undertake variance analysis to validate the assumptions.

Banks can also put in place certain prudential limits to avoid a liquidity crisis.

- Cap on interbank borrowings, especially call borrowings
- Purchased funds vis-à-vis liquid assets
- Core deposits vis-à-vis core assets (i.e., cash reserve ratio, liquidity reserve ratio, and loans)
- Duration of liabilities and investment portfolio
- Maximum cumulative outflows. Banks should fix cumulative mismatches across all time bands
- Commitment ratio—track the total commitments given to corporations/banks and other financial institutions to limit the off-balance sheet exposure
- Swapped funds ratio (i.e., extent of domestic currency raised out of foreign currency sources)

3.8.3.4.6 Alternate scenarios

The liquidity profiles of banks depend on the market conditions, which influence the cash flow behavior. Banks have to evaluate the liquidity profile under normal conditions, bank-specific crisis, and market crisis scenario. Banks should establish a benchmark for normal situations with respect to cash flow profile of on/off-balance sheet items and managing net fund requirements. Estimating liquidity under bank-specific crisis situations provides the worst-case benchmark. In this scenario, purchased funds are assumed not to be rolled over easily and core deposits could be closed prematurely along with substantial nonperforming assets. Market scenario analysis is done with respect to extreme tightening of liquidity conditions arising out of market disruptions, failure of major banks, financial crisis, and contagion. In this situation, the rollover of high-value customer deposits and purchased funds is assumed to be extremely difficult along with flight of volatile deposits. Banks are also entailed to incur a huge capital loss due to the sale of investments at huge discounts. Banks should prepare contingency plans to withstand any bank-specific or market crisis situation.

The general framework of the liquidity risk management process involves managing liquidity under normal scenarios and stress conditions. Some of the industry-standard liquidity management tools are as follows:

(a) Static funding gap

It is calculated as the net asset position over total liabilities. Basically, it defines the short fall in maturing liabilities required to service maturing assets. It is usually calculated on a maturity bucket basis.

(b) Dynamic cash flow gap

It is a measurement based on maturing assets and liabilities plus assumed marketable asset liquidation over a given period.

(c) Liquidity assets ratio

It is the ratio of liquid assets to total liabilities. The liquid assets include cash and cash equivalents, trading account securities, and repo investments into government securities.

(d) Concentration ratios

This ratio reassures the funding from a particular source compared to assets/liabilities or capital.

(e) Liquidity stress measurement

Ratios are used for measurement under different stress scenarios.

3.8.3.4.7 Challenges of liquidity management

Funding liquidity risk embedded in the balance sheet remains the major challenge for ALM units. The business maturity transformation process results in liquidity, interest rate, and currency mismatches. Since the subprime mortgage crisis, the maturity transformation process consisting of funding of long-term mortgages and other securitized assets with short-term liabilities has grown in relevance. It is high time that banks assess the buoyancy of funding and liquidity sources through the ALM process.

3.8.3.5 Operational risk

Basel II defines operational risk as the "risk of loss resulting from inadequate processes, people and systems or from external events." Operational losses result from internal fraud, external fraud, employment practices, workplace safety, clients, products, and business practices, damage to physical assets, business disruptions and system failures, and execution, delivery, and process management. Operational risk consists of breakdowns in internal controls and corporate governance. These risks lead to financial loss through error, fraud, or failure to perform. Operational risk can also be considered as risk that arises from various types of human or technical error. It also includes loan fraud and embezzlement that affect its day-to-day business.

Measuring operational risk requires estimating the probability of an operational loss event and the potential size of the loss. The process of operational risk assessment has to address the effect of operational risk on business objectives and options to manage and initiate actions to reduce or mitigate operational risks. The operational risk monitoring system focuses on operational performance measures such as volume, turnover, settlement facts, delays, and errors.

A McKinsey Research[6] report has shown that a decline in market value following an operational crisis is far greater than the financial loss. Financial institutions need to understand the different kinds of operational risk faced and the amount of potential losses to reduce their exposure. From 2001 to 2005, risk-related losses in financial services at the top 12 US banks represented 4-5% of their net income.[7]

---

[6]Robert S Dunnet, Cindy B Levy, Antonio P Simoes, (2005) Managing operational risk in banking, Mckinsey Quarterly Number 1, 21-24.
[7]Cindy B Levy, HamidSamandri, Antonio P Simoes, (2006) Better operational risk management for banks, Mckinsey on Corporate and Investment Banking Number 2.

3.8.3.5.1 Operational risk management

The management of operational risk essentially requires the ability to track and monitor performances of specified operational processes and systems. The operational risk management system also has to maintain databases of operational loss experiences. Internal controls and internal audits are used as the primary means to mitigate operational risk. Banks could also explore setting up operational risk limits, based on the measures of operational risk. Banks should have well-defined policies on operational risk management. A well-established internal control system includes segregation of duties and clears management reporting lines and adequate operating procedures. Most operational risk events are associated with weak links in internal control systems or laxity in complying with existing internal control procedures. There should be self-assessment of the internal control environment.

The worst operational risk crisis is associated with embezzlement, loan fraud, deceptive sales practices, antitrust violations, and noncompliance with industry regulations. It is observed that banks with better operational risk practices enjoy improved market sentiments and higher share prices.

All First is a Baltimore-based subsidiary of Allied Irish Bank. All First lost $691 million because of a single rogue trader whose practices went undetected for five years until he was caught in 2002. In 2011, Switzerland's biggest bank received a huge blow when the bank lost around $2 billion (£1.3 billion) at the hands of a rogue trader.

3.8.3.6 Other perspectives of risk

3.8.3.6.1 Residual risk

Residual risk is the likelihood of the occurrence of adverse effects on a financial result and on a bank's capital because their credit risk mitigation techniques are less efficient than anticipated or their implementation does not sufficiently reduce the risks to which the bank is exposed.

3.8.3.6.2 Dilution risk

Dilution risk is the possibility of the occurrence of adverse effects on a bank's financial result and its capital due to the reduced value of purchased receivables as a result of cash or noncash liabilities of the former creditor to the debtor.

3.8.3.6.3 Settlement risk

Settlement/delivery risk is the possibility of adverse effects on a bank's financial results and capital arising from unsettled transactions or the counterparty's failure to deliver in free delivery transactions on the due delivery date.

3.8.3.6.4 Compliance risk

Compliance risk is the risk to current or anticipated earnings or capital arising from violations of or nonconformance with laws, rules, regulations, prescribed practices, internal procedures, or ethical standards. Compliance risk also arises as a result of failure to comply with procedures for the prevention of money laundering and the financing of terrorism. Compliance risk encompasses any risk of sanctions by regulatory authority, risk of financial losses, and reputational risk. In short, it can be stated that this risk encompasses noncompliance with all laws and regulations, prudent ethical standards, and contractual obligations. It also includes the exposure to litigation often known as legal risk.

3.8.3.6.5 Strategic risk

Strategic risk deals with the adverse effects on a bank's performance owing to the absence of adequate policies and strategies. Strategic risk arises on account of the failure of banks to respond strategically to economic, technological, competitive, regulatory, and other environmental changes. Strategic risk arises from adverse business decisions.

3.8.3.6.6 Reputational risk

A reputational risk is the risk that the intangible asset of a stakeholder's perception about the bank will lose value and result in financial losses. It is the risk to the current or anticipated earnings or enterprise value because of negative public opinion. Adverse media coverage also results in reputational risk. Reputational risk impairs the institution's strategic pursuit to establish new relationships or services along with the impact on existing services. Reputational risk may also expose a bank to litigation. It is observed that banks having diversified asset management divisions are more likely to have higher reputational risk.

3.8.3.6.7 Concentration risk

Concentration risk refers to groups of exposures with a similar risk category such as economic sectors, geographic areas, types of products, and other exposures. Concentration risk arises from maturity and currency mismatches of credit-hedging instruments. Concentration risk can be managed through the active management of a credit portfolio.

3.8.3.6.8 Country risk

Country risk refers to political, economic, and transfer risks. Transfer risks imply the possibility of losses arising from a bank's inability to collect receivables in a currency owing to restrictions enacted by the government. In this case, restrictions on payment of obligations to creditors from other countries may exist. Country risks can be related to the effects of government action or political force majeure.

3.8.3.6.9 Foreign exchange risk

The risk profile of a bank's balance sheet is affected by the volatility in forex rates. It is the risk that a bank may suffer losses on account of adverse exchange rate movements, which have an impact on open-currency positions. Thus, foreign exchange risk arises from a mismatch of currency and assets with liabilities. Foreign exchange risk is also related to interest rate risk and liquidity risk. Setting appropriate limits in open positions and gaps is essential for forex risk management. Maturity and position (MAP), interest rate sensitivity (SIR), and VaR are some of the approaches to measuring foreign exchange risk.

3.8.3.6.10 Delivery risk

Delivery risk encompasses operational, technological, new product, and strategic risk. Operational risk is the ability of a bank to deliver its financial services in a profitable manner. Technological risk arises as the delivery system becomes inefficient due to new delivery systems. New product risk is associated with the delivery of new products and services. Strategic risks refer to the ability of banks to select geographic and product areas that will be profitable in a complex environment.

3.8.3.6.11 Price risk

Price risk is the risk to current or anticipated earnings or capital arising from changes in the value of their trading portfolios or other obligations, which are part of distributing risks. These portfolios are typically subject to daily price movements and are accounted for primarily on a market-to-market basis.

These risks are highest from market making, dealing and position taking in interest rates, foreign exchange, equity, commodities, and credit markets.

Price risk also arises in banking activities whose value changes are reflected in the income statement, such as in lending pipelines and mortgage servicing rights. The risks to earnings or capital arising from the conversion of a bank's financial statements from foreign currency translation should also be assessed under price risk.

RISK MANAGEMENT SYSTEM FAILURE: THE CASE OF LTCM

Risk management has become a critical challenge to financial institutions all over the world. In the modern context, banks have to give greater importance to credit risk management. The implementation of the Basel Accord has made banks move toward the quantitative risk evaluation of their loan products. Banks face quantitative challenges with respect to the calculation of default probabilities for the loan default by client, loss rate estimation, and the issues related to structural elements of a credit deal. Sophisticated risk management techniques for managing credit, operational, and market risk have to be put in place by banks to cover up their potential losses. The importance of risk management techniques for banks have become more relevant in the last two decades, particularly in the context of huge losses suffered by financial institutions such as Long Term Capital Management (LTCM), Barings Bank, and Metallgesellschaft.

The year 1988 witnessed the collapse of LTCM, the world's largest hedge fund. The primary factor contributing to LTCM's failure was its poor risk management techniques. In addition to hedge funds, LTCM also relied heavily on convergence arbitrage, which was a reflection of its poor fund investment strategy. LTCM failed to estimate the fund's potential risk exposure correctly through VaR analysis.

In the late 1990s, LTCM emerged as one of the most highly leveraged hedge funds in the world through its modern hedging strategies. The fund performed exceedingly well for most of its life, with investors earning 20% in 10 months in 1994, 43% in 1995, 41% in 1996, and 17% in 1997. In August and September of 1998, following the default of Russia on its ruble-denominated debt, world capital markets were in crisis and LTCM lost most of its capital.

The financial institution had a capital base of $3 billion with assets worth $100 billion and derivative assets valued at over $1.25 trillion. LTCM used different VaR techniques to measure market risk exposure. Its VaR analysis showed that investors might experience a loss of 5% or more in about one month in five, and a loss of 10% or more in about one month in ten. Only one year in 50 should it lose at least 20% of its portfolio. LTCM observed that a decline of approximately 45% in its equity value with a 10 standard deviation was a near impossible thing for the company. The heavy reliance on its VaR estimates proved to be a terrible mistake for LTCM. In fact, LTCM believed that historical trends in securities movements were an accurate predictor of future movements, which led the company to sell options in which the implied volatility was higher than the historical volatility. The reliance on a risk model that underestimated the probability of a large downward movement in securities prices led LTCM to be overly optimistic in its hedging strategies. In August 1998, the VaR models used by LTCM failed to detect nonlinearity events such as the Russian default on its sovereign debt and the liquidity crisis in the global financial markets. The LTCM VaR models had estimated the fund's loss would be no more than $50 million of capital. But in reality, the fund soon found itself losing $100 million every day. Fearing that LTCM's collapse would create havoc in the global financial system based on its highly leveraged derivative positions, the Federal Reserve pumped in a $3.6 billion bailout package.

By August 1998, LTCM faced the dilemma between reducing risk and raising additional capital. LTCM faced harsh liquidity positions when its investments began losing value. LTCM's actual exposure to liquidity and solvency risks was not factored into by its VaR models. LTCM relied too much on VaR models and too little on stress testing, gap risk, and liquidity risk. The lessons learned from this crisis signify the importance of imposing stress loss limits on portfolios to protect against extreme shocks. In short, LTCM severely underestimated its risk. The trading positions were undiversified, thereby exposing the company to liquidity, credit, and volatility spreads.

References

(1) Mete Feridun, (2006) Risk Management in banks and other financial institutions: Lessons from the crash of Long Term Capital Management (LTCM). Banks and Bank Systems, 1, 3, 132-141.

(2) R. Lowenstein, (2000) When Genius Failed: The Rise and Fall of Log-Term Capital Management. New York: Random House, 21-45.

MANAGING RISK FAILURES

It is often said that risk metrics is the cornerstone of risk management as it determines what top management learns from risk managers about the overall risk position of the firm. Basically there are five types of risk management failures: Failure to use appropriate risk metrics, mismeasurement of known risks, failure to take known risks into account, failure in communicating risks to top management, and failure in monitoring and managing risks (Rene, 2008). The choice of an appropriate risk metric is a critical factor to avoid risk management failures. VaR is the most modern basic technique used to estimate risk exposure but exclusive focus on VaR could lead risk managers to ignore other critical dimensions of risk.

Top management has to analyze long-run indicators and implications of risk. VaR doesn't have the ability to analyze catastrophic losses with a small probability of occurrences. Risk managers could also falter in terms of choosing the correct distribution, assessing the probability of a large loss, and determining the size of loss given that the event takes place. Statistical modeling techniques are effective in estimating the distribution of known risks based on the availability of historical data. But historical data is of limited use in situations where the risk has not manifested itself in the past. For example, there had been no instances of a downturn in the real estate market in the context of large amounts of securitized subprime mortgages prior to the subprime mortgage crisis. In this case, the distribution of losses associated with the sharp downturn of real estate prices couldn't be correctly modeled based on historical data. Risk managers also tend to ignore a known risk because it is not significant in their assumptions or it may be difficult to incorporate it in risk models. For example, traders have an option such as payoff compensation whereby they receive a significant share of the profits they generate, but they do not have to pay back the losses. This model of compensation creates incentives for traders to take more and more risks.

By monitoring some of the risks, they can increase their expected compensation by increasing the risks that are not monitored. Some firms prohibit trading of new financial instruments citing reasons for proper modeling of risks. But this involves costs, as it is often extremely valuable for traders to be active at the start of a new market. It is pertinent for risk managers to develop a methodological approach to identifying and anticipating unknown risks in its scenario planning exercises. Communication failures have been identified as a major reason for many risk management failures in recent years. Timely information to the board and to top management is essential for assessing the consequences of retaining or laying off risks. The effectiveness of risk monitoring and control depends on a firm's culture and incentives.

Reference
Rene M. Stulz, (2008) Risk Management Failures: What are they and when do they happen? *Journal of Applied Corporate Finance*, 20, 4, 58-67.

FINANCIAL CRISIS 2008 AND RISK MANAGEMENT FAILURE OF MAJOR BANKS

The financial meltdown of 2008 that spurred the largest economic downturn since the Great Depression was the result of excessive risk taken by banks and neglect by financial regulators. Regulators, politicians, and bankers were to blame for the 2008 financial slowdown. The International Monetary Fund (IMF) estimated that the scale of losses that started in 2007 exceeded US$4 trillion.

UBS suffered among the largest losses of any European bank during the subprime mortgage crisis. Before the crisis, UBS was considered to be a conservative and solid international bank with exemplary risk management practices. Approximately 3000 people were employed in the risk assessment section. The group CEO and vice president of the board of directors were members of the risk committee. Internal and external audits were conducted on a regular basis. In 2007 and 2008, UBS suffered losses of US$19 billion from positions in mortgaged-backed securities alone. UBS's total losses in the mortgage market were in excess of US$37 billion. It was the largest write-down by any bank since the credit crunch began. Earlier, UBS was convinced that it had predominantly first-class subprime positions on its books. Two years preceding the crisis saw the bank's growth in asset-backed securities outpacing other sectors in the fixed income market. The greatest part of the UBS losses was incurred on securities that had been given the highest rating (AAA). UBS's reputation changed dramatically. Normally based on VaR estimates, UBS should have experienced about two or three exceptions (i.e., 1% of 250 days). Instead, UBS suffered 27 exceptions during the year 2007. The crisis had resulted from the bank's actions that combined a predilection for risk taking with an overestimation of its own ability.

Continued

FINANCIAL CRISIS 2008 AND RISK MANAGEMENT FAILURE OF MAJOR BANKS–cont'd

The in-house hedge fund Dillon Read Capital Management (DRCM), which operated as an independent division within the UBS Group, invested heavily in low-quality paper. As a result, it began showing a loss as early as the first quarter of 2007. UBS went on purchasing highly rated subprime paper while other banks were quickly unloading their positions. In May 2007, UBS announced the closure of DRCM. In the same year, the bank received a large capital injection from the government of Singapore Investment Corporation, the bank's largest shareholder.

Another example of the pivotal role of mortgage-backed securities in the credit crisis is evident in the collapse of Bear Stearns, the fifth-largest investment bank in the United States. Bear Stearns was one of the biggest underwriters of complex investments linked to mortgages. Two of its hedge funds that heavily invested in subprime mortgages became the major casualty of the financial crisis. The firm spiraled from being healthy to practically insolvent within a short period. Bear's investors became increasingly reluctant to do business with the investment bank. In March 2008, faced with a slew of withdrawals from clients and pullback from lenders, the firm had less than $3 billion in cash on hand. Bear Stearns failed because its investors no longer believed that it could repay its loans—even its short-term, overnight loans. Bear Stearns's web of intertwined agreements with other banks and investment houses couldn't prevent the collapse of the company. JPMorgan Chase bailed out Bear Stearns for $236 million to prevent filing of bankruptcy; this was just $2 a share to take over the investment bank, which a year previously was trading as high as $170 a share. The Federal Reserve, which engineered the emergency bailout of Bear, provided up to $30 billion for Bear Stearns's less liquid assets.

The subsequent sudden failure of Lehman Brothers in mid-September 2008 was a watershed moment in the global financial crisis. With over $639 billion in assets and $613 billion in liabilities, the Lehman Brothers's bankruptcy was the largest in US history. Lehman's insolvency resulted in more than 75 separate and distinct bankruptcy proceedings. Some of the causes leading to the crisis were the overreliance on the market for credit default swaps (CDOs), misrepresentation of financial statements, complex structuring of the company, and unethical values in top management. Lehman used financial engineering to temporarily shuffle $50 billion of assets off its books in the months before its collapse to conceal its dependence on leverage, or borrowed money. The company had had negative cash flows for three years prior to the crisis despite healthy-looking balance sheets and income statements.

Banks such as Merrill Lynch had bought pools of mortgages and bundled them into securities, eventually making them into CDOs. Merrill Lynch paid upfront for the mortgages, but this outlay was quickly repaid as the bank made the securities and sold them to investors. The origins of Merrill's crisis came at the beginning of 2006 when the giant insurer AIG decided to stop buying the assets known as "super seniors." The super senior was the top portion of a CDO, meaning investors who owned it were the first to be compensated as homeowners paid their mortgages and the last in line to take losses should the homeowners become delinquent. During 2008, Merrill sustained huge losses, forcing its sale to Bank of America in a deal worth $50 billion.

The financial crisis highlighted the importance of transparency of internal controls and effective risk-mitigation strategies. The crisis also highlighted the need to aggressively address the contractual, operational, and technical challenges posed by counterparty risk, particularly on bilateral derivative trades.

References

(1) Tobias Straumann, (September 2010) The UBS Crisis in historical perspective, University of Zurich Institute for Empirical Research in Economics.

(2) http://www.bbc.co.uk/news/business-12297002?

(3) http://www.riskmanagementmonitor.com/the-financial-crisis-was-a-failure-of-risk-management-says-the-federal-government/

(4) UBS, (April 2008) Shareholder Report on UBS's Write-Downs, p. 24.

(5) John Waggoner, David J. Lynch, Red flags in Bear Stearns Collapse.

(6) http://www.usatoday.com/money/industries/banking/2008-03-17-bear-stearns-bailout_N.htm

(7) http://www.economist.com/node/13226308

(8) Lehman Brothers Bankruptcy Filing, http://www.rediff.com/money/2008/sep/16lehman.pdf. Accessed 07 April 2009.

(9) http://www.msnbc.msn.com/id/31066137/media-kit/

3.9 RISKS IN MAJOR NONBANKING FINANCIAL INSTITUTIONS

3.9.1 RISKS IN INSURANCE

There are two categories of risk in insurance—speculative or dynamic risks and pure or static risk. Speculative risk arises as a result of various decisions such as venturing into a new market, purchasing new equipment, and investing in stocks/bonds where the end result may be either profit or loss. Speculative risk is uninsurable. Pure (static) risks involve conditions of loss or no loss as compared to loss or profit with speculative risk. Examples of pure risks include premature death, occupational disability, and medical expenses. Private insurance companies usually insure only pure risks. The major types of pure risk are classified as personal risks, property risks, and liability risks. The major personal risks that directly affect an individual are premature death, old age, poor health, and unemployment. Personal risks lead to loss or reduction of income and elimination of financial assets. Fundamental risks, which affect the entire economy, include inflation, economic crisis, and natural disasters. Particular risks affect only individuals.

The risks in the insurance business sector can be classified as technical, asset, and other risks. Technical risks derive from the nature of the business of the insurance sector. Underpricing, unforeseen or inadequately understood events, and insufficient reinsurance are examples of technical risks. The calculation of insurance liabilities is based on statistical probability or actuarial techniques. If the calculations go wrong then liabilities would be understated or premiums would be undercharged. Insurers also face market risk, credit risk, and, to some extent, liquidity risk.

Banks are considered to be risk averse and not suited to take on general insurance risks. Banks and life insurance companies differ in the respect that the maturity of liabilities in banks is generally shorter than those of life insurance companies. Hence, life insurance companies can play a larger role in long-term financing. Life insurance is less prone to liquidity crisis.

3.9.1.1 Underwriting and investment risk

Underwriting and investment are two important and related business activities of insurance companies. The management of underwriting and investment risks is a major aspect of an insurer's operation. Underwriting risk refers to the loss on underwriting activity in the insurance or securities industry. Underwriting risk may arise from an inaccurate assessment of the risks entailed in writing an insurance policy. In underwriting, insurers take on risks in exchange for premiums. The difference between earned premiums and the sum of claims and expenses represent the insurer's underwriting profit. Underwriting risk arises when actual insurance claims and expenses incurred deviate from the expected values that had determined the premium level, which leads to fluctuation of underwriting profit. In other words, underwriting risk is the risk related to entering into insurance contracts in which the premiums charged do not adequately cover the claims the company has to pay.

Underwriting risk in property casualty insurance is the risk of insured losses in the property casualty business (insurance and reinsurance) being higher than expected. In other words, underwriting risk is the risk related to entering into insurance contracts. The significant risks in property casualty insurance are the premium and reserve risks. The underwriting risks in the life or health business are the risks that insured benefits payable in life or health business (insurance and reinsurance) may be higher than expected. Investment risk is the risk of volatility in financial markets that will impact the results of operations and finance. Investment assets and provisions for claims are exposed to interest rate changes.

3.9.1.2 Other risks in the insurance business

Market risk is the risk of economic losses that results from risk of economic losses resulting from price changes in capital markets.

Credit risks incur as a result of changes in the financial situation of a counterparty such as an issuer of securities. Credit risks also arise out of investments and payment transactions with clients. Operational risks are potential losses that result from inadequate processes, technical failure, internal procedures, breakdown of infrastructure, IT security, and the like. Liquidity risk arises when insurance companies are unable to meet payment obligations.

Provisioning risk relates to the provisions for claims made to cover future payments on claims incurred. This risk arises from exposure to changes in inflation, interest rates, disbursement patterns, economic trends, legislation, and court decisions.

3.9.2 RISK IN PENSION FUNDS

Defined benefit plans are generally more certain about the amount of the promised retirement benefits than the defined contribution plans. The major risks in defined benefit plans are firm-specific risks and funding risks. The other risks include investment risks, plan termination risks, compliance risk, and additional plan risks. The firm-specific risk arises when the plan sponsor faces financial distress and is unable to pay the promised pension. The financial condition of the sponsor affects its ability to fund its pension obligations as well as places employees at risk for their jobs. Another major risk is associated with the funding status of the plan, which, in turn, depends on the investment performance of plan assets. Investment risks are thereby dependent on the investment performance of the plan, which relies on asset allocation, security selection, and market performance. Plan termination risk arises when pension corporations terminate their defined benefit plans to reduce funding costs or regain excess pension assets. Compliance risk arises when pension plans violate antidiscrimination laws of the Internal Revenue Service (IRS). When this happens, the contributions to the pension plan or the earnings from the plan are immediately taxed. Defined pension plans also face risks on additional aspects such as changes in the taxation policy of pensions, use of the sponsor's own securities to fund the plan, and revisions to the plan document. Successive governments may adopt changes in the level of tax-deductible contributions to defined benefit pension plans. These changes reduce the attractiveness of such defined benefit plans, which may then be converted into defined contribution plans.

Defined contribution plans guarantee no fixed benefit; the ultimate retirement benefit is determined by the rate of return earned on funds contributed to the account and the total amount contributed. There is no funding risk in a defined contribution plan as it is always fully funded. The sponsor shifts all of the funding risks to employees. Investment risk is present in a defined contribution plan as participants' rate of return earned on funds depends on the various investment options decided by participants. Some defined contribution plans face liquidity risk stemming from provisions in the plan document, which allows loans for plan participants. In such cases, the plan is under obligation to provide the funds. If the economic situation is unfavorable (e.g., rising interest rates or falling share prices) then the plan may have to liquidate securities at unfavorable prices and incur huge losses on the pension portfolio. The plans are compelled to hold large liquid assets to minimize these liquidity risks, but this, in turn, results in lower investment returns. To provide a safety net for employee retirement benefits, Congress passed the Employee Retirement Income Security Act (ERISA) in 1974, which set mandatory funding requirements for defined benefit pension plans and established minimum vesting requirements.

3.9.2.1 Risk management of pension funds

Risk management has become a sophisticated function within financial institutions. Pension fund risk is defined in terms of a trade-off between risk and return on the assets built against their fund obligations.

In defined benefit pension funds, the major steps in risk management consist of measurement and assessment of pension fund risks. The design, monitoring, and revision of the fund's parameters (e.g., contributions, benefits, and investments) are made in line with the objectives of the funds. Defined benefit pension plans are subject to investment, inflation, and longevity risks. Plan members are exposed to the risk that pension fund assets will not cover benefit promises if the plan is terminated.

Asset liability modeling is (ALM) is a key strategic tool used by pension fund managers for risk management. The ALM method involves developing mathematical formulas for pension fund assets and liabilities based on certain assumptions of economic, financial, and biometric variables that affect the evolution of assets and liabilities. Monte Carlo simulations and other stochastic models are capable of generating a number of scenarios simulating assets and liabilities. Traditional ALM models focus on asset optimization with deterministic view on liabilities. New risk immunization techniques such as liability driven investment (LDI) strategies consider the stochastic nature of liabilities of investors.

3.9.3 RISK IN MUTUAL FUNDS

The level of risk in a mutual fund depends on the type of investment. The higher the potential returns, the higher the risks. Stock-based mutual funds are riskier than bond-based mutual funds. All types of investments are affected by market risk in mutual funds due to the decline in the value of investments. All types of investments are affected by liquidity risk because the fund will not be able to sell an investment that declines in value because there are no buyers. Fixed income securities are affected by credit risk, and the investment will have no value if the bond issuer can't repay bonds.

Call risk is one of the types of risk in mutual funds. When the rate of interest falls, the party who issued the bond will redeem or otherwise go for the call option. The issuer has the right to redeem it before its maturity date. Investments of fixed income securities are also affected by interest rate risk in asmuch as the value of fixed income securities decline when interest rates rise. Mutual funds' investments are also affected by country and currency risks.

3.10 SUMMARY

The recent economic crisis and turmoil in credit markets underscores important principles for financial institutions' risk management, including the value of proper risk identification and measurement. The major steps financial institutions need to take to identify risk are identifying, measuring, monitoring, and controlling risks. The major risks faced by financial institutions include credit risks, interest rate risks, market risks, and operating and liquidity risks. The three basic strategies involved in mitigating risk are avoidance or elimination of risk by simple business practices, transfer of risk to other participants, and active management of risk at the firm level. Financial institutions such as banks face major challenges with respect to organizational structure, decentralization of resources, poor integration of systems, and lack of transparent reporting systems. The major tools of the risk management systems used by banks are stress testing and asset and liability management. The major risks faced by banks are credit risk, counterparty risk, interest rate risk, market risk, liquidity risks, and operational risks. Other risks are residual, dilution, settlement, compliance, concentration, country, foreign exchange, strategic, and reputational risks. The different forms of interest rate risk are gap or mismatch risk, basis risk, embedded option risk, yield curve risk, price risk, and reinvestment risk, among others. The instruments for credit risk management consist of estimating expected loan losses, multitiered credit approval systems, prudential limits, risk ratings, risk pricing, portfolio models, and loan review mechanisms. The instruments for measurement of interest rate risk are maturity gap analysis, duration gap analysis, and simulation analysis. The basic model for measurement of market risk is VaR. Liquidity risks are measured through various ratios. The risks in major nonbanking financial institutions such as insurance include underwriting and investment risks along with market, credit, and provisioning risks. Pension fund risks consist of firm-specific risks, funding risks, investment risks, plan termination risks, and compliance risks. Mutual fund risks consist of market risks, liquidity risks, call risks, and currency risks.

QUESTIONS FOR DISCUSSION

1. What are the basic risk mitigation strategies?
2. Explain the structure of the risk management framework in banks.
3. Discuss risk management systems.
4. Explain credit risk.
5. Explain how credit risk is managed.
6. What are the different types of interest rate risks?
7. How is interest rate risk measured?
8. Discuss market risk management.
9. Discuss liquidity risk and its management.
10. Discuss operational risk and its management.
11. List other types of risks.
12. What are the major risks in nonbanking financial institutions?

REFERENCES

Buehler, K., Pritsch, G., 2003. Running with risk. Mckinsey Quarterly 4, 40–49.
Risk Management Systems in Banks. http://rbidocs.rbi.org.in/rdocs/notification/PDFs/9492.pdf.
Bogoslaw, 2009. How banks should manage their risks. http://www.businessweek.com/investor/content/sep2009/pi20090914_336015_page_2.htm.
Technical Assistance Consultant's Report. Risk management and asset and liability management in banks, Focus Paper, Asian Development Bank.
Bank Supervision and Examination Process, Large Bank Supervision, Comptrollers Handbook, January 2010. Comptroller of the Currency Administrator of National Banks.
Mark, C., Rene S., 2006. The Risk of Financial Institutions, National Bureau of Economic Research, volume ISBN: 0-226-09285-2. University of Chicago Press. URL: http://www.nber.org/books/care06-1.

Blome, S., et al., 2007. Pension fund regulation and risk management: results from an ALM optimization exercise. OECD Working Papers on Insurance and Private Pensions, No 8. OECD Publishing, http://dx.doi.org/10.17 87/171755452623 1OECD.

McLeod, R.W., Moody, S., Phillips, A., 1992. Risks of pension plans. Financial Services Review 1057-08102 (2), 131–156.

Oldfield, G.S., Santomero, A.M. 95-05-B, 1995. The Place of Risk Management in Financial Institutions, Wharton Financial Institutions Centre.

Santomero, A.M., 1995. Financial risk management: the whys and hows. Financial Markets, Institutions and Instruments 4 (5), 1–14.

Guidance for stress testing for banking organizations with total consolidated assets of more than $10 billion, May 14, 2012. http://www.federalreserve.gov/bankinforeg/srletters/sr1207a1.pdf.

What is bank stress test? IMF Survey Online, July 29, 2010. http://www.imf.org/external/pubs/ft/survey/so/2010/pol072910a.htm.

MONEY MARKETS, BOND MARKETS, AND MORTGAGE MARKETS

4.1 INTRODUCTION

A *financial market* can be considered as any marketplace where buyers and sellers engage in the trade of assets such as equities, debt instruments (e.g., bonds), currencies, and derivatives. Financial markets are characterized by transparent pricing and basic regulations on trading, costs, and fees. Investors have access to a number of financial markets and exchanges that represent a vast array of financial products. The capital market is the place where individuals and institutions trade financial securities. Capital markets consist of money market, bond market, mortgage market, stock market, spot or cash market, derivatives market, foreign exchange market, and interbank market.

The money market is an integral part of the financial market in which financial instruments with high liquidity and short maturities are traded. In the money market, borrowing and lending take place for a short period of time, which ranges from several days to less than a year.

The bond market consists of various debt instruments used by corporate state governments, municipalities, and foreign governments to finance a number of activities. Bonds are bought and sold by investors on credit markets throughout the world. The bond market is also known as a debt, credit, or fixed-income securities market. Mortgage markets are markets where mortgage loans and servicing rights are traded between different participants including mortgage originators, mortgage aggregators (securitizers), and investors. Mortgage originators are basically financial institutions such as saving institutions and mortgage companies. Mortgages are security instruments that are used to finance real estate purchases.

The stock market allows investors to buy and sell shares in publicly traded companies. Stock markets are classified into primary and secondary markets. Cash markets are those financial markets in which goods are sold for cash and are delivered immediately. The prices are settled in cash on the spot at current market prices.

Derivative markets are marketplaces where derivative contracts are traded. A derivative is a contract that derives its value from its underlying asset or assets. For example, the value of an option on a stock depends on the price of the stock in the market. The major derivatives are forwards, futures, options, and swaps. There are derivative markets for structured products and collateralized obligations usually in the over-the-counter (OTC) market.

The foreign exchange market is where trading of currencies takes place. The foreign exchange market is the largest and most liquid financial market in the world. The interbank market is a part of the financial system where trading of currencies takes place between banks and financial institutions.

Capital markets are further segregated into primary and secondary markets. Primary markets are also known as new issue markets where investors can participate in the new security issuance. The issuing company receives cash funds from the sale of securities. In the United States, the Securities and Exchange Commission (SEC) is responsible for registering securities prior to their primary issuance. The secondary market is where investors purchase securities or assets from other investors. Primary securities issued are listed and traded in the secondary market on stock exchanges such as the New York Stock Exchange (NYSE), Nasdaq, or Tokyo Stock Exchange. The OTC market is a type of secondary market that is often referred to as a dealer market. These stocks do not trade on organized stock exchanges such as the NYSE. The stocks are traded on the OTC bulletin boards or pink sheets. Markets also exist where OTC transactions take place between broker-dealers and large institutions.

4.2 FINANCIAL MARKET INSTRUMENTS

Financial market instruments consist of money market and capital market instruments. Money market instruments are involved in short-term borrowing, lending, buying, and selling with original maturities of one year or less. Capital market instruments generate funds for corporations, companies, and governments. Capital markets are also known as securities markets because long-term funds are raised through trade on debt and equity securities.

4.2.1 MONEY MARKET INSTRUMENTS

The market for money market instruments are OTC and wholesale in nature. Money market instruments include Treasury bills, commercial paper, banker's acceptances, deposits, certificates of deposits, bills of exchange, repurchase agreements, federal funds, and mortgage- and asset-backed securities. The major money market instruments involve interbank lending, which involves mutual borrowing and lending by means of commercial paper and repurchase agreements. Money market instruments are basically benchmarked to the London Interbank Offered Rate (LIBOR) for a fixed period and an amount of currency. A money market is in fact an OTC market comprising an informal network of banks and traders linked by communication devices (e.g., telephones, computers, and fax machines). Money market instruments have maturities ranging from one day to one year and are extremely liquid. Money market instruments have the highest liquidity and lowest risk. Money market instruments are avenues where corporates with temporary cash surplus can invest their funds to earn a return with the least risk. Similarly, corporations that face a temporary cash shortfall can sell securities or borrow funds on a short-term basis. The money market acts as a repository for short-term funds.

The major money market instruments are:

- Certificate of deposits
- Repurchase agreements
- Commercial paper
- Eurocurrency deposits
- Federal agency short-term securities
- Municipal notes
- Treasury bills
- Foreign exchange swaps
- Short-lived mortgaged and asset-backed securities

4.2.1.1 Types of money market instruments
4.2.1.1.1 Treasury bills
Treasury bills (T-bills) were first issued by the United States during the World Wars to contain the unprecedented high public debt. Treasury bills issued by the government are short-term notes with a maturity of 90,180, or 360 days. T-bills can be purchased directly through auctions or indirectly through secondary markets. The shorter duration T-bills of 90 and 180 days can be auctioned on a weekly basis while T-bills of longer than 360 days' duration can be auctioned monthly. The face value of a T-bill is called its par value. Treasury bills are purchased always at discounted face value. Earlier Treasury securities were available in increments of $1000 from 1998. Now all Treasury marketable bills, notes, bonds and Treasury inflated-protected securities (TIPS) are available to the public in increments of $100.

Treasury bills can be purchased in electronic form at a bank, through a dealer or broker, or through the website Treasury Direct. These bills are issued through an auction-bidding process that can be either competitive or noncompetitive. In noncompetitive bidding, a buyer agrees to accept whatever interest rate is decided at the auction. In other words, the buyer is guaranteed that full amount of the bill, but is unaware of the interest rate that would be received until the auction closes.

In competitive bidding, usually carried out by corporations, the interest expected is specified. The buyer's bid will be accepted only if the rate of interest specified by the buyer is less than or equal to the highest accepted yield set by the auction. If the bid is higher than the rate set by the auction, then the bid would be rejected. It is through this competitive bidding process that the discount rates for an auction are decided. In a single auction a buyer can buy a maximum of $5 million in bills by a process of noncompetitive bidding, whereas the maximum given to an investor by competitive bidding amounts to 35% of the total amount. Treasury bills are highly liquid forms of investment that can be traded in the secondary market and converted into cash. Treasury bills are considered to be the most risk-free form of investment as they are backed by the government.

The regular weekly T-bills have maturity dates of 28, 182, and 364 days. Treasury bills are sold by single-price auctions held weekly.

4.2.1.1.2 Federal agency notes
Federal agency securities are minimum credit risk investment products that are backed or sponsored by federal agencies. The agency discount notes are sold at a discount and mature to face value in short-term intervals. The federal agencies are direct arms of the US government. The issuing federal agencies include the Government National Mortgage Association (GNMA), Export Import Bank, Federal National Mortgage Association (FNMA), Federal Home Loan Mortgage Corporation (FHLMC), Federal Farm Credit Bureau (FFCB), and Federal Home Loan Bank (FHLB). These agency securities are considered suitable investments for banks and are frequently purchased for investment portfolios by banks and by corporations. They offer higher yields than T-bills.

4.2.1.1.3 Tax-exempt state and municipal short-term notes
These instruments are tax-exempt, short-term notes issued by state and municipal governments. They are riskier than T-bills and have lower yields.

4.2.1.1.4 Certificates of deposit
A certificate of deposit (CD) is issued by a bank acknowledging a deposit in that bank for a specified period of time at a specified rate of interest. CDs are essentially a form of negotiable time deposit.

Banks collect deposits from corporations for a fixed period of time and agree to repay with specified interest at the end of the time period. The maturity rates on the CDs range from 30 days to 6 months or longer. A penalty exists for early withdrawal of funds. Certificates of deposits of larger denomination ($100,000 or more) pay higher interest rates than smaller denominations. CDs with broker involvement carrier higher interest rates and offer greater liquidity than CDs purchased directly from banks.

4.2.1.1.5 Types of CDs

4.2.1.1.5.1 Traditional CD. In a traditional CD, the interest rate is fixed over a specific period of time. On maturity the amount can be withdrawn or rolled over to another CD. Early withdrawal results in a huge penalty.

4.2.1.1.5.2 Bump-up CD. In bump-up certificates of deposits, the CD's interest rate can be swapped for a higher interest rate if new CD rates during the same period rise during the investment period. Most financial institutions permit the bump-up of a CD once during the term.

4.2.1.1.5.3 Liquid CD. In a liquid CD, the option exists for the investor to withdraw part of the deposit without paying a penalty. The interest rate on this CD is lower than a normal CD.

4.2.1.1.5.4 Zero coupon CD. Instead of an annual interest payout, a zero coupon CD reinvests the payments to earn interest on a higher total deposit. The interest rate offered is slightly higher than other CDs but is taxable.

4.2.1.1.5.5 Callable CD. A callable CD can be recalled by the bank after a stipulated period after returning the deposit plus any interest owed. Callable CDs offer higher interest rates. Banks recall the CDs when the interest rates fall significantly below the initial rate offered. These CDs are offered through brokerages.

4.2.1.1.5.6 Brokered CD. These CDs carry higher interest rates and are offered by brokerage firms. Brokerages have access to a bank's CD offerings including online and small banks. They carry a higher rate of interest.

4.2.1.1.6 Commercial papers

Commercial papers are unsecured short-term promissory notes with maturity mostly not exceeding 270 days. They are issued by large corporations to meet short-term obligations. In terms of dollar volume, commercial paper occupies the second position in the money market after Treasury bills. Commercial papers are used typically by large creditworthy corporations with unused lines of bank credit and have a low default risk. Credit rating agencies provide ratings for these commercial papers. The role of banks is to act as agents for the issuing corporations, but they are not obligated for the repayment of commercial paper.

Commercial paper is usually sold at a discount from face value and carries higher interest repayment rates than bonds. Commercial papers can be issued in two ways. Corporations can market the securities directly to buy and hold investors like money market funds. Or the commercial paper is sold to a dealer who sells the paper in the market. Dealers include large securities firms and subsidiaries of bank-holding companies. The yield for commercial paper holders is the annualized percentage difference between the price paid for the paper and the par value using a 360-day year.

US commercial paper markets are credit rated into the categories of AA nonfinancial, A2/P2 nonfinancial, AA financial, and AA asset backed. Table 4.1 highlights US Commercial paper market statistics with respect to number of issues and average amount during the period 2010-2012. Table 4.2 provides the value of commercial paper issued in the major currencies US dollar, euro, and pound sterling during 2011-2012.

Table 4.1 US Commercial Paper Market Statistics		
Period	**Number of Issues**	**Average Amount (in Millions of US Dollars)**
2010	2962	84,343
2011	2813	90,293
2012 (up to Sept)	2427	75,034
Source: http://www.federalreserve.gov/releases/cp/volumestats.htm#total_mkt		

Table 4.2 Commercial Papers: Currency Segregation (in Billions of US Dollars)		
	December 2011	**June 2012**
US dollar	179.3	176.8
Euro	252.4	245.2
Pound sterling	111.9	105.1
Source: BIS.org		

4.2.1.1.7 Bankers' acceptances

A bankers' acceptance is a money market instrument issued by a nonfinancial corporation guaranteed by the bank. Bankers' acceptances are issued by firms as part of commercial transactions. They are traded at a discount from face value on the secondary market. Bankers' acceptances are used to finance foreign trade, purchases of goods on credit, or for financing of inventory. The maturity period ranges between 30 and 180 days. Bankers' acceptances are typically sold in multiples of US $100,000.

4.2.1.1.8 Repurchase agreements

Repurchase agreements are also known as repos or buybacks. These are Treasury securities that are purchased from a dealer with the agreement that they will be sold back in the future for a higher price. In other words, in a repurchase agreement, one party sells assets or securities to another and agrees to purchase them back later at a set price on a set date. Many central banks use repos and reverse repos in government debt as a part of their open-market operations. Repurchase agreements are liquid as their duration ranges from 24 h to several months.

There are three types of repo maturities. In overnight repos, the securities are sold for one day and bought back the next day. Open repos don't have a specific end date. In repos, the repurchase price is greater than the original sale price, which, in fact, is the interest on the loan when expressed as an annualized percentage of sales price, known as the repo rate. The party that originally buys the securities effectively acts as a lender. The party that originally sells the securities acts as the borrower who, in fact, is using their security as collateral for a secured cash loan at a fixed rate of interest. Reverse repos are used to acquire securities by traders engaged in short selling. A repo is equivalent to a spot rate combined with a forward contract. Traders use repos to finance long positions, cover short positions in securities, and obtain access to cheap funds. Most repurchase agreements involve US government securities issued by government-sponsored enterprises.

4.2.1.1.9 Types of repos

4.2.1.1.9.1 Hold in custody repo. In a hold in custody repo, the collateral pledged by the (cash) borrower is placed in an internal account (held in custody) by the borrower for the lender during the time period of agreement rather than delivery to the cash lender. Large institutions are involved in such transactions.

4.2.1.1.9.2 Tri-party repo. In a tri-party repo, a custodian bank or international clearinghouse acts as the tri-party agent or intermediary between the two parties to the repo. The intermediary undertakes the administration of the transaction, which includes collateral allocation and marking-to-market.

4.2.1.1.9.3 Reverse repo. Reverse repos are agreements where securities are bought for resale at a later period. On the settlement date of the repo, the buyer acquires the relevant security on the open market and delivers it to the seller. In such transactions, the seller expects the relevant security to decline in value between the date of the repo and the settlement date.

4.2.1.1.9.4 Other types of repos. In whole loan repos, the transaction is collateralized by a loan or other form of obligation such as mortgage receivables, rather than security. Equity repos are repos on equity securities. A sell/buy back is the spot sale and forward repurchase of a financial asset. The forward price is set relative to the spot price to yield a market rate of return. A buy/sell back is the equivalent of a reverse repo.

The US repurchase agreement (repo) market is a large financial market where participants provide collateralized loans to one another. The collapse of Lehman Brothers and Bear Stearns during the economic crisis of 2008 could be attributed to the central role played by this market. The current US repo market is estimated to be $3035 billion in value. At the same time the market value of the reverse repo market is estimated to be $2446 billion.[1] The current European market for repos is estimated at €5647 billion.[2] The US repo market is considered to have a daily turnover of more than $4 trillion.[3]

4.2.1.1.10 Eurodollar deposits

Generally, a Eurodollar deposit is a short-term CD with a fixed interest rate in US dollars outside the jurisdiction of the Federal Reserve. These deposits help corporations and individuals hedge against short-term fluctuations in US dollar exchange rates.

Eurocurrency is the general term for any currency deposited in bank branches outside the countries in which it is the national currency. The beginning of the Eurodollar market was during the Cold War era when dollars were held in Europe. The funds came to be known as Eurodollars and deposits were Eurodollar deposits. The banks started to lend the deposited dollars. Eurodollars are an attractive investment as they are not subject to US banking regulations. European banks expanded their Eurodollar operations globally in the context of financial regulations in the US. Now a bank in Asia or Europe may accept dollars and call them Eurodollars. A euromarket exists for other currencies such as the sterling, yen, and others. Eurodollar deposits offer different types of interest rates, including long-term, short-term, fixed, and variable interest rates, Some Eurodollar deposits are overnight.

---

[1] Federal Reserve Bank of New York data, June 25, 2012.
[2] http://www.icmagroup.org/Regulatory-Policy-and-Market-Practice/short-term-markets/Repo-Markets/repo
[3] SIFMA fact sheet.

Table 4.3 International Money Market Instruments Data (in Billions of US Dollars)		
	December 2011	June 2012
Total issues	895.7	999.6
Commercial papers	578.4	563.8
Other instruments	317.2	435.8
Source: BIS.org.		

4.2.1.1.11 Foreign exchange swaps

A foreign exchange swap is the simultaneous purchase and sale of identical amounts of one currency for another with two different value periods. Foreign exchange swaps can be unsecured, secured, or overnight, and have very short-term maturity periods. Table 4.3 provides the value of international money market instruments issued during 2011-2012.

4.2.1.2 Participants in the money market

The major participants in the money market are governments, commercial banks, corporations, government-sponsored enterprises, money market mutual funds, dealers, and the Federal Reserve.

4.2.1.2.1 Governments

Treasury bills are the most actively traded among all money market instruments. The US Treasury raises significant amounts of funds in the money market through the issue of Treasury bills, which helps the government raise funds to meet short-term expenditures. The Federal Reserve is a key participant in the money market. The Federal Reserve conducts open-market operations by buying and selling Treasury bills to bring demand supply in equilibrium. The Federal Reserve controls the supply of reserves available to banks and other depository institutions primarily through the purchase and sale of Treasury bills, either outright in the bill market or on a temporary basis in the market for repurchase agreements.

4.2.1.2.2 Commercial banks

Banks play a major role in the money market. Banks borrow in the money market to fund their loan portfolios and to acquire funds to satisfy the reserve requirements as stipulated by central banks such as the Federal Reserve. Banks are the major participants in the market for federal funds, which are very short term in nature, mainly overnight. Here, funds are transferred between banks within a single business day. The fund market distributes the reserves throughout the banking system. The federal funds rate is the rate at which borrowing and lending of reserves takes place. Banks are also the major issuers of negotiable CDs, bankers' acceptances, and repurchase agreements. Banks are active participants on the borrowing side of the repurchase market. Banks also raise funds by acquiring funds in the Eurodollar market and acting as dealers in the market for OTC interest-rate derivatives. OTC interest-rate derivatives involve the exchange of cash payments based on changes in the interest rates. Banks also act as middlemen in swap transactions as a counterparty to both sides of the transaction. Banks provide commitments that help ensure that investors in money market securities will be paid on a timely basis. Banks provide commitments through backup lines of credit and letters of credit, which are widely used by commercial paper issuers and issuers of municipal securities.

4.2.1.2.3 Corporations

Nonfinancial and financial corporations raise large amount of funds from the money market by issuing commercial papers. Financial and nonfinancial businesses also participate in bankers' acceptances.

4.2.1.2.4 Government-sponsored enterprises

Government-sponsored entities including Farm Credit System, FHLB System, and FNMA borrow funds from money markets to invest primarily in the farming and housing sectors of the economy.

4.2.1.2.5 Money market mutual funds

Intermediaries such as money market mutual funds purchase large pools of money market instruments and sell shares in these investments to investors. This enables them to earn yields available on money market instruments.

4.2.1.2.6 Broker-dealers

Dealers and brokers play a significant role in marketing new issues of money market instruments. Dealers can act as intermediaries between different participants in the repurchase agreement market. Brokers also play a major role in linking borrowers and lenders in the federal fund market. Table 4.4 highlights the various money market instruments and the principal borrowers of these instruments.

4.2.2 CAPITAL MARKET INSTRUMENTS

The securities market consists of primary and secondary markets. The primary market is intended for new issues, whereas the secondary market is geared toward trading existing issues. There are three different markets where stocks are used as the capital market instruments, namely, the physical, virtual, and auction markets. The bond market is also known as a debit, credit, or fixed-income market. The largest securities market in the world in terms of trading volume is the US Treasury market.

The capital market, also known as the securities market, helps corporations and governments raise long-term funds. The capital market consists of both a primary market where new issues are sold to investors and a secondary market where existing securities are traded. The primary market is the market

Table 4.4 Money Market Instruments and Borrowers	
Instrument	**Principal Borrower**
Treasury bills	US government
Federal funds	Banks
Negotiable certificates of deposit	Banks
Eurodollar time deposits	Banks
Repurchase agreements	Government, securities dealers, banks, nonfinancial corporations
Municipal notes	State and local governments
Commercial paper	Nonfinance and finance companies
Bankers' acceptances	Nonfinance and finance companies
Government-sponsored enterprise securities	Farm credit system, FHLB system, FNMA
Shares in money market instruments	Money market funds, short-term investment funds

for new long-term capital; it is the market where the securities are sold for the first time (also called the new issue market (NIM)). The company receives the money and issues new security certificates to investors. The primary market performs the crucial function of facilitating capital formation in the economy. The secondary market is the financial market for trading of securities that have already been issued in an initial private or public offering.

In stock market trading of company stocks (collective shares), other securities and derivatives take place. Commodities and financial assets are traded in the commodities market. In 2012 the size of the worldwide bond market was estimated at $45 trillion. The size of the stock market was estimated at about $51 million. The world derivatives market was estimated at about $300 trillion. Stocks are listed and traded on stock exchanges, which are entities that specialize in the business of bringing buyers and sellers of stocks and securities together.

4.2.2.1 Types of capital market instruments
4.2.2.1.1 Treasury notes
Treasury notes (called notes or T-notes) in denominations of $1000 usually mature in 2 to 10 years and have a coupon payment every six months. T-notes and T-bonds are quoted on the secondary market at a percentage of par value in 32nds of a point ($n/32$ of a point, where $n = 1, 2, 3, \ldots$).

4.2.2.1.2 Treasury bonds
Treasury bonds (also called T-bonds) have the longest maturity span of 20 to 30 years. As with T-notes, the coupon payment occurs every six months. The T-bond secondary market is highly liquid and often the latest T-bond offering is used as a proxy for long-term interest rates. T-bonds are in high demand from such investors as pension funds and institutional investors.

4.2.2.1.3 Treasury inflation-protected securities
TIPS are inflation indexed bonds issued by the US Treasury whose principal is adjusted to the consumer price index. Though the coupon rate is constant, the investor receives a different amount of interest as it is multiplied by the inflation adjusted principal, thus safeguarding the investor against inflation. TIPS have maturity durations of 5, 10, and 30 years.

4.2.2.1.4 Separate trading of registered interest and principal securities
Separate trading of registered interest and principal securities (STRIPS) are T-notes, T-bonds, and TIPS whose interest and principal portions have been stripped or separated and sold in the secondary market. STRIPS are created by investment banks or brokerage firms. Table 4.5 provides the list of countries that hold the maximum of the US Treasury.

Table 4.5 Top Holders of US Treasury Securities as of May 2012		
SL	Country	$US Billion
1	China	1169.6
2	Japan	1105.2
3	Oil exporters	260.9
4	Brazil	243.4
5	Caribbean banking centers	229.8
Source: http://www.treasury.gov/resource-center/data-chart-center/tic/Documents/mfh.txt.		

There are several types of nonmarketable Treasury securities including state and local government series (SLGS), government account series debt issued to government-managed trust funds, and savings bonds.

4.2.2.1.5 Municipal bonds

Municipal bonds are issued by state or local authorities. The interest income received by holders of municipal notes are often exempt from federal and state income taxes. Basic municipal bonds consist of general obligation bonds and revenue bonds. In the case of general obligation bonds, the principal and interest bonds are secured by the credit of the issuer. Revenue bonds are issued for financing public projects such as toll roads, bridges, airports, and water and sewage treatment facilities.

4.2.2.1.6 Secured premium notes

Secured premium notes (SPNs) are secured debentures that are redeemable at premiums issued along with a detachable warrant, which is redeemable after a few years. The warrants give holders the right to get allotted shares on the condition that the SPN is fully paid. There is a lock-in period for SPNs during which no interest is paid for an invested amount. The SPN holder has an option to sell back the SPN to the company at par value after the lock-in period.

4.2.2.1.7 Corporate bond market

The bond market, also known as the credit or fixed income market, is the financial market where participating firms can issue new debt known as the primary market or buy or sell debt securities known as the secondary market usually in the form of bonds. In terms of total face value of bonds outstanding, the corporate bond market is much bigger than each of the markets for municipal bonds, Treasury securities, and government agencies securities.

4.2.2.1.8 Corporate bonds

Corporate bonds are debts issued by industrial, financial, and service companies to finance capital investments. There is wide range of choices for corporate bonds in terms of bond structures, coupon rates, maturity dates, credit quality, and industry exposure. A short-term corporate bond has a maturity of less than 5 years, an intermediate bond has a maturity of 5-10 years, and long-term bond have a maturity of 10 years.

Corporate bonds are rated by one or more primary rating agencies, including Standard and Poor's, Moody's, and Fitch. Bond ratings are based on various financial parameters of the company that issues the bond. The rated bonds fall into two categories: investment grade or noninvestment grade (high-yield bonds). Bonds that are considered to carry a minimal likelihood of default are labeled "investment grade" and are rated Baa3 or higher by Moody's, or BBB− or higher by Standard and Poor's and Fitch ratings. High-yield bonds have a rating of BB (Standard and Poor's, Fitch Ratings) or Ba (Moody's) and are considered speculative as they have a greater risk of default than investment-grade bonds. Such bonds have to offer higher coupon rates to attract investors. These bonds are issued by new or startup companies. Investment bonds have maturities of over 10 years as compared to the shorter maturities of high-yield bonds. The corporate bond market is one of the largest OTC financial markets in the world.

4.2.2.1.9 Types of corporate bonds

The different types of corporate bonds are described below.

4.2.2.1.9.1 Fixed-rate coupon bonds. Fixed-rate coupon bonds are the most common form of corporate bonds in which the coupon remains fixed throughout the bond's life. Straight bonds are the corporate market's "plain vanilla" bond, offering a fixed coupon rate of interest that is paid in cash, usually in semiannual payments, through the maturity or call date.

4.2.2.1.9.2 Zero coupon bonds. Zero coupon corporate bonds are issued at a discount from face value (par) with the full value, including interest paid at maturity. The prices of zero coupon bonds tend to be more volatile than bonds that make regular interest payments.

4.2.2.1.9.3 Floating rate bonds. Floating rate bonds have variable coupon rates that can change over multiple times per year. The coupon payment is fixed to a predetermined benchmark such as the spread above the yield on a six-month Treasury or price of a commodity.

4.2.2.1.9.4 Variable and adjustable rate. In these bonds coupons are tied to a long-term interest rate benchmark and are typically only reset annually.

4.2.2.1.9.5 Callable and putable bonds. In callable bonds, the issuer of the bond has the right to redeem the security on a set date prior to maturity and pay back the bondholder either the par value or a percentage of par. The call schedule lists the precise call dates of when an issuer may choose to pay back the bonds. In putable bonds, the holder has the right to give the bond back to the issuer and receive the par value of the bond.

4.2.2.1.9.6 Step-up and step-down corporate bonds. In step-up corporate bonds, a fixed rate of coupon is paid until the call date and if the bond is called up, then the interest rate increases. These are also known as split coupon bonds. In step-down bonds, a fixed rate of interest is paid until the bond is called up, and if the bond is not called, then the coupon rate decreases.

4.2.2.1.9.7 Convertible bonds. Convertible bonds are bonds that can be exchanged for a specific amount of common equity of the issuing company. The price at which the bonds are convertible into shares (conversion price) is set at the time of issue and represents a premium to the market price of the equity at that time. The conversion option may be exercised at one specified future date or within a range of dates.

4.2.2.1.9.8 Pay in kind bonds. Pay in kind (PIK) bonds allow the issuer the option of paying the bondholder interest either in cash or in additional securities.

4.2.2.1.9.9 Floating-rate and increasing-rate notes. Floating-rate and increasing-rate notes (IRNs) pay fluctuating or adjusted rates of interest based on an interest rate benchmark or a schedule of payments.

4.2.2.1.9.10 Extendable reset notes. Extendable reset notes give the issuer the option of resetting the coupon rate and extending the bond's maturity at periodic intervals or at the time of specified events. In exchange for these options, the bondholder receives the right to sell, or "put," the bond back to the issuer.

4.2.2.1.9.11 Deferred-interest bonds. This bond pays no interest to the bondholder until a future date.

4.2.2.1.9.12 Multi-tranche bonds. Multi-tranche bonds offer bondholders several tiers of investments within the same issue. The tiers may vary in their targeted maturities and credit quality.

4.2.2.1.9.13 Asset-backed securities and mortgage-backed securities. These securities are created through securitization. Securitization is the process of creating securities by pooling together various cash flow-producing financial assets. These securities are then sold to investors. Securitization covers residential and commercial mortgages, automobile loans, credit card financing, equipment loans and leases, asset-backed commercial paper, and more.

4.2.2.1.9.14 Junk bonds. Corporate bonds that are perceived to have very high risk are known as junk bonds. A junk bond is a high-yield bond issued by a corporation with a lower than investment-grade rating. It is a major component of the leveraged finance market.

4.2.2.1.10 Fundamentals of corporate bonds

The face value or par value of a bond is the principal amount of a bond that is repaid at the end of the maturity term. The stated interest payment made on a bond is called a coupon. Coupons are paid semi-annually or annually. The maturity period is the specified date on which the principal amount of a bond is paid. As the time period changes, the interest rate changes in the market. But the cash flows from a bond will remain the same. As a result of this relationship, the value of the bond will fluctuate. The present value of a bond will decrease when interest rates increase and will increase when the interest rate falls. The interest rate required in the market on a bond is called the yield to maturity (YTM) of a bond. When a bond sells for less than face value, it is said to be a discount bond. When a bond sells for more than a face value, it is called a premium bond. Bond value is the sum of the present value of the coupon plus the present value of the face value. The risk that arises for bond owners from fluctuating interest rates is called the interest rate risk. The longer the time to maturity, the greater the interest rate risk. The lower the coupon rate, the greater the interest rate risk.

4.2.2.1.11 Bond features

Indenture is a written agreement between the corporation that is the borrower and its creditors. It is also known as the deed of trust. This legal document consists of provisions for basic terms of bonds, total amount of bonds, the collateral used as security, repayment provisions, call provisions, and details of protective covenants.

Corporate bonds usually have a face-value denomination of $1000. Corporate bonds are usually in a registered form in which the registrar of a company records the ownership of each bond, and the payment is made directly to the owner of the record. In bearer form, the bond is issued without record of the owner's name, and payment is made to whomever holds the bond.

Collateral are securities that are pledged as security for payment of debt. Mortgage securities are secured by a mortgage on the real property of the borrower. A debenture is an unsecured bond for which no collateral is pledged.

The face value of a bond is repaid at maturity, and the bondholder will receive the stated or face value of the bond. In some other cases, the face value may be paid in part or in whole before maturity.

A sinking fund refers to an account managed by the bond trustee for the purpose of repaying the bond. The company makes an annual payment to the trustee who then uses the fund to retire a portion of the debt. Sinking funds are of different kinds. For example, some sinking funds begin about 10 years after the initial issuance. In some other cases, the sinking fund establishes equal payments over the life of the bond.

A call provision is an agreement that gives a corporation the option to repurchase a bond at a specified price prior to maturity. The amount by which the call price exceeds the par value of the bond is the call premium.

Protective covenants in an indenture stipulate certain actions the company must undertake during the term of the loan. Covenants can be classified as positive and negative covenants. A positive covenant specifies an action a company must abide by, such as maintaining working capital at some specified level or publishing an annual audited financial statement and maintaining collaterals. Negative covenants prohibit or limit the actions that companies undertake. Examples of negative covenants include limitations on the amount of dividends paid and no further issue of additional debt. Negative covenants can also place restrictions, stipulating, for example, that the firm cannot sell or lease any major assets to other lenders or participate in merger or acquisition activity.

4.2.2.1.12 Bond ratings

Credit rating agencies, such as Moody's, Standard and Poor's, and Fitch Ratings, assign credit ratings to debt securities such as bonds. Credit ratings are financial indication to potential investors of the debt instruments. These rating agencies assign letter grades such as AAA, BB, or CC based on the quality of the bond. AAA ratings indicate bonds of highest quality. Bond ratings below BBB or Baa are considered to be of noninvestment grade and are called high-yield or junk bonds. Bonds in a default category for nonpayment of principal and/or interest are rated D.

Investment Quality Ratings of Bonds			
Moody's	**Standard and Poor's**	**Fitch**	**Remarks on Creditworthiness**
Aaa	AAA	AAA	Highest ratings. Capacity to pay principal and interest is extremely strong.
Aa1	AA+	AA+	
Aa2	AA	AA	Capacity to pay is very strong. Along with the highest rating, this group constitutes the high-grade bond class.
A1	A+	A+	
A2	A	A	
A3	A−	A−	A ratings indicate capacity to pay interest and repay principal as strong but susceptible to adverse economic conditions.
Baa1	BBB+	BBB+	
Baa2	BBB	BBB	
Baa3	BBB−	BBB−	Debt rated Baa and BBB have adequate capacity to repay principal and interest but susceptible to changes in economic environment.
Ba1	BB+	BB+	
Ba2	BB	BB	
Ba3	BB−	BB−	These ratings are less speculative or vulnerable than other lower ratings.
B1	B+	B+	
B2	B	B	
B3	B−	B−	They are predominantly speculative.

Ratings in the category C have the highest degree of speculation. Debt rated D is in the default category.

Quantification is integral to rating analysis. The rating for a bond issue is based on the synthetic ratings of a firm. It uses one of the financial ratios or a score based on multiple ratios such as earnings before interest and taxes (EBIT), interest coverage ratio, earnings before interest, taxes, depreciation, and amortization (EBITDA), interest coverage ratio, funds flow/total debt ratio, free operating cash flow to total debt ratio, return on capital, operating income to sales, and long-term debt to capital ratios. For example, if the interest coverage ratio is above 8.5, the firm's bond issue may be rated AAA. Different measures are used for different industries and different external influences play ranging roles in credit rating processes. Ratings are not only based on a defined set of financial ratios; comprehensive qualitative elements are also an integral part of credit rating processes. Specific risk factors weighted in a given rating will vary considerably by sector.

The sovereign credit rating is the credit rating of a national government by the credit rating agency. The rating indicates the risk level of the investing environment of a country. In 2011, four nonfinancial US companies had a better rating than the sovereign rating for the United States, based on S&P: Automatic Data Processing, Exxon Mobil, Johnson & Johnson, and Microsoft had AAA ratings when the United States had an AA rating. In 1983, there were 32 nonfinancial companies that were rated AAA.[4] Berkshire Hathaway, General Electric, and Pfizer lost their AAA ratings during the financial crisis of 2008.

4.2.2.1.13 Major corporate bond issues

In 2013, Apple made the biggest corporate bond issue, valued at $17 billion, which was used to finance a $100 billion share buyback scheme. The Apple bond offering included six-part benchmark maturities of 3-year, 5-year, 10-year, and 30-year fixed rate bonds, along with 3-year and 5-year floating rate notes.[5] Apple's bond issue was rated AA+ by Standard and Poor's Ratings Services and Aa1 by Moody's Investors Service. Goldman Sachs and Deutsche Bank were the bankers for the deal. The biggest global corporate bond offering previous to this was Roche Holding's $16.5 billion sale in 2009, followed by France Telecom with a $16.4 billion deal in 2001.

4.2.2.2 *Debt instruments in international financial markets*

There has been phenomenal expansion among international financial markets over the last few decades. The modern era of international financial markets came about with the emergence of Eurodollar markets. Banks have been actively involved in international financial intermediation through the underwriting of securities, short-term international bank loans, and the sale of foreign bonds by governments and corporations. The 1960s witnessed the emergence of the Eurobond market, which was the result of regulations imposed by the US government. Eurobond markets facilitated borrowers in Europe to issue bonds for their international investors. Institutional innovations such as the private use of both the European Currency Unit (ECU) and the Special Drawing Rights (SDR) for Eurobonds, bank deposits, and euro credits along with the establishment of a clearinghouse mechanism for international bonds and euro certificates of deposit facilitated the growth of international financial markets. These instruments are typically structured in an unregulated environment. The Eurobond market was characterized by the absence of regulatory norms, including the registration requirements and disclosure rules that exist in domestic markets. The absence of reserve requirements and interest rate ceilings provided a distinct competitive advantage for financial institutions, especially banks, to operate in the Eurodollar market.

---

[4]http://money.cnn.com/2011/08/08/news/companies/aaa_companies/index.htm
[5]Michael Mackenzie, Vivianne Rodrigues, Apple cleans with $17 billion US bond issue, http://www.ft.com/intl/cms/s/0/3ce27f5a-b19e-11e2-9315-00144feabdc0.html#axzz2TlaaI2uS.

4.2.2.2.1 Syndicated euro credit loans

Syndicated credit loans have become one of the most important international debt sources for multi-billion projects throughout the world. The potential borrower gives the mandate to the lead bank to act as the syndication manager for syndicating the amount of funds. Two or more reputable banks are involved in the syndicate. It is the responsibility of the syndicated managers to market the participation in syndication to other financial institutions and to structure and price the deal. In a syndicated loan market, there is a reciprocity code wherein banks underwrite each other's deals. The syndicated loans usually permit multiple drawdowns to allow borrowers to accommodate loan disbursements for their financial needs. Eurodollar loans are basically priced at a certain spread over the LIBOR or any other interbank offered rates (e.g., SIBOR, Euribor, etc.). Euro credit loans are usually denominated in US dollars. Multicurrency options are also given to borrowers.

4.2.2.2.2 Euro commercial papers

Euro commercial paper is a short-term debt instrument issued by corporations and financial institutions in any major currency to investors around the world outside the country of origin of the borrowers. For example, a euro commercial paper can be denominated in yen and sold to investors throughout the world except in Japan. Euro commercial paper is sold at a discount and has a maturity period of less than one year. Institutional investors and corporations invest short-term cash surpluses in euro commercial papers. Euro commercial papers are low cost, offer flexibility, and have a simple structuring process. Euro commercial papers are offered in an unregulated environment and are not subject to registration requirements.

4.2.2.2.3 Euro notes

Euro banknotes (or euro notes) are short- to medium-term debt instruments sold in the Eurocurrency market. Euro notes are similar to euro commercial papers with the difference that issuers of euro notes don't have sufficient creditworthiness to issue normal euro commercial paper. Euro notes are backed by guarantee facilities such as a note issuance facility (NIF) or a revolving underwriting facility (RUF). In a NIF, a group of banks gives a purchase guarantee or backup credit guarantee to an issuer in case they are not able to sell the euro notes. Euro notes can also be issued under an RUF guarantee facility under which the guarantor bank provides the backup euro note purchase facility while an investment bank handles the marketing of euro notes. The other euro note guarantee facilities include multiple options facility (MOF), global note facility (GNF), and transferable RUF. In the case of an MOF, if the issuer is unable to sell the euro notes, it can make use of the option to access six-month financing by different financial products, including the bank loan facility or banker's acceptances. GNF offers borrowers the option of switching between US and euro commercial paper markets. In a transferable RUF setup, each guarantor bank with prior consent of the borrower can transfer the underwriting obligations to another bank.

4.2.2.2.4 Euro medium-term notes

Euro medium-term notes (EMTNs) are directly issued to markets with maturities of less than five years and are offered continuously rather than all at once, as with a bond issue. There is no underwriting syndicate for typical EMTNs issues. EMTNs are noncallable, unsecured senior debt securities. In structured EMTNs, a borrower issues EMTNs and simultaneously enters into one or more derivative agreements to transform the cash payments. For example, a borrower who issues floating-rate EMTNs along with a swap agreement can create synthetically a fixed note because floating rate payments can be swapped for a fixed rate payment.

4.2.2.2.5 Eurobonds

Eurobonds are medium to long-term marketable securities sold in any major currency to investors throughout the world, except to investors in the country of the domicile of the borrowers. A Eurodollar bond that is denominated in US dollars and issued in Korea by a French company can also be considered a Eurobond. Eurobonds carry the name of the currency in which it is denominated. For example, a euro yen is denominated in Japanese yen.

The Eurobond market has grown quickly ever since its inception during the post-World War II period. Eurobonds are traded electronically with facilities provided by clearing systems such as Euro Clear and Clear Stream. Eurobonds can be denominated in any major currency and have differential maturity periods for fixed and floating rate bonds. Fixed rate Eurobonds have maturities up to 15 years whereas floating rate bonds have maturities up to 30 years. Eurobonds are issued in large amounts ranging between $100 million and $500 million. Supranational organizations such as the World Bank and corporations are major issuers in the Eurobond market. Eurobonds are bearer bonds because they are not registered centrally in one location. The Eurobond market is a largely wholesale institutional market with bonds held by large institutions.

4.2.2.2.6 Types of Eurobonds

There are different types of Eurobonds, including conventional or straight bonds, floating rate bonds, zero coupon bonds, convertible bonds, and high yield bonds. Conventional or straight Eurobonds have a fixed coupon paid on an annual basis and a maturity date when all the principals are paid. Floating rate bond notes (FRN) are short- to medium-term bonds where the coupon interest rate is linked to a benchmark rate plus some additional "spread" of basis points. Each basis point is 100th of 1%. The reference benchmark rate is usually the LIBOR or Euribor (Euro interbank offered rate) or US Treasury bond market yield curve. The spread added to the reference rate depends on the credit quality of the issuer. Zero coupon bonds don't have to pay interest payments. In convertible Eurobonds, the bonds are convertible into shares of the issuing company. The coupon payable is usually less than that offered for other bonds. Banks and brokers help investors buy and sell Eurobonds.

4.2.2.2.7 Special types of Eurobonds in financial markets

Convertible bonds can, at the option of the bondholder, be converted into equity of the issuing company. Convertible bonds generally pay a coupon higher than the dividend rate of the underlying equity at the time of issue.

Exchangeable bond permits the holder to exchange the bond for shares of a company in which the issuer has an ownership position but not in stocks of the issuing company. Equity warrant bonds are debt securities that give the holder the option to purchase equity in the issuer, i.e., the parent company or in another company, during a predetermined period on one particular date at a fixed contract price.

Index linked bonds are bonds in which payment of income on the principal is related to the consumer price index or another specific price index. Commodity-linked bonds are bonds in which the payment meant for investors is dependent to a certain extent on the price level of a commodity such as crude oil, silver, or gold at maturity. Debt warrant bonds are securities that allow holders to buy additional bonds from the issuer at the same price and yield as the initial bond.

Liquid yield option notes combine the features of zero coupon bonds with convertibility into a fixed number of shares of common stock. The bond is issued at a large discount on the par value. It is puttable by the holder and callable by the issuer, according to the respective exercise prices.

Dual currency bonds are characterized by principal payments in one currency and coupon payments in another currency. In this type of bond, the issuer issues the bond in a foreign country but the principal payments are made in the currency of the issuer's country of residence and the coupon payments in the foreign currency.

Foreign currency-linked bonds are linked to changes in foreign currency. In this case, all amounts paid are linked to the foreign currency exchange rate.

4.2.2.2.8 Floating rate notes

Floating rate notes (FRNs) are bonds in which the coupon rate depends on the market interest rate. The coupon paid to bondholders at regular intervals consists of market interest rate plus a spread, which is the rate fixed when the prices of bonds are fixed. Most floating rate notes pay interest at intervals of three months. Floating rate notes are suited for investors who believe that the market interest rates will go up. In the United States, the major issuers of floating rate notes are the FHLBs, FHLMC, and FNMA. In primary markets, floating rate notes are traded through dealers.

4.2.2.2.9 Types of FRNs

4.2.2.2.9.1 Perpetual FRNs. The principal amount of this type of FRN never matures. The coupon payments are perpetual in nature and are refixed periodically on a fixing date with reference to an interest base rate such as a three- or six-month US dollar LIBOR. This type of debt instrument is issued primarily by financial institutions such as banks. Basel recommendations stipulate consideration of perpetual FRNs as upper-tier 2 capital or lower-tier 2 capital, based on terms of transaction for capital adequacy considerations.

4.2.2.2.9.2 Fake perpetual FRNs. This type of FRN has a call option that stipulates that if the issuer does not call the bond within the specified period of time, then the margin over the applicable base rate increases. Fake perpetual notes are issued by banks to raise subordinated debt. The Basel committee considers fake perpetual FRNs as part of tier 2 capital for capital adequacy considerations.

4.2.2.2.9.3 Variable rate notes. Variable rate notes (VRNs) differ from normal FRNs in that FRNs carry a fixed spread over a base rate such as the US dollar LIBOR; the spread on VRNs varies over time depending on the change in the issuer's risk perception. The spread is typically reset at a fixed interval of three months, normally with mutual consent between the issuer and the arranging institution. VRNs also have a provision of a put option, which gives the option to the holder of the notes to sell the notes back to the lead manager of the issuing syndicate.

4.2.2.2.9.4 Reverse FRNs. In reverse FRNs (also known as inverse FRNs) the principal redemption/coupon payments will fall if the reference index/asset/spread rises and vice versa. A typical coupon can be calculated as a fixed coupon minus the floating reference index. For example, 6.5% minus three-month LIBOR. These notes combine an FRN and an interest swap.

4.2.2.2.9.5 Collared FRNs. A collared FRN (also a called minimax FRN) is a specific type of floating rate note with an embedded collar. It is the combination of floored FRN and capped FRN in which the coupon rate will not fall below the predefined minimal guaranteed coupon (floor) and rises above the predefined maximal coupon (cap). The sale of cap(s) results in more premium than what investors pay for the floor(s) rate, making it a common floating rate note variation when short rates are low and the yield curve rises steep.

4.2.2.2.9.6 Step-up recovery FRNs. A step-up recovery floating rate note is an FRN in which the interest rate paid to the bondholder is increased over the interest prevailing in the market as time goes.

4.2.2.2.9.7 Interest rate differential notes. These types of FRNs pay the investor the difference between two different interest rate indices. For example, a CMT-Euribor differential note pays the difference between the CMT rate and a short-term LIBOR index.

4.2.2.2.9.8 Leveraged FRNs. In a leveraged FRN the coupon rate is leveraged based on a certain formula. The coupon rate will rise in relation to a rise in the reference index, which can be in any asset class under the condition that the rise is in a ratio greater than 1. Leveraged FRNs allow speculation on the volatility of interest rates.

4.2.2.2.9.9 Ratchet FRNs. FRNs combined with a ratchet option pay higher floating coupons subject to the condition that the coupon cannot rise by more than an amount fixed from the previous coupon level nor fall below the previous coupon. The issuer of the note will be in an advantageous position if the implied forward interest rates over the life of the issue are high and the actual market rates are unlikely to fall through the floor level.

4.2.2.2.9.10 Corridor floating rate notes. FRNs with embedded corridor options are known as corridor floating rate notes. In this type of bond, the principal and/or coupons are linked to a number of days (or percentage) in a specified period of time during which some reference index such as LIBOR (or spreads) is above, below, or in between a range.

4.2.2.2.10 Foreign bonds

Foreign bonds are debt securities issued in a domestic capital market by nonresident issuers and in the currency in which the bond is denominated and then sold. A bond denominated in US dollars that is issued by a corporation in Japan is a foreign bond. There are a large number of foreign bonds in international markets, such as Yankee bonds, Samurai bonds, Shogun bonds, Bulldog, Dragon bonds, Olympic bonds, and many others.

4.2.2.2.11 Global bonds

Global bonds are a combination of Eurobonds and foreign bonds. A global bond is a bond offered within several different markets at the same time. The first global bond was issued by the World Bank in 1989. Global bonds are denominated basically in US dollars, Japanese yen, Canadian dollars, and Australian dollars. Global bonds are issued by large international corporations with high credit ratings.

4.2.2.2.12 Sovereign bonds

Sovereign bonds are debt securities issued by national governments. These bonds can be denominated in either local currency or global currency such as the US dollar or euro. Sovereign bond yields are the interest rates governments pay on their debts.

4.2.2.3 Trends in global bond market

According to the Bank of International Settlements Data, the total size of the global debt securities market in 2012 was $78 trillion. Nonfinancial companies constitute approximately 12% of the debt market. The US corporate bond market is the most developed and liquid corporate bond market in the world. The majority of corporate debt outstanding is issued by US residents, which accounts for approximately 61% of the total debt outstanding. The Eurozone accounted for 10% of the global debt market. Japanese and UK residents account for 11% and 8% of global debt securities. Approximately 70% of corporate bonds are denominated in US dollars and 20% denominated in euros. Figure 4.1 highlights the percentage of debt securities issued by government, financial and nonfinancial corporations.

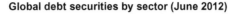

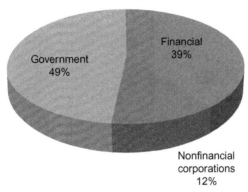

Global debt securities by sector (June 2012)

FIGURE 4.1

Global debt securities by sector.

Source: Data from Bank of International Settlements, http://www.bis.org/publ/qtrpdf/r_qa1212.pdf.

4.2.2.4 Bond market participants

Institutions, investors, governments, traders, and individuals are the major participants in the bond market. Individual investors constitute only a minor portion of the bond market owing to the high minimum denominations of most issues. The three major groups in the bond market are issuers, underwriters, and purchasers. The issuers (governments, banks, and corporations) sell bonds or other instruments to fund their operations. Central governments, including the US government, are the biggest issuers in the bond market. In fact, the United States is the biggest issuer of domestic government bonds. The second largest government bond market in the world is Japan. Government-sponsored entities, such as Fannie Mae, are also major players in the mortgage-backed securities (MBS) market. Banks are also a major issuer in the bond market. In the corporate bond market, corporations are the major issuers. The underwriting segment of the bond market is made up of investment banks and other financial institutions that facilitate the sales of the bond issue. Purchasers of bonds include governments, banks, corporations, and individual investors. Governments play a major role as they borrow and lend money to other governments and banks. A number of financial institutions invest in the bond market. Life insurance companies basically invest in corporate bonds and have some part in Treasury and agency securities. Commercial banks invest in government bonds, Treasuries, and municipal bonds. Government and private pension funds invest heavily in corporate bonds but also in Treasury and agency bonds.

4.2.2.5 Secondary bond markets

Secondary bond markets exist for both government and corporate bonds. US government bonds are traded by bond dealers who specialize in Treasury bonds or agency bonds. In the United States Treasury bonds are traded by a set of primary dealers that includes banks and large investment banks (e.g., Goldman Sachs and Morgan Stanley). The main market makers in the secondary municipal bond markets are banks and investment banks that underwrite the issues. All corporate bonds are traded OTC by dealers who are large investment banks. Table 4.6 gives the amounts outstanding of international bonds and notes during 2011-2012.

Table 4.6   International Bonds and Notes Statistics, Amounts Outstanding (in Billions of US Dollars)

	December 2011	June 2012
Total issues	27,573.3	27,940.4
Floating rate bonds	7687.2	7373.7
Straight fixed rate	19,398.7	20,089.1
Equity related	487.4	477.7
Total	55,146.6	55,880.9

Source: www.bis.org.

4.2.2.6 Bond investment strategies

Portfolio managers of financial institutions follow a specific strategy for investing in bonds. Diversification is a principal strategy in bond investment. Bond portfolio investment strategies can be classified into passive, active, matched funding, contingent, and structured strategies. Passive strategies consist of buy and hold strategies and indexing.

4.2.2.7 Passive strategies

4.2.2.7.1 Buy and hold strategy

The simplest strategy is to buy and hold bonds with desired levels of credit quality, coupon rate, term to maturity, and indenture provisions. In this type of strategy, the investor need not be concerned about the impact of interest rates on a bond's price or market value. If the interest rate rises and the market value of the bond falls, there will not be any effect until the strategy is changed to sell the bond. But because the bond is held, the investor may not be able to invest the principal at higher market rates. In callable bonds there is a risk of having the principal amount returned before maturity.

Buy and hold investors can also manage interest rate risk by laddered and barbell strategies.

4.2.2.7.2 Laddered strategy

In a laddered strategy, investors can manage interest rate risk by creating a laddered portfolio of bonds with different maturities of, say, 1, 3 or 5 years. The principal amount of a laddered portfolio is repaid at regular defined intervals. An institutional investor can create a laddered portfolio in which when one bond matures, it can be reinvested at the longer term end of the ladder. In cases where interest rates are rising, the maturing principal can be invested at higher rates. For example, consider a case where one fourth of funds is invested in 5-, 10-, 15-, and 20-year bonds. In 5 years when the bond with a 5-year maturity is redeemed, the amount can be used to buy 20-year bonds. This investment creates a new investment, which, in turn, achieves the same maturity structure that existed when the portfolio was created.

4.2.2.7.3 Barbell strategy

In a barbell strategy, investments are made in bonds with short-term maturity and long-term maturity. Investments in short-term/long-term bonds provide liquidity if the investor desires to sell the bonds for cash. The long-term bonds will provide higher coupon rates. Hence this strategy aims to provide higher return and liquidity.

4.2.2.7.4 Indexing strategy

Instead of a buy and hold strategy, investors may prefer to hold a bond portfolio designed to replicate a selected fixed income index. In an indexing strategy, there is full replication of the index or stratified sampling. For example, Vanguard's Total Bond Index Fund replicates the performance of the Barclays Capital US Aggregate Index.

4.2.2.8 Active strategies

In active bond portfolio strategies, the fixed income manager will form a portfolio of bonds that will attempt to produce superior risk-adjusted returns compared to the index against which the performance of the portfolio is measured. This strategy relies on uncertain forecasts of future interest rates. The duration of the portfolio is altered to preserve capital when an increase in interest rate is expected and to realize attractive capital gains when interest rates are expected to decline. The portfolio duration is reduced when interest rates are expected to increase and increase the portfolio duration when a decline in yield is expected.

In valuation analysis, the portfolio manager selects bonds based on their intrinsic value, which is based on bond and market characteristics. A credit analysis strategy involves detailed analysis of the bond issuer to determine expected changes in the default risk. The major determinants of the active global bond investing strategy are such interrelated factors as the local economy of each country, the impact of total demand and domestic monetary policy on inflation and interest rates, and the effect of inflation and interest rates on exchange rates.

4.2.2.9 Match funding strategies

In matching strategies, investors create a bond portfolio that will generate periodic income that can match their periodic expenses. Dedicated portfolios are an example of a matched funding strategy. For example, in a pure cash matched dedicated portfolio, a portfolio of bonds is selected that will provide a stream of payments from cash flows, such as coupons and principal repayments, that will exactly match the specified liability schedules. The aim is to build a portfolio that will generate sufficient funds in advance of each scheduled payment.

In an immunization strategy, the aim is to derive a specified rate of return similar to current market returns during a given investment horizon irrespective of what happens to the future level of interest rates. Horizon matching is a combination of both cash matching dedication and immunization strategies.

4.2.2.10 Contingent and structured strategies

In this strategy, contingent procedures are adopted to manage bond portfolios. This strategy allows bond managers to realize higher returns through active strategies while focusing on bond immunization techniques to ensure a minimal return over the investment horizon.

4.2.2.11 Other specific strategies

4.2.2.11.1 Maximizing income

To maximize interest income, it would be beneficial to invest in longer-term bonds. Coupon rates on corporate bonds are higher than Treasury bonds. Corporate bonds with lower credit ratings give higher coupon rates. High-yield or junk bonds offer above-market coupon rates and yields.

4.2.2.11.2 Rolling down yield curve

This strategy involves buying long-duration bonds and selling them after a duration of two to three years to profit from their rise in value during that time. This strategy depends on the shape of the yield curve. The rolling down yield curve investment strategy can be profitable based on the assumption that long-term bonds pay more interest than short-term bonds and the former will rise in value over time. This strategy works for corporate bonds because the spreads between longer and shorter term bonds are wider than for Treasury bonds.

4.3 **MORTGAGE MARKETS**

Mortgages are securities or loans used to finance real estate purchases such as homes or land. An important characteristic of mortgage debt is that it is secured by the property, which acts as collateral to the mortgage loan. In other words, if the property owner fails in his or her payment obligations, the creditor can then seize the property. Usually the mortgage agreement envisages a part of the purchase price known as a down payment to be made to the financial institution. Generally a 20% down payment is required. The mortgage represents the difference between the down payment and the face value of the mortgage. Mortgages held by financial institutions that are federally insured are called federally insured mortgages; otherwise they are conventional mortgages. Mortgages usually have an original maturity of either 15 or 30 years. Mortgage refinancing is done when the mortgage borrower takes out a new mortgage and uses the funds obtained to pay off the current mortgage.

The main criteria used to measure the creditworthiness of a prospective borrower are the borrower's credit history, payment ability measured in terms of income, and amount of down payment made by the borrower. Mortgages are classified into prime and subprime mortgages. A subprime mortgage is offered when a borrower doesn't meet the traditional lending standards. The borrowers of these subprime loans are charged higher appraisal fees and interest rates to compensate for the risk of default.

Mortgage markets consist of primary mortgage and secondary mortgage markets. In the primary mortgage market, the four categories of mortgages issued by financial institutions are home, multifamily dwelling, commercial, and farm. Home mortgages refer to loans to purchase single- to four-family dwellings. Multifamily dwelling mortgages are used to finance the purchase of apartment complexes, townships, or other large units. Commercial mortgages are intended for constructing office buildings, shopping malls, and the like. Farm mortgages are meant for financing farm purchases.

The secondary mortgage market refers to the market for the sale of securities or bonds collateralized by the value of mortgage loans. The loans from the primary mortgage market are grouped together by mortgage lender and commercial bank and sold as collateralized mortgage obligations (CMOs) or MBS to investors who can include pension funds, insurance companies, and hedge funds. Secondary mortgage markets were established to boost up the US economy after the Great Depression of the 1930s. In 1930, the government established the Federal National Mortgage Association (FNMA or Fannie Mae). In 1960, the Government National Mortgage Association (GNMA or Ginnie Mae) and FHLMC (Freddie Mac) were established to promote housing expansion by means of creating MBS.

According to the Federal Reserve Bulletin 2012, the number of home loans reported by covered lenders declined from 7.9 million in 2010 to less than 7.1 million in 2011. In 2011, there was about $13.7 trillion in total US mortgage debt outstanding. There was about $8.5 trillion in total US mortgage-related securities, of which $7 trillion was sponsored by government-backed enterprises and the remaining $1.5 trillion pooled by private mortgage entities.[6]

---

[6]Federal Reserve Statistical Release, 2012 Securities Industry and Financial Markets Association Statistical Release.

4.3.1 PARTICIPANTS IN THE MORTGAGE MARKETS

Commercial banks and saving institutions play a major role in both primary and mortgage markets. These institutions originate and service commercial and residential mortgages and maintain mortgages within their investment portfolios. They are also involved in buying and selling of MBS. Credit unions and finance companies also originate and maintain mortgages in their investment portfolios. Mortgage companies contribute to both primary and secondary markets. Mutual funds are involved in the construction of portfolios of MBS. Securities firms sell MBS and facilitate institutional investors in mortgage hedge against interest rate risk. Insurance companies purchase mortgages and sell MBS.

4.3.2 TYPES OF MORTGAGES

4.3.2.1 Fixed rate mortgages

A fixed rate mortgage locks in the borrower's interest rate over the life of the mortgage. The required periodic payment over the life of the mortgage remains constant irrespective of changes in market interest rates. In this case, financial institutions are exposed to interest rate risk because they use funds obtained from short-term customer deposits to make long-term mortgage loans. Borrowers are insulated from any rise in interest rates but at the same time they fail to benefit from declining rates.

4.3.2.2 Adjustable rate mortgages

In adjustable rate mortgages (ARMs), the interest rate is linked to the market interest rate or interest rate index, which reflects market conditions. The monthly payment will change over the life of the mortgage. Many ARMs specify a maximum allowable fluctuation in the mortgage rate per year and over the mortgage life irrespective to changes in market interest rates. These caps are usually 2% per year and 5% for the mortgage's lifetime.

4.3.2.3 Graduated payment mortgages

Graduated payment mortgages (GPMs) allow the borrower initially to make small payments on the mortgage. Then the payment increases on a graduated basis over the first 5-10 years, and finally the payments level off at the end of the mortgage period.

4.3.2.4 Automatic rate reduction mortgages

In automatic rate reduction mortgages, the lender financial institution automatically lowers the rate on an existing mortgage when the prevailing market interest rate falls. However, in this system of payments, the rate cannot be increased if the market rate increases. The automatic rate reduction system enables mortgage lenders to prevent their customers from refinancing their mortgages with other mortgage lenders when mortgage rates fall.

4.3.2.5 Growing equity mortgages

In growing equity mortgages (GEMs), initial payments are basically low but increase over a part or the entire life of the mortgage. The incremental increase in monthly payments quickly reduces the principal on the mortgage. GEMs facilitate borrowers to pay off their mortgage in a shorter period of time than originally stipulated in the contract.

4.3.2.6 Second mortgages

Second mortgages are loans secured by collateral that is already used to secure a primary mortgage. The interest rate on the second mortgage is higher because it is riskier, as its priority claim against the collateral property in the event of default is less than that of the first mortgage. In other words, in case of default, the second mortgage holder is paid off after the settlement for the first mortgage.

4.3.2.7 Shared appreciation mortgages

Shared appreciation mortgages (SAMs) allow home buyers to obtain mortgages at below-market interest rates in exchange for shares for lenders in any price appreciation in home property values. The lender financial institution will have a share in the portion of the gain if, in the future, the property is sold for more than the original purchase price.

4.3.2.8 Equity participation mortgages

In equity participation mortgages (EPMs), an external investor shares in the appreciation of the property rather than the financial institution that issued the mortgage.

4.3.2.9 Reverse annuity mortgages

A reverse annuity mortgage is one in which a homeowner's equity is gradually depleted by a series of payments from the mortgage holder to the homeowner. Reverse annuity mortgages increase in size as the annuity payments continue. A reverse annuity mortgage is used primarily by elderly homeowners who wish to convert the equity in their homes into a stream of retirement income payments.

4.3.2.10 Amortization and balloon payment mortgages

With respect to payment schedule, mortgages can be either amortized or categorized into balloon payments. In amortization, the fixed monthly payment made by the mortgage borrower consists of part principal and part interest. In amortization, principal and interest is fully paid off by the maturity date. If the payments are set up to cover the full balance over the life of loan, it is known as a fully amortized loan. In balloon payments, a fixed monthly interest payment for a certain period is required and the full payment of the mortgage principal is made at the end of the period. This leaves a balloon payment, or a very large amount due at the end of the mortgage.

4.3.3 MORTGAGE-BACKED SECURITIES

MBS are groups of mortgages or loans that are sold by banks, securities firms, and other issuing financial institutions and then packaged together into "pools" or "tranches" and sold as a single security. This process is known as securitization. The cash flows (interest and principal payment) the borrowers of the mortgage make pass through the MBS and flow to bondholders. There is a fee for the financial institutions that originate the mortgages. The issuer of the MBS assigns a trustee who holds the mortgages as collateral for the investors who purchase the securities. These trusts are often called real estate mortgage investment conduits (REMICs). The issuers of the MBS hire rating agencies such as Moody's, Standard and Poor's, or Fitch to assign ratings for the securities for sale. The mortgages in a highly rated tranche are generally expected to receive more favorable payments. Mortgage pools are created mainly by the three quasi-governmental agencies: the Government National Mortgage Association (GNMA or Ginnie Mae), Federal National Mortgage (FNMA or Fannie Mae), and Federal

Home Loan Mortgage Corp (Freddie Mac). Mortgage pools are also created by private entities. These "private label" MBS are issued by homebuilders or financial institutions through subsidiaries and are supported by residential loans that do not conform to the agencies' requirements.

Investors can buy individual MBS through a broker. Investors can also opt for mutual funds or exchange traded funds that have exposure to this sector or are dedicated solely to MBS. Examples of exchange traded funds that invest in MBS include Barclays Agency Bond Fund, ishares Barclays MBA Fixed Rate Bond Fund, and ishares Barclays GNMA Bond Fund.

Mortgages are among the most actively traded securities in the US bond market.

Steps in the Creation of MBS

1. A mortgage lender such as a bank extends a loan to a home buyer.
2. The bank sells these loans to government-sponsored enterprises (GSE) such as Fannie Mae or Freddie Mac or to a bank, finance company, or other private entity.
3. The agency bundles or packages the purchased mortgage loans into pools or tranches. The number of individual mortgages in the tranche can vary from a few to thousands of loans. Based on the monthly payments from homeowners, the pool of mortgages generates regular cash flows.
4. The agency then sells the claims on the cash flow generated on mortgages in the form of bonds to investors. After the initial sale, MBS are traded on the open market.
5. The mortgage payments consisting of interest and principal passe through the mortgage servicer and flow to bondholders.

4.3.3.1 Risks in mortgage investments and MBS

Investors face credit risk in the mortgage business when borrowers delay payment or default. Some of the amount can be recovered through foreclosure and resale of the home for which the loan has been issued, but the process is costly and does not guarantee the recovery of the whole principal amount. The probability that a borrower will default depends on economic conditions and borrower's creditworthiness as measured by income level and credit history. Mortgages are subject to interest rate risk because the value of a mortgage tends to decline in response to increases in interest rates. Mortgages are long term in nature but are commonly financed with short-term deposits. Hence, investments in mortgages lead to high exposure to interest rate risk.

One of the distinctive risks in MBS is the prepayment risk. This risk arises when investors decide to pay back the principal on their mortgages ahead of the payment schedule. For investors, this means that there is an early return of principal. As a result, the principal value of the underlying security gets reduced over a time period, which leads to reduction in interest income. Prepayment risk is highest when interest rates fall, which motivates home borrowers to refinance their mortgages. In this scenario, the owner of MBS also faces the risk of reinvestment of the returned principal at a lower rate.

Fundamentally there is an inverse relationship between interest rates and bond prices. When interest rates rise, bond prices drop, and when interest rates drop, bond prices increase. Bonds that exhibit negative convexity show fewer price increases when the interest rate drops compared to bonds with normal convexity. MBS exhibit negative convexity. Hence MBS have greater interest rate risk compared to other bonds. This happens when the investor wants to sell MBS in the secondary market. MBS tend to have smaller gains when the bond price rises and bigger falls when bond prices goes up. Hence, MBS offer higher yields than US Treasuries on account of the higher risk.

4.3.3.2 Types of MBS

4.3.3.2.1 Pass-through securities

These basic MBS are also known as participation certificates. Pass-through securities are collateralized by pools of similar mortgage loans. They are issued or guaranteed by Ginnie Mae, Fannie Mae, or Freddie Mac. The cash flow consisting of promised payments of principal and interest on pools of mortgages is passed through to MBS investors.

4.3.3.2.2 Collateralized mortgage obligations

CMOs are MBS that are separated and issued as different classes of mortgage pass-through securities with different risks, terms, and interest rates. In other words, the cash flows from MBS are categorized as tranches or pools into many classes of securities with different maturities and payment schedules. CMOs typically have three or more bond classes termed *tranches*. In other words, tranches are different classes of bonds with different maturity terms. Each tranche will have its own expected maturity and cash flow pattern. The payments in CMOs consisting of both principal and interest are made monthly or quarterly, unlike other bonds. The different tranches of securitized loans are offered to different types of investors. For example, pension funds, insurance companies, and other institutional investors invest in the most highly rated tranches with AAA or AA ratings. Institutional investors such as hedge funds require higher yields and hence invest in tranches with higher risks.

There are different types of CMOs, including sequential pay tranches, planned amortization tranches (PAC), targeted amortization type tranches (TAC), companion tranches, and z tranches, principal only (PO) securities, interest only (IO) securities, and floating rate tranches.

In a sequential CMO (a plain vanilla offering) the tranches are paid sequentially with no overlap. In a PAC CMO, there is a main and support tranche. The presence of a main tranche provides investors with a more certain cash flow. TACs are similar to PACs, but the principal payment is specified for only one prepayment rate. Companion tranches are available with CMOs that have PAC or TAC, as they will be able to absorb variable prepayment rates. Z tranches are characterized with no interest until the lockout period ends. Principal only (PO) securities are paid only with principal payments. In PO, the investor buys the bond at a deep discount from face value and it is redeemed through scheduled payments. In IO types of CMO, the principal amount is notional with a no par value. The IO cash flows decline as the notional principal declines in value. Floating rate tranches are CMOs in which the interest rate is tied to an interest rate index such as LIBOR or cost of fund index (COFI).

4.3.3.2.3 Asset-backed securities

Asset-backed securities (ABS) are also created through the process of securitization in which loans are packaged and sold as securities. The types of loans that are typically securitized include credit card receivables, auto loans, and student loans. When consumers take a loan, the debt amount becomes an asset on the balance sheet of the lender. The lender sells these assets to a trust or a special-purpose vehicle, which packages them into an asset-backed security that can be sold in the market. The issuer of an ABS benefits from the new source of funding as a result of the issue of ABS while the buyer of ABS benefits from the higher yield from ABS and facilitates portfolio diversification.

4.3.3.2.4 Collateralized debt obligation

Collateralized debt obligation (CDO) is an asset-backed security that is issued by a special purpose vehicle (SPV) or trust. CDOs provide a means to create fixed income securities from a pool of diversified debt instruments with differing yields and risks. CDOs differ from CMOs in the context of the credit quality of tranches. The senior tranches have the highest credit quality with the lowest yield. Next in line is the mezzanine tranches with lower credit quality and higher yield, while the subordinate or equity tranches receive residual tranches and are of lowest credit quality with the highest yield.

CDOs are classified based on their underlying debt. CDOs based on bonds are known as collateralized bond obligations (CBOs). They include corporate bond-backed CDOs, structured finance-backed CDOs where the underlying assets are residential MBS, commercial MBS, and ABS or real estate investment trust (REIT) debt. Collateralized loan obligations (CLOs) are CDOs based on bank loans. Usually subprime loans are pooled and sold as CLOs. CDOs can also be classified as cash CDOs and synthetic CDOs. Cash CDOs are backed by cash market debt instruments, whereas synthetic CDOs are backed by other credit derivatives.

4.3.3.3 Subprime mortgage crisis

It is a known fact that the subprime mortgage market disproportionately contributed to the severity of the recent economic crisis. At the time of the crisis, almost 30% of Fannie Mae's and Freddie Mac's direct purchases were considered subprime. Government-sponsored Fannie and Freddie were in fact the largest single investor (holding almost 40%) of subprime private-label MBS.

From 2000 to 2003, the size of the mortgage market increased by almost 400%.[7] This is in contrast to the early 1990s, which witnessed a period of stability in the mortgage market. The 30-year rates began a slow decline from over 10% in 1990 to just below 7% in 1998, which was the lowest in the decade. The late 1990s witnessed a peak of growth of the mortgage market. The mortgage market then started shrinking in the face of a housing market expansion phase. This could be because the increase in mortgage rates led to a lower demand for refinancing. During 2003-2004, the refinancing volumes dropped by 40%. Mortgage market participants such as Fannie and Freddie collect a major chunk of income from fee income or gains realized upon sale of a mortgage or mortgage-backed security along with mortgage payments from borrowers. The decline in refinancing volume more than offset the increase in new purchase volume, reducing fee income across the mortgage industry.

After 2003, the yield curve representing the difference between short-term and long-term rates was showing a flattening trend. When the spread between short-term and long-term rates are wide, mortgage firms can profit by floating short-term debt and buying back their own MBS. With the narrowing down of the spread, the arbitrage profits from mortgage firms' portfolio trading activities came down. From 2003 to 2005 net interest income fell by 45%. The declining fee income and reduced interest spread compelled mortgage participants to enhance their income by lowering the credit quality of the loans.[8]

There are no statutory or regulatory restrictions on the credit quality of mortgages that can be purchased. During the bubble years, Fannie's subprime direct purchases equaled between $100 billion and $200 billion annually.[9] The majority of Fannie Mae and Freddie Mac activity in the subprime market was through the direct purchase of whole mortgages. The purchase of private-label subprime MBS

---

[7] Origination Estimates, http://www.mbaa.org/files/Research/HistoricalWAS/HistoricalMortgageOriginationEstimates102610.xls.
[8] Mark Calabria, (March 2011) Fannie Freddie and the subprime mortgage market, Cato Institute Briefing Papers.
[9] Wallison and Calomiris, (September 2008) The Last Trillion-Dollar Commitment: The Destruction of Fannie Mae and Freddie Mac, *AEI Financial Services Outlook.*

also helped fuel the housing bubble. In addition to being the largest players in the subprime mortgage market, both Fannie Mae and Freddie Mac were also the drivers of the market.

Different stakeholders including mortgage originators, credit rating agencies, and financial institutions that packaged, purchased, and insured MBS were responsible for the crisis. Mortgage originators were aggressively increasing their business of home lending without properly checking on the credit quality of buyers. Credit rating agencies overrated many MBS and CDOs to further their businesses. Financial institutions such as securities firms and commercial banks who packaged the MBS also failed to take into account the riskiness of these investments. Financial institutions that pooled funds from individual investors to invest in these MBS failed in their own assessments of the credit quality of MBS. The credit crisis had a contagious effect such that many homeowners lost their homes and financial institutions thereby lost the funds on their mortgage investments. Mortgage insurers also suffered heavy blows because of foreclosures, whereby the collateral was worth less than the amount owed on the mortgage. Several financial institutions and home builders went bankrupt. Thousands lost jobs and the economic crisis set in. In 2008, Fannie Mae and Freddie Mac reported losses of more than $14 billion. By September 2008, the US government took over the management of Fannie Mae and Freddie Mac.

4.4 SUMMARY

The financial market is where buyers and sellers engage in the trade of assets. Capital markets consist of money markets, bond markets, mortgage markets, stock markets, spot or cash markets, derivatives markets, foreign exchange markets, and interbank markets. The money market is an integral part of the financial market in which financial instruments with high liquidity and short maturities are traded. The bond market is also known as the debt, credit, or fixed income securities market. Mortgage markets are where mortgage loans are traded. The money market instruments consist of Treasury bills, federal agency notes, certificates of deposit (CDs), commercial papers, bankers' acceptances, and repurchase agreements (repos).

The major participants in the money market are governments, commercial banks, corporations, government-sponsored enterprises, money-market mutual funds, brokers, dealers, and the Federal Reserve.

The securities market consists of primary and secondary markets. The primary market handles new issues, whereas the secondary market handles trading of existing issues. The capital market instruments include Treasury notes, Treasury bonds, municipal bonds, and corporate bonds. The corporate bonds consists of zero coupon bonds, floating rate bonds, and convertible bonds. Bond ratings are assigned by credit rating agencies such as S&P and Moody's. The major debt issued in the international market includes euro notes, Eurobonds, euro medium-term notes, global and foreign bonds. The three major groups in the bond market are issuers, underwriters, and purchasers. The issuers (e.g., governments, banks, and corporations) sell bonds or other instruments to fund their operations. Secondary bond markets exist for both government and corporate bonds. Bond portfolio investment strategies can be classified into passive, active, matched funding, contingent, and structured strategies. Mortgages are securities or loans used to finance real estate purchases for homes or land. Commercial banks and saving institutions play a major role in both primary and mortgage markets. MBS are created through the process of securitization. The different types of MBS include pass-through securities and CMOs.

QUESTIONS FOR DISCUSSION

1. Discuss the structure of financial markets.
2. Discuss the different types of money market and capital market instruments.
3. Explain the fundamentals of a bond.
4. What is an indenture?
5. Explain credit ratings.
6. What are the major debt instruments issued in the international debt market?
7. Distinguish between Eurobonds, foreign bonds, and global bonds.
8. Discuss the different types of Eurobonds.
9. What are the different types of floating rate notes?
10. What are the different bond investing strategies?
11. Explain mortgage markets.
12. What are the different types of MBS?
13. Explain the following: (a) MBS and (b) CMOs.

REFERENCES

Treasury Inflation-Protected Securities (TIPS). TreasuryDirect.gov. 7 April 2011. http://www.treasurydirect.gov/indiv/products/prod_tips_glance.htm. Retrieved 27-04-2011.

http://www.inc.com/encyclopedia/money-market-instruments.html.

Treasury Broadens Savings Opportunities for More Investors, New $100 Minimums for Treasury Marketable Securities to Debut in April. http://www.treasurydirect.gov/news/pressroom/pressroom_100mktmin.htm.

http://guides.wsj.com/personal-finance/banking/what-is-a-certificate-of-deposit-cd/.

Veale, S.R., 2001. Stocks, Bonds, Options, Futures. New York Institute of Finance. http://www.investopedia.com/terms/b/bankersacceptance.asp#ixzz27nBLDWx4.

http://glossary.reuters.com/index.php?title=Repurchase_Agreement&action=edit.

Buljevich, E.C., Park, Y.S., 1999. Project Financing and International Financial Markets. Kluwer Academic Publishers.

http://www.investinginbonds.eu/Pages/LearnAboutBonds.aspx?id=6368.

http://www.altiusdirectory.com/Finance/floating-rate-notes.php.

http://www.montegodata.co.uk/educate/ComplexSwaps4.htm.

Cook, T., LaRoche, R.K., The Money Market (Chapter 1). Federal Reserve Bank of Richmond, 1998.

http://www.richmondfed.org/publications/research/special_reports/instruments_of_the_money_market/pdf/chapter_01.pdf.

http://climatebonds.net/2013/02/9-useful-facts-bond-markets/.

Prosser, M., One of the most profitable strategies in bond investing, http://www.forbes.com/sites/marcprosser/2013/02/04/one-of-the-most-profitable-strategies-in-bond-investing/2/04/2013.

Reilly, F.K., Brown, K.C., 2012. Bond portfolio management strategies. Analysis of Investments and Management of Portfolios. 10th ed. South Western Cengage Learning pp. 669-702 (Chapter 19).

http://thismatter.com/money/bonds/types/cdo.htm.

STOCK MARKETS, DERIVATIVES MARKETS, AND FOREIGN EXCHANGE MARKETS

5.1 STOCK MARKETS AND INSTRUMENTS

5.1.1 INTRODUCTION

Stock markets play a vital role in the growth of the industry and commerce of any country. The stock market is the primary source for any company to raise funds for business expansions. Through the primary market of stock exchanges, companies can issue shares to the public and get funds for business purposes. To issue shares to investors, a company needs to get listed in a stock exchange. The secondary function of the stock exchange is to provide a platform for liquidity for buyers and sellers of the stocks that are listed in the stock market. In the secondary market of stock exchanges, the retail and institutional investors buy and sell the stocks. Table 5.1 gives the market value of equities outstanding issued by various entities as of March 2013.

5.1.2 STOCK MARKET INSTRUMENTS AND CHARACTERISTICS

5.1.2.1 Common stock

Basically, corporate stocks are of two types: common stock and preferred stock. Stocks are equity capital, giving the owners of stock part ownership in the corporation. One of the important characteristics of common stock is the limited liability feature of common stocks, which means that common stockholder losses are limited to the amount of their original investment in the company. The main features of common stock include shareholder rights. Stockholders are the real owners of a company. Common stockholders have a fundamental privilege of voting rights. Stockholders control the corporation through the right to elect the directors. Directors of corporations are elected at an annual shareholder meeting by a vote of the majority of shareholders. The voting can be either cumulative or straight voting. In cumulative voting, the shareholder may cast all votes for one member of the board of directors. In cumulative voting, the number of votes assigned to each stockholder equals the number of shares held multiplied by the number of directors to be elected. In straight voting, shareholders cast all of their votes for each candidate for the board of directors. Through this procedure the directors are elected one at a time. Most shareholders don't attend annual shareholder meetings. For that reason corporations mail proxies (voting ballots) to shareholders prior to the annual meeting. A proxy is a grant of authority by a shareholder allowing the representatives of the shareholder to vote on their behalf. The typical rule is one vote per share of common stock. However, some firms are classified as dual-class firms in which two classes of common stock are

SL	Entities	2008	2012
	Table 5.1 Corporate Equities Outstanding, Market Value (Billions of US Dollars)		
1	Nonfinancial corporations	10,016.6	16,199.4
2	Financial corporations	2875.4	4960.9
3	Rest of world	2748.4	4745.7
	Total	15,640.4	25.906

Source: Federal Reserve Flow of Funds, Z.1 March 7, 2013.

issued with differential voting rights assigned to each class. For example, Google has two classes of common stock, A and B. The A class shares are held by the public and each share has one vote. The class B shares are held by company insiders and each class B share has 10 votes. The Ford Company has class B shares that are held by Ford family interests and are not publicly traded. These class B shares represent about 40% of the voting power though they constitute only 10% of the total number of shares outstanding.

Common stockholders have residual claim on the firm's assets in the event of the liquidation of the firm. They have only residual claims on the cash distribution after the priority claims of senior lenders such as bank loans and bondholders.

Another distinctive feature of common stock is related to dividend payments. Dividends are payments made by a corporation to shareholders in either cash or stock. The payment of dividends is at the discretion of the board of directors. Dividends are not a liability for a corporation unless it is declared by the board of directors of a corporation. Dividends are paid out of a firm's after-tax profits. Payment of dividends is not a business expense and is not deductible for corporate tax purposes. Individual stockholders are taxed for the dividends received.

Usually stockholders have the right to share proportionally in any new stock issue, which is called preemptive right.

5.1.2.2 Preferred stock

Preferred stocks are hybrid securities that have the characteristics of both bonds and stocks. Preferred stocks have dividend priority over common stock. The holders of preferred shares receive dividends before the holders of common shares. Preferred stockholders generally do not have voting rights in the company. Dividends payable on preference shares can be cumulative or noncumulative. Preference dividends are cumulative in the sense that if they are not paid in one particular year, they will be carried forward as arrears and must be paid before dividends are given to common stockholders. In noncumulative preference dividends, if dividends are missed they are never paid. Preferred stocks are also classified as participative and nonparticipative. In the former category the dividends paid in any year may be greater than the stated dividends. In the latter category the dividend is fixed irrespective of any increase or decrease in the firm's profits. Dividends paid on preferred stock are not a tax-deductible expense.

5.1.2.3 Primary stock market

The primary stock market is the market in which firms float new stocks to the public. New stock issues can be divided into initial public offerings (IPOs) and seasoned equity offerings (SEOs).

An IPO involves a firm selling its common stock to the public for the first time. At the time of IPO there is no existing public market for the stock. SEOs are new shares offered by firms that already have stocks outstanding. New issues (seasoned or IPOs) are typically underwritten by investment bankers.

5.1.2.3.1 IPO process
Underwriting is an integral part of the IPO process. The process of underwriting involves formulating the method used to issue securities, price and sell new securities. The process involves the acquisition of the total issue from the company and selling the securities to interested investors. The issuing company and investment bank will negotiate the deal. The details include the amount of funds to be raised, the type of securities to be issued, and the underwriting agreement details. The underwriting process takes the forms of negotiated, competitive bids, or best efforts arrangements. Sometimes the underwriting is taken up by a syndicate of underwriters in which the lead underwriter leads the syndicate and others sell a part of the issue.

A registration document is filed with the US Securities and Exchange Commission (SEC) by the investment bank. The registration gives details about the company—information such as financial reports, management background, and information about the prospective offering. The SEC investigates and determines whether all material information has been disclosed. The SEC then approves the IPO and the stock is offered to the public.

The underwriter prepares an initial prospectus called a red herring, which contains all information about the company and offer issue except the offer price and effective date of issue. The red herring prospectus is distributed to potential equity buyers. The underwriter and the company promote the stock offerings through road shows.

Typically an IPO is priced either through a fixed price method or a book-building process. In the fixed price method, the company, with the help of its lead manager, fixes a price for the issue. In the book-building process, the price is determined through the analysis of confidential investor demand data that is compiled by the book runner (lead manager).

In IPOs there is usually a lockup period, which is a predetermined time period following an IPO where large shareholders are restricted from selling their shares.

5.1.2.3.2 Shelf registration
In 1983, the SEC adopted Rule 415, which permits shelf registration. Shelf registration allows a company to offer multiple issues of stock over a 2-year period. Securities can be shelved for up to 2 years until the firm is ready to issue them. Only investment-grade rate companies are eligible for shelf registration.

5.1.2.3.3 Private placements
Instead of public offerings, equity securities can be sold privately to small groups of financial institutions. This arrangement is called private placement. The placement need not be registered with the SEC. The investors involved in private placements are large banks, insurance companies, mutual funds, and pension funds.

5.1.2.3.4 Green shoe option
A green shoe option embedded in an underwriting agreement gives the underwriter the option of allocating shares in excess of the shares included in the public issue. The option includes the operations of a

post-listing price-stabilizing mechanism for a period not exceeding 30 days. This overallotment option is normally done if the demand for a security issue is higher than expected. According to the agreement the overallotment is a maximum of 15% of the issue size. A green shoe option aims to provide additional price stability to a security issue because the underwriter can smooth out price fluctuations when demand increases.

5.1.2.3.5 Flipping shares

Investors who engage in a flipping strategy have no plans for investing in the firm over the long run. This process involves the practice of buying initial public offerings at the offering price and then reselling them once trading is initiated for profit gains. This practice is followed by institutional investors who get most of the IPO shares at offering price. Flipping becomes profitable particularly in a hot IPO market when the price of an IPO rises over the offering price in the first day of listing.

5.1.2.3.6 Underpricing of IPOs

An IPO is said to be underpriced if the price of the newly listed shares in initial trading exceeds the offer price at which it was sold to investors. Academic researchers suggest that underpricing is often used by insiders to retain control of the firm. Insiders have incentives to underprice to ensure oversubscription and rationing in the share allocation process. This rationing allows discrimination between applicants for shares and limits the block size of new shareholdings. It is argued that underpricing and subsequent oversubscription is meant to discriminate the rationing process against large applicants. The average underpricing for IPOs in the United States was 14.8% for 1990-1998 and 12.1% for the 2001-2009 period. According to information asymmetry theory, IPO pricing is the result of information disparities. Companies intentionally underprice IPOs as a rational behavior to induce uninformed investors to participate in the market, thereby raising the demand for the issues. Moreover, the price of the IPO must be low enough to induce the investment bank to act in the issuing firm's best interest.

This situation arises because underwriters need uninformed investors to bid for the issue since there are not enough informed investors. The underwriter reprices the IPO so that uninformed investors bid, which results in underpricing. Table 5.2 lists the largest IPOs in the world.

5.1.2.4 *Secondary stock markets*

In secondary stock markets, called exchanges, investors trade among themselves. In this market investors trade previously issued and listed securities without the involvement of issuing companies. The secondary stock markets can be further divided into auction and dealer markets. Auction markets are also referred to as order-driven markets. In a pure auction market, interested buyers and sellers submit bid and ask prices (buy and sell orders) for a given stock to a central location where the orders are matched by a broker who acts as a facilitating agent. The New York Stock Exchange (NYSE), the largest stock market in the world, is a classic example of an auction market. This auction system is price driven because the shares of stock are sold to the investor with the highest bid price and are bought from the seller with the lowest offering price. The other major trading system is known as a dealer market, which is also referred to as a quote-driven market. In this system dealers buy and sell shares of stock for themselves. Dealers earn profits through the differences in the bid and ask prices of their securities. There are numerous trading dealers who compete against each other to provide the highest bid prices when selling and lowest ask prices when buying the stock.

Table 5.2   Biggest IPO Issues

SL	Corporation	Stock Exchange	Sector	Deal Value (Billions of US Dollars)	Year
1	Agricultural Bank of China	Hong Stock Exchange/ Shanghai Stock Exchange	Finance	19.23	2010
2	Industrial and Commercial Bank of China	Hong Stock Exchange/ Shanghai Stock Exchange	Finance	19.09	2006
3	NTT Mobile	Tokyo Stock Exchange	Communications	18.1	1998
4	Visa	New York Stock Exchange	Finance	17.86	2008
5	AIA	Hong Kong Stock Exchange	Finance	17.82	2010
6	Enel SpA	New York Stock Exchange	Energy	16.45	1999
7	General Motors	New York Stock Exchange	Automotive	15.8	2010
8	NTT	Tokyo Stock Exchange	Communications	15.3	1987
9	Deutsche Telekom	New York Stock Exchange	Communications	13.03	1996
10	Bank of China	Hong Kong Stock Exchange/ Shanghai Stock Exchange	Finance	11.19	2006

Collated from various sources.

Many over-the-counter (OTC) markets are classified as dealer markets. The National Association of Securities Dealers Automated Quotation (NASDAQ) stock exchange is a dealer market. Most bonds are traded in dealer markets.

Trading activity in a stock market is classified into call markets and continuous markets. In a call market, the market is called at a certain time, called the trading session. All the traders need to be present to trade at that time. A call market is very liquid during a trading session. A call market may trade all the securities at the same time or the securities may be called one after another in rotation. If there are fixed trading hours in a session, then the call market may call as many securities as possible in the given time period. Call markets are also used to sell debt securities such as bonds, notes, and bills. Examples of a call market are Deutsche Bourse and Euronext Paris Bourse.

In a continuous trading market, traders consisting of buyers and sellers continuously place their orders and match on a continuous basis. Most of the stock exchanges, foreign exchange markets (forex markets), and derivatives exchanges are continuous trading markets. Most continuous markets typically start the trading session with a call market auction. Some markets close with a call market auction.

5.1.2.5 Stock market transactions and strategies

To place an order to buy or sell a specific stock, an investor contacts a brokerage firm. The brokerage firm acts as a financial intermediary between buyers and sellers of the stock in the secondary market. The broker provides a bid quote if the investor wants to sell a stock or an ask quote if the investor wants to buy a stock.

The different types of market orders are market buy/sell orders, limit orders, special orders, margin transactions, and short selling, described in the following sections.

5.1.2.5.1 Market orders

This is the most common type of order in which an order is given to buy or sell a stock at the best possible current price. A market sell order indicates that the investor is willing to sell at the highest bid available at the time on the exchange. A market buy order indicates the investor's willingness to pay the lowest offering price for a stock trading in the exchange.

5.1.2.5.2 Limit orders

Investors placing a limit order or stop order specify the buy or sell price. In other words, a limit order is an order that sets the maximum or minimum price at which the investor is willing to buy or sell a particular stock. The primary advantage of a limit order is that it guarantees that the trade will be made at a particular price. The brokerage firm will probably charge a higher commission for the limit order. It has to specify how long the limit order will be outstanding. A limit order can be instantaneous. In a kill order the order is immediately canceled. In a fill order, the order is immediately filled.

5.1.2.5.3 Special orders

A stop loss order is a particular type of limit order in which the investor specifies a selling price that is below the current market price of the stock. For example, say a stock is bought at $40 and it is expected to go up. But if it doesn't the investor wants to limit his or her losses. So a stop loss order is given at $35. Then if the stock drops to $35, the specified stop loss order, being a market seller order, will indicate the stock be sold at the prevailing market price. A stop buy order is a type of limit order in which the investor specifies a purchase price that is above the current market price. Suppose a stock is sold short at $60 expecting it to decline at $50. To hedge for increases in price the stop buy order can be used to purchase the stock using a market buy order if it reaches a price of $65.

5.1.2.5.4 Margin transactions

In trading transactions, investors can buy stock with cash or leverage a part of the transaction cost. The leverage process involves buying on margin in which the investor pays for the stock with some cash and borrow the rest through the broker, using the stock as collateral. The interest rate charged on these loans by the brokerage firms is usually 1.50% above the rate charged by the bank making the loan. The minimum margin requirement involving cash is variable with about 40% of the total transaction. There is also a minimum amount of equity that must be maintained in a margin account, which is called the maintenance margin. Typically the minimum required level of margin specified by the NYSE is 25% of the total market value of the securities in the margin account. Some brokerages have a higher maintenance margin requirement of 30-40%. If the stock price declines to a level such that the investor's equity market value drops below 25% of the total value position, then the investor receives a margin call to provide more equity.

5.1.2.5.5 Short selling
Short selling is a technique by which investors place an order to sell a stock that they don't own. Investors short a stock when they expect the price of the stock to decline. In short selling the investor borrows the stock from another investor through the broker and sells it in the market. Then the stock is replaced by buying it at a price lower than the price at which it had been sold. This is known as covering the short position. The short seller must pay any dividends due to the investor who had lent the stock.

Suppose an investor decides to sell short 100 shares of a company as she thinks that the earnings will drop and as a result stock prices will decline. The investor's broker would borrow shares from another investor with the promise to return them back later. The investor then sells the borrowed shares at the current market price. If the expectation comes true and the price drops, the investor "covers the short position" by buying back the shares and the broker returns them to the lender. The net gain for the investor is the difference between the sell price and buy price minus the broker's commission and interest for borrowing.

5.1.2.6 Facilitators in stock transactions
Floor brokers, market makers, and specialists are the major participants in stock transactions.

5.1.2.6.1 Floor broker
Floor brokers execute orders for their clients. Floor brokers do not execute orders on their own accounts. A floor broker represents client orders at the point of sale on stock exchanges such as the NYSE. A floor broker's clients include banks, broker dealers, hedge funds, mutual funds, and pension funds. A floor broker earns a commission for each share traded.

5.1.2.6.2 Market maker
A market maker is a broker-dealer who facilitates the trading of shares by posting bids and ask prices along with maintaining an inventory of shares. Many foreign exchange trading firms and banks act as market makers. The market maker sells to and buys from its clients.

5.1.2.6.3 Specialist
A specialist is a member of a stock exchange whose role is to facilitate trading in certain stocks. The specialist's function is to make a market in the stock traded by displaying the best bid and ask prices to the market during trading hours. A specialist is a type of market maker. The NYSE has seven specialist firms while NASDAQ has nearly 300 market makers. Specialists in the NYSE perform the roles of auctioneer and agent.

5.1.2.7 Innovations in trading systems
In the mid-1970s, centralized transactions from national and regional stock exchanges were introduced, which was followed by the introduction of the Intermarket Trading System (ITS) that linked regional national exchanges. In the 1990s, designated computerized trading platforms, including electronic communications networks (ECNs), were introduced and enabled the availability of quotes to the public markets. In 2000, the SEC replaced price quotes in eighths to decimal pricing. Earlier the system

of quoting in eights (1/8, 3/8, 5/8, 7/8) ensured wide bid ask spreads and high profits for dealers. The NYSE created a new trading order "Direct +" that allowed member firms to trade up to 1099 shares electronically every 30 s without allowing an order to get in front of the order submitted. In early 2000, algorithmic trading was introduced to help firms develop computer programs (algorithms) to divide large orders into small orders. Smart order routing algorithms were developed to minimize transaction costs. As a result of these innovations, the number of transactions grew exponentially from 545 million in 2002 to more than 2 trillion in 2008.

In 2005, the national market system was implemented wherein electronically various exchanges were linked into one electronic market. Later, algorithmic trading was extended to create the high frequency trading (HFT) algorithm to process thousands of orders daily and recognize a news event and respond with an order in microseconds.

5.1.2.8 New trading systems

Technological systems, such as Super DoT, facilitated the trading process in exchanges such as the NYSE. SuperDOT is the electronic system used by the NYSE to route market orders and limit orders from investors or their agents to a specialist located on the floor of the exchange. It is very useful for keeping track of market activity in a specific security. The SuperDOT-like Opening Automated Report Service (OARS) reports the opening price for each security to the originating broker. OARS can accept member firms' preopening market orders up to 30,099 shares and automatically pair the buy and sell orders and provide information about the imbalances to the specialist before the opening of the stock trading. In 2009, SuperDOT was replaced by the new NYSE Super Display Book System for processing orders. The Display Book is an electronic workstation where specialists on the exchange execute and manage order flow.

In the NASDAQ, the major order processing systems are the Small Order Execution System (SOES) and SelectNet. After the stock market crash of 1987, the NASDAQ introduced the SOES to facilitate automatic order execution for individual traders with orders less than or equal to 1000 shares. The aim was to provide liquidity for small investors and traders. This system is now phased out. SelectNet is a service provided by the NASDAQ that allows member firms to buy or sell orders in NASDAQ securities in the system. This system functions by directing those orders to a single market maker (directed orders) or broadcasting the order to market participants (broadcast orders). The trades executed through SelectNet are submitted for clearing as locked-in trades.

5.1.2.9 Regulation in the stock market

The aim of the SEC is to protect investors, maintain fair, orderly, and efficient markets, and facilitate capital formation. The SEC requires public companies to disclose financial and other information to the public. The SEC oversees key participants in the stock market, which includes stock exchanges, securities brokers and dealers, investment advisors, mutual funds, and other financial institutions. The main objective of the SEC is to promote the disclosure of important market-related information, fair dealings, and protection against fraud. The Edgar database contains the disclosure documents that public companies are required to file with the SEC.

The major laws that govern the securities industry are:

- Securities Act 1933
- Securities Act 1934
- Trust Indenture Act 1939

- Investment Company Act 1940
- Investment Advisers Act 1940
- Sarbanes-Oxley Act 1940
- Dodd-Frank Act 2010

5.1.2.10 Participants in the stock market

The major participants include individual retail investors, institutional investors such as mutual funds, banks, insurance companies and hedge funds, and publicly traded corporations. Households are the single-largest holders of corporate stock holdings. Mutual funds and pension funds are also major players in the stock market.

5.1.2.11 Stock market indexes

A stock market index measures the pulse of the entire stock market and tracks the market's changes over time. A market index is a tool used by investors and managers to measure performance indicators of specific stock exchanges. These indexes allow investors to compare the performance of individual stocks with more general market indicators. The major stock market indexes are discussed in the following sections.

5.1.2.11.1 Dow Jones Industrial Average

The Dow Jones Industrial Average (DJIA) is the oldest and the best-known price-weighted index. It is the price-weighted average of 30 large blue-chip American industrial stocks. General Electric has the longest presence in the index. Some of the major companies in the index include Walmart, Proctor & Gamble, JPMorgan Chase, ExxonMobil, DuPont, Coca-Cola, AT&T, American Express, and 3M.

5.1.2.11.2 NYSE Composite Index

The NYSE Composite Index measures the performance of all common stocks listed on the NYSE, which includes American depository receipts (ADRs), real estate investment trusts (REITs), and listings of foreign companies. But exchange-traded funds (ETFs), closed-end funds, and derivatives are excluded from the index. It is a value-weighted index that is calculated on both price return and total return basis. The NYSE Composite Index is made up of issues consisting of more than 1900 companies, including more than 1500 US companies and over 330 non-US companies with a total float adjusted market cap of over $19 trillion. It is a globally diversified index with US stocks constituting approximately 64% and non-US companies comprising 36% of the NYSE Composite Index market capitalization. The index represents stocks from 38 countries. The constituents in the Composite Index represent 10 industrial sectors as defined by the Industry Classification Benchmark. Some of the largest companies included in the index include ExxonMobil, Proctor & Gamble, AT&T, General Electric, Chevron, BP, Walmart, Novartis, and Pfizer.

5.1.2.11.3 NASDAQ Composite Index

The NASDAQ Composite Index measures all NASDAQ domestic and international-based common type stocks listed on the NASDAQ stock market. The NASDAQ Composite is measured using a market capitalization-weighted methodology. The index came into existence in 1971 and currently includes over 3000 securities. Close-end funds, convertible debentures, preferred stocks, ETFs, and other derivative securities are not included in the index.

5.1.2.11.4 Standard & Poor's 500

The Standard & Poor's (S&P) 500 Index is a market value-weighted index of stock prices of 500 large US firms. The index includes both growth and less-volatile value stock. The S&P 500 focuses on the large-cap sector of the market. The S&P MidCap 400 represents the mid-cap range of companies, and the S&P SmallCap 600 represents small-cap companies. The three indexes are combined and calculated together as the S&P Composite 1500.

5.1.2.11.5 Nikkei 225 or Nikkei

The Nikkei is a stock market index for the Tokyo Stock Exchange (TSE). It is a price-weighted index with the unit being yen. Another major index in the TSE is Topix. Nikkei 225 represents sectors including foods, automotive, textiles, chemicals, construction, banking, retail, and pharmaceuticals.

5.1.2.11.6 Emerging markets

The emerging markets are in countries such as Brazil, Russia, India, and China (BRIC). Markets in countries such as Turkey, Indonesia, Mexico, and Philippines (TIMPs) are also considered to be developing markets. These regions are witnessing favorable demographics and show signs of strengthening economies and political institutions.

5.1.2.12 Investing in foreign stocks

Different methods are used to purchase foreign stocks. These can include direct purchases, international mutual funds, international ETFs, ADRs, and global depository receipts (GDRs), described in the following sections.

5.1.2.12.1 Direct purchases

Through direct purchases, investors can invest in stocks of foreign companies that are listed in local stock exchanges in limited sets. Foreign stocks that are not listed on local stock exchanges can be purchased through the foreign offices of brokerage firms.

5.1.2.12.2 International mutual funds

Investments in foreign stocks can also be made through the purchase of shares of international mutual funds, which consist of portfolios of international stocks managed by various financial institutions.

5.1.2.12.3 International exchange-traded funds

International ETFs represent any ETF that invests in foreign-based securities. These funds are passive funds that mimic an underlying index. Investors have access to a large number of company stocks through the ETFs. The focus of the ETFs are either global or regional in nature.

5.1.2.12.4 American depository receipts

Purchase of foreign equity is also possible through ADRs and GDRs. Through ADRs, large numbers of foreign companies are actively traded on major US equity markets including the NYSE, AMEX, and NASDAQ. An ADR is a certificate that represents shares of a foreign stock owned and issued by a US bank. The foreign shares are held in bank custody overseas and the certificates traded in the United States. Sponsored programs are organized directly by the company who signs the depository agreement with the bank that acts as the depository and transfers the underlying equity securities to the depository bank for the purposes of arrangement of the ADR program.

In an unsponsored program, a dealer acts as a market maker for the issue and arranges the program in conjunction with the depository bank that issues the ADR. Investors purchase ADRs from brokers or dealers. The dealers either purchase already issued ADRs on a US exchange or purchase the shares of the issuing company from the issuer's home market. The US dealer then deposits those shares in the bank branch in that market. The bank then issues ADRs representing those shares to the dealer's custodian. ADRs are issued and dividends are paid in US dollars. Hence, domestic investors get the opportunity to own shares of a company without the risk of exchange of currencies. The company pays the dividends in its home currency and the issuing bank distributes the dividends in dollars net of exchange costs and foreign taxes.

5.1.2.12.5 Global depository receipts

GDRs are negotiable certificates issued by depositary banks that represent ownership of a given number of a company's shares that can be listed and traded independently from the underlying shares. These instruments are typically used by companies from emerging markets. A GDR is basically used to access two or more markets, usually the United Kingdom and the United States.

5.1.2.13 *Common stock portfolio management strategies*

Active and passive strategies are the two broad methods of managing common stock portfolios. Active strategies focus on attempts to outperform markets by actions that include timing market transactions, which are used in technical analysis and identification of undervalued or overvalued stocks using fundamental analysis. Active strategies also involve the selection of stocks according to one of the market anomalies such as pricing inefficiencies. The conceptual background for the passive strategy is based on modern portfolio theory and capital market theory. The portfolio theory suggests that the market portfolio offers the highest level of return per unit of risk in a market that is price-efficient. Hence a portfolio of financial assets similar to the market portfolio will capture the pricing efficiency of the market. There are two types of passive strategies: the buy and hold strategy and the indexing strategy. In a buy and hold strategy a portfolio of stocks based on some criterion is chosen and held to the end of investment time. In other words, there is no active buying and selling of stocks once a portfolio is created. The indexing strategy is the most commonly followed passive strategy. In indexing, a portfolio is designed to replicate the performance of a benchmark index referred to as an indexed portfolio.

5.1.2.14 *Stock market trends*

According to the World Federation of Exchanges (WFE) Report 2012,[1] the global stock market capitalization witnessed a 15.1% growth rate to approximately $55 trillion. The total number of listed companies in the WFE exchange was 46,332. According to WFE Report 2013, the global market capitalization amounted to 64.195 trillion registering a growth rate of 17%. The best performance in the stock market was observed in the Americas followed by the Asia Pacific region and the Europe Africa Middle East region. The value of share trading in these stock exchanges amounted to $49 trillion. Table 5.3 gives the equity market capitalization amounts region wise. Table 5.4 provides the values of equity market capitalization in different exchanges.

---

[1] Focus 2012 Market Capitalization Trend, Focus No 239, January 2013, World Federation of Exchanges.

Table 5.3 **Domestic Equity Market Capitalization**

Region	Billions of US Dollars
Americas	28,297
Asia Pacific	18,415
Europe Africa Middle East	17,483
Total	64,195

Source: 2013 Market Capitalization Trend Report, World Federation of Exchanges Report.

Table 5.4 **Largest Domestic Equity Market Capitalization 2013**

SL	Exchange	Billions of US Dollars
1	NYSE Euronext (US)	17,950
2	NASDAQ OMX (US)	6085
3	Tokyo Stock Exchange	4543
4	London Stock Exchange	4429
5	NYSE Euronext (UK)	3584
6	Hong Kong Exchange	3101
7	Shanghai SE	2497
8	TMX Group	2114
9	Deutsche Borse	1936
10	Six Swiss Exchange	1541

Source: 2013 Market Capitalization Trend, World Federation of Exchanges Report.

5.1.2.15 Bull and bear markets

A bull market is associated with the expectation of future price increases (capital gains) as a result of increased investor confidence. The US stock markets witnessed bullish characteristics during the periods 1925-1929, 1953-1957, and 1993-1997. The Bombay Stock Exchange Index SENSEX, representing the Indian stock market, witnessed a bullish trend during the period 2003-2008 when the index rose from 2900 to 21,000 points.

A bear market represents a general decline in the stock market over a period of time. During the stock market crash of 1929, the DJIA market capitalization fell by 89%.

5.1.2.16 Major stock exchanges in the world
5.1.2.16.1 New York Stock Exchange Euronext

In 1817, as a result of the Buttonwood Agreement, the New York Stock Exchange Board was established. In 1863, the name was shortened to New York Stock Exchange. In 2006, the NYSE became public. The NYSE operates in four business divisions: global market data, trading solutions, exchange solutions, and global connectivity. NYSE Group Inc. and Euronext NV merged in 2007 to form the New York Stock Exchange Euronext (NYX). The NYX is the only stock exchange operator in the Fortune 500 list. The NYX is the world's leading operator of financial markets and provider of innovating trading technologies. The stocks traded in the NYX constitute one third of equities traded worldwide. The NYX is also one of the world's

Table 5.5   Listing Requirements in the NYX

Criteria	Requirements	Worldwide
Distribution	Round lot holders	5000
	Total shareholders	
	Public shares	2.5 MM
	Public market value	$100 MM
Financials	Aggregate pretax income for the past three years	$100 MM
	Minimum pretax income in each of the preceding two years	$25 MM

Source: http://usequities.nyx.com/listings/list-with-nyse/worldwide-listing-standards.

leading futures and options trading exchanges and offers derivative products on commodities, foreign exchange, equities, bonds, and swaps. The NYX constitutes 70 of the largest 100 global corporations and 90% of the DJIA. The NYSE Euronext's equities division consists of the NYSE, NYSE Euronext, NYSE MKT, NYSE Alternext, and NYSE Acra. About 2800 companies, with a global market capitalization of about $18 trillion, are listed on the NYSE. In 2008, NYSE Euronext acquired the American Stock Exchange for $260 million in stock. Stocks worth $37 billion are exchanged daily on the floor of the NYSE EuroNext.

The NYX allows two sets of standard worldwide and domestic under which non-US companies may qualify to list. The list include both distribution and financial criteria. Table 5.5 gives the listing requirements in the NYSE.

5.1.2.16.2 National Association of Securities Dealers Automated Quotation System

The NASDAQ OMX Group is the world's largest electronic OTC exchange company, which operates in 24 markets, three clearinghouses, and five central securities depositories spanning six continents. These divisions support the trading of equities, options, fixed income, derivatives, commodities, futures, and structured products. Around 3600 companies worth $5.2 trillion in market capital are listed in the NASDAQ. In the United States, the NASDAQ has three marketplaces: the NASDAQ Global Select Market, the NASDAQ Global Market, and the NASDAQ Capital Market. The global technology platform of NASDAQ can handle more than 1 million messages per second at sub 80 microsecond average speeds. It is the largest single liquidity pool for US equities. Technology stocks such as Facebook, Microsoft, and Intel are listed in the NASDAQ.

5.1.2.16.3 London Stock Exchange

Around 3000 companies from 70 countries are listed in the London Stock Exchange (LSE). There are 400 member firms in the LSE, which are primarily investment banks and stockbrokers. In 2007, the LSE merged with Borsa Italiana to create Europe's diversified exchange market called the London Stock Exchange Group. A comprehensive range of real-time FTSE indexes are available from the London Stock Exchange. In 2010, €20.8 billion was raised on the London stock market of which €17.9 billion was raised from the main market of the LSE. The listing requirement at the LSE requires firms to provide audited accounts that cover at least 3 years and a final balance sheet that is not more than six months before the date of the prospectus. There should be evidence of revenue earning that supports at least 75% of the company's business.

5.1.2.16.4 Tokyo Stock Exchange

In 2011, the TSE acquired the Osaka Securities Exchange (OSE) to form the Japan Exchange Group. These exchanges are licensed to operate financial instruments exchanges under the Financial Instruments and Exchange Act. The exchange trades securities and derivatives, publishes stock prices, ensures fair trading of securities and other financial instruments, and carries out other activities. The security listing requirement for stocks in the TSE includes criteria such as more than 800 shareholders and market capitalization of 2 billion yen. Another requirement is that the listing company should have at least 500 million yen as profit. TSE listed stocks are classified as first section, second section, Mothers (market of high growth and emerging stock), and PRO (Tokyo PRO Market). There are 2320 companies listed under these categories in the TSE of which 10 are foreign firms.

5.2 DERIVATIVES MARKET AND INSTRUMENTS

5.2.1 INTRODUCTION

Derivatives have become an integral part of the financial market as they deal with multieconomic functions. Derivatives are complex and controversial in nature. Derivatives have become an effective tool to reduce business risks, expand product offerings, and manage capital and funding costs. Commercial and investment banks are the major players in the OTC derivatives market. They are often the market makers and developers of new products. Banks have active roles in foreign exchange derivatives, interest rate derivatives, equity derivatives, commodity derivatives, and credit derivatives.

The uniqueness of derivatives is in their close relationship between their values and values of their underlying assets. It is easier to take a short position in a derivative than in other assets. Exchange-traded derivatives are more liquid and have lower transaction costs than other assets. Derivatives can be constructed to closely match specific portfolio requirements. Derivatives are useful for hedging and speculating purposes.

Derivatives such as swaps, futures, and options form a significant share of total assets at large banks. Most derivatives are based on one of four types of assets: foreign exchange, interest rates (debt securities), commodities, and equities. Derivatives are traded either on organized exchanges or on the OTC market. Exchange-traded contracts are standardized contracts that have standardized features and do not cater to individual needs. In the OTC market a derivative investor is exposed to the risk that his counterparty may default on the contract.

Derivatives have emerged as a central element of modern financial markets. Derivatives offer various types of risk protection and investment strategies. The two segments in the derivative market are the off-exchange or OTC and exchange-traded segments. The OTC market accounts for approximately 80% of the derivatives market.

5.2.2 CLASSIFICATION OF DERIVATIVES

Basically, derivatives are classified by type of derivative and marketplace, type of underlying, and type of product. Derivatives are traded bilaterally through the OTC market as individual customized contracts or multilaterally on exchanges as standardized contracts. The underlying assets in derivatives can be financial instruments themselves or physical assets. The examples are fixed income, foreign exchange, credit risk, equities, and equity indexes or commodities. There are three basic types of derivatives: forwards or futures, options, and swaps.

5.2.3 **USERS OF DERIVATIVES**

Corporations and financial institutions are the major users of derivatives. Corporations and financial institutions use derivatives to protect themselves against changes in raw material prices, exchange rates, and interest rates. These derivatives serve as insurance against unwanted price fluctuations and reduce the volatility of company cash flows. About 92% of the world's largest companies manage their price risks using derivatives.[2] Derivatives can also be used as channels of investment rather than investing directly in assets. If a creditor defaults on its bonds, credit derivatives provide compensation benefits. Weather derivatives provide compensation if a temperature at a particular location rises or falls below a predefined reference temperature. Derivatives also allow investors to take positions against the market if they expect the underlying asset to fall in value.

5.2.4 **VOLUME OF BANK EXPOSURE IN DERIVATIVES TRADING**

The notional value of banking holding in derivatives rose from $1.4 trillion to $8.6 trillion during 1986-1992. In 2012, the value of the derivatives market was estimated to be $600 trillion according to a BIS statistics report. It is said that the world's GDP is only about $65 trillion, which is roughly 10.83% of the worldwide value of the global derivatives market.

In the United States, the nine largest banks have in excess of $220 trillion of derivatives exposure.[3] This can be described as more than three times the size of the global economy. In the United States, the four biggest banks (JPMorgan Chase, Citigroup, Bank of America, and Goldman Sachs) hold about 95% of the industry's total exposures to derivatives. JPMorgan is the largest commercial bank with maximum exposure in derivatives. In 2012, Morgan Stanley had a derivative exposure of $1.722 trillion. Wells Fargo has a derivative exposure of $3.332 trillion. Bank of New York has a derivative exposure of $1.375 trillion. HSBC has a derivative exposure of $4.321 trillion.

Before the economic recession, banks made enormous gains by selling complex derivatives directly to the public. In the United States, regulatory reforms, including the Dodd-Frank Act, have mandated the trading of derivatives through clearinghouses that bear the risk, and the role of big banks and financial institutions is to simply broker the transactions. In 2010, JPMorgan had a loss of $2 billion in derivatives trading. Table 5.6 gives the amounts and market values of the global OTC derivatives market.

5.2.5 **MAJOR DERIVATIVES EXCHANGES**

5.2.5.1 *CME Group*

CME was founded in 1898 as a not-for-profit corporation. The CME Group consists of the Chicago Mercantile Exchange (CME), Chicago Board of Trade (CBOT), New York Mercantile Exchange (NYMEX), Commodity Exchange (COMEX), and Kansas City Board of Trade (KCBT). In 1994, COMEX and NYMEX merged together to form the world's largest physical futures trading exchange. In 2007, CME holdings merged with CBOT Holdings and was renamed the CME group. CBOT is a major marketplace for trading agricultural and US Treasury futures as well as options on futures. In 2008, the CME Group acquired Credit Market Analysis Limited along with its three subsidiaries,

---

[2]The Global Derivatives Market – An Introduction. Deutsche Borse Group. http://www.math.nyu.edu/faculty/avellane/global_derivatives_market.pdf.
[3]http://seekingalpha.com/article/600231-the-banks-and-derivatives-too-big-to-fail-or-too-exposed-to-be-saved

Table 5.6   Global OTC Derivatives Market (Billions of US Dollars)

Instruments	Notional Amounts Outstanding		Gross Market Value	
	December 2010	December 2012	December 2010	December 2012
Total contracts	601,046	632,580	21,296	24,740
Foreign exchange contracts (A)				
Forwards and forex swaps	28,433	31,718	886	803
Currency swaps	19,271	25,420	1235	1247
Options	10,092	10,220	362	254
Total (A)	57,796	67,358	2483	2304
Interest rate contracts (B)				
FRA	51,587	71,353	206	47
Interest rate swaps	364,377	369,999	13,139	17,080
Options	49,295	48,351	1401	1706
Total (B)	465,259	489,703	14,746	18,833
Equity linked contracts (C)				
Forwards and swaps	1828	2045	167	157
Options	3807	4207	480	448
Total (C)	5635	6252	647	605
Commodity contracts	2922	2587	526	358
Credit default swaps	29,898	25,069	1351	848
Unallocated	39,536	41,611	1543	1792

Source: BIS Statistics Report 2012.

which provide credit derivatives, market data. In 2008, the CME Group acquired NYMEX and COMEX. The CME Group offers a wide range of derivatives products, including major asset classes based on interest rates, equity indexes, foreign exchange, energy, agricultural products, metals, weather, and real estate. The group deals with both exchange-traded and OTC derivatives. NYMEX deals with energy futures and option contracts for crude oil, natural gas, heating oil, and gasoline. COMEX is the major marketplace for metal futures and options contracts for gold, silver, and copper. Energy and interest rate derivatives contributed approximately 27% and 26% of the clearing and transaction fees revenues for CME in 2011. The notional value of products traded amounted to US $1068 trillion. CME generated revenues of approximately $3280 million in 2011. Approximately 84% of the volume trading was electronic in 2011.

5.2.5.2 Eurex Exchange

The Eurex Exchange is one of the world's leading derivatives exchanges. Eurex is a public company wholly owned by Deusche Borse AG. Eurex operates the Eurex exchanges, Eurex Clearing, the ECNs (electronic communication networks), Eurex bonds, and Eurex Repo. Trading volume at Eurex exceeds 1.5 billion contracts a year. Market participants are connected from 700 locations worldwide. The key products traded in Eurex consist of fixed income, money market, equity derivatives, equity index derivatives, dividend derivatives, volatility index derivatives, ETFs derivatives, inflation, commodities, weather, and property derivatives.

5.2.5.3 NYSE Euronext LIFFE

The London International Financial Futures and Options Exchange (LIFFE) set up in 1982 is the international derivatives business division of NYSE Euronext. The NYSE LIFFE connects five European derivatives markets through a single electronic platform called the LIFFE CONNECT. The LIFFE offers more than 1000 different derivatives contracts, which include derivatives in short-term interest rates, bonds, swaps, equities, and commodities. In the 1990s, the LIFFE merged with the London Options Market (LTOM) and London Commodity Exchange (LCE). In 2002, Euronext took over the LIFFE. In 2008, the NYSE launched a US future exchange called the NYSE LIFFE, which offers a range of US derivatives contracts.

5.2.6 DERIVATIVES INSTRUMENTS

Derivatives are instruments whose values depend on the value of the underlying securities. The fundamental products of derivatives include agriculture commodities, energy, precious metals, currencies, common stocks, and bonds.

5.2.6.1 Forward contracts

Forward contracts are the most basic derivatives products available. It is a contract to buy or sell an asset at a certain future time for a price fixed today. Forward contracts are viewed as trade agreements negotiated directly between two parties for future transactions. A forward contract agreement is usually an OTC agreement between two financial institutions or between a financial institution and one of its clients. Many large banks employ both spot and forward foreign exchange traders. Forward contracts are basically used to hedge foreign currency risk. It is a private contract between two parties and is not standardized. It is settled at the end of the contract and when delivery or final cash settlements usually take place. Forward contracts do not require collaterals. Hence, forward contracts have credit (or default) risk.

5.2.6.2 Futures contracts

Futures contracts are similar to forward contracts wherein agreements are entered to buy or sell an asset for a fixed price. Futures contracts are traded on exchanges. The largest exchanges on which futures contracts are traded are the CBOT and the CME. Futures contracts are characterized by margin requirements, daily settlement procedures, and delivery procedures. A futures contract is settled daily and the contract is usually closed out prior to maturity. The margin accounts are held by the exchange's clearinghouses and are marked to market, which involves adjustment for contract price movements. It also involves virtually no risk.

5.2.6.2.1 Treasury bond futures

Treasury bond futures are one of the most popular long-term interest rate futures contracts and are traded on the Chicago Board of Traders. Treasury notes and Treasury bond futures contracts are very widely used. T-bond and T-note futures contracts are called interest rate futures.

5.2.6.2.2 Stock index futures

Stock index futures provide general hedges against stock market movement and can be applied to either whole (diversified) portfolios or individual stocks.

5.2.6.2.3 Eurodollar futures

Eurodollar futures are one of the most popular interest rate futures contracts in the United States and are traded on the CME. The Eurodollar is the dollar deposited in a US-based or foreign bank outside the United States. The Eurodollar interest rate is the rate of interest earned on Eurodollars deposited by one bank with another bank.

5.2.6.3 *Options contracts*

Options are derivatives that are traded on both exchanges and the OTC markets. A call option gives the holder the right to buy an underlying asset by a certain price. A put option gives the option holder the right to sell an underlying asset by a certain date for a certain price. American options can be exercised at any time up to expiration date. European options can be exercised only on the expiration date itself.

5.2.6.3.1 Equity options

These are options on the common stock of individual companies. The largest exchange for options is the Chicago Board Options Exchange (CBOE). In 2011, the CBOE accounted for about 27% of the options market. The Philadelphia Stock Exchange (PHLX) is the second-largest options market. Options on these exchanges are traded with a typical contract for 100 shares of the stock.

5.2.6.3.2 Stock index and index ETF options

The popular options on stock indexes include American and European Options on the S&P 100, European options on the DJIA (DJX), and European options on the NASDAQ 100. Options on stock indexes such as the S&P 500 are patterned closely after equity options. Index options can only be settled in cash. ETF options are designed like regular stock options and permit physical delivery.

5.2.6.3.3 Currency options

Currency options are traded in the OTC market. Currency options are tailored to meet the requirements of corporate treasurers according to their specifications for strike prices and expiration dates. Foreign currency options are contracts that allow for the sale or purchase of a set amount of foreign currency at a fixed exchange rate. Foreign option contracts exist for several major currencies, including the euro, Australian dollars, Japanese yen, Canadian dollars, British pounds, and Swiss francs. The majority of currency options trade in OTC markets.

5.2.6.3.4 Options on futures contracts

Options on future contracts are also known as futures options. These options give the holder the right—not an obligation—to enter into a futures contract on an underlying security or commodity at a later date and at a predetermined price.

5.2.6.3.5 Swaptions

Options are usually embedded in a swap agreement. In an extendable swap, one party has the option to extend the life of the swap beyond the specified period. In a puttable swap, one party has the option to terminate the swap early.

5.2.6.3.6 Futures options

A futures option is the right without obligation to enter into a futures contract at a certain futures price. Futures options are basically American in nature.

5.2.6.3.7 Options on interest rate futures

The most actively traded interest rate options offered by exchanges include Treasury bond futures, Treasury note futures, and Eurodollar futures. An option on Eurodollar futures is an option to enter into a Eurodollar futures contract. Financial institutions offer a variety of options products to their clients.

5.2.6.4 Forward rate agreements

Forward rate agreements (FRAs) are the most basic OTC interest rate contracts. They are the contracts where two parties agree today to a future exchange of cash flows based on two different interest rates. The cash flow, which is based on a fixed rate, is decided at the deal's origination while the other cash flow, which is based on a floating rate, is fixed at a later stage.

5.2.6.5 Swaps

Swaps are agreements in which companies exchange cash flows based on specified dates. Swap transactions involve exchange of cash flows on several dates. The most common of all swaps is the plain vanilla interest rate swap. In this type of swap, the agreement stipulates the payment by company cash flows equal to interest at a predetermined fixed rate on a notional principal for a number of years. In return, the company receives the interest at a floating rate on the same notional principal for the same period of time. The London Interbank Offered Rate (LIBOR)[4] is the most widely used floating rate in interest rate swap agreements.

5.2.6.5.1 Currency swaps

A currency swap involves an exchange of principal and interest payments in one currency for principal and interest payments in another. The principal amount that is specified in each of the two currencies is usually exchanged at the beginning and end of the swap. There are different types of currency swaps.

5.2.6.5.2 Amortizing swaps

In an amortizing swap the principal reduces in a predetermined pattern. In a *step-up swap*, the principal increases in a predetermined pattern.

5.2.6.5.3 Deferred swaps

Deferred swaps, also called *forward swaps,* are characterized by the fact that parties do not exchange interest payments until some future date.

5.2.6.5.4 Constant maturity swaps

A constant maturity swap is an agreement to exchange a LIBOR rate for a swap rate.

5.2.6.5.5 Compounding swaps

In a compounding swap, there is only one payment date at the end of the life of the swap. The interest rate is compounded forward to the end of the life of the swap according to preagreed rules.

---

[4]LIBOR is the rate of interest at which a bank deposits money with other banks in the euro currency market. One month, 3 months, 6 months, and 1 year LIBOR are all quoted in major currencies.

5.2.6.5.6 Accrual swaps

In an accrual swap, the interest rate on one side of the swap accrues only when the floating reference rate is in a certain range.

5.2.6.5.7 Cross-currency interest rate swaps

A *cross-currency interest rate swap* combines a fixed-for-floating interest rate swap and a fixed-for-fixed currency swap. In a floating-for-floating currency swap, the floating rate of one currency is exchanged for a floating rate in another currency.

5.2.6.5.8 Equity swaps

Equity swaps are equivalent to portfolios of forward contracts calling for exchange of cash flows based on two different investment rates. An equity swap is an agreement to exchange the total return (dividends and capital gains) realized on an equity index for either a fixed or floating rate of interest.

5.2.6.5.9 Commodity swaps

Commodity swaps are a series of forward contracts on a commodity with different maturity dates and the same delivery prices. In a volatility swap, there are a series of time periods.

5.2.6.5.10 Interest rate swaps

An interest rate swap can also be considered as a portfolio of forward-rate agreements. In this type of swap, investors and borrowers are exposed regularly to interest rate movements at regular intervals over an extended period of time, such as with a floating rate note (FRN) that resets its coupon rate twice annually for several years.

5.2.6.5.11 LIBOR in arrears swaps

A plain vanilla interest rate swap that is designed so that the floating rate of interest observed on one payment date is paid on the next payment date.

5.2.6.5.12 Accrual swaps

Accrual swaps are swaps where the interest on one side accrues only when the floating reference rate is within a certain range.

5.2.6.5.13 Cancelable swaps

A cancelable swap is a plain vanilla interest rate swap where one side has the option to terminate on one or more payment dates.

5.2.6.6 Packages

A package is a portfolio of standard European calls, standard European puts, forward contracts, cash, and underlying assets.

5.2.6.6.1 Forward start options

Forward start options are options that will start at some time in the future.

5.2.6.6.2 Compound options

Compound options are options on options. There are four main types of compound options: a call on a call, a put on a call, a call on a put, and a put on a put.

5.2.6.6.3 Barrier options
Barrier options are options where the payoffs depend on whether the underlying asset price reaches a certain level during a certain period of time.

5.2.6.6.4 Binary options
Binary options are options with discontinuous payoffs.

5.2.6.6.5 Lookback options
The payoffs from lookback options depend on the maximum or minimum asset price reached during the life of the option.

5.2.6.6.6 Shout options
A shout option is a European option where the holder can "shout" to the writer at one time during its life. At the end of the life of the option, the option holder receives either the usual payoff from the European option or the intrinsic value at the time of the shout, whichever is greater.

5.2.6.6.7 Asian options
Asian options are options where the payoff depends on the average price of the underlying asset during at least some part of the life of the option.

5.2.6.7 *Weather derivatives*
Energy companies are the most active and sophisticated users of derivatives. In energy derivatives markets, the trading of crude oil, natural gas, and electricity derivatives takes place.

5.2.6.8 *Insurance derivatives*
Insurance derivatives provide protection against adverse events. Insurance companies use these derivatives when they hedge their exposure to prevent large losses from catastrophic events.

5.2.6.9 *Commodity derivatives*
In commodity derivatives, the underlying asset is a commodity, such as cotton, gold, copper, wheat, or spices. Commodity derivatives were originally designed to protect farmers from the risk of under- or overproduction of crops. Commodity derivatives are investment tools that allow investors to profit from certain commodities without possessing them. The buyer of a derivatives contract buys the right to exchange a commodity for a certain price at a future date. The buyer may be buying or selling the commodity. The buyer does not have to pay the full value of the amount of the commodity in which investment is made. He only needs to pay a small percentage, known as the margin price. On agreement, the seller gives the owner the ownership of the commodity at the agreed future date along with the physical delivery. Based on the spot price of the commodity the buyer makes profit or loss. Exchanges facilitate the contract settlements and clearing.

5.2.6.10 *Asset-backed securities in the securitization market*
Securitization is considered to be a modern financial innovation. The main essence of securitization is the issuance of securities that derive their cash flows from underlying assets. One of the unique characteristics of securitization is that the performance of the security is determined by the cash flows of the pledged collateral and not on the financial strength of the asset issuer.

These structured finance techniques can be classified as agency mortgage-backed securities (MBS) and nonagency-backed securities. Agency mortgage markets originated in the United States when the Government National Mortgage Association (Ginnie Mae) and other agencies started pooling government-sponsored mortgage loans in the 1970s. These types of securitization were later adopted by entities such as the Federal Home Loan Mortgage Corporation (Freddie Mac) and the Federal National Mortgage Association (Fannie Mae).

Nonagency-backed securities came into existence in the US market by the mid-1980s to satisfy investors' need for varied mortgage securities with different maturities and interest rates. According to the Securities Industry and Financial Markets Association (SIFMA), asset-backed securities (ABS) encompass a number of consumer finance assets, including automobile loans, credit card receivables, consumer loans, student loans, and other financing receivables structures. The ABS class also includes home equity loans and home equity lines of credit products. Securities backed by mortgages are known as MBS. Security structures backed by commercial real estate loans are known as commercial mortgage-backed securities (CMBS). Collateralized debt obligations (CDOs) are backed by debt instruments. CDOs backed by corporate loans or bonds are referred to as collateralized loan obligations (CLOs) or collateralized bond obligations (CBOs). One of the recent structured derivatives products that have emerged is the synthetic CDO. Synthetic CDO relies on credit derivatives, particularly credit default swaps (CDSs), to transfer risks and cash flow payment between investors and issuers. Instead of creating a portfolio of corporate bonds, the originator of the CDO forms a portfolio consisting of short positions in CDSs. The credit risks are then passed on to tranches.

The collateral cash flows of ABS are basically distributed into different tranches having different risk ratings and maturities. The components of each security have a number of senior tranches with high ratings of AAA, subordinated tranches with ratings below AAA, and unrated residual equity tranches. The senior tranches receive overcollateralization protection. Other ancillary enhancements are also put in place to protect investors from default and other risks. This includes exchange and interest rate swaps.

5.2.6.11 *Credit derivatives*

The most common forms of credit derivatives are CDSs, total return swaps (TRSs), credit spread options, and credit-linked notes (CLNs). A CDS is a contract in which a buyer (also known as the protection buyer) purchases protection from a seller (the protection seller) against the risk of default by a reference entity on a reference asset. The protection buyer pays a regular fee or premium to the protection seller for the life of the swap or until a credit event occurs. In return, the protection seller pays the protection buyer an agreed amount only if a specified credit event occurs during the life of the swap. The agreed-upon amount the protection seller provides the protection buyer depends on whether the transaction will be cash settled or physically settled.

If the swap is cash-settled, the buyer receives the difference between par value and fair market value of the reference asset. If the swap is physically settled, the buyer will deliver to the seller an agreed-upon deliverable obligation and, in return, receives par value (or another agreed-upon reference price) from the seller.

TRSs are a type of credit derivative that involve agreements to exchange the total return on a bond (or any portfolio of assets) for LIBOR plus a spread. The total return includes coupons, interest, and the gain or loss on the asset over the life of the swap.

Credit spread options are important tools for managing the risks associated with low-rated bonds and debt. In a credit spread option strategy, the premiums received from the short leg(s) of the spread are greater than the premiums paid for the long leg(s) resulting in funds being credited into the option trader's account when the position is entered.

A CLN is a special form of repackaging that is often directly issued by a corporate issuer. CLN is an interest-bearing debt security whose interest payments and repayment are contingent on the financial solvency of the underlying debtor.

5.2.7 DERIVATIVES RISKS IN BANKS

Counterparty credit risk is a major risk for OTC derivatives. Counterparty risk belongs to the same category of risks that banks face for their investment banking activities. The potential exposure of derivatives is a huge challenge for banks, as the derivatives contract has no net value in the initiation stages, but value and the bank's potential loss may vary over the life of the contract. Banks are also subjected to market price risk wherein the value of the derivatives position changes over time. Banks also face liquidity risks. Derivatives investors face settlement risk. A common settlement risk arises when one party pays out funds or delivers assets before receiving assets or payment from its counterparty. Another type of settlement risk arises when derivative contracts are settled on terms that depend on the prices of particular assets at settlement time. Banks dealing with derivatives instruments are also affected by cross-market disturbances. Banks involved in derivatives activity also face the challenge of operational risk. Participation in derivatives markets requires highly sophisticated and reliable internal control mechanisms. One of the major aspects of a bank's internal controls is the maintenance of accurate valuation of derivatives holdings.

5.2.8 FUNCTIONS OF FINANCIAL INSTITUTIONS IN DERIVATIVES MARKETS

Banks performs two major functions in the derivatives market segment—one as a derivatives dealer and the other as an end user. Banks that sell derivatives products to their customers are known as dealers. There are two types of dealers: Tier I and Tier II. A Tier 1 dealer performs the role of a market maker who provides the quotes for other dealers and brokers. Tier I dealers may also assume proprietary positions in derivatives owing to expected changes in prices. Tier 1 dealers are also involved in the development of new derivatives products. Tier 1 dealers are characterized by large portfolios with high transaction volume and complex contracts. Tier II dealers are not market makers and deal with a select customer base. Banks also become end users in the derivatives markets. Banks use derivatives for cash market investments and interest rate risk management.

Derivatives are also big business on Wall Street. Banks collect many billions of dollars annually in undisclosed fees associated with these instruments. Commercial banks use interest rate products as derivatives. Commercial banks use credit derivatives to manage their credit risk exposure. Banks can transfer the credit risk of a portfolio of exposures to investors via securitization transactions such as CLOs.

A commercial bank can use credit derivatives to manage the risk of its loan portfolio. An investor, such as an insurance company, asset manager, or hedge fund, can use credit derivatives to align its credit risk exposure with its desired credit risk profile. An investment bank can use credit derivatives to manage the risk it incurs when underwriting securities. By the adoption of credit derivatives, the underwriter might be able to hedge some of the credit risk more easily.

Banks act as intermediaries in the OTC market. This function is performed in two ways. First banks act as brokers, matching parties with offsetting needs. This function enables banks to act as counterparties taking the other side of the contracts with their clients. It would be difficult for nonfinancial firms to find suitable counterparties without the help of intermediaries. Banking intermediaries contribute toward the liquidity of the OTC market.

Intermediation activities contribute revenue to banks. These revenues come through transaction fees, bid offer spreads, and trading profits. For executing trades, banks often charge end users transaction fees. Banks also charge implicit fees by having a spread between their bid and offer quotes. If a bank is involved as a broker matching two end users, the seller of the contract receives less than the amount paid by the buyer, and the bank profits from the bid-offer spread. When a bank acts as a counterparty, it may offer to pay less and demand more than what end users pay and receive. These series of trade activities become a source of income for banks.

Banks also profit from their trading positions when there is disequilibrium in asset prices. In this role as market maker, banks build up positions in derivatives and take profits through arbitrage, which involves risk. But as a result of these positions, banks are exposed to financial market risk. To hedge these risks, banks engage in offsetting trades just as end users trade in derivatives for hedging the risk of their portfolios. For example, a bank that is a market maker for an interest rate swap may become an end user to enter into an offsetting swap. Banks are viewed as end users of credit securitization and credit derivatives. Banks have different incentives for the application of credit derivatives. They use credit derivatives to hedge dynamic counterparty credit exposure in their derivatives portfolios, reduce future funding costs, and manage credit risk of their loan portfolios.

5.2.8.1 Role of financial institutions in forwards, futures, and options contracts

Large investment banks have their own specialized traders to deal with forwards and futures for proprietary trading and external customers. Banks assume the role of speculators and hedgers in the forwards and futures market.

Options play a very vital role in the modern financial system. Banks and hedge funds are the biggest traders of options. Banks use option hedging to insure against adverse price movements. Banks, along with institutional investors, are the main professional speculators in options. Most of the trading is conducted by proprietary desks, trading for the bank's own accounts.

5.2.8.2 Role of financial institutions in swaps

Swap banks are financial institutions that act as intermediary agencies when conducting currency or interest swaps between two parties. A swap bank is actively involved in identifying and arranging for the two parties involved to discuss the terms of the exchange, as well as to help execute the actual swap. For the execution of the business deal, the swap bank normally receives some type of compensation from one or both parties.

Banks play a vital role in currency and interest rate swaps, which ranges from client service to proprietary trading. Banks also act as counterparties to the swap arrangement by matching their client's currency or interest rate exposure with that of another banks' client or another client. Banks also act as market makers for their clients' transactions. Banks are also involved in proprietary trading for their own account by entering into swaps as a position in a particular currency.

Currency swaps play a vital role in providing foreign currency liquidity to the banking system. During the recent economic crisis, currency swaps played a key role following the events after Lehman

Brothers' collapse. Banking systems produce synthetic foreign currency funding from international funds with the help of currency swap transactions. Investment banks hold large swap positions.

5.2.8.3 Role of financial institutions in asset securitization

The major facilitators in the securitization process include the issuer, underwriter, rating agency, servicer, and trustee. The sponsor/originator or issuer has the role of bringing together the collateral assets for the asset-backed security. Structured finance offers channels for banks, mortgage companies, and other financial institutions to sell their assets by becoming loan originators of the portfolio of securitized assets. The pooled assets are generally sold to a special purpose vehicle (SPV). The SPV buys the assets from the issuer with borrowings from the buyers of the security tranches issued by the SPV. The SPV transfers the asset to another entity called the trustee, which issues the security shares backed by those assets. The servicer is responsible for processing payments and interaction with borrowers along with implementation of collection measures as prescribed by pooling and servicing agreements. The servicer basically has three fiduciary responsibilities: collection of payments generated from underlying assets, the transfer of payments to accounts managed by the trustee, managing deposits, and investments of revenues streams on behalf of trustees.

ABS underwriters fulfill the traditional role of issuer. The underwriter analyzes investor demand and designs the structure of the security tranches in tune with the investor risk preferences. Rating agencies have played a vital role in the development of structured finance instruments because institutional investors and regulated firms are required to hold mostly investment grade assets.

The role of the issuer and lender often overlap. Consumer auto finance lenders and large retail banks are major issuers in the auto securitization markets. Commercial banks, investment banks, and mortgage lenders have sponsored most MBS and home equity issues.

The CDO collateral includes business loans, leveraged loans, credit facilities, term loans, and corporate bonds. In a synthetic CDO, the SPV and its investors derive cash flows from the premiums paid by the CDS protection buyers, which is typically a commercial or investment bank. Large banks with maximum exposures in syndicated lending and bond underwriting play an active role as CDO collateral managers. Investment banks act as underwriters for the ABS. Commercial banks act as information specialists that can bridge the certification gap between issuers and investors.

5.2.8.4 Role of banks in credit derivatives

Credit derivatives have provided banks with a whole range of instruments for selling loans and transferring loan risk. Pure derivatives such as CDS or TRSs allow banks to buy protection on a single exposure or on a basket of exposures. CDOs enable banks to sell risks from their entire loan portfolio. Financial institutions such as banks, insurance companies, investment banks, corporations, hedge funds, pension funds, mutual funds, and government/export credit agencies use credit derivatives. Two of the most important reasons for banks in particular to use credit derivatives are to manage credit risk and regulatory capital. Through credit derivatives, financial institutions are able to retain legal title in spite of transferring credit risk. Credit derivatives also help financial institutions to trade and manage portfolios, economic capital, and individual lines of credits.

5.2.8.4.1 Players in the derivatives market

There are three types of participants in the derivatives market: hedgers, speculators, and arbitrageurs. Hedgers are the investors who use derivatives as a hedging tool to reduce their futures risk. A hedge is an investment made to reduce the risk of adverse price movements in a security by taking an offsetting position in a related security. For example, an airline firm becomes a hedger by buying a futures contract in jet fuel. Speculators try to gain by making profits in a fluctuating market. Speculators take higher risks to get a higher return in a short span of time. Speculators are the persons who don't invest any money but make money by speculating on up-and-down movements of stocks and indexes. Arbitrageurs profit from the price differential in two different markets by simultaneous operating in both markets. Arbitrageurs buy low in one market and sell the same at a high price in the market.

5.2.8.4.2 Hedging with derivatives

Financial institutions and corporations use derivative financial instruments to hedge their exposure to different risks, including commodity risks, foreign exchange risks, and interest rate risks. Basically hedging consists of taking a risk position that is opposite to an actual position that is exposed to risk. A company that takes variable-interest, short-term loans or that reissues commercial paper as it matures faces interest rate risk. In such cases, the firm might hedge its position by entering into a transaction that would produce a gain of almost the same amount as the potential loss if interest rates do increase. Forwards, futures, and options can be used to hedge exposure to the effects of changing interest rates. Foreign exchange futures contracts can be used by firms to hedge foreign exchange risks. Interest rate swaps, which form a major chunk of derivatives, is used to hedge interest risk. In interest rate swaps, the fixed interest payments are exchanged for floating rate payments or vice versa without exchanging the underlying principal amounts. Derivatives hedging techniques using interest rate swaps and interest rate caps can help institutions retain core longer-duration assets to manage interest rate risk.

5.3 FOREIGN EXCHANGE MARKET AND INSTRUMENTS

5.3.1 INTERNATIONAL MONETARY SYSTEMS

The international monetary system refers to the operating system of the financial environment, which consists of financial institutions, multinational corporations, and investors. The international monetary system provides the institutional framework for determining the rules and procedures for international payments, determination of exchange rates, and movement of capital.

The major stages of the evolution of the international monetary system can be categorized into the following stages.

5.3.1.1 The era of bimetallism

Before 1870, the international monetary system consisted of bimetallism, where both gold and silver coins were used as the international modes of payment. The exchange rates among currencies were determined by their gold or silver contents. Some countries were either on a gold or a silver standard.

5.3.1.2 Gold standard

The international gold standard prevailed from 1875 to 1914. In a gold standard system, gold alone is assured of unrestricted coinage. There was a two-way convertibility between gold and national currencies at a stable ratio. No restrictions were in place for the export and import of gold. The exchange rate between two currencies was determined by their gold content.

The gold standard ended in 1914 during World War I. Great Britain, France, Germany, and many other countries imposed embargoes on gold exports and suspended redemption of bank notes in gold. The interwar period was between World War I and World War II (1915-1944). During this period the United States replaced Britain as the dominant financial power of the world. The United States returned to a gold standard in 1919. During the intermittent period, many countries followed a policy of sterilization of gold by matching inflows and outflows of gold with changes in domestic money and credit.

5.3.1.3 Gold exchange standard

The Bretton Woods System was established after World War II and was in existence during the period 1945-1972. In 1944, representatives of 44 nations met at Bretton Woods, New Hampshire, and designed a new postwar international monetary system. This system advocated the adoption of an exchange standard that included both gold and foreign exchanges. Under this system, each country established a par value in relation to the US dollar, which was pegged to gold at $35 per ounce. Under this system, the reserve currency country would aim to run a balance of payments (BOPs) deficit to supply reserves. If such deficits turned out to be very large then the reserve currency itself would witness crisis. This condition was often coined the Triffin paradox. Eventually in the early 1970s, the gold exchange standard system collapsed because of these reasons. From 1950 onward, the United States started facing trade deficit problems. With development of the euro markets, there was a huge outflow of dollars. The US government took several dollar defense measures, including the imposition of the Interest Equalization Tax (IET) on US purchases of foreign stock to prevent the outflow of dollars. The international monetary fund created a new reserve asset called special drawing rights (SDRs) to ease the pressure on the dollar, which was the central reserve currency. Initially, the SDR were modeled to be the weighted average of 16 currencies of such countries whose shares in the world exports were more than 1%. In 1981, the SDR were restructured to constitute only five major currencies: the US dollar, German mark, Japanese yen, British pound, and French franc. The SDR were also being used as a denomination currency for international transactions. But the dollar-based gold exchange standard could not be sustained in the context of rising inflation and monetary expansion. In 1971 the Smithsonian Agreement signed by the Group of Ten major countries made changes to the gold exchange standard. The price of gold was raised to $38 per ounce. Other countries revalued their currency by up to 10%. The band for exchange rate fluctuation was increased to 2.25% from 1%. But the Smithsonian agreement also proved to be ineffective and the Bretton Woods System collapsed.

5.3.1.4 Flexible exchange rate regime

European and Japanese currencies became free-floating currencies in 1973. The flexible exchange rate regime was formally ratified in 1976 by IMF members through the Jamaica Agreement. The agreement stipulated that central banks of respective countries could intervene in the exchange markets to guard against unwarranted fluctuations. Gold was also officially abandoned as the international reserve asset. In 1985, the Plaza Accord envisaged the depreciation of the dollar against most major currencies to solve US trade deficit problems.

In general there are many flexible exchange rate systems. In a free-floating or independent-floating currency, the exchange rate is determined by the market, with foreign exchange intervention occurring only to prevent undue fluctuations. For example, Australia, the United Kingdom, Japan, and the United States have free-floating currencies. In a managed-floating system, the central monetary authority of countries influences the movement of the exchange rate through active intervention in the forex market with no preannounced path for the exchange rate. Examples include China, India, Russia, and Singapore. In a fixed-peg arrangement, the country pegs its currency at a fixed rate to a major currency or to a basket of currencies. For example, many GCC countries such as UAE and Saudi Arabia have pegged their currencies to the US dollar.

5.3.2 EUROPEAN MONETARY SYSTEM

In 1979, the European Monetary System (EMS) was introduced with the motto of establishing a zone of monetary stability in Europe. The aim was to coordinate the exchange rate policies and establish the European Monetary Union. In the EMS, member countries collectively manage their exchange rates. The band for exchange rate fluctuations was widened to a maximum of plus or minus 15%. Central banks are allowed to intervene in the forex market to keep the market exchange rate within the band. The Maastricht Treaty signed by the European countries was aimed at closely coordinating the fiscal, monetary, and exchange rate policies. The treaty also paved the way for the adoption of a single European currency, the euro.

On January 1, 1999, 11 of the 15 European countries adopted the euro as their common currency. These countries are Austria, Belgium, Finland, France, Germany, Ireland, Italy, Luxembourg, Netherlands, Portugal, and Spain. Greece joined the euro group in 2001. Denmark, Sweden, and the United Kingdom have not adopted the euro. Each national currency of the euro countries was irrevocably fixed to the euro at a conversion rate as of January 1, 1999. The European Central Bank (ECB), with its headquarters in Frankfurt, Germany, maintains the monetary policy of the members of the euro 12 group. The national central banks of these countries, along with the ECB, form the European System of Central Banks. The major benefits from euro adoption were reduced transaction costs and elimination of exchange rate uncertainty. European companies have been able to save millions of dollars since exchange rate uncertainty was removed.

5.3.3 BALANCE OF PAYMENT

A BOP is the statistical record of a country's international transactions over a certain period of time. In this double-entry bookkeeping system, any receipt from a foreigner is recorded as a credit and payments to foreigners are recorded as debits. The three major divisions of a BOP are the current account, capital account, and official reserves account. The current account includes the exports and imports of goods and services. The current account is further subdivided into merchandise trade, services, factor income, and unilateral transfers. Merchandise trade represent exports and imports of tangible goods. Trade in services include payments and receipts for service-related activities such as financial services, transport services, law, accountancy, management consultancy, and tourism. Factor income consists of payments and receipts of interest, dividends, and the like. Unilateral transfers include payments such as gifts and foreign aids.

The capital account measures all the short-term and long-term monetary transactions between a country and the rest of the world. The capital account consists of direct investment, portfolio investment, and other investments. Direct investment refers to money that follows across national boundaries for investment purposes. Portfolio investment refers to investments in foreign stocks and bonds. Other services include bank deposits, currency investments, and net government borrowings from foreigners.

Official reserves consists of a country's reserve assets such as gold, foreign exchange reserves, and SDRs.

Because a BOP is based on double-entry bookkeeping, the sum of all debits or payments must be equal to the sum of all credits or receipts. A country with a current account deficit will have a capital account surplus and the country with a current account surplus will have a deficit in its capital account.

5.3.4 DETERMINANTS OF EXCHANGE RATES

Exchange rates are basically determined by the demand and supply of a particular currency as compared to other currencies. Inflation is a major factor that affects exchange rate. If a country has low inflation, its domestic currency will appreciate in value as the purchasing power of the currency increases as compared to other currencies. Inflation and interest rates are highly correlated. Higher inflation will lead to higher interest rates in an economy. Interest rate is also a critical determinant of changes in exchange rates. A current account deficit or negative BOP indicates that there is excess demand for foreign currency, which would lead to lower value of a country's currency.

5.3.4.1 International parity relationships

Relationships exist between exchange rates, interest rates, and inflation and forward rates. International parity relationships, such as purchasing parity, interest rate parity, and the Fischer effect, have implications in the field of international finance.

5.3.4.1.1 Law of one price

The law of one price states that the prices of identical commodities that are exchanged in two or more markets must be the same. In an efficient market, there must be only one price for commodities regardless of where they are traded. Identical goods must have identical prices. For example, an ounce of gold must have the same price expressed in terms of dollars in London as it does in Tokyo. Otherwise, it would result in arbitrage[5] opportunities. Competitive markets will equalize the price of identical goods in two countries when prices are expressed in the same currency with the assumption that transportation and transaction costs are absent.

5.3.4.1.2 Purchase power parity

The purchase power parity (PPP) theory states that the exchange rates between currencies of two countries should equal the ratio of the two countries' price level of a fixed basket of goods and services. PPP states that the exchange rates between currencies are in equilibrium when the purchasing power in each of the two countries is the same. The basis for PPP is the "law" of one price. This law states that in equilibrium conditions, when a country's domestic price level increases, then the currency must depreciate for maintaining parity. This parity relationship is also known as absolute PPP. Another version, relative PPP, states that the rate of appreciation or depreciation of a currency is equal to the difference in inflation rates between the foreign and home country.

5.3.4.1.3 Interest rate parity

The interest rate parity (IRP) or the covered interest parity theory states that the interest rate differential between two currencies will be reflected in the discount or premium for the forward exchange rate on

---

[5] Arbitrage is defined as the simultaneous buying and selling of the same security for two different prices.

the foreign currency if there is no arbitrage opportunity. The size of the forward premium or discount on the foreign currency must be equal to the interest rate differential between the countries in comparison. The uncovered IRP states that the forward exchange rate must be an unbiased predictor of the future spot exchange rate.

5.3.4.1.4 Fisher effect

The Fisher effect states that the nominal interest rate is equal to the real interest rate plus compensation for expected inflation.

5.3.4.1.5 International Fisher effect

The international Fisher effect (IFE) states that the expected change in the current exchange rate between any two currencies is approximately equal to the difference between the two countries' nominal interest rates at that time.

5.3.5 FOREIGN EXCHANGE MARKET AND INSTRUMENTS

The foreign exchange market or forex market is the market where currencies are traded. The forex market is the world's largest financial market where trillions are traded daily. It is the most liquid among all the markets in the financial world. Moreover, there is no central marketplace for the exchange of currency in the forex market. It is an OTC market. The currency market is open 24 hours a day, five days a week, with all major currencies traded in all major financial centers. Trading of currency in the forex market involves the simultaneous purchase and sale of two currencies. In this process the value of one currency (base currency) is determined by its comparison to another currency (counter currency). The price at which one currency can be exchanged for another currency is called the foreign exchange rate. The major currency pairs that are traded include the EUR/USD, USD/JPY, GBP/USD, and USD/CHF.[6] The most popular forex market is the euro to US dollar exchange rate (EUR to USD), which trades the value of euros in US dollars.

Foreign exchange markets can be considered as a linkage of banks, nonbank dealers, and forex dealers and brokers who all are connected via a network of telephones, computer terminals, and automated dealing systems. Electronic Broking Services and Reuters are the largest vendors of quote screen monitors used in trading currencies.

The forex market consists of three major segments: Australasia, Europe, and North America. Australasia includes the major trading centers of Bahrain, Sydney, Tokyo, Hong Kong, and Singapore. Europe includes Zürich, Frankfurt, Paris, Brussels, London, and Amsterdam. The North America region includes New York, Montreal, Toronto, Chicago, San Francisco, and Los Angeles.

5.3.5.1 Exchange rate quotation

The two basic quotations are direct and indirect quotes. In direct quotation, the cost of one unit of foreign currency is given in units of local or home currency. In indirect quotations the cost of one unit of local or home currency is given in units of foreign currency.

For example, consider EUR as the local currency. Then

Direct Quote: 1 USD = 0.773407 EUR
Indirect Quote: 1 EUR = 1.29303 USD

---

[6]CHF—Swiss Franc; JPY—Japanese Yen; GBP—Great Britain Pound; EUR—Euro; USD—US dollar.

5.3.6 TYPES OF FOREIGN EXCHANGE MARKETS

To allow the buying and selling of currencies, the foreign exchange market has a network of different currency traders who work around the clock to complete the forex transactions. The main types of foreign exchange markets are spot market, forward, future, currency swaps, and currency options. The spot and forward exchange markets are OTC markets.

5.3.6.1 Spot market

In the spot market, currencies are traded for immediate delivery or for delivery in the near future. The trades in the spot market are settled on the spot. Spot market transactions constitute approximately 40% of the total market transactions in the foreign exchange market. The trades conducted in spot markets are termed forex contracts and are settled electronically. In a spot market, a specified amount of currency is transferred against the receipt of a specified amount of another currency based on an agreed exchange rate (spot rate) within two business days of the date in which the deal was finalized. The most widely traded currency in volume in the spot market is the US dollar. The other major currencies are the euro, Japanese yen, British pound, and Swiss franc. In a spot market, information regarding open interest and volume is unavailable because the currency transactions are carried in the OTC markets and not through exchanges. Most currencies in the interbank spot market are quoted in European terms in which the US dollar is priced in terms of the foreign currency. In an interbank foreign exchange market, traders buy currency for inventory at bid price and sell from inventory at the higher offer or ask price. The difference between the bid and ask price is called a bid-ask spread.

5.3.6.2 Currency forward market

A forward foreign exchange (FX) transaction consists of the purchase of one currency against the sale of another for delivery on an agreed date in the future. It is similar to a spot deal except that the settlement is specified at a later date of say, one month, six months, and so on. FX contracts are used by market participants to lock in an exchange rate on a specific date. The forward forex currency market comprises forward outright deals and swaps. An outright forward deal is a binding obligation for the physical exchange of funds at a future date for an agreed exchange rate. There is no payment upfront for an outright forward contract. Nondeliverable forwards (NDFs) are similar in nature, but hedging of currencies is allowed in cases where government regulation restricts foreign access to local currency. NDFs are usually settled against a fixed rate at maturity with the net amount in some fully convertible currency.

An outright forward locks in an exchange rate known as the forward rate for an exchange of specified funds at a future delivery date. The forward rate is based on the spot rate at the time the deal is fixed with an adjustment for the forward points, which represents the interest rate differential between the two currencies concerned. In other words, a forward rate is obtained by multiplying the spot rate with interest rate differential.

A swap is a combination of a spot and a forward outright deal. Forward foreign exchange markets are decentralized wherein different participants enter into different types of forex deals through forex brokers.

5.3.6.3 Currency futures market

The futures market consists of standardized currency contracts called currency futures, which are derivatives instruments. Currency future prices are fundamentally spot prices, which are adjusted by the forward swaps based on interest rate differential. Currency futures are traded and cleared at major exchanges such as CME, which is the largest market for exchange-traded currency futures. The most popular currency futures market is the EUR futures market, which deals with the euro-to-US dollar exchange rate and GBP (British pound-to-US dollar) futures market. They have centralized pricing and clearing mechanisms so that the market price is the same regardless of the brokerage being used. Currency future contracts are worth a specific amount of underlying currency. For example, the EUR futures contract is worth $125,000. Each currency contract specifies the contract value, minimum price change, and price change value. The typical duration for currency futures are three months. Differences exist in the quoting convention in spot and future markets. In a currency future market, currency futures are quoted as the foreign currency directly against the US dollar. For example, the euro is quoted as the foreign currency directly against the US dollar (euro/USD) unlike the USD/euro in the spot forex market.

Gaps, volume, and open interest are important technical analysis tools available in the futures markets. Open interest and volume are tools to gauge market sentiments in currency futures markets. Open interest refers to the total number of contracts entered into but not yet offset by a transaction or delivery. Open interest refers to a trader's position wherein a buyer buys a contract to establish a long position and a seller establishes a short position.

5.3.6.4 Currency swap market

The basic currency swap involves the exchange of principal and fixed interest payments on a loan in one currency for principal and fixed interest payments on a similar loan in another currency. The parties in a currency swap will exchange principal amounts at the beginning and end of the swap. Each party uses the repayment obligation to its counterparty as collateral and the amount of repayment is fixed at the foreign exchange forward rate as of the start of the contract. Foreign exchange swaps can be viewed as risk-free collateralized borrowing and lending. Financial institutions, exporters, and importers use foreign exchange swaps to raise foreign currencies. Institutional investors use foreign exchange swaps to hedge their positions.

A cross-currency swap contract involves one party borrowing one currency from another party and simultaneously lending the same value, at current spot rates, of a second currency to that party. Cross-currency swaps are used to fund foreign currency investments by financial institutions and multinational corporations.

5.3.6.5 Currency options market

A foreign currency option is a contract giving the option purchaser (the buyer) the right, but not the obligation, to buy or sell a fixed amount of foreign exchange at a fixed price per unit for a specified time period. Foreign currency options are available on the OTC markets and on organized exchanges. The main advantage of OTC options is that the options are tailored to meet the specific needs of a firm. Financial institutions hedge their positions by buying and selling currency options in the OTC market. Currency options are also traded on organized stock exchanges such as the PHLX and London International Financial Futures Exchange (LIFFE). The NASDAQ OMX offers US dollar settled options on the Australian dollar, British pound, Canadian dollar, euro, Japanese yen, Swiss franc, and more.

5.3.7 MARKET TRENDS IN FOREIGN EXCHANGE MARKETS

According to BIS Survey reports, the global foreign exchange market turnover was 20% higher in April 2010 than in April 2007, with an average daily turnover of $4.0 trillion compared with $3.3 trillion in 2007. The increase was driven by the 48% growth in turnover of spot transactions, which represent 37%

of foreign exchange market turnover. Spot turnover rose to $1.5 trillion in April 2010 from $1.0 trillion in April 2007.[7] According to the survey report, the foreign exchange trading activity of other financial institutions (e.g., investment banks, hedge funds, mutual funds, insurance companies) amounted to $1.9 trillion in 2010, which represented a 42% increase when compared to the amount of $1.3 trillion in April 2007.

The turnover of foreign exchange currency products, such as outright forwards, foreign exchange swaps, currency swaps, and currency options in the OTC market, was much larger than the volumes traded in the organized exchanges. The daily turnover for currency instruments on organized exchanges was $168 billion, which was less than 7% of the $2.5 trillion average daily turnover in the OTC markets.[8]

The US dollar continues to be the major currency of transactions but this is slowly changing. The US dollar share of transactions was 90% of all transactions in 2001 after the introduction of the euro. By April 2010, the US dollar's share had fallen to 85%. Table 5.7 provides the amount of global foreign exchange market turnover by type of instrument.

Foreign exchange swaps constitute the major share of the global foreign exchange turnover. Table 5.8 shows the value of OTC foreign exchange derivatives.

5.3.8 FOREIGN EXCHANGE RISK MANAGEMENT

Foreign exchange risk is also known as exchange rate risk or currency risk. This risk arises from unanticipated changes in the exchange rate between two currencies. Multinational companies, export import businesses, and investors making foreign investments face exchange rate risks. When a currency falls in value in relation to other currencies, the currency is said to depreciate in value, and when the currency rises in value relative to other currencies, it is said to appreciate in value. Goods and services in countries where the currency has depreciated will become cheaper for foreign buyers. In the case of currency appreciation, a country's goods and services become more expensive for foreign buyers.

Table 5.7   Global Foreign Exchange Market Turnover by Type of Instrument

Daily Averages in April (Billions of US Dollars)				
Instrument	**1998**	**Percent**	**2010**	**Percent**
Spot transactions	568	37.20	1490	37.43
Outright forwards	128	8.38	475	11.94
Foreign exchange swaps	734	48.07	1765	44.34
Currency swaps	10	0.65	43	1.09
Options and other products	87	5.70	207	5.20
Total	1527	100	3981	100

Source: Triennial Central Bank Survey, Report on Global Foreign Exchange Activity in 2010, Monetary and Economic department, Bank for International Settlements.

[7] Triennial Central Bank Survey, Report on global foreign exchange activity in 2010, Monetary and Economic department, Bank for International Settlements.

[8] Triennial Central Bank Survey, Report on global foreign exchange activity in 2010, Monetary and Economic department, Bank for International Settlements.

Table 5.8   Amount of OTC Foreign Exchange Derivatives (Billions of US Dollars)[a]

	Notional Amounts Outstanding		Gross Market Value	
	December 2010	December 2012	December 2010	December 2012
All currencies	57,796	67,358	2482	2384
Canadian dollars	2421	3099	101	80
Euro	21,913	23,797	887	759
Japanese yen	12,574	14,111	688	827
Pound sterling	6584	7825	254	207
Swedish krone	1589	1453	50	36
Swiss franc	4213	3832	294	154
US dollar	48,741	57,600	1956	1868
Other	17,556	22,999	735	676

Source: BIS, statistical data 2012.
[a]The notional amount on a financial instrument is the nominal or face amount that is used to calculate payments made on that instrument. Gross market value, a BIS measure of credit exposure in the OTC derivatives market.

Foreign exchange risks can be classified into economic and translation exposure. Economic exposure refers to risks in which changes in economic conditions will adversely impact the investments or operations of a firm. For example, sovereign debt default by a country would affect the exchange rate of the currency. Economic exposure leads to possible changes in the firm's cash flows. The unexpected changes in the exchange rate will affect the market value of the firm. Economic exposure is the combination of transaction exposure and operating exposure. Transaction exposure arises when the future cash flows of the firm are affected by changes in the currency exchange rate. It is the gain or loss arising when converting the currencies. Companies involved in imports and exports face transaction exposure. Managing transaction exposure is an integral part of the Treasury risk management function of corporations. Operating exposure is the degree of risk that a company is exposed to when shifts in exchange rates affect the value of certain assets of the business thereby impacting the overall profitability of the company.

Translation exposure is also known as accounting exposure. Accounting exposure measures the impact of changes in exchange rate on the financial statements of a company. Translation exposure arises when the financial statements of overseas subsidiaries are consolidated into a parent company's financial statement. The performance of an overseas subsidiary in home-based currency can be affected to a greater extent if the exchange rate fluctuation happens in relation to the currency in which the subsidiary cash flows occur.

5.3.9 MANAGEMENT OF TRANSACTION EXPOSURE

Transaction exposure hedging consists of internal and external techniques.

5.3.9.1 Internal techniques

The basic internal techniques are hedging through invoice currency, leading and lagging, and matching.

5.3.9.1.1 Hedging through invoice currency

Through this technique a firm can shift, share, or diversify exchange rate transaction risk. The invoice in home currency strategy implies that all import and export transactions be denominated in home currency. This strategy is, however, unrealistic in a competitive environment. This method involves shifting exchange rate risk by invoicing foreign sales in home currency. Thus, a firm can shift exchange rate risk by invoicing foreign sales in home currency. A firm can share exchange rate risk by prorating the currency of the invoice between foreign and home currencies. A firm can diversify exchange rate risk by using a market basket index.

5.3.9.1.2 Leading and lagging

If a currency is expected to appreciate, the payment of bills denominated in that currency must be paid early. If currency depreciation is expected, then the receipts of the bills must be collected early. In the event of expectation of currency depreciation, an importer must attempt to delay the payment. If an exporter expects that currency in which receipts are denominated will depreciate, efforts must be made to collect the receipts immediately.

5.3.9.1.3 Matching

The matching method involves matching the receipts and payments in the same foreign currency. Then it is only required to focus on the forex market for the unmatched portion of the total transactions.

5.3.9.2 External techniques

The external techniques used to hedge transaction risks consist of using derivatives products such as forward contracts, future contracts, money market hedges, options, and currency swaps. Bilateral and multilateral netting are basically matching techniques.

5.3.9.2.1 Forward contracts

Forward contracts specify a price at which the firm can buy or sell the foreign currency at a specified future date. This enables the conversion of uncertain future home currency values of the liability (asset) into a certain home currency value to be received on the specified date.

5.3.9.2.2 Futures contracts

These exchange-traded contracts are characterized by certain sizes, maturities, and currencies. As a result it is not possible to get an exact offsetting position to totally eliminate the transaction exposure.

5.3.9.2.3 Money market hedges

Money market hedging involves the use of borrowing and lending transactions in foreign currencies to lock in the home currency value of a foreign currency transaction. It is also known as a synthetic forward contract. The basic principle of a money market hedge is based on the covered IRP, which states that the forward price must be equal to the current spot exchange rate times the ratio of the two currencies' riskless returns. Consider the case of an importer firm that has to pay foreign currency at a future specified date. The firm can determine the present value of the amount of foreign currency payable at the foreign currency lending rate and convert the appropriate amount of home currency at the given current spot exchange rate and lend it for the said period. This process converts the commitment into home currency payables and eliminates the exchange risk. Similarly, a firm that has to receive foreign currency at a specified date in the future will borrow the present value of the foreign currency receipts at the foreign currency borrowing rate and convert it into home currency at the current spot exchange rate.

5.3.9.2.4 Options

Foreign currency options are contracts that give the owner the right but not the obligation to trade domestic currency for foreign currency or vice versa in specified quantities at a specified price over a stated period of time. There are different kinds of options based on the exercise time, the determination of the payoff price, and the possibility of payoff. Among these the Asian (lookback) and basket rate options are popular methods for hedging transaction risks. In the lookback option, the payoff price in the option is the average spot price over the life of the contract. In the basket rate option, a firm can buy options based on some weighted average of currencies that matches the transaction trend instead of individual currencies.

5.3.9.2.5 Bilateral and Multilateral Netting
Netting of cash flows or obligations is a means of reducing credit exposure to counterparties. With bilateral netting, two counterparties agree to net with one another. Multilateral netting occurs between multiple counterparties. Typically, it is facilitated through a membership organization such as an exchange.

5.3.10 MANAGEMENT OF OPERATING EXPOSURE
5.3.10.1 Marketing strategies
Operating exposure is managed basically through marketing, production, and financial strategies. Marketing strategies focus on market selection, pricing, and promotion policies. Market selection and segmentation provide the basic parameters in which a company can adjust its marketing mix to manage operating exposure due to exchange rate fluctuations. Pricing policies are also critical decisions with respect to exchange rate fluctuations that would impact the market share and profitability. The promotional budgets planned must also incorporate scenarios of exchange rate fluctuations.

5.3.10.2 Production strategies
Product mix, product sourcing, and plant location decisions are the basic production strategies aimed at hedge operating exposure. Diversifying operations create a natural hedge against exchange rate fluctuations. Diversifying activities such as clubbing the production and export of manufactured goods with the import of competitive consumer goods from foreign producers can offset exposures to exchange rate fluctuations. In the event of home currency appreciation, diversifying sources of inputs into overseas markets can also be a viable strategy as long as the material inputs are not priced in integrated markets. Having production locations in different countries can become an effective strategy to hedge operating exposure. Different foreign plant locations give the firm flexibility to shift production among the plants in response to real exchange rate changes.

5.3.10.3 Financial strategies
The financial strategies for managing operating exposure include use of options, swaps, and the like. The firm can also reduce the impact of exchange rate fluctuations on firm value by denominating debt in foreign currencies.

5.3.11 MANAGEMENT OF TRANSLATION EXPOSURE
Translation exposure arises from the need to restate the foreign subsidiaries financial statement, which is stated in foreign currency into the parent's reporting currency while preparing the consolidated financial statements. This process of restating the financial statements may affect the parent company's net worth.

5.3.11.1 Measures of translation exposure
The two methods generally used to measure translation exposure are the current rate method and the temporal method.

Current rate method

- All assets and liabilities are translated at the rate in effect on the balance sheet date.
- All items on the income statement are translated at an appropriate average exchange rate or at the rate prevailing when the various revenues, expenses, gains, and losses were incurred (historical rate).
- Dividends paid are translated at the rate in effect on the payment date.
- Common stock and paid-in capital accounts are recorded at historical rates.
- Gains and losses resulting from translation are reported in a special reserve account on the consolidated balance sheet.

Temporal method

- Monetary assets (cash, marketable securities, accounts receivables) and monetary liabilities (current liabilities and long-term debt) are translated at the current exchange rate prevailing on the balance sheet date.
- Nonmonetary assets (inventory, fixed assets, etc.) and nonmonetary liabilities are translated at their historical rate.
- Income statement items are translated at the average exchange rate over the period, except for items that are associated with nonmonetary assets or liabilities, such as inventory and depreciation of fixed assets, which are translated at their historical rate.
- Dividends paid are translated at the rate in effect on the payment date.
- Equity items are translated at their historical rate.

In temporal method translation, gains and losses on monetary accounts are presumed to be meaningful components of expenses or revenue because monetary accounts closely approximate market values. Translation gains and losses on nonmonetary accounts are less meaningful because nonmonetary accounts reflect historical costs.

5.3.12 MARKET PARTICIPANTS IN THE FOREIGN EXCHANGE MARKET

Central banks, global funds, retail clients (individual retailers), and corporations are the major participants in the foreign exchange market. The commercial banks and investment banks together form the interbank market. The interbank market is the largest market that operates in the foreign exchange market. Essentially the foreign exchange market is divided into whole (interbank) and retail (client) markets. The interbank market consists of a network of corresponding banking relationships in which large commercial banks maintain corresponding banking accounts with one another by maintaining demand deposit accounts. The Society for Worldwide Interbank Financial Telecommunication (SWIFT) HELPS international commercial banks communicate these transactions. The Clearing House Interbank Payments System (CHIPS) in association with the US Federal Reserve Bank System (Fedwire) provides a clearinghouse for the interbank settlement between international banks. Forex brokers match dealer orders to buy and sell currencies for fees.

Nonbank dealers include large nonbank financial institutions such as investment banks, pension funds, and hedge funds. Participants can be speculators or hedgers in the foreign exchange market. Most interbank trades are speculative transactions. Basically multinational companies are hedgers in the foreign exchange market. Multinational companies with numerous worldwide operations engage in a number of international financial transactions with vendors and suppliers in a number of countries.

Table 5.9   Global Foreign Exchange Market Turnover by Counterparty

Daily Averages in April (Billions of US Dollars)				
Counterparty	**2007**	**Percent**	**2010**	**Percent**
Interbank dealers	1392	42	1548	39
Other financial institutions	1339	40	1900	48
Nonfinancial customers	593	18	533	13
Total	3324	100	3981	100

Source: Triennial Central Bank Survey, Report on Global Foreign Exchange Activity in 2010, Monetary and Economic department, Bank for International Settlements.

The central bank controls the supply of the respective country's currency in the forex market. The central bank performs such functions as fixing overnight lending rates, purchase and sale of government securities, among other functions. Table 5.9 provides global foreign exchange market turnover by counterparty.

5.4 SUMMARY

The stock market is an important part of the economy of a country. It is the primary marketplace where corporations can raise funds. A stock market consists of primary and secondary stock markets. In the primary stock market, companies sell shares to the public to raise funds. The main stock market instruments are common stock and preferred shares. New stock issues are divided into public offerings (IPOs) and seasoned offerings (SEO). An IPO involves a firm selling its common stock to the public for the first time. SEOs are new shares offered by firms that already have stocks outstanding. The process of underwriting involves formulating the method used to issue securities, PRICE and SELL new securities. The secondary stock market is where investors trade can further be divided into auction and dealer markets. The market participants in the stock market are retail investors, mutual funds and other institutional investors, banks, insurance companies, and hedge funds.

A stock market index measures the pulse of the entire stock market and tracks the market's changes over time. The DJIA, NYSE Composite Index, NASDAQ Composite Index, and Standard & Poor's are the major stock indexes. Foreign stocks can be purchased through international mutual funds, international ETFs, ADRs, and GDRs. Active and passive strategies are the two broad methods of managing common stock portfolios. The NYSE is the biggest stock market in the world.

Derivatives have become an effective tool to reduce business risks. Derivatives are traded bilaterally through OTC markets as individual customized contracts or multilaterally on exchanges as standardized contracts. Corporations and financial institutions are the major users of derivatives. Most derivatives are based on one of the four types of assets: foreign exchange, interest rates (debt securities), commodities, and equities. The major derivatives exchanges are the CME Group, Eurex Exchange, and NYSE Euronext LIFFE. Forwards, futures, options, and swaps are the major derivatives instruments.

The main essence of securitization is the issuance of securities that derive their cash flows from underlying assets. MBS, CDOs, and CLOs are instruments of securitization. The most common forms of credit derivatives are CDSs, TRSs, credit spread options, and CLNs. Banks perform two major functions in derivatives market segments: one as a derivatives dealer and the other as an end user. Hedgers, speculators, and arbitrageurs are the main players in the derivatives markets. Financial institutions and corporations use derivatives financial instruments to hedge their exposure to different risks, such as commodity risks, foreign exchange risks, and interest rate risks.

International monetary systems refer to the operating system of the financial environment and consist of financial institutions, multinational corporations, and investors. The international monetary system has evolved from the era of bimetallism into the gold standard, gold exchange standard, and finally into a flexible exchange rate system. The aim of the EMS was to coordinate the exchange rate policies and to establish the European Monetary Union. International parity relationships, such as purchasing parity, IRP, and the Fisher effect, have implications in the field of international finance. The foreign exchange market or forex market is the market where currencies are traded. The forex market is the world's largest financial market where trillions are traded in daily volume. The foreign exchange market consists of currency spot, forwards, futures, options, and swap markets. The foreign exchange risk consists of economic and translation exposure. Economic exposure consists of transaction and operating exposure. Both external and internal techniques are used to manage transaction exposure. Operating exposure is managed through marketing, production, and financial strategies. The current rate method and temporal method are two methods of measuring translation exposure. Central banks, global funds, retail clients (individual retailers), and corporations are the major participants in the foreign exchange market.

QUESTIONS FOR DISCUSSION

1. Discuss the main characteristics of common stock.
2. Explain the process of an IPO.
3. Explain the green shoe option.
4. Distinguish between an auction and dealer market.
5. What are the different types of market orders in a stock market?
6. What is short selling?
7. Discuss the different methods used to purchase foreign stocks.
8. Distinguish between active and passive strategies.
9. What are derivatives?
10. Explain the various types of basic derivatives.
11. Discuss the various types of futures and options contracts.
12. What are the different types of swaps?
13. Explain weather, commodity, and insurance derivatives.
14. What are ABS?
15. What are the major functions of financial institutions in the derivatives markets?
16. Distinguish between hedgers, speculators, and arbitrageurs.
17. What is hedging?
18. Discuss the salient features of the international monetary system.

19. Discuss the salient features of the EMS.

20. What are the components of a BOP?

21. Explain PPP and IRP theories.

22. What is the Fisher effect?

23. How do you explain the foreign exchange market?

24. What are the different types of foreign exchange markets?

25. Discuss the different types of risks in foreign exchange markets.

26. How do you manage transaction and translation exposure?

27. How do you manage operating exposure?

REFERENCES

Karlis, P.L. IPO underpricing. http://www.iwu.edu/economics/PPE08/peter.pdf.

Michael, B., Franks, J., 1997. Underpricing, ownership and control in initial public offering of equity securities in the UK. Journal of Financial Economics 45, 391–413.

Brown, R., 2012. Securities markets, organization and operation. Analysis of Investment and Management of Portfolios. South Western Cengage Learning (pp. 99–111, Chapter 4).

http://www.alcopartners.com/RegulatoryDox/Controller_derivatives.pdf.

Protess, B. Banks increase holdings in derivatives. http://dealbook.nytimes.com/2011/09/23/banks-increase-holdings-in-derivatives/.

Pales, J., Kuti, Z., Csavas, C., 2011. Magyar Nemzeti Bank. MNB Occasional papers 90.

Cetorelli, N., Peristiani, S. The Role of Banks in Asset Securitization. http://www.newyorkfed.org/research/epr/12v18n2/1207peri.pdf.

Becketti, S., 1993. Are derivatives too risky for banks? Economic Review Third Quarter, 1–16. http://www.kansascityfed.org/PUBLICAT/ECONREV/econrevarchive/1993/3q93beck.pdf.

http://www.law.harvard.edu/programs/about/pifs/llm/sp33.pdf.

Milton, F., 1953. Essays in Positive Economics. University of Chicago Press, Chicago.

Robert, S., 1982. The International Monetary System, 1945-1981. Harper & Row, New York.

Cheol, E., Bruce, R., 2011. The market for foreign exchange. International Financial Management, fourth ed. McGraw-Hill International Edition (pp. 106–131, Chapter 5).

Cheol, E., Bruce, R., 2011. International monetary system, International Financial Management, fourth ed. McGraw-Hill International Edition (pp. 25–58, Chapter 2).

Financial Accounting Standards Board, December 1981. Foreign Currency Translation. Statement of Financial Accounting Standards No 52. Financial Accounting Standards Board, Stamford, Connecticut.

William, F., 1972. Decision analysis for exchange risk management. Financial Management Winter, 101–112.

George, A., Weston, J., 2001. The use of foreign currency derivatives and firm market value. Review of Financial Studies 14, 243–276.

Michael, A., Dumas, B., 1984. Exposure to currency risk: definition and measurement. Financial Management Spring, 41–50.

Eugene, F., Lessard, D., 1986. On the measurement of operating exposure to exchange rates: a conceptual approach. Financial Management 25–37.

STRATEGIES OF DEPOSITORY INSTITUTIONS

6.1 COMMERCIAL BANKS AND THRIFT INSTITUTIONS

6.1.1 INTRODUCTION: COMMERCIAL BANKS

The commercial banking industry provides commercial, industrial, and consumer loans and accepts deposits from individual and institutional customers. These deposits are then used to extend credit to other customers. The deposits are used to support economic activity through business loans, mortgages, auto loans, and home repair loans. Commercial banks offer a wide range of financial services that specifically address the needs of private enterprise. Commercial banking covers services such as cash management, credit services, deposit services, and foreign exchange. Cash management activities include money transfers, payroll services, and bank reconcilement. Credit services include asset-based financing, lines of credit, commercial loans, or mortgage loans. Deposit services include checking or savings account services. Banks also provide loans in the form of credit cards and render local services that include safe deposits, notary services, and merchant banking. Generally depository institutions consist of commercial banks, foreign banks, and thrift institutions. Commercial banks are generally used to refer to any banking division that deals with deposits and loans of business organizations.

Commercial banks process payments through a variety of means that include telegraphic transfers, Internet banking, and electronic funds transfer. Commercial banks issue bank checks and drafts as well as accept money on term deposits. Commercial banks also act as moneylenders by way of installment and overdrafts. Commercial banks also deal with a number of export-import trading documents including letters of credit, performance bonds, security underwriting commitments, and various types of balance sheet guarantees. Commercial banks also provide safe deposit boxes for valuables and documents. The relevant departments in large commercial banks provide currency exchange functions.

Commercial banks earn margins by earning more in interest from borrowers than they pay in interest to depositors. In other words, banks collect interest on loans and interest payments from the debt securities they possess and pay interest on the deposits, certificates of deposits, and short-term borrowings. The difference is known as the spread or the net interest income. Net interest margin is found out by dividing the net interest income by the bank's earning assets.

The term *commercial bank* is used to differentiate from investment banks, which are engaged in financial market-related activity. Commercial banks are also differentiated from retail banks that cater to individual clients only. Investment banking covers a wide set of services from asset securitization, mergers and acquisitions, security underwritings, equity private placements, and placements of debt securities with institutional investors. As a result of the 1999 repeal of the Glass-Steagall Act, many commercial banks entered into nontraditional investment banking activities. On account of globalization and financial deregulation, there has been convergence between investment and commercial bank activities. Currently, it is observed that investment and commercial banks compete directly in areas including money market operations, insurance business, portfolio management private placements, project finance, bonds underwriting, and financial advisory services. Commercial banks such as Citicorp and JPMorgan Chase have investment banking divisions.

6.1.1.1 Global commercial banking trends

Globalization has made the world's biggest banks complex financial organizations with billions of dollars in cash and assets. There are approximately 6.2 billion deposit accounts in the world, more than one for each adult in the world.[1]

The commercial banking industry reached its pinnacle of growth in 2007. Then the economic crisis slowed down the growth of the commercial banking industry, which was followed by slow recovery, and then again impacted by the eurozone crisis. The eurozone banking sector is under major duress from the European debt crisis. With the eurozone breakup and eurozone debt exposure along with the sovereign bond rating soaring, many commercial banks are facing a worse crisis. Many core European banks continue to face severe challenges because of their significant exposure to peripheral bond holdings and declining confidence in the interbank market. The symptoms of private-sector deleveraging hamper assets and loan growth, which could lead to an economic slowdown.

The financial crisis has compelled banks to reassess such business fundamentals as profitability, client relationships, and cross-selling capabilities. Banks are shifting the focus from a product-centric approach to a client-centric approach. There is greater focus on managing the fundamental assets of customer, staff, and capital than on product innovation. Banks have a renewed focus on increasing risk transparency and staff efficiency. Banks are also deploying client profitability analytics to enhance profitability at multiple levels and are accelerating the use of algorithmic approaches to complex back-office tasks.

The US commercial banking industry was forecast to have total assets of $18.9 trillion in 2013. Loans to customers accounted for 57.6% of the total assets for the US commercial banking industry. The United States generates 37.3% of the global commercial banking industry's total assets.[2] The number of banks in the US industry has declined by 15% in the past five years but, the bigger banks in the United States are getting bigger. About two thirds of all US commercial banks' assets are located at five banks: Wells Fargo, Bank of America, Citigroup, US Bancorp, and Sun Trust Banks. Since 1993, the shares of big banks have increased manifold times while smaller banks shares have declined.

The UK commercial banking industry witnessed a compound growth rate of 13.4% during the period 2004-2008. Loans to customers proved the most lucrative for the UK commercial banking industry, generating 62.1% of total assets.[3] European banks have been affected by the eurozone sovereign debt crisis to a great extent. Among the emerging markets, China is in the leading position in the context of banking dominance. Hong Kong is the world's leading international finance center in terms of total foreign-owned banking assets.[4]

[1]Jake Kendall, Nataliya Mylenko, Alejandro Ponce (March 2010). Measuring Financial access around the world. The World Bank Financial and Private Sector Development. http://elibrary.worldbank.org/deliver/5253.pdf?itemId=/content/workingpaper/10.1596/1813-9450-5253&mimeType=pdf

[2]Reference Code: 0072-2218, Commercial banking in United States, Industry profile, Data Monitor Report 2009.

[3]Reference Code: 0183-2218, Commerical banking in United Kingdom, Data Monitor Report 2009.

[4]http://www.thebanker.com/Banker-Data/Bank-Trends/Hong-Kong-home-to-largest-international-bank-assets

Deregulation, globalization, and integration of financial institutions along with the adoption of new technologies have created a competitive environment in the banking sector. The economic recession led to banks in matured markets writing off assets worth more than $2.1 trillion by year-end 2010. At the same time, for Asian banks the equivalent figure was just $115 billion.[5] Banks in emerging markets are well capitalized and reflect the shift from mature to emerging markets. The growing significance of the emerging market is reflected in the growth of Chinese banks, which account for a large share of the global banking industry. China's banking industry is dominated by big four state-owned banks. The other emerging markets are Brazil, India, Russia, and South Africa. Singapore, Turkey, and South Korea have banks with market values of over $20 billion.

After the economic recession banks in developed economies, especially in the United States, initiated actions to restructure the balance sheets. Banks in the euro-area region face significant structural challenges in many ways, such as high funding costs, declining asset quality, and low profitability. European and US banks have substantially increased their regulatory and capital ratios. According to an IMF report in 2013,[6] the asset quality of banking systems in Sweden and the United Kingdom is stable with some balance sheet weakness. The report says that the banking systems in Japan, Switzerland, and the United States have better loss-absorption capacity and asset quality. Another significant trend observed is that banks are changing their funding models to face countercyclical and structural pressures. Also banks are changing the liabilities side of their balance sheet to reduce the use of wholesale, short-term, and cross-border funding in response to wholesale funding runs, higher costs of wholesale funding, and Basel III liquidity requirements.[7] The strong deposit growth and weak loan demand of US banks have reduced their reliance on wholesale funding. New regulations stipulate that affiliates of foreign banks have to hold more capital and liquidity locally. Table 6.1 highlights the financial parameters of the top five global banks in the year 2012.

After the meltdown, many banks began revising their fundamental banking strategies in general. Now there is widespread acceptance of economic capital and risk adjusted return on capital (RAROC) as the primary means to test the success of the lending activities of a bank. The rapid development of

Table 6.1   Top Five Banks in 2013 (Millions of US Dollars)

Bank	Tier 1 Capital	Total Assets	Profits	CAR (%)	ROA (%)
ICBC	160,645	2,788,905	49,075	5.7	1.76
JPMorgan Chase	160,002	2,359,141	28,917	6.78	1.23
Bank of America	155,461	2,212,004	3071	7.03	0.14
HSBC holdings	151,048	2,692,538	20,649	5.61	0.77
China Construction Bank Corp	137,600	2,221,435	39,974	6.19	1.80

Source: http://www.thebankerdatabase.com.

[5] *Global Financial Review*, International Monetary Fund, April 2010.
[6] IMF Global Financial Stability Report, Old risks, New Challenges April 2013.
[7] IMF Global Financial Stability Report, Old risks, New Challenges April 2013.

the secondary markets, especially the credit derivatives market, as additional channels to manage risk is another significant strategic development.

In the 1990s, the concept of economic capital had great impact on corporate banking as it created a common analytical framework for lenders to assess portfolio performance and client-level profitability. Some of the significant developments that contributed to the changing focus are detailed below.

The development of the commercial paper market altered the role played by banks in the credit market. Banks were compelled to become backup lines of credit as the strong financial position of the highly rated large corporate customers enabled them to raise capital from the financial markets directly.

The emergence of universal bank models is another noteworthy trend of universal banking strategies. On account of the lucrative fees of the investment banking sector, corporate banking institutions acquired more than 45 investment banks valued at $106 billion during the period 1990-2000.[8] This strategy turned out to be a bust for the majority of US and European banks.

The explosive growth of secondary loan and credit markets altered the shape of the corporate banking industry. The adoption of active loan portfolio management is the result of this change process. Markets of credit default swaps and collateralized loan obligations thrived which, to a greater extent, contributed to the subprime mortgage crisis. These markets provided a new means for corporations to hedge loan exposure and benchmark pricing for standalone credits. This mechanism enabled banks to change the profile of their loan books.

6.1.1.2 Challenges in the commercial banking industry

Commercial banks face challenges with respect to additional revenue generation by means of attracting new customers and expanding commercial loan portfolios. There are also challenges of regulatory issues. Banks in mature markets face the challenges of low demand for loans, economic uncertainty, low interest rate environments, and high cost of liquidity.

Today, the commercial banking industry is facing an enormous challenge with respect to evaluating creditworthy small businesses. The economic slowdown has taught consumers and small businesses to adopt a conservative approach while managing risks and debt levels. But this trend is detrimental to banks whose main source of income is derived from loans.[9] It has become a challenge for banks to attract, evaluate, and monitor good credit opportunities. Banks face challenges with respect to managing information regarding risk allocation across portfolios. It is noteworthy that around 160 million adults in developed countries have no bank account (19% of all adults) whereas 2.7 billion adults (72% of the adults) in developing countries are without banks. Table 6.2 provides the historical statistics of the commercial banking industry during the period 1970-2011.

The commercial banking industry has witnessed drastic changes during the last five decades. In the 1970s, there were approximately 13,500 banking institutions. By 2011, the total number of commercial banks was reduced to 6291. At the same time, the number of branches increased by almost four times. The net income of FDIC-insured commercial banks in the United States and other areas was approximately 110 billion. The net income of commercial banks increased by approximately 6%

---

[8]John Walenta (May 2003). Rethinking large corporate banking: Part 1 What the past decade teach us? RMA Journal.
[9] http://www.banktech.com/core-systems/22900089, Addressing Commercial Finance Challenges, Trends in Commercial banking industry.

Table 6.2   Commercial Banking Highlights, Historical Statistics 1970-2011 (Billions of US Dollars)

Year	Number of Institutions	Number of Branches	Net Income	Total Interest Income	Total Noninterest Income	Total Assets	Total Deposits
1970	13,511	21,839	4.84	30.51	4.20	570.16	482.51
1980	14,434	38,738	14.01	176.42	14.35	1855.69	1481.16
1990	12,347	50,885	15.99	320.48	54.90	3389.49	2650.15
2000	8315	64,900	70.80	428.15	154.25	6245.56	4179.57
2011	6291	83,209	110.88	455.37	212.97	12,639.74	9253.87

Source: Historical Statistics on banking FDIC.

during the last decade. The total assets of the commercial banking sector increased by approximately by 100% during the period 2000-2011.The total deposits almost more than doubled in 2011 compared to the deposits in 2000.

6.1.1.3 Functions of commercial banks

Banks provide safety to customers. Customers no longer need to keep large amounts of currency on hand. They can use checks, debit cards, or credit cards. Banks also act as payment agents within a country and between nations. Banks facilitate payment through checks, wire transfers, and various types of electronic payments. Banks play a major role as financial intermediaries. Banks collect money from depositors and lend it to borrowers. Banks are basically involved in maturity transformation. Banks transform debts with very short maturities (deposits) into credits with very long maturities (loans). In the process banks are exposed to risk owing to increases in short-term funding costs that may rise at a faster rate.

Banks are also involved in money creation in an indirect way through the process of fractional reserve banking. Banks keep only a fraction of their deposits in the form of cash or liquid marketable securities. The rest is lent out to customers as loans or is used to acquire stocks or bonds of other companies. This is known as the money multiplier and can be expressed as the $m = 1$/reserve requirement. Thus, banks facilitate an increase in their money supply.

Thus, major functions of commercial banks are to accept deposits, provide loans, facilitate overdrafts, discount bills of exchange, invest funds, buy or hold securities, perform agency functions, as well as other miscellaneous functions.

6.1.1.3.1 Accept deposits

The most important function of commercial banks is to accept deposits from the public. The three basic types of deposits are current (sight/overnight), fixed/time deposits (certain duration before maturity), and savings deposits (redeemable at an agreed notice). Deposits are made by residents or nonresidents of a country.

(a) *Current deposits*

The depositors of current deposits (also called demand deposits) can withdraw and deposit money whenever they want. These deposits have either no interest or very low rates of interest. Such deposit accounts are highly useful for traders and big business firms because they need to make payments and accept payments many times in a day.

(b) *Fixed deposits*

Fixed deposits are deposited for a definite period of time. This period is generally not less than one year and, therefore, these are called long-term deposits. Fixed deposits cannot be withdrawn before the expiration of the stipulated time and, as such, they are also called time deposits.

(c) *Savings deposits*

In savings deposits, money up to a certain limit can be deposited and withdrawn once or twice in a week. In savings deposits, the rate of interest is very small. Savings deposits are basically meant to mobilize small savings in the form of deposits.

The deposit product segment consists of a comprehensive range of products meant for consumers and small businesses. These products include savings accounts, money market savings accounts, certificates of deposits, individual retirement accounts (IRAs), and interest checking accounts. These deposit accounts provide the main source of funding and liquidity for commercial banks. Through asset and liability management activities and investing deposits in earning assets, banks earn interest revenues. Through deposits, banks generate various account fees such as fund fees, overdraft charges, and account service fees. Deposits are by far the largest product segment for banks, accounting for approximately 60% of the industry.

6.1.1.3.1.1 Significance of deposits. Deposits are the most stable and significant source of funding for any commercial bank. Deposits act as an intermediary between savers and borrowers. Banks provide savers the opportunity to earn interest on surplus funds. At the same time, banks provide funds to firms for investment or consumption purposes. The different sources of deposits include other banks, financial institutions, households, businesses, and governments.

6.1.1.3.1.2 Nature of deposits. Current/checking accounts are short term in nature. These are also referred as core deposits. Many banks pay no interest at all on checking account balances. The interest rate is low for savings bank accounts. Wholesale deposits refer to funds such as interbank CDs. Banks usually focus more on core deposits than on wholesale funds to become more competitive. This could be attributed to the fact that wholesale funding involves higher costs, thereby resulting in narrower interest spreads and lower profits.

6.1.1.3.2 Provide loans

The major function of banks is to advance loans to customers. Banks charge interest from borrowers and this forms the main source of their income. The process of credit creation by commercial banks involves the creation of loans out of deposits and deposits out of loans. Banks demand proper security or collateral while advancing loans. Evaluation of the creditworthiness of borrowers is an integral part of the loan process.

Consumer lending is a major component of bank lending of which residential mortgages constitute a major share. Mortgages are typically for 30-year repayment periods, and interest rates may be fixed, adjustable, or variable. Automobile lending also forms a major part of secured lending for many banks. Auto loans are typically offered for shorter durations compared to mortgage loans and they have higher interest rates. Credit cards are another significant lending type, which are, in essence, personal lines of credit. Major credit cards, such as Visa and MasterCard, facilitate proprietary networks through which money (debits and credits) is moved around between a shopper's bank and the merchant's bank after a transaction.

The loans provided by commercial banks are segregated into secured loans, unsecured loans, and mortgage loans.

6.1.1.3.2.1 Secured loans. A secured loan is one in which the borrower provides a certain property or asset as collateral against the loan. In a situation in which the borrower is unable to pay back the loan amount, the bank has the right to use the property in any way to recover the amount due.

6.1.1.3.2.2 Unsecured loans. Unsecured loans have no collateral and hence command higher interest rates. Unsecured loans include credit cards, corporate bonds, and bank overdrafts.

6.1.1.3.2.3 Mortgage loans. Mortgage loans are similar to secured loans but are specifically used to buy real estate property for commercial purposes. In this case, usually the bank holds a lien on the title to the particular property purchased with the loan. If the borrower is unable to pay the loan back, the bank leverages this item against the loan to generate funds or recover the principal. Mortgage products and services are generally offered through the bank's retail network. Mortgage business models include the origination, fulfillment, sale, and servicing of first mortgage loan products. Banks often manage these mortgage portfolios by repackaging them into products and selling them to investors in secondary mortgage markets in the form of securitization and collateralized debt obligations. The Home equity products include lines of credit and home equity loans.

6.1.1.3.2.4 Business lending. There are a number of lending-related products and services. These products include commercial and corporate bank loans. The commitment facilities offered by banks include business banking clients, middle market commercial clients, and large multinational corporate clients. Real estate lending products are offered to public and private developers and real estate firms. Indirect consumer loans are offered through products in automotive, marine, and motorcycle categories.

Business lending includes commercial mortgages (loans intended to purchase buildings), equipment lending, loans secured by accounts receivables, and loans for expansion purposes. The residential construction industry has been a major user of bank loans in many countries. Business lending also consists of mezzanine financing, project financing, or bridge loans.

The following types of loans can also be differentiated.

(a) *Cash credit*

In cash credit schemes banks provide loans to their customers on the basis of bonds, inventories, and other approved securities. Under this scheme banks enter into an agreement with their customers by which money may be withdrawn several times during a year. The bank sets up open accounts for their customers and deposits the loan money.

(b) *Demand loans*

Demand loans can be recalled on demand by the banks. The entire loan amount is paid in lump sum by crediting it to the loan account of the borrower. As a result, the entire loan becomes chargeable to interest with immediate effects.

(c) *Short-term loan*

These loans may be given as personal loans, loans to finance working capital, or as priority sector advances. These are made against some security and the entire loan amount is transferred to the loan account of the borrower.

6.1.1.3.3 Overdraft services

Banks usually advance loans to their customers up to a certain amount through overdrafts if there are no funds in the account. For this function banks demand security from customers and charge a very high rate of interest.

6.1.1.3.4 Discounting of bills of exchange

This method is the most important method of advancing loans to traders for short-term purposes. Banks advance loans to traders and business firms by discounting their bills. This method facilitates traders to obtain loans on the basis of their bills of exchange before the time of maturity.

6.1.1.3.5 Fund investment

Banks invest their surplus funds in government securities, Treasury bills, savings certificates, and the like. Surplus funds are also invested in state and municipal bodies.

6.1.1.3.6 Buy/hold securities

Banks often use their capital to acquire investment securities. Regulations in different countries require banks to hold some percentage of capital as reserves. The banking sector is a major buyer of government debt securities. Banks are also buyers of municipal bonds. The investment securities issued by national, state, and local governments are treated as safe as cash by regulators. Banks earn income from these investments.

6.1.1.3.7 Agency functions

Banks perform a number of agency functions such as collection of checks, drafts, and bills of exchange for customers. Many banks collect dividends for customers declared by companies. Banks facilitate payment of insurance premiums for their customers.

6.1.1.3.8 Miscellaneous functions

Banks are involved in collecting useful statistics related to trade and industry. Banks also provide lockers for the safe custody of valuable assets. Banks facilitate foreign trade by selling and purchasing foreign exchange. Banks provide loans for consumer durables and issue letters of credits.

6.1.1.4 *Sources of funds for commercial banks*

The major sources of funds (liabilities) for commercial banks are equity capital provided by promoters and stockholders, deposits and nondepository funds (borrowed or liability funds).

Equity capital is an important part of a bank's capital. Primary capital consists of common stock, preferred stock, and retained earnings. Secondary capital consists of subordinated notes and bonds. Banks also issue preferred shares to raise capital in times of crisis or to facilitate acquisitions. These types of shares are generally callable, which means that banks have the right to buy back shares at a time when the capital position is stronger.

Depository accounts consist of current, savings, time, and money market deposit accounts (MMDAs). Noninterest-bearing demand deposits and interest-bearing checking accounts are collectively called transaction accounts. An interest-bearing checking account is called a negotiable order of withdrawal (NOW) account. Examples of time deposits include retail certificates of deposit (retail CD) and negotiable certificates of deposit (NCD) offered by large banks to corporations. The minimum deposit requirement is $100,000. MMDAs are more liquid than retail CDs and do not specify a maturity. These accounts offer lower interest rates compared to CDs.

The nondepository sources of funds consist of federal funds, Federal Reserve borrowings, repurchase agreements, Eurodollar borrowings, and bond issues. Banks can take out loans from the federal fund market to cope with imbalances in the short-term. Such loans are typically mature in 1-7 days with the provision of a rollover. This rollover can result in a series of 1-day loans. The federal fund rate is the interest rate charged in the federal funds market. The federal fund rate is typically quoted on an annualized basis and is generally in the range of 0.25-1% above the Treasury bill rate.

The Federal Reserve System and other central banks also provide a temporary source of funds to commercial banks. The interest rate charged on the loans is called a primary credit lending rate. The maturity of Federal Reserve loans varies from 1 day to a few weeks. Banks also use repurchase agreements (repos) as short-term sources of funds. In a repo, the seller of a security agrees to buy it back at a specified price and time. The seller pays an interest rate called a repo rate when buying back the securities. The commercial bank sells part of its government securities holdings, such as Treasury bills, to a corporation that has excess short-term funds and buys them back after a short time. The government securities offered act as collateral for the repo transaction.

Commercial banks also access Eurodollar borrowings from banks outside the country where the bank is domiciled. Commercial banks also issue bonds for long-term investment needs, such as the purchase of fixed assets such as land, buildings, etc.

6.1.1.5 *Uses of funds by banks*

The major uses of funds (assets) include cash, bank loans, investment in securities, federal funds loaned out, repurchase agreements, and Eurodollar loans. Cash reserves requirements for commercial banks are stipulated by the Federal Reserve and other central banks. The cash assets of the bank include vault cash, cash items in process of collection, balances due from depository institutions, and Federal Reserve banks. Vault cash is coin and currency that banks hold to meet customer withdrawals. Bank loans can be classified as business loans, consumer loans, and real estate loans.

6.1.1.5.1 Business loans

Business loans are classified as working capital loans and term loans. Working capital loans, which are short term in nature, are designed to provide funds for the working capital needs of a company. Term loans are primarily used to finance the purchase of fixed assets such as machinery. Term loans are sanctioned with protective covenants that stipulate conditions of "dos and don'ts" for the borrower. In amortized term loans, the borrower makes fixed periodic payments over the life of the loan. The principal amount of the loan may also be paid off in one lump sum amount called a balloon payment at a specified date in future.

In a direct lease loan, the bank purchases the required asset for a company and leases it to the firm. A line of credit denotes an informal agreement between a bank and a business firm in which the bank allows the firm to borrow up to a certain limit of money provided the bank has funds available. In times of credit crunch, the lender bank has no obligation to lend the money. Many businesses use lines of credit to build up inventories. An alternative to a line of credit is a revolving charge or credit loan. It is a formal short-term financing agreement in which the bank guarantees to advance the money when the borrowing firm requires it. Commercial banks also finance leveraged buyouts (LBOs). An LBO is an acquisition of a company financed predominantly with debt.

6.1.1.5.2 Loan syndication

In loan syndication, a consortium of banks join together to fund a large single project. In the syndication process a lead bank negotiates the deal and is responsible for arranging the documentation process, disbursement, and payment structure of the loan. Other banks in the consortium provide the funds required for the borrower.

6.1.1.5.3 Consumer loans

Commercial banks provide consumer loans for personal, family, or household purposes. These consumer loans are monitored by government regulatory agencies that focus on consumer protection regulations, such as the Truth in Lending Act. Commercial banks provide loans to finance purchases of cars and household products. A mortgage loan is used by an individual to purchase a house. Banks have the lien on the title to the house until the mortgage is fully paid off. Special types of consumer loans include home equity loans, student loans, and automobile loans. Home equity loans are also known as second mortgages. In second mortgages, the difference between the amount paid for the house and its current market value is used to secure the loan. Banks also provide real estate loans. The maturity for a residential real estate loan usually is between 15 and 30 years.

6.1.1.5.4 Investment in government securities and bonds

Commercial banks invest excess cash in government Treasury securities, including Treasury bills and securities issued by agencies of the federal government such as Fannie Mae and Freddie Mac. Commercial banks also invest in investment-grade corporate and municipal bonds. Commercial banks also invest in mortgage-backed securities (MBS).

6.1.1.5.5 Other uses of funds

Commercial banks often lend funds to other banks in the federal funds market. Banks also act as a lender in the repo transaction by purchasing a corporation's securities and selling them back at a specified period. Commercial banks also provide Eurodollar loans to companies.

6.1.1.6 Commercial bank statistics

The bank credit of commercial banks in the United States was $10.05 trillion during May of 2013, according to the Federal Reserve FRB H.8 Release. The total assets of US commercial banks as of May 2013 amounted to $13.52 trillion. The total deposits of commercial banks amounted to $9.38 trillion as of May 2013.The total liabilities amounted to $12 trillion. Time deposits accounted for almost 84% of the total deposits. Deposits form 78% of the total liabilities and borrowings accounted for 22% of the total liabilities. Table 6.3 gives the value of assets of US commercial banks as of May 2013. Table 6.4 gives the value of the liabilities of US commercial banks as of May 2013.

6.1.1.7 Off-balance sheet activities

The off-balance sheet activities of commercial banks consist of a variety of items, including loan commitments, certain letters of credit, and revolving underwriting facilities. The notional values of derivatives instruments such as swaps, futures, forwards, and options are off-balance sheet activities. The fair values are recorded on the balance sheet. Letters of credit are also considered as off-balance sheet activities. A letter of credit is a document issued by a bank on behalf of its customer authorizing a third party to draw drafts on the bank up to a stipulated amount with specified terms and conditions. A traveler's letter of credit is addressed by the bank to its correspondents authorizing drafts by the person named in accordance with the specified terms. These letters are generally sold for cash. A commercial letter of credit is issued to facilitate trade or commerce. A standby letter of credit (SBLC) is an irrevocable commitment on the part of the issuing bank to make payment to a designated beneficiary. It obligates the bank to guarantee or stand as surety for the benefit of a third party. A formal loan commitment is a written agreement, signed by the borrower and lender, detailing terms and conditions under which a loan of up to a specified amount will be made.

Table 6.3   Assets of Commercial Banks in the United States (2013)

Assets	Amount (Billions of US Dollars)
Securities in bank credit	2750
Treasury and agency securities	1860.1
Mortgage-backed securities (MBS)	1367.7
Commercial and industrial loans	1550
Real estate loans	3541.4
Consumer loans	1134.1
Other loans and leases including Fed funds and reverse repos	1077.9
Cash assets	2092.2
Trading assets including derivatives	543.4
Other assets	1124.1

Source: Federal Reserve Board (FRB: H.8 Release) May 2013.

Table 6.4   Liabilities of Commercial Banks in the United States (2013)

Liabilities	Amount (Billions of US Dollars)
Large time deposits (A)	1536.50
Other deposits (B)	7845.4
Total deposits (A+B)	9381.9
Borrowings	1549.8
Trading liabilities	270.50
Net due to related foreign offices	349.9
Other liabilities	448.6
Total liabilities	12,000.7

Source: Federal Reserve Board (FRB: H.8 Release) May 2013.

The commitment will have an expiration date and, for agreeing to make the accommodation, the bank may require a fee to be paid and/or require the maintenance of a stipulated compensating balance by the customer.

Commercial banks also engage in other fee-generating activities such as trust services and correspondent banking. Trust services include estate assets and pension fund assets. Banks manage pension funds as trustees for bonds held by pension funds and act as transfer and disbursement agents for pension funds. Commercial banks also generate fees by providing services such as check clearing and collection, foreign exchange trading, and hedging services to other banks. This process is called correspondent banking.

6.1.1.8 Types of commercial banking customers
The retail customers market is the largest segment of a commercial banks' customer base. Retail customers are offered the primary banking products, including mortgage products, credit cards, and fund

management services. Banks also serve small business, corporate and institutional clients. These clients deal in much larger scale of transaction value. Generally larger corporate and institutional clients deal with commercial banks whose assets are greater than $1 billion. This market segment is generally considered to account for approximately 35% of the industry (IBISWorld). Commercial banks also provide loans to and accept deposits from government clients. Customers are also involved in student loan services, retirement services, auto finance, and more. Retail banks focus on individual consumer banking relationships. Wholesale banks deal with commercial customers.

6.1.1.9 Special characteristics of commercial banks

As with other financial intermediaries, commercial banks facilitate the flow of funds from savers to borrowers. Depository institutions such as commercial banks own only few fixed assets as their function is financial in nature and thereby have very low operating leverage. Commercial bank deposits are insured by the FDIC. Each depositor is insured up to $250,000 per insured bank. Liabilities of banks, such as deposits, are often payable on demand. As the market interest rate changes, depositors can renegotiate the deposit rates. This will lead to asset allocation and pricing problems as interest expense changes occur in the short run.

6.1.1.10 Components of income statements

6.1.1.10.1 Interest income

Interest income is the sum of the interest and fees earned on all assets, including loans and deposits held at other financial institutions.

Components of Interest Income	Details
Income on loans and leases	Interest and fees on loans, income from lease financing
Investment interest income	US Treasury and agency securities, mortgage-backed securities
Other interest income	Interest due from banks, interest on Fed funds sold and resales, trading account income

6.1.1.10.2 Interest expense

Interest expense is the sum of the interest paid on all interest-bearing liabilities, including current, time, savings deposits, and other borrowings.

Components of Interest Expense	Details
Interest expense on deposits	Interest on deposits held in foreign offices, interest on certificates of deposits, other deposits
Other interest expenses	Interest on Fed funds purchased and resales, interest on trade liabilities and other borrowings, interest on mortgages and leases, interest on subordinated notes and debentures

6.1.1.10.3 Net interest income

Net interest income (NII) is found out by subtracting total interest expense from total interest income.

6.1.1.10.4 Noninterest income

Noninterest income is derived primarily from noncore activities such as fees collected from investment banking, venture capital, and trading activities.

Components of noninterest income	Fiduciary activities, deposit service charges, trading revenue, venture capital revenues, securitization income from trading securities, off-balance sheet derivatives, investment banking, advisory, brokerage and underwriting fees and commissions, insurance commission fees and income from underwriting insurance and from the sale of insurance, net servicing fees from servicing real estate mortgages, and credit cards

6.1.1.10.5 Provision for loan losses

The provision for loan losses is a noncash tax-deductible expense. This provision is the current period's allocation to the allowance for loan losses listed on the balance sheet.

6.1.1.10.6 Net income

Net income refers to the operating profit less all federal, state, and local income taxes plus or minus any accounting adjustments and extraordinary items.

6.1.1.11 Framework for bank performance evaluation

The framework for a bank's performance can be analyzed along six dimensions.

(a) Deposit mobilization

This is fundamental for the success of any financial institution. Deposits facilitate sustainability and mobilization of investment resources. Deposits are the most common source of loanable funds for banks.

(b) Quality of lending

The quality of lending is an integral part of the financial evaluation process. The main aspects to be considered while evaluating the quality of lending are formal credit, risk concentration, portfolio classification, interest accrual, and provisions for loan losses.

(c) Capital adequacy analysis

This analysis determines the quality of assets and adequacy of provisions. In this analysis capital is expressed as a percentage of total risk-weighted assets. This analysis reflects the margin of protection available to both depositors and creditors against unexpected losses incurred by banks.

(d) Liquidity analysis

This analysis assesses the capacity of banks to meet their debt obligations as they occur. It reflects the bank's ability to convert assets without loss and raise loans in the market to meet debt obligations.

(e) Earnings performance analysis

This analysis determines if the banks' operations are generating adequate returns on the assets and equity.

(f) Loan growth

Loan growth is similar to revenues growth for industrial companies. Loan growth is an important yardstick for evaluating a company's performance. Above-average loan growth indicates attractive new market segments. Above-average loan growth also means a bank prices its money more cheaply and loosens its credit standards.

6.1.1.12 Analysis of bank performance

6.1.1.12.1 Profitability measures

6.1.1.12.1.1 Return on equity. A return on equity (ROE) is a major profitability model used to analyze a bank's performance. It measures the overall profitability of the bank per dollar of equity.

ROE = Net income/Total equity capital

6.1.1.12.1.2 Return on assets. A return on assets (ROA) is the ratio of net income to total assets.

ROA = Net income/Total assets

6.1.1.12.1.3 Equity multiplier. The equity multiplier (EM) is the financial leverage measure that links the ROE with ROA. Increasing EM values lead to increasing amounts of debt financing relative to stockholder equity. EM is the ratio of total assets to total equity. A high value of EM increases ROE when the net income is positive, but it also indicates high capital or solvency risk.

EM = Total assets/Total equity capital
ROE = (Net income/Total assets) × (Total assets/Total equity)
ROE = ROA × EM

6.1.1.12.1.4 Profit margin. The profit margin (PM) measures the ability to pay expenses and generate net income from interest and noninterest income.

PM = Net income/Total operating income

6.1.1.12.1.5 Asset utilization. Asset utilization (AU) measures the amount of interest and noninterest income generated per dollar of total assets.

AU = Total operating income/Total assets
ROA can be expressed in terms of PM and AU.
ROA = PM × AU

AU ratio measures the extent to which the bank's assets generate revenue. AU ratio can be expressed in terms of interest income ratio and noninterest income ratio.

AU = Interest income ratio + Noninterest income ratio
Interest income ratio = Interest income/Total assets
Noninterest income ratio = Noninterest income/Total assets

6.1.1.12.2 Other profitability ratios

6.1.1.12.2.1 Net interest margin. Net interest margin (NIM) is a measure of the net return on the bank's earning assets, which include investment securities, loans, and leases. It is the ratio of interest income minus interest expense divided by earning assets.

NIM = Net interest income/Earning assets
Net interest income = Interest income − Interest expense

6.1.1.12.2.2 Spread. A spread is the measure of the difference between lending and borrowing rates. Spread is the difference between the average yield of the earning assets and the average costs of interest-bearing liabilities. Both NIM and spread are important measures to evaluate a bank's ability to manage interest rate risk. A bank's interest income and interest expense will change as the market interest rate changes. The higher the spread the better the profitability position of the bank.

6.1.1.12.2.3 Efficiency ratio. An efficiency ratio measures a bank's ability to control noninterest expense relative to net operating income. Net operating income is the net interest income plus noninterest income.

Efficiency ratio = Noninterest expense/Net operating income

6.1.1.12.2.4 Overhead efficiency ratio. Overhead efficiency ratio is the ratio that measures a bank's ability to generate noninterest income to cover noninterest expenses. The higher the ratio, the better the efficiency position of the bank.

Overhead efficiency = Noninterest income/Noninterest expense

6.1.1.12.2.5 Risk adjusted return on capital. Large banks evaluate line of business profitability and risk through risk adjusted return on capital (RAROC).

RAROC = Risk adjusted income/Capital

6.1.1.12.2.6 Expense ratios. Profit margin represents a bank's ability to control expenses. Various expense ratios can be derived from profit margin.

Interest expense ratio = Interest expense/Total operating income
Provision for loan loss ratio = Provision for loan losses/Total operating income
Noninterest expense ratio = Noninterest expense/Total operating income
Tax ratio = Income taxes/Total operating income

The lower the values of these expense ratios, the higher the bank's profitability as measured by profit margin ratio.

6.1.1.12.2.7 Productivity ratios. The main productivity ratios used in analyzing a bank's performance is asset per employee and average personnel expense.

Assets per employee = Average assets/Number of employees
Average personnel expense = Personnel expense/Number of employees
Net income per employee = Net income/Number of employees

6.1.1.12.2.8 Leverage ratios.

Capital to assets ratio

This ratio measures the ratio of a bank's book value of primary or core capital to the book value of its assets. Core capital consists of a bank's equity, cumulative preferred stock, and minority interests in equity accounts of consolidated subsidiaries.

Capital asset ratio = Core capital/Assets
Total risk-based capital ratio = Total capital (Tier I plus Tier II)/Risk-adjusted assets
Tier I (core) capital ratio = Core capital (Tier I)/Risk-adjusted assets

6.1.1.12.3 CAMEL rating system

CAMEL is an internal supervisory tool for evaluating the soundness of a financial institution. The CAMEL-based rating reviews different aspects of a bank with respect to a financial statement, funding sources, macroeconomic data, and cash flow. CAMEL is an acronym for five components of bank factors;

- Capital adequacy
- Asset quality
- Management quality
- Earning ability
- Liquidity

A sixth factor that measures the sensitivity to market was included later in the rating system.

Each component in the CAMEL model is scored from 1 to 5. After computing the rating for each of the elements, the composite rating is the average of the sum of five elements. Banks with ratings of 1 or 2 are considered to present few, if any, supervisory concerns, while banks with ratings of 3, 4, or 5 present moderate to extreme degrees of supervisory concern.

6.1.1.12.3.1 *Capital adequacy.* Maintaining an adequate level of capital is a critical element that is essential to maintaining balance along with a bank's risks exposure (e.g., credit risk, market risk, operational risk etc.) for the purpose of absorbing potential losses. The capital base of financial institutions facilitates depositors in forming their risk perception about the banking institutions.

The most widely used indicator of capital adequacy is the capital to risk-weighted assets ratio (CWRA), commonly known as CAR. The other ratio is capital to assets. According to the Basel Committee, a minimum of 9% CRWA is required. A ratio below the standard specified indicates that the bank is not adequately capitalized to carry out the expansion of business.

Tier 1 capital (core capital) is shareholder equity capital. Tier 2 capital (supplementary capital) is the bank's loan loss reserves plus subordinated debt, which consists of bonds sold to raise funds. Risk-weighted assets are the weighted total of each class of assets and off-balance sheet exposures with weights related to the risk associated with each type of asset.

With respect to rating of capital adequacy, a rating of 1 indicates a strong capital relative to the bank's risk. A rating of 5 indicates a deficiency level of capital.

6.1.1.12.3.2 *Asset quality.* Poor asset quality is a major contributing factor for bank failures. The asset quality of banks can be analyzed by assessing the credit risk and evaluating the quality of loan portfolio. Nonperforming loans (NPLs) and the provisions for loan losses are often considered as important asset quality indicators. Under general classification, loans are divided into five categories: standard, special mention, substandard, doubtful, and loss. The latter three categories are classified as NPLs. A loan is considered an NPL if default of interest payments happens for 90 consecutive days. In some countries, regulators allow a longer period of 180 days.

In the context of asset quality, a rating of 1 indicates a strong asset quality and minimal portfolio risks.

The ratios to gauge asset quality are:

Gross NPL ratio

This ratio indicates whether the bank adds fresh stock of bad loans.
Gross ratio = Gross NPL/Total loan

Net NPL ratio

A high net NPL ratio is indicative of the high probability of a large number of credit defaults that affect the profitability. The higher the ratio, the higher the credit risk.

6.1.1.12.3.3 *Management quality.* The management quality can be assessed by the total asset growth rate, loan growth rate, and earnings growth rate and comparing it to nominal GNP growth.

The ratios that can be used to assess the management efficiency are as follows:

Total advance to total deposit ratio

This ratio measures the efficiency and ability of banks to convert the deposits available with the banks (excluding other funds such as equity) into high-earning advances. Total deposits include demand deposits, savings deposits, term deposits, and deposits of other banks. Total advances include the receivables.

Business per employee ratio

Revenue per employee is a measure of how efficient is the employees of a bank. This ratio indicates the productivity potential of the human resources of the bank.

Business per employee = Total income/No. of employees

Profit per employee

This ratio indicates the surplus earned per employee. The higher value for this ratio is indicative of the efficiency of the management.

Profit per employee = Net profit/Number of employees

6.1.1.12.3.4 *Earning ability.* Strong earnings and profitability profile of banks reflect the ability to support present and future operations. Consistency in profits helps banks to absorb loan losses and provide sufficient provisions. It also increases shareholder value. The profitability ratios measure the ability of a bank to generate profits from revenues and assets.

The single best indicator used to gauge earning is the return on assets (ROA), which is net income after taxes to total asset ratio. Return on equity is another measure of earnings, which is the ratio of net income to total equity.

Net interest income margin

The net interest income margin ratio can be used to gauge the earning ability of a bank.

Operating profit to average working fund

This ratio for the operating profit to average working fund indicates how much a bank can earn from its operations net of the operating expenses for every amount of money spent on working funds. Average working funds are the total resources (total assets or total liabilities) employed by a bank. The higher the ratio, the better the earning potential of the bank. This ratio determines the operating profits generated out of the working funds employed.

Net profit to average asset

Net profit to average asset indicates the efficiency of banks in using their assets for generation of profits. A higher ratio indicates better income-generating capacity of assets and better efficiency of management. It is determined by dividing the net profit by average assets.

Interest income to total income

Interest income is a basic source of revenue for banks. The interest income to total income indicates the ability of the bank to generate income from its lending. In other words, this ratio measures the income from lending operations as a percentage of the total income generated by the bank in a year.

Other income to total income

Fee-based income accounts for a major portion of a bank's other income. The bank generates higher fee income through innovative products and adapting technology for sustained service levels. A higher ratio indicates an increasing proportion of fee-based income.

6.1.1.12.3.5 *Liquidity.* Fund management practices should ensure an institution is able to maintain a level of liquidity sufficient to meet its financial obligations in a timely manner.

The ratios suggested to measure liquidity under the CAMEL model are as follows.

Liquidity asset to total asset

Liquidity is essential for banks to meet their financial obligations as they come due. The proportion of liquid assets to total assets indicates the overall liquidity position of the bank. Liquid assets include cash in hand, balance with central banks, and money at call and available at short notice.

Liquidity asset to demand deposit

The liquidity asset to demand deposit ratio measures the ability of a bank to meet the demand from deposits in a particular year. Demand deposits offer high liquidity to the depositor and hence banks have to invest these assets in a highly liquid form.

Liquidity asset to total deposit

The liquidity asset to total deposit ratio measures the liquidity available to the deposits of a bank. Total deposits include demand deposits, savings deposits, term deposits, and deposits of other financial institutions.

6.1.1.12.3.6 *Sensitivity to market risk.* Sensitivity to market risk refers to risk factors due to changes in market conditions that would adversely impact earnings and/or capital. Market risk arises from changes in interest rates, foreign exchange rates, commodity prices, and equity prices. Sensitivity analysis is used to analyze a bank's exposure to interest rate risk, foreign exchange volatility, and equity price risks. Risk sensitivity is evaluated in terms of management's ability to monitor and control market risk.

6.1.1.13 Key banking rates/ratios

6.1.1.13.1 Bank rate

A bank rate is the rate at which the central bank of a country allows financing to commercial banks. The central bank uses the bank rate for short-term purposes. Any upward revision in the bank rate is an indication that banks should also increase deposit rates as well as base rate/benchmark prime lending rates.

6.1.1.13.2 Repo rate

The repo (repurchase) rate is the rate at which central banks lend short-term money to banks against securities. Borrowing from central banks becomes expensive when the repo rate increases.

6.1.1.13.3 Reverse repo rate

Reverse repo rate is the rate at which banks place their short-term excess funds with the central banks. An increase in the reverse repo rate means that the central bank is borrowing money from the banks at a higher interest rate.

6.1.1.13.4 Cash reserve ratio

In many countries banks are required to hold a certain proportion of their deposits in the form of cash; this is called the cash reserve ratio (CRR). Usually these reserves are deposited with central banks of the country. This is a tool used by central banks to control liquidity in the banking system. The central banks in developing nations such as India use CRR either to drain excess liquidity or to release funds for growth of the economy.

6.1.1.13.5 Statutory liquidity ratio
In different countries banks are required to maintain a minimum proportion of their net demand and time liabilities as liquid assets in the form of cash, gold, and approved securities. The ratio of liquid assets to demand and time liabilities is the statutory liquidity ratio (SLR). The increase in SLR restricts the bank's leverage position to circulate more money into the economy.

6.1.1.13.6 Credit to deposit ratio
The credit to deposit ratio is the proportion of loan assets created by banks from the deposits received. This ratio indicates how much of the advances lent by banks is accounted for by deposits. The higher the CDR, the higher the loan assets created from deposits. Deposits include current savings as well as term deposits.

6.1.1.13.7 Nonperforming assets to loans (advances)
Net nonperforming assets (NPAs) to loans (advances) is used as a measure the overall quality of a bank's loan book. NPA refers to those assets for which interest is overdue for more than 3 months. Net NPAs are calculated by reducing the cumulative balance of provisions outstanding at a period end from gross NPAs. A higher ratio reflects a bad quality of loans.

6.1.1.13.8 Provision coverage ratio
The provision coverage ratio indicates the cumulative provision balances of a bank to gross NPAs. This ratio measures the extent to which banks have made provisions against the loan portfolio.

6.1.1.13.9 Rate paid on funds
The rate paid on funds (RPF) is determined by dividing total interest expense by total earning assets. This indicates what percentage or rate of interest is paid from assets.

6.1.1.13.10 Gross yield on earning assets
The gross yield on average earning assets measures the total average return on a bank's earning assets. The gross yield on earning is the RPF plus the net interest margin.

6.1.1.14 Credit appraisal at commercial banks
Loans are the most dominant asset of depository institutions (commercial banks) and generate the largest share of operating income. Bank credit is the primary source of available debt financing for different types of borrowers. Interest rate risk arises from credit decisions. Loan maturities, pricing, and the form of principal repayment affect the timing and magnitude of a bank's cash inflows. When a customer requests a loan, the bank officials conduct a credit analysis to determine the borrower's ability and willingness to pay back the loan amount. A typical credit analysis consists of the five Cs of credit: character, capital, capacity, condition, and collateral. *Character* refers to the borrower's honesty and trustworthiness. *Capital* refers to the borrower's wealth position based on financial soundness and market standing. *Capacity* refers to the ability of borrower to repay the loan amount. A borrower must have identifiable cash flow to repay the debt amount. *Condition* refers to the economic environment or business cycle

that influences a firm's operations. *Collateral* is the lender's secondary source of repayment in case the borrower defaults. The credit analysis procedure involves collecting information such as the borrower's credit history. The borrowing company's management policies are evaluated along with external factors such as the operating environment of the industry in which the borrower operates. A financial statement analysis of the borrower is done and the cash flows are projected to determine the ability to repay the debt. In this credit analysis process, the collateral is also evaluated. The loan officer evaluates the credit file, which contains background information on the borrower, and other aspects such as call report summaries, past financial statements, credit reports, and supporting schedules for inventory, equipment, and insurance coverage. If the credit is approved, the borrower is apprised of the preliminary credit terms such as the loan amount, maturity, pricing, collateral requirements, and repayment schedule.

6.1.2 THRIFT INSTITUTIONS

Thrift institutions consisting of mutual savings banks, savings and loan (S&Ls) associations, and credit unions are financial intermediaries that raise funds through time and savings deposits and invest in residential mortgages and loans. During the 1800-1900 period, these thrift institutions were established to satisfy the unmet demand for small savings accounts and home mortgages at a time when commercial banks were not involved in this line of business. The focus of thrift institutions is on consumer accounts and loans and not on business accounts and loans.

Mutual savings banks and S&Ls associations were established in the 1800s to provide low-cost mortgage loans to the working-class population. Credit unions were established in the early 1900s to provide members with low-cost personal loans. Thrift institutions generally don't offer checkable deposits. S&Ls associations, known as building and loan societies, were established to facilitate wage earners to obtain funds to purchase or build homes. Mutual savings banks were established to encourage savings by the lower-economic sections of society. The balance sheet of a mutual savings bank consisted of savings deposits on the liability side and consumer loans and residential mortgages on the asset side. In the case of S&Ls associations, the liability side has savings shares and the asset side has residential mortgages. In the 1980s, the relaxation of federal restrictions enabled thrift institutions to have greater portfolio diversification. Through the enactment of the Deregulation and Monetary Control Act of 1980 and Depository Institutions Act of 1982, the federal government removed regulatory barriers that prevented thrift institutions from offering the same services as traditional banks. These acts were aimed at reducing the interest rate risk faced by S&Ls associations by allowing them to expand their range of assets and liabilities beyond the traditional ones of mortgages and time deposits. To become competitive, thrift institutions were compelled to pay higher rates on deposits. Table 6.5

Table 6.5　Highlights of Savings Institutions (2013)	
Number of FDIC-insured institutions	971
Number of FDIC supervised	437
Total assets	$1062 billion
Total loans	$633 billion
Domestic deposits	$810 billion
Source: FDIC Statistics.	

		Total	Total Real				
Year	Number of Institutions	Loans and Leases	Estate Loans	Loans to Individuals	Total Assets	Deposits	Net Income
1984	3418	737.66	720.47	44.16	1144.24	944.73	1.15
1990	2815	821.93	755.72	47.94	1259.17	987.14	−4.7
2000	1589	827.82	722.85	65.19	1217.33	735.19	10.7
2010	1128	780.34	616.09	89.76	1253.45	908.59	8.1
2012	987	647.75	480.51	93.45	1059.69	803.23	10.9

Table 6.6   Highlights of FDIC-Insured Financial Institutions (Billions of US Dollars)

Source: FDIC Statistics: HSOB Saving Institutions.

highlights the statistics of US savings institutions. Table 6.6 gives the statistics of FDIC-insured financial institutions during the period 1984-2012.

The number of FDIC-insured savings institutions declined during the 1984-2012 period. In 1984 there were 3418 savings institutions. By 2012, the number was reduced to 987. The total of loans, leases, and deposits is also showing a declining trend. The total number of loans and leases peaked during 2005 with a value of $1.3 trillion. The total assets peaked in 2007 with a value of $1.86 trillion.

6.1.2.1 New regulations for thrift institutions

New regulatory oversight requires thrifts to reevaluate the current methods of operation. The major regulators of thrift institutions are the Federal Reserve System, National Credit Union Administration, Federal Home Loan Bank System, and Federal Deposit Insurance Corporation.

In 2011, the Dodd-Frank Act reforms stipulated the treatment of thrift institutions similar to bank-holding companies. The Collin Amendment to the Dodd-Frank Act states that bank-holding corporations (BHCs) and savings and loan holding corporations (SLHCs) must adhere to the same capital requirements as insured depository institutions. SLHCs are now required to file the same applications and follow the same procedures as BHCs. Mutual savings banks must also follow new rules on application processing, dividend waivers, and the submission of offerings or proxy materials and stock repurchases. The Dodd-Frank Act abolished the Office of Thrift Supervision (OTS) and transferred regulatory jurisdiction of approximately 670 federal thrifts and 60 state-chartered thrifts, and their parent SLHCs, to the other federal banking agencies (FBAs), including the Office of the Comptroller of the Currency (OCC), the Federal Reserve Board (FRB), and the Federal Deposit Insurance Corporation (FDIC). Subsidiaries of thrift institutions, such as service corporations, can engage in a number of financial activities such as residential real estate development and real estate brokerage companies. Repurchase agreements with affiliates are subject to collateralization requirements. The Dodd-Frank Act imposes new sanctions for the failure by a savings association to comply with the Qualified Thrift Lender (QTL) test. The 1-year grace period to return to compliance was removed through the revised regulations. Federal law requires savings institutions to meet a QTL test.

6.1.2.1.1 Qualified thrift lender test

To be a QTL, an institution must either meet the Home Owners' Loan Act (HOLA) QTL test or the Internal Revenue Service (IRS) tax code Domestic Building and Loan Association (DBLA) test.

Under the QTL test, an institution must hold qualified thrift investments (QTIs) equal to at least 65% of its portfolio assets. The ratio of an institution's QTI divided by its portfolio assets is the institution's actual thrift investment percentage (ATIP). A QTI must fall into one of the two categories:

- Assets that are includable in QTI without limit
- Assets limited to 20% of portfolio assets

Portfolio assets are total assets minus goodwill and other intangible assets, office property, and liquid assets not exceeding 20% of total assets. An institution ceases to be a QTL when its ratio of QTI (numerator) divided by its portfolio assets (denominator) falls, at month end, below 65% for 4 months within any 12-month period.

The principal types of QTIs include unrestricted amounts of residential real estate loans, home equity loans, MBS, credit card and credit card account loans, small business loans, and education loans, and a basket of other consumer loans and certain types of other assets not to exceed 20% of total assets.

Federal thrifts are subject to a statutory lending limit for commercial loans equal to 20% of their total assets. This limitation serves as a significant impediment for a thrift seeking to diversify its asset portfolio or change its business strategy to increase its focus on commercial lending.

6.1.2.2 *Types of thrift institutions*
6.1.2.2.1 Mutual savings banks
Mutual savings banks were established to provide members with low-cost home mortgage loans and to promote savings among members. The first mutual savings bank in the United States was chartered in Boston in 1816 to uplift the poor and working classes. Mutual savings banks have characteristics of both credit unions and S&Ls associations. They are nonprofit cooperatives, like credit unions which pool members' savings, and the primary lending activity of providing mortgage loans resembles that of S&Ls associations. The capital of a mutual savings bank is in the form of savings deposits, and depositors of a savings bank is are voting members. The average Tier I capital ratio for all mutual banks is 12.36% and the average risk-based capital ratio is 25.30%. During the financial crisis, it is said that 12 mutual savings banks failed with total assets of $2 billion approximately.

6.1.2.2.2 Savings and loan associations
The first US savings and loan association was established in 1831. The primary objective of the establishment of S&Ls associations is to assist homeowners with low-cost mortgage loans using savings deposits. They provide loans for the construction, purchase, repair, or refinancing of houses. The Federal Home Loan bank system was bestowed with the administrative responsibility of S&Ls in 1932. S&Ls associations can be either state or federally chartered and must fulfill the state requirements to be incorporated.

6.1.2.2.3 Credit unions
These nonprofit depository institutions were established to provide services to members of a specific group, for example, the employees of a company. Credit union membership is based on a common bond, a linkage shared by savers and borrowers who belong to a specific community, organization, religion, or place of employment. Credit unions pool their members' savings deposits and shares to finance their own loan portfolios rather than rely on outside capital. Members benefit from higher returns on savings,

lower rates on loans, and fewer fees on average. Credit unions enable members to have access to low-cost personal loans and higher interest rates on deposits than are offered by traditional banks. Credit unions are prohibited from providing services to the general public. Employees can become members of a credit union by investing in the shares of the credit union. Each share has a minimum value ranging from $5 to $10. Credit union deposits are insured by the National Credit Union Share Insurance Fund. National Credit Union Administration is the primary regulator of credit unions. In 2009 there were more than 7500 US credit unions with membership of 90 million American citizens and total assets of $1 trillion.[10]

Because credit unions are nonprofit institutions, they are not subject to taxation as is the case with banks. According to analysts, after the enactment of the Dodd-Frank Act, credit unions became a competitive alternative for banks in terms of low-cost loans. Owing to regulatory changes banks have increased fees and added restrictions to free checking accounts to offset loss in revenues. Analysis shows that the rate on new car loans at credit unions in 2012 averaged 3.4% or 1.5 percentage points less than at banks. Similarly, the rate on gold and platinum credit cards was 9.8% or about 1.4 percentage points lower.[11] Table 6.7 provides statistics on global credit unions.

The Navy Federal Credit Union is a $54-billion credit union that is affiliated with the armed forces and is the largest credit union in the world. Table 6.8 provides the value of assets and liabilities of US credit unions during the period 2007-2012. Table 6.9 lists the largest credit unions in the US along with their asset sizes.

Table 6.7   Statistics on US Credit Unions

Number of credit unions	55,952
Members	200.243 million
Penetration	7.72%
Savings and shares	$1293.256 billion
Loans	$1083.818 billion
Reserves	$161.810 billion
Assets	$1693.949 billion

Source: Statistical Report, 2012, World Council of Credit Unions, http://www.woccu.org/.

Table 6.8   Assets and Liabilities of Credit Unions in the US (Billions of US Dollars)

	Year					
	2007	**2008**	**2009**	**2010**	**2011**	**2012**
Assets	696	740.6	791.7	871.1	906.1	958.9
Liabilities	625.4	679	738.3	806.3	807.6	856.9

Source: Federal Reserve Statistics.

---

[10] http://advice.cuna.org/download/uscu_profile_yearend09.pdf for summary data from the 2005-2009 period.
[11] Ashok Robin and Patricia Wollan (Winter 2012). Credit union performance in the post credit union membership access act 0f 1998 era. Southern Business Review, 1-18.

Table 6.9 Largest Credit Unions in the US	
Credit Union	**Assets (Billions of US Dollars)**
Navy Federal CU	55.5
State Employees CU	27.11
Pentagon CU	16.84
Boeing Employees CU	11.90
Schools First CU	9.87
Source: SNL Financial, 2013.	

6.1.2.3 Risk management in thrift institutions

Savings institutions face liquidity, credit, and interest rate risk. Savings institutions finance long-term assets with short-term liabilities. These institutions depend on new additional deposits to cover withdrawal requests. If new deposits are not sufficient to match withdrawal requests, savings institutions face liquidity crisis. Liquidity risks are managed through repurchase agreements and borrowed funds from the Fed funds market. Savings institutions also can sell their short-term Treasury securities or mortgages in the secondary market to raise funds to manage liquidity risks. Credit risk in savings institutions arises due to the fact that the primary assets in savings institutions are mortgages. Insurance is the tool for managing credit risk in these institutions.

Thrift institutions are particularly prone to interest rate risk due to the very nature of their business. Excessive interest rates affect the earning and capital of thrift institutions. Changing interest rates affect thrift institutions' assets, liabilities, and off-balance sheet activities. Savings and loan associations face interest rate risk in the form of repricing risk, yield curve risk, basis risks, and options risks. Repricing risk arises from the timing differences in the maturity and repricing of assets and liabilities. The income of thrift institutions declines when thrift institutions fund long-term fixed-rate loans with short-term deposits. The cash flows on the loans are fixed while the interest paid on the deposits is variable. Yield curve risk also arises when unexpected shifts of the yield curve cause adverse effects on savings institutions' economic value. Savings institutions are also subject to basis risks owing to differences in the rates earned and paid on different financial instruments with other. Savings institutions also face option risks from options embedded in many financial instruments. Savings institutions have to establish board-approved limits on interest rate risks, which are defined in terms of net portfolio value. Institutions also set risk limits that are expressed in terms of interest rate sensitivity of projected earnings.

Savings institutions use such methods as adjustable rate mortgages, interest rate futures, and interest rate swaps to manage interest rate risks. Through adjustable rate mortgages wherein interest rates are linked to market determined rates such as 1-year Treasury bills, savings institutions are able to maintain a stable spread between interest revenues and interest expenses.

Savings institutions participate in futures, options, and swap markets to hedge interest rate risks. Savings institutions use bond futures contracts to hedge their fixed rate mortgages. By selling bond futures contracts, savings institutions benefit if the interest rate rises. This benefit can be attributed to the difference in the market value of the bond futures, which the savings institution sells, and the value when it purchases the securities in the future when the interest rate rises. (The value of a bond falls when the interest rate rises.) Hedging in futures markets enables savings institutions to reduce the spread between interest revenues and expenses in times of increasing interest rates. Savings institutions also hedge interest rate risk by participating in options markets through the purchase of put options on interest rate futures.

Interest rate swaps are used by savings institutions to swap the outflow of fixed rate payments for an inflow of variable rate payments. The fixed rate payments from the swap can be matched against the fixed rate mortgages. The variable rate payments from the swap can be matched against the variable cost of funds. When the interest rate rises, the fixed flow payments from the swap agreement remain fixed. At the same time, the variable rate inflow payments on account of swap agreements will increase. In a declining interest rate environment, the interest rate swap will not have a favorable impact as the variable inflow component will decrease while the fixed outflow payments due to the swap remain the same.

6.1.2.4 Participation of savings institutions in financial markets

Savings institutions participate in money markets, mortgage markets, bond markets, and derivatives markets. Savings institutions issue commercial papers in the money market for sources of deposit funds. Savings institutions sell mortgages in the secondary mortgage market and issue MBS. They participate in bond markets by purchasing bonds and selling bonds for long-term funds. Finally, savings institutions also participate in the derivatives markets, including future markets, options markets, and swap markets to hedge their interest rate risks.

6.2 SUMMARY

Depository institutions are broadly classified into commercial banks and thrift institutions. The commercial banking industry provides commercial, industrial, and consumer loans and accepts deposits from individual and institutional customers. Commercial banking covers services such as cash management, credit services, deposit services, and foreign exchange. The commercial banking industry reached its pinnacle of growth in 2007. The explosive growth of secondary loan and credit markets altered the shape of the corporate banking industry. Commercial banks face challenges with respect to additional revenue generation in the event of economic uncertainty, regulatory issues, high-liquidity costs, and low demand for loans.

The basic functions of commercial banks are to accept deposits and provide loans. Other functions include providing overdraft facilities, discounting bills of exchange, funding investments, and performing agency functions. The major sources of funds (liabilities) for commercial banks are equity capital provided by promoters and stockholders, deposits and nondepository funds (borrowed or liability funds). The major uses of funds (assets) include cash, bank loans, investment in securities, federal funds loaned out, and repurchase agreements. Off-balance sheet activities of commercial banks consist of a variety of items, including loan commitments, certain letters of credit, and revolving underwriting facilities. A commercial bank's performance can be evaluated along the dimensions of deposit mobilization, quality of lending, capital adequacy analysis, liquidity, earnings, and loan growth. The major profitability measures used to evaluate a bank's performance are return on assets, net interest margin, and RAROC. The CAMEL rating system is a supervisory tool for evaluating the soundness of a financial institution. Thrift institutions consist of mutual savings banks, S&Ls associations, and credit unions. These financial intermediaries raise funds through time and savings deposits and invest in residential mortgages and loans. Savings institutions face liquidity, credit, and interest rate risk.

QUESTIONS FOR DISCUSSION

1. Discuss the major services offered by commercial banks.
2. What is net spread?
3. What are the trends and challenges faced by the commercial banking industry?
4. What are the main functions of commercial banks?
5. Discuss the major sources and uses of funds for commercial banks.
6. What are the off-balance sheet activities of commercial banks?
7. How can a commercial bank's performance be evaluated?
8. What are the different types of thrift institutions?
9. Explain the highlights of major regulations for thrift institutions.
10. Explain risk management in thrift institutions.

REFERENCES

http://www.ibisworld.com/industry/global/global-commercial-banks.html.

http://www.economywatch.com/banks/commercial-banks/.

http://www.investopedia.com/terms/c/commercialbank.asp#ixzz1yyxGuN95.

Simpson, S.D. The Banking System: Commercial Banking-What Banks Do. http://www.investopedia.com/university/banking-system/banking-system1.asp#axzz1ytSZM65p.

ftp://ftp.fao.org/docrep/fao/007/ae362e/ae362e00.pdf.

Beck, T., Demirguc-Kunt, A., Levine, R., 2003. Bank concentration and crises. NBER Working Paper 9921.

Bikker, J.A., Haaf, K., 2002. Competition, concentration and their relationship: An empirical analysis of the banking industry. Journal of Banking & Finance 26 (11), 2191–2214.

Koch, T.W., MacDonald, S., 2010. Evaluating commercial loan requests and managing credit risk. Bank Management. seventh ed. South West Cengage Learning (pp. 587–653, Chapter 14).

Thrift Institutions after Dodd Frank, The new regulatory framework, 2011. Morrison Forester.

http://blogs.law.harvard.edu/corpgov/2012/01/17/new-dodd-frank-regulatory-framework-for-thrift-institutions/.

http://www.mofo.com/files/Uploads/Images/111208-Thrift-Institutions-User-Guide.pdf.

http://www.occ.gov/static/news-issuances/ots/exam-handbook/ots-exam-handbook-270.pdf.

http://www.paulhastings.com/assets/publications/1839.pdf.

U.S. League, Chicago, 1987. U.S. League of Savings Institutions, 87 Savings and Institutions Sourcebook.

INVESTMENT BANKS AND FINANCE COMPANIES

7.1 INTRODUCTION TO INVESTMENT BANKING

Investment banks have emerged as one of the most powerful financial institutions in the world. In short, investment banks trade and issue equity and debt and offer a range of investment activities for clients.

Technological revolution in the last four decades has facilitated the advent of low-cost information and communication technologies that have changed the nature and mode of delivery of financial products and services. The integration of the global financial industry has facilitated the creation of innovative financial products and services. The 1980s witnessed widespread deregulation, technological revolution, and consolidation in the form of mergers and acquisitions. These changes led to integration of investment banks. Investment banks perform multiple services including underwriting and brokerage services, and focus on the commercial side of business. Those firms that focus only on one area such as security trading or securities underwriting are generally known as securities firms.

7.1.1 FUNCTIONS OF INVESTMENT BANKING

An investment bank offers services in equity capital markets, leveraged debt capital markets, commercial real estate, asset finance and leasing, and corporate lending services. Investment bank services are in the form of arrangements for debt facilities and the supply of liquidity. Equity capital market services include initial public offerings (IPOs), right issues, and more. Trading on stocks and bonds and M&As advisory services are other major functions of investment banks. Investment banks manage assets and investment portfolios and are also primary dealers in government securities and underwriters of corporate bonds and equities.

In short, the services provided by investment banks include a complete range of cash management, trade finance, Trust and Securities services, and capital market sales. The asset finance and leasing division of investment banks provide structured financing solutions, and advisory and arranging services for high-value assets such as aircraft, ships, real estate, infrastructure, renewal energy, and other assets such as patents.

Taking a theoretical perspective, an investment bank is involved in two lines of business: one is on the sell side and the other is on the buy side. Market making and trading securities are activities carried out by investment banks on the sell side. Underwriting and research activities are performed as an insider function. On the buy side, investment banks offer asset management services for pension funds, mutual funds, and hedge funds.

7.1.1.1 *Raising funds*

Investment banks help companies raise funds by means of selling financial instruments in the capital market. These securities include common stocks, preferred stocks, and bonds. An investment bank assists clients in raising funds through three major stages. The first phase is the investigation stage and consists of legal and market analysis. In legal analysis, the legal framework for the creation of a security, such as an equity or bond, is undertaken and submitted to the regulatory agency for clearance. The regulatory agency grants the authorization for the issue of sale subject to the condition that relevant financial details are disclosed to prospective investors. In the market analysis phase, the investment banker determines the fair price for the securities. The investment banker facilitates the preparation of the prospectus (financial disclosure brochure) and advertises the issue. In bond issues, the investment banker decides on the coupon rate for the bonds.

In the second phase known as underwriting, investment banks assume the risk of loss due to non-subscription by underwriting the securities offerings. Investment banks perform the underwriting function by buying the entire block of securities at a discounted price from the concerned company. Then the investment bank attempts to sell the securities to investors at the maximum retail price. Often investment banks borrow money from its commercial financing division to buy the issues. If the stock price falls during the period of sale, investment banks will sell the stock at a much lower price, thereby exposing it to great risk. Sometimes an underwriting syndicate is formed with lead investment banks and other banks. The final phase involves selling the issue. Additional brokerage firms may be enlisted to sell the issues.

Investment banks help organizations to raise capital for projects. Investment banks also offer advisory services in the context of proper avenues of investments. Unlike commercial banks where customers directly deposit and withdraw money, investment banks indirectly help investors to invest money in a chosen market. Investment banks sell shares of corporations to raise funds for investment projects.

The top investment bank underwriters include JPMorgan, Barclays Capital, Citigroup, and Deutsche Bank.

7.1.1.2 *Asset management*

The asset management function of investment banks involves managing the funds of corporate institutional investors by investing in stocks, fixed-income securities/bonds, derivatives investments, and other types of investments. The asset management division deals with institutional investors, retail investors, and alternate funds on the basis of investor and investment types. The asset management division helps corporate clients in long-term investment of assets. The asset division provides investment advice and products to pension funds, insurance companies, and other investors. The asset management division also develops products tailored to retail investors, which are marketed through retail banks or financial advisors. Real estate and hedge funds constitute the alternate funds segment. Real estate helps investors to make decisions concerning domestic, commercial, or industrial property. In a nutshell, the asset management division of an investment bank performs the basic functions of investment management and sales and distribution. The function of investment management involves investing a client's funds in specific asset classes, such as equities and fixed income as well as hedge funds. There are portfolio managers for specific funds such as growth funds, value funds, and domestic funds. The sales and distribution division of an investment bank is responsible for creating a marketing strategy for creating, positioning, and selling the investment products of the investment bank.

7.1.1.3 Mergers and acquisitions advisory services

Investment banks are actively involved in mergers and acquisitions. These banks perform the functions of deal making, advising, and underwriting. Investment banks find potential targets and carry out due diligence valuation analysis. They play a vital role in packaging a deal on behalf of a company for strategic and financial buyers. During the sale process, investment banks perform a range of activities. They develop an initial estimation on the current valuation and suggest methods of transaction structuring. Also during the sale process, investment banks refine the valuation parameters, develop a comprehensive list of strategic and financial buyers, organize meetings with potential buyers, and manage the due diligence and bidding processes. Investment banks also facilitate negotiation of term sheets and closing documents. Other functions are to facilitate leveraged buyouts and raise large amounts of funds from capital markets.

7.1.1.4 Facilitation of arbitrage

Some investment banking firms associate with securities arbitrage firms to facilitate arbitrage activity by buying undervalued shares and reselling them at a higher price. Pure arbitrage involves buying an asset in one market at one price and selling it immediately in another market at a higher price. Risk arbitrage involves buying securities in expectation of some impending event. Investment banks also raise funds for arbitrage firms. Investment banks receive fee income through advisory services offered to arbitrage firms and also receive commission on bonds issued to support arbitrage activity. Investment banks also receive fees from divestiture activity.

7.1.1.5 Brokerage services

Some securities firms provide brokerage services to customers by executing buy or sell orders for primarily institutional investors. Full-service brokerage firms provide information and personalized advice and execute orders. Discount brokerage firms only execute orders upon request and don't provide advisory services. Brokerage services generate income for securities firms through management fees, trading commissions, and margin interest. Management fees are obtained by managing the client firm's securities portfolio. Trading commissions are fees generated for executing securities trades. Margin interest is interest charged to investors who buy securities on margin.

7.1.1.6 Market making

Market making is the process of creation of a secondary market in an asset by securities or investment bank. Investment banks, known as market makers, stand prepared to buy or sell stocks on a regular and continuous basis at a publicly quoted price. Market makers provide sufficient liquidity by reducing volatility in prices to maintain a fairly and orderly market for stocks. Generally market makers must be ready to buy or sell at least 100 shares of a stock in which they make a market. Hence, a large order from an investor can be filled by the participation of a number of market makers at potentially different prices. Market makers on the New York Stock Exchange are referred to as *jobbers* and those on the London Stock Exchange are referred to as *specialists*.

7.1.2 STRUCTURE OF INVESTMENT BANKS

The finance divisions of investment banks are generally segregated into business area control, legal entity control, and group risk control. The business area control divisions calculate, analyze, and report risk to the trading desks. The legal entity control divisions present financial results to corporate centers. The group risk control divisions are responsible for risk measurement and reporting. The global valuation groups deal with pricing of exotic investment funds. The global banking divisions consist primarily of corporate finance and global transaction banking.

The transaction banking sections of investment banks deal with areas of cash management, trade finance, and trust and securities services. The cash management sections manage the investment of cash flows to maximize short-term liquidity. The trade finance divisions offer comprehensive solutions for structured trade and export finance along with risk-mitigation products.

The trust and securities divisions provide administrative services for securities transaction deals. The capital market sales divisions of investment banks provide clients with asset, liability, and risk-management solutions across a wide range of different asset classes such as foreign exchange, interest rates, equities, commodities, and credit.

The global markets divisions of investment banks deal with sales, trading, and structuring. Sales teams are responsible for raising capital and placing bonds and shares with investors. Trading teams make prices, book trades, and manage risks. Structuring teams design complex over-the-counter structured products. Structured products consist of equity, debt, money markets, foreign exchanges, and derivatives.

7.1.3 ACTIVITIES OF INVESTMENT BANKING

The role played by investment banks can be segregated as front-office, middle-office and back-office activities. In the front-office role, investment banks help in raising capital for corporate clients through IPOs, right offerings, and private placement. The front office also plays a vital role with respect to financial advice, monitoring, and researching. The equity research division reviews company reports and assists traders in trading operations. The traditional business of investment banks is corporate finance, which involves raising funds in capital markets and mergers and acquisitions advisory services. Usually the investment banking division is divided into industry coverage and product coverage groups. The industry coverage group focuses on specific industries such as health care and industrials, whereas product-coverage groups focus on financial products, leveraged financing, public financing, asset financing and leasing, and structured finance.

The middle-office roles are related to sales and trading, investment management, and merchant banking divisions. With respect to sales and trading activities, an investment bank performs the function of buying and selling products on behalf of the bank and its clients. In market making, traders buy and sell financial products. The middle-office division focuses on risk management, Treasury management, internal controls, and corporate strategy. Risk management involves managing the market and credit risk. The corporate treasury is responsible for investment banks' funding, capital structure management, and liquidity risk monitoring. The financial control division tracks and analyzes the capital flows of the firm.

The back-office division include operations, technology, and the like. Investment banks do have considerable amounts of in-house software.

The other business services division provides cash management, custody services, lending, and securities brokerage service to institutions.

7.1.3.1 Securities underwriting

This is the process by which investment banks raise investment capital from investors in the form of equity and debt capital on behalf of companies and government authorities. In other words, this is the process of selling a newly issued security such as stocks or bonds to investors. When a firm decides to issue securities, it usually hires an investment bank as an intermediary. The issuing firm pays a commission or gross spread and receives the net proceeds when the securities are issued. Underwriters profit from the underwriting spread, which is the price they pay issuers and the amount they collect from the investors or broker-dealers who buy the issue offerings. For large stock or bond issues, an underwriting syndicate consisting of a number of investment banks underwrites the issues. Through the formation of a syndicate, underwriters can reduce their risks by an allocation of shares to other investment banks. Syndication also has the scope for expanding the marketing of company shares through other investment banks.

7.1.3.2 Equity underwriting

Underwriters offer a set of services for IPOs or seasoned equity offerings. Investment banks advise their corporate clients regarding the appropriate structure of financial statements, preparation of offering statement and size, and timing of the issue. Underwriting investment banks conduct the due diligence of a firm. The underwriter is involved in a marketing role by accompanying an issuer's senior management on the road to provide information to potential investors. The underwriter prices the shares based on an assessment of demand and its own financial analysis. The underwriter contractual agreement also involves issues of overallotment options, lockup periods, and the prospect of price stabilization in the aftermarket. Investment bankers also structure deals in which securities are sold to institutional investors such as pension funds and private equity funds. This process is referred to as private placement.

Managing underwriters may underwrite the IPO on either a firm commitment or on a best efforts basis. In a firm commitment offering, underwriters will purchase shares at a discount and resell them for the full public offering price to institutional and individual investors. In contrast, a best efforts offering means that underwriters are only committing their best efforts to sell the shares. In a best efforts deal, investment bankers do not undertake any guarantees with respect to the quantity of securities that will be sold or prices for the securities. In other words, the risk associated with unsold or overpriced securities lies with the issuer. But in firm commitment deals, the risk associated with unsold or overpriced securities are carried by the investment bankers. The underwriting fees are higher in firm commitment deals than in a best-efforts deal.

Investment bankers cannot sell securities at a price above the stated offer price. Although if the issue fails to sell out at the offer price, the underwriter may sell at a lower price. From 1982 onward, the US regulator—the SEC—began permitting publicly traded firms to issue securities without distributing a prospectus. SEC Rule 415 states that by filing a letter with the SEC disclosing the intention of selling additional securities within the next 2 years, a firm can sell the securities whenever it wants. This process is known as shelf registration. Existing disclosures such as quarterly financial statements provide sufficient information to investors. The securities can be taken off the shelf and sold, thereby becoming known as shelf issues.

7.1.3.3 Methods of IPO pricing

Two methods are generally used for pricing an IPO. In the fixed price method, the issuing firm fixes the price with the help of the lead manager. In the book building process, the lead investment bank determines the price through the analysis of confidential investor demand data. The book building process is a mechanism by which underwriters set an offer price for the issue by canvassing potential buyers. A significant fact of the book building process is that the underwriter has complete discretion in allocating shares. The investment banker usually facilitates a marketing campaign in the form of "road shows" where presentations about the issue are made to institutional investors and money managers. Once demand is stimulated, underwriters try to set an offer price and allocate securities to investors based on different criteria.

It is often stated that where book building is used, investment bankers may underprice IPOs to induce regular investors to reveal information during the preselling period, which can be used to assist in pricing the issue.

7.1.3.4 Stabilization activities

In many markets, such as in the United States, regulation allows manipulated activities for stabilization or price support at the time of securities offerings. These practices include allowing underwriters to overallot securities and then cover the resulting short position by retiring the securities or through the process of exercising an overallotment option known as the green shoe option. The green shoe option is a clause in the underwriting agreement of an IPO that allows selling additional shares (usually 15%) to the public if the demand exceeds expectations and the stock trades above its offering price.

7.1.3.5 Compensation for underwriting

The direct compensation that underwriters receive for IPO issues are in the form of the underwriting discount or gross spread. In most countries, including the United States, the firm selling the securities to the public pays investment bankers both buying and selling commissions so that buyers do not have to pay commissions when buying a new issue.

IPOs are usually underwritten by a syndicate of investment banks, the largest of which is the lead underwriter. The lead underwriter, the comanagers, and the syndicate members all receive compensation from the company for being involved in the IPO process. This compensation comes from the gross spread—the difference between the price at which the securities are bought from the issuer and the price at which they are delivered to the public. The underwriting spread in an IPO typically consists of a manager's fee, an underwriting fee, and a concession. A member of the syndicate is entitled to an underwriting fee and concession. A broker-dealer who is not a member of the syndicate but sells shares would receive only the concession. Usually the lead underwriter, known as the book runner, takes the highest proportion of the gross spread. The lead underwriter receives a fee for his efforts, which is typically 20% of the gross spread. The second portion of the spread is the selling concession and is the amount paid to the underwriter and other syndicate members for actually selling the securities. This is typically equal to 60% of the gross spread. Each syndicate member receives a selling concession based on the amount of the issue it sells to its customers.

Public offerings are sold to both institutional investors and retail clients of the underwriters. More than one law firm is also involved in an IPO process to facilitate an array of legal requirements. The initial preliminary prospectus is known as a red herring prospectus. Brokers can take indications of interest after issue of the prospectus.

The letter of intent protects the underwriter against any uncovered expenses in the event the offer is withdrawn either during the due diligence and registration stage or during the marketing stage. The letter of intent contains a clause requiring a company to reimburse the underwriter for any out-of-pocket expenses incurred during the process, either during the due diligence and registration stage, or during the marketing stage. Another element of the letter of intent is the gross spread or the underwriting discount. The letter of intent also includes a commitment by the underwriter to enter into a firm commitment agreement with the issuer firm to cooperate in the due diligence process and a commitment by the company to grant a 15% overallotment option to the underwriter. There is no guarantee of the final offering price in a letter of intent. The registration and marketing process takes several months and it would be impossible for underwriters to include certain information such as final IPO prices as price discounts to dealers would be in the initial filing stages with the SEC.

Universal banks are permitted to perform both commercial and investment banking functions in Europe. However, in the United States, the Glass-Steagall Act separated commercial and investment banking functions from the 1930s to the 1990s. The ban on underwriting securities was first relaxed for debt securities and later on for equity securities. In 1999, the Glass-Steagall Act was repealed except for deposit insurance schemes.

7.1.3.6 Debt instruments underwriting

The debt capital markets services division of investment banks solicits structures and executes investment-grade debt and related products, including new issues of public and private debt.

The underwriter helps government entities bring bond issues to market. The underwriter buys the bonds from the issuer and resells them to investors. The difference between the purchase price paid by the underwriter to the issuer and the price at which the bonds are resold to investors represents the underwriter's profit or discount. The underwriter's discount depends on factors such as the interest rate and accurate pricing of the bonds. The profit made by the underwriter depends on the market movement of interest rates. Municipal bond underwriting is one of the functions performed by investment banks. In January 1989, JPMorgan Securities underwrote the first public corporate bond issue by a commercial banking organization since the Glass-Steagall Act.

Competitive bidding and negotiated sales are two common ways by which governments issue debt through bonds. Underwriters are involved in both types of processes to determine the price of a new issue. Bonds are also sold through private placements. In private placements, issuers may sell bonds to investors directly or through a placement agent.

Also in bond underwriting, a syndicate of underwriters can be formed comprising a lead manager and comanagers. The syndicate determines the pricing and distribution of the issue. The lead manager is responsible for coordinating the deal. For competitive as well as negotiated deals, there are requirements related to advertising the sale of bonds and circulation of disclosure document.

7.1.3.6.1 Process of competitive sales

In the process of competitive sales, underwriters submit a sealed bid for purchasing the bonds to the issuer at a specific time on a specified date. The bidder who offers the lowest interest cost based on the time value of money to the issuer will be awarded the bid. The syndicate of underwriters purchases the bonds and resells them to retail investors. Once the issuer has structured the offering and completed the relevant legal and financial aspects, an official note of sale structured as the advertising document is published. The notice of sale is sent out to potential bidders. The notice of sale includes information on amount of debt or bonds being issued, the structure of deal, type of bonds, and bidding specifications.

7.1.3.6.2 Process of negotiated sales

In a negotiated sale, the underwriter is selected by the issuer prior to the public sale date. The issuer may also select comanagers from competing firms to work as a part of the syndicate. The first step in a negotiated sale is the request for proposal (RFP), which is sent to selected underwriters. The RFP solicits information on the firm's experience with underwriting the type of issue, management fees and estimated expenses, and initial ideas about the structure of the deal. The selected underwriter has the exclusive right to purchase the bonds at an agreed price. The manager sets a preliminary pricing schedule, which is later revised.

7.1.3.6.3 Private placements

Private placements are also known as direct purchases. These are direct transactions between the issuer and investors without an underwriter. Here the placement agents act as intermediaries between the issuer and investors.

7.1.4 INVESTMENT BANK PARTICIPATION IN FINANCIAL MARKETS

Investment banks have active participation in the money, bond, mortgage stock, and derivatives markets. Many investment banks through money market mutual funds invest in money market securities. Investment banks also underwrite commercial papers. Investment banks actively participate in the bond market through underwriting bond issues in the primary market and provide advisory services for clients for bond purchases and sales. Investment banks also play a role in the bond market by facilitating the raising of funds for corporate restructuring activities such as mergers and acquisitions, leveraged buyouts, and other activities. Investment or securities firms also play a role in the mortgage market by underwriting securities that are backed by mortgages for various financial institutions. In stock markets, the investment banks play the major roles of underwriters in the primary market, advisors and brokers in the secondary market. In derivatives markets of futures, options and swaps, investment banks act as financial intermediaries or brokers.

Commercial banks and thrift institutions are major competitors for investment banks in providing brokerage and merger advisory services. Some investment banks own mutual funds. Mutual funds also depend on securities firms such as investment banks for advisory services related to the execution of stock trades. Investment banks provides advisory services to insurance companies for executing securities transactions and hedging risks. Pension funds also receive advisory services from investment banks with respect to securities transactions related to buying and selling securities. Pension funds and insurance funds invest in new issues, which are underwritten by securities firms.

7.1.5 REGULATION OF SECURITIES INDUSTRY

The regulation of the securities industry vests with the Securities and Exchange Commission. The SEC sets the rules governing securities firms' underwriting and trading activities. The SEC supervises stock exchanges for the prevention of unfair or illegal practices to ensure orderly trading. The Securities Investor Protection Corporation (SIPC) offers insurance on cash and securities deposited at brokerage firms. The SPIC acts as a trustee to recover funds and enables customers of failed brokerages to receive all nonnegotiable securities that are registered in their names. Funds from the SIPC are available to satisfy the remaining claims of each customer up to a maximum of $500,000. The SEC enacted the Regulation Fair Disclosure (FD) in the year 2000, which requires all firms to disclose any significant information related to market participants. The SEC rule on shelf registration allows large corporations to register their new issues with the SEC up to 2 years in advance.

7.1.6 **RISK IN INVESTMENT BANKING**

The major risks faced by investment banks are market, credit, operational, legal, and reputation risks. Market risk is the loss incurred as the result of fluctuations in exchange rates and interest rates. Investment banks' exposure to exchange rate risk arises when translating assets and liabilities denominated in foreign currencies into the home currency as a result of consolidation.

Interest rate risk affects investment banks as the market value of the bonds held as investments will increase when interest rates decline and vice versa. Investment banks that facilitate bridge loans to corporations face credit risk. Securities firms are subject to market risks as their services offered are related to the stock market environment. In a bull market, a higher volume of trading activity would prove beneficial to these investment banks. The mutual funds subsidiaries of investment banks benefit from a bullish market. When the stock market is bearish, the business activity of investment banks is reduced. Table 7.1 lists the largest global investment banks.

7.1.7 **CHALLENGES FOR INVESTMENT BANKS**

Demographic challenges of an aging population and life-saving cycles have an impact on the growth of investment banking, particularly in terms of asset management. Emerging markets provide immense opportunities for growth in investment banking. Investment banking faces huge operational and risk challenges in the context of emerging technology commoditization.

Resource constraints are leading to rising input costs for businesses and banking activity universally.

The post-economic crisis wave of regulation presents a major compliance challenge for all investment banks. In the context of regulations, investment banks face the challenges of robust risk management. In the changed scenario proprietary trading operations are limited by regulators and successful client franchises emerges as a critical factor for sustainability of investment banks. In the context of crisis, regulatory shifts are observed and regulatory practices are being strengthened as evident from new regulations such as the Dodd-Frank Act, Basel III, and Capital Requirements Directives 2 and 3, along with OTC derivatives clearing regulations. There is increased focus on strategic risk management and establishment of control frameworks. The Dodd-Frank Wall Street Reform and Consumer Protection Act 2010 introduced an extensive set of new regulations to reduce counterparty risk and increase transparency.

Table 7.1	Largest Investment Banks
SL	**Company**
1	JPMorgan
2	Bank of America/Merrill Lynch
3	Goldman Sachs
4	Morgan Stanley
5	Credit Suisse
6	Deutsche Bank
7	Citi
8	Barclays Capital
9	UBS
10	BNP Paribas

The OTC derivatives market, which accounted for almost 90% of the global $605 trillion derivatives market, was viewed as the catalyst of the financial crisis. The new derivatives regulations intend to clear OTC derivatives through central counter parties (CCPs). This action is supposed to bring transparency to the OTC markets.

The process of commoditization following electronification led to massive volume growth of over 400% during the 10-year period of 2000-2010. In this context, investment banks face challenges of developing clearing capabilities or outsourcing this service to third-party providers. Investment banks face the challenges of developing a client offering that protects existing revenue bases while at the same time capitalizing on new market opportunities. Securing connectivity to marketwide tools along with automation in core trade processing will emerge as a key requirement for investment banks.

Investment banks face the challenge of regaining their focus on client relationships. Before the economic crisis, investment banks had moved away from their traditional roles as financial intermediaries to focus on development of complex products, thereby increasing risk through proprietary trading activity. The majority of investment banks have neglected client service-based investments. Investment banks also face the challenge of meeting the varied needs of different client segments. There is a growing demand for integrated service offerings across products and channels covering different regions due to the proliferation of electronic trading platforms, the rise in multi-asset trading, and the growth of emerging markets. Harnessing innovative technologies also remains a challenge for investment banks.

7.1.8 GLOBAL INVESTMENT BANKING STATISTICS

According to a Data Monitor report, the global investment banking and brokerage sector grew by 9% in 2010 to reach a value of $72.3 billion. Mergers and acquisitions is the largest segment of the global investment banking and brokerage sector, accounting for 42.2% of global investment banking in 2010. The Americas account for 49.2% of the global investment banking and brokerage sector value.[1]

The global investment banking and brokerage sector declined by 11.7% in 2011, to reach a value of $63.9 billion, representing a compound annual rate of change (CARC) of −6.7% for the period spanning 2007-2011. In 2011 the mergers and acquisitions advisory segment was the investment sector's most lucrative sector with total revenues of $31.1 billion, equivalent to 48.7% of the sector's overall value. The investment banking sector is expected to have a compound annual growth rate of 6% during the period 2011-2016, with a value amounting to $85.6 billion by the end of 2016.[2]

According to a McKinsey & Company report, due to declining returns, 13 of the largest investment banks announced plans to cut US$15 billion in expenses, including compensation, and US $1.03 trillion in risk-weighted assets. Merger activity in the US consumer industry steeply rose to $93 billion of announced deals in 2012 compared to $28.5 billion in the year 2011. Centreview Partners and Goldman Sachs emerged as the top financial advisers for US consumer mergers and acquisitions deals with a value of $52.17 billion and $51.50 billion. The former made five deals and the latter made 17 deals during 2012.[3] JPMorgan remains the leading investment bank in the world.

---

[1] Global Investment banking & brokerage, DATA MONITOR, Reference Code: 0199-2308, April 2011.
[2] http://www.businesswire.com/news/home/20120628005980/en/Research-Markets-Global-Investment-Banking-Brokerage-Sector
[3] Investment Banking: Size Matters. But What Is the Right Size, 14 March 2013. http://tabbforum.com/opinions/investment-banking-size-matters-but-what-is-the-right-size.

7.1.8.1 Emerging markets

According to a McKinsey report,[4] the post-economic crisis outlook for investment banking services is bright in emerging Asia and Europe, the Middle East, and Latin America. China, India, and UAE also have increasing demands for sophisticated investment banking services. Global banks dominate most ASEAN corporate and investment-banking markets. Table 7.2 gives the statistics on mergers and acquisition fees earned by investment banks during 2013.

7.1.9 ROLE OF INVESTMENT BANKS IN THE GLOBAL ECONOMIC CRISIS

The strategic changes in the nature of investment banks have often been cited as a reason for the economic crisis that crippled the global economy. The transition from fee-generating activities into highly leveraged investment activities increased the risk profile of investment banks. Investment banks made huge investments in highly complicated mortgaged-backed securities and credit default swaps. At the same time these investment banks were highly leveraged. In times of economic boom, this high risk-taking strategy helped senior managers earn huge bonuses. But as the asset value declined, this new scenario led to the collapse of many investment banks. Many investment banks also failed on the asset liability management front. Banks such as Lehman Brothers were financing their long-term investments in risky assets through short-term commercial papers. When the risk-prone assets failed, Lehman Brothers defaulted on its commercial paper obligations. Many commercial banks were also affected by the crisis as these investment banks were the subsidiaries of bank holding companies. The crisis led to consolidation and restructuring in the financial industry; for example, the acquisition of Bear Stearns by JPMorgan, the sell-off of Lehman Brothers, and the acquisition of Merrill Lynch by Bank of America. Goldman Sachs restructured to become a bank in order to receive Troubled Asset Relief Program (TARP) funds. Investment banks have undergone paradigm shifts on account of unprecedented global credit and solvency crises. Two of the five leading investment banks have collapsed.

Table 7.2	Mergers & Acquisitions Fees in 2013	
	Banks	**Fees in Millions of US Dollars (Imputed)**
1	Goldman Sachs	1659.58
2	JPMorgan	1294.66
3	Morgan Stanley	1235.80
4	Bank of America/Merrill Lynch	1041.96
5	Citi	836.61
6	Barclays	778.48
7	Credit Suisse	750.41
8	Lazard	720.95
9	Deutsche Bank	586.25
10	Rothschild	557.32

Source: Thomson Reuters/Freeman Consulting.

---

[4]Markus Buhume, Dianele Chiarella, Matthieu Lemerle. Mckinsey Report Corporate and Investment Banking, Number 7 September 2008.

Many universal banks have had to scale down their capital market businesses. Worldwide, Asian banks are better off than their Western counterparts.

Looking ahead, investment banks will have to continue to face the challenges and constraints of increased regulations. In light of stricter regulations, higher capital costs, and reduced leverage, investment banks must reorient their strategies with respect to their business mix, their target client focus, their capital allocation, their operating model, and their financial structure.

7.2 FINANCE COMPANIES

Finance companies are specialized financial institutions that make loans to individuals and corporations for the purchase of consumer goods and services. Finance companies do not accept deposit accounts. The sources of funds are short-term and long-term debt, such as commercial paper and bonds to finance the loans. Finance companies are less regulated than commercial banks as they don't rely on deposits as sources of funds. Finance companies generally charge higher interest rates than do depository institutions such as savings banks and credit unions. Loans approved by finance companies are secured by collateral. Finance companies are far less regulated than banks and thrifts. Because finance companies don't take deposits from the public, no government deposit insurance is involved. The only exception is when the finance company acts as a bank holding company or is a subsidiary of a bank holding company. Regulation Z—the "truth in lending" regulation—stipulates that banks and finance companies have to disclose the annual percentage rate charged on loans in correct terms. Finance companies must also disclose the total interest cost of credit over the life of the loan. The level of interest rates that finance companies can charge is limited by usury statutes.

In the United States, finance companies have become America's second largest source of business credit behind banking institutions.

7.2.1 TYPES OF FINANCE COMPANIES

The major types of finance companies are consumer or personal finance companies, business or commercial finance companies, sales finance companies, and captive finance companies.

7.2.1.1 Consumer finance companies

Consumer finance companies are also known as small loan or direct loan companies. The primary business of consumer finance companies is to provide credit to consumers. Consumer finance companies' core business includes secured and unsecured personal loans, home equity loans, and sales financing. Consumer finance companies also focus on retail credit cards. Large retailers operate their own credit card programs either in-house or through finance subsidiaries. Smaller retailers usually contract with a finance company. Examples of consumer finance companies include Household Finance Company, Person Finance Company (owned by Citicorp), E*Trade, the Motley Fool, and Intuit.

7.2.1.2 Commercial finance companies

Commercial finance companies or credit companies provide loans to manufacturers and wholesalers. These loans are secured by accounts receivables, inventories, and equipment. Commercial finance companies provide a variety of loans, including factoring, working capital loans, equipment financing and leasing, specialized equity investments, and collateral-based financing. Factoring is a very common practice in the apparel industry. Commercial finance companies offer services in leasing equipment such as railroad cars, planes, and computers.

Banks usually require a 7-year repayment schedule on term loans and 15-year schedules for loans on commercial property. But finance companies' payment schedules range from 10 years for term loans and up to 25 years for loans on commercial real estate. Examples of commercial finance companies include the Money Store and AT&T Small Business Lending Group.

7.2.1.3 Sales finance companies

Sales finance companies, also known as acceptance companies, purchase retail and wholesale papers from consumer and capital goods dealers. Sales finance companies engage primarily in buying installment credit contracts, which are secured by automobiles or other consumer goods from retailers. A sales finance company engages in the business of purchasing retail installment contracts, obligations, or credit agreements made between other parties. They can purchase installment contracts from dealers or finance retail sales at a discount. Finance companies work with merchants who sell goods rather than with consumers. The retail installments of receivables consist of automobile sales, industrial equipment, farm equipment, household appliances, and other durable goods sold on installment payable plans. Sales finance companies also finance inventories of dealers who sell them their consumer credit contracts. Sales finance companies can provide funds to retailers and provide factoring services.

7.2.1.4 Captive finance companies

A captive finance company is a subsidiary of a manufacturer established to support sales through granting loans to dealers to finance stocks or grant loans to consumers. A credit card company that provides store charge cards can be considered a captive finance company. Department stores also often offer store cards to their customers. For example, Sears Roebuck Acceptance Corporation finances consumer purchases at Sears's stores. The three major captive finance companies in the auto sector are General Motors Acceptance Corporation (GMAC) now known as Ally Financial, Chrysler Financial, and Ford Motor Credit Company. They are all the subsidiaries of the three major car manufacturers. Captive finance companies focus on creating attractive financial products to stimulate the sales of new and used automobiles.

7.2.2 ASSETS AND LIABILITIES OF FINANCE COMPANIES

The main assets of finance companies are loan portfolios, which include consumer, business, and real estate loans. Given that finance companies don't accept deposits, the major sources (liabilities) of funds are commercial papers, money market instruments, and bank loans. Captive finance companies raise funds directly from the parent company.

The primary source of income for finance companies is the interest income from its loan portfolio and income from loan origination fees. Credit insurance is also a source of income for captive finance companies.

7.2.3 RISK OF FINANCE COMPANIES

Finance companies face credit risks when customers default on their loans. The probability of default increases as consumer finance companies lend to borrowers who couldn't get credit from other sources. The delinquency rates of finance companies are higher than they are for banks or thrifts. Finance

Table 7.3　Financial Highlights: Assets of Finance Companies (Billions of US Dollars)

Assets	2008	2009	2010	2011	2012
Consumer loans	836.6	702.1	827.7	817.1	833.6
Real estate loans	502	447.9	317.8	276.6	180.1
Business loans	573.3	463.6	407.7	410.0	421.8
Total	1911.9	1613.6	1553.1	1503.8	1435.6

Source: Federal Reserve Statistical Release, May 2013.

Table 7.4　Financial Highlights: Liabilities of Finance Companies (Billions of US Dollars)

Liabilities	2008	2009	2010	2011	2012
Open market paper	123.5	100.9	62.1	111	121
Corporate bonds	974.1	924.5	837.5	1078.4	1039.8
Depository institutions	182	174.9	144.5	91.5	102.1
Miscellaneous liabilities	669.9	680.2	586.3	308.9	299.9
Total	1949.5	1880.5	1630.4	1589.8	1562.8

Source: Federal Reserve Statistical Release Z.1, Financial Accounts of US, June 6, 2013.

companies cushion off the higher probability of losses from bad loans by charging very high interest rates compared to those charged by banks. Finance companies are also subject to liquidity risks. Liquidity problems arise when customers withdraw their funds all at once. For small finance companies, the liquidity problem is greater because their assets, consisting of consumer and business loans, are not easily sold in the secondary financial markets. Finance companies face interest rate risk as their loan assets are not as interest rate sensitive as their liabilities (borrowings). Banks and thrifts face greater interest rate risk than finance companies do as they hold more long-term assets (loans). Table 7.3 provides the value of assets of US finance companies during the period 2008-2012.

In 2012, consumer loans accounted for 58% of the total loans issued by finance companies. At the same time business loans accounted for 29% of the total loans. During the 5-year period 2008-2012, the total loans of finance companies decreased by approximately 25%. Table 7.4 lists the liabilities of US finance companies during the period 2008-2012.

In 2012, corporate bonds accounted for approximately 67% of the total liabilities. Open market paper was the second-largest source of funds for finance companies.

7.3 SUMMARY

Investment banks offer services in equity capital markets, leveraged debt capital markets, commercial real estate, asset finance and leasing, and corporate lending services. The major functions of investment banks are raising funds, asset management, mergers and acquisitions advisory services, brokerage services, and market making. Investment banks help companies with sourcing funds by selling financial instruments in the capital market. These securities include common stocks, preferred stocks, and bonds. The asset management function of investment banks involves managing the funds of corporations and investing in stocks, fixed-income securities/bonds, derivatives investments, and other types of investments. Investment banks are actively involved in mergers and acquisitions by performing the functions of deal making. The finance divisions of investment banks are generally segregated into business area control, legal entity control, and group risk control. The role played by investment banks can be segregated as front-office, middle-office, and back-office activities. Securities underwriting is the process by which investment banks raise investment capital from investors in the form of equity and debt capital on behalf of companies and government authorities. Underwriters offer a set of services for IPOs or seasoned equity offerings. The methods used for IPO pricing are the fixed price method and book building process. The debt capital markets services divisions of investment banks solicit structures and execute investment-grade debt and related products, which include new issues of public and private debt. Investment banks actively participate in the money, bond, mortgage stock, and derivatives markets. The strategic changes in investment banks has often been cited as a reason for the economic crisis that crippled the global economy.

Finance companies are specialized financial institutions that make loans to individuals and corporations for the purchase of goods and services. The major types of finance companies are consumer finance, business or commercial finance, and sales finance companies.

QUESTIONS FOR DISCUSSION

1. What are the major functions of investment banks?
2. Explain equity underwriting and debt underwriting.
3. What is the book building process?
4. What are the main challenges in investment banking?
5. What are the different types of finance companies?

REFERENCES

Brigham, E.F., Ehrhardt, M.C., 2010. Initial public offerings, investment banking and financial restructuring. Investment Banks and the Global Economic Crisis Financial Management: Theory and Practice. 13th ed. (Chapter 20).

http://www.finextra.com/community/fullblog.aspx?blogid=559.

The 10 top challenges for investment banks 2011, Accenture Report.

http://campus.murraystate.edu/academic/faculty/lguin/FIN330/IB%20Functions.htm.

The Unofficial guide to investment banking. http://85.195.122.57/files/M225825_20080206_153755/pdf_en/DB_UGIB_Investmentbanking.pdf.

Ritter, J. Investment banking and securities issuance. http://bear.warrington.ufl.edu/ritter/publ_papers/investment%20banking%20and%20securities%20issuance.pdf.

Aggarwal, R., 2000. Stabilization activities by underwriters after initial public offerings. Journal of Finance 55, 1075–1103.

Loughran, T., Ritter, J.R., 2003. Why has IPO underpricing changed over time? Working Paper (University of Notre Dame; University of Florida).

http://www.servinghistory.com/topics/investment_banker:sub::Core_Investment_Banking_Activities.

http://www.antiquemr9.blogspot.com/2012/03/role-of-investment-banking.html.

http://financecareers.about.com/od/investmentbanker/a/underwriting.htm.

Roten, I.C., Mullineaux, D.J. Equity underwriting spreads at commercial bank holding companies and investment banks. http://www.uky.edu/~icrote2/Equity.pdf.

IPO Basics: Investment Bankers, Underwriters, and Other Key Players. http://www.inc.com/articles/1999/11/15746.html.

http://www.publicbonds.org/major_players/underbasics.htm.

Andresky Fraser, J., March 1997. Show Me the Money: You Can Look for Money in All the Wrong Places. Inc.

Sherman, A.J., 1997. The Complete Guide to Running and Growing Your Business. Times Books.

http://wps.aw.com/wps/media/objects/2095/2146070/CH26.pdf.

MUTUAL FUNDS, INSURANCE, AND PENSION FUNDS

8.1 MUTUAL FUNDS

8.1.1 INTRODUCTION

The vast majority of investment companies are mutual funds, both in terms of number of funds and assets under management (AUM). A mutual fund is a fund set up and operated by an investment management company that raises capital for investing in financial instruments. It is a professionally managed collective investment vehicle that collects money from investors and invests in traded financial securities. Mutual funds have become a typical investment for consumers and institutional investors. Mutual funds represent the second largest pool of private capital in the world after the banking industry. A mutual fund enables investors to make diversified investments across a large number of firms. In other words, a mutual fund allows investors to buy a portfolio of shares in small increments. They have relatively lower risks than individual stock purchases. Mutual funds are invested in almost every traded financial instrument. Institutional households and institutional investors such as pension funds hold accounts in mutual funds. Mutual funds have to be registered with the regulatory authority of the respective countries where they are located.

8.1.2 ORGANIZATION OF MUTUAL FUNDS

A mutual fund is organized as a corporation or business trust, which is also called a statutory trust. The fund's board plays a major role in the functioning of the mutual fund. The fund operations are supervised by officers and directors if the fund is in the form of a corporation and by trustees if the fund takes the form of a business trust.

Mutual funds are required to establish a written compliance program that highlights the detailed procedures and internal controls meant to ensure compliance with relevant laws and regulations governing the mutual funds industry. The compliance program is overseen by the chief compliance officer (CCO).

8.1.3 STAKEHOLDERS OF MUTUAL FUNDS

8.1.3.1 Shareholders

Shareholders have specific voting rights to elect directors and approve changes in the terms and conditions of the fund's contract with its investment adviser.

8.1.3.2 Board of directors

The board of directors or board of trustees is entrusted with the responsibility to hire the fund managers and other service providers for the fund. The board of directors has an active role in ensuring that the fund is managed in the best interests of the investors of the fund. The internal oversight mechanism is entrusted with the board of directors. External oversight is provided by the US Securities and Exchange Commission (SEC), the Financial Industry Regulatory Association (FINRA), and certified public accounting firms. The board of directors reviews and approves major contracts with service providers and approves policies and procedures that ensure the fund's compliance with the securities laws governing the financial services industry. The Investment Company Act of 1940 stipulates that at least 40% of the members of a fund board have to be independent members who don't have any significant business relationship with the mutual fund's adviser or underwriter.

8.1.3.3 Sponsors

The fund manager or the investment management company is also known as the fund sponsor or the fund management company. The main role of the fund manager is to trade the fund's investments based on the investment objectives of the fund. The fund manager is a registered investment advisor. The sponsors of the fund are entrusted with the responsibility of coordinating the arrangements for the launch of the fund. Sponsors facilitate selection of directors and people to manage and operate the fund. "Fund family" or "fund complex" refers to funds that are managed by the same fund manager. The major steps in initiating a mutual fund involve registration of the fund with the SEC as an investment company and registration of the fund shares for sale to the public in accordance with the Securities Act of 1933. The seed capital or initial investment minimum amount of $100,000 as stipulated by the Investment Company Act is usually contributed by the sponsor or adviser.

8.1.3.4 Advisers

The investment portfolios of mutual funds are managed by entities known as investment advisers, which are registered with the SEC. Investment advisers buy and sell securities in the fund's portfolio consistent with the fund's investment objectives and policies. Many advisors, in addition to managing the fund's portfolio, also provide various administrative back-office services.

8.1.3.5 Administrators

Administrators are responsible for handling administrative services such as back-office functions for a fund. Administrators provide office space, clerical help, and fund accounting services, bookkeeping, internal auditing, and clerical and fund accounting services for the fund. Fund administrators also maintain compliance procedures and internal controls under the supervision of the fund's board and CCO.

8.1.3.6 Underwriters

Underwriters are known as the fund's distributors through whom investors buy and redeem shares directly or indirectly. The principal underwriter enters into a contract with the mutual fund to purchase and resell fund shares to the public. Underwriters have to be registered as broker dealers with the SEC.

8.1.3.7 Transfer agents

Transfer agents maintain records of the mutual fund's shareholders' account and calculate and distribute dividends and capital gains. These agents prepare and mail statements for shareholder transactions and account balances. They also maintain customer service departments such as call centers.

8.1.4 **KEY FEATURES OF MUTUAL FUNDS**

A mutual fund is established by an investment company with a specific investment strategy and objectives. Objectives include short-term capital appreciation or long-term returns or focus for specific sectors such as an energy fund or specific financial instrument. Investment management companies typically manage several mutual funds to attract a wider customer base. These companies generate revenue from mutual funds by charging investors management fees, including purchase (front-end loaded) or redemption (back-end loaded) fees. Most institutional investors such as pension funds rely on advisors to identify investments. Mutual fund investors also rely on tracking services such as Morning Star and Lipper Analytical to rate funds based on historical performance.

8.1.5 **CLASSIFICATION OF MUTUAL FUNDS**

Based on the registration, mutual funds consist of open-ended, closed-ended, and unit investment trusts.

8.1.5.1 *Open-ended funds*

In open-ended funds, unit shares can be issued and redeemed at any time. An investor usually buys shares directly from the fund itself rather than from existing shareholders. An initial front-end load is charged on the purchase of shares or units. Most open-ended funds are actively managed. The net asset value (NAV) is calculated by dividing the fund's assets minus liabilities by the number of shares outstanding. It is calculated at the end of each trading day.

> NAV = Market value of fund/Number of shares
>
> Market value of funds[1] = (Number of shares * Current share price) + Interest and dividends received today − Expenses incurred today

8.1.5.2 *Closed-end funds*

Closed-end funds generally issue a fixed number of shares that are listed on the stock exchange or are traded in the OTC market. The market price of closed-end fund shares is determined by the supply and demand in the marketplace. Closed-end funds offer a fixed number of shares to investors during an initial public offering. These funds can also make subsequent public offerings of shares for raising additional capital. After the issue, the shares of a closed-end fund are not typically purchased or redeemed directly by the fund. Instead they are bought and sold by investors in the open market. A closed-end fund need not maintain cash reserves or sell securities to meet redemptions. Hence, closed-end funds have the flexibility to invest in less liquid portfolio securities. The price per share will be different from the NAV per share of the investments held by the fund. It could be at a discount or premium to the NAV. Closed-end funds can use leverage to enhance returns by raising additional investment capital by auction rate securities, long-term debt, and reverse repurchase agreements. At the same time the fund has limited flexibility to borrow against its assets. According to the ICI (Investment Company Institute) Fact Book of 2012, the total net assets of closed-end funds was $265 billion. Predominantly, the bond funds accounted for a large share of assets in closed-end funds. Bond funds with a value of $163 billion accounted for 62% of closed-end fund assets in 2012.

---

[1]Consider a mutual fund that has issued 100 million shares to its investors. It uses the proceeds to buy stocks of, say, 50 different companies. The total market value is the sum of the respective share prices multiplied by the number of shares invested in each company.

8.1.5.3 Unit investment trusts

Unit investment trusts (UITs) are exchange-traded mutual funds that offer an unmanaged portfolio of securities with a fixed life. The main types of UITs are stock (equity) trusts, which provide capital appreciation and/or dividend income, and bond (fixed-income) trusts, which provide regular income. UITs are hybrid in nature with characteristics of both open- and closed-end funds. As with closed-end funds, UITs issue only specific and fixed numbers of shares called units. As with open-end mutual funds, the units are redeemable. But the sponsor of the UIT maintains a secondary market in the units. UITs don't actively trade their investment portfolios. UIT investors generally buy and hold a set of particular investments until a stipulated period after which the trust is dissolved and the proceeds are paid off.

8.1.6 SOURCES OF REVENUE FOR INVESTORS IN A MUTUAL FUND

Mutual funds generate returns for investors in three ways. The income received from dividends or coupon payments are paid as dividends to shareholders. The capital gains that result from the sale of securities within the fund are also a source of revenue for investors. Shareholders receive returns when the mutual fund's share price increases. When the NAV of a fund increases, the shareholder gains by selling the mutual fund shares.

Dividend distributions are received from interest and dividends earned by the securities in a fund's portfolio and net short-term gains. Long-term capital gains are gains resulting from the sale of securities held in its portfolio for more than one year. The SEC requires mutual funds to disclose standardized information after tax returns for 1-, 5-, and 10-year periods. Investors who sell mutual fund shares usually incur capital gains or losses in the year the shares are sold.

8.1.7 MUTUAL FUND EXPENSES AND LOAD FEES

Mutual funds investors incur two types of expenses and fees: ongoing expenses and sales loads. The ongoing fund expenses cover portfolio management, fund administration, daily fund accounting and pricing, distribution charges (12b-1fees), and other costs of operating funds. The fund's expense ratio is the fund's annual operating expenses expressed as a percentage of fund assets. Investors pay these expenses indirectly as expenses are paid from the fund's assets. Sales loads are one-time fees that are paid directly by investors either at the time of share purchase (front-end loads) or when shares are redeemed (back-end load).The maximum limit on front-end loads is 8.5%, but, on average, mutual funds charge 5.75% or less. Mutual funds with front-end load fees usually offer breakpoint discounts to investors. These breakpoint discounts involve volume discounts in which the percentage load will be less if the investor invests more. Bank-end loads or rear loads range between 5% and 6% for the first year and then generally decline by a certain percentage each subsequent year. The 12b-1 fees are distribution fees charged by mutual funds on shareholders. In 1980, the SEC adopted Rule 12b-1 under the Investment Company Act of 1940 in which shareholders are permitted to provide compensation for financial professionals and intermediaries through asset-based fees. These fees, known as distribution fees, provide a means for investors to pay indirectly for services received from brokers, discount brokerage firms, and the like. The 12b-1 fees can also be used to pay for a fund's advertising and marketing expenses. Load classes serve investors who own fund shares purchased through financial professionals whereas no-load fund classes serve investors who purchased shares without the help of a financial professional or who prefer to compensate the financial professional separately.

Share classes for funds are sold through brokers. Class A shares usually charge a front-end sales load together with a small 12b-1 fee. Class B shares have a contingent deferred sales charge that gradually declines over a period of time along with 12b-1 fees. Class C shares have high 12b-1 fees and a small contingent deferred sales charge for 1 or 2 years. No-load funds have two classes of shares: Class I shares that do not charge a 12b-1 fee and Class N shares that charge a 12b-1 fee of no more than 0.25% of fund assets.

The ICI report states that expense ratios averaged 77 basis points for equity fund investors during 2012 compared to 99 basis points in 1990.

8.1.8 REGULATION OF MUTUAL FUNDS

The Securities Act of 1934 empowered the SEC with authority over the securities industry. The Investment Company Act of 1940 regulates mutual funds on disclosures and information about investment objectives, investment company structure, and operations. The regulations are related to transparency, liquidity, audited track records, and safety of mutual funds. Details of the mutual fund's holdings must be publicly available. Shares of mutual funds are redeemed by the fund company, which assures liquidity for investors. Mutual funds are bound by regulations to publish audited financial reports. For safety purposes it has to be ensured that fund shareholders receive an amount of cash that equals their portion of ownership in the fund. Mutual funds are expected to disclose information on performance in comparison to a broad market index and details of portfolio managers in the prospectus. The prospectus must contain information on the minimum amount of investment required, the objectives of the mutual fund, the various types of risk for mutual funds, and the returns on the fund for the past 1, 3, and 5 years. The Insider Trading and Securities Fraud Enforcement Act of 1988 stipulates that mutual funds develop systems and procedures to prevent insider trading. The Market Reform Act introduced in 1990 permitted the SEC to introduce circuit breakers to halt program trading during periods of extreme volatility. The National Securities Markets Improvement Act 1996 was aimed at promoting more efficient management of mutual funds, protecting investors, and providing more effective and less burdensome regulation. If a mutual fund distributes at least 90% of its taxable income to shareholders the fund is exempt from taxes on dividends, interest, and capital gains. In 2010, the SEC reformed Rule 2a-7, which deals with the regulation of money market funds. The new rules require money market funds to hold significant liquidity and have stricter maturity limits.

The Investment Company Act of 1940 prohibits complex capital structures and limits funds' use of leverage. The Investment Company Act imposes limits on the issuance of senior securities and borrowing. Mutual funds and exchange-traded funds (ETFs) are permitted to borrow if the fund has at least 300% asset coverage. In other words, the fund's total net assets are at least three times the total aggregate borrowings. According to the Investment Company Act of 1940, closed-end funds are permitted to use debt and preferred stock with conditions that include asset coverage requirements of 300% for debt and 200% for preferred stock.

The Investment Company Act stipulates strict custody of fund assets. Funds usually use domestic banks and international banks serve as custodians for domestic securities and international securities. The major custodian services include safekeeping and maintaining accounts for a fund's assets, settling securities transactions, receipts of dividends, providing foreign exchange services, and paying funding expenses. The Investment Company Act also prohibits direct transactions between funds and affiliates.

8.1.9 CATEGORIES OF MUTUAL FUNDS

Mutual funds are classified by their principal investments. The four main categories of funds are stock or equity funds, bond or fixed-income funds, money market funds, and hybrid funds.

8.1.9.1 Stock funds

Stock funds are characterized by style in terms of market capitalization. Large-cap stock funds invest in shares of companies with large market capitalization, generally greater than $11 billion. Mid-cap stock funds invest in stocks of corporations of mid-size capitalization, generally between $2.5 billion and $11 billion. Small-cap stock funds invest in stocks of corporations of small-size capitalization of generally between $750 million and $2.5 billion.

On the basis of objectives, stock funds are categorized as growth stock and value funds. Growth stock funds invest in growth stocks that have higher growth rates in earnings compared to the industry average. Value stock funds invest in value stocks whose intrinsic value is more than the market value and are considered undervalued. Capital appreciation funds consist of stocks that have the potential for abnormal growth.

A sector fund is one that invests in one particular industrial sector. An equity income fund focuses on current income over growth. These funds invest in stocks of companies that pay regular dividends. Option income funds invest in securities on which options may be written and earn premium income from writing options.

International and global stock mutual funds invest primarily in stocks of companies located in different countries around the world. These types of mutual funds are an essential part of a diversified portfolio. There are also region-specific mutual funds, including Europe-, Asia Pacific- or Latin America-based stock mutual funds. Another category of mutual fund is an emerging markets fund that focuses on stocks issued by companies based in emerging markets. Specialty funds focus on a group of companies from a specific sector such as energy, pharmaceuticals, and high technology. Index mutual funds are designed to replicate the performance of an existing stock index.

8.1.9.2 Bond funds

The different bond funds consist of government bond funds that invest in various types of US Treasury bonds, municipal bond funds that invest in different types of municipal bonds, and corporate bond funds that invest in various bonds issued by corporations. Bond funds are also categorized into long-term and short-term bond funds. Investment-grade corporate bonds are issued by high net-worth corporations to raise capital. These bonds are typically rated BBB and above by S&P or Baa and above by Moody's. Investment-grade corporate bond mutual funds allow investors to gain access to a diversified group of corporate bonds. High-yield bond mutual funds invest in junk bonds. Treasury inflation-protected securities (TIPS) bond mutual funds invest in TIPS bonds that are issued by the US Treasury and pay a coupon based on an inflation-adjusted principal of the bond. International bond mutual funds invest in bonds issued by foreign companies. Income funds are also a part of bond funds. Income funds consists of corporate, Treasury, and bonds backed by government agencies such as the Government National Mortgage Association (GNMA or Ginnie Mae). According to the ICI Fact Book for 2013, the assets of bond mutual funds amounted to $304 billion.

8.1.9.3 Money market funds

A money market fund is an open-ended fund that invests in short-term fixed-income securities such as US Treasury bills and commercial papers. Money market funds seek to limit exposure to losses from credit, market, and liquidity risks. Money market funds aim to maintain a stable value of $1 per share. In 2011, according to the ICI Fact Book, there were 632 money market funds in operation with total assets of nearly US $2.7 trillion. Money market funds consist of institutional money funds and retail money funds. Institutional money funds are marketed to corporations and government bodies. These funds are characterized by high minimum investment and low-expense share classes. The largest institutional money market fund is the JPMorgan Prime Money Market Fund with over $100 billion in assets. Retail money funds are offered to individuals and exist in the form of government-only funds, nongovernment funds, and tax-free funds. The largest money market mutual fund is Fidelity Investments Cash Reserves with assets exceeding US $110 billion. Safety and liquidity are the most important advantages of the money market funds.

Ultrashort bond funds are mutual funds, similar to money market funds, that invest in bonds with extremely short maturities. Money market funds consist of retail money market funds and institutional money market funds. Institutional money market funds are used by businesses, pension funds, state and local governments, and large account investors.

8.1.9.4 Hybrid funds

Hybrid funds invest in both bonds and stocks or in convertible securities. Balanced funds invest in stocks for capital appreciation and bonds for income. Asset allocation funds split investments between growth stocks, income stocks/bonds, and money market instruments or cash for stability. Funds of funds are mutual funds that primarily hold and invest in shares of other mutual funds. Hybrid funds are the most popular funds of funds. In 2012, the number of funds of funds was 1156 with asset value of $1.3 trillion.

8.1.9.5 Active/index funds

Active funds are run by fund managers and analysts who attempt to beat the market by choosing investments that can earn returns higher than the market index. Fidelity Magellan Fund is an example of this type of fund.

Index funds invest in securities that track a market index such as the S&P 500. These funds invest in the same securities in the same proportion. According to an ICI report from 2013, 373 index funds managed total net assets of $1.3 trillion.

8.1.10 OTHER TYPES OF FUNDS

There are a variety of other types of investments funds, including ETFs, venture capital funds, private equity funds, hedge funds, and real estate investment trusts.

8.1.10.1 Exchange-traded funds

An ETF is an investment company whose shares are traded intraday on stock exchanges at market-determined prices. As in the case of a listed company, investors can buy or sell ETF shares through a broker or in a brokerage account. Most ETFs are structured as open-ended investment companies or UITs. Other types of ETFs invest in commodities, currencies, and futures. There are also indexed-based ETFs that track the performance of specific indexes. Actively managed ETFs create a mix of investments according to investor objectives. According to the ICI Fact Book, in 2012 the total number of index-based and actively managed ETFs in the United States was 1194 with net assets of approximately $1.3 trillion.

The sponsor of the ETF chooses the investment objective. For an index-based ETF, the sponsor chooses both the index and the method of tracking its target index. The target index is tracked through either replication or representative sampling. In replication, the index-based ETF invests in all assets in the index proportionate to their respective weights in the index. In the representative sampling method, the ETF chooses a representative sample of securities in the target index. An active ETF trades its portfolio securities regularly. ETFs are required to publish information about their portfolio holdings daily. Each business day, the ETF publishes a "creation basket" that contains details about the securities such as their names and quantities of securities. ETF shares are created when the authorized participant (e.g., large institutional investor such as a market maker or broker dealer) deposits the daily creation basket or cash with the ETF. A typical creation unit contains large blocks of shares in the range of 25,000-200,000 shares. The authorized participant may be charged a transaction fee to offset any transaction expenses of the fund. The creation unit is liquidated when the authorized participant returns the specified number of shares in the creation unit to the ETF. In exchange, the authorized participant receives the daily "redemption basket," a set of specific securities and other assets within the ETF portfolio, which is basically the mirror image of the creation basket.

As with a mutual fund, ETF funds have to conform to investor protection mechanisms that include daily valuations and liquidity requirements, limitations on leverage, and disclosure requirements.

With regard to differences between ETFs and mutual funds, the retail investor can buy and sell ETF shares on a stock exchange through a broker dealer, as would be done for any other type of stock. Mutual fund shares are not listed on stock exchanges, and retail investors buy and sell mutual fund shares through various distribution channels including financial advisers, broker-dealers, or directly through a fund company. Differences also exist with respect to pricing. In the case of mutual funds, investors who place orders to buy or sell shares throughout the day have the same price as the closing NAV of the day. But the price of an ETF share is continuously determined on a stock exchange. In 2011, assets in ETFs amounted to $118 billion, which accounted for about 8% of the total net assets managed by investment companies.

The first ETF was introduced in 1993 as a broad-based domestic equity fund tracking the S&P 500 index. Primarily the price of an ETF is influenced by supply and demand. The portfolio transparency and the ability of authorized participants to create or redeem ETF shares ensure that the price of an ETF share is approximately equal to its underlying value. Investors usually buy ETF shares and/or sell the underlying securities when the ETF is trading at a discount. An increase in demand for the ETF should raise its share price and lower the price of the underlying securities due to selling the underlying securities. If the ETF is trading at a premium to its underlying securities, then the ETF shares are sold and the underlying securities bought. As a result, the ETF share price decreases and the price of the underlying securities bought rise. In 2012, large-cap domestic equity ETFs accounted for the largest proportion of ETF assets, amounting to $293 billion.

8.1.10.2 Venture capital funds

Venture capital funds are pooled investments that manage money from investment banks or wealthy investors to invest in start-up, small, and medium-size enterprises that are characterized as high-risk/high-return opportunities. Many technology firms such as Apple, Microsoft, and Oracle were supported initially by venture capital funds. The mushrooming of dot-com companies was attributed to the growth of venture capital. A vulture capitalist fund is a type of fund that focuses on buying distressed firms at very low prices. This usually happens when the firm files for bankruptcy.

Under Rule 203(I)-1(a) of the SEC, a venture capital fund has to meet five criteria to qualify as a venture capital fund: (1) The fund has to be a private fund; (2) the fund must hold itself out to investors and potential investors as pursuing a venture capital strategy; (3) no more than 20% of the fund's assets may be invested in assets other than qualifying investments or short-term holdings; (4) a fund cannot borrow, issue debt obligations, provide guarantees, or otherwise incur leverage in excess of 15% of its aggregate capital contributions and uncalled committed capital; and (5) the fund must only issue securities that do not provide investors with any right (except in extraordinary circumstances) to withdraw, redeem, or require the repurchase of such securities.

Venture capital is basically the second or third stage of a traditional start-up financing sequence. In the first stage, the entrepreneur invests his or her own funds called seed capital. Then an angel investor brings in additional funds for first stage existence and expansion. Venture capital funds are then utilized to establish the firm. These venture capital firms obtain their investment funds from wealthy individuals, investment banks, endowments, pension funds, insurance companies, and other financial institutions. The fundraising involves circulating a prospectus to potential investors. The first round and second round of venture capital funding involves substantial cash investments and managerial assistance. Venture capital fund managers receive annual management fees (usually 2% of invested capital) and a part of the fund's net profit. Venture capitalist funds select companies to invest in after an extensive due-diligence process. Firms are selected based on criteria in which opportunities exist for venture capital funds to grow their investments rapidly and to exit within a designated time frame. The exit process, known as the harvest strategy, takes place within 3-10 years, usually through an initial public offering (IPO) or merger or sale of the company.

Major venture capital firms include Intel Capital, Felicis Ventures 3i, Accel Partners, Sequoia Capital, First Round Capital, and SV Angel.

8.1.10.3 Private equity funds

Private equity funds are investment vehicles established by sponsors (investment managers) in order to raise funds to make multiple investments in a specified industry sector or geographic region. Private funds are passive investments in which investors make a commitment to invest a set amount of capital over time and entrusting the fund's sponsor to source, acquire, manage, and divest the fund's investments. The key economic incentives for sponsors are management fees and profit share on the fund's investments. The key economic incentive for investors is the expected returns on the invested capital through access to a portfolio of investments sourced and managed by an investment team that specializes in specific sectors or geographic areas. Private equity funds are structured as closed-end investment vehicles.

Private equity funds have long lives. The term of a fund begins following the first fund closing and typically runs for 10-12 years.

8.1.10.4 Hedge funds

A hedge fund is an alternative investment vehicle that is a pool of underlying securities. An unregulated hedge fund can invest in a wider range of securities than can mutual funds. In addition to traditional securities such as stocks, bonds, commodities, and real estate, these funds invest in sophisticated and risky investments. Hedge funds use long positions and short positions as the investment strategy. Hedge funds also invest in options and futures. Hedge funds are typically not as liquid as mutual funds. Unlike mutual funds, hedge funds generate returns over a specific period of time called the lockup period during which investors cannot sell their shares. Mutual fund managers are paid fees regardless of their funds' performance. Hedge fund managers receive a percentage of the returns they earn for investors. Popular hedge fund investment strategies include convertible arbitrage, options strategy, and macro.

8.1.10.5 Real estate investment trusts

A real estate investment trust (REIT) is a corporation that owns and manages a portfolio of real estate properties and mortgages on behalf of shareholders. Investors can buy shares in a publicly traded REIT. An investment in REIT provides liquidity and diversity for investors as the investment is in a portfolio of properties and the shares can be easily sold.

REITs are required to distribute at least 90% of their taxable income to investors. REITs have to gain pass-through entity status in order to qualify as an REIT. A pass-through entity status enables the REIT to pass the responsibility of paying taxes onto its shareholders. REITs are managed by a board of directors or trustees. An REIT must hold at least 75% of total investment assets in real estate. REITs are also required to pass the 95% income test in which it is stipulated that at least 95% of an REIT's gross income must come from financial investments such as rents, dividends, and capital gains. REITs are basically classified in equity, mortgage, and hybrid categories. Equity REITs own and manage real estate properties, such as office buildings, malls, and apartments. These REITs earn dividends from rental income as well as capital gains from the sale of properties. Unlike equity REITs, which invest in properties, mortgage REITs (known as MREITs) provide loans for mortgages to real estate owners or purchase mortgages or mortgage-backed securities. The main source of revenue for MREITs is the interest earned on mortgage loans. REITs are also classified into closed-end and open-ended REITs. Open-ended REITs can issue new shares and redeem shares at any time. Closed-end funds can issue shares to the public only once.

REITs can also be classified as private REITs, publicly traded REITs, and non-exchange-traded REITs. Private REITs are not registered or traded with the SEC and are subject to less regulation.

Publicly traded REITs collect funds via an IPO from investors. Investors own a portion of a managed pool of real estate. The income generated through renting, leasing, or selling the properties is distributed directly to REIT investors. The dividends are also distributed to investors.

8.1.11 MUTUAL FUND INDUSTRY TRENDS

According to the 2012 ICI Fact Book, the value of the global mutual fund industry is estimated to be $23.8 trillion. The US mutual fund market with $11.6 trillion in assets is the largest mutual fund market in the world. In year-end 2011, the United States accounted for 49% of the global mutual fund industry, whereas Europe, Asia and Africa, Asia/Pacific region, and the other Americas constituted 30%, 13%, and 8%, respectively, of the global market share. In the United States, segregation on the basis of funds reveals that domestic equity funds and world equity funds constituted 33% and 12% of mutual fund assets, whereas bond funds, money market funds, and hybrid funds constituted 25%, 23%, and 7%, respectively, of mutual fund assets in the US market. In 2011, approximately 650 sponsors managed mutual fund assets in the United States.

According to the ICI Fact Book of 2012, worldwide assets invested in mutual funds amounted to $26.8 trillion. US investment companies accounted for 28% of each of the shares of US corporate equities and municipal securities. At the same time, US investment companies' share of the commercial papers market is 42%. Investment companies are the largest investors in the US commercial paper market. The number of individuals owning mutual funds in the United States is 92.4 million.[2] The total number of US investment companies in 2012 was 16,380, out of which 8752 were mutual funds and

---

[2]2013 ICI Fact Book, Investment Company Institute.

5787 were UITs. The US mutual industry with $13 trillion in assets is the largest in the world, which accounted for 49% of mutual fund assets worldwide. More than 700 sponsors managed mutual fund assets in 2012. Table 8.1 highlights the value of assets of different types of US funds as of the year 2013.

In 2012, US mutual funds' assets were approximately $13 trillion. Overall, mutual funds reported $196 billion of net inflows in 2012. Households are the largest group of investors in funds and registered investment companies and constituted approximately 23% of households' financial assets in 2012. Table 8.2 gives the total value of net assets of investment companies on the basis of types during 1995-2012.

Table 8.1   Highlights of Different Types of Funds

Funds	US Dollars (Value of Assets)
Mutual funds	$13 trillion
Exchange-traded funds	$1.3
Closed-end funds	$265 billion
Unit investment trusts	$72 billion

Source: Investment Company Institute. 2013. 2013 Investment Company Fact Book: A Review of Trends and Activity in the Investment Company Industry. *Washington, DC: Investment Company Institute. http://www.icifactbook.org/.*

Table 8.2   Investment Company Total Net Assets by Type (1995-2012) (Billions of US Dollars)

Year	Mutual Funds	Closed-End Funds	ETFs	UITs	Total
1995	2811	143	1	73	3028
1996	3526	147	2	72	3747
1997	4468	152	7	85	4712
1998	5525	156	16	94	5790
1999	6846	147	34	92	7119
2000	6965	143	66	74	7247
2001	6975	141	83	49	7248
2002	6383	159	102	36	6680
2003	7402	214	151	36	7803
2004	8095	253	228	37	8613
2005	8891	276	301	41	9509
2006	10,398	297	423	50	11,167
2007	12,001	312	608	53	12,975
2008	9604	184	531	29	10,348
2009	11,113	224	727	38	12,152
2010	11,832	238	992	51	13,113
2011	11,627	243	1048	60	12,979
2012	13,045	265	1337	72	14,719

Source: Investment Company Institute. 2013. 2013 Investment Company Fact Book: A Review of Trends and Activity in the Investment Company Industry. *Washington, DC: Investment Company Institute. http://www.icifactbook.org/.*

Table 8.3 **Number of Investment Companies by Type (1995-2012) (Billions of US Dollars)**

Year	Mutual Funds	Closed-End Funds	ETFs	UITs	Total
1995	5761	499	2	12,979	19,241
1996	6293	496	19	11,764	18,572
1997	6778	486	19	11,593	18,876
1998	7489	491	29	10,966	18,975
1999	8003	517	30	10,414	18,958
2000	8370	481	80	10,072	19,003
2001	8518	491	102	9295	18,406
2002	8511	544	113	8303	17,471
2003	8426	583	119	7233	16,361
2004	8415	619	152	6499	15,685
2005	8449	635	204	6019	15,307
2006	8721	646	359	5907	15,633
2007	8746	663	629	6030	16,068
2008	8880	642	743	5984	16,249
2009	8612	627	820	6049	16,108
2010	8540	624	950	5971	16,085
2011	8678	632	1166	6043	16,519
2012	8752	602	1239	5787	16,380

Source: Investment Company Institute. 2013. 2013 Investment Company Fact Book: A Review of Trends and Activities in the Investment Company Industry. *Washington, DC: Investment Company Institute. http://www.icifactbook.org/.*

During the period 1995-2012, the total assets of investment companies rose almost fivefold. Table 8.3 lists the number of investment companies by types during the period 1995-2012.

8.1.12 CHALLENGES FACED BY THE MUTUAL FUND INDUSTRY

In spite of being a diversified investment solution, mutual fund investments do not guarantee any return. The issue of fluctuating returns is one of the major challenges faced by the mutual fund industry. The mutual fund industry is a highly competitive industry that is quite sensitive to the fees paid. The changing business scenario and regulatory environment create new challenges for asset management companies. ETFs continue to challenge the dominance of open-ended mutual funds. Mutual fund companies also get involved in overdiversification. Smaller margins and slower growth will lead to a wider gap between industry winners and losers.

8.1.13 PARTICIPATION OF MUTUAL FUNDS IN FINANCIAL MARKETS

Mutual funds participate in the money, bond, capital, mortgage, and derivatives markets. Money market mutual funds invest in money market instruments, including Treasury bills, commercial papers, bankers' acceptances, and certificates of deposits. Bond mutual funds invest in government bond markets and mortgage markets by investing in Treasury bills and bonds issued by government mortgage agencies such as Ginnie Mae. Stock mutual funds purchase various stocks. Various mutual funds also take positions in futures, options, swaps, and other derivatives markets to hedge against interest rate risk. Some commercial banks have investment company subsidiaries that offer mutual funds. Mutual funds also invest in commercial papers issued by finance companies. Stock mutual funds invest in stocks issued by insurance companies. Pension funds also invest in mutual funds.

Biggest Mutual Funds Companies

Vanguard

American Fund

Fidelity

PIMCO

T. Rowe Price

JPMorgan Chase

Franklin Templeton

Black Rock

8.2 INSURANCE

8.2.1 INTRODUCTION

Insurance is a way to reduce potential financial loss by means of covering the cost of unexpected events such as property damage, theft, or illness. An insurance policy is a contract between the client and the insurance company in which the client pays the premium fee, and in exchange, the insurance company agrees to pay a certain amount of money if the event the insurance covers occurs during the term of the policy. The details of the insurance protection, such as which events are covered and the amount, are specified in the insurance contract. Insurance companies provide various forms of insurance and investment services to individuals and charge a fee called a premium.

The primary purpose of the insurance business is to spread risk. The major activities of insurance companies include underwriting insurance policies, collection of premiums, investigation, and settling of claims made under policies. Another integral function is investing and managing the portfolio of funds. Investing activities are important for both life/health insurers and property and casualty insurers. Investment income is a major source of revenue for property and casualty insurance due to the time gap between the receipt of premiums and the payment of claims.

Insurance companies face the problems of adverse selection and moral hazard. Adverse selection in the insurance industry is the tendency of high-risk individuals and companies with higher-than-average potential for claims to seek insurance coverage to a greater extent than low-risk individuals or companies. People with chronic health problems, for example, have strong incentives to purchase health insurance. Similarly, workers employed in high-risk occupations are inclined to buy workers' compensation coverage. Adverse selection is related to health and life insurance. To manage adverse selection, insurers resort to selective underwriting and adjusting premiums for risk factors such as setting high life insurance premiums for smokers. Insurers try to gain additional information through measures such as requiring medical examinations for life insurance. Insurance companies cannot identify good and bad risks. The person getting insured has more information about the quality of his or her health than the insurance company.

The problem of moral hazard can be applied to the insurance industry. Moral hazard refers to the tendency of insurance protection to alter an individual's motive to prevent loss. Moral hazard in insurance relates to the tendency of the insured to engage in more risky activities than they would if they had no insurance. It also refers to the possibility that an insured person may deliberately cause an insured event or pretend that such an event occurred to obtain insurance payments. For example, after getting insurance, a policyholder may become more careless about his or her health. Moral hazard concerns are mitigated by insurance companies through selective underwriting, insurance deductibles, policy exclusions, and contingent pricing.

8.2.2 MAJOR TYPES OF INSURANCE

The insurance industry is basically classified into two major groups: life and property insurance. Life insurance provides protection in the event of untimely death, illness, and retirement. Life insurance is a guaranteed promise to pay money directly to your beneficiaries. Property insurance provides protection against personal injury and liability due to accidents, theft, fire, and other unforeseen events.

8.2.2.1 Life insurance

Life insurance protects individuals and beneficiaries against the risk of loss of income in the event of death or retirement. The two distinct businesses of the life insurance industry consist of selling life insurance policies to consumers and investing funds derived from the premiums for these policies. On the basis of the type of policy, life insurance guarantees the insured consumer a predetermined monetary sum if the client dies before a certain age or has a lifespan beyond a certain age limit.

In countries such as the United States, life insurance annuity policies were a primary vehicle for retirement savings before the advent of Social Security and pension funds. The life insurance industry derives revenues by charging premiums that are calculated to exceed claims and by the accumulation of interest and capital gains derived from the invested amount of capital. Currently, life insurance companies sell annuity contracts, manage pension plans, and sell accident and health insurance. Life insurance companies derive their funds from two sources: (1) They receive premiums that must be used to pay out future claims when the insurer dies, and (2) they also receive premiums paid into pension funds managed by life insurance companies.

The two main types of life insurance are term and permanent life insurance.

8.2.2.1.1 Term life insurance

Term life insurance provides coverage if the covered person dies within a specified period of time unless the premium amount is not paid. Term life insurance premiums are generally less expensive than permanent life insurance premiums. Premiums are usually paid for a fixed length of the term, often in intervals of 5 or 10 years. Premiums are subject to increase when the policy is renewed. Most life insurance policies are subject to a maximum age limit. In life insurance, the death benefit is paid to the beneficiary if the policyholder dies before the policy expires. Term insurance policies do not accumulate cash value. Basic term life is an employer-paid benefit that provides beneficiaries with essential protection and a cost-effective financial safety net in times of necessity. Supplemental term life is an employee-paid benefit that offers extra protection. Dependent term life provides coverage for dependents (e.g., spouse and children).

8.2.2.1.2 Permanent life insurance

Permanent life insurance provides coverage throughout one's lifetime unless the policyholder defaults on the payment of premiums. The premiums for permanent life insurance are usually higher than the premiums for term life insurances during the initial years but are lower than the term premiums in later years. Permanent life insurance policies usually accumulate cash value, which is added to the face value of the policy and is paid at the time of death or returned to the policyholder if the policy is canceled. Permanent life insurance allows policyholders to take a loan against the cash value of the policy.

The major types of permanent insurance are whole life and universal life policies. Whole life insurance policies guarantee the amount of premiums, and the policies have guaranteed minimum cash values. The death benefit amount is also guaranteed. Universal life insurance policies combine life insurance with an investment account. The investment account has cash value. Loans and withdrawals are permitted from the investment account. This type of insurance policy also permits the increase or decrease of premiums based on the limits specified in the insurance policy. There is also flexibility to decide how to invest the premium. The death benefits and cash value of the investment account may increase or decrease depending on the type of investments. The premium for the policyholder may increase if the returns on the chosen investments fall.

A universal life policy allows the insured the flexibility to customize the coverage and premium, unlike traditional policies. Variable universal life is a type of permanent life insurance that offers both a death benefit and an investment feature. The premium amount for variable universal life insurance is flexible according to customer needs. The investment feature allows variable universal life insurance to build a cash value that can be invested in money, equity, or bond mutual funds. This exposure provides the opportunity for an increased rate of return over a normal universal life or permanent insurance policy.

Permanent life insurance provides lifetime coverage, income protection with an additional tax-advantaged investment opportunity, and flexible funding options. Permanent life insurance tends to be more expensive than term life coverage. In this type of insurance, the employee can keep the coverage even if changing employers. Permanent life insurance also provides a tax-deferred investment opportunity in which, in addition to the premium, there is an option to contribute more money to the coverage with tax-deferred growth opportunity.

Ordinary life insurance policies are marketed on an individual basis, usually in units of $1000. The policymakers make periodic premium payments in return for insurance coverage.

8.2.2.1.3 Group life insurance

Group life insurance coverage is provided by employers to a group of people who are usually employees of the same company. This insurance covers a large number of insured persons under a single policy. Group life insurance policies incur lower costs than the policies offered to individuals due to tax cuts offered to the insurer and the sharing of expenses. Group life insurance is generally offered as a piece of a larger employer or membership benefit package. The organization purchasing the policy for its workers retains the master contract.

8.2.2.1.4 Credit life insurance

Credit life insurance is generally bought by mortgagors. The amount of the policy matches the loan balance at any given time, and it is designed to pay off a borrower's debt if the borrower dies.

The face value of a credit life insurance policy decreases proportionately with an outstanding loan amount as the loan is paid off over time. Credit life insurance also has provisions to protect a person's dependents.

8.2.2.1.5 Other life insurance products

A number of other life insurance products are available to consumers, including annuities and pension plans.

8.2.2.1.5.1 Annuity. An annuity is a tax-deferred contract that is issued by an insurance company to provide income for a specified time period. There are basically two types of annuities. In deferred annuities, an asset's taxes are deferred, and account balances are converted into income payments at a later date. In immediate annuities, income payments are received no later than 12 months after issue. Annuities are classified as variable annuities, fixed annuities, and income annuities.

A variable annuity is a contract between the investor and the insurance company whereby the investor purchases the annuity by making one or more payments. The money is invested in a variety of investment options that are similar to mutual funds. The insurance company pays the investor a stream of income payments that could last a specific period of time. Fixed annuities offer more safety and predictability than variable annuities. The principal amount is guaranteed in fixed annuities. There is no accumulation period with an income annuity. In an income annuity, assets are not put into investment options. One or more payments to the insurance company is made in exchange for the promise of a lifetime of income payments.

8.2.2.1.5.2 Pension plans. Life insurance companies play a significant role in supplying retirement saving products. They supply personal and group pension schemes. Life insurance companies provide group pensions in a more intensive package of services including investment, administration, and actuarial services. Insurance companies offer many alternative pension plans to private employers to attract businesses.

8.2.2.2 Property and casualty insurance

Property/casualty insurance (PC) is insurance on homes, cars, and businesses. Property insurance protects a person or business with an interest in physical property against its loss of income-producing abilities. Casualty insurance mainly protects a person or business against legal liability for losses caused by injury to other people or damage to the property of others.

The property and casualty insurance industry consists of underwriting risk and investment management business. The underwriting business involves examining the frequency and severity of potential damage to physical assets (property) or injury to persons (casualty).

The primary components of the PC industry consist of primary issuers, reinsurers, and excess insurers. The primary carriers write policies for firms and individuals to insure themselves against known and identified potential risks. Reinsurers cover the aggregate pool of large group of policies collected by the primary issuer. Excess insurers tend to offer coverage above the levels of US$10 million to US$100 million.

8.2.2.2.1 Major products of PC insurance

The major products under property and casualty insurance consist of auto insurance, homeowner's insurance, worker's compensation, professional liability, renter's insurance, fire and allied insurance, marine insurance, liability insurance, and fidelity insurance.

Automobile insurance provides coverage for personal injury, automobile damage sustained by the insured, and liability to third parties for losses caused by the insured.

Homeowner's insurance covers the structure of the insured's house and personal property included in the house. There is an option to purchase homeowner's insurance that covers either the actual cash value or replacement costs.

Worker's compensation provides employee benefit payments for work-related injuries, death, and diseases.

Professional liability insurance covers physicians, dentists, engineers, accountants, directors, and other professionals from liabilities arising from failure to provide professional services.

Renter's insurance provides the same coverage as a homeowner's policy but to a renter. It protects the renter from theft and damage to personal items (e.g., furniture, electronics, clothing, etc.).

Fire and allied insurance provides coverage against damage from fire, windstorm, hail storm, and the like.

Marine insurance covers inland and ocean marine issues. The inland marine policy covers property involved with transportation through inland water sources. Ocean marine policies provide coverage for ships, cargos, and freight.

Liability insurance provides coverage for accidents and health due to loss from sickness or accidental body injury. Liability insurance protects an insured person when others claim to be hurt or injured as a result of something you did or did not do. Liability insurance generally pays medical bills or provides compensation to anyone who can prove you were negligent or acted improperly.

Fidelity insurance protects employers against loss from embezzlement or misappropriation of funds by an employee.

8.2.2.3 *Other classifications*
8.2.2.3.1 Health insurance
Health insurance, also called medical insurance, helps policyholders protect themselves and family from expensive or unexpected health care-related expenses. Health insurance are designed to estimate the overall risk of health-related expenses and supplement health care-related costs. Most insurance policies do not cover all healthcare costs. These include co-payment and co-insurance costs. Co-payments, premiums, and out-of-pocket expenses depend on the type of health insurance. A plan called a PPO (preferred provider organization) tends to have more out-of-pocket costs than an HMO (health maintenance organization). But PPOs offer more flexibility when choosing a doctor and other services.

Disability insurance is a type of medical coverage that pays part of the income for a policyholder if he or she becomes ill or injured and requires an extended period of time to recover. Medicare is another type of health insurance program provided to people over the age of 65 with certain health conditions. Medicaid is a type of federal health insurance that pays healthcare costs for low-income citizens of all ages. Long-term care insurance helps clients cover costs for long-term care assistance.

8.2.2.3.2 Business insurance
Business insurance is the coverage available to business owners to protect against losses and to insure operations of the business. Different types of insurance for businesses include coverage for property damage, legal liability, and employee-related risks. Companies evaluate their insurance needs based on potential risks, which depend on the type of environment in which the company operates.

8.2.2.3.3 Bond insurance

Bond insurance is a financial guarantee insurance in which an insurance company guarantees scheduled payments of interest and principal on a bond in the event of a payment default by the issuer of the bond or security. The insurance company is paid a premium by the issuer or owner of the security to be insured. The premium for insurance on the bond is a measure of the expected risk of failure of the issuer. Bond insurers generally insure only securities that have ratings in the investment grade category. Securities, such as municipal bonds, infrastructure bonds, asset-backed securities, residential mortgage-backed securities, and CDOs, have bond insurance. Aaa-rated insurers have historically insured mostly general obligation and essential service bonds. During the credit crisis of 2008, the credit ratings of large insurance companies were downgraded and many insured bonds suffered major losses.

8.2.2.3.4 Mortgage insurance

Mortgage insurance is an insurance policy that protects the mortgage lender or titleholder if the borrower defaults on payment or is unable to meet the contractual obligations of the mortgage. In other words, it is a financial guarantee that reduces the loss to lenders or to an investor in the event the borrower does not repay the mortgage. Using mortgage insurance enhances the quality of assets. Mortgage insurance is generally intended to cover the lender's losses when the lender is compelled to sell for less than the prevailing mortgage amount. Mortgage insurance is also known as private mortgage insurance or mortgage title insurance. Investors such as Fannie Mae and Freddie Mac have set parameters for mortgages before they are purchased. One such parameter is that mortgages must have a loan to value ratio of at least 80%, which means that borrowers must make a 20% down payment. To overcome this requirement, mortgage insurance was created to help more consumers afford home ownership.

Mortgage insurance can be purchased at different stages of the mortgage cycle. It is most commonly purchased during the origination process of the mortgage when the loan originator takes the loan application or when the processor completes the loan file. Mortgage insurance serves as the interlink for low-down-payment loans for delivery into the secondary market. In other words, mortgage insurance enables the mortgage cycle to progress from origination to the secondary market. Some insurance companies provide mortgage insurance in the form of a credit default swap. If default occurs, an insurance company pays the income stream of the mortgage.

8.2.3 UNDERWRITING CYCLE

The underwriting cycle is the tendency of property and liability insurance premiums, profits, and availability of coverage to rise and fall with some regularity over time. This cycle lasts typically for 5-7 years. A cycle generally begins when insurers tighten their underwriting standards and sharply raise premiums after a period of severe underwriting or investment losses. This results in an increase in profits and accumulation of capital due to stricter standards and high premium rates. This increase in underwriting capacity leads to increased competition from existing or new players for market expansion. This leads to relaxation of underwriting standards and drives premium rates downward, leading to underwriting losses and thereby setting the stage for repetition of the cycle. Managing the underwriting cycle is a major challenge in the insurance industry.

8.2.4 INSURANCE PRICING

Insurance is a financial transaction on losses. When a policy is written, the insurer estimates the expected losses. Over time this estimate develops as more information becomes available. Log normal distribution is used to aggregate losses. Insurance is priced as discounted cash flows. The higher the interest rate, the lower the price. Financial theory views insurance policies as financial instruments traded in markets whose price is determined by forces of supply and demand. Financial models can be applied to insurance pricing. Asset pricing models view insurance firms as levered corporations with debt and equity capital. The insurer raises debt capital by issuing insurance contracts. Insurance contracts are roughly analogous to the bonds issued by nonfinancial corporations. Insurance policies are more risky than conventional bonds because both the payment time and amount are stochastic. Financial theory considers insurance underwriting and pricing decisions as capital budgeting decisions based on rules that include net present value (NPV) and internal rate of return (IRR). Insurance pricing models are based on the capital asset pricing model, the intertemporal capital asset pricing model, arbitrage pricing theory, and options pricing theory.

Buying insurance can also be regarded as buying a call option on losses. Selling insurance is the equivalent of selling a call option on losses. The insured has an option on losses that pays only if losses exceed a certain specified threshold. For an option, the higher the interest rate the higher the price of the option. When interest rates rise, the price of insurance will rise as all other things remain equal. Current actuarial pricing does not account for the optionality offered by insurance contracts. It is loss estimation rather than pricing.

8.2.5 DISTRIBUTION CHANNELS

In general an insurance distribution system can be categorized as direct and independent writing. Direct writing consists of companies that sell through direct marketers, exclusive agents, or through the Internet or telephone. In this method the insurer owns the customer list. In independent writing, the independent agency or broker becomes the representative of competing products of many insurance companies and usually has the ownership rights to the customer list. Today insurance companies are using multiple distribution channels.

8.2.6 REGULATION

In advanced countries such as the United States, there are a number of regulatory laws to protect policyholders. Insurance companies file annual statements with regulatory authorities, such as the National Association of Insurance Commissioners (NAIC), in accordance with Statutory Accounting Principles (SAP). The three basic regulatory systems used to monitor insurers' solvency are the Insurance Regulatory Information System (IRIS), Financial Analysis and Solvency Tracking (FAST), and Risk Based Capital (RBC). Regulatory insurance authorities use IRIS-based ratios to scrutinize the financial condition of insurance companies. FAST is also a regulatory solvency system designed to evaluate the performance of insurance companies based on detailed financial analysis. This system focuses on identifying probable insurance firms with financial difficulties. Financial analysis in this system is based on an insurance company's financial statements. RBC measures stipulated by NAIC determine the minimum statutory capital and reserve requirements of insurance companies based on the profile and line of business. For life insurance companies RBC stipulates capital requirements related to assets, assets/liability mismatches, underwriting risks, credit risks, and interest rate risks. For property and casualty companies RBC includes asset risk, underwriting, reserve risks, credit risk, and other factors. An RBC ratio of 70-100% is not satisfactory, and so regulators initiate actions for control.

The McCarran Ferguson Act of 1945 empowers the state insurance authority to regulate insurance premium rates. This act has special focus on personal lines and products such as automobiles and homeowners. Insurance guaranty funds adopted by all US states compensate policyholders for losses that result from insurance company insolvencies.

8.2.7 RISK MANAGEMENT IN INSURANCE

8.2.7.1 Types of risk

The three fundamental risks faced by insurance companies are underwriting, market, and regulatory risks.

8.2.7.1.1 Underwriting risk

Insurance premium prices are based on estimates and assumptions of expected claim costs, which are the costs incurred to issue and administer the policy. These estimates may prove wrong because of wrong assumptions, changes in the regulatory environment, increased life span, or even uncontrollable variables such as natural weather catastrophes. In this scenario underwriting risks arise because the premium collected will not cover the cost of coverage. Underwriting risks increase when competition among insurers leads to aggressive pricing of policies. Underwriting risk for life insurers arise due to longevity risk, whereas for PC insurers it could be attributed to catastrophe risks.

8.2.7.1.2 Catastrophe risk

Catastrophe risk results from catastrophic events such as hurricanes and tropical storms. The insurance service office (ISO) defines a catastrophe as an event that causes $25 million or more in insured property losses. Catastrophic risks affect a large number of PC policyholders and insurers. According to Insurance Information Institute data, in 2012 Hurricane Sandy caused an $18.75 billion in losses of insured property. The most costly hurricane to date was in 2005 with Hurricane Katrina, which resulted in insured losses of approximately $47 billion in current exposure terms.

8.2.7.1.3 Longevity and mortality risk

Longevity risk arises from the underestimation of the mortality projections calculated by actuaries for price and reserve life-contingent annuities. Longevity risk is associated with annuities in which the expected cost to the insurer increases with the policyholder's life expectancy. Insurers offering annuities bear excessive risk and charge high premiums.

8.2.7.1.4 Market risk

Market risk arises due to economic losses as result of adverse changes in the market value of financial instruments, assets, and liabilities, resulting from changes in macroeconomic variables such as interest rates and stock prices. Property casualty insurers' exposure to market risk arises from investment portfolios. Life and health insurance companies have exposure to market risk because of their reserve liabilities and asset management income along with exposure to investment portfolio. The primary sources of market risk are interest rate risk, prepayment and extension risk, credit risk, liquidity, and equity price risk. The market value of fixed rate investments fluctuates from changes in market interest rates. Prepayment risk arises when borrowers redeem loans or borrowed funds before the maturity period to take advantage of a decline in interest rates. Extension risk arises when borrowers repay at a slower pace than expected when interest rates increase. Credit risk arises due to fluctuations in the value of investments resulting from issuer or borrower default or changes in the likelihood of default or recovery rates. Liquidity risk refers to the possibility of insufficient liquid resources to meet claims. The frequency and magnitude of PC liquidity claims are more volatile compared to life or health insurance claims. Equity price risk results from the probable economic loss that results from adverse changes in stock prices. Life and health insurers face equity price risk because of guarantees provided on variable life insurance and annuities. Equity price risks also arise for life insurance insurers as the fee income generated for managing AUM depends on portfolio sizes and performance of equity markets.

8.2.7.1.5 Downgrade risk

Ratings given by rating agencies such as S&P, A.M., and Moody's also determine the risks faced by insurance companies. One of the determinants of the quality of insurance policies is the rating for long-duration (long-tail) policies. A rate downgrade will severely affect the financial stability of insurers. The primary determinant of ratings is the capital adequacy ratio based on factors of investment risk, credit risk, and underwriting risk. Rating agencies such as Moody's determine capital ratio on the basis of Monte Carlo simulations to assess investment, reinsurance, reserve, and underwriting risk.

8.2.7.1.6 Regulatory risk

Insurance companies face regulatory risk including rate regulation, participation in involuntary markets, assessment risk, restrictions on dividends, limits on underwriting, and reinsurance requirements.

Rate regulation risk arises when state regulatory agencies may not approve insurance rates or when they reduce existing rates, which could result in lower profits from underwriting operations.

Insurers may have statutory obligations for participation in involuntary insurance schemes, including automobile and workers' compensation. Insurers are also mandated to participate in Fair Plans or Windstorm Plans, which offer basic property coverage to the insured. This type of participation might undermine underwriting profitability.

Assessment risk arises due to insurance guaranty funds that compensate policyholders for losses arising from insolvencies of insurance companies. These guaranty funds are required to pay certain claims against the insolvent insurer.

Premiums are based on statutory capital plus surplus. Investment losses may result in restrictions on underwriting.

State insurance regulators place restrictions on repatriation of dividends from underwriters to parent holding companies. As a result, parent companies find it difficult to obtain funds from their insurance subsidiaries.

Reinsurance risk arises when insurers are obligated to purchase reinsurance from a mandatory reinsurance fund. The changing cost of reinsurance under the program may lead to reduction in profits from underwriting operations.

8.2.7.2 Risk measurement in insurance

Value at risk (VaR) and expected shortfall (ES) are two major metrics used to measure and manage financial risks in insurance. The VaR is the loss during an N day period that at a confidence level of X% will not be exceeded. The ES, also known as tail conditional VaR, is the expected loss conditional on incurring a loss greater than the VaR. In addition to measuring risk, these tools are used to determine economic capital, setting up insurance deductibles and reinsurance cedance levels, along with estimation of expected claims and losses. Economic capital is the amount of capital required to absorb potential losses. VaR and ES are also alternate approaches for risk adjustment in accounting for insurance contracts.

8.2.7.3 Risk mitigation strategies in insurance

8.2.7.3.1 Internal measures

The internal measures that can be adopted by insurance companies to mitigate risks include the process of diversifying insurance exposures and designing policies that limit the exposure. Diversification of insurance to cover wide geographic regions, industries, and policy types is useful for mitigating credit risk. A balanced portfolio consisting of term insurance and annuity business can be used as a natural hedge for mortality risk. Insurance exposures can also be diversified by participation in underwriting pools. Proper asset liability management helps to mitigate inflation and interest rate risks.

8.2.7.3.2 Reinsurance

Reinsurance is also a major risk mitigation strategy. Reinsurance is the transfer with indemnification of all or part of underwriting risk from one insurer to another for a portion of the premium. Usually in reinsurance contracts, the primary underwriter insurer and the reinsurer either share proportionately all insured losses known as quota share contracts or unproportionately known as excess of loss contracts. Reinsurances reduce the burden on regulatory capital by reducing exposures and increasing surplus.

8.2.7.3.3 Financial market instruments

PC insurers use financial instruments (e.g., catastrophe bonds) and derivatives instruments (e.g., catastrophe futures, weather derivatives, and credit derivatives) to manage insurance risks. Life insurers use mortality catastrophe bonds, long-term longevity bonds, and related solutions to hedge risks. Longevity-linked swaps and forward contracts are also used to hedge insurance risks. Credit derivatives (e.g., credit default swaps) are used to hedge the risk of a reinsurer's insolvency. Life insurance companies use derivatives to hedge exposures due to various annuities and life guarantees. Equity derivatives are often used to manage exposure owing to fluctuations in fee income. Financial market solutions have lower costs and greater underwriting capacity compared to reinsurance.

8.2.7.3.4 Letters of credit

Letters of credit are also used to manage exposures that result from catastrophic events. Letter of credit agreements help the insurance company obtain funds immediately without liquidating portions of the investment portfolio.

8.2.7.3.5 Increased capital and contingent capital

Insurance companies can reduce solvency risks by increasing capital. Capital can be increased by issuing shares or subordinated debt. Contingent capital contracts are options or hybrid securities in which capital is obtained through issuing preferred shares or subordinated debt if a covered event results in a financial loss.

8.2.7.4 Sources and uses of funds by insurance companies

Premiums are the major source of funds for insurance companies. The most significant liabilities for insurance companies are insurance reserves. Insurance reserves consist of liability for future policy benefits and claim reserves. The future policy benefits are for life and health insurance, whereas the claim reserves are for PC and life and health insurance. PCs refer claim reserves as the liability of loss reserve, whereas life and health insurers considered it the liability for policy and contract claims. Capital raised by insurance companies is also a source of funds for investment purposes in fixed assets.

The largest asset class for insurance companies is investments. Insurance companies are major investors in financial institutions. Insurance companies also invest in government securities and corporate securities, as well as mortgage markets and collateralized loan obligations. Property and casualty insurers have substantial reinsurance assets and receivables.

The loss reserve represents the estimated liability for PC claims that have been reported to the insurer but are not yet settled. The liability for policy and contract claims measures the estimated ultimate cost of settling claims related to incurred but not reported death, disability, and long-term care as well as claims that have been reported but not yet settled.

8.2.7.5 Valuation of insurance companies

The performance of insurance companies can be measured by parameters such as growth in the number of policies, market share growth, growth in number of branches, and other parameters. The average number of policies per agent reflects the efficiency of the insurance company. The financial indicators used to evaluate the performance of insurance companies include growth in gross and net premiums, profit from underwriting, average profit per branch and employee, average annual cost per employee, and, most importantly, return on investment. Insurers have four primary sources of revenue: net premiums earned, net investment income, fee income, and realized gains and losses.

Major Valuation Ratios	
Return on equity (ROE)	Income available to shareholders/common equity
Combined ratio	Loss ratio + loss expense ratio + underwriting expense ratio + policyholder dividend ratio
Loss ratio	Losses/net premium earned
Loss expense ratio	Loss expenses/net premium earned
Underwriting expense ratio	Underwriting expenses/net premium earned
Policyholder dividend ratio	Policyholder dividends/net premium earned

The combined ratio highlights the underwriting profitability of a PC insurance company. The loss and loss expense ratio indicates the average cost of insurance protection per dollar of net premiums earned during the period. The underwriting expense ratio indicates the operational efficiency in underwriting. Underwriting expenses include commissions to agents and brokers, taxes, salaries, employee benefits, and other operating costs.

The combined ratio highlights the cost of protection and the cost involved in generation and maintenance of business. When the combined ratio is under 100%, underwriting results are considered profitable and if it is over 100% the underwriting results are considered unprofitable. The disadvantage of the combined ratio is that it does not reflect the investment profits generated by insurers.

The operating ratio measures the overall operational profitability from underwriting and investment activities. An operating ratio of greater than 100% suggests that the insurance company will not be able to generate profits from its underwriting and investment activities. Net investment income is earned primarily on funds obtained.

Operating ratio	Combined ratio − Net investment income ratio
Net investment income ratio	Net investment income/Net premiums earned
Net investment income	Investment income − Investment expense

8.2.7.5.1 Underwriting leverage

Underwriting leverage measures the efficiency of the use of capital resources by an insurance company to generate business. Insurers with low underwriting leverage have more potential for growth. Policyholder surpluses measure the cushion available to absorb such losses.

Underwriting leverage = Net premiums written/Policyholder surplus

8.2.7.5.2 Investment yield

This ratio measures the profitability of investments.

Investment yield = Net investment income/Investment assets. High-risk investments have high yields, whereas low-risk investments have low yields. In general, PC insurers invest in short-term higher credit quality investments and hence reap lower investment yields.

8.2.7.5.3 Investment return

Investment return consists of investment yield and net capital gains. Investment return measures current performance.

8.2.7.5.4 Growth

In addition to earnings, dividends, and assets, other growth metrics, such as growth in AUM, are important indicators of future revenues for life insurers. Premium revenue being the primary source of revenue is an important indicator of the growth potential of an insurer. Asset growth is a leading indicator of revenue and earnings growth.

8.2.7.5.5 Risk ratios

Insurance-related risks can be evaluated by examining business lines and exposure to high-risk coverage such as commercial liability lines, catastrophe losses, and other factors. Investment risks can be evaluated by analyzing the portfolio mix. Risks can be evaluated using combined ratio and premium growth. A low value of combined ratio indicates that underwriting profits are available to absorb unexpected losses. A high premium growth may be due to potential mispricing. Other risk ratios include the premium leverage, i.e., the ratio of gross loss reserve to the net loss reserve and the reserve leverage, i.e., the ratio of gross loss reserve to the net loss reserve.

The value of operations of an insurance company can be measured using fundamental valuation models that focus on free cash flow and relative valuation, which focuses on comparison of market prices and the performance of the insurer with peer companies. Discounted cash flow valuation is rarely used to value financial service companies.

8.2.7.6 Participation of life insurance companies in financial markets

Life insurance companies as investment managers manage the assets of pension funds. Life insurance companies invest their funds in money market, bond market, mortgages, and stock markets. Insurance companies purchase money market securities, including Treasury bills, commercial papers, bonds, and other capital market securities. Insurance companies also participate in derivatives markets such as futures, options, and swaps to hedge interest rate risks.

8.2.7.7 Global insurance market trends

Insurers are among the top three institutional investors worldwide, along with pension funds and investment funds. According to an OECD Global Insurance Market Trends[3] report, insurance premium

---

[3]Global Insurance Market Trends OECD. http://www.oecd.org/insurance/insurance/49108065.pdf.

growth in the direct life insurance industry generally displayed greater strength across countries in comparison with the nonlife insurance in the period 2010-2011. Premium growth in the nonlife sector was affected by low economic growth, unemployment, and lower incomes in many countries. Growth in life insurance underwriting activity was positive in many countries. In a number of markets, the recovery of unit-linked insurance business, along with growth in annuity insurance products and other savings products containing a guarantee component, contributed importantly to the positive performance of life insurance.[4]

According to a Global Insurance Data Monitor report from 2011, life insurance is the largest segment of the global insurance market, accounting for 57.6% of the market's total value. The global insurance market grew by 4.7% in 2010 to reach a value of $4.073 trillion. By 2015, the global insurance market is forecast to have a value of $5.128 trillion, an increase of 25.9% since 2010.[5]

With respect to investment allocation, most insurers invest the largest proportion of their portfolio in government bonds and fixed-income private bonds. In most countries, the life insurance industry has an aggregate less than 10% of assets invested in equities.

One of the challenges faced by insurance companies is the persistently low interest rate in a number of countries. Sovereign default risk is viewed as a major risk for the insurance sector, particularly in those countries with substantial exposures to government debt. Financial market volatility is another major risk for insurers as it would have an impact on capital planning as institutional investors.

In the context of the global financial and economic crisis, nonlife insurers have refocused their strategies to reduce expenses related to claims, operations, and distributions. These developments have led to renewed focus on underwriting business. Insurers in developed markets face the challenges of growth prospects, particularly in the context of high insurance penetration (premiums as a percentage of GDP) and density (premium per capita). Insurance products are highly commoditized and people are heavily customized.

The insurance industry has to meet diverse consumer needs for new insurance products and develop enhanced distribution systems to meet consumer demand. The insurance industry also has to gear up to meet regulatory challenges.

According to Swiss Re's study the world's insurance premiums amounted to $4.6 trillion in 2011. Life and nonlife insurance premiums excluding cross-border businesses accounted for 6.6% of the world's GDP in 2011. Premiums accounted for 17% of the GDP in Taiwan, followed by the Netherlands where premiums accounted for 13.2% of the GDP. In 2011, the United States accounted for 26.2% of the world's premiums with $1.2047 trillion. Japan accounted for 14.26% of the world's premiums with $655.408 billion.[6]

In terms of premiums written in PC insurance, private auto insurance contributes the most followed by homeowner's insurance. In life insurance the focus is on annuities. Among traditional life insurance venues, universal and term life and group life insurances are the major contributors to premiums. Table 8.4 provides the statistics on world premiums during the period 2009-2011. Table 8.5 provides a list of the top global insurance companies by revenues. Table 8.6 gives a list of the top insurance companies based on market capitalization in 2011.

---

[4]Global Insurance Market Trends OECD. http://www.oecd.org/insurance/insurance/49108065.pdf.
[5]Global Insurance, Data Monitor, 0199-2087, 2010.
[6]International Insurance Fact Book 2013, Insurance Information Institute.

Table 8.4 World Premium Statistics (Billions of US Dollars)

Year	Life	Nonlife	Total
2009	2367.442	1742.193	4109.635
2010	2516.377	1819.310	4335.687
2011	2627.168	1969.519	4596.687

Source: Swiss Re, sigma No. 3/2012, Insurance Information Fact Book 2013.

Table 8.5 Top Global Insurance Companies by Revenues

Rank	Company	Revenues (Billions of US Dollars)	Country	Industry
1	Japan Post Holdings	211.019	Japan	Life/health
2	Berkshire Hathaway	143.688	United States	Property/casualty
3	AXA	142.712	France	Life/health
4	Allianz	134.618	Germany	Property/casualty
5	Assicurazioni Generali	112.628	Italy	Life/health
6	Nippon Life Insurance	90.783	Japan	Life/health
7	Munich Re	90.137	Germany	Property/casualty
8	Meiji Yasuda Life	77.463	Japan	Life/health
9	American International Group	71.730	United States	Property/casualty
10	MetLife	70.641	United States	Life/health

Source: Insurance Institute Information Fact Book 2013

Table 8.6 Top Insurance Companies Based on Market Capitalization, 2011

Country	Insurance Company	Market Cap (Billions of US Dollars)
United States	American International Group (AIG)	172.24
France	AXA Group	66.12
Germany	Allianz Worldwide	65.55
Canada	Manulife Financial	50.52
Italy	Generali Group	45.45
United States	Prudential Financial	39.70
United States	MetLife	37.94
United Kingdom	Aviva	33.10
Germany	Munich Re	30.99
Netherlands	AEGON	26.40

Source: http://worldsten.blogspot.com/2011/08/top-10-insurance-companies-of-world.html.

8.3 **PENSION FUNDS**

8.3.1 **INTRODUCTION**

A pension fund is established by an employer based on the contributions made by the employer and employees. The objective of this common asset pool is to provide pensions for employees at the time of their retirement based on the growth of funds. Pension funds are operated by intermediary financial institutions on behalf of the company or in-house pension funds of the company. Pension funds are large institutional investors who invest in the shares of companies. Pension funds can be open-ended or close-end. In open-ended pension funds, there is no restriction on membership, whereas closed-end pension funds support pensions that are limited to certain employees. There are different types of closed pension funds, including single-employer pension funds, multiemployer pension funds, related member pension funds, and individual pension funds.

A pension or retirement income plan refers to a legally binding contract having an explicit retirement objective, and the benefits are paid only when the beneficiary reaches a certain legally defined retirement age.

8.3.2 **TYPES OF PENSION PLANS**

8.3.2.1 Public pension and private pension plans

The public pension plan is the Social Security plan administered by central, state, or local government as well as other public-sector bodies. Private pension plans are administered directly by private-sector employers who function as plan sponsor, private pension fund, or private-sector provider.

8.3.2.2 Occupational and personal pension plans

Occupational plans are established by employers or groups such as industry associations or labor or professional associations. The plan may be administered directly by the plan sponsor or by an independent entity. Occupational plans are either mandatory or voluntary in nature. In mandatory plans, employers are obliged to participate in the pension plan by law. In voluntary plans, the establishment of plans is voluntary for employers. In some countries, employers can on a voluntary basis establish occupational plans that provide benefits that replace at least partly those of the Social Security system.

Personal pension plans are established and administered directly by a pension fund or a financial institution acting as a pension provider. These plans are not related to employment relationships and individuals can purchase these plans independently. The employer may nonetheless make contributions to personal pension plans. These plans are also classified as mandatory and voluntary plans. In mandatory personal pension plans, individuals must join or are eligible to receive mandatory pension contributions. In other words, individuals are required to make pension contributions to the pension plans of their choice, which is normally within a certain range of choices. In voluntary personal pension plans, individual participation is voluntary and individuals are not required to make any pension contributions to the pension plan. But this type of plan also includes those plans that individuals must join if they choose to replace part of their Social Security benefits with those from personal pension plans.

8.3.2.3 Defined contribution and defined benefit occupational plans

This categorization is in compliance with IASB accounting standards.

Occupational plans also can be categorized as defined contribution (DC) and defined benefit (DB) plans. Under a DC occupational plan, the plan sponsor pays a fixed contribution and has no legal encumbrances to pay further contributions to an ongoing plan in the event of an unfavorable plan event. In a DC plan, the contributions are specified, not the benefits. In this individual account plan, each participant accrues benefits only on the amount contributed to the account and any income, expenses, and investment gains or losses to the account.

Plans other than DC plans are called DB plans. Traditional DB, hybrid DB, and mixed DB are the three types of DB plans. In traditional DB plans, the benefits are linked through a formula to the members' wages or salaries or other factors such as length of employment. In a hybrid DB plan the benefits depend on a rate of return on the basis of contributions. The rate of return is either specified in the plan rules, in terms of index market rates, salary, or profit growth or is defined with reference to the actual return of any supporting assets and a minimum return guarantee specified in the plan rules. Mixed DB plans consist of two separate DB and DC components that are treated as part of same plan. A DB plan specifies either the benefit that will be paid to a plan participant or the method of determining the benefit. The plan sponsor's contributions to the plan vary from year to year depending on the plan's funding requirements. Benefits are often based on average pay and years of service.

8.3.2.4 Protected and unprotected pension plans

Both occupational and personal pension plans are covered under this category. An unprotected pension plan does not offer any investment return or benefit guarantees covering the whole plan, whereas the protection plan provides benefit guarantees covering the whole plan.

8.3.2.5 Funded pension plans versus unfunded pension plans

Funded pension plans are occupational or personal pension plans that accumulate assets to cover the plan's liabilities. In book-reserved pension plans, the provisions for occupational pension plan benefits are entered as reserves in the balance sheet of the plan sponsor. The unfunded pension plans are financed directly from the contributions of the plan sponsor or provider of the plan participant.

8.3.2.6 Pension funds versus pension contracts

In pension funds, the plan/fund members have a contractual claim over the assets of the pension. Pension funds are in the form of a special-purpose legal entity, such as a trust, foundation, corporate entity, or legally separated fund managed by a pension fund management company on behalf of the plan/fund members.

Pension contracts are insurance contracts that specify the amount of pension plan contributions in exchange for which pension plan benefits are paid on attainment of a specified retirement age or an earlier exit of members from the plan.

8.3.3 PENSION FUND CLASSIFICATION

Pension funds are classified as open pension funds and closed pension funds. Open pension funds support at least one plan with no restriction on membership. At the same time, open-ended pension plans support only pension plans that are limited to certain employees. Closed pension funds are further classified into single-employer and multiemployer pension funds. In single-employer pension funds, assets of pension plans established by a single sponsor are pooled together. Multiemployer pension funds are funds that pool the assets of pension plans established by various plan sponsors. Multiemployer pension funds are further classified into group pension funds, industry pension funds, and collective pension funds. Group pension funds are set up for related employers of companies that are financially related or owned by a single holding group. In industry pension funds, plans are intended for unrelated employers who belong to the same trade or industry sector. Collective pension funds are meant for unrelated employers that may be in different trades or businesses.

8.3.4 TYPES OF PRIVATE PENSION FUNDS

Private pension funds consists of private defined benefit and defined contribution pension funds. These include 401(k), 403(b), and individual retirement accounts (IRAs).

A 401(k) is a qualified plan established by an employer to which employees make salary deferral or salary reduction contributions on a post-tax or pretax basis. A 401(k) is a feature of a qualified profit-sharing plan that allows employees to contribute a portion of their wages to individual accounts. The earnings in this plan accrue on a tax-deferred basis. The 403(b) plan (also known as a tax-sheltered annuity (TSA)) is a retirement plan for employees of public schools and certain tax-exempt organizations. Individual accounts in a 403(b) plan can be an annuity contract provided through an insurance company or a custodial account invested in a mutual fund. IRAs are a form of individual retirement plan. The most important features of an IRA are the tax-deferred growth and the potential tax deduction. In a traditional IRA, an investor gets tax deduction for the savings contributed to the account.

8.3.5 KEY FEATURES OF PENSION FUNDS

The governance and investment policies of a pension fund are the critical factors for determining its investment decision in terms of portfolio investment in diversified stocks, bond, real estate, and other assets. Pension funds have a long-term investment time on account of the fact that they have relatively stable and known inflows (contributions) and outflows (benefits). Traditionally pension funds have been managed passively by investments in highly stable stocks and bonds as they cannot take excessive risks because these funds represent individual savings for retirement. But it is observed that due to regulatory changes and change in capital market conditions, pension funds have diversified into higher risk and international investments. Pension funds are highly regulated in advanced countries such as the United States. Each pension fund has specific operating and investment guidelines.

Basically there are two types of autonomous pension funds. In the institutional type, the fund is an independent legal entity with its own internal governing board. This type of fund exists in countries such as Japan and in European countries including Norway, Poland, the Netherlands, Switzerland, Denmark, Finland, Italy, and Austria. In the contractual type of pension fund, assets are segregated and pooled without a legal entity-like structure and are governed by a separate financial institution such as a pension fund management company, bank, or insurance company. This type of fund exists in Mexico, Portugal, the Czech Republic, Slovakia, and Turkey. Pension funds that are in the form of a trust have the characteristics of both institutional and contractual types.

8.3.6 CHALLENGES FACED BY THE GLOBAL PENSION FUND INDUSTRY

Global pension plans are operating in a highly regulated environment. The complex impact of regulations and reforms have affected large pension plans. Pension funds face challenges with respect to governance and risks. Currently more focus should be given to investment risk reporting. After the recent economic crisis, pension plans are changing their business and operational models. Defined contribution schemes face challenges from members for accessing real-time information on their investments and retirement benefits with transparency and cost reductions.

Pension funds face the challenges of member engagement, particularly in the context that savings for retirement is still a low priority for younger generations. It is a known fact that engagement levels for retirement savings in pensions schemes are activated only when individuals are close to the retirement period. This delay will not lead to increased benefits. On account of lack of adequate growth in the pension sector, the consolidation of large schemes and service providers has become an ongoing trend. These consolidations are basically focused on achieving cost savings and investments in large-scale products such as infrastructure.

Public and government pension funds face the challenges of managing their investment portfolios. Pension funds faces the challenges of direct investment strategies for improved portfolio construction, investment control, and cost reduction. Inflation is among the challenges faced by pension funds as many pension schemes are inflation linked. Many pension schemes hedge the risk by buying index-linked bonds. For public pension funds, the underfunding trends of the government force the funds to alter their investment strategies to maximize returns by assuming increased risks. Pension funds have increased allocations in alternative investments such as venture capital, private equity, real estate, and hedge funds.

8.3.7 RISK IN PENSION FUNDS

In DC plans, only contributions into the fund are predetermined, not the benefits. The contributions made by individuals or sponsors such as employers are invested to have a cumulative balance at the time of retirement and are later withdrawn to purchase an annuity or a related retirement product. In the case of a DC plan, the individual members bear the risks inherent in the plan. Investment risks and longevity funding risks are the major risks faced by pension funds. In DB plans the risks are considered within the assessment of the solvency of the fund or plan. With respect to DB plans, the supervisor has to focus on funding and solvency issues. With DC systems the supervisory focus is on processes rather than outcomes as benefits are not guaranteed. Funding risk is a major risk faced by DC plans. Funding risk arises when the pension funds provide relative guarantees of performance or provide life annuities, life assurance, or medical insurance. The funds need to be insured. Pension funds have to be capitalized sufficiently to meet the costs that are not chargeable to the members.

The most important risk faced by members of DC funds is investment risk as no form of guarantee is given by the pension provider. The control mechanisms for investment risk in pension funds include internal risk-management techniques, quantitative investments, and VaR. Internal risk-management techniques can include thematic reviews and inspections, litigation for nonpayment of contributions, and more. Transparency and education for members is vital for managing risk within DC pension systems. Liquidity risk is also prevalent in DC pension plans. Liquidity risk arises when plans don't have sufficient liquidity to pay out balances or benefits to members without incurring losses. Costs and fees are also important for DC plans. Operational risk, which consists of risk associated with security and accuracy of the management information system, also exists with respect to the operations of pension funds.

DB plans are faced with market-related and liability risk. Market risk consists of asset liability mismatch, interest rate, credit risk, and equity and currency risk. Liability risk consists of longevity, early retirement, and other demographic factors.

8.3.8 GOVERNANCE STRUCTURE OF PENSION FUNDS

The corporate governance of pension funds is vested with the governing body. The governing body must be accountable to pension plan members, beneficiaries, and supervisory boards. The governing board depends on the support of subcommittees. An auditor independent of the pension fund entity performs audit functions. An actuary performs the professional or legal duties with respect to DB plans financed through pension funds. With respect to disclosure function, the governing body discloses relevant information to pension plan members, beneficiaries, plan sponsors, and supervisory authorities.

8.3.9 PARTICIPATION OF PENSION FUNDS IN FINANCIAL MARKETS

Pension funds participate in all major financial markets. They participate in the major markets, including money, bond, mortgage, stock, and derivatives markets. Pension funds invest a portion of funds in liquid money market instruments and bonds. The portfolio of investments for pension funds also consists of stocks and mortgages. Pension funds invest in derivatives instruments such as futures contracts, stock options, and interest rate swaps to hedge their interest rate risks.

8.3.10 REGULATION OF PENSION FUNDS

The Employee Retirement Income Security Act of 1974 (ERISA) provides a comprehensive framework for the regulation of employee pension and welfare benefit plans offered by private pension funds. There are various provisions in ERISA aimed at protecting the rights of plan participants and beneficiaries in employee benefit plans. ERISA sets standards that pension plans must meet with respect to participation, vesting period, and funding. ERISA requires plans to provide participants with plan information that contains the plan features and funding. ERISA sets fiduciary standards that require employee benefit plan funds to inform participants of their rights under the plan and the financial status of the plans. The fiduciary guidelines give participants the right to sue in federal courts for benefits and breaches of fiduciary duties. ERISA also established the Pension Benefit Guaranty Corporation (PBGC) to ensure that plan participants receive promised benefits up to a statutory limit if the plan terminates for lack of sufficient assets to pay for the promised benefits. Congress has granted certain tax deductions and deferrals to qualified plans to motivate employers to establish pension plans. ERISA stipulates that DB plans must be fully funded. The assets held in the pension fund must be sufficient to pay the benefits plan participants have earned. The employer bears the investment risk for the assets held by the DB plan. If the assets decrease in value or liabilities increase the plan sponsor must make additional contributions to the pension fund. The investment risk in a DC plan is borne by the employee. DC plans are not insured by the PBGC. ERISA imposes two general vesting requirements based on age and length of service. All plans must provide employees' rights to their normal retirement benefits upon attainment of normal retirement age. ERISA stipulates that a qualified DB plan must meet vesting provisions based on an employee's years of service to the employer. A participant's benefits are fully vested after 5 years of service, known as 5-year cliff vesting, or based on a graded vesting schedule.

The Pension Protection Act of 2006 (PPA) established new funding requirements for defined-benefit pension plans and introduced reforms that affected the cash balance of pension plans, DC plans, and deferred compensation plans for highly compensated employees. The Protection Act introduced new rules for calculating plan assets and liabilities and eliminated deficit reduction contributions for underfunded plans. When it is fully phased in, the plan funding must be equal to 100% of the plan's liabilities.

Under the PPA, a plan sponsor's minimum required contribution is based on the plan's target normal cost and the difference between the plan's funding target and the value of the plan's assets.

8.3.11 GLOBAL PENSION FUND TRENDS

The global trend shows that the allocation of pension funds to public equities has decreased and interest in DC plans has accelerated. According to OECD calculations, an employee who has saved for retirement for 40 years in a pension plan investing 60% in equities and 40% in long-term government bonds and retired at the end of 2010 would have experienced an annual investment performance of 2.8% in Japan, 4.2% in Germany, 4.4% in the United States, and 5.8% in the United Kingdom.[7] According to an OECD Report, global pension funds had US$20.1 trillion in total assets in 2011. During the economic recession of 2008, the global pension markets lost $3.4 trillion in market value. The OECD weighted average asset-to-GDP ratio for pension funds increased from 67.3% of the GDP in 2001 to 72.4% of the GDP in 2011, with the Netherlands achieving the largest ratio in 2011, at 138%. The United States has the largest pension fund market with assets worth US$10.6 trillion among the OECD countries in 2011. The United Kingdom and Japan are the other big markets in pension funds with assets of $2.1 trillion and $1.5 trillion in 2011. All the OECD private pension markets including occupational and personal were valued at $29.5 trillion in 2011. Total pension fund assets in the OECD area grew by 85% between 2001 and 2011, or about 6.4% annually.

According to a global pension assets study in 2013 by Towers Watson covering 13 major pension markets, the total assets of the global pension market was estimated to be US$29.754 trillion. The largest pension markets were in the United States, Japan, and the United Kingdom with 56.5%, 12.5%, and 9.2% of the total pension assets. The defined contribution assets constituted 45.4% of the total pension assets. According to the study, the average global asset allocation of the seven largest markets was 47.3% in equities, 32.9% in bonds, 1.2 % in cash, and 18.6% in other assets including property. According to the Towers Watson report, the weighted average portfolio for the top 20 funds showed that 50% of the total assets was invested in fixed-income securities. Table 8.7 gives the total

Table 8.7 Pension Funds Total Investment: Select OECD Members (Billions of US Dollars)		
Country	**2001**	**2011**
United States	7205.8	10,584.2
United Kingdom	1040.5	2129.5
Japan	756	1470.3
Netherlands	411.3	1157.3
Australia	268.2	1340
Canada	375.6	1106.1
Source: OECD Global Pension Statistics.		

---

[7] http://www.oecd.org/daf/financialmarketsinsuranceandpensions/privatepensions/PensionMarketsInFocus2012.pdf

Table 8.8   Largest US Corporate Pension Plans

	Corporation	Total Assets (Billions of US Dollars)
1	IBM	91.688
2	General Motors	83.626
3	Ford	64.108
4	Royal Dutch Shell	72.935
5	General Electric	54.440
6	Boeing	56.178
7	AT&T	45.060
8	Exxon Mobil	30.722
9	Lockheed Martin	309.24
10	United Tech	299.28

Source: Citi Research.

Table 8.9   Regional Indicators: Value in Billions of US Dollars

	2001	2011
Total OECD	10,732.3	20,112.7
Total G20	9859.9	17,535.7
Euro area	676.1	1956
Latin America	35.6	694.1
Asia	813.9	1828.8
Total world	10,870.8	20,719.3

Source: OECD Global Pension Statistics.

Table 8.10   Assets of Private Pension Funds (Billions of US Dollars)

Year	2007	2008	2009	2010	2011	2012
DB plans	2515.7	1894.9	2129.1	2389.6	2450.7	2547.4
DC contribution plans	3592.5	2673.2	3313.6	3753.5	3851.6	4088.6
Total	6108.2	4568.1	5442.7	6143.1	6302.3	6636

Source: Z.1 Financial accounts of the United States, Federal Reserve Statistical Reserve, June 6, 2013.

investments of pension funds during the period 2001 and 2011 by country. Table 8.8 lists the largest US corporate pension plans in terms of total assets. Table 8.9 provides details of pension investments by region. Table 8.10 highlights the assets of private pension funds in the US. Table 8.11 highlights the value of financial assets of other pension funds in the US.

Table 8.11   Financial Assets of Other Pension Funds (Billions of US Dollars)

Year	2007	2008	2009	2010	2011	2012
State and local government employee retirement funds	3285.9	2428.6	2722.2	2949.3	2872.6	3193.5
Federal government retirement funds	1197	1222.3	13,247	1425.4	1509.6	1582.3

Source: Z.1 Financial accounts of the United States, Federal Reserve Statistical Reserve, June 6, 2013.

8.4 SUMMARY

Mutual funds, insurance, and pensions funds are major financial intermediaries. A mutual fund is a professionally managed collective investment vehicle that collects money from investors and invests in traded financial securities. Mutual funds represent the second-largest pool of private capital in the world after the banking industry. Mutual funds are classified as open-ended, closed-end, and UITs. In open-ended funds, unit shares can be issued and redeemed at any time. Closed-end funds generally issue a fixed number of shares that are listed on the stock exchange or traded in the OTC market. UITs are exchange-traded mutual funds that offer an unmanaged portfolio of securities with a fixed life. The Investment Company Act of 1940 regulates mutual funds regarding disclosures and information about investment objectives, investment company structure, and operations. The main categories of funds are stock or equity funds, bond or fixed-income funds, money market funds, and hybrid funds. Other types of funds include ETFs, venture capital funds, private equity funds, hedge funds, and REITs.

Insurance is a way of reducing potential financial loss by means of covering the cost of unexpected events such as property damage, theft, or illness. The insurance industry is basically classified as life or property insurance. The two main types of life insurance are term and permanent life insurance. There are also other life insurance products such as group life insurance, credit life insurance, annuities, and pension plans. Property/casualty insurance is insurance on homes, cars, and businesses. Other types of insurance include health insurance, business insurance, bond insurance, and mortgage insurance. The three fundamental risk faced by insurance companies are underwriting, market, and regulatory risk. VaR and ES are two major metrics used to measure and manage financial risks in insurance. The major risk mitigation measures in insurance consist of internal measures, reinsurance, and use of financial market instruments and letters of credit. Premiums are a major source of funds for insurance companies. The performance of an insurance company can be evaluated using ratios such as the combined ratio, operating ratio, and underwriting leverage ratio.

Pension funds established by an employer based on the contributions made by an employer and an employee provide pensions for employees at the time of retirement. Pension funds are classified as different types: public and private pension plans, occupational and personal pension plans, DC and DB plans, protected and unprotected pension plans, funded versus unfunded pension plans, and single- and multiple-employer pension funds. Private pension funds consists of 401(k), 403(b), and IRAs. Traditionally pension funds have been managed passively by investments in highly stable stocks and bonds. Pension funds face challenges with respect to governance and risks. Investment risk, longevity, and funding risk are the major risks faced by pension funds.

QUESTIONS FOR DISCUSSION

1. Discuss the roles of the major stakeholders of a mutual fund.
2. Discuss the different types of mutual funds.
3. Explain the different mutual fund expenses and fees.
4. What are major categories of mutual funds?
5. What are alternative types of funds?
6. Explain the problems of adverse selection and moral hazard in the insurance industry.
7. Discuss the major types of insurance.
8. What are the different types of property and casualty insurance?
9. Explain the underwriting cycle.
10. What are the major risks faced by insurance companies?
11. What are the risk mitigation strategies in insurance?
12. What are the sources and uses of funds in insurance?
13. Explain the significance of valuation of insurance companies with ratio analysis.
14. What are the different types of pension plans?
15. Discuss the major regulations for mutual funds, insurance, and pension funds.

REFERENCES

Investment Company Fact Book, 2011. Investment Company Institute. http://www.icifactbook.org/. Retrieved 2012-08-02.

Investment Company Fact Book, 2012. Tables 37-39, pp. 170-172

Investment Company Fact Book, 2012 (Chapter 2).

American Insurance Association. http://www.aiadc.org.

National Association of Insurance Commissioners (NAIC). http://www.naic.org.

http://ok.gov/sde/sites/ok.gov.sde/files/PFLModule_11.2.pdf.

World Insurance Report, 2012. Capgemini EMFA.

http://www.oecdlibrary.org.

Global Insurance Market Trends OECD. http://www.oecd.org/insurance/insurance/49108065.pdf.

Madsen, C., Pedersen, H., December 2002. An examination of insurance pricing and underwriting cycles. http://www.actuaries.org/AFIR/Colloquia/Maastricht/Madsen_Pedersen.pdf.

Cummins, D. Asset Pricing models and insurance ratemaking. http://www.actuaries.org/LIBRARY/ASTIN/vol20no2/125.pdf.

Nissim, D. Analysis and Valuation of Insurance Companies. Industry Study No 2, Centre for excellence in accounting and security analysis, Columbia Business School. http://www.columbia.edu/~dn75/Analysis%20and%20Valuation%20of%20Insurance%20Companies%20-%20Final.pdf

Baranoff, E.G., Sager, T.W., 2002. The relations among asset risk, product risk, and capital in the life insurance industry. Journal of Banking and Finance 26 (6), 1181–1197.

http://www.iii.org.

Private Pensions: OECD Classification 12 and Glossary. ISBN 92-64-01699-6, © OECD 2005.

http://thismatter.com/money/banking/nondepository-institutions.htm.

Financial Services: Global pension Industry Depth, Knowledge and depth. www.kpmg.com.

http://www.kpmg.com/IL/en/IssuesAndInsights/ArticlesPublications/PublicationSeries/Documents/Global_Pensions_Industry_Depth_Knowledge_and_Insight_October_2011.pdf.

OECD, 2012. Pension Markets in Focus. September 2012, Issue 9.

http://www.oecd.org/daf/financialmarketsinsuranceandpensions/privatepensions/PensionMarketsInFocus2012. pdf.

OECD Global Pension Statistics.

Ganzi, J., Seymour, F., Bueffet, S., Dubash, N., 1998. Leverage for the Environment: A Guide to the Private Financial Services Industry. World Resources Institute, Washington, DC.

Ashcroft, J., Stewart, F., 2010. Managing and supervising risks in defined contribution pension system. International Organization of Pension Supervisors Working Paper 12.

Global Pension Assets Study, 2013. towerswatson.com.

Puracell, P., Staman, J., May 2009. Summary of the Employee Retirement Income Act (ERISA). Congressional Research Service. http://www.aging.senate.gov/crs/pension7.pdf.

Puracell, P., 2006. CRS Report for Congress. Summary of the Pension Protection Act of 2006. Congressional Research Service. http://401kpsp.com/indexes/pension%20act%20summary.pdf.

CHAPTER

PRIVATE EQUITY AND HEDGE FUNDS

9

9.1 PRIVATE EQUITY
9.1.1 INTRODUCTION

Private equity (PE), often categorized along a broader category called private capital, refers to any ownership interest in an asset that is not tradable in a public market. PE is a type of equity investment in private companies that is not listed on the stock exchanges. The PE investment will generally be made by a private equity firm, a venture capital firm, or an angel investor. PE funds invest in assets that are not publicly owned or the PE fund buys the publicly traded assets and then takes the company private.

These companies provide funds to new companies for expansion, new product development, or restructuring operations. PE companies generally invest in new companies that do not have sufficient operating histories to issue common stock on a public exchange. Venture capital is a type of private equity that focuses on startup companies. Venture capital funds provide sources of financing in stages classified as seed financing, done in the early stage and at a later stage. Investors at the seed stage, known as angels, provide financial sources to develop an innovative plan. Early stage financing occurs when business plans and part of the management team is in place. Later stage financing provides financing when the infrastructure is in place and a viable product is ready to be introduced. Buyouts involve the acquisition of a product line, a set of assets, or a business. The primary aim of investment by the PE firm is to get involved in the business, increase the value, and sell their shares in the business to get the desired payoff.

Private equity funds invest in companies that have the potential to provide huge returns. They aim to magnify returns on investment through extensive use of debt. A PE firm will look for high growth, competitive products and services. The PE investor then brings capital but will only profit if the company grows. When an entrepreneur seeks a PE investor, the expectation is for a long-term partnership for the next few stages of growth of the company.

A typical PE investment process involves the stages of investment through a majority stake; the PE investor sees improvement in the performance of the company and then exits the investment after making huge gains. PE firms make use of borrowed funds to conduct leveraged buyouts (LBOs).

Big banks are the largest lenders to PE firms. Investment banks provide bridge loans to cover the costs of PE acquisition until permanent sources of funds are obtained. ExxonMobil, Royal Dutch Shell, and Chevron Texaco are some of the major corporations that have benefitted from PE deals. Some of the world's largest PE firms include Kohlberg, Kravis and Roberts (KKR), Blackstone, Bain Capital, Carlyle Group, TPG Capital, and Goldman Sachs.

One of the most-often cited PE deals was the buyout of RJR Nabisco by KKR in the 1980s. In 2007, in another high-profile deal, KKR & Co. (formerly Kohlberg Kravis Roberts & Co.) bought TXU Corporation for $45 billion.

9.1.2 STRATEGIES OF PRIVATE EQUITY FIRMS

The role of a PE firm is basically to provide capital to support long-term, illiquid investment strategy. Private equity strategies involve LBOs, venture capital, growth capital, distressed investments, and mezzanine capital. In LBOs, the PE firm acquires the stock or assets of a target company financed largely by borrowing. The buying group may be sponsored by a buyout specialist (e.g., KKR). As part of the ongoing private transaction, the buyout group delists the firm and makes it private. In an LBO, debt financing typically represents 50% or more of the purchase price.

Basically there are four stages in an LBO operation. The first stage of operation consists of raising the cash required for the buyout and devising a management incentive system. In the second stage, the organizing sponsor buys all the outstanding shares of the company and takes it private or purchases all the assets of the company. In the third stage, management tries to increase profits and cash flow by cutting operating costs and changing marketing strategies. In the fourth stage, the investor may take the company public again if the performance of the company improves. This second public offering is known as the secondary initial public offering (SIPO).

Growth capital strategies are often minority investments in mature companies by PE firms to expand or restructure an operation or to finance a major acquisition. Mezzanine capital or subordinated debt financing are used by PE firms to finance LBO. Venture capital is a type of private equity investment for the promotion of new technology, new marketing concepts, and new products. Distressed or a special category of turnaround strategies are used by PE firms for the purpose of corporate restructuring. A PE firm's strategies can also be involved in investments in real estate, infrastructure, energy, and power sectors.

9.1.3 ORGANIZATION STRUCTURE OF PRIVATE EQUITY FUNDS

Private equity funds are, in short, investment vehicles established by sponsors (investment managers) whose primary function is to raise capital for a specific industry sector or geographic region. Passive investors who invest an amount of capital over time pass on the responsibility to manage and divest the fund's investments to sponsors of the fund. Sponsors of the fund receive management fees and profit participation in the fund's investments. Investors are expected to receive a high rate of return on their invested capital. Figure 9.1 gives the general structure of a PE business.

Private equity funds are established as limited partnerships (LPs) or limited liability companies (LLCs). The liability of limited partners of an LP or LLC are limited to its capital commitments and its share of investment funds. The main advantage is that such partnerships are considered to be "pass-through" entities and are not subject to corporate income tax.

Private equity funds are generally structured as closed-end investment funds. The period for raising funds normally varies from 12-18 months. Sponsors of the fund invite investors to make capital commitments during this period. In the United States capital funds for PE are normally raised through the process of private placements. Private placements are made to financial institutions, government and corporate pension plans, university endowments, foundations, sovereign wealth funds, funds of funds,

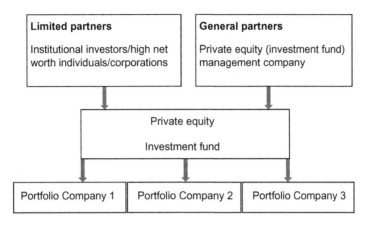

FIGURE 9.1

Structure of private equity business.

and insurance companies. In other words, PE firms (also known as PE management companies or general partners (GPs)) establish investment funds that collect capital from investors known as LPs. The capital funds collected are invested in high-potential companies that are known as portfolio or investee companies. The GP or manager has the legal power to act on behalf of the investment fund. A management company or investment adviser affiliated with the GP provides investment advisory services. The investment fund or GP enters into an investment advisory agreement with the investment advisor for providing the services of investment professionals, an evaluation of potential investment opportunities, and other investment advisory services. The fund pays the management fees to the investment advisor. The PE funds for investment purposes outside the United States in offshore jurisdictions such as the Cayman Islands or Channel Islands are also formed as LPs or LLCs.

9.1.3.1 Exit strategy
The fund manager (sponsor) runs the investment operations and prepares exit strategies depending on market conditions and the agreements drawn up in advance with entrepreneurs.

The investor's capital commitment is not funded all at once but is made as separate capital contributions according to the company's needs. The divestment period ranges from 4-6 years following the investment period. The capital recovered from the exit along with capital gains is redistributed to the original investors by the fund sponsor on a pro rata basis, depending on the size of the initial investment.

A trade sale or merger and acquisition is the most popular type of exit strategy. It is also referred to as the sale of company shares to industrial investors. A management team repurchase is also an important exit strategy. The sale of the investment to another financial purchaser (known as the secondary market investor) is also a part of the exit strategy. Exiting through an IPO is also a widely adopted exit strategy for a PE firm.

9.1.4 TYPES OF PRIVATE EQUITY FUNDS
There are different types of PE funds based on the life cycle of a firm. These funds can be LBO funds, venture capital funds, growth equity funds, and special situation funds.

9.1.4.1 Leveraged buyout funds

LBO funds typically acquire controlling stakes either alone or in partnership with other PE firms of mature, cash-flow stable companies. The financing of these transactions is done predominantly with debt in the form of bank loans, term loans, subordinated or mezzanine debt. Examples of LBO funds include KKR, Carlyle, TPG, Blackstone, and Apollo.

9.1.4.2 Venture capital funds

Venture capital funds invest in minority stakes in startup companies in high-growth sectors such as IT, biotech, and healthcare technologies. Seed financing is used to research, assess, and develop an idea or initial concept before the startup phase. In this stage investors are business angels who are basically entrepreneurs. Startup financing is used for product development and initial marketing. Venture capital funds invest in the very early stages or later stages of a project. In early stage funding, venture capital is invested in companies that have technical talent to invent and commercialize new technologies. In later stage funds, the strategy is to help portfolio companies maximize their growth potential through enhancing managerial capabilities. Examples of venture capital funds include Kleiner Perkins, Sequoia, Accel, August Capital, and Andreessen Horowitz.

9.1.4.3 Growth equity funds

Growth equity funds provide capital for expansion purposes. These funds invest in later-stage, pre-IPO companies or in private investment in public equity (PIPE) transactions with public companies. Examples of growth equity fund companies include Summit Partners, JMI, and TA Associates.

9.1.4.4 Special situation funds

Special situation funds are also called distressed funds. They invest in debt securities of financially distressed companies at a large discount. These funds invest in mezzanine or mid-layer debt capital, which provides more protection than equity financing in the event of default. These funds specialize in turnaround investments. Some special funds focus on specific geographic regions or specific sectors.

9.1.5 DETERMINANTS OF PRIVATE EQUITY

From the perspective of a growing company, raising capital through PE can be a viable alternative to fundraising. PE funds invest in the most dynamic companies with the highest potential for growth. Sectors like software, telecommunications, and Internet services focus on PE investments for expansion purposes. The increasing demand for PE must also be viewed in the context of increasing regulation of public markets. Raising of funds through PE also helps the company have control over the operations as shareholders are limited. With an increase in PE deals, the value of a company may increase in the stock market. Companies that are the target of PE buyouts have witnessed stock prices rise.

9.1.6 PRIVATE EQUITY MARKET TRENDS

The PE industry has witnessed a cycle of ups and downs during the last three decades. The equity market had its lows during the junk bond crisis of the 1980s, the dot-com crisis of the 1990s, and the recession of 2008. According to Bain and Company's Global Private Equity Report of 2012, over US$2 trillion of assets are managed by PE firms. The same report states that funds available for investment totaled $949 billion. According to a Deloitte report, the assets under management of PE firms amounted to $3 trillion in 2012.

The PwC Private Equity Market Trend Report of 2012 has cited a number of trends. According to the report, health care and related services are viewed by PE funds as offering growth potential because of shifting demographics in Western markets. It is expected that technological innovations will trigger many social responses that will act as sources of opportunity for PE firms. Buyout funds or non-venture-equity funds have emerged as a significant force in the global corporate restructuring arena. Knowing the local markets is the biggest challenge of PE markets worldwide. Exit strategies are well defined in Western markets. Also, in developed market mergers, IPOs, management buyouts, or recapitalization have well-established exit modes with financial infrastructure, although challenges exist in developing markets.

Private equity firms are rapidly establishing footholds in the growing market of African continents such as Nigeria, Ghana, and Kenya. According to an E&Y report in 2012 called "Private Equity Round Up Africa," PE firms are attracted to the region's high growth rates and its shift away from commodities and agrarian-based economies to consumer economies, which are driven by a growing middle class.

9.1.7 REGULATION

Private equity funds are regulated by or exempted from regulations by a myriad of US federal legislation. Private equity funds are exempted from registration as investment companies provided that the PE firm is owned by not more than 100 persons and doesn't make public offerings. Sponsors of PE funds can avoid registration with the US SEC under the Advisers Act through the exemption that investment advisers with fewer than 15 clients need not register. The Dodd-Frank Act of 2010 amended the Advisers Act to eliminate the private investment adviser exemption. Now PE funds with assets under management of $150 million or more must register with the SEC as investment advisers. The Dodd-Frank Act imposes additional recordkeeping and reporting requirements for investment advisers. The Securities Exchange Act stipulates the registration of issuing firms with total assets exceeding $10 million and 500 or more investors in case of a US issuer. Hence, most PE funds seek to limit the number of record owners to up to 499 investors to circumvent the registration provision under the Exchange Act. The ERISA Act of 1974 places restrictions on PE funds if the fund holds "plan assets" under ERISA. If the fund qualifies as a venture capital operating company or a real estate operating company, exemptions to the above rules prevail.

9.1.8 CHALLENGES

Private equity firms face challenges of regulatory compliances and tax issues. They also have challenges with respect to achieving target compliance to meet new established standards. Economic instability in the markets of the United States and Europe as well as emerging markets like India and China is putting pressure on the top-line revenue growth of PE firms. According to the Wharton Private Equity Review Report,[1] during the boom period of 2005-2007, PE deals were completed with 15% of equity financed and the rest accounted for by debt financing through LBOs. After the

---

[1] Wharton Private Equity Review Navigating the challenges ahead, http://knowledge.wharton.upenn.edu/papers/download/072809_PrivateEquity09.pdf.

economic meltdown of 2007, approximately 35-40% of equity was required. For a smaller buyout, the equity requirement accounts for 50-75%. This changing pattern of capital structure creates new challenges for PE financing.

One of the major challenges faced by PE firms in the United States buyout market is the sharp rise in purchase price multiples being paid for high-value companies. This can be attributed to the increase in the number of PE firms competing for high-quality deals. The major challenges faced by PE firms in the European buyout market is the difficulty in finding a feasible way to exit boom-year deals through exit routes such as public markets, trade sales, and secondary sales. Regulatory issues in major emerging markets such as China are impediments for the growth of PE markets. There are also sectors that are not accessible to foreign investors and offshore funds. Regulatory risk is also a challenge. As a result of the implementation of Basel III and the Dodd-Frank Act, banks are being forced to exit or decrease their level of activity in private equity and leveraged lending.

9.2 HEDGE FUNDS

9.2.1 INTRODUCTION

A hedge fund is an alternative investment fund that is available to institutional investors and high-net-worth individuals with significant assets. Like mutual funds, hedge funds are pools of underlying securities, and they can invest in a number of securities. Hedge funds use advanced investment strategies such as long and short positions, and leveraged and other derivative positions in domestic and global markets to earn higher rates of returns. Hedge funds are highly leveraged and invest in high-risk financial derivatives. Generally, hedge funds trade in liquid securities in public markets. They use arbitrage strategies to buy and sell undervalued securities, trade options, or bonds. Hedge funds are set up as open-ended private investment partnership funds with large minimum initial investments. They are expected to have a net worth of more than $1 million. Pension funds, endowments, insurance companies, private banks, high-net-worth individuals, and insurance companies invest in hedge funds to minimize portfolio volatility and enhance returns.

Hedge funds can be used by investors to reduce overall portfolio risk exposures. They can accomplish this by providing effective diversification for investment portfolios and by using a number of risk management tools to reduce the downward risk. Investors use funds for capital preservation, as they offer higher risk-adjusted returns than traditional investments. Hedge funds employ various investment tools that can increase returns. Most are structured as open-ended funds, issuing new shares to investors on an ongoing basis. Hedge funds typically charge investors a management fee, usually 1-2% of the assets managed. Most also charge an incentive (or performance) fee that ranges between 10% and 20% of fund profits.

9.2.2 MARKET TRENDS

In 1990, there were approximately 640 hedge funds worldwide with assets of $39 billion. By 2007, the number rose to 9700 hedge funds under management, with more than $1.7 trillion in assets. By 2012, the size of the global hedge industry had reached $2.13 trillion[2] with an estimated 8350 active funds.

---

[2]Chung, Juliet (19 April 2012). Hedge-Fund Assets Rise to Record Level. *The Wall Street Journal*. http://online.wsj.com/article/SB10001424052702304331204577354043852093400.html?mod=googlenews_wsj.

According to a Global Hedge Fund Industry Report, investors allocated $15.2 billion of net new capital to hedge funds in the first quarter of 2013. These funds have experienced capital inflows in 14 of the last 15 quarters.

Most hedge funds are established in offshore financial centers to take advantages of tax benefits. The Cayman Islands is the main center for hedge funds; an estimated 34% of the global hedge fund industry is based there.

According to a study by the Centre for Hedge Fund Research in 2012,[3] hedge funds significantly outperformed traditional asset classes such as equities, bonds, and commodities over a 17-year period. The report found that hedge funds returned approximately 9% on average after fees between 1994 and 2011 compared to 7.18% for global stocks, 6.25 % for global bonds, and 7.27% for global commodities.

9.2.3 STRUCTURE OF HEDGE FUNDS

Most hedge funds are organized as LPs and are considered pass-through entities for tax purposes. The typical fund structure is a two-tiered organization. The hedge fund manager (portfolio manager) is the GP in a hedge fund organized as an LLC. The other entity is the limited partner in the organizational setup. The hedge fund manager performs the day-to-day operations and administrative responsibilities of the hedge fund and receives the management fees paid by the limited partners.

The key players in a hedge fund are the portfolio managers, prime brokers, administrators, distributors, and auditors. The portfolio manager determines the investment strategy and makes the investment and allocation decisions. Funds must secure their loans with collateral to gain margin and secure trade. The prime broker or securities firm with the help of a risk matrix determines how much to lend to each of its clients. The prime broker is involved in prime brokerage services such as lending money, acting as a counterparty to derivatives contracts, and lending securities for short selling. Auditors ensure fund compliance. The administrator is involved in the valuation of assets and other related back-office functions. The distributor is responsible for marketing the fund to potential investors. Legal advisors, registrars, and transfer agents are the other service providers involved in the fund.

Many hedge funds set up feeder funds for foreign and US tax-exempt investors. Feeder funds are established in foreign jurisdictions, usually tax-haven regions, with investment partnership interests in the United States. Figure 9.2 gives the general structure of hedge funds.

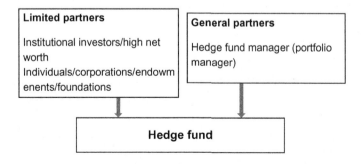

FIGURE 9.2

Structure of hedge funds.

---

[3]The Value of the Hedge Fund Industry to Investors, Markets and the Broader Economy, Centre for Hedge Fund Research 2012, Imperial College London, AIMA, KPMG.

9.2.4 DIFFERENCE BETWEEN MUTUAL FUNDS AND HEDGE FUNDS

Mutual funds are regulated by the SEC. Although hedge funds are in the process of becoming regulated, currently unregulated hedge funds can invest in a wider range of securities than mutual funds. In addition to conventional securities such as stocks, bonds, commodities, and real estate, hedge funds invest in more sophisticated and risky investments. They use long and short strategies, which involve long positions (buy stock) and sell positions (sell stocks with borrowed money and buy back stocks when prices fall). Hedge funds also invest in derivatives products such as futures and options.

Hedge funds are not as liquid as mutual funds. While mutual fund shares can be sold any time, since their net asset value (NAV) is calculated every day, hedge funds generally have a lockup period during which investors cannot sell their shares.

There are also differences in the way the two types of fund managers are compensated. Mutual fund managers are paid fees irrespective of their fund's performance. Hedge fund managers, in contrast, receive a percentage of the returns they earn for investors along with a management fee, which ranges from 1% to 4% of the NAV. The risk involved is therefore higher for hedge fund investors since managers focus on generating higher returns by taking excessive risks. US laws stipulate that hedge fund investors must have a net worth of more than $1 million and significant investment knowledge. Hence, they are typically open to only a limited range of investors.

9.2.5 REGULATION

In the United States, hedge funds are regulated by the SEC and Commodity Futures Trading Commission (CFTC). Fund managers can accept investment capital only from accredited investors or qualified purchasers such as public employee retirement plans, corporate employee retirement plans, university endowments, foundations, family offices, and high-net-worth individuals. Accredited investors consist of individuals, financial institutions, and executive officers or directors of such institutions. Individuals with more than $1 million in assets or joint income of more than $3 million are accredited investors. Financial institutions (banks), insurance companies, pension funds with profits exceeding $5 million in investments, or individuals with investments of at least $25 million are qualified purchasers. These accredited investors or qualified purchasers had been exempt from registration with SEC. Regulations were not stringent for hedge funds until the 2008 credit crisis. New regulations introduced in the United States and the European Union as of 2010 require hedge fund managers to report more information, for greater transparency. The Dodd-Frank Wall Street Reform Act contains provisions that require hedge fund advisers with US$150 million to register with the SEC. Most commodity pool operators and commodity trading advisers must register with the CFTC. The Jumpstart Our Business Startups (JOBS) Act of 2012 removed a prior ban on general solicitation and advertising by companies conducting private offerings including hedge funds with the condition that the funds be sold only to investors with a net worth of over $2.5 million.

9.2.6 HEDGE FUND STRATEGIES

Hedge funds use different strategies based on investment style and risk return characteristics. The prospectus highlights key aspects such as a fund's investment strategy, type, and leverage limit for potential investors.

Hedge funds typically use long short strategies, which involve long and short positions. They also use the investment technique of leverage as a strategy to increase returns by taking high risks.

Popular hedge fund strategies can be categorized as equity-based strategies, arbitrage-based strategies, opportunistic strategies, and multiple strategies. In equity-based strategies, hedge managers take long positions in undervalued stocks and short positions in overvalued stocks. In equity-neutral strategies, managers take offsetting long and short positions. Arbitrage strategies are undertaken for fixed-income securities, convertible securities, and possibilities of mergers. Opportunistic strategies involve investment in high-yield and distressed and global macro strategies, as well as managed futures.

Hedge funds also invest in emerging market funds. Emerging market strategies specialize in investments of securities of emerging market countries. Hedge funds can mix and match different hedge funds and other pooled investment vehicles. This blend of different strategies and asset classes aims to provide more stable long-term investment return for individual funds. Hedge funds also invest in bonds, with a primary focus on yield or current income rather than on capital gains, and they often invest in equities for realizing higher returns, especially small-cap stocks. The investment theme of hedge funds is also subject to changes in the context of events such as IPOs, earnings announcements, and other corporate activities such as mergers, acquisitions, and LBOs.

The major investment strategies of hedge funds are discussed in the following.

9.2.6.1 Equity long strategy

An equity long short strategy involves taking a long position in undervalued stocks and a short position in overvalued stocks. This strategy aims to minimize general market exposure and gain from the spread between stocks. Equity long short strategies that hold equal value of long and short positions are termed market neutral strategies. There are also skewed or long bias strategies like 130/30 strategies in which hedge funds have 130% exposure to long positions and 30% exposure to short positions.

9.2.6.2 Fixed income strategy

A fixed income arbitrage strategy is based on the pricing differential between fixed income securities. This type of arbitrage involves the simultaneous purchase and sale of two similar securities. The hedge fund trader will sell (short) the overvalued security and buy the undervalued security. Once the prices revert to the true value, the trade is closed at a profit gain.

9.2.6.3 Convertible arbitrage strategy

A convertible arbitrage is a type of equity long short strategy in which instead of buying and shorting stocks, the hedge fund takes a long position in convertible securities and simultaneously takes a short position in the same company stock. This strategy aims to profit from the pricing differential in which convertible bonds may be priced inefficiently compared to common stock. In a typical convertible arbitrage, a hedge fund buys a company's convertible bonds and shorts the common stock of the company. If the stock price falls, the hedge fund benefits from the short position but the convertible bonds value may not decline and the bonds are not converted into stocks. If the stock price rises, the hedge fund will convert the bonds into stocks and sell them at market value, thereby gaining from the long position. Convertible arbitrage becomes riskier when unpredictable events such as a market crash happen, which will result in a decline in the value of securities. In 2005, many arbitrageurs who had long positions in General Motors convertible bonds and short positions in GM stock suffered huge losses due to downgrading of the company bonds by credit-rating agencies.

9.2.6.4 Fund of funds strategy

A fund of funds (hedge funds) is the strategy involving construction of a portfolio of a number of hedge funds. The fund of funds is a collective investment that holds a portfolio of other investment funds instead of investing directly in securities like stocks, bonds, and derivatives. This strategy aims at diversification and varied management experiences. The hedge fund manager aims to select the best performing hedge funds in a portfolio. Considering that the initial investment criteria is very high for each hedge fund, the fund of hedge funds strategy enables investors to have access to a number of good-performing hedge funds. A fund of funds usually charges an incremental fee structure.

9.2.6.5 Investments in distressed securities

Some hedge funds focus on investing in distressed securities. A company's debt is considered distressed when its yield to maturity is more than 1000 basis points above the risk-free rate of return or if it is rated CCC or below by any major credit-rating agency. The company may file for bankruptcy.

9.2.6.6 Global macro strategy

A global macro strategy adopted by hedge funds focuses on investing in instruments whose price fluctuates from changes in the macroeconomic policies and flow of capital around the world. Global macro strategies use macroeconomic scenario analysis to identify trends and opportunities for investment. Directional investment strategies identify market movements and trends for investment decisions. The global macro strategies consist of currency, interest rate, and stock index strategies. Currency traders focus on the relative strength of one currency versus another, which fluctuates owing to a number of factors. Leverage can be employed to trade in currencies. The various currency instruments include spot transactions, futures contracts, options, and forward rate agreements. In a global macro strategy, the hedge the fund manager also focuses on interest rate trading. The fund invests in sovereign debt instruments such as Treasury bills, government bonds, and the like.

Hedge portfolio managers use equity indexes to create investment portfolios. Equity indexes are available in futures exchanges, options exchanges, and exchange traded funds.

9.2.6.7 Merger arbitrage strategy

Hedge funds also focus on merger arbitrage. This is an event-driven investment strategy that aims to gain from the pricing inefficiencies that exist before or after corporate events involving restructuring, such as mergers, acquisitions, or spin-offs. For example, in a merger arbitrage involving acquisition of a company using stock, the hedge fund buys the stock of the target company and shorts the stock of an acquiring company. It is generally seen that the target firm's stock price gain and the acquirer firm's stock price lose after the merger announcement. On completion of the merger, the target firm's stocks are converted into the acquiring firm's stock. The merger arbitrageur gains as he or she is able to cover the short position.

9.2.6.8 Relative value arbitrage

Large institutional investors like hedge funds, investment banks, and PE firms are the major users of relative value arbitrage. The relative value arbitrage is an investment strategy that aims to exploit the price differential between related financial instruments. This process involves buying and selling different securities and profits from the diverging price differential between two securities. When the price of one security rises and the other falls, the relative value arbitrageur buys one security and shorts the other. When prices converge again, the relative value arbitrageur closes the trade.

9.2.6.9 Managed futures strategy

Managed futures is one of the oldest styles of investment strategy practiced by hedge funds. Through managed futures, hedge funds take short and long positions in futures contracts of equity indexes, commodities, metals, foreign currency, and government bond futures. The hedge fund manager focuses on highly liquid regulated exchange-traded instruments and foreign exchange markets. Portfolios are marked to market every day. Managed futures can reduce risk through portfolio diversification.

9.2.7 CHALLENGES

Hedge funds face the challenge of developing a sound organizational structure to fit into investors' perception of institutional quality. They also face the challenge of meeting institutional requirements for stepping up reporting and transparency in the context of a changing regulatory environment. Hedge funds face enormous challenges as investors demand more solid returns with a robust operating model and lower overall risk profile. Compliance has become a major challenge for hedge funds given the increasing regulatory burden and push by investors for additional transparency.

Biggest Hedge Funds

Bridgewater Associates
Man Group
JPMorgan Asset Management
Brevan Howard Asset Management
Och-Ziff Capital Management

9.3 SUMMARY

Private equity is a type of equity investment into private companies that are not listed on stock exchanges. The primary aim of investment by a PE firm is to get involved in the business, increase the value, and sell its shares in the business to get the desired payoff.

Private equity strategies involve LBOs, venture capital, growth capital, distressed investments, and mezzanine capital.

Private equity funds are established as LPs or LLCs. Private equity funds are basically structured as closed-end investment funds. In the United States the capital funds for PE are normally raised through the process of private placements. Mergers and acquisitions or trade sales, management buyouts, and IPOs are the three main exit strategies adopted by venture capitalists. The different types of PE funds are categorized as leverage buyout funds, venture capital funds, growth equity funds, and special situation funds. Venture capital is a type of PE investment for promotion of new technology, new marketing concepts, and new products.

A hedge fund is an alternative investment fund that is available to institutional investors and high-net-worth individuals with significant assets. Hedge funds are highly leveraged and invest in high-risk financial derivatives. Most hedge funds are organized as LPs.

Popular hedge fund strategies can be categorized as equity-based strategies, arbitrage-based strategies, opportunistic strategies, and multiple strategies. Some of the major investment strategies of hedge funds are equity long strategies, fixed-income strategies, convertible arbitrage strategies, fund of funds strategies, global macro, relative value arbitrage, and managed futures.

QUESTIONS FOR DISCUSSION

1. Discuss private equity and hedge funds.
2. Explain the structure and strategy of PE funds.
3. What are the different types of PE funds?
4. Differentiate between mutual funds and hedge funds.
5. Explain the different strategies adopted by hedge funds.

REFERENCES

Data Monitor Report, 2012.

http://www.investopedia.com/terms/h/hedgefund.asp#ixzz2Au9soxeK.

Friedland, D. Magnum Funds. http://www.magnum.com/hedgefunds/abouthedgefunds.asp.

Anson, M.J.P., 2006. The Handbook of Alternative Assets. John Wiley & SonsISBN: 0-471-98020-X p. 123.

Hedge Funds: How They Serve Investors In U.S. and Global Markets, Hedge Fund Facts.org. Coalition of Private Investment Companies, 2009. http://www.hedgefundfacts.org/hedge/wp-content/uploads/2009/09/Hedge_Funds.pdf.

http://www.imf.org/external/pubs/ft/fandd/2006/06/basics.htm.

Bain Global Private Equity Report 2012.

Private Company Knowledge Bank. Privco.com. http://www.privco.com/knowledge-bank/private-equity-and-venture-capital. Retrieved 18 May 2012.

Weston, F. et al., 1990. Going Private and Leveraged Buyouts. Mergers Restructuring and Corporate Control (Chapter 16, p. 394).

http://www.bloomberg.com/apps/news?pid=20601102&sid=abPIOg0EYQy0&refer=uk.

2013 Private Equity Fund Outlook In search of firm footing Deloitte Report.

http://www.deloitte.com/assets/Dcom-CaymanIslands/Local%20Assets/Documents/2013_Private_Equity_Fund_Outlook.pdf.

Guide on Private Equity and Venture Capital for Entrepreneurs. An EVCA Special paper, November 2007. http://www.evca.eu/uploadedFiles/Home/Toolbox/Introduction_Tutorial/EVCA_PEVCguide.pdf.

Naidech, S.W. Chadbourne and Parke LLP, 2011. Private Equity Fund Formation. Practical Law Publishing Limited and Practical Law Company.

10 Challenges facing the private equity industry in 2013. Altius Associates. http://www.altius-associates.com/downloads/AA_Q1-2013_whitepaper.pdf.

http://www.barclayhedge.com/research/educational-articles/in-depth-articles/hedge-funds-future-prospects-are-bright.html.

Díaz, G.G., 2011. A basic outlook on hedge fund structure and taxation issues. http://www.uprblj.com/wp/wp-content/uploads/2011/12/2-UPRBLJ-264.pdf.

ISLAMIC INFLUENCE

10.1 INTRODUCTION

The sharia, which is the interpretation of the religious law of Islam, lays down four main prohibitions to distinguish Islamic finance from conventional finance. One of the most important principles of Islamic finance is the scriptural injunction against interest or *riba*. The sharia principles also consider uncertainty (*gharar*), gambling (*masir*), and use of certain products such as pork or alcohol as unislamic. There are *fiqh* academies composed of Islamic legal and religious scholars who generate fatwas or legal rulings on various issues. For each financial institution, a sharia advisory committee comprised of Islamic jurists oversees the operation of each institution. It is the responsibility of the committee to determine the nature of business and finance to be either permissible (*hallal*) or unlawful (*haram*).

Islamic finance has more than US$800 billion in assets worldwide. The basic concept of Islamic finance is driven by the guiding principle of extending religious doctrine in the sharia to financial agreements and transactions. The Islamic finance industry had been growing at an average rate of 15% because of huge demand for sharia-compliant products. Islamic banks have increased their presence in conventional financial systems by either opening up Islamic banking activities or offering specific Islamic financial products. Islamic banks and institutions with elements such as profit-and-loss sharing contracts can be considered as alternative financial intermediaries, which aim to bring in more stabilization and efficiency in resource allocation.

10.2 FEATURES OF ISLAMIC FINANCE

Islamic finance is based on the Islamic principles and jurisprudence. Islamic financial institutions aim to ensure that all their contracts adhere to Islamic legal requirements as well as to state requirements. The contracts prescribed in Islamic law provide a significant part of the principles and procedures explicitly laid down in the *Fiqh* or Islamic jurisprudence which has to be observed for sharia compliance. Islamic finance prohibits speculation, which is similar to gambling, whereby one gains by chance rather than by means of productivity. Hence, contracts that involve speculation (*maysir*) are prohibited (*haram*) under Islamic laws. Contracts in which one party gains at the expense of others through unjustified means are considered void in the Islamic system. The payment and receipt of interest (*riba*) is prohibited under the Islamic principles. The basic principle is that the returns on funds provided by the lender must be earned through profits derived from commercial risks undertaken by the lender. The contracts that contain the element of uncertainty (*gharar*) in factors such as content, price, and time for delivery are considered void in Islamic finance. For example, the sale of building prior to construction is forbidden because of the uncertainty of its existence at the time of contract. Islamic banks have a board of sharia scholars. The board of sharia scholars plays a supervisory role to ensure the Islamic products offered by banks adhere to sharia-compliant Islamic principles.

10.3 RELEVANCE OF ISLAMIC FINANCE IN THE GLOBAL ECONOMY

According to current data, the Islamic banking industry has assets worth more than US$800 billion. Islamic banks were able to withstand the 2008 economic crisis mainly due to greater focus on collateralization, less reliance on excessive leverage, and absence of derivatives instruments such as mortgage-backed securities. Until the onset of the credit crisis in 2007, the Islamic banking industry was growing at an average rate of 15%. Conventional banking has increasingly been focusing on sharia-compliant Islamic products. Islamic banking commands approximately 25% of the banking market in the Gulf Cooperation Council (GCC). Statistics indicate that global Islamic banking and finance reached $1.3 trillion in 2012 and is expected to reach $1.8 trillion by 2015.[1] It is considered to be one of the fastest growing sectors in the financial industry. Considering its size, there is no real competition between the conventional finance and Islamic finance industries. According to a global Islamic finance report in 2011, Islamic finance assets stood at $1.14 trillion. Islamic finance has grown at a compounded annual rate of 15-20% over the past decade. There are approximately 275 Islamic financial institutions with a presence in 75 countries. The GCC accounts for two thirds of Islamic financial assets. Malaysia leads in terms of maturity and sophistication. The *takaful* industry constitutes only 1% of the global insurance market even though Muslims account for 20% of the world's population.

10.4 CHALLENGES

Islamic banks face challenges of liquidity management owing to limited availability of tradable money market instruments. There is no sharia-compliant short-term Islamic money market in any local currency or in the US dollar. Similarly, a Islamic repo market has not yet been developed. Governance issues, such as sharia compliance of products and services, constitute a major challenge for the Islamic finance industry. A lack of sharia expertise is one of the challenges that face regulators of the Islamic financial industry. The Islamic finance industry faces asset concentration risk due to limited eligible asset classes. There are also no uniform reporting and rating standards.

The emergence of Islamic banking within the conventional financial system raises the challenge of how to incorporate Islamic activities into existing juridical and supervisory frameworks. With respect to the legal system, the challenge is how existing laws in the secular jurisdiction allow financial transactions to be governed by sharia principles.

10.5 REGULATION

In 2002, central banks and monetary authorities of Islamic countries established the Islamic Financial Services Board (IFSB) to develop international finance standards consistent with sharia principles. In 2008, the IFSB issued regulatory standards on capital adequacy and risk management for Islamic institutions.

---

[1]http://gulftoday.ae/portal/2b84bd06-7527-4b5e-b36a-b495220cf977.aspx

10.6 **FINANCING METHODS IN ISLAMIC FINANCE**
10.6.1 **FIXED CLAIM INSTRUMENTS**
10.6.1.1 *Murabaha (cost plus financing)*
Murabaha is one of the most popular and common means of Islamic financing. It is also known as markup or cost plus financing. It is a contract of sale in which the seller is obligated to inform the buyer the cost price of the asset and the profit the seller makes. *Murabaha* is a contract of sale between the bank and the client for the purpose of the sale of goods at a price plus an agreed profit margin for the bank. In the process of *murabaha*, initially the client approaches an Islamic bank for funding the purchase of a specific commodity. Being an Islamic bank, the bank cannot offer interest rate loans to its clients. However, some part of the total amount required may be offered by interest-free loan. In the *murabaha* model the Islamic bank purchases the commodity by cash and sells it to the customer at a profit. The client buys the commodity from the bank on the basis of a deferred payment. In this way, the client gets the intended commodity and the Islamic bank makes a profit by buying and selling the commodity to the client. In technical terms, in a *murabaha* model contract of sale the seller declares his cost and profit. Some schools of thought have questioned the legality of this financing method as it is similar to *riba* or interest. An important requirement for a *murabaha* sale is that the two sales contracts in which a bank acquires the goods and the other through which it sells them to the client should be separate and real transactions. Usually *murabaha* contracts are used to provide consumer finance for the purchase of consumer durables, housing finance, and purchase of fixed assets, including machinery, equipment, and current assets such as raw materials. *Murabaha* contracts are also used to issue letters of credit and provide financing to import trade.

10.6.1.2 *Ijara*
Ijara is basically designed as an installment leasing agreement. An *ijara* contract involves providing products or services on a lease or rental basis. It is similar to a conventional lease agreement wherein the owner or lessor rents or leases property or goods to a lessee for a specific period.

The main differentiating features of *ijara* are (1) the lessor must own the assets for the full lease period; (2) no compound interest is charged to the lessee if the lessee defaults or make delayed payments; and (3) the leased assets use is specified in the *ijara* contract.

According to sharia principles, there are three kinds of *ijara* arrangements, as follows.

10.6.1.2.1 *Operating lease* (*operating* ijara)
In an operating lease the lessee can return the fixed asset back to the lessor at the end of the contract, but the lease rental covers only part of the lease's asset value. This setup is basically a hire arrangement with the lessor. The lease contract doesn't contain any promise to buy or sell the assets. But in certain cases, the bank may offer a verbal unilateral promise of transfer of ownership or offer a purchase schedule for the asset. At times, the lessee is also allowed to make a verbal unilateral promise of transfer of ownership to purchase the asset. In that case, the purchase price is ultimately decided by the market value of the asset or by a negotiated price.

10.6.1.2.2 Ijara wa iqtina (*lease and ownership*)
The lease can also be in the form of a hire purchase known as *ijara wa iqtina* (lease and ownership) in which the lessee agrees to buy the asset at the end of the lease period.

10.6.1.2.3 Ijara mawsoofa bil thimma (*forward lease*)

Ijara mawsoofa bil thimma is a combination of a construction finance (*istisna*) and redeemable leasing agreement. This type of lease is executed at a future date. It is called forward leasing. The forward leasing contract buys out the construction project as a whole at its completion or in tranches of the project.

10.6.1.3 Mukarada

Mukarada is a bond issued by an Islamic bank to finance a specific project. The investors have proportional interest in profits of the projects but no voting rights. Investment certificates are known as *mukarada*.

10.6.1.4 Salam (forward contract)

Salam is a transaction whereby the seller agrees to supply some specific goods to the buyer at a future date in exchange for immediate payment. *Salam* is basically used to finance agricultural products. In other words *salam* is a type of sales contract in which the price known as the *salam* capital is paid at the time the contract is fixed and the delivery of the product to be sold known as *al-Muslam Fihi* is deferred. In moral terms, the seller is obligated to deliver the goods at the said date. The *salam* cannot be canceled once signed. In a *salam* contract, the seller and buyer are known as *Muslam Ilaihi* and *al-Muslam* or *Rabb al-Salam*. Parallel *salam* occurs when the seller enters into another separate *salam* contract with a third party to acquire goods whose specifications correspond to that of the commodity specified in the first *salam* contract.[2]

10.6.1.5 Istisna

Istisna is a sharia mode of financing used to finance the construction of buildings, residential towers, and manufacture of aircrafts, ships, and machinery. *Istisna* means "asking someone to manufacture." *Istisna* is a sale contract between the seller and buyer for the sale of an asset as specified in the sales contract before the goods are manufactured. To satisfy the terms of the contract, the seller can either manufacture or construct the asset itself or get it manufactured by someone else to deliver it to the buyer on the specified date in the sales contract. The option exists in the contract for the buyer to pay the sales price in a lump sum or in different payment schedules. The contract is irrevocable after the commencement of manufacture except when the delivered goods do not meet the contracted terms. *Istisna* differs from *ijara* in that the manufacturer must procure its own raw materials.

10.6.1.6 Sukuk

Sukuk is an asset-backed trust certificate (bond) representing ownership of an asset or its *usufruct* (earnings) based on the principle of sharia. Unlike conventional bonds, a *sukuk* has an underlying tangible asset transaction either in ownership or in a master lease agreement. *Sukuk* certificates are an integral part of Islamic capital markets. On the basis of sharia standards, *sukuk* are classified as tradable and nontradable. The different types of *sukuk* certificates are based on *alsalam, murabaha, musharakah, mudarabah,* and *ijara*.

10.6.1.6.1 Differentiating sukuk *from conventional bonds*

Sukuk certificates differ from conventional bonds in terms of asset ownership, investment criteria, issue price and unit, investment rewards and risks, and effect of costs. *Sukuk* certificates give partial

---

[2] AAOIFI *Shariah* standards (2005).

ownership in the asset to the investor, unlike conventional bonds which are debt obligations to the bond holder. Conventional bonds can be used to finance any asset or project. But *sukuk* bonds can only finance assets that are sharia compliant. Ordinary bonds represent a share of debt while *sukuk* represent a share of the underlying asset. Conventional bondholders receive coupon payments and a principal amount at the bond's maturity date. *Sukuk* holders receive shares of profits from the underlying asset. Bondholders are not affected by costs related to assets and projects. However, *sukuk* holders are affected by costs related to underlying assets.

10.6.1.6.2 *Islamic financing through* sukuk
In the *sukuk* scheme, the originator sells a certain asset to a special-purpose vehicle that, in turn, buys out the asset using sources of funds obtained from the issue of *sukuk*. The owner of a *sukuk* certificate has a property share in the given asset and has the right to a part of the income. Figure 10.1 reflects the mechanism of financing through *sukuk*.

10.6.1.6.3 Sukuk *market*
The Islamic Fiqh Academy of the Organisation of Islamic Cooperation (OIC) in 1988 legitimized the concept of *sukuk*. In 2001, the first international sovereign *sukuk* was issued by the government of Bahrain. This issue was a US$100 million *ijarah sukuk* with a fixed rate of 5.25% and 5-year maturity. Malaysia has the world's largest *sukuk* market. *Sukuk* is used by the corporate sector and states for raising funds. *Sukuk* has become an important Islamic financial instrument for raising funds for long-term project financing. Approximately 87% of global *sukuk* issues are of sovereign and quasi-sovereign types, and the remaining 13% are issued by corporations. The *sukuk* market grew from US$7.2 billion in 2004 to US$39 billion by year-end 2007.[3] By 2011, more than $19 billion had been raised through 30 issues of *sukuk* bonds on the London Stock Exchange.[4] In 2011, a total of $84.4 billion *sukuks* were issued worldwide, which was 62% more than in 2010. According to Kuwait Financial Centre statistics, the Middle East and North Africa accounted for 23% of all the issuances with a combined value of $9.66 billion.

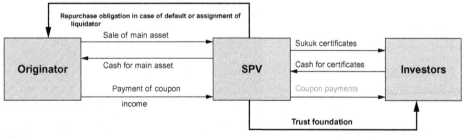

FIGURE 10.1

Financing through *sukuk*.

Source: http://www.goodhillinvest.com/Securitization.html.

---

[3] Moody's Investors Service, 2008.
[4] http://lexicon.ft.com/Term?term=sukuk-(Islamic-bonds)

In 2012, the global issuance of *sukuk* amounted to $138 billion. The value of new *sukuk* (Islamic bonds) was expected to reach $100 billion in 2013, with GCC issuers dominating the market. Although the *sukuk* bond market is still a small segment of the global fixed income market,[5] the global *sukuk* market is expected to grow more than 140% to reach $292 billion in issuances by 2016, according to a trade Arabia report. Malaysia was the top *sukuk* issuer with $31 billion, followed by Saudi Arabia ($6.4 billion) and Indonesia ($3.4 billion) in 2012. Malaysia accounted for 71% of total issuances.[6]

Arab countries have not yet developed a sophisticated bond market. The bond and *sukuk* markets of the region lack the salient features of a well-developed debt capital market, including credit ratings, transparency, market making, and a broad spectrum of institutional market participants. The Saudi market is the largest debt market in the GCC region. The *sukuk* market in the Middle East was dominated by UAE with 69% of all issuance and was focused on logistics and real estate in 2011. The Arab region accounted for 40% of the total value of US$19.15 billion worth of global *sukuk* bonds issued in 2009. Saudi Arabia overtook UAE to become the largest issuer of *sukuk* in the first quarter of 2012 in the GCC, according to Zawya reports. Saudi Arabia raised $6.4 billion compared to $1.9 billion by the UAE in the first quarter of 2012.

The largest individual *sukuk* issue worldwide was the Qatar Sovereign Sukuk 2014 with a value of $9.06 billion with 3-year tenor. The second-largest issue was the Malaysian sovereign *wakala* global *sukuk*. The increasing demand for *sukuk* could be attributed to factors such as the heightened volatility of global equity markets and the Eurozone debt crisis. The *sukuk* market is dominated by the Asian and GCC regions.

10.6.2 EQUITY-LIKE INSTRUMENTS

10.6.2.1 Mudarabah (profit sharing)

In this type of equity-like investment, one partner provides the capital investment (*rabb ul maal*) to another partner (*mudarib*) who is responsible for operations and management of the business. The partners have to determine the distribution of profit based on the actual profit earned by the enterprise. The proportion of profit distributed is not a function of the percentage of capital contribution. Basically there are two types of *mudarabah*. In restricted *mudarabah* or *al- mudarabah al -mugayyadah*, the capital provider (*rabb- ul- maal*) may specify the businesses in which to invest. In the case of no specification of the nature of business it is called unrestricted *mudarabah*. The *mudarabah* contract can be terminated by either of the two parties as per the notice period in the contract.

10.6.2.2 Musharakah (joint venture)

Musharakah is a type of joint venture (*shirkah-ul-amwal*). *Musharakah* is a profit-and-loss-sharing partnership contract. Under the Islamic jurisprudence, *musharakah* means the formation of a joint enterprise for the conduct of business in which the partners share the profit based on the agreement of the parties, but loss is subject to the ratio of investment. An Islamic bank may enter into a *musharakah* with a customer to provide a sharia-compliant financing option to a customer on a profit-and-loss sharing basis. The proportion of profit to be distributed among the partners must be determined and agreed on at the time of the contract. Usually the customer is the managing partner in such a contract.

---

[5]Global *sukuk* issuance to top $100 billion in 2013, http://www.tradearabia.com/news/BANK_232107.html.
[6]http://www.emirates247.com/news/region/saudi-top-sukuk-issuer-in-gulf-2012-04-07-1.452594

The *musharakah* contract can be constant in nature wherein the shares of the partners in the capital structure remain fixed throughout the period of the contract. In alternate form the *musharakah* contract can be diminishing in nature wherein the Islamic bank agrees to transfer its share gradually to the other partner, which would lead to a diminishing share of the Islamic bank. Finally, the customer becomes the sole proprietor of the venture.

10.6.2.2.1 *Comparison of* mudarabah *and* musharakah

In *mudarabah* the whole investment comes from the *rabb-ul-maal* partner, whereas in *musharakah* the investment comes from all parties. Similarly, all the partners participate in the management of *musharakah*, whereas it is the responsibility of *mudarib* in *mudarabah*. In *musharakah* all the partners share the loss to the extent of the ratio of their investment, while in *mudarabah* the loss, if any, is suffered by the *rabb-ul-mal* only, because the *mudarib* does not invest anything. The liability of the partners in *musharakah* is normally unlimited. In *musharakah*, the assets are jointly owned by all the partners. But in the case of *mudarabah*, the goods purchased by the *mudarib* are owned by the capital provider (*rabb-ul-maal*) and the *mudarib* can earn his share in the profit only if he sells the goods profitably.

10.6.3 INVESTMENT FUNDS

An investment fund is a fund in which investors contribute their surplus money to earn *halal* profits, which are based on the precepts of Islamic sharia. Investors receive ownership certificates or units. These investors receive pro rata profits earned by the fund. Some of the commonly used Islamic funds are *ijarah* funds, commodity funds, *murabaha*, and mixed funds.

10.7 MODELS USED IN ISLAMIC BANKS

The first model is the two-tier *mudārabah* model that replaces interest by profit-sharing modes on both the liability and asset sides of the bank. This model of Islamic banking also takes the role of an investment intermediary, rather than being a commercial bank only. The second model of Islamic banking is the one-tier *mudārabah* with multiple investment tools. This model evolved because Islamic banks faced practical and operational problems in using profit-sharing modes of financing on the asset side. As a result the industry opted for fixed-income modes of financing.

10.8 RISK IN ISLAMIC

10.8.1 DIFFERENT TYPES OF RISK IN ISLAMIC FINANCE

Islamic financial institutions face both general risks and unique risks. Like traditional financial institutions, Islamic institutions face credit risk, benchmark risk, market risk, liquidity risk, and operational risk. Counterparty risk, however, exists because of the unique nature of the asset and liability structure of Islamic institutions.

10.8.1.1 Credit risk

Credit risk in Islamic institutions arises due to settlement or payment risks on account of *salam/istisna* contracts or *murabahah* contracts. In *murabahah* and *musharakah* contracts, credit risk arises due to nonpayment of the share amount of the bank by the debtor when it becomes due. In *murabahah* contracts, credit risk arises in the form of counterparty risk because of nonperformance of parties to the contract.

10.8.1.2 Benchmark risk

Islamic financial institutions usually use a benchmark rate to price different financial instruments. For example, in a *murabahah* contract the markup pricing is determined by adding the risk premium to the benchmark rate, which is usually the LIBOR. The markup rate is fixed during the duration of the contract. If the benchmark rate changes, then the markup rate cannot be changed; hence, Islamic financial institutions face market interest rate risk in the form of benchmark risk.

10.8.1.3 Liquidity risk

Liquidity risk is a major risk faced by Islamic financial institutions. Islamic banks are constrained to borrow funds to meet liquidity requirements as interest-based loans are prohibited by sharia. Raising funds through debt-based assets is also not an option for Islamic financial institutions.

10.8.1.4 Operational risk

Operation risk arises in Islamic financial institutions due to the scarcity of qualified and trained Islamic financial professionals who lack the expertise to conduct Islamic financial operations. According to IFSB, operational risk is associated with loss resulting from inadequate or failed internal processes, people, and systems, or from external events, including losses that result from sharia noncompliance and failure in fiduciary responsibilities.

10.8.1.5 Legal risk

Islamic financial systems face legal risk due to the fact that there are no standard forms of contracts for various financial instruments or a standardized litigation system to resolve problems. Uncertainty in regulation can also account for legal risk since regulatory changes affect the legality of certain Islamic financial instruments.

10.8.1.6 Fiduciary risk

Fiduciary risk arises in Islamic banks due to breach of contracts by Islamic banks, which occurs due to noncompliance with sharia. According to IFSB the risk of losses that arises from such events as negligence, misconduct, or breach of investment mandate is basically characterized as fiduciary risk. Fiduciary risk is an indication of failure to perform in accordance with explicit and implicit standards applicable to fiduciary responsibilities. Fiduciary risk can create a huge impact on a bank's costs and access to liquidity. Negligence on the part of an Islamic bank during due diligence in its selection of projects under *mudarabah* or *musharakah* contracts can also create fiduciary risk.

10.8.1.7 Counterparty risk

Murabahah contracts face counterparty risk as the contract is a promise to buy; it is not a sales contract. On account of the unsettled nature of contract litigation, problems can a rise in *murabahah* contracts. Late payments by counterparties leads to counterparties risk and loss to banks. Counterparty risk also exists in *salam* financing because of failure to supply goods during the stipulated period. *Salam* contracts result in physical deliveries and as a result Islamic banks face storage and price risks. In *istisna* financing, buyer default risk is a major risk. There can also be risks involving contract failure regarding the quality and time of delivery.

10.8.2 RISK MANAGEMENT IN ISLAMIC FINANCIAL INSTITUTIONS

Credit risk mitigation strategies involve estimation and minimization of expected credit losses. The expected credit losses is a function of probability of default, maturity of facility, loss given default (LGD), exposure at default, and sensitivity of assets' value to systematic and nonsystematic risks. Islamic banks are required to maintain mandatory loan loss reserves subject to regulatory requirements in different jurisdictions. Islamic banks also use collateral as a means of protection against credit losses. According to sharia principles, assets can be used as security in deferred obligations (*al rahn*). Cash, tangible assets, gold, silver, and other precious metals as well as shares in equities can be used as collateral according to the Islamic sharia. In a contractual risk mitigation strategy, clauses that contain agreements between parties to lock in price levels are required in contracts such as *salam*. Nonavailability of financial derivatives is a major hindrance for Islamic banks to manage market risk compared to conventional banks. GAP analysis is a major technique used to measure interest rate risk. Net *murabahah* income of a Islamic bank is exposed to markup price risk. GAP analysis techniques can be used to mitigate the *murabahah* markup price risk. In a two-step contract, an Islamic bank can play the role of a guarantor in facilitating funds to users.

10.9 *TAKAFUL*

Takaful is commonly referred to as Islamic insurance. *Takaful* means "the act of a group of people reciprocally guaranteeing each other." It is based on the concept of mutual cooperative insurance. *Takaful* insurance is thereby based on the cooperative principle and the principle of separation between funds and operations of shareholders. In the process, the ownership of *takaful* (insurance) funds and operations are passed on to policyholders.

10.9.1 WORKING OF GENERAL *TAKAFUL*

The investor pays a premium as a participative contribution (*tabarru*) to the common fund called *takaful*. The salient feature of *takaful* is that members devise schemes in which they themselves are insured and are insurers. The contributions collected from policyholders are considered as donations and form the source through which claims are reimbursed. The *takaful* operator is an insurance company that manages the *takaful* fund. In *takaful* policyholders are joint investors with a *takaful* operator who acts as a *mudarib* (manager or entrepreneurial agent). The policyholders share in the investment pool's profits as well as losses. After the close of the financial year any remaining cash surplus after deduction of expenses is returned to policyholders in the form of cash dividends or distributions. Losses are divided and liabilities spread according to a community pooling system. In *takaful* the uncertainty with respect to subscription and compensation is eliminated. The funds are invested in sharia-compliant instruments.

10.9.2 DIFFERENCE BETWEEN CONVENTIONAL INSURANCE AND *TAKAFUL*

Conventional insurance involves the elements of excessive uncertainty (*gharar*) compared to Islamic insurance. *Takaful* differs from conventional insurance companies in that risks are assessed and how the *takaful* funds are managed. Another major difference between *takaful* and conventional insurance is that policyholders solely benefit from the profits generated from *takaful* and investment assets and not just the shareholders as in conventional insurance.

In conventional insurance risk is transferred from the policyholder (insured) to the insurance company (the insurer) with the insurance premium that is paid by the policyholder. *Takaful* is based on the concepts of mutuality in which risk is not transferred but is shared by the common pool of participants. The role of the insurance company (*takaful* operator) is to manage the funds of participants.

From an Islamic perspective, conventional insurance involves an element of gambling. The insured pays a premium in the expectation of gain or compensation against the claim. If the expected event does not materialize, the policyholder loses the amount paid as premium. If the event occurs, the insured gains and the insurer loses as the amount paid will be much larger than the amount collected as a premium. In conventional insurance, funds are invested in fixed interest-bearing financial instruments. In *takaful* insurance, funds are invested only in non-interest-bearing financial instruments. In conventional insurance, the surplus or profits belong to shareholders. The insured policyholder is covered during the policy period and is not entitled to any return at the end of such period. In *takaful*, the profits belong to participants and are shared in proportion to their contributions to the fund at the end of every year.

10.9.3 MODELS OF *TAKAFUL*

There are basically two models in *takaful*: the *al mudharabah* and the *al wakala* models.

10.9.3.1 Al mudharabah model

In this model, the *takaful* operator accepts payment of the contribution from the participants and the profit is shared between the policyholder and *takaful* operator in a predetermined manner. The sharing of the profit approved by the sharia board will be in a ratio such as 50/50, 60/40, and so on based on the development stage of the company. The sharing of surplus due to the operations of *takaful* is carried out after fulfilling the obligations of the participants of the fund.

10.9.3.2 Al wakala model

In this model, the *takaful* operator acts as an agent or representative of the participants or policyholders. The *takaful* operator earns a fee for the services as a *wakeel* or agent and does not participate in the profits or share in the underwriting results. Under this model, the surplus or deficit belongs to the participants. The *takaful* operator may charge a fund management fee or a performance incentive fee. The *takaful* operator assumes the business risks in developing and operating the *takaful* business on behalf of participants but does not participate in the mutual underwriting losses.

10.9.4 OTHER MODELS

10.9.4.1 Cooperative insurance (ta'awuni model)

The *ta'awuni* model is based on the concept of pure *mudharabah* in which the *takaful* operator (insurance company) and policyholders share the direct investment income. The policyholder is entitled to 100% of the surplus with no deduction made prior to the distribution. This model basically is applied to the family *takaful* in which the fund is entirely distributed to the participants.

10.9.4.2 Nonprofit model

This model of *takaful* is practiced by social and governmental organizations that operate on a nonprofit basis. The *tabarru* donations from participants are given to the weaker sections among the pool of participants.

10.10 SUMMARY

Islamic finance is based on Islamic principles and jurisprudence. Payment and receipt of interest (*riba*) are prohibited under Islamic principles. Contracts that involve speculation (*maysir*) and uncertainty (*gharar*) are considered void in Islamic finance. Islamic banks face the challenges of liquidity management due to limited availability of tradable money market instruments. Financing instruments in Islamic finance consist of equity-like and debt-like instruments. Fixed-claim instruments include *murabaha*, *ijara*, *salam*, and *istisna*. *Murabaha* is a contract of sale between the bank and the client for the purpose of sale of goods at a price, plus an agreed profit margin for the bank. An *ijara* contract involves providing products or services on a lease or rental basis. *Salam* is a transaction whereby the seller agrees to supply specific goods to the buyer at a future date in exchange for immediate payment. *Istisna* is a sales contract between the seller and buyer for the sale of an asset as specified in the sales contract before the goods are manufactured. *Sukuk* is an asset-backed trust certificate (bond) representing ownership of an asset or its usufruct (earnings) based on the principles of sharia.

Equity instruments include *mudarabah* and *musharakah*. In *mudharabah* one partner provides the capital investment (*rabb ul maal*) to another partner (*mudarib*) who is responsible for operations and management of the business. *Musharakah* is a profit-and-loss sharing partnership contract.

Islamic financial institutions face various risks such as credit risks, benchmark risks, liquidity risks, operational risks, legal risks, and fiduciary risks. *Takaful* is commonly referred to as Islamic insurance. The two basic models of *takaful* insurance are the *al mudharabha* and *al wakala* models.

QUESTIONS FOR DISCUSSION

1. What are the main features of Islamic finance?
2. Explain the different debt instruments in Islamic finance.
3. What are the different types of equity-like instruments in Islamic finance?
4. Explain the different types of risk in Islamic finance.
5. Distinguish between *takaful* insurance and conventional insurance.

REFERENCES

Latif, Q., Crawford, S. Introduction to islamic financial risk management products, QFinance. www.qfinance.com.

Jobst, A. The international role of islamic finance. www.qfinance.com.

Rasul, B. Identifying the main regulatory challenges for Islamic finance. www.qfinance.com.

El-Gamal, M.A., 2000. A basic guide to contemporary islamic banking and finance. http://www.ruf.rice.edu/~elgamal/files/primer.pdf.

Kumaran, S., 2012. Risk management and mitigation techniques in islamic finance a conceptual framework. International Research Journal of Finance and Economics, EuroJournals Publishing Inc. (98), 83–96.

http://www.islamic-finance.com/item_ijara_f.htm.

Jamaideen, F. Islamic Finance for dummies, Leasing or renting (ijara) in Islamic finance. http://www.dummies.com/how-to/content/leasing-or-renting-ijara-in-islamic-finance.html.

http://islamicfinanceaffairs.wordpress.com/2007/05/25/islamic-finance-basics-what-is-murabaha-ijara-and-musharakah-mudarabah/.

Izhar, H., March 2010. Identifying operational risk exposures in islamic banking. Kyoto Bulletin of Islamic Area Studies 3 (2), 17–53.

Bring on the bonds: More expected from the world's second largest sukuk issuer. The Report: Qatar 2012. http://www.oxfordbusinessgroup.com/news/bring-bonds-more-expected-world%E2%80%99s-second-largest-sukuk-issuer.

http://cief.wordpress.com/2006/04/02/mudarabah.

http://www.islamic-banking.com/basis_and_principle_of_takaful.aspx.

http://www.takaful.com.pk/TakafulVsConventional.html.

http://www.takaful.coop/index.php?option=com_content&view=article&id=5&Itemid=23.

http://www.financialislam.com/takaful-business-models.html.

Faria, W. Islamic banking industry to touch $1.8 trillion mark by 2015. http://gulftoday.ae/portal/2b84bd06-7527-4b5e-b36a-b495220cf977.aspx.

http://www.standardandpoors.com/spf/upload/Ratings_EMEA/Slide_Deck_Dubai_IF_Conference.pdf?elq=44373115fa0248cc8c81d6760c72dbef.

CONSOLIDATIONS IN FINANCIAL INSTITUTIONS AND MARKETS

11.1 INTRODUCTION

Financial consolidation in the financial sector occurs mainly for cost savings and revenue enhancement. Mergers and acquisitions (M&As) occur in the banking sector for economies of scale. Various types of synergies are at play in the financial sector's M&As. Among the major contributing factors are advances in information technology, financial deregulation, and globalization of financial markets. Technological innovation has facilitated enhanced consolidation in the sector. These technological developments make it feasible for financial service firms to provide a wider array of products and services to a larger number of clients across different geographic regions. The removal of legal and regulatory barriers in many countries has facilitated cross-border consolidation activity. Advances in telecommunications and computing have facilitated lowered transaction costs.

In the past, M&As in the financial sector were segmented along distinct lines of banking, insurance, and securities in line with official regulations and industry practice. With structural reforms the boundaries separating these sectors are becoming increasingly blurred. As a result, financial institutions now offer all types of products and services that compete not only against those offered by similar institutions but also against offerings by other categories of service providers. Financial service firms are using a consolidation strategy to reorient their product mixes to expand into new profitable avenues. In particular, they are using M&As to achieve growth and gain complementary skills in many geographic markets. Many established banks have acquired smaller investment banks to become global investment banks.

During the 1980s and 1990s, ownership linkages and alliances were established between insurance companies and investment banks. This resulted in the concept of "one-stop shopping." The trend of insurance firms merging with banking companies is known as *bancassurance*. Through these strategic deals, bank acquirers have been able to expand their retail banking product lines and insurers have obtained access to an established distribution network through bank branches.

From 1990 to 2001, more than 10,000 financial firms were acquired in the developed nations. The 1990s saw some of the largest mergers in banking history in the United States. The proportion of banking assets accounted for by the 100 largest banking organizations rose from over 50% in 1980 to nearly 75% in 1997. The basic reasons cited for this trend were the emergence of a new statutory environment that allowed interstate ownership, competitive pressure, and geographical diversification. The number of US banks declined by more than a third from 1980 to 1997. During the period 1994-2002, more than 1300 new banks were opened in the United States in direct response to a perceived decline in services resulting from bank mergers. During the 1980s and 1990s, banking mergers accounted for 60% of all financial mergers and 70% of the value of those mergers. From 1980 to 2003, the number of banking organizations overall decreased from 16,000 to about 8000. During this same period, the share of industry assets held by the 10 largest commercial banking organizations as ranked by assets rose from 22% to 46%, whereas the share of industry deposits held by the 10 largest banks increased from 19% to 41%.[1] A comparable trend was occurring in Europe where from 1985 to 1999, the number of European banks decreased from 12,670 to 8295.

In the United States, financial mergers have been heavily concentrated in banking over the last few decades. In comparison, Australia, the Netherlands, and the United Kingdom witnessed greater M&As activity in insurance, securities, and other segments of the financial industry.

The largest European banking groups (BNP Paribas in France, IntesaBsci in Italy, Banco Santander Central Hispano and Banco Bilbao Vizcaya Argentaria in Spain, and NatWest/Royal Bank of Scotland in the United Kingdom) were formed as a result of megadeals that happened between 1999 and 2002. The year 1998 witnessed four mcgamergers of the US banking industry: Citicorp/Travelers, Bank America/NationsBank, BankOne/First Chicago, and Norwest/Wells Fargo.

M&As have become a compelling strategy for financial-sector firms in times of boom as well as bust. During the economic recession of 2008, many financial services firms had to suffer significant write-downs and became targets for acquisitions. Barclays Bank acquired the assets of Lehman Brothers. Bank of America acquired Merrill Lynch, while JPMorgan Chase acquired Bear Stearns and Washington Mutual. In 2009, Wells Fargo acquired Wachovia. In Europe, the eurozone crisis placed the focus on M&A activity in the European financial services industry.

11.2 MEGAMERGERS AND ACQUISITIONS IN THE BANKING AND OTHER FINANCE SECTORS

One of the biggest banks in the world, Bank of America focused on a series of M&As over a period of time. In 1998, NationsBank and Bank America Corporation merged to form Bank of America. This merger resulted in the union of the second-largest financial institution based on deposits with the largest bank in the US Southeast. NationsBank had undertaken a series of acquisitions to become the largest and fastest growing financial institution in North Carolina. The merger between NationsBank and Bank America Corporation established the first coast-to-coast interstate retail and commercial retail lending giant in US history. Technically the deal was a purchase of Bank America Corporation by NationsBank, but the deal was structured as a merger with NationsBank and the new entity was renamed Bank of America. The deal was valued at approximately $64.8 billion. The new combined bank had assets of approximately $570 billion as well as 4800 branches in 22 states at the time of merger. In 2004, Bank of America acquired FleetBoston for $47 billion in a stock swap deal. This acquisition created a bank with 33 million customers. With this deal, Bank of America acquired the largest FDIC deposit market share in the United States and became the second-largest US bank behind Citicorp. In 2006, Bank of America acquired MBNA, the credit card company, in a deal valued at $35 billion. This acquisition transformed Bank of America into one of the world's largest credit card issuers. The combination of the powerful distribution channel of Bank of America

---

[1] Steven J. Pilloff, Bank Merger Activity in the United States, 1994-2003, Staff Study 176, 2004, Board of Governors of the Federal Reserve System.

with the customer base of MBNA products resulted in significant growth opportunities. In 2007, ABN Amro, the parent company of LaSalle Bank, sold LaSalle to Bank of America in a deal valued at $21 billion. The acquisition gave Bank of America an additional 411 branches, 17,000 commercial banking clients, 1.4 million retail customers, and 1500 ATMs. In 2008, during the subprime mortgage crisis, Bank of America bought out the crisis-ridden Countrywide Financial Corporation for about $4 billion. Countrywide faced a severe crisis on account of rising defaults among subprime borrowers. This acquisition gave Bank of America about 9 million borrowers to whom the bank could sell other products. Bank of America had to write-down the value of Countrywide assets by 10% owing to lower housing values. During the economic crisis of 2008, Bank of America purchased the world's largest retail brokerage firm Merrill Lynch in an all-stock deal valued at $50 billion. Merrill Lynch had been battered by $52.2 billion in losses and write-downs from subprime-mortgage-contaminated securities, and its stock value had plunged more than 80% from its peak of $97.53 in 2007. This buyout gave Bank of America a salesforce of 16,690 brokers who managed $1.6 trillion assets in value.

In 2007, a consortium led by the Royal Bank of Scotland (RBS) acquired the Dutch Bank in a deal that became the largest financial services merger in history. The consortium consisted of RBS, Fortis Group of Belgium, and Santander Central Hispano of Spain. In 2008, the Dutch state replaced Fortis as a stakeholder in RFS Holdings. In 2010, ABN AMRO and Fortis Bank Nederland merged to form the current ABN AMRO Bank NV. ABN AMRO is now owned by RBS, Santander, and the Dutch government.

Citicorp, which was established in 1812, is a global diversified financial services holding company that provides business services to consumers, corporations, governments, and institutions. Citigroup consists of two primary business segments: Citicorp and Citi Holdings. Citigroup made 315 acquisitions and took stakes in 242 companies during the period from 1981 to 2011. In 1998, Citicorp and Traveler's Group merged to form the world's biggest financial services company named Citigroup, offering banking, insurance, and investment operations in over 100 countries. With approximately $698 billion in assets and $135 billion in market capitalization, the new combined group became the largest financial firm in the world. The merger deal was driven by the logic of creating financial services one-stop shopping for customers by offering traditional banking, investment banking, brokerage, and insurance services under one umbrella throughout the world. In the year before the merger, Traveler's Group had acquired Salomon Brothers in a stock deal valued at $9 billion.

JPMorgan Chase is a product of a series of M&As. In 2000, Chase Manhattan Corp. merged with JPMorgan and Co., thereby combining four of the largest and oldest money center banking institutions in New York City (Morgan, Chase, Chemical, and Manufacturers Hanover) into one firm, known as JPMorgan Chase and Co. The Chase Bank had been the product of the union of three New York banks that had combined in the previous decade and Chemical Bank, which purchased Chase Manhattan in 1996 and Manufacturers Hanover in 1991. In this merger deal, Chase bought out its rival in a $34 billion all-stock deal. At the time of the deal, the combined bank became the third-largest bank holding company in the United States after Citigroup and Bank of America, with assets of approximately $660 billion. In 2004, JPMorgan Chase took over Bank One in a $58 billion deal. JPMorgan was able to consolidate its position in the retail and credit card segment as Bank One, which was the world's largest Visa card issuer. The merger also facilitated the cross-selling of each other's products.

Table 11.1   Biggest Banking Sector Deals

SL	Buyer	Seller	Price (Billions of US Dollars)	Year
1	Royal Bank of Scotland	ABN Amro Holdings	95.6	2007
2	Citicorp	Travelers Group	72.66	1998
3	NationsBank	Bank of America	61.63	1998
4	JPMorgan Chase	Bank One Corporation	58.76	2004
5	Bank of America	Merrill Lynch	50	2008
6	Bank of America	Fleet Boston Fin Corp.	47	2004
7	Mitsubishi Tokyo	UFJ Holdings	41.43	2005
8	Bank of America	MBNA	35.81	2005
9	CitiGroup	Associates First Capital	31	2000
10	Unicredito Italiano	Capitalia	29.9	2007

Wachovia Corporation was a diversified financial services company that provided a broad range of banking and investment banking products. In 2001, First Union Corporation merged into Wachovia Corporation. In 2004, Wachovia purchased SouthTrust Corporation in a $14.3 billion deal that gave Wachovia entry into the fast-growing Texas market. In 2006, Wachovia acquired Westcorp and Golden West Financial Corporation. In 2007, Wachovia purchased AG Edwards for $6.8 billion to create the US's second-largest retail brokerage firm. In 2009, Wachovia itself was purchased by Wells Fargo and Co., the diversified financial services company, for $12.7 billion. The Wells Fargo deal occurred during a turbulent period when banks and financial firms were in the midst of the 2008 credit crisis.

In 2005, UFJ Holdings, the fourth-biggest bank, was acquired by Mitsubishi Tokyo Financial Group to create the world's biggest bank. The merged bank was renamed the Mitsubishi UFJ Financial Group.

In 1998, Price Waterhouse and Coopers, the fourth and the sixth largest of the Big Six audit firms, combined to form PricewaterhouseCoopers. The merger resulted in a professional services firm second only to Arthur Andersen in consulting income. The revenues for the new combined company were $15.3 billion in 1998. PricewaterhouseCoopers went on to acquire several European consulting firms such as France-based SV&GM Group, the Italian consulting firm Galgan and Merli, and Belgium-based KPMG Consulting. The Berkshire Hathaway's deal to buy HJ Heinz in 2013 for $27.4 billion was the largest private equity deal of 2013. Table 11.1 highlights the biggest banking sector mergers and acquisition deals.

11.3 CONSOLIDATION IN THE INSURANCE SECTOR

M&As activity has been dominant in the insurance sector for years. According to the Insurance Information Institute, the number of M&As transactions ranged between 255 and 522 in the US insurance industry from 1999 to 2008. Consolidation activity takes place in the insurance sector basically to increase geographical reach and product range, which should result in benefits from scale and scope economies. The number of insurance company mergers has grown since the early 1990s.

Table 11.2   Biggest Property and Casualty Insurance Mergers

Year	Acquirer	Target	Value (Billions of US Dollars)
2006	Cerberus	GMAC	14
2007	Berkshire	Equitas	7
2008	Liberty Mutual	Safeco	6.2
2008	Tokyo	Philadelphia	4.7
2010	FairFax Financial Holdings	Zenith National Insurance	1.4

Source: Property—Casualty Insurance Mergers and Acquisitions, Deals and Drivers. Conning Research and Consultancy, Strategic Study Series, 2010.

The maximum number of insurance mergers has taken place in the United States followed by the United Kingdom. Table 11.2 gives the list of biggest property and casualty insurance mergers.

11.4 STOCK MARKET MERGERS

During the last decade, a major trend observed is the merger of international stock exchanges. The reasons for consolidation in stock exchanges can be attributed to a number of factors. Stock exchanges are facing the pressures of increasing competitiveness and cost cutting. The increased competition has resulted from transformation of the securities market. Many exchanges that were cooperatives converted their ownership structures into standard corporations.

From 2000 to 2008, a number of megamergers occurred. The New York Stock Exchange bought out Euronext. NASDAQ merged with the OMX Group. The Chicago Mercantile Exchange bought out the Chicago Board of Trade for $8 billion and then acquired the New York and Chicago Mercantile Exchanges in 2008.

NYSE Euronext (NYX) is the holding company and the first cross-border exchange group created by the historic combination of NYSE Group and Euronext NV in 2007. The deal was valued at $10.2 billion. The combination was by far the largest of its kind and the first to create a truly global marketplace. Euronext is one of Europe's largest stock exchanges with subsidiaries across Europe in Belgium, France, Portugal, and the United Kingdom.

Some other major stock market mergers include:

- In 2011, the London Stock Exchange (LSE) merged with TMX Group of Canada, which owned the Toronto Stock Exchange and the Russian exchanges MICEX and RTS.
- The Tokyo Stock Exchange merged its cash equities business with a derivative platform of the Osaka Securities Exchange in 2011.
- In 2013, NYSE Euronext merged with ICE in a $8.2 billion deal to create one of the largest derivative exchanges by contracts traded. The combined ICE-NYSE became the third-largest exchange globally behind Hong Kong Exchanges and Clearing and CME Group.

The major hurdles for consolidation in financial stock markets are the political and regulatory barriers. For example, Singapore faced stiff resistance from Australian lawmakers over the combination of their two stock exchanges.

11.5 SUMMARY

The major contributing factors for M&As in the finance sector can be attributed to advances in information technology, financial deregulation, and globalization of financial markets. Consolidation has led to a one-stop shopping concept in the finance sector. The trend of insurance firms merging with banking companies is known as *bancassurance*. From 1990 to 2001, more than 10,000 financial firms were acquired in the developed nations. The 1990s saw some of the largest mergers in banking history in the United States. US financial mergers have been more heavily concentrated in banking over the last few decades. In comparison, Australia, the Netherlands, and the United Kingdom witnessed greater M&As activity in insurance, securities, and other segments of the financial industry.

QUESTIONS FOR DISCUSSION

1. Discuss the basic reasons for consolidation in the finance sector.
2. Discuss the major mergers that occurred in the banking sector.

REFERENCES

The Deal: ICE-NYSE Unexpected Merger Success, 8/07/2.

Lumbkin, S., 2000. Mergers and Acquisitions in the Financial Services Sector, 2000: Insurance and Private Pensions Compendium for Emerging Economies. OECD Publications, Japan (Book I Part 1:5c).

de Souza, I., Adolph, G., Gemes, A., Marchi, R., 2009. Perils of Financial Sector M&A: Seven Steps to Successful Integration. Booz & Co. report.

Group of Ten, 2001. Report on Consolidation in the Financial sector. www.OECD.org.

PwC, 2011. Sharing Deal Insight Report, Q1.

http://message.bankofamerica.com/heritage/#/merger-history.

Annual Report, Bank of America.

http://media.corporate-ir.net/media_files/irol/71/71595/reports/2010_AR.pdf.

http://blogs.wsj.com/deals/2011/06/29/bank-of-america-countrywide-worst-deal-in-history.

http://news.bbc.co.uk/2/hi/business/7033176.stm.

B

CASES ON UNIVERSAL BANKING

1.1 BANK OF AMERICA

Bank of America (BoA), headquartered in Charlotte, NC, is one of the world's largest financial institutions; it provide a full range of banking, investing, asset management, and other financial and risk products and services. BoA has a rich tradition of more than 200 years. According to BoA statistics, the bank serves approximately 51 million consumer and small businesses, with approximately 5300 retail banking offices and 16,350 ATMs. The online division of the bank has 30 million active users and more than 13 million mobile users. BoA, through its various banking and nonbanking subsidiaries, operates in more than 40 countries. BoA is listed on the New York Stock Exchange and is a component of the Dow Jones Industrial Average.

BoA is a global leader in corporate and investment banking and trading with broad portfolios of asset classes. It is also one of the world's leading wealth management companies. Whereas Merrill Lynch Wealth Management and US Trust have more than 18,800 clients for personalized financial advice, BoA supports more than 3 million small business owners.

1.1.1 MAJOR DIVISIONS

BoA serves people, companies, and institutional investors. The diversified range of banking and financial services is provided through the following major divisions:

- Consumer and Business Banking (CBB)
- Consumer Real Estate Services (CRES)
- Global Commercial Banking (GB)
- Global Banking and Markets (GBM)
- Global Wealth and Investment Management (GWIM)

Consumer and Business Banking, which comprises deposits, card services, and business banking, offers a diversified range of credit, banking, and investment products and services to consumers and businesses. The franchise network of this division provides approximately 5500 banking centers, 16,300 ATMs, call centers, and online and mobile platforms.

Consumer deposit activities consist of comprehensive products such as traditional savings accounts, money market savings accounts, CDs, IRAs, noninterest-bearing checking accounts, as well as investment accounts and products. Deposits also generate fees such as account service fees, overdraft charges, and ATM fees as well as investment and brokerage fees from Merrill Edge accounts.[1] The deposit products

---

[1] Merrill Edge is the integrated investing and banking services unit that caters to clients with less than $250,000 in investable assets.

remain the stable source of funding and liquidity for the bank. Card services is the major leading issuer of credit and debit cards to consumers and small businesses. Card services generate interchange revenue from credit and debit card transactions as well as annual credit card fees and other miscellaneous fees.

In the mass retail segment, there are 40 million customers with small account balances who account for 25% of deposits. According to the BoA website, approximately 0.5 million checks are deposited via mobile devices at BoA, which accounts for 3% of its check deposits. There are 8 million preferred customer clients (having more than $50,000 in deposits and multiple accounts) who account for 57% of BoA's deposits.

The business banking unit provides a wide range of lending-related products and services, integrated working capital management, and treasury solutions to clients.

Consumer Real Estate Services consists of home loans, legacy assets, and servicing. The home loan unit provides loan production activities. Legacy assets and servicing is responsible for mortgage servicing activities. Through home loan operations, CRES generates revenue through fixed- and adjustable-rate first-lien mortgage loans for home purchases and refinancing needs, home equity lines of credit (HELOCs), and home equity loans. First mortgage products are either sold into the secondary mortgage market to investors or held on the balance sheet for asset and liability management (ALM) purposes. CRES mortgage banking income is classified into production and servicing income.

The Global Commercial Banking division includes Global Corporate and Global Commercial banking, and investment banking provides global Treasury services and business-lending services. Global Treasury Services include deposits, Treasury management, credit card, foreign exchange, short-term investment, and solutions for corporate and commercial banking clients. The business-lending activities include various loan-related products and services (e.g., commercial loans, leases, commitment facilities, trade finance, real estate lending, and direct/indirect consumer loans). The investment banking products and services involve debt and equity underwriting, merger, and other advisory services. The fees of investment banking activities are shared between the Global Banking and Global Markets divisions, based on the contribution of each segment.

The Global Banking Markets division provides sales and trading services and research services to institution clients across various asset classes including fixed-income, credit, currency, commodity, and equity businesses. The products offered are securities and derivatives in both primary and secondary markets. GBM provides services such as market making, financing, securities clearing, settlement, and custody services to institutional clients. GBM also provides risk management products using derivatives instruments based on equity, interest rate, credit, currency, commodity, and mortgage-related products. Sales and trading revenue is composed of fixed income (government debt obligations, corporate debt obligations, commercial mortgage-backed securities, residential mortgage-backed securities, and collateralized debt obligations), currencies (interest rate and foreign exchange contracts), commodities (derivatives such as forwards, swaps, and options), and equity (equity derivatives).

Global Wealth and Investment Management is composed of Merrill Lynch Global Wealth Management and Bank of America Private Wealth Management (US Trust). Merrill Lynch's advisory services are provided to clients with over $250,000 in total investable assets. The advisory services consist of brokerage, banking, and retirement products.

US Trust along with Merrill Lynch Private banking unit provides comprehensive wealth management solutions to high-net-worth individuals. The major services provided by Merrill Lynch Wealth Management include Investment Management, Wealth Management Banking, concentrated stock strategies, tax and estate planning, and retirement services. US Trust is involved in analyzing a wide range of asset classes that includes hedge and private equity funds and global investment opportunities. The specialty asset management at US Trust concentrates on nonfinancial assets such as farm and ranchland, timberland, oil and gas properties, real estate, and private businesses.

"All Other" consists of ALM activities, equity investments, liquidating businesses, and others. ALM activities cover the whole-loan residential mortgage portfolio, investment securities, interest rates, and foreign currency risk management.

BoA has contractual obligations to make future payments on debt and lease agreements. BoA securitizes first-lien residential mortgage loans in the form of mortgage-backed securities (MBS) guaranteed by the government-sponsored enterprises (GSEs) or by GNMA (Ginnie Mae). Legacy companies and subsidiaries sold pools of first-lien residential mortgage loans and home equity loans as private-label securitizations. BoA extends credit to customers in the form of loan commitments, standby letters of credit (SBLCs), and commercial letters of credit.

1.1.2 ASSETS AND LIABILITIES OF BANK OF AMERICA

The assets for BoA consist of federal funds sold, securities borrowed or purchased under agreement to resell, trading account assets (government, corporate fixed-income securities, equity, and convertible instruments), debt securities (US Treasury and agency securities, MBS, foreign bonds, corporate bonds, and municipal debt). These debt securities portfolios are primarily used to manage interest rate and liquidity risks. Loans and leases as well as other assets also form a major part of BoA's assets.

The liabilities consist of deposits, fed funds purchased and securities loaned, trading account liabilities (short positions in fixed-income securities), commercial paper, long-term debt, and other liabilities. Deposits are generated primarily by the CBB, GWIM, and GBM segments.

Statistics from 2012 reveal that approximately 68% of the US commercial loan portfolio excluding small business was in the global banking sector. The commercial real estate portfolio, consisting of loans made to the public, private developers, and commercial real estate firms, is predominantly managed by the global banking division. Approximately 20% of the consumer portfolio is made up of home equity loans, which are HELOCs, home equity loans, and reverse mortgages.

In 2012, the bank's long-term/short-term senior debt ratings and outlooks expressed by the rating agencies are as follows: Baa2/P-2 (negative) by Moody's, A-/A-2 (negative) by S&P, and A/F1 (stable) by Fitch.

1.1.3 STRATEGY OF BANK OF AMERICA

BoA provides services for people, companies, and institutional investors. People are provided products and services. Companies are provided financing and advisory needs for commercial and investment clients. The institutional investors are provided trading guidance and research expertise to clients in more than 100 countries.

BoA is focused on transforming into a more efficient bank by selling noncore assets, reducing risk exposure, and building capital. BoA was able to improve its Tier 1 common capital ratio under Basel I by about 3% points during the last 3 years and twice what it was before the crisis. In 2011, the Tier 1 common capital ratio was 9.86%, up 126 basis point at the end of 2010.

BoA has divested more than $60 billion of assets in noncore activities, which has had no real impact on core earnings. During 2011-2012, BoA reduced long-term debt by approximately $100 billion while maintaining excess liquidity of $372 billion. In 2012, the number of 60-days-plus delinquent loans declined by 33%. BoA has modified more than 1 million mortgage loans since 2008.

In 2011, the assets it calls Global Excess Liquidity amounted to $378 billion. The "time to required funding" (which measures the length of time the parent bank could pay all unsecured contractual obligations without tapping external sources) was improved to 29 months. In 2011, the risk-weighted assets were decreased by $171 billion to $1.28 trillion.

BoA entered into strategic agreements with Fannie Mae and Freddie Mac to resolve representations and warranties and to repurchase claims that involved certain residential mortgage loans sold to them by entities related to Countrywide Financial. In 2012, BoA became one of the largest US mortgage service providers to reach global settlements to resolve federal and state investigations on certain origination, servicing, and foreclosure practices.

1.1.3.1 Focus on small, medium, and large companies

BoA serves more than 30,000 companies with revenues of $50 million to more than $2 billion.

BoA and its subsidiaries provide a comprehensive range of services for all types of companies ranging from small businesses to multinational companies. The major services include capital raising and advisory, lending and financing, card solutions, merchant services, payments/receivable management, equipment financing/leasing, liquidity management, retirement and benefit plan services, investment solutions and management, trade services, mergers and acquisitions, interest rate, currency risk, and commodity risk management.

In 2011, BoA extended $17.7 billion in credit to small businesses across the United States. During the last 5 years, BoA purchased $10 billion in products and services of small, medium, and diversified businesses. According to bank statistics, more than 2 million small business customers use online banking services, and the mobile banking services used by clients have exceeded 0.5 million. Approximately 8000 Merrill Lynch Financial Advisors serve the retirement plan needs of small business owners.

BoA provides services of capital raising, capital management, and Treasury solutions for medium and large companies. The clients are served through a network of offices, client relationship teams, and product specialists. Institutional investors and corporate clients are provided financial products, advisory services, financing securities clearing, and settlement and custody services. BoA is a global leader in the distribution of fixed income, currency, and energy commodity products and derivatives.

The Bank of America's Merrill Lynch Global Banking and Markets division serves institutional, corporate, and commercial clients globally with a wide range of products, services, and client solutions. BoA's client base consists of 98% of US Fortune 100 and 85% of the Global Fortune 500 companies.

Merrill Lynch Global Research provides trading strategies and market guidance for all asset classes. The unit with 740 analysts in 20 countries focuses on global equities, global credit research on fixed income, global economics, global commodities and asset allocation, and global currencies and exchange rates. The analysts offer insights and guidance on more than 3300 stocks, 860 corporate bond issuers, 40 currencies, 60 economies, and 20 commodities. Merrill Lynch also provides a fixed-income index platform, which is based on 5000 fixed-income bonds. The unit also provides investable commodity indexes based on 500 commodities and sector equity and equity derivatives indexes based on more than 100 equities.

The Global Capital Markets and Global Corporate and Investment Banking (GCIB) divisions focus on underwriting services in equity and debt capital markets and merger and acquisition (M&A) financial advisory services worldwide. The divisions serve more than 12,000 institutional clients in different parts of the globe.

Affluent clients are provided a full set of investment management, brokerage, banking retirement, wealth structuring, and trust services through the Merrill Lynch Global Wealth and Investment Management, US Trust, and Merrill Edge businesses. The long-term flow of assets under management has grown to $28 billion. In 2011, BoA Merrill Lynch was ranked as the top global research firm of 2011 by *Institutional Investor* magazine.

The growth opportunities for BoA exist in the emerging markets of China, Brazil, and Russia, as a large number of clients do business in this region.

As an innovative step, BoA has eliminated overdraft fees for everyday debit card transactions at point of sale and has introduced easy-to-read banking statements. BoA launched the ambitious Project New BAC, which is a two-phase enterprisewide initiative meant to simplify and streamline workflows and processes for achieving operational excellence. This cost-cutting strategy was aimed at reducing expenses by $5 billion by year-end 2013. The Phase I evaluation was completed in 2011. The project approved more than 2000 ideas suggested by employees for improving customer services. In the first quarter after the BAC initiative was activated, the number of employees was reduced by 3100.

1.1.4 CORPORATE SOCIAL RESPONSIBILITY ACTIVITIES

During the past 8 years BoA contributed toward the economic health of communities by financing more than 114,000 units of affordable housing in low-income communities. During 2012, the bank provided more than $22 million in housing grants. In 2012, BoA provided $19.1 billion in total credit to small businesses, customers, local communities, and nonprofit organizations. BoA generated $36.5 billion in commercial real estate loans in 2011. The bank has helped more than 1.3 million customers avoid foreclosure, which included modifications of 1 million home loans. BoA was involved in the creation of a consumer financial protection bureau, and invested $4 billion in environmental business. The investments included distributed solar deals and launching of socially responsible investment portfolio for wealth management clients.

1.1.5 GROWTH THROUGH MERGERS AND ACQUISITIONS

The BoA growth strategy has been focused on a series of M&As over a period of time. In 1960, the Security National Bank of Greensboro and American Commercial Bank of Charlotte merged to form the North California National Bank (NCNB). In 1981, NCNB acquired First National Bank of Lake City Florida. In the 1980s and 1990s, NCNB grew through a series of mergers and acquisitions. In 1986, NCNB acquired Banker's Trust. In 1988, NCNB acquired the First Republic Bank. By early 1990, NCNB became the tenth-largest US bank. In 1991, NCNB acquired the C&S/Sovran of Atlanta and Norfolk and changed the name to NationsBank. In 1993, NationsBank acquired MNC Financial. Barnett Bank was acquired in 1997.

In 1997, NationsBank acquired Boatmen's Bank. By acquiring the fifth-largest bank, NationsBank became the leading financial institution in three leading geographic regions and served more than 13 million customers in 16 states. In 1998, NationsBank acquired California-based Bank America Corp.

and became BoA. With the acquisition of BoA, the new financial institution became the first coast-to-coast retail banking franchise in the United States. In 1999, Fleet Financial Corporation acquired BankBoston Corporation to form the fifth-largest bank named FleetBoston Financial. In 2004, BoA acquired FleetBoston Financial. In the same year, BoA acquired National Processing Company, which was engaged in the processing of Visa and MasterCard transactions.

With the acquisition of MBNA in 2006, BoA became the worldwide leading credit card issuer. In 2007, BoA acquired US Trust and expanded its services to high-net-worth individuals. Again in 2007, BoA gained a strong foothold in the Midwest through the acquisition of Chicago-originated LaSalle Bank. With the acquisition of Countrywide Financial Corporation, BoA became the largest mortgage lender and loan service provider in the United States. In the midst of the economic crisis of 2008, BoA acquired Merrill Lynch and extended its reach to retail brokerage and wealth management divisions.

As a result of its mergers and acquisitions, BoA became the world's largest issuer of credit, debit, and prepaid cards based on purchase volume. BoA is the largest consumer and small business bank in the United States.

1.1.6 RISK MANAGEMENT AT BANK OF AMERICA

BoA has a defined risk framework that is approved annually by the corporation's board of directors. Risk management planning is integrated with strategic, financial, and customer/client planning. The risk-adjusted returns of each business segment is assessed. The board comprises a majority of independent directors who oversee the management of the corporation through the governance structure, which includes board committees and management committees. The standing committees that oversee risks are the Audit and Enterprise Risk Committee and Credit Committee. All employees have accountability for risk management in categories of businesses, governance and control, and corporate audit. Governance and control functions comprise global risk management, global compliance, legal, and enterprise control functions. The global risk management unit is led by the chief risk officer who has the mandate to ensure that appropriate risk management practices are in place. Global risk management contains two risk teams: enterprise risk teams and independent business risk teams. Enterprise risk teams set and establish enterprise policies, programs, and standards. They also provide enterprise-level risk oversight and monitor systemic and emerging risk issues. Independent business risk teams establish policy limits, controls, and thresholds within defined corporate standards. The credit committee identifies and manages credit exposures on an enterprisewide basis.

BoA uses risk management process tools such as risk and control self-assessments (RCSAs) for risk identification and assessment of control environment, monitoring, reporting, and quality assurance. Management conducts enterprisewide stress tests on a periodic basis to conduct sensitivity analysis on balance sheet, earnings, capital, and liquidity in different economic and business scenarios.

Strategic risk is assessed within the strategic plan in the context of the overall financial condition each year. Such parameters as forecasted earnings, returns on capital, the current risk profile, liquidity requirements, and stress-testing results are assessed when considering strategic risks. Proprietary models are used to measure capital requirements for credit, country, market, operational, and strategic risks. The economic capital measurement process provides a risk-based measurement of the capital required for unexpected credit, market, and operational losses over a 1-year time horizon at a 99.97% confidence level. The bank's primary market risk exposures are in its trading portfolio and equity investments.

Global funding and liquidity risk management activities are centralized within the corporate treasury. The enterprise-risk committee approves the corporation's liquidity policy and contingency funding plan, including establishing liquidity risk-tolerance levels. The Asset Liability Management Risk Committee (ALMRC) is responsible for managing liquidity risks and maintaining exposures within the established tolerance levels. BoA uses assets called Global Excess Liquidity sources as the primary means of liquidity risk mitigation. These liquidity sources are in the form of cash and high-quality liquid unencumbered securities. The bank's Global Excess Liquidity sources were $372 billion and $378 billion in 2012 and 2011, respectively. The bank uses the metric Time to Required Funding to evaluate the appropriate level of excess liquidity. This debt coverage measure indicates the number of months the bank can continue to meet its unsecured contractual obligations as they come due using its Global Excess Liquidity sources without any additional new debt.

Credit risk is managed based on the risk profile of the borrower or counterparty, repayment sources, and the nature of underlying collateral. The portfolios are classified as either consumer or commercial for monitoring credit risk. On account of the changing economic environment, the underwriting and credit management practices are often refined. To manage credit risk based on consumer business, there are collection programs, loan modifications, and customer assistance infrastructures. A number of actions are undertaken to mitigate losses in commercial business, which include portfolio monitoring and hedging activity.

From 2008 to 2012, BoA and Countrywide completed approximately 1.2 million loan modifications. The bank also reviews and manages concentrations of credit exposure by industry, product, geography, customer relationship, and loan size.

BoA purchased credit protection to cover funded and unfunded portions of certain credit exposures. Based on fair value option, the amount was $19.4 billion and $14.74 billion in 2011 and 2012, respectively. BoA faces commodity risk owing to exposures to instruments traded in petroleum, natural gas, power, and metal markets. The hedging instruments used to mitigate this risk include options, futures, and swaps.

Market risk is inherent in financial instruments such as loans, deposits, securities, short-term borrowings, long-term debt, trading accounts, and derivatives. The risk of adverse changes in the economic value of nontrading positions is managed through ALM activities. Hedging instruments such as options, swaps, futures, and forwards are used to manage mortgage risks. Equity market risk is mitigated through options, futures, swaps, convertible bonds, and cash positions. The Global Markets Risk Committee monitors significant daily revenues and losses by business and analyzes the primary driving factors for gains and losses. Value at Risk (VaR) is a key statistic used to measure market risk. The accuracy of the VaR methodology is reviewed by back testing, which is a comparison of the VaR results from historical data against the actual daily profit and loss. Trading portfolio stress testing is also conducted to estimate the value change in the trading portfolio that would result from abnormal market movements. Various situations that are categorized as historical or hypothetical are regularly run and reported for overall trading portfolios and individual businesses.

Interest rate risk also contributes to significant risk exposure. Interest rate derivatives are used to hedge the variability of cash flows of assets and liabilities.

The operational risk management programs use key tools such as personnel management practices, data reconciliation processes, fraud management units, transaction processing monitoring and analysis, and business recovery planning, along with enterprise risk management tools such as loss reporting and scenario analysis to identify, measure, control, and review operational risks. Table 1.1 gives the business segment results of BoA during the period 2010-2012. Table 1.2 shows the details of noninterest income of BoA during the period 2010-2012. Table 1.3 gives the financial highlights of BoA during the period 2008-2012. Table 1.4 highlights the comparative key statistics of BoA during the period 2011-2012. Table 1.5 gives the key details of the long-term debt issuances of BoA.

REFERENCES

1. Annual Reports, Bank of America
2. http://www.bankofamerica.com

Table 1.1   Business Segment Results 2010-2012 (Millions of US Dollars)

Business segment	Total Revenues			Net Income (Loss)		
	2010	2011	2012	2010	2011	2012
Consumer and business banking (deposits and card services)	35,902	32,880	29,023	1362	7447	5321
CRES	10,329	(3154)	8759	(8947)	(19,529)	(6507)
GCB	11,226	17,312	17,207	3218	6046	5725
GBM		14,798	13,519		988	1054
GWIM	16,289	16,495	16,517	1340	1718	2223
Others	9695	16,095	(790)	1472	4712	(3628)
Total	111,390	94,426	84,334	(2238)	1446	4188

Source: Annual Reports

Table 1.2   Noninterest Income 2010-2012 (Millions of US Dollars)

	2010	2011	2012
Card income	8108	7184	6121
Services charges	9390	8094	7600
Investment and brokerage services	11,622	11,826	11,393
Investment banking income	5520	5217	5299
Equity investment income	5260	7360	2070
Trading account profits	10,054	6697	5870
Mortgage banking income	2734	(8830)	4750
Insurance income	2066	1346	(195)
Gains on sale of debt securities	2526	3374	1662
Other income	2384	6869	(1839)
Net impairment losses	(967)	(299)	(53)
Total	58,697	48,838	42,678

Source: Annual Reports

Table 1.3   Financial Highlights 2008-2012 (Millions of US Dollars)

	2008	2009	2010	2011	2012
Net interest income	45,360	47,109	51,523	44,616	40,656
Noninterest income	27,422	72,534	58,697	48,838	42,678
Total revenue net of interest expense	72,782	119,643	110,220	93,454	83,334
Total loans and leases	910,871	948,805	940,440	926,200	907,819
Total assets	1,843,985	2,443,068	2,264,909	2,129,046	2,209,974
Total deposits	831,157	980,966	1,010,430	1,033,041	1,105,261
Long-term debt	231,235	446,634	490,497	421,229	275,585
Total shareholder equity	164,831	244,645	228,248	230,101	236,956
Performance ratios					
Return on average assets (%)	0.22	0.26	n/m	0.06	0.19
Market capitalization	70,645	130,273	134,536	58,580	125,136
Capital ratios					
Risk-based capital					
Tier 1 common (%)	4.8	7.81	8.6	9.86	11.06
Tier 1 (%)	9.15	10.40	11.24	12.40	12.89

Source: Annual Reports

Table 1.4   Key Statistics 2011-2012

	2011	2012
Total deposit spread (%)	2.12	1.81
Client brokerage (millions of US dollars)	66,576	75,946
Online banking active accounts (in thousands)	29,870	29,638
Mobile banking active accounts (in thousands)	9166	12,013
Banking centers	5702	5478
ATMs	17,756	16,347

Source: Bank Website

Table 1.5   Recent Biggest Long-Term Debt Issuances

Currency	Note	Rate	Pricing (bps)	Date	Size (Billions of US Dollars)
USD	10 year	Fixed	T+150/147	1/13	4.3
USD	5 year	Fixed	T+125/122	1/13	3
USD	10 year	Fixed	T+378/325	1/12	2.3
EUR	7 year	Fixed	DBR+164	07/13	2

Source: Bank Website

1.2 JPMORGAN CHASE AND COMPANY

JPMorgan Chase is one of the largest and oldest financial institutions in the world. The bank's legacy dates back to 1799, whose foundation is based on more than 1200 predecessor institutions.

JPMorgan Chase and Co. is the holding company that serves customers and clients under its Chase and JPMorgan brands. The Chase brand includes consumer and commercial banking businesses. The consumer businesses include branch ATM, online banking, credit cards, small business, home finance, home equity loans, auto finance, education finance, retirement and investing, retail checking, and merchant services. Commercial banking consists of middle-market banking, business credit, equipment finance, commercial term lending, and community development banking. The commercial banking business also includes corporate client banking, not-for-profit, health care banking, real estate banking, and international banking.

The businesses under the 160-year-old JPMorgan brand include investment banking, asset management, Treasury services, worldwide securities services, and private banking. JPMorgan Asset Management is a leading asset manager for institutions, individuals, and financial intermediaries.

JPMorgan Investor Services is a global leader in providing solutions and helping institutional investors and broker-dealers in more than 100 markets. JPMorgan offers Treasury services to more than 135,000 corporations, financial institutions, governments, and municipalities in more than 180 countries. JPMorgan spends over $8 billion on systems and technology yearly. There are 6500 professionals who provide insights on more than 4000 companies and 40 developed and emerging markets. The bank has about 4000 risk and credit officers to manage exposures that include on average $3.4 billion new lending and $1 trillion in trading activities every day. Approximately 80% of Fortune 500 companies are the clients of JPMorgan Chase. The massive scale at which JPMorgan Chase operates is highlighted by the fact that the bank arranges $450 billion of syndicated loans for clients and processes up to $10 trillion a day in transactions around the world. In 2012, JPMorgan Chase provided credit worth $1.8 trillion dollars of which $20 billion was provided for small businesses. JPMorgan Chase also originated more than 920,000 mortgages and provided credit cards to 6.7 million people. With 260,000 employees, the company serves more than 50 million customers daily and has about 2.2 million middle-market and small businesses in the United States. Worldwide, the company has businesses with 5000 issuer and 16,000 investor clients.

In March 2012 JPMorgan Chase passed the Federal Reserve Board's Comprehensive Capital Analysis and Review (CCAR) stress test, which allows firms to increase dividends.

JPMorgan Chase has provided approximately $85 billion in credit for nearly 1500 nonprofit and government entities, which includes states, municipalities, hospitals, and universities. In 2012, loans to middle-market companies amounted to $50.7 billion, which registered 14% compound annual growth. The investable assets for high-net-worth individuals amounted to $42 billion in 2011.

1.2.1 BUSINESS DIVISIONS

The major business segments are Consumer and Community Banking (CCB), Corporate and Investment Bank, Commercial Banking, and Asset Management along with a Corporate/Private Equity segment.

1.2.1.1 Consumer and Community Banking

In 2012, Chase combined its three retail businesses—CBB, mortgage banking, card merchant services and auto finance—into one unit, CCB. The consolidation of businesses in the group has resulted in an increase in revenues of approximately $14 billion from cross-selling and synergies across businesses.

JPMorgan Chase						
Consumer Business			**Wholesale Businesses**			
Consumer and Community Banking			**Corporate and Investment Bank**		**Commercial Banking**	**Asset Management**
Consumer and Business Banking	Mortgage Banking	Card, Merchant Services and Auto	Banking	Markets and Investor Services	Middle-Market Banking	Private Banking
Consumer Banking	Mortgage Production	Card Services Credit card	Investment Banking	Fixed-Income Markets	Commercial Term Lending	Investment Management
Business Banking	Mortgage Servicing	Merchant Services	Treasury Services	Equity Markets	Corporate Client Banking	High Bridge/ Gavea
Chase Wealth Management	Real Estate Portfolios	Auto Finance Student Loans	Lending	Securities Services	Real Estate Banking	
				Credit Adjustment and Others		

CCB offers various deposits, investment products, and services to consumers and lending, deposit, cash management, and payment solutions to small businesses. Mortgage banking originates and services activities and portfolios that consist of residential mortgages, home equity loans, and purchased credit impaired (PCI) portfolios accounted by Washington Mutual. The card segment issues credit cards to consumers and small businesses and facilitates payment services to corporate and public-sector clients through its commercial card products.

As of 2012, JPMorgan is the number-one issuer of credit cards, the number-two mortgage originator, and the number-three mortgage service company in the United States. More than half of JPMorgan Chase's earnings comes from US consumers. In 2012 mortgage banking had a net income of $3.3 billion as compared to a net loss of $2.1 billion in 2011; the improvement is credited to improved residential real estate portfolio and strong mortgage loan originations.

JPMorgan was the among the first banks to roll out a full range of mobile solutions across different products. In 2012, approximately 12 million customers used mobile banking services and $18 billion dollars was transacted in mobile payments.

JPMorgan has the largest ATM network in the United States and the second-largest branch network. In May 2012, the bank launched its first prepaid card called Chase Liquid. Currently 50% of Chase deposits are made with a teller and the rest are done through ATMs, online, and mobile devices. The number of mobile users is increasing roughly by 350,000 a month.

The mortgage banking unit introduced the My New HomeSM app, which is the only application in the market that enables customers to search for and compare homes, calculate payment, and connect with a local Chase mortgage banker from a mobile device. It was the top-performing bank according to an FDIC 2012 survey.

1.2.1.2 Corporate and Investment Banking

In 2011, JPMorgan's Investment Bank (IB) and Treasury and Securities Services (TSS) divisions were combined to form the Corporate and Investment Bank (CIB). CIB focuses on three major segments:

banking, markets, and investor services. The CIB division of JPMorgan Chase offers a variety of investment banking, prime brokerage, Treasury and securities products and services to a global client base consisting of corporations, financial institutions, and municipal corporations. The division offers a complete range of investment banking products and services in all major capital markets. Treasury services focus on cash management, liquidity solutions, and trade finance products. The Markets and Investor services segment is a global market maker in cash securities, derivatives instruments offering risk management solutions, and prime brokerage. This segment also consists of a securities services business that services securities, cash and alternative investments, and a depository receipt program.

On account of Basel III regulations, the allocated capital to CIB was increased to $56.5 billion in January 2013. The division employs around 52,000 people in 60 countries and serves 7600 clients. The assets under custody amounted to $18.8 trillion. The division was ranked number one in investment fees in 2012.

1.2.1.3 Commercial Banking

The Commercial banking (CB) segment consists of middle-market banking, commercial term lending, corporate client banking, and real estate banking. Middle-market banking provides services to corporations, municipalities, financial institutions, and other nonprofit entities with annual revenues ranging between $20 million to $500 million. Commercial term lending provides term financing to real estate investors for multifamily properties as well as financing office and industrial properties. Corporate client banking provides services to clients with annual revenue of between $500 million and $2 billion. Real estate banking provides full-service banking to investors and developers of institutional-grade real estate properties. Commercial banking provides finances to real estate investors and owners. In partnership with other businesses, the segment offers lending, Treasury services, and investment banking services to clients. The bank extended $126 billion in new and renewed financing. The strategy of the bank is to focus on differentiating services and capabilities as the fundamentals of the multifamily housing market improve.

1.2.1.4 Asset Management

The Asset Management (AM) division is a global leader in investment and wealth management with client assets of $2.1 trillion. The segment offers investment management services across all major asset classes. AM also provides retirement products, brokerage and banking services such as loans, mortgages, and deposits. Global Investment Management and Global Wealth Management franchises have clients composed of the "world's largest high-net-worth individuals," a majority of top pension funds, sovereign wealth funds, central banks, endowment family offices, and approximately 3000 global financial intermediary firms who invest in banks' funds on behalf of their clients. In 2011, JPMorgan Chase celebrated the 110th anniversary of one of its private client families. Approximately 215 of the bank's public mutual funds are ranked 4 or 5 stars by Morningstar.

The Corporate/Private Equity segment consists of private equity, Treasury, and chief investment office, which measures, monitors, reports, and manages the firm's liquidity and funding.

1.2.2 CORPORATE SOCIAL RESPONSIBILITY ACTIVITIES

JPMorgan Chase contributes approximately $200 million every year to help the poor and disadvantaged. The bank dispensed over $1 billion in cash through branches and ATMs at the time of Hurricane Sandy. In 2012, JPMorgan Chase provided $20 billion in new credit to American small businesses. From 2009 to 2012, the bank added more than 1000 small business bankers. The bank gave $990 million in loans and over $1 billion in equity to build more than 31,000 units of housing for low- and moderate-income families in over 200 US cities. JPMorgan Chase provided more than $85 billion in capital or credit to approximately 1500 government entities, including states, municipalities, hospitals, universities, and nonprofit organizations.

JPMorgan Chase also invested $1 million in clean water programs in rural villages across India, Vietnam, Indonesia, and the Philippines. To promote sustainability, the bank deployed over $5 billion of capital for alternative energy and clean technology companies and projects. The bank has collaborated with the Brookings Institution to launch the Global Cities initiative to focus on metropolitan communities.

1.2.3 CAPITAL STRATEGY

The capital strategy at JPMorgan Chase emphasizes long-term stability for investing in leading businesses in highly volatile environments. Senior management considers the implication of the firm's capital strength before making decisions on business activities. The Regulatory Capital Management Office (RMCO) provides the overall capital governance framework and is responsible for reviewing, approving, and monitoring the implementation of the bank's capital policies and strategies. The firm assesses capital based on regulatory capital requirements, economic risk capital assessment, and line of business equity attribution. The bank measures economic capital basically based on four risks; credit market, and operational and private equity risk. Private equity risk capital is the capital allocated to privately held securities, third-party fund investments, and private equity portfolios within the Corporate/Private Equity segment to cover potential loss associated with the decline in equity markets.

1.2.4 ACQUISITIONS BY JPMORGAN CHASE BANK

JPMorgan Chase is a product of a series of mergers and acquisitions. All four of JPMorgan Chase's major New York City heritage firms—JMorgan and Co., The Chase Manhattan Bank, Manufacturers Hanover Trust Co., and Chemical Bank—grew through mergers in the 1950s and 1960s.

Merger Highlights: 1990-2010	
Year	**Deals**
1991	Manufacturers Hanover Corp. merged with Chemical Banking Corp., which was then the second-largest banking institution in the United States
1995	First Chicago Corp. merged with NBD Bancorp to form First Chicago NBD
1996	Chase Manhattan Corp. absorbed Chemical Banking Corp.
1998	Bank One Corp. merged with First Chicago NBD under the name of Bank One Corp.
2000	JPMorgan & Co. merged with Chase Manhattan Corp. to form JPMorgan Chase & Co.
2004	JPMorgan Chase & Co. acquires Bank One Corp.
2008	JPMorgan Chase & Co. acquires The Bear Stearns Companies
2008	JPMorgan Chase & Co. acquires the deposits, assets, and certain liabilities of Washington Mutual banking operations
2010	JPMorgan Chase acquired full ownership of its UK joint venture JPMorgan Cazenove

1.2.4.1 JPMorgan and Chase Manhattan merger

In 2000, the Chase Manhattan Corp. merged with JPMorgan and Co., in effect combining four of the largest and oldest money center banking institutions in New York City (Morgan, Chase, Chemical, and Manufacturers Hanover) into one firm called JPMorgan Chase and Co. The Chase Bank is the product of the union of three New York banks that combined in the last decade: Chemical Bank, which purchased Chase Manhattan in 1996 and Manufacturers Hanover, which Chemical bought in 1991. In this merger deal, Chase bought out its US rival in a $34-billion all-stock deal. The combined bank became the third-largest bank holding company in the United States after Citigroup and BoA with assets of $660 billion. The merger motive was to satisfy Chase's goal of acquiring a major investment banking firm. The merger resulted in cost savings of approximately $1.5 billion, which came from real estate, systems integration, and reduced staffing. The new bank consolidated its ranking position in asset management and wealth management. In 2007, the bank became the largest US hedge fund firm.

1.2.4.2 Merger of Bank One with JPMorgan Chase

In 2004, JPMorgan Chase took over Bank One in a $58-billion deal. The newly combined company became the United States' second-biggest bank, with $1 trillion of assets and 2300 branches in 17 states centered in the Midwest and Northeast regions. The deal combined the investment and commercial banking strength of JPMorgan Chase with the consumer banking operations power of Bank One. This model of integration was expected to lead to less volatile earnings and higher market valuation. JPMorgan Chase was able to consolidate its position in the retail and credit card segment as Bank One had been the world's largest Visa card issuer. The merger also facilitated the cross-selling of each other's products. Cost-cutting was one of the strategic aims of the deal. The merger eliminated about 10,000 jobs as a part of an effort to attain cost savings of $2.2 billion within a 3-year period. Though technically the deal was a takeover of Bank One by JPMorgan Chase, the new board consisted of equal members from each bank.

1.2.5 RISK MANAGEMENT AT JPMORGAN CHASE

The bank's chief executive officer is responsible for setting the overall firm's appetite for risk. Each line of business risk committee is responsible for decisions with respect to business risk strategy, policies, and controls.

The risk management function is headed by the firm's chief risk officer. The risk management organization is composed of a risk operating committee and risk management business control committees. The risk operating committee sets risk management priorities and risk issues highlighted by line of business CEOs and cross-line business risk officers. There are three business control committees with risk management function. The Model Risk and Development unit within the risk management function provides oversight of the firmwide model risk policy guidance with respect to a model's appropriate usage and conducts independent review of models. Legal and Compliance has oversight for legal risk. The bank uses a firmwide Valuation Governance Forum (VGF) to oversee the management of risks.

The bank uses risk management models, such as VaR and stress models, for the measurement, monitoring, and management of risk positions.

The bank manages liquidity and funding using a centralized global approach to monitor exposures and identify constraints on the transfer of liquidity within the firm. The firm has a liquidity governance framework to review, approve, and monitor implementation of liquidity risk policies. For managing liquidity, Treasury is responsible for defining and implementing funds and transferring pricing across all lines of business.

The bank has a stable source of funding through its diversified deposit franchise through each of its lines of business. Funding markets are accessed regionally through hubs in New York, London, and Hong Kong by means of which the bank can cater to client needs in the framework of local market dynamics.

In 2012, the rating agencies rated JPMorgan Chase as follows: A2 by Moody's, A by S&P, and A+ by Fitch Ratings for long-term issues.

The firm's exposure to credit risk is through its lending, capital market activities, and operating services businesses. The methodologies used to measure probable and unexpected credit losses depend on the characteristics of the credit exposure. The scored portfolio is generally held in CCB and includes residential real estate loans, credit card loans, business banking loans, and student loans. The probable credit losses that are inherent in a portfolio are estimated using portfolio modeling, credit scoring, and decision support tools, which consist of loan-level factors such as delinquency status, credit scores, and collateral values.

The risk rates portfolios are included in the CIB, CB, and AM divisions. The probable and unexpected credit losses for the risk-rated portfolios are based on estimates of the probability of default and loss severity given a default. The probability of default is estimated for each borrower, and a loss given default is estimated considering the collateral and structural support for each credit facility. Stress testing is conducted to measure and manage credit risk in the firm's credit portfolio. The risk management practices also evaluate the delinquency and other trends against business expectations, current and forecasted economic conditions, and industry benchmarks. Loss mitigation strategies such as interest rate reductions, term or payment extensions, principal, and interest deferral are employed to minimize losses in residential real estate portfolios. The wholesale credit risk is managed through loan underwriting and credit approval process, loan sales and securitization, loan syndications, credit derivatives, and master netting agreements. The mortgage loans consisting of prime, subprime, and loans held for sale amounted to $84.5 billion in 2012.

Products across fixed income, foreign exchange, equities, and commodities are sources of market risk in CIB. Market risks also arise from activities in mortgage production, mortgage servicing, and more. The bank uses various statistical metrics such as VaR and economic value stress testing to measure market risk. The nonstatistical risk measures include loss advisories, profit and loss drawdowns, risk identification for large exposures, and nontrading interest rate-sensitive revenue at risk stress testing. VaR is calculated assuming a one-day holding period and an expected tail loss methodology, which approximates a 95% confidence level.

The bank runs weekly stress tests on market-related risks across the different lines of business using multiple scenarios with the assumption of changes in key risk factors such as credit spreads, equity prices, interest rates, currency rates, or commodity prices.

The market risk is controlled primarily through a series of limits set in the context of the market environment and business strategy in consultation with each line of business. The bank takes into account factors such as market volatility, product liquidity, and accommodation of client business and management experience.

The interest rate risk exposure for the bank arises from trading activities and traditional activities such as extension of loans, credit facilities, taking deposits, and issue of debt. The ALCO establishes the bank's interest rate risk policies and sets risk guidelines.

The firm manages interest rate exposure related to assets and liabilities on a consolidated corporate-wide basis. The interest rate risks of business units are transferred to treasury through a transfer pricing system. This system takes into account such factors as asset and liability balances, contractual rates of interest, contractual principal repayment schedules, interest rate reset dates, and more. The firm manages interest rate risk through its investment securities portfolio and derivatives. The firm evaluates its non-trading interest rate risk exposure through stress testing of earnings at risk, which measures the extent to which changes in interest rate will affect the bank's core net income. The bank also conducts simulations of changes in nontrading interest rate-sensitive revenue under a variety of interest rate scenarios.

The bank is exposed to country risk through wholesale lending, investing, and market-making activities. The country risk management group uses signaling models and ratings indicators to identify potential country risk concerns.

Operational risk is measured using an operational risk capital model based on a loss distribution approach. The bank's operational risk framework is supported by Phoenix, which integrates the individual components of the operational risk management framework into a unified web-based tool.

The fiduciary risk management is a part of the relevant line of business risk committees. JPMorgan Chase has established a new Firmwide Oversight and Control group to make decisions and keep control while undertaking major acquisitions. Table 1.6 gives the value of total client assets of JPMorgan Chase during the period 2006-2012. Table 1.7 provides the financial highlights of JPMorgan Chase during the period 2008-2012. Table 1.8 shows the revenues and net income of the various business segments of JPMorgan Chase during the 3-year period 2010-2012.

REFERENCES

1. Annual reports of JPMorgan Chase & Co.
2. http://www.jpmorganchase.com/
3. Andrew Garfield, Chase acquires JP Morgan for $34bn, but 10,000 jobs may go, http://www.independent.co.uk/news/business/news/chase-acquires-jp-morgan-for-34bn-but-10000-jobs-may-go-699819.html
4. Thor Valdmanis, Christine Dugas and Adam Shell, JPMorgan, Bank One to join, http://www.usatoday.com/money/industries/banking/2004-01-14-jpmorgan-bankone_x.htm
5. http://www.smh.com.au/articles/2004/01/15/1073877965942.html

Table 1.6   Assets Management: Total Client Assets (Trillions of US Dollars)

Year	Value
2006	1.3
2007	1.6
2008	1.5
2009	1.7
2010	1.8
2011	1.9
2012	2.1

Source: Annual Reports

Table 1.7   Financial Highlights 2008-2012 (Millions of US Dollars)

Parameters	2008	2009	2010	2011	2012
Net revenue	67,252	100,434	102,694	97,234	97,031
Noninterest expense	43,500	52,352	61,196	62,911	64,729
Net income	5605	11,728	17,370	18,976	21,284
ROE IN (%)	2	6	10	11	11
Tier 1 capital ratio	10.9	11.1	12.1	12.3	12.6
Tier 1 common capital ratio	7.0	8.8	9.8	10.1	11
Market cap	117,695	164,261	165,875	125,442	167,260
Trading assets	509,983	411,128	489,892	443,963	450,028
Loans	744,898	633,458	692,927	723,720	733,796
Total assets	2,175,052	2,031,989	2,117,605	2,265,792	2,359,141
Deposits	1,009,277	938,367	930,369	1,127,806	1,193,593
Long-term debt	302,959	289,165	270,653	256,775	249,024
Total stockholder equity	166,884	165,365	176,106	183,573	204,069
Nonperforming assets	12,780	19,948	16,682	11,315	11,734
Number of employees	224,961	222,316	239,831	260,157	258,965

Source: Annual Reports

Table 1.8   Business Segments Revenue Highlights 2010-2012 (Millions of US Dollars)

Segment	Total Net Revenues			Net Income		
	2010	2011	2012	2010	2011	2012
Consumer and community banking	48,927	45,687	49,945	4578	6202	10,611
Corporate and investment bank	33,477	33,984	34,326	7718	7993	8406
Commercial banking	6040	6418	6825	2084	2367	2646
Asset management	8984	9543	9946	1710	1592	1703
Corporate/private equity	7414	4135	(1152)	1280	822	(2082)

Source: Annual Reports

1.3 CITIGROUP

Citigroup (or Citi) was founded in 1812 with the establishment of the City Bank of New York. Citi's footprint exists in 1000 cities spanning 160 countries. The Citigroup regions consist of North America, Europe, Middle East, Africa (EMEA), Latin America, and Asia.

1.3.1 MAJOR ACHIEVEMENTS AND MILESTONES

Citigroup is credited with originating some innovative ideas for the global community. Citi pioneered the concept of paying interest on every savings account. Citigroup is credited with facilitating the project that led to the invention of the cargo container. In 1865, Citi funded the transatlantic cable initiative. In the 1940s, Citigroup provided underwriting services for credit generation for the first passenger jet. Citigroup played a role in rebuilding Europe after World War II by means of arranging for commercial letters of credit for shipments to affected countries receiving aid under the Marshall Plan. Citi was also involved in financing the Panama Canal project, which facilitated international trade. In 2011, Citi teamed up with Google and MasterCard PayPass to pioneer Google Wallet, which was a significant milestone enabling Citi to emerge as a global powerhouse in digital banking. Citigroup, which pioneered its first ATM in 1977, currently has 26,000 ATMs around the world. Citigroup made a huge leap in digital banking with the introduction of Citi Smart Banking, an integrated system with workstation access to online banking. Through Citi Smart Banking, customers can obtain market information on wall displays and customer services via video chat. The Citi News App aims to set new standards for digital banking by offering customers investment information at their fingertips. For space technology programs, Citi is a leading lender for joint ventures involved in the operation of space vehicles. In 2002, Citigroup played a role in the development of equator principles advocated by the World Bank for mitigating social and environment risks in project financing.

Approximately 96% of the world's Fortune 500 companies are served by Citi's Transaction Services (CTS). In 2012, Citi introduced a new platform called Rainbow for core banking technology. Citigroup currently has about 250,000 full-time employees.

1.3.2 STRUCTURE OF CITIGROUP

Citigroup consists of Citicorp and Citi Holdings. Citicorp is Citi's core franchise consisting of its Global Consumer Banking businesses and Institutional Clients Group. The Institutional Clients Group includes securities, banking, and transaction services. In 2012, Citicorp had $1.7 trillion of assets and $863 billion of deposits, which account for 92% of Citi's total assets and 93% of its deposits. In 2012, Institutional Clients Group had approximately $1.1 trillion of assets and $523 billion of deposits. Citi Holdings consists of brokerage, asset management, local consumer lending, and special asset pools (SAPs).

1.3.2.1 Global Consumer Banking

Citi's Global Consumer Banking business, known as Citibank, is one of the largest retail banks in the world, serving more than 100 million clients in 40 countries. GCB is strategically positioned in the world's top cities with the highest consumer banking growth capabilities. The collective GCB businesses in 2012 amounted to $337 billion in deposits, $295 billion in loans, and $154 billion in assets under management in retail banking. The primary business units within the Global Consumer banking division are the Retail Banking, Citi Branded Cards, CitiMortgage, Citi Commercial Bank, and retail services, which operates in key markets of North America, Latin America, EMEA, and Asia. Global operations outside the United States account for half of consumer banking's total loans, deposits, revenues, and net income.

1.3.2.1.1 Retail banking

Citi's network of global retail banks consists of more than 4600 branches, holding deposits of more than $300 billion. Citibank offers a full range of consumer banking services, including checking, savings accounts, loans, small business, and wealth management. Citi's Banamex franchise serves close to 21 million customers. The wealth management segment provides investment and financial advisory services, which includes managed portfolios, stocks, bonds, mutual funds, insurance products, and retirement solutions. Citigold International combines banking with wealth management to provide personalized services and access to globally connected clients.

1.3.2.1.2 Credit cards

According to a Nelson Report, Citi is the largest credit card issuer in the United States with 134 million accounts accounting for $363 billion in annual purchase sales and $150 billion in receivables across Citi Branded Cards and Citi Retail services credit cards. Citi Branded Cards have more than 55 million consumer and small business users in 38 countries. This segment had annual purchase sales of $292 billion and a loan portfolio of $111 billion in 2012. Citi became the first nondomestic credit card issuer in China. A joint venture with Telcel called Banamex enables millions of customers to have bank accounts with service functionality delivered entirely through mobile phones.

Citiprice Rewind is a complimentary benefit for members. The feature automatically credits a refund if a lower price is found on a purchase within 30 days.

1.3.2.1.3 Citi Retail Services

Formerly known as Retail Partner Cards, Citi Retail Services is one of the largest providers of consumer and commercial credit card products, services, and retail solutions to major national and regional retailers. The segment serves approximately 79 million accounts for a number of major brands, which include Home Depot, Macy's, Sears, Shell, and ExxonMobil.

1.3.2.1.4 Citi Commercial Bank

Citi Commercial Bank serves approximately 100,000 small to medium-size companies in 32 countries. The segment provides tailored-made solutions for cash management, foreign exchange, lending, and trading. Citi Commercial Bank also offers secure web-based solutions for clients to manage their operations from anywhere via the Internet.

1.3.2.1.5 CitiMortgage

CitiMortgage has approximately 2 million customers in 29 countries. The segment offers loans for home purchase and refinance transactions. CitiMortgage's free SureStart preapproves potential homeowners to establish their price range before they shop for a home. In 2012, Citibank originated $58 billion in mortgages.

1.3.2.2 Citi's Institutional Clients Group

1.3.2.2.1 Corporate and investment banking

Citi's Institutional Clients Group (ICG) is among the leading global corporate and investment banks. It provides a broad range of strategic and financing products, services, and consultancy to multinational and local companies, municipalities, financial institutions, government, and privately held businesses in more than 160 countries. The client teams of Citi's corporate and investment banking are categorized by industry and country. The client teams are segregated into strategic coverage team and corporate banker teams. The strategic team is responsible for M&As, equity, and related financing. The corporate banking team along with capital market product partners focus on corporate banking and finance services to global, regional, and local clients. Citi has been the investment advisor for high-profile deals, for example, Express Scripts' acquisition of Medco Health Solutions for $34 billion. Citi also provided a $7 billion bridge loan for the deal. Citi was also a coadvisor for Eaton's $12 billion acquisition of

Cooper Industries and was among the two banks to provide a $6.75 billion senior unsecured bridge loan facility to finance Eaton. Citi was the lead advisor for the AMC Entertainment sale to China's Dalian Wanda Group for $3 billion.

Citi's Capital Markets origination business group focuses on raising debt and equity. Citi has underwriting leadership in debt capital market transactions across a range of currencies and markets. In 2012, Citi facilitated Petrobas's $7 billion mutlitranche bond offering, which was the largest emerging market corporate bond offering in an international market. Citi was the lead manager for the five discrete equity transactions for the sale of AIG, and was the joint bookrunner for the $850 million private placement project bond for Topaz Solar Farm, which when completed will be the largest solar project in the United States. Citi was the lead advisor for the leveraged buyout deal of Apollo Global Management's acquisition of El Paso's exploration and production business for $7.5 billion. Citi was also the investment advisor for such deals as securitization for Ford Credit, bond issue for VimpleCom, yen bond issue for Panasonic, senior bond issue for CapitalOne, and equity issue for AIB/MetLife.

1.3.2.2.2 Citi Markets

Citi Markets provide a range of financial products and solutions across a broad range of asset classes through underwriting, sales and trading, distribution and research activities. The products offered include equities, commodities foreign exchange products, derivatives instruments such as credit, futures, G10 rates, municipals, and securitized products. The investment research and analysis division provides insights to institutional clients on companies, sectors, economic regions, market, and product analysis. The bank has trading floors in more than 80 countries and 400 connections that offer cash and clearing security systems to institutional clients. The Citi Velocity platform provides clients with access to Citi's capital market intelligence and services across equities, futures, FX, emerging markets, rates, commodities, and securitized markets. Through Citi's web, mobile, and trading applications clients can access proprietary data and analytics. Citi research segment provides sophisticated post-trade analysis tools.

1.3.2.2.3 Citi Private Bank

Citi Private Bank offers a wide range of products and services to cover capital market, managed investments, portfolio management, trust and estate planning, investment finance, banking and art, aircraft, and sports advisory services. The bank has about $250 billion in assets under management. The comprehensive services are offered to entrepreneurs, single and multifamily offices, senior corporate executives, law firms, and the like.

1.3.2.2.4 Citi Transaction Services

CTS provides cash management, trade, securities, and fund services to multinationals, financial institutions, government, and public-sector organizations in more than 140 countries. CTS serves 81% of Fortune 500 companies. CTS daily transacts more than $3 trillion in financial, commercial, and capital flows, and caters to the needs of clients through sustained investment in technology and digital innovation. The unit consists of Citi treasury and trade solutions, and Citi's Securities and Fund Services (SFS).

Citi Digital Working Capital uses digital and mobile platforms, tools, and analytics to provide a comprehensive set of Treasury and trade solutions (e.g., cash management, payments, receivables, liquidity and investment services, prepaid card programs, trade finance services).

Citi's SFS segment provides customized solutions to clients for investment and transaction. The services offered include investment administration, portfolio and fund services, investment and financing solutions.

The CitiDirect BE Mobile platform is used by 400,000 corporations to authorize and release payments as well as to run real-time account enquiries. The platform has surpassed $20 billion in transaction value amount, accounted by transactions in 112 languages and 87 countries.

1.3.2.3 Citi Holdings

Citi Holdings consists of brokerage and asset management, local consumer lending, and SAP. Citi has announced plans to divest Citi Holding. The brokerage and asset management includes Citi's remaining interest in its Morgan Stanley Smith Barney joint venture. Citi Holdings' local consumer lending covers residential, commercial real estate, personal, and consumer branch lending. The SAP consists of a portfolio of securities, loans, and other assets that Citigroup intends to divest through asset sales over a period of time.

1.3.3 ASSETS AND LIABILITIES OF CITIGROUP

Citi's assets include cash and deposits with banks, fed funds sold and reverse repos, trading account assets, investments, and loans. The fed funds sold consist of unsecured advances to third parties of excess balance in reserve accounts held at Federal Reserve banks. The trading account assets include debt and marketable equity securities, derivatives in net receivable position, residual interests in securitizations, and physical commodities inventory. Investments consist of debt and equity securities. Debt securities include bonds, notes, redeemable preferred stocks, certain mortgage- and asset-backed securities, and structured notes. Loans represent the largest share of Citi Bank's assets. Corporate loan growth is basically driven by transaction services, securities, and banking segments. Consumer loan growth was driven by its Global Consumer Banking division. Other assets include brokerage receivables, goodwill, intangibles, and mortgage servicing rights.

The liabilities consist of deposits, federal funds purchased and repos, trading account liabilities, debt, and other liabilities. The federal funds purchased consist of unsecured advances of excess balances in reserve accounts at Fed reserve from third parties. The trading account liabilities consist of securities in short positions and derivatives in net-payable positions. Debt consists of short-term and long-term borrowings. Short-term borrowing consists of commercial paper and borrowings from other banks and market participants. The long-term borrowing includes senior notes, subordinated notes, trust preferred securities, and securitizations. Other liabilities include brokerage payables.

Citigroup's off-balance sheet items include special-purpose entities such as credit card receivables, leases, and letter of credits. Citigroup enters into various derivatives transactions such as futures, forwards, swaps, and options for trading and hedging activities.

1.3.4 STRATEGY

Citigroup is focused on providing best-in-class products and services to customers and leveraging the company's global network, including many of the world's emerging economies. Citigroup's strategy is based on the current trends of globalization, urbanization, and digitization. Growth strategy is increasingly focused on emerging markets. Citi investment plans cover more than 150 cities, which account for 32% of global GDP. In 2012, Citi reduced the size of Citi Holdings by approximately 31%. Citi Holdings' net loss was $6.6 billion compared to a net loss of $4.2 billion in 2011.

Citi plays a variety of roles in asset securitization, which includes acting as underwriter of asset-backed securities, depositor of the underlying assets into securitization vehicles, trustee to securitization vehicles, and counterparty to securitization vehicles under derivatives contracts.

Citi generates capital through earnings from its operating businesses. Capital is supplemented through issuance of common stock, perpetual preferred stock, and equity. Citi has to face significant regulatory changes in the context of uncertainties in the United States and in other global markets in which it operates. The Eurozone debt and economic crisis have created new challenges for Citigroup.

1.3.4.1 Mergers and acquisitions by Citicorp

Citigroup made 315 acquisitions and took stakes in 242 companies during 1981 to 2011.[2] In 1998, Citicorp and Travelers Group merged to form the world's biggest financial services company, offering banking, insurance, and investment operations in more than 100 countries. Travelers Group was a New York-based financial services firm whose companies included Salomon, brokerage firm Smith Barney, Travelers Life and Annuity, and Primerica Financial Services. Over several decades Citicorp has developed a strong global retail franchise along with worldwide corporate banking business. Through the merger with Travelers, Citicorp gained access to an expanded client base of investors and insurance customers. Travelers, in turn, was able to market mutual funds and insurance to Citicorp's retail customers. The merger made investment products such as stocks and bonds more accessible to middle-class customers.

With approximately $698 billion in assets and $135 billion in market capitalization, the new combined group became the largest financial firm in the world, ahead of Tokyo-Mitsubishi Bank Ltd. The combined group had revenues of about $50 billion and operating income of approximately $7.5 billion at the time of the merger. At the time of the merger, Citicorp was the largest issuer of credit cards in the world. The deal was valued at $70 billion.

Over a period of years Citicorp has also acquired stakes in international banks and brokerage firms including Nikko Beans, a Japanese online brokerage firm; Bank Handlowy Warszawie, a leading corporate bank in Poland; Mexico's Banacci; and Diner's Club of Europe. By acquiring European American Bank in 2001, Citigroup added 97 branches in the New York area. Citicorp also acquired an additional 352 branches and 1.5 million new customers in California and Nevada markets by purchasing Golden State Bancorp.

In 2000, Citigroup bought the Associates First Capital Corporation, the largest American consumer finance company in a stock deal valued at $31.1 billion. With this acquisition, Citigroup became the fifth-largest consumer finance company in Japan, which was the world's second-largest market for consumer lending. The acquisition improved Citigroup's position in the credit card and commercial leasing business. The combined companies had about 2000 retail branches across the United States, and Citigroup became the top US provider of credit cards, home equity loans, and commercial leasing services. Associates First was the fifth-largest consumer finance company in Japan and operated private-label credit card programs for several gas station operators and retailers such as Radio Shack. Even prior to the merger, Citicorp had the biggest market share in credit card business through its Citibank Visa and MasterCard products.

---

[2]http://www.alacrastore.com/mergers-acquisitions/Citigroup_Inc-1003632

1.3.5 **CORPORATE SOCIAL RESPONSIBILITY ACTIVITIES**

Through the Citi Microfinance, Citi Community Development, and Citi Foundation units, Citigroup develops initiatives to serve underprivileged sections of society. Citi has invested $12 million in mobile banking initiatives across Africa, which has provided benefits to more than 100 million people. About 1.65 million people are said to have benefited from Citi-funded programs during the past decade. Citi Microfinance is involved in developing commercial relationships with microfinance institutions, networks, and investors. In 2007, Citi initiated plans to invest $50 billion in initiatives such as wind energy, solar power systems, and promotion for clean technology to mitigate climate change. The Citi for Cities initiative aims to assist urban cities with modernizing their infrastructure and job creation. The bank was the official sponsor of the US Olympic and *Paralympic* teams in 2012. Citi's Road to Recovery tour spanned to 35 markets to offer assistance to distressed CitiMortgage homeowners. Citi Microfinance partnered with Citi's Environmental Products trading and origination team to purchase 1.17 million metric tons of carbon credits from social enterprise Micro Energy credits.

1.3.6 **RISK MANAGEMENT**

Citi has an independent risk management structure that facilitates in managing the principle risks of credit, market, and operations across the dimension of businesses, regions, and critical products. Citi has deployed a broad and diversified set of risk management and mitigation processes and strategies along with risk models to analyze and monitor various risks. Citi fosters a risk culture, which is based on its policy of "Taking Intelligent Risk with Shared Responsibility, without Forsaking Individual Accountability." The chief officer with the oversight from the Risk Management and Finance Committee of the board of directors is responsible for establishing core standards for management, measurement, and monitoring of risks. Each of Citi's major business segments has a business chief risk officer who is the central point of risk decisions such as setting risk limits or approving transactions in business. Regional chief risk officers are accountable for risks in their respective geographic areas. Product chief risk officers are responsible for critical areas such as real estate.

The business, regional, and product chief officers report to Citi's chief risk officer who, in turn reports to the head of franchise risk and strategy, a direct report to the CEO.

Firmwide stress tests are conducted to measure the potential impact to component businesses of Citi owing to changes in various types of risk factors such as interest rates and credit spreads.

Risk capital is the amount of capital required to absorb potential unexpected economic losses that result from extreme severe events over a 1-year period. Citi calculates and allocates risk capital across various business divisions. Citi is obligated to perform stress testing on a periodic basis for a number of regulatory exercises such as Fed Reserve's Comprehensive Capital Analysis (CCAR) and Dodd-Frank Act Stress Testing (DFAST). The risk capital framework is reviewed on a regular basis in the context of market developments and evolving practices. Citi also faces legal and regulatory risks.

Credit risk arises in many of Citigroup's business activities such as wholesale and retail lending, capital market derivatives exposure, structured finance, repurchase agreements, and reverse repurchase transactions. Other sources for credit risk are from settlement and clearing activities. Concentration risk also exists whereby the risk is associated with having credit exposure concentrated within a specific client, industry region, or other category. Credit risk is managed by actions such as setting a defined risk appetite, credit limits, and credit policies both at a business and firm level. The processes and policies include watch lists, portfolio review, updated risk ratings, and classification triggers. For managing risks in settlement and clearing activities, the intraday client use of lines are monitored against limits. Typically, the clients are moved to a secured (collateralized) operating model. For managing concentration of risk, a framework that consists of industry limits, obligor limits, and single name triggers is in place. Citigroup uses credit derivatives to hedge credit risks in its corporate credit portfolio in addition to outright asset sales.

With respect to liquidity risks, the maintenance of adequate liquidity depends on market disruptions and increases in Citi's credit spread. Citi's aggregate liquidity resources are managed by the Citi treasurer. The chief risk officer is responsible for the overall risk profile of Citi's aggregate liquidity resources. The Asset Liability Management Committee (ALCO) sets the strategy of liquidity portfolio and monitors its performance. Liquidity stress testing is performed for each of Citi's major divisions and segments.

Citi has a market risk limit framework to identify risk factors within the parameters of Citi's overall risk tolerances. These limits are monitored by various committees such as independent market risk, asset and liability committee, and global finance and asset and liability committee.

To manage interest rate risk, Citi adopts such actions as modifications on pricing of new customer loans and deposits and off-balance sheet derivatives transactions with opposite risk exposure. Citigroup uses stress testing to measure the impact of nonlinear interest rate movements on balance sheet items, analysis of portfolio duration, and volatility.

Citigroup uses swaps as interest rate hedging. For example, Citigroup issues fixed-rate long-term debt and then enters into a fixed-pay variable-rate interest rate swap with the same period and notional amount to convert the interest payments to a net variable rate basis.

Price risk in Citi's trading portfolio is monitored by VaR, stress testing, and factor sensitivity. For VaR, Citi uses Monte Carlo simulation, which involves approximately 300,000 market factors making use of 180,000 time series with sensitivities updated daily and model parameters updated weekly.

Citigroup maintains a system of policies and a framework for assessing and communicating operational risk across businesses. An operational risk council consisting of members of Citi's franchise risk and strategy provides oversight for operational risk management. The enterprise risk management within Citi's independent risk management is responsible for the effectiveness of controls and managing operational risks across different business lines.

In addition to the principal risks, Citi has a number of risks associated with the global and emerging markets owing to its extensive global network. Citigroup is subject to country risks and cross-border risks. Country risk arises when an event within a country will impair the value of Citi's franchise or will adversely affect the ability of obligors within the country to honor their obligations to Citi. Cross-border risk arises with foreign exchange controls of foreign government such as restrictions on convertibility and remittances outside the country. Citi operates in countries such as Argentina and Venezuela with strict foreign exchange controls that limit its ability to convert local currency into US dollars and/or transfer funds outside the country. Since 2011, the Argentine government has been tightening its the foreign exchange controls. Since 2003, the Venezuelan government has also enacted foreign exchange controls. Table 1.9 reflects the ratings of Citi's debt issuances in year 2012. Table 1.10 provides the financial highlights of Citigroup during the period 2008-2012. Table 1.11 shows the revenue highlights of the various business segments of Citicorp during the period 2010-2012. Table 1.12 gives the income highlights of the various business segments of Citicorp during the period 2010-2012.

Table 1.9 Citi's Debt Ratings, December 2012

| Citi Debt Rating | Citigroup | | Citibank NA | | Citigroup Global Markets |
	Senior Debt	Commercial Paper	Long Term	Short Term	Long Term
Fitch Ratings	A	F1	A	F1	NR
Moody's	Baa2	P-2	A3	P-2	NR
S&P	A-	A-2	A	A-1	A

Source: Bank Reports

Table 1.10   Financial Highlights Citigroup 2008-2012 (Millions of US Dollars)

	2008	2009	2010	2011	2012
Net revenues	51,599	80,285	86,601	78,353	70,173
Net income	(27,684)	(1606)	10,602	11,067	7541
Total assets	1,938,470	1,856,646	1,913,902	1,873,878	1,864,660
Total deposits	774,185	835,903	844,968	865,936	930,560
Long-term debt	359,593	364,019	381,183	323,505	239,463
Total Citigroup stockholder equity	141,630	152,700	163,468	177,806	189,049
Employees (in thousands)	323	265	260	266	259
Return on average assets (%)	(1.28)	(0.08)	0.5	0.6	0.4
Tier 1 Common (%)	2.3	9.6	10.75	11.8	12.67
Tier 1 Capital (%)	11.92	11.67	12.91	13.55	14.06

Source: Bank Report

Table 1.11   Business Segment Revenue Highlights 2010-2012 (Millions of US Dollars)

Citicorp	2010	2011	2012
Global Consumer Banking	39,369	39,195	40,214
Securities and Banking	23,122	21,423	19,743
Transaction Services	10,085	10,579	10,857
Corporate/others	1754	885	192
Total Citicorp	74,330	72,082	71,006
Total Citi Holdings	12,271	6271	(8330)
Total Citigroup revenues	86,601	78,353	70,173

Source: Bank Report

Table 1.12 Business Segment Income Highlights 2010-2012 (Millions of US Dollars)

Citicorp	2010	2011	2012
Global Consumer Banking	4969	7672	8104
Securities and banking	6551	4913	4495
Transaction services	3622	3349	3495
Corporate/others	242	(728)	(1625)
Total Citicorp	15,384	15,206	14,469
Total Citi Holdings	(4433)	(4103)	(6560)
Total Citigroup net income	10,602	11,067	7541

Source: Bank Report

REFERENCES

1. Mitchell Martin, Citicorp and Travelers Plan to Merge in Record $70 Billion Deal: A New No. 1: Financial Giants Unite, http://money.cnn.com/1998/04/06/deals/travelers/
2. Patrick McGeehan, Citigroup to buy Associates First for $31 billion, http://www.nytimes.com/2000/09/07/business/citigroup-to-buy-associates-first-for-31-billion.html?pagewanted=all&src=pm
3. Annual Reports Citigroup
4. http://www.citigroup.com

1.4 BARCLAYS

Barclays is one of the major global financial service providers with a presence in more than 50 countries in the markets of Europe, Americas, Asia, and Africa. Barclays has a rich history of over 300 years, originating as a goldsmith banker in Lombard Street in London in 1690. In 1819, Barclays funded the Stockton and Darlington Railway, which became the world's first industrial stream railway. In the 1900s, Barclays financed two of the fastest passenger ships in the world. In War World II, despite bomb damage, Barclays branches remained opened during the blitz. In 1966, the United Kingdom's first credit card was launched by Barclays. In 1967, Barclays unveiled the world's first ATM from its branch in London. In 1986, Barclays established an investment banking operation named Barclays Capital, which manages large corporate and institutional businesses. In the same year Barclays became the first UK bank to get listed in both the New York Stock Exchange and the Tokyo Stock Exchange.

In 2008, Barclays completed the integration of the acquisition of the North American businesses of Lehman Brothers. In 2012, Barclays provided £44 billion in gross new lending to UK households and businesses. Barclays also facilitated the creation of 112,000 new businesses in the United Kingdom. Barclays continues to innovate services; for example, through its Pay Tag platform, Barclays enables more than 750,000 mobile phone users to make contactless payments across three countries. Barclays' tax amounted to £3.2 billion in 2012.

1.4.1 BUSINESS STRUCTURE

The major division of Barclays bank consists of retail business and banking, Barclays card, investment banking, corporate banking, and wealth and investment management.

1.4.1.1 Retail Business and Banking

The Retail Business and Banking unit consists of segments in the United Kingdom, Europe, and Africa. The retail sector provides retail banking services and general insurance to individuals and businesses of small and medium enterprises (SMEs). The European retail sector provides retail banking services to affluent individuals and business banking services to SMEs. The African segment of retail banking serves customers and clients in 12 countries with a range of banking and bancassurance solutions. The UK-based Retail Business and Banking unit provides a customer referrals service for platforms in wealth and investment management, corporate banking, and the Barclays card and retail banking sector. UK Retail Business and Banking has more than 15 million personal customers and the segment serves over 750,000 businesses. The current account platform, Features Store, enables customers to access free and paid-for features and to personalize their debt card. Barclays Mobile Banking app Pingit and text alerts facilitate customers in their everyday banking; they can track payments and send and receive funds at any time.

The African division facilitated the partnership deals of Kenya Airways and Barclays Bank of Kenya. Major deals included the $500 million Zambia Sovereign benchmark issuance, and a project financing of $1.5 billion to Exxon Mobil/NNPC to develop 27 oil wells in Nigeria. In 2012, life insurance products in the framework of the bancassurance model were introduced in African countries such as Botswana, Mozambique, Zambia, and Ghana. Barclays was the leading provider of loans to UK households and businesses under the National Loan Guarantee Scheme (NLGS) and Funding for Lending Scheme (FLS).

1.4.1.2 Barclaycards

It is the international payment business of Barclays that offers payment and lending services to individuals and businesses, which also include card issuing and payment acceptance services. Barclays is rated as having the world's eighth-largest payment business, serving 29 million retail and business customers. In 2012, Barclaycards received awards such as the Moneyfacts Best Card Provider 2012 award in the United Kingdom and Forrester Voice of the Customer award in the United States. Barclaycards include Freedom and Cashback consumer cards in the United Kingdom, Google Adwords for UK SMEs, Barclaycard Plus for online spending in Germany, and a social media credit card called Barclaycard Ring in the United States.

1.4.1.3 Investment Banking

Barclays' Investment Bank division serves large corporate clients, financial institutions, governments, and institutional investors in the areas of financial advisory, capital raising, financing, and strategic risk management services. The services include underwriting debt and equity issuance, advisory services for mergers and acquisitions, restructuring, making active markets for securities across global debt, and more. The investment bank is aiming to become the "go-to" bank for corporate and institutional clients. The investment bank provides client-focused services for retail, wealth, and corporate customers.

The market team segment provides services of execution and risk management for a full range of asset classes, which includes equity and fixed income, currency, and commodity (FICC) products.

The segment facilitates client transactions on stock, options, and futures exchanges and also provides prime brokerage service such as clearing, financing, and securities lending to institutional clients. The market segment also acts as market makers for securities across all asset classes. Barclays facilitates companies to hedge their exposures to movements in interest rates, currencies, and commodity prices through derivatives products. The multiasset research team focuses on providing insights about global companies and trends in markets and economy to clients. In 2012, the investment bank was the fourth-largest provider of financing whereby over £830 billion was financed for businesses and governments.

1.4.1.4 Universal Banking
Barclays' Universal Banking division provides integrated cash management, financing, and risk management solutions to large corporate clients, multinationals, and financial institutions. Barclays' corporate banking division provides services to more than 40,000 corporations, including multinationals and financial institutions. The division through its Barclays Africa arm provides integrated corporate banking across Africa. In 2012, the unit rolled out its cash management platform Barclays.net. The division also made investments in trade finance hubs in important markets. Corporate banking division lent £1.5 billion through its Cashback finance scheme under the NLGS allocation.

1.4.1.5 Wealth and Investment Management
The Wealth and Investment division provides a full range of wealth management services to affluent and high-net-worth global clients. The services include banking, credit, investment management, advisory services, fiduciary services, and brokerage. Recently, the division launched a new digital client portal.

1.4.2 STRATEGY
Barclays Bank faces the challenges of a prolonged period of lower global growth, tough regulatory environments, and increased client expectations. The bank focuses on 39 of its 75 businesses to innovate, invest, and grow. The bank plans to strategically realign 15 businesses that generate income of approximately £4 billion. There are 17 businesses that generate over £2 billion, and the bank plans to reposition or divest them over a period of time.[3]

Barclays' focus is on investments in the United Kingdom, the United States, and Africa. The bank has plans to restructure Barclays' European retail operations to focus on a mass affluent customer segment. In the context of changing market opportunities, Barclays is involved in repositioning Barclays' European and Asian equities and investment banking decision. The bank also aims to invest in high-return businesses such as UK mortgages, Barclaycards, and wealth management. The bank also has plans to exit from structured capital market businesses. The bank will focus on the fixed-income, currency, and commodities business of the largest business division Investment Banking, which constituted 63% of the investment bank's income in 2012. The bank also plans to put more focus on less capital-intensive businesses of equities and investment banking.

Africa is the primary emerging market for Barclays. The European retail and business banking faces macroeconomic, sovereign, and regulatory challenges. The bank aims to generate £1.7 billion in cost savings, primarily by reducing operating expenses, by 2015. To satisfy the Basel III requirement of target capital position through the cycle Core Tier 1 ratio of 10.5%, the bank focuses on

---

[3] Barclays' Strategic Review, Executive Summary, Becoming the Go to bank 12 Feb 2013.

reduction of the risk-weighted assets. The Core Tier 1 ratio was 10.9% in 2012 compared to 11% in 2011. The decline in Core Tier 1 capital to £42.1 billion was partially offset by 1% reduction in risk-weighted assets to £387 billion.

Rising unemployment and higher interest rates would reduce the debt service ability in the retail sector with a negative impact on corporate credit. The strategic concept of the "go-to" bank was based on the three components of turnaround, return acceptable numbers, and sustain forward momentum.

1.4.3 CORPORATE SOCIAL RESPONSIBILITY ACTIVITIES

The bank invested a total of £64.5 million in community programs globally in 2012, with active participation of 68,000 employees. Barclays Money Skills helped 1 million people manage their funds. Barclays Apprentice Program was launched to help tackle the problem of youth unemployment in the United Kingdom. Barclays' employees invested 458,000 h of volunteering and raised £30m for charities through fundraising initiatives.

1.4.4 RISK MANAGEMENT AT BARCLAYS

In Barclays, each key risk is managed by the group key risk owner within the framework of principal risk policy. The Board Citizenship Committee known as the Board Conduct, Reputation and Operational Risk Committee has the oversight of conduct risk, reputation risk, and operational risk. The Financial Risk Committee has the oversight of credit and market risk. The Treasury Committee has the oversight of funding risk. Tax risk is managed by the Tax Risk Committee.

Barclays' Board Risk Committee focuses on credit, market, capital, and funding risk. The funding risk arises due to a failure to maintain capital ratios to support business activity and regulatory requirements. Funding risk consists of capital risk, liquidity, and structural risk. The bank also faces pension fund risk.

Barclays' board approves medium-term planning (MTP), which is performed yearly. The planned performance of each business depends on the ability of the business to manage its risks. Groupwise stress tests and the annual review of risk appetite are integral parts of MTP. Reverse stress testing is also used for ongoing risk management.

Barclays' groups face credit risk mainly from wholesale and retail loans and advances, trading activities including debt securities, settlement balances with market counterparties, and reverse repurchase agreements. The counterparty credit risk arises from derivatives contracts entered into with clients. The group buys and sells financial instruments that are traded or cleared on exchanges, including futures, options on futures, and interest rate swaps. Diversification is achieved through setting maximum exposure guidelines to individual counterparties. The group offers forbearance programs through agreements to help distressed clients. Barclays employs three basic strategies to mitigate credit risks: netting and set off, collateral, and risk transfer. The netting and set off technique is used mainly in derivatives and repo transactions with financial institutions. Barclays enters into standard master agreements with counterparties for derivatives transactions. In the event of default, these agreements allow for the netting of credit exposure to a counterparty against Barclays' obligation to the counterparty, thereby resulting in a lower net credit exposure. Collaterals are also used to mitigate credit risks. For home loans, collaterals are in the form of houses and apartment buildings. For wholesale lending, the fixed charge over commercial property is the collateral. For credit cards and other retail lending, charges over motor vehicles and physical assets are collaterals. Instruments such as guarantees, credit insurance, credit derivatives, and securitization are used to transfer credit risk from one counterparty to another. When risk is transferred to a counterparty who is more creditworthy, overall credit risk will be reduced.

The counterparty risk under derivatives transaction is adjusted through credit value adjustment. The credit value adjustment for derivatives positions is calculated as a function of the "expected exposure," which is the average of future hypothetical exposure values for a single transaction or group of transactions by the same counterparty and the credit default spread for a given horizon.

During 2012, the Barclays Bank PLC rating was downgraded by Moody's from Aa3/P-1/C to A2/P-1/C-.

Market risk consists of traded market risk, nontraded risk, and pension risk. Traded risk is basically accounted for by investment banking services. Nontraded market risk is found in retail and business banking, corporate banking, wealth and investment, and treasury. A reduction in client activity in investment banking could lead to lower fees and commission income, which leads to decreased market liquidity.

The other market risk consist of pension and asset management structural risk. Pension fund risk arises due to factors such as the decline of investment returns or the market value of pension funds, or the increase in the market value of pension liabilities. Asset management structural risk, basically found in the wealth and investment management, arises when the fees and commission income earned by asset management products are affected by a change in market level. Wherever possible, the Treasury acts as a central internal clearinghouse for nonbehavioral interest rate risk netting-off positions.

Barclays uses technical tools, such as Daily Value at Risk (DVaR), expected shortfall, primary and secondary stress testing, and combined scenario stress testing, to measure market risk. The three main contributors to total DVaR are credit, spread, and interest rate risk.

Barclays Group is exposed to two kinds of foreign exchange risk, namely the transactional and transnational foreign currency exposure. The group's strategy is to minimize the volatility of the capital ratios caused by foreign exchange movements by using the Core Tier 1 capital movements to broadly match the revaluation of the group's foreign currency risk-weighted assets exposures.

Barclays also faces operational, legal, and reputational risk. The bank faced legal exposure owing to proceedings in the Lehman Brothers' case, as well as residential mortgage-backed securities, and a certain series of preference shares issued in the form of American Depository Shares and civil actions.

Barclays manages the composition and duration of the balance sheet through the transfer of liquidity premium directly to business units.

Barclays Group uses economic capital as an internal measure of the risk profile of the bank, expressed as the estimated stress loss at 99.98% confidence level. The group basically assigns the economic capital to risk categories of credit risk, market risk, operational risk, property and equipment risk, and pension risk. The economic capital framework uses default probabilities during average credit conditions. Barclays uses economic capital as part of the Group's Internal Capital Adequacy Assessment Process (ICAAP) for assessing the group's financial volatility within the risk-appetite framework.

Barclays has a comprehensive liquidity risk management framework for managing liquidity risk. The Liquidity Risk Appetite (LRA) is the level of liquidity risk that the group chooses to meet regulatory obligations in alignment with business objectives. The LRA runs three primary liquidity stress scenarios: a 3-month marketwide stress event, a 1-month Barclays-specific stress event, and a combined 1-month marketwide and Barclays' specific stress event. Primarily, the group focuses on 1-month Barclays' specific stress scenario, which leads to the maximum net outflows of each of the liquidity stress tests.

Barclays focuses on maintaining a long-term strategic funding plan for reducing structural funding risk and optimizing interest costs. The operational risk at Barclays consists of risk such as cybersecurity risk, external suppliers, fraud, taxation, technology, and transaction operations. Barclays also has a dedicated environmental risk management team that considers environmental issues in credit risk assessment and facilitates environmental risk policies. Table 1.13 provides the financial highlights of Barclays Bank during the period 2008-2012. Table 1.14 gives the income highlights of Barclays Bank during the period 2010-2012.

Table 1.13   Financial Highlights 2008-2012 (Millions of UK Pounds)

	2008	2009	2010	2011	2012
Total net income	21,199	29,123	31,440	32,292	24,691
Profit after tax	5287	10,288	4549	3951	(236)
Total assets	2,052,980	1,378,929	1,489,645	1,563,527	1,490,321
Deposits	116,545	77,912	79,296	92,085	78,583
Loans and advances to banks and customers	509,522	461,359	465,741	479,380	466,218
Total shareholder equity	47,411	58,478	62,262	65,196	62,957
Core Tier 1 ratio (%)	5.6	10	10.8	11	10.9
Tier 1 ratio (%)	8.6	13	13.5	12.9	13.3

Source: Annual Reports

Table 1.14   Total Income Analysis by Business 2010-2012 (Millions of UK Pounds)

	2010	2011	2012
UKRRB	4518	4656	4421
Europe RBB	1164	1226	915
Africa RRB	3512	3571	3157
Barclaycards	4024	4095	4170
Investment bank	13,209	10,335	11,722
Corporate banking	3162	3108	2918
Wealth and investment management	1560	1744	1815
Head office and other operations	291	3557	(4427)
Total	31,440	32,292	24,691

Source: Annual Reports

REFERENCES

1. Barclays' Strategic Review, Executive Summary, Becoming the Go to bank 12 Feb 2013
2. http://group.barclays.com/about-barclays/about-us#about-us
3. Various Annual Reports of Barclays Bank

1.5 **BNP PARIBAS**

BNP Paris is a French-based leading banking institution in the euro region with a presence in 80 countries and employing nearly 190,000 employees, of which 76% are based in Europe. The BNP Paribas Group was formed from the merger of BNP and Paribas in 2000. BNP, the first French bank, was established in 1848, whereas Paribas, an investment bank, was founded in 1872.

The group's four domestic markets in Europe are Belgium, France, Italy, and Luxembourg. The bank has one of the most extensive global banking networks. The strategic focus of the bank is on the areas of retail banking, corporate and investment banking, private banking, and asset management. The bank provides integrated banking solutions with a network of 150 business centers in 23 European countries. BNP Paribas is a European leader in private banking, consumer credit, cash management, and equipment financing for businesses.

BNP Paribas has strategic growth plans in the Mediterranean basin countries through its retail banking integrated model. The Corporate and Investment Banking and Investment Solutions division of BNP Paribas is a major player in the European markets with a strong position in the American region and the fast-growing markets of the Asian Pacific.

1.5.1 **CORE BUSINESS DIVISIONS**

1.5.1.1 *Retail Banking*

BNP Paribas' Retail Banking division plays a vital role in the bank's strategy of global expansion. The retail banking division follows a unique integrated business model that fosters cross-selling between the various segments of the division. The retail banking division consists of domestic markets, international retail banking, and BNP Paribas Personal Finance. In 2012, the retail banking sector contributed 61% of the total revenues of the group. The retail banking sector has 7150 branches in 41 countries, constituting 70% of the total workforce in the group.

1.5.1.1.1 Domestic markets

The domestic markets consist of the retail banking networks of BNP Paribas in France (FRB), Italy (BNL bc), Belgium (BNP Paribas Fortis), and Luxembourg (BGL BNP Paribas), along with specialized divisions of BNP Paribas Leasing Solutions and BNP Paribas Personal Investors. The domestic markets operate in 26 countries. The French retail banking unit has 6.9 million customers, which include 136,000 wealth management clients. FRB also has approximately 80,000 corporate and institutional clients.

BNP Paribas Leasing Solutions offer businesses and individuals a range of solutions using multichannels such as direct sales, sales via referrals, or via partnerships. There are four international business lines within equipment solutions, categorized by assets and specific leasing solutions. Arval and BNP Paribas Leasing Solutions are the two specialist companies. Arval is involved in the long-term leasing of company vehicles with services, and Arval leased 689,000 vehicles in 2012. BNP Paribas Leasing Solutions include financing for equipment sales and investments for both corporate and individual clients. Technology solutions deal with services related to office equipment, hardware and software, and telephone and medical equipment. Equipment and logistics solutions cover agricultural equipment, goods handling, construction and public works, and industrial vehicles. BNP Paribas is the leader in cash management in Belgium, Italy, and France according to *Euromoney*. BNP Paribas Leasing Solutions has €19.4 billion outstanding under management.

BNP Paribas Personal Investors is the online savings and trading segment, which provides financial advisory and brokerage services to affluent clients in Europe and Asia. The major brands of BNP Paribas Personal Investors are Cortal Consors, B*capital, and Geojit BNP Paribas. Cortal Consors provides online savings and brokerage advice, with personalized advisory services to over 1 million clients in Germany, France, and Spain. B*capital is the investment company that provides services across various asset classes of equities, bonds, and derivatives. Geojit BNP Paribas is one of the leading retail brokers in India and also operates in the Middle East. The division had 1.4 million customers as of 2011. There are also two online communities for the personal investors brand portfolio. Approximately 64% of the business is done online in this division.

The Wealth Management division develops the private banking model for domestic markets.

1.5.1.1.2 BNP Paribas Personal Finance

BNP Paribas Personal Finance provides consumer credit, mortgage activities, and hybrid mortgage/loan consolidation products for individual customers. In Europe, BNP Paribas Personal Finance is the leader in personal loans, which comprise consumer credit and mortgage financing businesses. The major brands include Cetelem, Findomestic, and AlphaCredit. These brands market a range of products available at the point of sale through its customer relations centers and online. The division also offers varied insurance and savings products to customers in France and Italy. BNP Paribas has partnerships with retail groups, web merchants, and financial institutions to offer integrated services. As of 2011, BNP Paribas Personal Finance had €123 billion in assets under management. This segment is present in 25 countries and has 12 million active customers.

1.5.1.1.3 International Retail Banking

This division consists of the group's retail banking segment outside the eurozone, which includes the United States and 14 countries in the European Mediterranean region. The three business lines are Retail Banking, Wealth Management in partnership with Investment Solutions and Corporate Banking. Corporate Banking provides local access to all BNP Paribas products through a network of 67 business centers, 22 trade centers, and 15 multinational desks. The division consists of five geographical regions of the United States, Turkey, the Mediterranean and Africa, Central and Eastern Europe, and Asia.

1.5.1.2 Investment Solutions

Investment Solutions provides a broad range of high value-added products related to the collection, management, development, protection, and administration of client savings and assets. Investment Solutions comprises BNP Paribas Cardif, BNP Paribas Securities Services, BNP Paribas Wealth Management, BNP Paribas Investment Partners, and BNP Paribas Real Estate. Cardif is a global player in the personal insurance field. Securities Services is a European leader in securities services for a clientele of asset managers, financial institutions, and corporations. BNP Paribas Wealth Management is the group's private banking arm, which serves a clientele of wealthy individuals and entrepreneurs. Investment Partners is the group's asset management arm. The Real Estate unit provides a comprehensive range of services including property development, transaction, property management, and investment management. Investment Solutions accounted for 15% of revenues in 2012.

1.5.1.3 Corporate and Investment Banking

Corporate and Investment Banking (CIB) provides financing, advisory, and capital markets services to clients worldwide. The division offers expert advisory services in a variety of asset classes including structured financing and derivatives. The division is strong in Europe and Asia, with 15,000 clients in 50 countries. In 2012, this division accounted for 24% of the group's income, generating €9.7 billion. CIB consists of corporate banking, corporate finance, global equity and derivatives, and fixed-income segments. CIB was the world's second-largest worldwide trade finance provider in 2012.

CIB provides all financing services from transaction banking to specialized financing solutions, which includes vanilla lending, structured financing, cash management, and international trade finance. The CIB finance team offers advisory services for M&As and primary equity capital market transactions. The primary capital market transactions include IPOs, equity issues, right issues, and convertible bond issues. The Global Equities and Commodity Derivatives (GECD) business offers equity, commodity, index and fund derivatives, financing solutions, and an integrated equity brokerage platform. The fixed-income business segment offers products and services to a diversified client base of asset managers, insurance companies, banks, corporates, governments, and supranational organizations. The business segment provides credit, currency, and interest rate products.

BNP Paribas Investment manages the group's portfolio of listed and unlisted investments.

CIB was involved in major issues with Ford Motor Credit Company, AT&T, Disney, Xerox, Time Warner, IBM, Lotte, LG, Dolphin Energy, and Teva, among others. BNP was credited with the first ever triple-currency hybrid capital transaction in Europe, euro-private placement listed in Paris, and the largest retail transaction.

In 2012, the ratings given by Standard & Poor's, Moody's, and Fitch were A+, A2, A+ for long-term credit of the bank.

1.5.2 CORPORATE SOCIAL RESPONSIBILITY ACTIVITIES

BNP Paribas is a major contributor or active member of United Nations Global Impact (advanced level), Global Impact France, UN Women's Empowerment Principles, UNEP Finance Initiative, Carbon Disclosure Project, Roundtable for Sustainable Palm Oil, and other associations. The group also designs solutions specific to the finance sector within the framework of the Equator Principles, Principle of Responsible Investment, and the institutional investors group on climate change and climate principles.

BNP Paribas was ranked number one in the banking sector for corporate social responsibility in the Vigeo World 120 index. BNP Paribas is the only French bank that is included in the Dow Jones Sustainability indexes. BNP Paribas was named 2012 Bank of the Year by the financial magazine *International Financing Review* (IIFR). BNP Paribas donated €103 million toward micro loans and financing for social entrepreneurship. The bank has committed €4.5 million a year to support disadvantaged sections of urban areas. BNP Paribas advised Sumitomo for a government-subsidized equity participation in the Desert Sunlight Solar Farm, one of the largest solar farms being built in California. The group's social responsibility is involved in areas of culture, social inclusion, education, health, and environment. The group supported 2167 projects with an investment commitment of €38.8 million.

1.5.3 **STRATEGY**

BNP Paribas strategy is centered around the business model of a diversified universal bank. The group focuses on investments in multichannel banking, distance banking, and online banking. The bank aims to capitalize on expansions in the fast-growing areas of the Asian Pacific, while maintaining its leading position across Europe. Domestic markets are strategically important for the group as they provide a large base of deposits and off-balance sheet savings that support both retail and business clients.

Innovation plays a critical role in identifying the growth strategy of the retail banking sector. Lease Offers is an online financing proposal and portfolio management tool provided by BNP Paribas Leasing Solutions to equipment distributors. French Retail Banking (FRB) has launched two applications: My Accounts for managing accounts on an iPad and My Transfers for transferring money free of charge using a mobile phone. FRB also has plans to invest in developing contactless mobile payments through its BNP Paribas Mobile package, which combines m-payment, m-banking, and telephony in partnership with Orange. Cortex FX, an advanced multiproduct platform offering a fully integrated trading environment, was launched in 2012. Approximately 630,000 BNP Paribas customers use mobile services for banking transactions, and BNP Paribas applications have been downloaded more than 2 million times.

The Originate to Distribute Model was introduced in 2012, offering global business lines such as Fixed Income and Corporate Banking, Investment Solutions.

In 2010, BNP Paribas initiated a program called One Bank for Corporates in Europe and Beyond, which was designed to provide seamless banking services to corporate clients throughout Europe from a single entry point. Currently, this program has an extensive network of 220 business centers in 36 countries with 1700 relationship managers specifically dedicated to corporate clients. There are a number of agreements with business networks and trade associations for strengthening relations. BNP Paribas met the Basel III regulatory requirements in 2012 without having to raise new capital. In 2012, the bank entered into strategic partnerships with Russian bank Sberbank, Cora hypermarkets, and Leclerc hypermarkets. Arval has developed several branded partnerships with well-reputed car manufacturers and dealerships.

In its pursuit of globalization strategy, BNP Paribas Securities Services launched a local custody service in the United States to provide postmarket services to financial institutions and institutional investors. Synergy between the different businesses is a key strength area of the group. For example, the Wealth Management segment derives synergy from the Corporate and Investment Banking division.

1.5.4 **RISK MANAGEMENT AT BNP PARIBAS**

The Group Risk Management (GRM) department is responsible for measuring and controlling risks at the group level. The independent GRM reports directly to the group's executive management. The front-line responsibility of managing risk lies with the divisions and business lines that undertake transactions. The Risk Management Committee, Capital Committee, and ALM Committee are responsible for management of risk, liquidity, and capital. The various risks faced by BNP Paribas are credit risk, counterparty risk, market risk, operational risk, compliance, and reputational risk.

The stress testing framework is an integral part of the risk management system at BNP Paribas. It is used in the major areas of risk management, capital planning, and regulatory requirements. Stress testing is done at the GRM and its business line or portfolio level is based on different types of risk.

The bank's lending activities are governed by the Global Credit Policy, approved by the risk committee, chaired by the chief executive officer. Specific policies are made to each type of business or counterparty. Decisions on retail banking exposures are based on the system of discretionary limits. A comprehensive risk monitoring system is organized to ensure that lending commitments comply with loan approval decisions. Daily exception reports provide warning signals of potential escalations of credit risks. BNP Paribas uses credit risk transfer instruments such as securitization or credit derivatives to hedge individual risks, reduce portfolio concentration, and more. The bank has a comprehensive internal rating system compliant with regulatory requirements regarding capital adequacy. The Internal Ratings Based Approach (IRBA) is also used for credit risk management. For exposures in the standardized approach, BNP uses external ratings assigned by S&P, Moody's, and Fitch.

Market risk monitoring and pricing is structured around several committees such as the Capital Market Risk Committee (CMRC), Product and Financial Control Committee (PFC), and Valuation Review Committee. Market risk is first analyzed by systematically measuring portfolio sensitivity to various market parameters. The results of these sensitivity analyses are compiled at various aggregate position levels and compared with market limits.

VaR is calculated using an internal model. It estimates the potential loss on a trading portfolio under normal market conditions over one trading day, based on changes in the market over the previous 260 business days with a confidence level of 99%. The group uses derivatives instruments to hedge interest rate risk that arises from fluctuations in income and expenses on account of floating rate assets and liabilities.

Liquidity and funding risk is managed through a global liquidity policy approved by Group Executive Management. The main liquidity risk mitigation techniques are building up a liquidity reserve, diversifying funding sources, and extending financing maturities.

Operational risk consists of legal risk, tax risk, and information security risk. Based on an approach structured by operational process and entity, a system of data collection of actual or potential incidents is developed by the operational risk management system. Legal risk is managed by executive legal affairs, global legal committee, and global litigation practice group. The group tax department along with the group finance legal risk monitors the global tax risks. Information security risk is managed by updating the procedural framework for each business line governing day-to-day practices.

For capital requirements calculated under the Advanced Management Approach (AMA), the bank develops an internal operational risk model based on internal and external loss data in the context of various scenario analysis. The Insurance Risk Management Committee oversees the risks of BNP Paribas Cardif. Table 1.15 gives the financial highlights of BNP Paribas during the 5-year period 2008-2012. Table 1.16 highlights the revenues of BNP Paribas by business segment during the 2-year period 2011-2012.

REFERENCES

1. http://invest.bnpparibas.com/en/pid5861/information-statement.html
2. Various Annual Reports of BNP Paribas
3. http://media-cms.bnpparibas.com/file/97/8/bnp_paribas-2013_information_statement.29978.pdf

Table 1.15   Financial Highlights 2008-2012 (Millions of Euros)

	2008	2009	2010	2011	2012
Revenues	27,376	40,191	43,880	42,384	39,072
Net income	3452	6474	9164	6894	7313
Loans and receivables due from credit institutions	69,153	88,920	62,718	49,369	40,406
Loans and receivables due from customers	494,401	678,766	684,686	665,834	630,520
Total liabilities	2,016,583	1,977,354	1,912,529	1,879,657	1,812,868
Consolidated equity	58,968	80,344	85,629	85,626	94,422
Capital ratios					
Total ratio (%)		14.2	14.5	14	15.6
Tier 1 ratio (%)		10.1	11.4	11.6	13.6

Source: Annual Reports

Table 1.16   Revenues by Business Segment 2011-2012 (Millions of Euros)

	2011	2012
Retail Banking		
French Retail Banking	6786	6797
BNL Banca Commercial	3163	3230
Belgian Retail Banking	3092	3183
Other domestic market activities	2309	2181
Personal Finance	5142	4982
International Retail Banking	3869	4199
Investment Solutions	5922	6204
Corporate and Investment Banking	9897	9715
Other activities	2204	(1419)
Total	42,384	39,072

Source: Annual Reports

1.6 CRÉDIT AGRICOLE GROUP

The Crédit Agricole Group had its origin when the first local bank was created in France in 1885. The Crédit Agricole Group is one of the largest banks in Europe and is the market leader in customer-focused banking in France. Crédit Agricole focuses on a range of retail banking businesses and specialized businesses such as corporate and investment banking, insurance, asset management, leasing, and consumer finance. The group comprises cooperative and mutual foundations, regional and local bank networks. Crédit Agricole has 150,000 employees, who serve approximately 51 million customers, 6.9 million mutual shareholders, and 1.2 million shareholders. The bank has a global presence in about 60 countries, with 11,300 branches in 11 countries (including 9000 in France and 900 in Italy). Crédit

Agricole S.A. is listed on Euronext Paris. Crédit Agricole has a number of subsidiaries that serve regional banks and banking networks in France and in other regions abroad.

In 2012, Crédit Agricole S.A. had a net loss of €6471 million. In the same year the group made two offers to buy back subordinated debt, which led to the buyback of $0.6 billion in nominal terms.

1.6.1 STRUCTURE OF CRÉDIT AGRICOLE GROUP

The Crédit Agricole Group includes Crédit Agricole S.A., all regional banks, local banks and their subsidiaries. There are 39 regional banks and 2512 local banks.

Crédit Agricole S.A.		
Retail Banking	**Specialized Business Lines**	**Corporate and Investment Banking**
• Crédit Agricole Regional Banks • LCL • International Retail Banking	• Specialized financial services, Crédit Agricole Consumer Finance, Crédit Agricole Leasing and Factoring • Savings Management Amundi, CACEIS, Crédit Agricole Assurances, Crédit Agricole Private Banking	Crédit Agricole CIB
Specialized Businesses and Subsidiaries		
Crédit Agricole Capital Investment and Finance, Crédit Agricole Immobilier, Uni-Éditions, Crédit Agricole Cards and Payments		

1.6.1.1 Business lines of Crédit Agricole S.A.

The following are the business lines for the group.

1.6.1.1.1 Retail banking

1.6.1.1.1.1 French Retail Banking: Regional Banks. The 39 Crédit Agricole regional banks provide a broad range of banking and financial products. The products and services include savings products such as money market, bonds, securities, life insurance investment products, home and consumer finance, corporate loans, loans to SMEs and farmers, personal services, and wealth management. The regional banks also provide property and casualty and life insurance products. They provide a full range of remote banking services such as interactive voice response, Internet and mobile phone services. The regional banks serve about 21 million customers with 7013 branches and 6667 in-store servicing points. The division is a market leader in France accounting for 23% of household deposits and 20.6% of household credit. Crédit Agricole is the leading financier of agriculture in France with a market share of approximately 78%. The bank is also a market leader for small businesses. The regional banks have approximately 900,000 customers in the small business segment.

1.6.1.1.1.2 French Retail Banking: LCL. Established in 2005, LCL is the only domestic network in France to focus exclusively on retail banking for customers, small businesses, and SMEs. The division consists of retail banking for customers and small businesses, private banking, and corporate banking. LCL serves about 6 million individual customers with innovative products in savings, investment, credit, insurance, and advisory services. LCL has a wide network of 2077 outlets and more than 6100 ATMs across France. Approximately 1090 specialist advisers serve as a single contact point for about 325,000 small business customers comprising tradespeople, small retailers, professionals, and farmers. LCL Banque Privée provides global relationships of high-net-worth banking and day-to-day banking to 150,000 customers in 70 privileged reception facilities. LCL Banque Privée is also the contact point for common banking transactions, including lending transactions involving property loans, asset-backed loans, and financing of stock options. SME banking consists of a national network of 88 business centers to serve approximately 27,300 customers. LCL offers a full range of payment instruments. LCL plays an active role in the construction of the Group Shared Payments platform for the group's payment system subsidiary Crédit Agricole Cards and Payments. LCL offers full structured remote-banking services via telephone and Internet. The LCL ala carte package has a specific tool that enables customers and advisors to construct personalized banking proposals around their plans.

1.6.1.1.1.3 International Retail Banking. The International Retail Banking line offers full retail banking services to more than 5.6 million customers in 10 countries in Europe and the Mediterranean Basin. The bank has a network of almost 2200 branches.

1.6.1.1.2 Specialized business lines

1.6.1.1.2.1 Crédit Agricole Consumer Finance. Crédit Agricole serves 23 markets in Europe. Consumer Finance offers a full range of consumer finance products such as personal loans, revolving credit, and leasing solutions. These products are supported by a set of insurance and service products such as cards, extended warranties, and loyalty programs. Crédit Agricole distributes its product range through distribution channels such as direct selling (Sofinco brand in France), retail points of sale, and partnerships with affiliates and nonaffiliates in the automotive, retail, and institutional sectors. The products are also offered in partnership with a network of brokers under the Interbank and Ribank brands in the Netherlands and under the Creditlift Courtage brand in France. Crédit Agricole Consumer Finance has subsidiaries in 14 countries. Consumer Finance is also a major international player in auto financing.

1.6.1.1.2.2 Crédit Agricole Leasing and Factoring. Crédit Agricole Leasing and Factoring (CAL&F) is a major player in specialized financing in France and Europe. In lease financing, CAL&F provides equipment finance leases, information system leases, property finance leases, sustainable development project financing, and local authority financing. CAL&F offers factoring services and management for financing of customer accounts. CAL&F is present in 11 countries in Europe and North Africa and has operational networks in Germany, Benelux, Spain, France, Italy, and Portugal.

1.6.1.1.3 Savings management

1.6.1.1.3.1 Asset Management, Securities and Investor Services. Asset management services are offered by the Amundi Group and its subsidiaries in 30 countries. Amundi is the second-largest European and ninth-largest global player in the asset management industry with €727.4 billion in assets under management. Amundi offers varied products in all asset classes and currencies. The investment solutions developed are offered to more than 100 million retail clients throughout the world.

The Securities and Investor Services (CACEIS) is the international banking group that specializes in asset services for institutional investors and corporations. CACEIS offers products and services such as custodianship, fund administration, middle office solutions, derivatives clearing, forex, stock lending, fund distribution support and services to issuers. CACEIS is the largest custodian bank and fund administrator in Europe with about €2500 billion in assets in custody and €1250 billion under administration.

The Crédit Agricole Assurances Group offers a comprehensive range of insurance products through Predica and Pacifica. The group is the largest bancassurer in France. Predica is the largest life insurance subsidiary of Crédit Agricole Assurances Group and the second-largest personal insurance provider in France. Predica is the leading player in the market for popular retirement savings plans. In property and casualty insurance, Pacifica has 9 million policies in the network of regional banks and about 1 million policies at LCL. The Assurances Group distributes its products through the Crédit Agricole regional banks and LCL. The group's subsidiary CACI specializes in creditor insurance. International insurance subsidiaries conduct business operations in seven countries.

1.6.1.1.3.2 Private Banking. The Crédit Agricole Private Banking unit has operations in 16 countries with €94 billion in financial assets under management. In France, Crédit Agricole Private Banking operates through its subsidiaries Indosuez Private Banking and Indosuez Gestion. The division offers a range of investment and wealth expertise services. Crédit Agricole Private Banking operates in European financial centers such as Switzerland, Luxembourg, and Monaco. Crédit Agricole also has a significant presence in the markets of Asia, the Middle East, and Latin America.

1.6.1.1.4 Corporate and investment banking

Crédit Agricole CIB has five business lines. They are Commercial Monitoring of Corporations and the International Network, Investment Banking, Corporate Banking, Capital Markets Activities, and, its newest offering, Debt Optimization and Distribution (DOD).

The first business line monitors the functioning of large French corporates, regional companies, and other local authorities. The investment bank mainly provides advisory services for mergers and acquisition activities and equity financing. CIB has been the investment advisor for deals such as the acquisition of Vermandoise de Sucreries by Cristal Union and the acquisition of CFAO by Toyota Tsusho Corporations. CIB was also the investment advisor for an additional equity issue for Alstom and convertible bond transactions for Faurecia and Unibail.

Corporate Banking deals with the origination, structuring, and financing of large exports and investment operations as well as complex structured loans. Capital Market Activities cover all the activities of trading and selling exchange market products for large corporations and financial institutions. A new business, Agroalimentaire, focuses on sustainable support of the food industry. Sodica is a company specializing in investment management and corporate finance activities. Crédit Agricole Immobilier, the property specialist line of DOD, was created to implement the distribute to originate model.

1.6.1.1.4.1 Subsidiaries of Crédit Agricole. CACIF (Crédit Agricole Capital Investissement and Finance), a wholly owned subsidiary of Crédit Agricole S.A., has investments in the four business lines of property development, property management, facility management, and property investment advisory services. In 2012, Immobilier sold 1544 homes in urban areas. Omnes Capital is a major player in the private equity market with a focus on small businesses. Crédit Agricole Cards and Payments is the Group's Flows and Payments subsidiary. Crédit Agricole S.A.'s press subsidiary Uni-Éditions is one of the top 10 magazine publishers in France.

1.6.2 **CORPORATE SOCIAL RESPONSIBILITY ACTIVITIES**

Crédit Agricole S.A.'s corporate social responsibility policy, established in 2011, is called the FReD approach and revolves around the RESPECT pillar along with seven themes: Recognition, Equality, Safety, Participation, Equity, Consistency, and Territory. The group features in the top three of Novethic's ratings for corporate social responsibility activities. The group is a signatory to the United Nations Global Compact and Climatic principles. The corporate and investment bank have adopted the Equator Principles. Crédit Agricole, in partnership with Grameen Bank, established Grameen Crédit Agricole Foundation with an endowment of €50 million. The foundation provides local microfinance institutions with loans, guarantees, and equity investments in Africa and Southeast Asia. The group trains approximately 10,000 young people each year. In 2012, Crédit Agricole launched a "green car" insurance program in which auto insurance policies were tied to a green auto loan for vehicles emitting less carbon. Crédit Agricole S.A. has been a constituent of the ASPI Eurozone index since September 2004. This index is composed of the 120 listed companies in the eurozone with the best social and environmental performance.

1.6.3 **STRATEGY**

Strategically Crédit Agricole is aiming to become the European leader in universal customer-focused banking. This customer-centric universal banking strategy combines the concept of a local retail bank with that of specialized financial services. The group aims to serve all market participants by giving them access to specialized businesses, including insurance, asset management, and corporate and investment banking.

The group is undertaking major transformation efforts in the context of slowing economic growth, the European sovereign debt crisis, and stringent regulatory requirements as stipulated by Basel III. Crédit Agricole is refocusing its banking investments in Europe, gradually disposing its investments in Bankinter in Spain. Regional banks are focusing on cross-border expansion into many European markets in Belgium, Spain, and Switzerland. Crédit Agricole is restructuring operations of its international retail banking for deployment of a full-service retail banking model. Crédit Agricole is adopting a unified approach in which various geographic locations of each business line facilitates the development of cross-selling and cross-border businesses. To manage the liquidity crisis and new regulatory requirements, Crédit Agricole adopted an adjustment plan that targeted reductions of debt of €50 billion and in risk-weighted assets of €35 billion by 2012. The Basel III rules set the minimum Core Tier 1 ratio by 7% by 2019. In 2012 Crédit Agricole Group's fully loaded Basel III, Core Tier 1 ratio was 9.3%.

To manage the regulatory constraints of liquidity, risk-weighted assets, and equity the CIB division has put focus on a portfolio of strategic customers consisting of large corporations and financial institutions. The division ceased its activities with equity derivatives and commodities and sold its equity brokerage segment CLSA of Citics and Cheureux to Kepler. In 2012, a new distribute to originate model was established to have additional gains from capital market activities in the bond and credit-restructuring areas along with global expertise of the structured and corporate finance and credit syndication. A new business line termed Debt Optimization and Distribution (DOD) was created to implement the model.

A leader in financing economy, Crédit Agricole has strategic priorities in sectors such as agriculture and agrifood housing, energy sources and environmental economics, and health.

1.6.4 **RISK MANAGEMENT AT CRÉDIT AGRICOLE**

The major risk at Crédit Agricole is classified as credit risk, market risks, structural asset/liability management risks, operational, legal, and noncompliance risk. The measuring and supervising risk is vested with dedicated Risk Management and Permanent Control (DRG-GRM department), which reports directly to the executive management. DRG organizes periodic review of the main credit risks and market risks through quarterly Risk Committee meetings. The Risk Committee addresses issues such as policies on risk takings, portfolio analysis, analysis of cost of risk, market limits, and concentration limit. DRG periodically informs the Crédit Agricole's Audit Committee about risk exposures and the methods to measure them. The risk strategies are adjusted according to the requirements of each business line, business sector, or country. CIB carries out active portfolio management to manage concentration risks.

The group uses credit derivatives or securitization mechanisms to diversify counterparty risk. Potential risk concentration mitigation is achieved by syndication of loans with outside banks and use of risk hedge instruments such as credit insurance and derivatives. In the context of recognition of risk, an impairment policy is implemented on an individual or portfolio basis.

1.6.4.1 *Credit risk*

A default is said to occur when a payment is generally more than 90 days past due. Each lending decision is based on risk return analysis. In CIB, an ex-ante calculation based on risk-adjusted return on capital is employed. All methods, procedures, and controls for the assessment of credit risk are covered by internal rating systems. The governance of the internal rating system is the responsibility of the Standards and Methodologies Committee (CNM) chaired by the group's head of Risk Management and Permanent Control. The committee reviews rules for identifying and measuring risks and estimates Basel II risk parameters. Each business line is responsible for defining, implementing, and substantiating its rating system for providing home loans and consumer finance for retail customers. The regional banks have common risk assessment models. The internal risk models of the group are statistical models based on explanatory behavioral variables.

CIB uses a specific internal methodology based on Monte Carlo simulations to estimate the risk of change in relation to derivatives instruments using a net portfolio approach for each customer. Credit stress scenarios are applied periodically to assess risk of loss and changes in capital requirement owing to changes in the environment.

The major credit risk mitigation mechanisms used to mitigate credit risk are collateral and guarantees received, netting contracts, and credit derivatives. The collaterals are notably used for financing of assets, property, aircrafts, and ships. Securities in the form of guarantees include public export credit insurance, private credit insurance, financial guarantee insurance, credit derivatives, and cash collateral. Through master contracts, Crédit Agricole and subsidiaries net their exposures to counterparties. Crédit Agricole also uses collateralization techniques such as deposits of cash or securities to manage risk positions. For managing banking books, the corporate and investment division uses credit derivatives and other risk transfer instruments such as securitization.

1.6.4.2 *Market risk*

Market risk comprises interest rate risk, exchange rate risk, price risk, and credit spread. Market risk is managed at two complementary levels, at the central and local group. At the central level, the GRM and Permanent Control department coordinates all groupwide market risk supervision and control issues. At the local level, the Risk Management and Permanent Control officer manages market risks from the business line. Group Risk Committee, Risk Monitoring Committee, and Standards and Methodology Committee are the three governing bodies involved in the management of market risk. The central element of the market risk measurement system is VaR. VaR includes a number of risk factors such as interest rates, foreign exchange, and asset prices. The VaR uses a confidence level of 1 day and 1 year of historical data. The main method used to measure VaR is the historical VaR method. The Monte Carlo method is used only for a marginal portion of Crédit Agricole CIB's commodity-related activities. A back-testing process is applied to check the relevance of the VaR model for each of the Crédit Agricole Group's entities with capital market activities. Stress scenarios are used to complement the VaR measure, which by itself cannot capture the impact of extreme market conditions. Crédit Agricole implemented "stressed VaR" in 2010 and Credit Valuation Adjustment (CVA) VaR to measure the potential loss arising from downfall of counterparties' credit ratings. CIB uses credit derivatives, which are managed through a system of market-risk indicators such as VaR, credit sensitivity, and sensitivity to interest rates.

Much of the group's exposure to global interest rate risk relates to retail banking. The company's exposure to global interest rate risk is managed regularly by Crédit Agricole S.A.'s Treasury and the ALM Committee. The group is primarily exposed to changes in interest rates in the eurozone. Each entity hedges its interest rate risks by means of financial instruments such as fair value hedging.

Foreign exchange risk consists of structural and operational foreign exchange risk. Structural foreign exchange risk arises from long-term investments by Crédit Agricole in assets denominated in foreign currencies. Operational foreign exchange risk arises mainly from revenues and expenses of all kinds that are denominated in currencies other than the euro. The group's policy is to borrow in the currency in which the investment is made to immunize that asset against foreign exchange risk. Operational currency exposure positions are updated monthly or daily for foreign exchange trading operations.

Fair value hedges and cash flow hedges are used for global interest rate risk management. For the protection of the group's net asset value, the matching of balance sheet and nonbalance sheet items are done by fair value hedges (derivatives instruments such as fixed-rate swaps, inflation swaps). If this neutralization is effected using derivatives instruments (mainly interest rate swaps), the derivatives instruments are classified as cash flow hedge.

Crédit Agricole uses a system underpinned by a series of limits, indicators, and procedures for assessing and monitoring liquidity risk. The system focuses on maintaining liquidity reserves, appropriate long-term refinancing time frame, and diversifying sources of refinancing. The management of short-term refinancing involves setting spreads on short-term funds raised under various programs such as negotiable CDs.

The governance of operational risk management vests with the operational risk committee. The group uses risk mapping to identify and qualitatively assess the risks. Table 1.17 gives the financial highlights of Credit Agricole Group during 2008-2012. Table 1.18 provides the income highlights of Credit Agricole segment-wise during the 5-year period 2008-2012.

REFERENCES

1. Crédit Agricole Group Website
2. Annual Report of Crédit Agricole

Table 1.17   Financial Highlights 2008-2012

	2008	2009	2010	2011	2012
Revenues (millions of euros)	15,956	17,942	20,129	19,385	16,315
Net income (millions of euros)	1266	1446	1752	(1198)	(6513)
Total assets (billions of euros)	1653.2	1557.3	1593.5	1723.6	1842.4
Gross loans (billions of euros)	436.9	463.6	499.6	521	460.9
Customer deposits (billions of euros)	607.8	643.4	671.7	674	634
Assets under management (in asset management, insurance and private banking) (billions of euros)	550.8	688.5	854.6	808.5	865.4
Market cap (billions of euros)	15.20	10.9	22.8	28.7	17.8
Tier 1 solvency ratio (%)				11.7	11.2
Total solvency ratio (%)				13.2	13.4

Source: Annual Reports

Table 1.18   Income by Business Line 2008-2012 (Millions of Euros)

	2008	2009	2010	2011	2012
Regional Banks	581	730	957	1008	824
LCL	691	574	671	675	663
International Retail Banking	(420)	(458)	(928)	(2458)	(4880)
Specialized Financing Services	460	457	536	91	(1613)
Savings Management	1392	1410	1509	951	1720
Corporate and Investment Banking	(1924)	(320)	975	(147)	(880)
Corporate Center	244	(1268)	(2457)	(1590)	(2305)

Source: Annual Reports

1.7 **HSBC**

HSBC is one of the largest banking and financial institutions with approximately 6600 offices in developed and emerging markets of the world. HSBC serves about 55 million customers in around 80 countries encompassing regions in Europe, Asia Pacific, Middle East, North America, and Latin America. The shares of HSBC Holdings plc are held by about 216,000 shareholders in 130 countries. HSBC is listed on London, Hong Kong, New York, Paris, and Bermuda stock exchanges. The four global businesses of HSBC are Retail Banking and Wealth Management, Commercial Banking, Global Banking and Markets, and Global Private Banking. Headquartered in London. HSBC Holdings is a public limited company incorporated in England and Wales. HSBC was established in Hong Kong and in Shanghai in 1865, as there was considerable demand for local banking facilities in Hong Kong and the China coast. The initial emphasis was on building presence in China and in the rest of the Asia Pacific region. In 1888, HSBC was the first bank to be established in Thailand where it printed the country's first banknotes. One of the key early strengths of HSBC was trade finance. In the 20th century, HSBC was actively involved in financing infrastructural projects in China.

In the later part of the century, HSBC transformed from a regional bank into a major financial service institution. In the late 1970s, HSBC conceived the strategy of the "three-legged stool" with its base in the three markets of Asia Pacific, the United States, and the United Kingdom. In the 1980s, HSBC acquired Marine Midland Bank in the United States. In the 21st century HSBC has renewed its growth strategy with a focus on growing businesses in China through strategic partnerships and organic growth.

1.7.1 BUSINESS DIVISIONS OF HSBC

1.7.1.1 Commercial Banking

The offerings of Commercial Banking include business banking, corporate banking, international products and services. The Commercial Banking division has its presence in 60 countries. Business banking provides a range of full-service packages from cash management to commercial mortgages. Corporate banking provides tailored systems and products, which includes foreign exchange, liquidity management, payments, and cash management. The international services provide cross-border products that include guarantees and structured debt for global transactions. This division serves more than 3 million customers, which range from small and medium-sized companies to multinational companies in more than 60 countries.

1.7.1.2 Global Banking and Markets

Global Banking and Markets is managed as two principal divisions of Global Markets and Global Banking. Global Markets offers operations of Treasury and capital market services. Global Banking offers financing, advisory, and transaction services.

The sector-focused client service teams of the division include the Corporate Sector Group, the Resources and Energy Group, and a Financial Institutions Group. The products and services offered are advisory, financing, prime services, research and analysis, securities services, trading and sales, and transaction banking.

The corporate sector covers all major industry sectors. The Corporate Sector Group is divided into industry or sector-specific teams that have offices in the major regions of the world. The Resources and Energy Group focuses on three primary sectors of oil and gas, power and utilities, metals and mining. The Financial Institutions Group is the client-sector group, which deals with financial institutions through the five subsectors consisting of banks and broker dealers, insurers, public sectors, asset managers, and hedge funds. The main products and services offered are credit and lending, equity capital market products, mergers and acquisition advisory, and leveraged finance.

HSBC's Global Advisory services provide financial advice on M&As and capital fund-raising for M&As, divestitures, joint ventures, and financial restructuring. The Asset and Structured Finance team provides asset and structured finance solutions for both corporate and institutional clients. The Credit and Lending team offers a wide spectrum of corporate banking services such as working capital arrangements, short- and medium-term acquisition finance. The team originates structure and executes equity and equity-linked issues such as initial public offerings (IPOs), secondary placements, right issues, convertible bonds, exchangeable bonds, and pre-IPO financing. The Leveraged and Acquisition Finance (LAF) team provides solutions for debt financing, which includes origination, arrangement, underwriting, syndication of leveraged buyouts, infrastructure financing, emerging market finance, project finance, and management buyouts and buy-ins. HSBC project and export finance team provides services in project finance, export finance, and global specialized finance. HSBC participates in project financing techniques to develop public-private partnerships (PPPs). The Export Finance team of HSBC is a global leader in the arrangement of Export Credit Agency Finance.[4] The Global Specialized Finance team is the arranger or provider of medium-term commercial trade financing to developing market financial institutions and government entities.

HSBC's Global Asset Management is one of the world's largest emerging-market asset managers offering a wide range of equity, fixed-income, liquidity, and alternative investment products. HSBC Group provides banking and wealth management services for more than 92 million customers in different markets covering Americas, Asia Pacific, Europe, the Middle East, and Africa.

HSBC provides online services consisting of e-solutions, HSBC net, and Prime Finance. e-trade solutions help companies bring in operational efficiencies such as reduction in trade cycles, automation of supply chain, and reduction of operating costs. The e-solutions include document tracker, document express, electronic advising, and Internet trade advising. Prime Finance offers a full-service prime brokerage based on a global custody platform. Prime Swap is a fully automated portfolio swap platform. These platforms offer fully integrated services to hedge funds and institutional asset managers. The key features of HSBC Prime Finance include flexible financing, equity financing and securities lending, cross-asset margining, foreign exchange hedging, global futures and options execution and clearing, and dedicated client service.

The Global Research division provides high-quality research and analysis to investors in areas of economics, currencies, equities, and fixed income. The division has 600 staff in 22 countries.

HSBC's Corporate Trust and Loan Agency (CTLA) provides a broad range of trustee, agency, and transaction management services. CTLA facilitates financing needs through debt capital market products such as bonds, medium-term notes, certificates of deposit, commercial papers, convertible bonds, exchangeable bonds, euro bonds, global bonds, floating rate notes, and private placements.

HSBC Securities Services (HSS) is a leading provider of fund services in the world, providing services to investment managers, sovereign wealth managers, asset managers, pension funds, and insurance companies. HSS has a custodian network in 88 markets. HSBC also offers products and services for fund administration such as accounting and valuation, transfer agency, investment operations, and corporate secretarial services. HSBC offers global tax services as well as comprehensive private-equity servicing solutions for accounting and valuation, financial reporting investor services, custody services, US tax reporting, and credit services. HSS Treasury offers CLS services to its funds and global custody clients through the bank's CLS settlement membership. HSS also offers services in venture capital, a fund of private equity funds, mezzanine funds, real estate funds, and leveraged buyout funds. HSBC Passive Hedging offers integrated service to protect clients from currency risk by steps such as automatic monitoring of cross-currency exposures, asset hedging, and share class hedging.

In trading and sales segments, HSBC has a strong sales and trading platform and acts as a market maker for gilt bonds offered by national governments, multilateral institutions, and corporations in various currencies. HSBC also acts as a market maker for gilt products, wholesale activities that are linked to STRIPS, and index-linked trading and repo markets. HSBC global equities provide

---

[4]Export credit agency finance is medium to long-term financing given to corporations project entities, and governments to finance the import of capital goods and services. Government-backed export credit agencies usually provide a guarantee or insurance policy to commercial banks that provide loans to the importer of capital goods.

cash and derivatives trading, sales and distribution, and equities finance expertise. HSBC offers a comprehensive range of Delta One products on a wide range of stocks and indexes. HSBC is an emerging markets secured financing specialist. Equity finance facilitates a number of activities such as long and short market access, Treasury management, inventory optimization, alpha generation, and collateralized financing. A wide range of products such as equity derivatives, swaps, low exercise price options (LEPOs), sector-linked products, listed and over-the-counter (OTC) dividend products, and exchange-traded funds (ETFs) are also offered. HSBC provides assistance for the future and option trading requirements of clients by offering brokers on specialist sales desks in all regions. The Chicago and Hong Kong desks operate for 24 h. HSBC offers a number of electronic trading solutions such as Bloomberg EMSX, Trading Technologies, Bloomberg Tradebook Trading Technologies, Fastfill, and in-house front-end order management systems, and HSBC Futures Direct. HSBC futures trade on all major futures and options exchanges. HSBC is the only OTC market maker with foundations in platinum, palladium, gold, and silver. HSBC is the largest metal custodian in the precious metals market with interest in sectors that include oil refining, petrochemicals, pharmaceuticals, glass, electronics, and jewelry. The money market team of HSBC manages deposits in all major currencies and most emerging market currencies. The services provided by the team include cash loans and deposits, certificates of deposit, commercial paper, and repo/reverse repo.

The HSBC Rates franchise consists of nearly 800 fixed-income specialists in more than 50 countries. The Rates franchise provides services such as debt issuance and advice, financing, innovative risk management, and investment solutions through vanilla and structured products. The products offered include index-linked, global government bonds, sovereign, agency and supranational bonds, inflation swaps, interest rate swaps, sovereign CDS, and more.

Transaction banking is also an important segment of HSBC. The Client Access program provides customized solutions to clients for cash management and Treasury operations. HSBC also offers an extensive range of trade and receivables finance.

1.7.1.3 Private Bank

HSBC Private Bank offers traditional banking services such as deposit products, short-term investments, trade services, and foreign exchange products with customized focus for high-net-worth individuals. HSBC Private Bank also provides individualized credit lines and loans, high-end residential mortgages and home equity loans, and letters of credit. Other products and service provided by Private Bank are online banking, portfolio management services, and discretionary services (e.g., solutions for fixed-income, conservative, balanced, growth, and equity-managed portfolios). HSBC Private Bank also provides advisory services in areas of emerging markets, fixed income and equities, structured products, foreign exchange, and commodity trading. The investment products include cash and foreign exchange, sovereign and corporate bonds, commodities, and structured products. The fund selection due diligence is managed by HSBC Multimanager and HSBC Private Bank's Fund Strategy Group. HSBC Private Bank's Alternative Investment Bank offers advisory services for clients in alternative investments of hedge funds, private equity, and real estate. HSBC Private Wealth Solutions provide wealth planning for high-net-worth individuals, entrepreneurs, and families. In 2011, the Private Bank had private client assets under administration of $203 billion. In wealth planning, the Private Bank provides trust and fiduciary services, wealth advisory, insurance, family office services, and specialist advisory services.

1.7.1.4 *Retail Banking and Wealth Management*

Retail Banking and Wealth Management offers a complete range of retail banking and wealth management services to about 54 million people worldwide. The retail banking products and services include loans, mortgages, life insurance, savings and current accounts. The four principal channels of Retail Banking and Wealth Management are HSBC Premier, HSBC Advance, Wealth Solutions, and Financial Planning and Basic Banking. HSBC Premier provides preferential banking services to affluent customers and their families. HSBC Advance offers a range of preferential products and services. Wealth Solutions and Financial Planning helps clients to manage wealth through investments and wealth insurance products. Basic Banking provides banking products using global product platforms.

HSBC Premier accounts can be accessed from a single log-on. HSBC Premier credit card entitles users to shopping and entertainment activities both at home and abroad. HSBC provides emergency support services to cover clients and their families. HSBC Premier customers are offered global view online banking services, which include fee-free, real-time money transfers with preferential exchange rates. HSBC provides services for expat banking. HSBC Premier also provides preferential banking services and specialist wealth management advice services. HSBC Premier provides a wide range of wealth management services in investment management, tax-efficient savings, traditional mutual funds, alternative investments, share dealing and brokerage, structured products, ETFs, insurance, retirement, and estate planning. HSBC also offers sharia-compliant investment funds in select markets. In 2012, the division made a profit before tax of US$9.6 billion.

1.7.2 STRATEGY

HSBC was founded in 1865 to finance trade between Asia and the West. HSBC is the world's largest global trade finance bank. Financing trade had been the core of HSBC's businesses. The bank aims to become the world's leading international bank.

HSBC focuses on the development of an international network connecting fast-growing emerging markets and developed markets. The emphasis is also on developing wealth management services, investment in retail banking, insurance, and asset management businesses. The four global businesses of HSBC serve varied clients from individuals and small businesses to governments and institutions. In the bank's commercial division, the strategic plan is to enhance international trade by focusing on fast-growing markets to facilitate trade and capital flows. Global Banking and Markets focuses on investments in the key strategic markets of Hong Kong, other Asia Pacific regions, and Latin America. This strategic initiative aims to leverage HSBC's extensive distribution network. The focus is on offering the delivery of an integrated suite of products and services for global clients.

HSBC focuses on the emerging markets that benefit from demographics and urbanization. The strength of HSBC lies in its massive networks and exposure to high-growth markets. The network of HSBC businesses is well connected to capture growing international financial flows. The bank focuses on capturing opportunities from social mobility and wealth creation in fast-growing markets. The plan for retail businesses is to invest only in markets where the bank can achieve profitable scale.

One of the priorities for the group is to grow the business organically based on six filters to find which businesses fit in the portfolio. A framework is used to assess investment opportunities based on strategic, financial, and risk criteria. With respect to implementing global standards the primary area of focus is customer due diligence, financial crime compliance, and financial intelligence. The bank also focuses on streamlining processes and procedures to generate sustainable savings.

In the private banking sector, the focus is on priority markets. In this context the division sold or closed a number of nonstrategic businesses and operations in Japan. The UK property advisory business was also closed down. HSBC eliminated redundant organizational layers and streamlined various processes to achieve a sustainable cost savings of US$2 billion. HSBC is in the forefront of initiatives to support the internationalization of renminbi as a major global trade and investment currency. In 2012, HSBC became the first bank to settle cross-border renminbi trade in 50 countries spanning six continents. HSBC has a leading position in infrastructural projects in Asia.

1.7.3 RISK MANAGEMENT AT HSBC

Credit risk arises from direct lending, trade finance, leasing businesses, guarantees, and derivatives. In derivatives contracts the measurement of exposure accounts for the current mark to market value to HSBC of the contract and the expected potential change in the value over time caused by movements in the interest rates. The credit risk is monitored within limits that represent the maximum exposure or loss to which HSBC could be subjected if the customer or counterparty fails to perform its contractual obligations. There is a risk control framework that provides policies, principles, and guidance for risk managers.

Liquidity risk basically arises from mismatches in the timing of cash flows. Funding risks arise when the liquidity needed to fund illiquid asset position cannot be obtained at the expected terms. Liquidity and funding risk is measured using internal metrics, which cover stressed operation cash flow projections, coverage ratios, and advances to core funding ratios. These risks are monitored by the regional Asset and Liability Management's (ALCO's), Group ALCO, etc., and managed on a standalone basis.

The exposure to market risk is segregated into trading and nontrading portfolios. The trading portfolios comprise positions that arise from market making and warehousing of customer-derived positions. The nontrading portfolios consist of positions that primarily arise from interest rate management of retail and commercial banking assets and liabilities, financial investments, and exposures from insurance operations. Market risk is measured in terms of VaR supplemented with stress testing to evaluate the potential impact on portfolio values. Market risk is monitored using measures that include sensitivity of net interest income and sensitivity of structural foreign exchange. Market risk is managed using risk limits.

Operational risk is measured using a top-risk analysis process and the risk and control assessment process. Operational risk is managed by global business and functional managers.

Compliance risk arises from rules, regulations, and group policies including those related to antimoney laundering, antibribery, and corruption. Compliance risk is measured by reference to identified metrics, incident assessments, and regulatory feedback. Compliance risk is managed by establishing and communicating appropriate policies and procedures and training employees.

Insurance risk arises from morbidity and mortality events. It is measured in terms of life insurance liabilities and nonlife written premiums for their respective contract types. The risk is managed both centrally and locally using product design, underwriting, reinsurance, and claims-handling procedures.

Fiduciary risk is managed within the designated businesses through a comprehensive policy framework. Reputational risk is monitored through a reputational risk management framework and is managed by every staff member within the framework of a number of policies and guidelines.

Pension risk is managed locally through the appropriate pension-risk governance structure. Sustainability risk is managed using sustainability risk policies covering project finance lending and sector-based sustainability policies.

HSBC faces significant macroeconomic and geopolitical risks as significant losses could result if one or more countries exit from the eurozone because of the economic crisis. HSBC exposure to European banks may come under stress, which would signal the potential for credit and market risk losses. Table 1.19 provides the financial highlights of HSBC during the period 2008-2012. Table 1.20 highlights the profit/loss before tax of global businesses of HSBC during the 3-year period 2010-2012. Table 1.21 gives the financial highlights of HSBC segregated on the basis of global business divisions.

REFERENCES

1. Annual Reports of HSBC
2. http://www.hsbc.com

Table 1.19   Financial Highlights 2008-2012 (Millions of US Dollars)

	2008	2009	2010	2011	2012
Total operating income	88,571	78,631	80,014	83,461	82,545
Net profit after tax	6498	6694	14,191	17,944	15,334
Return on equity (%)	4.7	5.1	9.5	10.9	8.4
Loans and advances to banks	153,766	179,781	208,271	180,987	152,546
Loans and advances to customers	932,868	896,231	958,366	940,429	997,623
Total assets	2,527,465	2,364,452	2,454,689	2,555,579	2,692,538
Deposits by banks	130,084	124,872	110,584	112,822	107,429
Customer accounts	1,115,327	1,159,034	1,227,725	1,253,925	1,340,014
Core Tier 1 ratio (%)	7	9.4	10.5	10.1	12.3
Total capital ratio (%)	11.4	13.7	15.2	14.1	16.1

Source: Annual Reports

Table 1.20   Profit/Loss Before Tax: Global Businesses 2010-2012 (Millions of US Dollars)

	2010	2011	2012
Retail Banking and Wealth Management	3839	4270	9575
Commercial Banking	6090	7947	8535
Global Banking and Markets	9215	7049	8520
Global Private Banking	1054	944	1009
Others	(1161)	1662	(6990)
Total	19,037	21,872	20,649

Source: Annual Reports

Table 1.21   Financial Highlights by Global Businesses 2012 (Millions of US Dollars)

	Retail Banking and Wealth Management	Commercial Banking	Global Banking and Markets	Global Private Banking	Others
Total operating income	46,218	18,353	18,289	3212	2332
Loans and advances to customers	378,040	288,033	283,842	45,213	2495
Total assets	536,244	363,659	1,942,470	118,440	201,741
Customer accounts	562,151	338,405	332,115	105,772	1571

Source: Annual Reports

1.8 INDUSTRIAL AND COMMERCIAL BANK OF CHINA

Industrial and Commercial Bank of China (ICBC) was established in 1984. The bank has a presence in 39 countries spanning six continents and provides a wide range of products and services to over 4.38 million corporate customers and 393 million personal customers. The bank has a wide distribution network consisting of 17,125 domestic institutions, 383 overseas institutions, and 1771 correspondent banks worldwide. By 2012, the bank had approximately 315 million e-banking customers with annual transactions that amounted to RMB332.6 trillion. Almost 75% of transactions were conducted through e-banking channels. In 2012, ICBC topped the Fortune Global 2000 list, which was the first by a Chinese company.

The bank has issued about 470 million credit cards, which had an annual consumption of RMB4.13 trillion, of which 77.13 million credit cards were issued with an annual consumption of RMB1.3 trillion. ICBC is ranked among the top four card-issuing banks in the world. It is one of the leading international settlement banks of the world with a business volume of US $2 trillion in 2012. Internet banking amounted to RMB300 trillion in 2012. The bank had 4.38 million corporate customers in 2012, and domestic branches disbursed an aggregate of US$146.1 billion in international trade finance.

1.8.1 BUSINESS SEGMENTS

1.8.1.1 Personal Banking

ICBC provides products and services to more than 250 million personal customers through a network of more than 16,000 branches in China, 190 overseas subsidiaries, and more than 1000 correspondent banks throughout the world.

The Personal Banking unit provides services in a wide spectrum of activities. ICBC Happy Loan is an ICBC brand of all personal loan services, which covers 20 or more personal loan products under three major categories of personal housing loans, personal consumer loans, and personal business loans. The other types of personal/private loans in this category include new and secondhand housing loans, car loans, pledge loans, credit loans, business loans, commercial housing, and vehicle loans. The personal banking unit also provides investment and financing services such as Smart Money Planner,

"Roll Over" account services,[5] personal insurance, and precious metal services, which include accumulation plan and metal trading. The other services provided by the personal banking division include convenient banking.

Link Express provides a range of innovative RMB wealth management products designed to meet the cash management needs of investors. Remittance Express enables investors to remit money at any ICBC outlet or via Internet banking, mobile banking (WAP), mobile banking (SMS), telephone banking, ATM, and self-service terminals (transfer/remittance device). Auto-Transfer is an ICBC service to make fund transfers as instructed by the client. ICBC also offers self-service bill payments. The bank's cross-border personal financial services include ICBC Currency Exchange, A/C Opening Services, Credibility Letter, Overseas Study Loan, overseas insurance services, and overseas financial services. The VIP services include private banking, wealth management services (e.g., wise gold services, platinum credit card services), and premium business services (e.g., aviation accident insurance and travel inconvenient insurance). The debit card services include Elite Club accounts. The bank has added a multicurrency ICBC credit card, ICBC QuickPay Card, and ICBC Money Fund Credit Card to its credit card product line. The bank was the first to launch the ICBC-AE Centurion Black Card in China to provide customized high-end services.

1.8.1.2 Corporate Banking

The different types of corporate deposits offered by ICBC include current deposits, time deposits, foreign exchange deposits, corporate agreement deposits, structured deposits, and group account deposits.

Loan financing consists of professional financing, working capital loans, project loans, domestic trade financing, real estate development loans, fixed assets support financing, and merging and acquiring loans. Professional financing consists of aircraft financing, commodity financing, lease financing, overseas M&A loan and global syndication, shipping financing and offshore engineering financing, export credit and overseas project financing, and natural resource-backed structured financing. ICBC plays a major role in financing the aviation market sector.

The Lease Finance division offers aircraft leasing, ship leasing, and equipment leasing. Bill services include bill discounting services such as discounting of banker's acceptances, bill rediscounting, and bill agency services.

ICBC has the largest market share in RMB settlement among all banks in China. ICBC settlements are carried out through electronic exchange, Internet banking, SWIFT-PCC system, and an all functional banking system (NOVA). Settlement services include corporate settlements, domestic settlements, agency services, and cash management.

The Corporate Wealth Management segment provides loans pledged under gold. The physical gold leasing facilitates qualified clients to lease gold from ICBC and pay leasing fees in RMB as agreed in the contract. In the agency gold-trading business, ICBC is a key market maker in China's gold market and is among the four gold-clearing banks designated by the Shanghai Gold Exchange. The OTC book-entry bond trading service provided by ICBC facilitates clients to trade RMB bonds. Corporate wealth management products include fixed-income and money market funds. In 2012, the total amount of precious metal business reached RMB1.09 trillion.

---

[5]Customers' current savings deposits are associated with low-risk funds such as money market and short-term debts for effective cash and investment management.

Corporate e-banking includes the Bank Enterprise Interlink, corporate Internet banking, and corporate telephone banking.

The Investment Banking segment provides various services such as restructuring, M&As services, banking syndicate loan management, private equity, structured financing consultancy, asset securitization, credit asset transfer, corporate listing consultancy, and institution financial consultancy. In the M&A field, ICBC has completed major strategic deals such as the merger of Bao and Bayi steel and the equity transfer of Changyu Group. ICBC has organized major banking syndicate loan projects such as the syndicate loan for Hynix ST Semiconductor for the amount $0.75 billion, CNOOC—Shell South China Petrochemical project with $2.6 billion, and the international syndicate loan for debt restructuring of the Yuehai Group involving HK$14 billion.

The asset custody services of the Corporate division offers safekeeping of customer's assets under their trust and services associate portfolios, which include settlement, account checking, valuation, and related services for investment management. ICBC is the largest asset custodian in China in terms of product offerings and services. Basic asset custody services include account opening, asset custody, investment settlement, accounts checking, asset valuation, and trading supervision. Value-added services include investment appraisal, performance evaluation, and advisory services.

The custody services are provided for securities investment funds, corporate annuity funds, pension insurance funds, trust funds, industry investments, and private equity funds.

In Institutional Banking, ICBC has more than 400,000 government clients providing services covering fiscal taxation, industrial and commercial customs, court and judiciary, social security, education, and research. Institutional Banking services are also offered to 7000 financial institutions, which includes banks, securities companies, insurance firms, trust companies, futures companies, and stock exchanges. The financial services provided to institutional clients cover more than 75 products under categories of assets, liabilities, and intermediaries. The integrated financial service solutions create a one-stop service model that is led by customer departments and supported by product and service departments. ICBC has a leading market share in key segments such as institutional deposit, third-party depository, property insurance, asset custody settlement, fiscal and bank futures transfer. The financial products and services to institutional customers are offered through 16,648 outlets across China, 239 overseas institutions, and a global network of 1669 correspondent banks.

The corporate annuity services include trusteeship management services, account management services, and trusteeship services. The Small Business Finance segment provides comprehensive financial services for small businesses including settlements and loans. The products include small business working capital loans, revolving loans, and online and trade financing for small businesses. ICBC is also involved in trust agency businesses of national development banks and agency trust businesses of the Chinese Export and Import Bank. ICBC undertakes underwriting of super short-term commercial papers, SME collective notes, and private placement notes.

1.8.1.3 E-banking

E-banking services cover both corporate and personal banking services. The Personal Banking@Home consists of personal Internet, telephone, and mobile banking. SMS banking is provided for account management, remittance service, wealth management, payment service, credit card, and security service. Corporate Internet banking provides account inquiry, transfer and settlement, and online payment services to corporate clients.

1.8.1.4 International Banking

The International Banking division of ICBC Global Services provides a collection of products and services related to the settlement, finance, and smart investment of RMB and foreign exchange. Global Services aims to minimize exchange risk and financial costs during international settlement and trade financing.

The two main services of ICBC Global Services are categorized as Services Mart and Commercial Package. Services Mart includes products such as Invitation to Tender, Contract Negotiation, Enter Agreement, Goods Collection, Production and Sales, Payment against Import, and Export Collection to Contract Completed. Also included are international settlement, trade financing, and foreign exchange guarantee services. Commercial Package is a product portfolio involved in export and import services.

1.8.2 STRATEGY

A key component of ICBC's growth strategy is business transformation. ICBC is in the process of implementing two 3-year plans. The economic boom and restructuring of China's economy provided a window of opportunity for ICBC to reorient its businesses. ICBC focuses on emerging businesses and intermediary business while limiting the scale of high capital-consuming businesses such as loans. Using diversified operations, the firm is aiming for capital savings and sustainable development. The bank is focusing on becoming the main linkage for promoting economic and trade relations between China and the rest of the world. The bank is actively involved in the promotion and development of sectors such as advanced manufacturing, service industry, cultural industries, and strategic emerging industries. The bank also focuses on financial services for small- and medium-sized enterprises. The bank facilitates corporations to have a wide range of financing tools that consist of investment banking, financial leasing, bond issuance, and syndicated loans. ICBC also has priorities in lending to local government financing vehicles and controlled loans to the real estate industry.

The bank has built an integrated production line-based centralized processing system. The bank is providing controlled lending to industries with high-energy consumption, high pollution, and overcapacity. The bank has also focused on improving the fund price management system to accommodate interest rate liberalization. The bank introduced more than 500 new products through independent R&D, which includes multiple currency credit cards and personal account-based foreign exchange trading. The bank is leveraging its advantages in integrated financial services such as corporate wealth management, cash management, e-banking, and asset custody to improve market competitiveness.

1.8.3 CORPORATE SOCIAL RESPONSIBILITY ACTIVITIES

In 2012, ICBC won several awards, including the Global Commercial Bank Transparency Gold award and the 2012 Best Corporate Governance Disclosure awards: H-Share Category Platinum award, the Hong Kong Corporate Governance Excellence award, and the Best Corporate Bank in China award by Global Finance. The bank actively supports the development of energy-efficient and environment-friendly sectors, providing total outstanding loans of RMB593.4 billion to the green economy sectors. During 2012, ICBC invested RMB12 million in a series of green poverty alleviation, sanitary poverty alleviation, and educational poverty alleviation programs.

1.8.4 **RISK MANAGEMENT**

The enterprise risk management system is a process in ICBC where the board of directors, senior management, and other employees of the bank are required to take effective control of all risks at various business levels.

The bank's credit risk arises from loans, Treasury operations such as dues from banks, reverse repurchase agreements, corporate bonds, and off-balance sheet activities that include guarantees, commitments, and financial derivatives. The Credit Risk Management Committee is the decision-making body of the bank with respect to important aspects of credit risk management.

ICBC implemented basic management rules for low-credit-risk business, loan guarantees, and unsecured loans. The bank formulated and implemented regional credit policies pursuant to the national strategic planning for key regions. The bank now puts emphasis on the green credit system by placing stringent limits on management for industry with excess capacity and supporting green industries that support energy savings and environmental protection. The bank has strengthened compliance management of personal loans and perfected its personal loan collection mechanism. ICBC has implemented a five-tier classification for measuring loan quality. These categories are pass, special mention, substandard, doubtful, and loss based on the possibility of collecting the principal and interest of loans.

The Market Risk Management Committee is the decision-making body with respect to market risk. Market risk is accounted for both by the banking and trading books. The bank's policy of managing interest rate risk is aimed at maximizing the risk-adjusted net interest income within the tolerable level of interest rate risk specified by its risk appetite. In 2012, the bank improved its consolidated management framework of interest rate risk at the group level.

ICBC mitigates exchange rate risk by limit management and hedging of risks. The bank carries out sensitivity analysis and stress testing of exchange rate risk on a quarterly basis and submits the report to the Market Risk Management Committee. The market risk in the trading book is measured by VaR, sensitivity analysis, and exposure analysis. The bank applies the historical simulation method to measure the VaR of the interest rate risk, foreign exchange rate risk, and commodity risk of fundamental commodity products and derivatives products of the trading books of the head office and all overseas branches.

Liquidity risk arises from such events as withdrawal of customer's deposits, drawing of loans by customers, mismatch of asset and liabilities, and difficulties in realization of assets. The decision-making system for liquidity risk management comprises the board of directors, special committees, the Asset and Liability Management Committee, and the Risk Management Committee. The bank's strategy is to establish a centralized liquidity risk management model based on the organizational structure and major business characteristics of the bank as well as regulatory policies.

The bank uses the scenario analysis method and the sensitivity analysis method to perform stress testing on liquidity risk. The bank applies the reserve ratio requirement, open market operations, and other monetary policies to regulate the money supply in the market for strengthening the liquidity management of the banking system.

The execution, delivery, and process management and the customers, products, and business activities constitute major sources of operational risk losses of the bank. ICBC strictly follows the requirements of the Guidance to the Operational Risk Management of Commercial Banks issued by the CBRC. The bank has formulated the Measures for Operational Risk Management, the Administrative Measures for Operational Risk, and Internal Control Self-Assessment. These measures were aimed at improving the three-tier policy and regulation system for operational risk management comprising the measures for operational risk management, relevant administrative measures, and detailed rules and manuals.

Legal risk arises due to legal sanctions, regulatory penalties, financial losses, and reputational losses or the failure of the bank to comply with relevant laws. The Legal Affairs Department of the Head Office is the functional department in charge of legal risk management across the bank. The bank has actively implemented the risk-based regulatory requirements in respect to antimoney laundering. The board of directors is responsible for formulating strategies and policies concerning the reputational risk management, which is in line with the strategic objectives to the bank. The bank manages and controls country risk through a series of management tools that include country risk assessment and ratings and country risk limits for the entire group. The bank uses stress tests to analyze and monitor country risk exposure. The country risk ratings and limits are reviewed by the bank at least once every year.

1.8.5 CAPITAL MANAGEMENT

ICBC implements a comprehensive capital management composed of capital adequacy ratio management, economic capital management, book capital management, and aggregate capital and structure management. The economic capital management of the bank includes three major procedures of measurement, allocation, and evaluation. The economic capital indicators include Economic Capital (EC), Risk-Adjusted Return on Capital (RAROC), and Economic Value-added (EVA). Table 1.22 provides the financial highlights of the Industrial and Commercial Bank of China during the 5-year period 2008-2012.

Table 1.22 Financial Highlights 2008-2012 (Millions of RMB)

	2008	2009	2010	2011	2012
Operating income	310,195	309,411	380,748	470,601	529,720
Net profit	111,226	129,396	166,025	208,445	238,691
Total assets	9,757,146	11,785,053	13,458,622	15,476,868	17,542,217
Total loans and advances to customers	4,571,994	5,728,626	6,790,506	7,788,897	8,803,692
Return on average total assets (%)	1.21	1.20	1.32	1.44	1.45
Nonperforming loans (%)	2.29	1.54	1.08	0.94	0.85
Core capital adequacy ratio (%)	10.75	9.90	9.97	10.07	10.62
Capital adequacy (%)	13.06	12.36	12.27	13.17	13.66

Source: Annual Reports

REFERENCES

1. http://www.icbc.com.cn
2. Various Annual Reports of ICBC

1.9 **DEUTSCHE BANK**

Deutsche Bank was established in Berlin, Germany in 1870. Deutsche Bank provides a wide range of products and services in investment, corporate, and retail banking, asset and wealth management. The bank has a strong competitive position in North America and emerging markets of Asia. Deutsche Bank also has an established presence in Japan, Asia Pacific, and Australia/New Zealand. Deutsche Bank is a leader in its German home market and has a formidable position in Europe. The share of capital held by private investors was 25% and institutional investors held 75% of the bank's total share capital.

1.9.1 **BUSINESS DIVISIONS**

Deutsche Bank consists of five corporate divisions: Corporate Banking and Securities (CB&S), Global Transaction Banking (GTB), Asset and Wealth Management (AWM), Private and Business Clients (PBC), and Noncore Operations Unit (NCOU).

1.9.1.1 *Corporate Banking and Securities*

The Corporate Banking and Securities (CB&S) division consists of the Markets and Corporate Finance Business segments. The Corporate Finance Business segment deals with sales, trading, and structuring of a wide range of financial market products, including bonds, equities, equity-linked products, exchange-traded products, money market instruments, and securitized instruments and commodities. The division also deals with M&As advisory, debt and equity issuance, and capital market coverage of large and medium-sized companies. The Corporate Finance division covers industry groups such as consumer, financial institutions group, health care, industrials real estate, and technology. Deutsche Bank provides a full range of advisory services that include M&As, industry specialization, regional expertise, and financial sponsors. The bank is also one of the leading global providers of investment banking services and products to financial sponsor clients. The Financial Sponsors Group offers derivatives products, equity products, industry expertise, leveraged finance, and M&As advisory services to private equity firms.

The Global Capital Markets consist of the Capital Markets and Treasury Solutions (CMTS), Equity Capital Markets (ECM), and Leveraged Debt Capital Markets (LDCM) groups. CMTS deals with Treasury-related needs of corporate, financial institutions, sovereign, and agency clients. ECM facilitates services in primary equity products such as IPOs, seasoned equity offerings, book-building processes, and convertible and exchangeable bonds. Deutsche Bank is credited with being the book runner for the world largest IPOs of the Agricultural Bank of China, General Motors, AIA Group, and the Industrial and Commercial Bank of China. The LDCM group originates, structures, underwrites, and distributes senior, mezzanine, and high-yield bonds and syndicated loans.

Deutsche Bank is a global leader in leveraged finance and delivers a full range of leveraged products and services. Deutsche Bank is one among the three top global underwriters for high-yield bonds. The full range of high-yield products offered includes bonds, floating rate notes, PIK notes, and zero coupon bonds.

Deutsche Bank's sales and trading activities exist in both physical and financial coal and freight markets. The bank provides integrated services consisting of financing, payment structures to hedge-embedded offtake agreements, and logistical support. Deutsche Bank Global Credit (GC) trades in a full range of credit products that include bonds, credit derivatives, and structured credit products. GC provides financing and risk management advice to all types of institutions. Deutsche Bank also provides solutions to the hedge industry by partnering with clients to provide multiasset financing solutions and global access.

1.9.1.2 Global Transaction Banking

The Global Transaction Banking (GTB) division consists of Trade Finance and Cash Management teams and Trust and Securities Services.

Trade Finance and Cash Management teams provide commercial banking products and services for corporations and financial institutions. The Cash Management team deals with the management and processing of domestic and cross-border payments and manages risk for international trade and ALM. The DB transaction solution facilitates Deutsche Bank as a partner for all local and international payment needs. Deutsche Bank has a broad network of international correspondent banks and is connected to all major clearing systems. The DB channel and information solutions provide a single platform for all clients' e-banking activities. Deutsche Bank's liquidity management solutions enable corporations to maximize earnings potential by reducing idle balances and optimize cash flow by centralization and pooling of funds. The DB financial supply chain solutions help businesses to have value-added services for all stages of the corporate supply chain. The DB trade solutions provide custom-made solutions for structured trade, commodity, and export finance. The trade solutions also provide comprehensive tools for performance tracking and reporting for risk management. Deutsche Bank offers solutions in the card payment sector in association with strategic partners such as American Express, Global Transaction Banking in Europe, and EVO payment international.

The Trust and Services team provides custody, clearing, and related services in more than 30 markets. This unit is one of the largest providers of administrative service providers for capital market instruments with around €1.7 trillion of assets under custody. The Global Equity Services provide depository services for American and global depository receipts. This unit also provides registrar and related service for German equities. Trust and Agency Services is one of the leading trustees and administrators in the securitization market. The unit is a leading trustee for bonds and other forms of debt financing.

The Private and Business Clients division provides a wide range of banking services to self-employed entrepreneurs, small- and medium-sized businesses and private individuals. The services provided include current accounts, deposits, loans, investment management, and pension products.

1.9.1.3 Asset and Wealth Management

Deutsche Asset and Wealth Management (AWM) offers traditional and alternative investments across all major asset classes. The AWM division also provides wealth management solutions and private banking services to high-net-worth clients. In 2012, AWM had €944 billion in invested assets with a presence in 35 countries. Maximum investments are made in fixed-income and money market investments. On behalf of clients, the division invests in assets of pension funds, national, and supranational institutions, insurance companies, charities, and foundations.

The division had €529 billion of assets under management in active strategies. Deutsche AWM provides a range of actively managed mutual funds to private investors. The division also provides investment and retirement solutions for pension funds, insurance companies, and corporations. The Asset

Management division provides institutional solutions with respect to strategic asset allocation and analytical solutions for institutional clients. In the passive management category the division is involved in the origination, issuance, and distribution of investment products in all asset classes, which includes warrants and certificates, ETFs, exchange traded commodities, and systematic funds. It also provides index-related strategies for institutional clients. The AWM division is a market leader in alternative investments with services in real estate, hedge funds, private equity, fund derivatives, retirement and hybrid solutions, and commodities investments. Deutsche Bank is also a global financial services provider of loans and deposits.

The AWM division comprises the Asset Management (AM) and Private Wealth Management (PWM) business segments.

The Wealth Management segment has 180,000 clients in 130 regions worldwide served by 900 relationship managers dedicated to high-net-worth individuals.

1.9.1.4 Private and Business Clients

The Private and Business Clients (PBC) division provides small businesses and individuals with a full range of traditional banking products that includes current accounts, deposits and loans, investment management products, and business banking services. The division operates in European markets and in emerging markets in Central and Eastern Europe along with markets in Asia. The bank also has a leader position in international foreign exchange, fixed income, and equities trading. PBC facilitates investors to access various markets through DB, with X-markets certificates, structured notes, funds and warrants, and other risk-optimized structures. The division provides loans for projects that focus on energy efficiency, renewable energies, and clean technologies.

1.9.1.5 Non-Core Operations Unit

The Non-Core Operations Unit (NCOU) was established to manage assets with the objective to reduce Basel III risk-weighted assets and balance sheet size. The aim is to increase the management focus on core operating businesses. Table 1.23 provides the number of clients by Deutsche Bank division during the period 2010-2012.

1.9.2 STRATEGY

Deutsche Bank supports sustainable activities such as renewable energy finance, microfinance, and impact investment funds. Deutsche Bank, with the formulation of Strategy 2015+, is focusing

Table 1.23   Number of Clients by Division 2010-2012

Division	2010	2011	2012
Corporate Banking and Securities	17,100	18,700	21,400
Asset and Wealth Management	2,770,700	2,803,200	2,941,700
Private and Business Clients	28,787,000	28,585,000	28,425,000

Source: https://www.db.com/medien/en/downloads/Deutsche_Bank_at_a_glance.pdf

on becoming a diversified universal bank through organic growth. Strategy 2015+ focuses on five critical levers such as capital, cost, competencies in core business, clients, and culture. In 2012, the bank raised its Basel III proforma core Tier 1 capital ratio to 7.8%. The proforma Basel III risk-weighted assets were reduced by €80 billion due to selling or hedging assets in the same period. The operation excellence program is aimed at saving €4.5 billion in operating expenses by 2015. As a part of strategic initiatives, a dedicated noncore operations unit was established to target derisking activities and improve operational excellence. The financial objectives of the Strategy 2015+ plan aims to achieve a post-tax return on average active equity of at least 12.5% and a Basel III, core Tier 1 target ratio of more than 10%. The other financial objectives include achieving a target cost income ratio of less than 65% and annual cost savings of €4.5 billion. Deutsche Bank's strategy is based on gaining capital strength. NCOU plays an important role in delivering this strategy. The Corporate Banking and Securities division leverages its strengths in fixed-income flow through platform integration.

Deutsche Bank has focused on M&As over the past few years. It is a leader in its German home market and enjoys an outstanding position in Europe.

Acquisition History	
Year	**M&As Activity**
1989	Acquired British Bank Morgan Grenfell
1991	All US activities merged under the holding company Deutsche Bank North America Holding
1993	Acquisition of Banco de Madrid and Banca Popolare di Lecco
1998	Acquisition of Crédit Lyonnais Belgium
1999	Acquisition and integration of Bankers Trust in the United States
2003	Acquisition of the Swiss Private Bank Rued, Blass & Cie
2004	Acquisition of the Russian investment bank United Financial Group
2006	Takeover of Berliner Bank and Norisbank
2010	Acquisition of Postbank and Sal. Oppenheim in Germany as well as parts of ABN AMRO in the Netherlands

1.9.3 CORPORATE SOCIAL RESPONSIBILITY ACTIVITIES

Deutsche Bank introduced an environmental and social risk framework to address environmental and social issues. The Asset and Wealth Management division manages €3.72 billion of assets for the promotion of sustainable financial products along the framework, which integrates environmental, social, and governance (ESG) issues. The ESG framework provides for carbon ratings and carbon tools. Deutsche Bank has launched a US$100 million global commercial microfinance consortium II fund that aims to help microfinance institutions to develop new products such as housing loans and facilitate fund investors to promote social enterprise in health care, education, energy, agribusiness, and biotechnology. The bank plays a leading role in the Banking and Environmental Initiative (BEI) to explore how valuation methods could stimulate clean energy investments. Deutsche Bank invested €82.7 million in social projects in 2012. Approximately 19,500 Deutsche Bank employees support community projects as corporate volunteers in sectors such as education, social investments, art, and music. In

2012, Deutsche Bank occupied a place in the carbon Disclosure Leadership Index consisting of 33 global companies.

1.9.4 RISK MANAGEMENT AT DEUTSCHE BANK

The major risk faced by Deutsche Bank include credit risk, operational risk, business risk, reputational risk, and liquidity risk. The key portfolio risk sensitivities are analyzed through a bottom-up risk assessment and a top-down macroeconomic and political scenario analysis. Every risk is approved within the risk management framework. The core risk management responsibilities are embedded in the management board and delegated to senior risk management committees for execution and oversight. The key targets for profit and loss, capital supply and capital demand, and key business areas for 3 years are approved by the management board.

Credit risk arises due to direct trading activity with clients such as OTC derivatives, FX forwards, and forward rate agreements. Credit risk is also accounted by traditional nontrading lending activities such as loans and contingent liabilities. Deutsche Bank categorizes credit risk as default risk, settlement, and country risk. The bank categorizes market risk as trading, trading default, and nontrading market risk. Trading market risk arises due to the market-making activities of the CB&S division taking positions in debt, equity, foreign exchange, and other derivatives. Trading default risk is inherent in rating migrations related to trading instruments. Nontrading risk consists of interest rate risk, credit spread risk, investment risk, and foreign exchange risk.

Deutsche Bank manages credit risk by actively managing and assessing a diversified credit portfolio to prevent undue concentration and large unexpected losses. The bank maintains conservative underwriting standards, and collateral agreements are used to secure a derivatives portfolio. The credit approval process involves a detailed risk assessment of each credit relevant counterparty. The rating methodologies are authorized for use within the advanced internal rating-based approach under applicable Basel rules. For credit portfolio management, two key credit risk measures are internal limits and credit exposure. Credit documentation with adequate terms and conditions are also in place. Netting and collateral agreements reduce credit exposure from derivatives and repo-style transactions. One of the key aspects of the overall risk management process involves risk transfers in various forms such as outright sales, portfolio hedging, and securitizations. Risk transfers are conducted by the respective business units and credit portfolio strategies group. The credit risk mitigating activities also include dedicated stress tests. The advanced internal rating approach is the most sophisticated approach within the regulatory framework for credit risk.

The market risk measurement metrics consist of VaR, stressed VaR, and the market risk standardized approach (MRSA).The different types of stress tests consist of portfolio stress testing, business-level stress testing, and event risk scenarios. Market risk is also managed by portfolio diversification and hedging activities. The economic capital for market risk measures the amount of capital needed to absorb severe unexpected losses over a period of 1 year.

In Deutsche Bank, operational risk is categorized as fraud risk, business continuity risk, regulatory compliance risk, information technology risk, outsourcing risk, and legal risk. The bank measures the regulatory and economic capital for operational risk using the internal advanced measurement approach (AMA). Day-to-day operational risk management activities are managed via key result indicators (KRIs) and self-assessment scores that focus on the business environment

Table 1.24 Financial Highlights 2008-2012 (Millions of Euros)					
	2008	**2009**	**2010**	**2011**	**2012**
Total assets	2,202,423	1,500,664	1,905,630	2,164,103	2,012,329
Loans	269,281	258,105	407,729	412,514	397,279
Total shareholder equity	30,703	36,647	48,819	53,390	54,003
Total noninterest income	1160	15,493	12,984	15,783	17,850
Net income	(3896)	4958	2330	4326	291
Basic EPS	(€6.87)	€7.21	€3.07	€4.45	€0.25
Cost/income ratio (%)	134.3	72	81.6	78.2	92.6
Core Tier 1 capital ratio (%)	7	8.7	8.7	9.5	11.4
Tier 1 capital ratio (%)	10.1	12.6	12.3	12.9	15.1
Source: Annual Reports					

and internal control factors. Stress testing is conducted on a regular basis to analyze the impact of extreme situations on capital and profit-and-loss accounts. Stress testing and scenario analysis play a vital role in the liquidity risk management framework. The Treasury function is responsible for management of the liquidity. The monthly stress test results are used to calibrate the short-term wholesale-funding profile limits. Table 1.24 gives the financial highlights of Deutsche Bank during the period 2008-2012.

REFERENCES

1. http://www.db.com
2. Annual Reports, Deutsche Reports

CASES ON MORTGAGE INSTITUTIONS AND CREDIT UNIONS

2.1 MORTGAGE INSTITUTIONS

2.1.1 FANNIE MAE

The Federal National Mortgage Association (FNMA), commonly called Fannie Mae, was established as a federal agency in 1938 and is the major source of residential mortgage credit in the US secondary market. The main function of Fannie Mae is to guarantee and purchase loans from mortgage lenders to facilitate people buying homes or refinancing purchases of homes. Fannie Mae's charter does not permit it to originate loans or lend money directly to consumers in the primary mortgage market. Instead, Fannie works with mortgage bankers, brokers, and other partners in the mortgage market, thereby ensuring that funds are lent to home buyers at affordable rates. Fannie Mae has three lines of businesses: the Single-Family, Multifamily, and Capital Markets. From January 2009 to June 2013, Fannie Mae provided $3.7 trillion in mortgage credit, which consisted of 3.1 million home purchases and 11.4 million in mortgage refinancing. Fannie Mae also facilitated financing for more than 1.9 million units of multifamily rental housing during the last 3-year period. The major activity of Fannie Mae is to securitize mortgage loans originated by lenders into Fannie Mae mortgage-backed securities, referred to as Fannie Mae MBS. Fannie Mae also purchases mortgage loans and mortgage-related securities.

Fannie Mae is playing an increasingly vital role in keeping the housing finance system liquid after the economic crisis of 2008. Fannie is supporting the home recovering process by helping families avoid foreclosure, which has accounted for 1.3 million homes since 2009. From 2009 to 2013, Fannie Mae refinanced more than 11.4 million mortgages, including loans refinanced through the Home Affordable Refinance Program (HARP).

2.1.1.1 Mortgage securitization

Fannie Mae promotes market liquidity by securitizing mortgage loans and Fannie Mae MBS are issued. The securitization of single-family and multifamily mortgage loans are categorized into lender swap transactions and portfolio securitizations. In lender swap transactions, mortgage lenders that operate in the primary mortgage market exchange pools of mortgage loans with similar characteristics for Fannie Mae MBS. The mortgage loans obtained in these lender swap transactions are placed in a trust separately from assets. On behalf of the trust, Fannie makes monthly distributions to Fannie Mae MBS certificate holders from the principal and interest payments on the underlying mortgage loans. In contrast, portfolio securitization transactions involve creating and issuing Fannie Mae MBS using mortgage loans and mortgage-related securities, which are held in Fannie Mae's mortgage portfolio. Fannie Mae serves as trustee for the MBS trusts, which are established for the sole purpose of holding mortgage loans separately from assets. The MBS trusts hold either single-family or multifamily mortgage loans or mortgage-related securities. In single-class MBS, investors receive principal and interest payments in proportion to their percentage of ownership of the MBS issuance. In multiclass MBS, which include real estate mortgage investment conduits (REMICs), the cash flows on the underlying mortgage assets are divided into several classes of securities, each of which represents an undivided beneficial ownership in the assets of the related MBS trust. The related holder is entitled to specific cash flow. Each of the classes in a multiclass MBS may have a different coupon rate, average life, repayment sensitivity, or final maturity.

2.1.1.2 Business segments

The three business segments of Fannie Mae are Single-Family Credit Guaranty, Multifamily, and Capital Markets.

The Single-Family business unit provides funds to the mortgage market by acquiring single-family loans through lender swap transactions and purchase of loans in collaboration with the Capital Markets group. Single-Family business is also involved in the pricing and managing of credit risk of the single-family guaranty book of business, consisting of single mortgage loans of Fannie Mae MBS and single-family loans held in the mortgage portfolio. The primary revenues are the guarantee fees for managing credit risk. A single-family loan is secured by a property with four or fewer residential units. The Single-Family business and Capital Markets groups securitize and purchase conventional single-family fixed-rate or adjustable-rate, first-lien mortgages, mortgage-related securities backed by these types of loans, loans insured by the Federal Housing Administration (FHA) and loans guaranteed by the Department of Veteran Affairs (VA) and the Rural Development Housing Program of Department of Agriculture. Mortgage servicers play a key role in the effective implementation of homeownership assistance initiatives and loss mitigation activities. They are the primary point of contact for borrowers.

The Multifamily business provides mortgage market liquidity for properties with five or more residential units consisting of apartment communities, cooperative properties, seniors housing, and manufactured housing communities. The Multifamily business unit facilitates funding to the mortgage market primarily by securitizing multifamily mortgage loans into Fannie Mae MBS and purchasing multifamily mortgage loans. The business unit also provides credit enhancement for bonds issued by state and local housing finance authorities to finance multifamily housing. Financing structures are also offered to facilitate construction loans. The multifamily market consists of a number of lending sources, which includes commercial banks, investment banks, life insurance companies, FHA, state, and local housing finance agencies, and the GSEs. The average size of loans in a multifamily book of business is $5 million. In 2012, the business unit executed multifamily transactions with 33 lenders. Multifamily loans typically have terms of 5, 7, or 10 years with balloon payments due at maturity, unlike a standard 30-year single-family residential loan. To promote product standardization in the multifamily market, Fannie Mae introduced the Delegated and Underwriting Services (DUS) for acquiring individual multifamily loans. Under this model, DUS lenders are preapproved and are delegated the authority to underwrite and service loans on behalf of Fannie Mae.

The primary function of the Capital Markets group is to manage investment activity in mortgage-related assets and other interest-earning nonmortgage investments. The investments are funded through the proceeds from the issuance of debt securities in domestic and international capital markets. Activities undertaken to promote liquidity include whole loan conduit, early funding, REMICS structured securitization, and MBS trading. Whole loan conduit activities involve purchase of single-family loans principally for the purpose of securitizing them. In the early funding program, the group purchases whole loans on an accelerated basis, which allows lenders to receive quicker payment for whole loans and pools, which replenishes their funds and provides the flexibility to originate more mortgage loans. The Capital Markets group also issues structured Fannie Mae MBS. In MBS trading, the Capital Markets division enters into purchase and sale transactions of mortgage-backed securities called agency MBS issued by Fannie Mae, Freddie Mac, and Ginnie Mae. The Capital Markets group also engages in issue of single-class and multiclass Fannie Mae MBS through portfolio securitization and structured securitization involving third-party assets.

Fannie Mae offers innovative online tools such as KnowYourOptions.com, which provides a one-stop resource for people who intend to get a mortgage refinance, a mortgage, or rent a home. The major services of the resource are highlighted below.

2.1.1.2.1 Rent services

Fannie Mae is the leading provider of financing to the US rental housing market. Fannie Mae provides services for multiple types of rental housing, which range from apartments and condominiums to single-family and multifamily units. Housing options are also designed specifically for students, senior citizens, and low-income groups.

The Protecting Tenants at Foreclosure Act (PTFA) was created to assist tenants when landlords face the danger of foreclosure. Under this law, valid tenants are permitted to stay in the residence until the end of their lease term. In the case of a month-to-month lease, tenants must be provided at least 90 days' notice before the termination of their lease. Qualified renters who occupy a Fannie Mae home at the time of foreclosure are eligible for the Tenant in Place program. The program offers two types of leases: Sign a new lease and Keep your current lease. In Sign a new lease, eligible renters who stay in a rental home owned by Fannie Mae that has been foreclosed are offered a new lease. The Fannie Mae lease options include month-to-month or term leases at market rate rent. In the current lease option, certain tenants who have the right to remain in the home until the lease period may be eligible for financial assistance for relocation. The rental rates under the new lease are market rental rates given the size and condition of the property subject to any legal rent control guidelines. Fannie Mae manages the property through a real estate broker or a property management company.

2.1.1.2.2 Buy services

Fannie Mae provides buying services to those interested in buying homes. Through the portal HomePath.com, Fannie Mae shows properties for sale for first-time home buyers. Fannie Mae also repairs many of its HomePath properties. Fannie Mae offers a special program called First Look, which permits home buyers who plan to occupy the property as a primary residence the opportunity to bid and purchase foreclosed properties 15 days before they are made available to investors.

2.1.1.2.3 Refinance services

In a refinance, the new mortgage with new terms, interest rate, and monthly payment replaces the current mortgage. Refinancing facilitates lower monthly payments and shortens the term of the loan, especially useful in an environment of high mortgage interest rates or adjustable-rate loans (ARMS). HARP is a federal refinance program that enables eligible borrowers with little to no equity in their homes to take advantage of low interest rates and other financing benefits. Fannie Mae works with a large number of lenders offering a variety of refinancing options.

2.1.1.2.4 Modify services
The Home Affordable Modification Program (HAMP) is designed to help homeowners who are facing financing difficulties. The loan undertaken by the homeowner is modified to make the monthly mortgage payment no more than 31% of gross (pretax) monthly income. In HAMP, modifications in mortgage loan type include changing an ARM to a fixed-rate mortgage or extending the term of the mortgage.

2.1.1.2.5 Avoid foreclosure services
Avoid foreclosure schemes involve options to stay in the home, leave the home, and reverse mortgages. The possible options under the stay in your home scheme include refinance, repayment plans, forbearance, modifications, and deed for lease schemes. The repayment plan is an agreement with the homeowner and mortgage company that allows the homeowner to pay the past due amount added to current mortgage payments over a specified period of time. Forbearance involves an offer by the mortgage company to temporarily suspend or reduce monthly mortgage payments for a specified period of time. Modification involves an agreement between the homeowner and the mortgage company to change the original terms of the mortgage, such as payment amount, length of loan, or interest rate. A deed for lease scheme involves the transfer of ownership of the home to the mortgage company, which is called deed-in-lieu of foreclosure, in exchange for a release from the mortgage and payments.

The possible leave home options are short sales, mortgage release, and foreclosure. A short sale involves the sale of a home for less than the balance remaining on the mortgage in agreement with the mortgage company. In a mortgage release, ownership of the property is transferred to the owner of the mortgage in exchange for a release from the loan and payments. Foreclosure is the legal process by which the mortgage company obtains ownership of the home. Foreclosure occurs when a homeowner defaults on payments or violates the terms of their mortgage loan.

In a reverse mortgage, the homeowner receives money from the mortgage company in the form of borrowing against the value of the home through a reverse mortgage. The payments along with accrued interest increase the loan's balance and decrease the equity in the property. Reverse mortgages are insured by the FHA as part of its Home Equity Conversion Mortgage (HECM).

2.1.1.3 Strategy
Fannie Mae is undergoing significant transformation. The Federal Housing Finance Agency's (FHFA's) strategic plan for Fannie Mae and Freddie Mac's conservatorships have identified three strategic goals. This plan involves building a new infrastructure for the secondary mortgage market, contracting Fannie Mae and Freddie Mac's dominant presence on the marketplace, and simplifying and shrinking their operations. The third goal involves maintaining foreclosure prevention activities and credit availability for new and refinanced mortgages. According to US Federal Reserve statistics, the total residential mortgage debt outstanding was $10.8 trillion in 2012, of which $9.9 trillion was single-family mortgage debt. Fannie Mae has an agreement with the US Department of Treasury in which Fannie Mae provides liquidity and stability to the housing and mortgage markets for capital injections from Treasury. Fannie Mae has provided approximately $3.3 trillion in liquidity to the housing market since the economic crisis. The agreement has covenants that restrict Fannie Mae's business activities. The bank was the largest single issuer of mortgage-related securities in the secondary market. Single-family loans acquired since 2009

constituted approximately 66% of the single-family guaranty book of business in 2012. Housing activity improved in 2012 compared to depressed levels in 2011. In 2008, the FHFA was appointed as conservator, which is a statutory process designed to preserve and conserve the assets and property of Fannie Mae.

2.1.1.4 Risk management

The enterprise risk governance structure consists of a board of directors, chief risk officers, and an Enterprise Risk Management division. Fannie manages risk using three lines of defense. The first line of defense is the active management of risk by the business unit. The second is the Enterprise Risk Management unit, which is responsible for ensuring compliance with risk framework. And the third line of defense is internal audit.

The two types of credit risk are mortgage credit risk and institutional counterparty risk. The housing crisis has led to this type of risk. Credit risk in a mortgage credit book arises when the mortgage assets are held in connection with the creation of Fannie Mae MBS. Single-family mortgage credit risk is managed through the four primary components of (1) the acquisition and servicing policies along with underwriting and servicing standards, (2) portfolio diversification and monitoring, (3) management of problem loans, and (4) REO (real estate owned) management. More focus is placed on loans with a higher risk of default, which includes loans associated with higher mark-to-market LTV (loan to value) ratios, loans to borrowers with lower FICO credit scores, and certain higher-risk loan product categories, such as Alt-A loans. Desktop Underwriter, a proprietary automated underwriting system, measures credit risk by assessing the primary risk factors of a mortgage and evaluating loans that are purchased or securitized. Loans with underwriting defects are identified early in their life cycle and feedback is provided to lenders, which may lead to systemic improvements in the loan origination process. Diversification within the single-family mortgage credit book of business by product type and loan characteristics is an important factor that influences credit quality. The key loan attributes are LTV ratio and product type. LTV is a strong predictor of credit performance. Regarding product type, adjustable-rate mortgages have exhibited higher default rates than fixed-rate mortgages.

Problem loan management strategies are primarily focused on reducing defaults to avoid losses. Various types of home retention solutions, including loan modifications, repayment plans, forbearances, and foreclosure alternatives, including short sales and deeds-in-lieu of foreclosure, are used. By 2012, about 13 Mortgage Help Centers had been established to accelerate response time for struggling homeowners with loans. Fannie Mae works with servicers to implement home retention and foreclosure prevention initiatives.

In its Multifamily Business unit, Fannie Mae uses various types of credit enhancement arrangements for multifamily loans, including lender risk sharing, lender repurchase agreements, pool insurance, subordinated participation in mortgage loans or structured pools, cash and letter of credit collateral agreements, and cross-collateralization/cross-default provisions. Among these, the most prevalent form of credit enhancement is lender risk sharing. Lenders in the DUS program typically share losses of up to 5% of the unpaid principal balance of the loan and share in the remaining losses up to a prescribed limit or share up to one third of credit losses on an equal basis.

Fannie Mae is exposed to institutional counterparty risk because of mortgage sellers or servicers who sell the loans to Fannie Mae or service the loans in Fannie Mae's investment portfolio. Other institutional counterparties include third-party providers of credit enhancement, custodial depository institutions, and derivatives counterparties.

Pool mortgage insurance coverage is also used to mitigate credit risk. As of 2012, six mortgage insurers, PMI, Triad, RMIC, Genworth, Radian, and MGIC, have provided a combined $70.3 billion in mortgage insurance coverage for Single-Family business.

One of the major market risks faced by Fannie is interest rate risk. Fannie Mae uses an integrated interest rate risk management strategy that allows for informed risk taking within predefined corporate risk limits. The bank actively manages interest rate risk by asset selection and structuring, which involves identifying or structuring mortgage assets with attractive prepayments and other characteristics. Other methods involve issuing a broad range of callable and noncallable debt instruments. Interest rate derivatives are also used to manage interest rate risk. The interest rate derivatives used are interest rate swaps, interest rate option contracts, foreign currency swaps, and futures. The interest rate risk is measured using fair value sensitivity of net portfolio to changes in interest rate levels and slope of yield curve and duration gap.

Liquidity risk management involves forecasting funding requirements, maintaining sufficient capacity to meet needs based on ongoing assessment of financial market liquidity, and maintaining capital regulatory requirements. The liquidity position is adversely affected by factors such as actions taken by the US Treasury, Federal Reserve, and various legislations. According to the FHFA, a portfolio of highly liquid securities to cover a minimum of 30 calendar days of net cash needs to be maintained by Fannie Mae.

The operational risk framework is based on the OFHEO/FHFA Enterprise Guidance on Operational Risk Management. This business resiliency program is designed to provide reasonable assurance for the continuity of critical business operations in the event of disruptions caused by the loss of facilities, technology, or personnel. The antifraud program provides a framework for managing nonmortgage-related fraud risk. Table 2.1 provides the financial highlights of Fannie Mae during the period 2008-2012.

REFERENCES

1. http://www.fanniemae.com
2. Annual Reports of Fannie Mae

Table 2.1 Financial Highlights 2008-2012 (Millions of US Dollars)					
	2008	2009	2010	2011	2012
Net revenues	17,436	22,494	17,493	20,444	22,988
Net income/loss	(58,707)	(71,969)	(14,014)	(16,855)	17,224
Investments in Fannie MBS	234,250	229,169	30,226	24,274	16,683
Other agency MBS	35,440	43,905	19,951	16,744	13,361
Total assets	912,404	869,141	3,221,972	3,211,484	3,222,422
Total nonperforming loans	119,955	222,064	253,579	251,949	250,897
Net interest yield	1.03%	1.65%	0.51%	0.60%	0.68%
Source: Fannie Mae Reports					

2.1.2 **FREDDIE MAC**

The Federal Home Loan Mortgage Corporation (FHLMC), also known as Freddie Mac, was established by Congress in 1970 to provide liquidity, stability, and affordability to the US housing market. Freddie Mac is regulated by the FHFA.[1] In 2008, the FHFA placed Freddie Mac into a conservatorship. The other regulatory agencies are the SEC, HUD, and Treasury. The US Department of Treasury has approval authority over issuance of notes, debentures, and new types of mortgage-related securities by Freddie Mac. The three lines of business are the Single-Family Credit Guarantee Business for home loans, Multifamily Business for apartment financing, and Investment Business for investment activity in mortgages and mortgage-related securities. Since 2009, Freddie Mac has financed 1.8 million family purchase borrowers, 7.2 million in refinancing, and provided 1.4 million units of multifamily rental housing. Freddie Mac focuses on the recovery of the housing market and the US economy. The primary objectives of Freddie Mac are to provide credit for mortgages, maintain foreclosure prevention activities, and minimize credit losses. Freddie Mac provides support for borrowers with a variety of conforming mortgage products, which include 30-year fixed-rate mortgages. Freddie Mac, Fannie Mae, and Ginnie Mae collectively guaranteed more than 90% of the single-family conforming mortgages during 2011-2012. In 2012, Freddie Mac purchased or issued guarantee commitments for single-family conforming mortgage loans that amounted to $426.8 billion, representing approximately 2 million homes. During the period 2009-2012, Freddie Mac helped about 785,000 borrowers avoid foreclosure. Freddie Mac's charter, like Fannie Mae's, does not permit it to originate mortgage loans or lend money directly to consumers in the primary mortgage market.

2.1.2.1 Business divisions

Based on types of business activities, the operations of Freddie Mac are categorized as Single-Family Credit Guarantee Business, Multifamily, and Investments.

2.1.2.1.1 Single-Family Credit Guarantee

The Single-Family Credit Guarantee segment funds millions of homes using mortgage securitization. In this business segment, single-family mortgage loans originated by sellers/servicers in the primary mortgage market are purchased. A mortgage securitization process is used to package the mortgage loans into guaranteed mortgage-related securities. This business segment guarantees the payment of principal and interest on mortgage-related securities in exchange for management and guarantee fees. Customers in the Single-Family guarantee segment are predominantly lenders in the primary mortgage market, such as mortgage banking companies, commercial banks, savings banks, credit unions, and more. In 2012, three mortgage lenders (Wells Fargo Bank, US Bank, and JPMorgan Chase Bank) each accounted for 10% or more of single-family mortgages. The Single-Family Credit Guarantee segment securitizes single-family mortgages, which are secured by one to four family properties. The segment earnings consist of management and guarantee fee revenues.

The Single-Family Credit Guarantee unit issues mortgage-related securities such as participation securities (PCs), REMICs, other structured securities, and other guarantee transactions. PCs are single pass-through securities, that represent undivided beneficial interests in trusts that hold pools of mortgages purchased by the Single-Family segment. Multiclass securities divide all of the cash flows of the

---

[1]The FHFA is an independent agency of the federal government responsible for oversight of the operations of Freddie Mac, Fannie Mae, and the FHLBs.

underlying mortgage-related securities into two or more classes based on investment criteria and portfolio requirements of different investors. Different classes of securities have varying maturities, payment priorities, and coupons. In single-family PCs, the mortgage loans of customers are exchanged for PCs in guarantor swap transactions. Institutional investors (e.g., pension funds, insurance companies, securities dealers, money managers, and REITs) purchase the PCs of Freddie Mac.

REMICs and other structured securities represent beneficial interests in pools of PCs and/or certain other types of mortgage-related assets. Other guarantee transactions involve the issue of mortgage-related securities to third parties in exchange for non-Freddie Mac mortgage-related securities. REMICs issue single-class and multiclass securities.

2.1.2.1.2 Multifamily business

Multifamily businesses involve a network of lenders to finance apartment buildings. Most loan acquisitions are financed through mortgage securitization. Multifamily segments have investments in securitization, guarantee activities in multifamily mortgage loans, and securities. Unlike family borrowers, multifamily borrowers are property developers and/or managers. The primary Freddie Mac guaranteed mortgage-related security is the single-class PC. The primary business model in the multifamily segment is to purchase held-for-sale multifamily loans for aggregation and then securitize them through multifamily K certificates. The multifamily segment conducts business in the US residential mortgage market and global securities market subject to the direction of the conservator FHFA. A significant portion of multifamily mortgage loans is acquired from large sellers or servicers such as CBRE Capital Markets and Berkadia Commercial Mortgage. Earnings in this segment consist of interest earned on assets related to multifamily investment activities and management and guarantee fee income.

2.1.2.1.3 Investments

Freddie Mac's Investment segment consists of activities related to investment, funding, and hedging activities. Freddie Mac invests in mortgage-related securities and single-family-performing mortgage loans, which are funded by other debt issuances and hedged using derivatives. The debt securities of the investment segment are bought by insurance companies, money managers, central banks, depository institutions, and pension funds. This segment uses a buy-and-hold strategy in mortgage-related securities and single-family-performing loans.

2.1.2.2 Strategy

The FHFA, like Fannie Mae, has identified three strategic goals for Freddie Mac. These involve building new infrastructures for the secondary mortgage market, contracting both Freddie Mac's and Fannie Mae's dominant presence in the marketplace, and maintaining foreclosure prevention activities and credit availability for new and refinanced mortgages.

Freddie programs are designed to help in housing recovery, promote liquidity and housing affordability, and expand foreclosure prevention efforts. The role of a conservator is to preserve and conserve the company's assets and property. Loan workout activities are a key component of the loss-mitigation strategy for managing and resolving troubled assets.

2.1.2.3 Risk management

Investment and credit guarantee activities expose the institution to three broad categories of credit and market risk in the form of interest risk and operational risk. The investment activity of Freddie Mac is significantly limited under the purchase agreement and the FHFA, and hence, there is a greater reliance on guarantee activities to generate revenues. Freddie Mac is subject to two types of credit risk: mortgage credit risk and institutional credit risk. The institution is primarily exposed to mortgage credit risk with respect to single-family and multifamily loans that are owned or guaranteed. Credit risk arises in as much as Freddie holds mortgage assets or has guaranteed mortgages in connection with the issuance of a Freddie Mac mortgage-related security or other guarantee commitment. Institutional credit risk arises when a counterparty in a business contract fails to meet its obligations with Freddie.

Single-family mortgage credit risk is influenced by factors such as the credit profile of the borrower, documentation level, number of borrowers, the purpose of the mortgage, occupancy type, the LTV ratio[2] of the loan, and other variables such as unemployment rates and home prices. Credit risk also arises because of significant exposure to the subprime, Alt-A, and option ARM loans that back nonagency mortgage-related securities. During the period of 2005–2007, financial institutions substantially increased their origination and securitization of higher risk mortgage loans such as subprime, option ARM, interest only, and Alt-A loans. Freddie Mac's condition also worsened due to exposure to these instruments.

Freddie Mac also faces institutional counterparty risk due to various counterparties, including mortgage sellers or services, mortgage insurers, derivative counterparties, mortgage investors, and title insurers. Single-family mortgages with LTV ratios above 80% at the time of purchase have to be covered by specified credit enhancements or participation interests.

The single-family loss mitigation strategy emphasizes early intervention by servicers in delinquent mortgages and provides alternatives to foreclosures. The loan workouts include forbearance agreements, repayment plans, loan modifications, short sales, and deed-in-lieu-of-foreclosure transactions.

In 2012, Freddie Mac helped approximately 169,000 home buyers either stay in their homes or sell their properties and avoid foreclosures through various workout programs, such as HAMP. In 2012, Freddie Mac completed 105,000 foreclosures. Under a 2005 agreement with the FHA, the institution prepares credit loss sensitivity. Institutional counterparty risk increased in magnitude due to industry consolidation and counterparty failures. Freddie Mac is exposed to institutional credit risk on account of exchange-traded derivatives as well as over-the-counter (OTC) derivatives. Freddie Mac is an active user of exchange-traded derivatives such as Treasury and Eurodollar futures.

Institutional credit risk also arises due to the potential insolvency of, or nonperformance by, mortgage insurers that insure single-family mortgages that Freddie purchases or guarantees. The exchange-traded and OTC derivatives of Freddie are exposed to institutional credit risk. Institutional credit risk is managed by a number of methods such as review of external rating analyses, implementing new standards for approving new derivatives counterparties, managing diversification mix among counterparties, master netting agreements, and collateral agreements along with stress testing to evaluate potential exposures under different adverse-market scenarios.

Freddie Mac uses master netting and collateral agreements to reduce credit risk exposure to active OTC derivatives counterparties for interest-rate swaps, option-based derivatives, and foreign-currency swaps. Liquidity management policies stipulate that the institution must maintain funds to cover maximum cash liquidity needs for at least 35 calendar days, assuming no access to the short- or long-term unsecured debt market.

Investments in mortgage loans and mortgage-related securities lead to exposure to interest rate and other market risk. Prepayment risk arises from the uncertainty as to when borrowers will

---

[2]Loan to value ratio—The amount of mortgage amount to the appraised value of a property.

pay outstanding principal balances of mortgage loans and mortgage-related securities. As a result, a potential mismatch exists between the timing of cash flow related to assets and payment of cash flow related to liabilities used to fund the assets. Credit guarantee activities also expose Freddie Mac to interest rate risk, as changes in the interest rate risk can cause fluctuations in the fair value of existing credit guarantees. Other market-related risks are duration risk, convexity risk, yield curve risk, volatility risk, basis risk, and foreign exchange risk. Duration risk arises as a result of the financial instrument's price sensitivity to changes in interest rates along the yield curve. Each financial instrument's duration is computed by applying an interest rate shock both upward and downward to the LIBOR curve and then evaluating the impact on the instrument's fair value. Convexity is the measure of how much a financial instrument's duration changes as interest changes. Volatility is the risk that a homeowner's prepayment option will gain or lose as the expected volatility of future interest-rate changes. Volatility risk arises from a prepayment risk, which is inherent in mortgages or mortgage-related securities. The basis risk is the risk that the interest rates in different market sectors will not move in tandem and adversely affect the fair value of net assets.

The risk management strategy for market risk mitigation involves matching the duration characteristics of assets and liabilities. Interest rate risk is mitigated by the use of a wide variety of callable and noncallable debt products. Duration risk and convexity risk are managed through asset selection and structuring. Option-based derivatives are used to manage prepayment risks. Option-based derivatives consist of call swaptions, which tend to increase in value when interest rates decline, and put swaptions, which tend to increase in value as interest rates increase. Interest rate swaps are also used to manage interest rate risk through rebalancing, in which the effective terms of the portfolio are changed.

Freddie Mac also faces legal risk. In 2011, the FHFA, as conservator for Freddie Mac and Fannie Mae, filed lawsuits against 18 corporate families of financial institutions seeking to recover losses and damages sustained by Freddie Mac and Fannie Mae as a result of their investments in certain residential nonagency mortgage-related securities issued or sold. Table 2.2 provides the financial highlights of Freddie Mac during the period 2010-2012. Table 2.3 provides the earning highlights of the different segments of Freddie Mac.

REFERENCES

1. Annual Reports Freddie Mac

Table 2.2 Financial Highlights 2010-2012 (Millions of US Dollars)			
	2010	**2011**	**2012**
Total mortgage loans	95,425	86,282	74,049
Total interest income	109,956	99,140	84,718
Net interest income	16,856	18,397	17,611
Net income/loss	(14,026)	(5266)	10,982
Total assets		2,147,216	1,989,856
Source: Annual Reports			

Table 2.3   Summary of Segment Earnings 2010-2012 (Millions of US Dollars)

Segments	2010	2011	2012
Investments	1251	3366	8212
Single-Family Guarantee	(16,256)	(10,000)	(164)
Multifamily	965	1319	2146
All others	15	49	788
Total	(14,025)	(5266)	10,982

2.1.3 GINNIE MAE

The Government National Mortgage Association (Ginnie Mae) has been an important cornerstone of the US housing finance system since its establishment in 1968. It was created as a wholly owned government corporation in the US Department of Housing and Urban Development for raising mortgage loans that were insured by other government agencies. Ginnie Mae remains the primary financing mechanism for all government-insured or government-guaranteed mortgage loans. Ginnie Mae offers traditional mortgage-backed pass-through securities and multiclass securities programs under REMICs and Ginnie Mae Platinum Securities. Ginnie Mae MBS provides funding for loans from the FHA, VA, and US Department of Agriculture (USDA) loans.

In 1970, Ginnie Mae introduced the first mortgage-backed security (MBS) used as a financial tool to raise funds from investors worldwide. The Ginnie Mae securities are the only securities that are explicitly backed by the full faith and credit of the US government. The main role of Ginnie Mae in the housing finance system is to guarantee principal and interest payments on securities and loans. Ginnie Mae does not create, buy, or sell mortgage loans and securities. Lenders have the complete responsibility for any servicing decisions. The basic difference between Ginnie Mae and other mortgage institutions such as Freddie Mac and Fannie Mae is that Ginnie Mae is a wholly owned government corporation, while the latter two are shareholder owned. Ginnie Mae makes explicit guarantees to investors, whereas Freddie and Fannie make implicit guarantees to lenders and investors. Ginnie Mae makes only government-insured loans, while Freddie and Fannie make conventional loans. By 2012, Ginnie Mae had guaranteed $1.7 trillion in MBS, thus providing housing opportunities for 7.1 million households since the subprime mortgage crisis of 2008. Ginnie Mae absorbs losses only after all other mortgage safeguards such as homeowner equity, mortgage insurance, and lender resources are exhausted, thereby minimizing risk to tax payers.

2.1.3.1 Major programs of Ginnie Mae

Ginnie Mae's HECM securities program is aimed as a financial solution to provide capital and liquidity for FHA-insured reverse mortgages meant for senior citizens. HECM loans are pooled into HECM mortgages-backed securities (HMBS) within the Ginnie Mae II MBS program. In 2012, the number of participations of the funded portion of HECM loans was approximately 2.018 million. The Manufactured Housing Program, insured by the FHA, provides guarantees for mortgage loans for the purchase of new or used manufactured homes. Ginnie Mae played a countercyclical role for housing finance in the secondary mortgage markets during the economic crisis.

Under the multifamily program, Ginnie Mae has guaranteed more than $165.2 billion in multifamily mortgage-backed securities, which provided financing to more than 2.7 million multifamily housing units.

Most Ginnie Mae securities are backed by single-family mortgages, which are originated through the FHA, VA, and the US Department of Agriculture's Rural Development and Public and Indian Housing programs. Ginnie Mae's single-family program is the conduit for government mortgage lending to capital markets all over the world.

Ginnie Mae's primary sources of cash are MBS and multiclass guaranty fee income, as well as commitment fee income.

2.1.3.2 Products

Platinum securities are multiclass securities that are formed by combining Ginnie Mae MBS pools with uniform coupons and original terms to maturity into a single certificate. The platinum securities are used for structured financings, repurchase transactions, and general trading. Smaller pools of Ginnie Mae can be combined into new or existing MBS, thereby creating larger Ginnie Mae platinum pools. Ginnie Mae provides guarantees for the timely payment of principal and interest on each Ginnie Mae Platinum pool, which is backed by the full faith and credit of the US government.

REMICs are multiclass securities that facilitate investors with different risk reward preferences, investment times, and asset liability management requirements to purchase MBS. These REMICs provide direct principal and interest payments from underlying mortgage-backed securities to classes with different principal balances, interest rates, prepayment characteristics, and final maturities.

Stripped mortgage-backed securities (SMBS) are also multiclass securities that represent interest in separate Ginnie Mae SMBS trusts. The timely payment of principal and interest on each class of SMBS is guaranteed by Ginnie Mae. SMBS consists of fully modified pass-through mortgage-backed securities that guarantee timely payment of principal and interest in accordance with various Ginnie Mae programs. The trust formed for each issue of SMBS is classified as the Grantor Trust.

Single-class securities consist of Ginnie Mae I and Ginnie Mae II. Ginnie Mae I MBS are modified pass-through mortgage securities in which the registered investors receive separate principal and interest payments on each of their certificates. These Ginnie Mae single-family pools are one of the most heavily traded MBS products. Single-family Ginnie pools have a 50 basis point (0.5%) guaranty and servicing fee. Ginnie Mae I also allows the securitization of multifamily mortgages. Ginnie Mae II MBS are modified pass-through mortgage securities, and the holders receive an aggregate principal and interest payment from a central paying agent. Under this program, multiple-issuer as well as single-issuer pools are permitted. Ginnie Mae II also permits securitization of ARMs. Ginnie Mae II MBS have a central paying and transfer agent involved in the collection of payments from all issuers.

Special initiatives involve the Servicemember's Civil Relief Act as well as targeted lending initiatives. Under the Civil Relief Act, Ginnie Mae will make payments of interest on pooled loans backing mortgage-backed securities to an issuer for interest in excess of 6% for payments. This targeted lending initiative was aimed at attracting more mortgage lending to traditionally underserved communities.

2.1.3.3 Risk management

Ginnie Mae programs regularly evaluate issuers and their performance in key areas of financial health, portfolio quality, onsite compliance field review, and insurance matching for mitigating risks. Financial health is analyzed through examining the issuer's net worth, liquidity, and profitability.

Table 2.4   Financial Highlights 2010-2012 (Millions of US Dollars)

	2010	2011	2012
Funds with US Treasury	6650.50	7210.3	7075.5
US government securities	3551.20	2126.80	2113.60
MBS program income	742.90	856.50	1165.1
Total revenues	1011.9	1064.6	1246.60
Total assets	17,063.3	18,851.10	23,729.6
Capital adequacy ratio	1.47%	1.30%	1.23%

Source: Annual Reports

Portfolio quality is monitored through early payment defaults, origination comparison ratios, and the like. Onsite compliance reviews test issuer and document custodian compliance with program requirements. Insurance matching via an automated verification process ensures insurance exists for all pooled loans. Operational risk is managed through the comprehensive program Contact Assessment Reviews (CARs). These reviews assess contractor compliance with the terms and scope of their contracts. In 2012, about 12 CARs were completed, covering a range of contracts that involved the institution's operations (e.g., master subservicing, pool processing, and field reviews). Ginnie Mae uses control structures such as enterprise risk policy, delegation of authority, and lean six sigma to enhance risk mitigation and control. Ginnie Mae manages internal operational risks using a combination of management oversight and technology. Table 2.4 shows the financial highlights of Ginnie Mae during the 3-year period 2010-2012.

REFERENCES

1. http://www.ginniemae.gov
2. Annual Reports 2012

2.2 THRIFT INSTITUTIONS—CREDIT UNIONS
2.2.1 NAVY FEDERAL CREDIT UNION

The Navy Federal Credit Union was established in 1933. The credit union has over 4 million members and $6 billion in reserves. The National Credit Union Administration (NCUA) insures savings up to $250,000 and IRA funds up to $250,000. The Navy Federal Union does not engage in subprime mortgage lending. The Navy Credit Union's business continuity plan is aimed at ensuring employee safety, safeguarding credit union assets, and member equity. The credit union has more than 50,000 ATMs throughout the world.

2.2.1.1 Products and services
2.2.1.1.1 Loans
Different types of loans such as mortgages, equity, motorcycle, boat, and collateral are provided by the Navy Federal Credit Union.

Different types of fixed-rate mortgages are offered for military personnel. These mortgages offer 100% financing. The fixed-rate mortgages offer 15- and 30-year terms with fixed monthly payments. Navy Federal services the entire life of the loan. VA mortgages are fixed-term mortgages guaranteed by the VA, which provides 100% financing for eligible veterans. Active Duty Choice Mortgages are fixed-term mortgages exclusively for active-duty members. HomeBuyers Choice Mortgages provide 100% financing for first-time home buyers. In this category, jumbo loan amounts are available up to $1 million. Refinance options are also available under this scheme. FHA mortgages, which are insured by the FHA, are meant for first-time home buyers who seek low down payments. FHA loans require a 3.5% down payment. FHA loans are also subject to an upfront mortgage insurance premium of 1.75% of the loan amount. Both fixed-rate and adjustable-rate mortgages are available under the FHA loan category. The Navy Federal Adjustable Mortgage begins with a low constant rate, then adjusts upward or downward regularly according to an index. Private mortgage insurance (PMI) is required if the loan to value ratio is over 80%. Other loans include interest-only loans, which provide the flexibility to delay the repayment of principal for 10 years. Fixed-rate and adjustable-rate interest-only loans are used for primary residences and second homes.

Equity loans consist of different loan types, including fixed-rate equity loans, interest-only fixed-rate loans, home equity lines of credit, and interest-only home equity lines of credit.

Interest-only fixed-rate loans begin with low interest-only payments, which then move to principal and interest payments starting in the sixth year. In home equity lines of credit, payments remain low during the 20-year draw time, thereby permitting the borrower to repay only the accumulated interest.

2.2.1.1.2 Checking and savings services
The Navy Federal Credit Union provides a number of checking and savings services such as basic savings, mobile banking, money market savings, IRA, Special EasyStartSM certificates, mobile and scan deposits. Mobile and scan deposits enable members to deposit personal and business checks safely and securely from anywhere with access to only a mobile device or scanner. In education savings, earnings are tax free if they are used for education expenses.

2.2.1.1.3 Credit cards
The credit cards offered by the Navy Federal Credit Union include cashRewards, Gorewards, Visa signature flagship rewards, nRewards, Platinum, and nRewards Secured. The debit card is the Visa check card. The Navy Federal Visa Gift card are other cards offered. The Visa Buxx card is a reloadable prepaid card for teens. Parents can load money onto Visa Buxx online or by phone.

2.2.1.1.4 Online and mobile banking
Mobile banking provides services with features of Android, iPhone, mobile web, and text banking.

2.2.1.1.5 Business services
Business services include checking and savings, loans, credit cards, retirement, insurance, and commercial real estate. Retirement and insurance services include 401(k) profit-sharing plans, Group Health-SMO, PPO, dental coverage, vision plans, and short-term health plans.

2.2.1.1.6 Investment and insurance
The Navy Federal Financial Group provides advisory services for investments in mutual funds, stocks, bonds, and annuities. The group also provides advisory services related to financial planning in ar-

Table 2.5   Financial Highlights June 2013 (Millions of US Dollars)

Assets	
Consumer loans	11,061.042
Mortgage loans	16,213.264
Credit card loans	7292.457
Home equity loans	676.170
Business loans	216.192
Total assets	54,442.042
Total interest income loans	1172.292
Net income	438.908

Source: Annual Reports

eas such as retirement planning, education planning, 401(k) rollovers, and TSP rollovers. The Navy Financial Group also offers life and accident insurance products. Trust services of Navy Federal deal with estate and financial planning. Table 2.5 gives the financial highlights of the Navy Federal Credit Union as of June 2013.

REFERENCES

1. http://www.navyfederal.org

2.2.2 STATE EMPLOYEES' CREDIT UNION

The State Employees' Credit Union (SECU) was established in 1937 to help North Carolina's state and public employees and families. The credit union was organized under the state laws of North Carolina. The cooperative model of credit unions is based on voluntary membership, democratic member control, members' economic participation, autonomy and independence, education, training, and information. The SECU serves approximately 1.8 million members with $25 billion in assets through 244 branch locations, 1100 no surcharge CashPoint ATMs, 24/7 contact centers, a voice response service, online member access, and convenient mobile access. SECU provides a variety of services and products, including checking and money market share accounts, share term certificates, individual retirement accounts, lending products, and financial advisory services. All services are available in SECU branches located in all 100 North Carolina counties.

2.2.2.1 Products and services
2.2.2.1.1 Loans
Loans provided by SECU consist of auto loans, mortgages, and personal loans. In the auto loans category, SECU provides Guaranteed Asset Protection (GAP) coverage on new vehicle loans for a flat fee of $250. GAP coverage is basically a debt cancellation product that aims to cover the difference between the insurance settlement amount and the outstanding loan balance if the vehicle is involved in a total loss claim. The Auto Power Program offers fixed-rate financing for new vehicles and finances up

to 100% of the manufacturer's suggested retail price with an additional 10% to cover other purchase-related expenses such as taxes and extended warranties. The credit union offers fixed-rate financing for used vehicles and also provides vehicle loan refinancing.

2.2.2.1.2 Mortgages

The credit union offers mortgage such as ARMs, biweekly mortgages, deed of trust and second mortgages, fixed-rate mortgages, and more. Second mortgages are used for debt consolidation or home improvement, which are usually secured by a primary residence, vacation home, or rental property. The SECU offers fixed-rate mortgages to purchase or refinance primary residences located in North Carolina. The maximum loan amount and interest rate depends on factors such as purpose of loan, type of mortgage, number of dwelling units, and occupancy status. Home equity lines of credit are secured open-ended loans in which borrowers can borrow up to 90% of the value of their home less the amount owed on their present mortgage. The SECU Mortgage Assistance Program is intended to help members who are having problems making their SECU mortgage payments. The program offers options of monthly payment alternatives, mortgage loan extensions, mortgage loan modifications, or refinancing. The credit union offers reverse mortgage loans in which the credit union provides cash to borrowers in the form of fixed monthly disbursements or single lump sum disbursements against prime residences. The amounts of lump sum only distributions are limited to the payoff of existing mortgages and other debt, medical expenses, and home improvement. The credit union also offers special mortgage programs such as first time home buyer's mortgages for members who have not owned a home in the past 3 years. The program also provides construction loans, manufactured home loans, and mortgage credit certificates.

Personal loans offered include variable rate open-ended unsecured loans, salary advance loans, share secured loans, student loans, and term notes.

2.2.2.1.3 Cards and accounts

The cards that SECU offers include CashPoints Global (CPG), which is a noninterest-bearing controlled spending account with electronic access through CPG. The credit union provides two types of debit cards, CashPoints and Visa Check. Credit cards include Visa credit cards and gift cards.

The SECU offers the Coverdell Education Savings Account (CESA) as a method of saving for elementary, secondary, and higher education expenses. The credit union also offers a health savings account (HAS) as a tax-deductible savings account with tax-free withdrawals for qualified medical expenses. Holiday cash accounts, individual retirement accounts, money market share accounts, and share-term certificate (STC) accounts are other deposit accounts offered by the SECU. The FAT CAT program promotes saving habits among children. The Zard program is geared toward teens. The credit union offers an Off to College/Off to Work program to members who are 18-25 who are entering college or the workforce. The Golden Circle Club account program caters to the needs of people over 50 years of age.

2.2.2.1.4 Estates, insurance, investments, and trusts

The SECU provides an Estate Planning Essential Program that allows members to meet with participating attorneys and have estate planning documents prepared at a predetermined price. The credit union has a partnership with AAA insurance to provide various personal insurance products. The credit union also provides term and whole life insurance and Medicare supplement plans. The SECU also provides investment accounts in mutual funds and offers revocable living trusts and special needs trusts.

Table 2.6   Financial Highlights (Millions of US Dollars)

	2011	2012
Net interest income	412.521	432.187
Net income	191.016	171.720
Loan to members	13,419.655	13,353.901
Total assets	23,061.183	25,097.326

Source: State Employees' Credit Union Reports

2.2.2.1.5 Services

The various services SECU offers include auto center services, automated services, branch services, and online services. Table 2.6 provides the financial highlights of SECU during the 2-year period 2011-2012.

REFERENCES

1. http://www.ncsecu.org

2.2.3 PENTAGON FEDERAL CREDIT UNION

The Pentagon Federal Credit Union (PenFed) was established in 1935 and serves about 1.2 million members, with $16 billion in assets. PedFed is composed of member owners and is headed by a volunteer board of directors. The credit union sponsors a trustee noncontributory-defined-benefit pension plan covering eligible employees. The credit union also sponsors a defined-benefit post-retirement plan.

2.2.3.1 Products and services

2.2.3.1.1 Credit cards

The credit union offers the PenFed Premium Travel Rewards American Express Card for services related to airfare purchases. The PenFed Platinum Rewards Visa Signature Card is used for complimentary 24/7 concierge services, special savings, and discounts from top retailers. The PenFed Promise Visa card, PenFed American Express card, and PenFed Gold Visa are other credit cards offered by PenFed. The Defender card provides 1.5% cash back on every purchase.

2.2.3.1.2 Loans

PenFed offers various types of loans such as new auto loans, used auto loans, and refinance auto loans. PenFed also provides a variety of home equity loans such as a home equity line of credit and 5/5 home equity line of credit. The key feature of the 5/5 home equity line of credit is that it is provided to owner-occupied homes with 75% or less loan to value or nonowner-occupied homes with 70% LTV. Education loans include an education line of credit and private student loan. In the former, a $500-25,000 line of credit is provided with a 9.9% APR. In private student loans, repayment can be deferred until 6 months after graduation. Loans are converted to a fixed-rate loan for more predictable payments for

Table 2.7 Financial Highlights (Millions of US Dollars)		
	2011	**2012**
Total assets	15,056.671	15,532.278
Total members accounts	11,906.258	12,237.028
Total interest income	648.410	589.218
Net income	121.517	145.984
Source: Pentagon Federal Credit Union Report		

repayment. Personal loans consist of bill consolidation loans and personal lines of credit. Bill consolidation loans simplify bill payments and convert a lot of credit card payment into one low monthly payment. In a personal line of credit, the limit is up to $25,000. The personal loans stipulate fixed monthly payments.

2.2.3.1.3 Checking and savings accounts
PenFed checking accounts provide complete-access checking and student checking. The services under complete-access checking include free bill pay, free Visa check card, and overdraft protection for qualified members. Student checking provides overdraft protection and requires a joint account holder. No minimum balance is required. Savings accounts consist of regular savings accounts and money market savings accounts. In the money market certificates, dividends are compounded daily and paid monthly for maximum returns. The option of automatic renewal is also available. The Coverdell Education Savings scheme provides savings for education purposes. PenFed IRAs consist of traditional IRAs, IRA premium accounts, Roth IRAs, and IRA certificates.

2.2.3.1.4 Mortgages
The 5/5 ARM conforming loans adjust only 1 in 5 years. Home purchases or external refinancing up to $4 million are provided under this scheme. 5/5 adjustable mortgage rate jumbo is another type of mortgage loan. There are also 20-year, 15-year, and 10-year fixed conforming loans, 15-year fixed jumbo loans, and 10-year balloon investment property products. The credit union also provides high-balance 15-year and 30-year fixed-rate mortgages. Jumbo loans include 5/5 ARM jumbo loans and 30-year fixed-rate jumbo loans. The 15-year and 30-year VA fixed loans are also offered. Table 2.7 gives the financial highlights of the Pentagon Federal Credit Union during the 2-year period 2011-2012.

REFERENCES
1. http://www.penfed.org

CASES ON INVESTMENT BANKS

3.1 INVESTMENT BANKS

3.1.1 CREDIT SUISSE

Credit Suisse is one of the world's leading financial services providers with headquarters in Zürich, Switzerland. This globally integrated financial institution provides advisory services, comprehensive solutions, and varied products to corporate, institutional, and government clients and high-net-worth individuals in more than 50 countries. The bank was founded in 1856 and presently employs 47,400 employees from 100 different nations. The global structure of Credit Suisse consists of regions of Switzerland, Europe, the Middle East, Africa, Americas, and Asia Pacific.

3.1.2 BUSINESS DIVISIONS

3.1.2.1 Private Banking and Wealth Management

The Private Banking and Wealth Management division consists of wealth management clients, corporate and institutional clients, and asset management businesses. The Wealth Management segment serves ultra-high-net-worth and high-net-worth individuals around the world and private clients in Switzerland. The Wealth Management Clients business is one of the largest players in the global wealth management industry and serves over 2 million clients.

The Corporate and Institutional Clients business offers expert advice and services to large corporate clients, small and medium enterprises, institutional clients, financial institutions, shipping companies, and commodity traders. This business segment serves more than 100,000 corporations and institutions in Switzerland. The Corporate Clients business provides a number of basic banking products such as traditional and structured lending, payment services, foreign exchange, capital goods, real estate leasing, and investment solutions. The Corporate Clients business also provides services in commodity trade finance, export finance, trade finance, and factoring. Product offerings include ship and aviation finance. Products and services for financial institutions include securities, cash and Treasury services. In collaboration with the investment banking division (IBD) the bank offers mergers and acquisitions (M&As) advisory services, syndications, and structured finance.

The Institutional Clients business provides a wide range of fund solutions and fund-linked services such as fund management and administration, fund design, and custody solutions to institutional clients such as pension funds and public-sector clients.

The Asset Management segment offers a wide range of investment products and solutions across diverse asset classes to pension funds, governments, foundations, endowments, corporations, and private individuals. Alternative investment offerings include hedge fund strategies, alternative beta, commodities, and credit investments. The bank has a strong presence in the area of multiasset class solutions in emerging markets. Other core investment strategies include an array of fixed-income funds, equity funds, and real estate businesses.

The legacy business includes exchange-traded fund (ETF) businesses, private equity businesses, and other investments targeted for sale.

3.1.2.2 Investment Banking

Credit Suisse's IBD provides a wide range of financial products and services, which includes global securities sales, trading, and execution, prime brokerage, capital raising services, corporate advisory and investment research to a client base consisting of corporations, institutional investors, hedge funds, and private individuals. The IBD offers customized financial solutions in close alignment with the Private Banking and Wealth Management divisions.

In debt capital markets, the IBD recently provided key financing for clients such as RedPrairie, Rank Group, Fortescue, and Kinetic Concepts.

The bank has provided M&As advisory services to a number of deals such as the Well Point acquisition of Amerigroup, the acquisition of the US natural gas company Southern Union by Energy Transfer Equity, the sale of Synthes to Johnson & Johnson, and the sale of Amylin to Bristol Myers Squibb. The equity capital market deals included initial public offerings (IPOs) for Cobalt International Energy, rights offerings for UniCredit Group, and active book runner for the Carlyle Group.

3.1.3 PRODUCTS AND SERVICES

The major activities of Credit Suisse are organized in broad functional areas of investment banking and global securities. The investment banking activities can be categorized along industry, product, and country groups. The major industry groups are energy, financial institutions, financial services, health care, media and telecom, real estate, and technology. The product groups are categorized as M&As and financing products. In global securities activities are focused on client-based and flow-based businesses. In global securities the bank engages in a broad range of activities involving fixed income currencies, commodities, derivatives, and cash equities. Loans are segregated into consumer loans and corporate and institutional loans. Consumer loans consist of classes of mortgages, loans collateralized by securities, and consumer finance. Corporate and institutional loans consist of real estate, commercial, and industrial loans. The group has defined benefit pension plans, defined contribution pension plans, and other post-retirement-defined benefit plans.

3.1.3.1 Investment banking products and services

Investment banking deals with equity and debt underwriting. The advisory services advise clients on all aspects of M&As, corporate sales and restructurings, divestitures, and takeover defense strategies. The Fund-Linked Products group deals with distribution of structured mutual funds and alternative investment products.

3.1.3.2 Global securities

Global securities provide a wide range of debt and equity securities, derivatives products, and financing opportunities. Global securities are structured into the following categories:

(a) Fixed-income business. Fixed-income business consists of government bonds, interest rate swaps, and options. The global rates product is a global market maker in cash and derivatives markets.

(b) Foreign exchange. Foreign exchange business consists of market making in products such as spot and options for currencies in many developed markets. Foreign exchange products also include proprietary market-leading technology.

(c) Credit. The credit products offered include standard debt issues, fund-linked products, derivatives instruments, structured solutions, and more. Credit Suisse is a leading dealer in flow trading of credit default swaps on individual credits, credit-linked notes, and index swaps. The investment-grade trades sovereign and corporate debt, nonconvertible preferred stock, and short-term securities such as floating rate notes and commercial paper. Leveraged finance provides capital raising and advisory services. Core leveraged credit products such as bank loans, bridge loans, and high-yield debt are provided for noninvestment-grade corporate and financial sponsor-backed corporates.

(d) Securitized products. These products trade, securitize, syndicate, underwrite, and provide research for residential mortgage-backed securities and asset-backed securities.

(e) Emerging markets. The Emerging Markets group offers a full range of fixed income instruments, local currency derivatives, and emerging-market investment products.

(f) Commodities. In the commodities category, trade is done in precious and minor metals, oil, gas, and other energy products. Commodity products also include benchmark indexes developed by Credit Suisse commodities.

(g) Equity. Cash equities offer a comprehensive range of offerings such as equity sales, which use research, offerings, and other products and services to cater to clients such as mutual funds, investment advisors, pension funds, hedge funds, and insurance companies.

(h) Sales trading provides a linkage of sales and position trading teams. Sales traders are primarily responsible for managing the order flow between clients and marketplace. Trading executes client and proprietary orders and makes markets in listed and over-the-counter (OTC) cash securities, exchange-traded funds, and programs. Advanced Execution Services (AES®) is a sophisticated suite of algorithmic trading strategies, tools, and analytics operated by Credit Suisse to facilitate global equity trading.

(i) Equity derivatives. Equity derivatives provide a wide range of equity-related products, investment options, and financing solutions.

(j) Convertibles. The Global Convertible Solutions business is a leading originator of new IPOs. Convertibles trading involves both secondary trading and market making along with the trading of credit default and asset swaps and distributing market information and research.

The Prime Brokerage services offer a wide range of services to hedge funds and institutional clients. Services include prime brokerage, start-up services, securities clearing, hedge fund administration, synthetics, and innovative financing solutions.

The arbitrage trading business focuses on liquidity, providing strategies in the major global equity and fixed income markets.

The equity research team uses in-depth analytical frameworks, proprietary methodologies, and data sources to analyze approximately 3000 global companies. The HOLT platform provides an advanced corporate performance, valuation, and strategic analysis frameworks, tracking more than 20,000 companies in over 60 countries.

3.1.4 STRATEGY

Credit Suisse operates as an integrated bank combining the expertise of global divisions of private banking and wealth and investment banking supported by shared services functions. The evolving regulatory framework and developments have changed the business and competitive landscape of the financial industry. One of the significant changes that affects the industry is the phasing-in of minimum capital requirements under Basel III in countries such as Switzerland. Credit Suisse is focused on strengthening the capital position, lowering the cost base, and reducing balance sheet assets in terms of total assets and risk-weighted assets (RWA). In 2012, Credit Suisse reduced Basel III RWA by CHF55 billion, added CHF12.3 billion of core capital and reduced the cost base by about CHF2 billion.

Credit Suisse created an integrated private banking and wealth management division to enhance revenues. The integrated Private Banking and Wealth Management division includes the Wealth Management Clients businesses and Asset Management business along with the Corporate and Institutional Clients' business in Switzerland. Asset Management businesses focus on liquid, scalable alternative investment products and multiasset class solutions in collaboration with other businesses. The Asset Management divisions have a strong position in the Swiss home market. Credit Suisse is also focusing on transforming the business model of investment banking and has become one of the first global banks to be Basel III compliant. The IBD realizes the importance of equities, underwriting, and advisory businesses and fixed-income business. The bank created combined shared services consisting of finance, operations, and information technology (IT) functions to realize the goal of establishing a common infrastructure for greater coordination and improvement of client accessibility. Credit Suisse has a target annual after-tax return on equity of 15% across the market cycle. The structured advisory process in Credit Suisse enables the business to be conducted compliant with applicable regulatory standards. The Swiss home market is a key area of focus for new services.

Credit Suisse has adopted a new client segmentation framework in the SME business, a redesigned sales management process, and integration of key organizational units.

In the bank's Asset Management division, the focus is on alternative investment strategies in emerging markets and on core investments that include asset allocation and traditional products. Credit Suisse has made strategic divestments with the sale of its ETF businesses, Aberdeen Asset Management and Wincasa AG.

Credit Suisse has realigned its asset management business into alternative investment strategies, core investments, and legacy businesses. Credit Suisse also has formed a joint venture focusing on investment strategies in the Middle East, Turkey, and other frontier markets.

In its Wealth Management division, services offered are based on a structured advisory process, client segment-specific value propositions, comprehensive investment services, and multishore platform. The ultra-high-net-worth and high-net-worth clients contributed 41% and 45% of assets under management in the Wealth Management Clients business. A specialized team offers tailor-made business and private financial solutions to ultra-high-net-worth individual clients. The multishore platform of global operations of Credit Suisse consists of 22 international booking centers in addition to its operations in Switzerland. The focus is on the targeted client segments in regions of the Americas, Asia Pacific, Europe, Middle East, Africa (EMEA), and home market of Switzerland.

Credit Suisse operates in two global business divisions of Private Banking and Wealth Management and Investment Banking. The operations are carried out in four market regions of Switzerland, EMEA, Americas, and Asia Pacific. The Asset Management business has a leading position in Swiss traditional business. In the EMEA region, Credit Suisse is active in 30 countries with approximately 9300 employees working in 75 offices. In the Americas, Credit Suisse has operations in the United States, Canada, Caribbean, and Latin America with 11,300 employees in 42 countries spanning 14 countries. Credit Suisse is present in 12 Asia Pacific markets with 7400 employees.

3.1.4.1 Liquidity and funding strategy

The liquidity and funding strategy is designed by the Capital Allocation and Risk Management Committee (CARMC) and overseen by the board of directors. The internal liquidity risk management framework is monitored by regulatory agencies such as the Swiss Financial Market Supervisory Authority (FINMA). The aim of the liquidity policy is to ensure that funding is available in times of stress either caused by market events or issues specific to Credit Suisse. The long-term funding that includes stable deposits is achieved through a conservative asset liability management strategy. A liquidity pool is maintained to address short-term liquidity stress. A Treasury-maintained liquidity pool consists of cash, high-grade bonds, and major market securities. A liquidity pool is also generated through reverse repurchase agreements. The bonds are eligible as collateral for liquidity facilities with various central banks such as the US Fed and European Central Bank. The Foreign exchange exposures, funding, liquidity, and capital in the banking book are managed centrally by the Treasury. The CARMC which includes the chief executive officers (CEOs) of the groups and divisions, the chief financial officer, the chief risk officer (CRO), and the treasurer, oversees the management of these functions. The liquidity contingency plan provides for specific actions to be taken in the event of a liquidity crisis.

The major funding sources are core customer deposits, long-term debt, and shareholder equity. Major portions of the balance sheet are match funded, in which the assets and liabilities have equal liquidity durations. Funding sources also consist of structured notes, which are linked to commodities, stocks, indexes, or currencies. The collateralized financings also include repurchase agreements and securities lending agreements. Capital market debt includes senior and subordinated debt issued in US-registered offerings and medium-term note programs. Investing activities include originating loans that are to be held to maturity, other receivables, and investment securities portfolios.

3.1.4.2 Capital management strategy

In 2012 Credit Suisse's position was strong with a BIA tier 1 ratio of 19.4%, which reflected a 7% decrease in RWA and an increase of CHF6.7 billion in Tier 1 capital. The capital adequacy standards of Basel are implemented by FINMA with some additional requirements for large Swiss banks known as Swiss finish. By year-end 2012, Credit Suisse had generated CHF12.3 billion in additional capital, resulting in a capital ratio of 9.3%.

Credit Suisse uses an advanced internal ratings approach (A-IRB) for measuring credit risk. Credit risk weights are determined by parameters such as probability of default (PD), loss given default (LGD), and transactional maturity. The capital requirements for market risk use models such as the standardized approach method. Based on the FINMA regulatory capital purposes within the Basel II.5 framework, Credit Suisse has implemented new risk measurement models such as incremental risk charge and stressed value at risk (VaR). The incremental risk charge is a regulatory capital charge for default and migration risk on positions in the trading books. Stressed VaR is a replicative VaR calculation on the group's current portfolio, which takes into account a 1-year observation period related to financial stress and facilitates the reduction of pro-cyclicality of minimum capital requirements for market risk. Noncounterparty risk arises from holding of premises, equipment, and investments in real estate entities.

3.1.5 **RISK MANAGEMENT**

The group is presently focusing on a less capital-intense business. The CARMC on a regular basis reviews risk exposures, concentration risks, and risk-related activities. The Risk Processes and

Standards Committee establishes the standards related to risk measurement and management. The Credit Portfolio and Provisions Review Committee reviews the quality of credit portfolios with a focus on development of impaired assets and assessment of related provisions and valuation allowances. The Reputational Risk and Sustainability Committee is responsible for setting policies, processes, and other issues related to reputational risk and sustainability issues. There are also divisional risk management committees within the organization. Credit Suisse classifies risk into management risk, chosen risk, and consequential risk. Strategic risk and reputational risk are part of management risk. The chosen risks consist of market risk, credit risk, and expense risks. The Consequential risk encompasses operational risk and liquidity risk. The CARMC is responsible for setting divisional risk limits. The limit measures used include VaR, economic capital, risk exposure, risk sensitivity, and scenario analysis. The economic capital is calculated separately for position risk, operation risk, and other risk. The position risk is used to assess, monitor, and report risk exposures. The other risks are expense risk, pension risk, and foreign exchange risk.

The principal market risk measurement methodologies used are VaR and scenario analysis. The additional risk measurement models include IRC and stressed VaR. The IRC is a regulatory capital charge for default and migration risk on positions in the trading book. Credit Suisse uses a 1-day holding period and 98% confidence level for VaR. The scenario analysis is based on key scenarios such as significant movements in credit spreads, interest rates, equity prices, commodity prices, foreign exchange rates, adverse changes in counterparty default, and recovery rates. The scenario analysis estimates specifically deal with the risk profile within particular businesses and limits. Stress testing is a critical element of the group risk control framework in which the results are monitored against limits. VaR is used to quantify market risk in the trading portfolio. Market risk associated with nontrading portfolios is measured and monitored using tools such as economic capital, scenario analysis, sensitivity analysis, and VaR. The Commodity risk on nontrading positions is measured using sensitivity analysis in which sensitivity to changes in value is observed for a 20% decline in commodity prices.

The credit risk exposure of Credit Suisse is disclosed for EU countries that are rated below AA or its equivalent by any one of the three major rating agencies or when the gross exposure exceeds the threshold of €0.5 billion.

The bank makes use of country limits and scenario analyses to analyze indirect sovereign credit exposures. The counterparty credit-risk stress-testing framework measures counterparty exposures in scenarios calibrated to the 99th percentile for the worst 1-month and 1-year observations in past. The scenario framework also analyzes extreme scenarios such as equity stock market crash and specific eurozone crises (e.g., the default of selected European countries such as Greece, Ireland, Italy, Portugal, and Spain). The gross credit risk exposure includes principal amount of loans, letters of credit issued, replacement value of derivatives instruments, netting agreements, notional value of investments in money market funds, and debt cash trading portfolios. The credit risk mitigation tools include credit default swaps (CDS), guarantees, insurance and collateral involving primarily cash, securities and real estate mainly for private banking, and wealth management exposure to corporations.

Credit risk arises from lending products, commitments, letters of credit, counterparty exposure from derivatives, foreign exchange, and other transactions. The major part of credit risk is concentrated in the wealth management and institutional client businesses within the private banking and wealth management division. The credit risk-exposure management consists of core components of individual counterparty rating systems, transaction rating systems, counterparty credit limit systems, country concentration limits, risk-based pricing methodologies, and active credit portfolio management. The ratings are based on internally developed rating models and processes. Credit officers use peer analysis, industry comparisons, external ratings, and opinions of credit experts to arrive at internal ratings. A PD is assigned to corporate and institutional counterparties based on internal risk estimates and RWA. The PD for corporations based in Switzerland and consumer loans is calculated by proprietary statistical rating models, which are composed of qualitative factors such as credit history reports from credit reporting bureaus and quantitative factors such as the borrower's income level for mortgage lending, balance sheet data, and ratios (e.g., loan to value (LTV). The potential credit loss is estimated using the expected loss on a transaction should a default occur (denoted as LGD) and counterparty credit rating. LGD takes into account structure, collateral, seniority of claim, and type of counterparty. Credit limits are used to manage individual counterparty risk and concentration risks in the portfolio. The credit risk concentration is regularly supervised by credit and risk management committees. The credit review process consists of regular asset and collateral quality reviews, financial statement analysis, economic and industry studies. Credit exposures are managed by utilizing credit hedges, collaterals, and guarantees.

Credit Suisse enters into derivatives contracts to mitigate interest rate, foreign exchange, and credit risk. Counterparty credit risk in forward contracts is mitigated by counterparty credit limits and established extension policies. The change in market value for futures contracts and options on future contracts are settled with a clearing broker in cash each day. Swap agreements consisting of interest rate swaps, CDS, currency and equity swaps are used for trading and risk management purposes.

Operational risk teams at the divisional and group levels are responsible for implementation of the operational risk management framework. Tools for management and reporting of operational risk include risk and control self-assessments, scenario analysis, reporting, and analysis of internal and external loss data. The RAR Operational Risk Modeling Team is responsible for the operational risk measurement methodology and associated capital calculations.

Reputational risk arises from a number of sources such as the nature of a proposed transaction or service, activity of a potential client, regulatory environment, and environmental or social impacts of a transaction. The Reputational Risk and Sustainability Committee is responsible for oversight of reputational risk and sustainability issues.

3.1.6 CORPORATE SOCIAL RESPONSIBILITY ACTIVITIES

Credit Suisse serves over 100,000 corporate clients in the Swiss home market. In other words, Credit Suisse serves one in every three Swiss companies with financial services and products. The integrated banks also provide risk capital to small- and medium-size Swiss companies. Credit Suisse focuses on microfinance and education as effective tools to promote economic growth and social development. The Disaster Relief Fund of the Credit Suisse Foundation offers emergency financial aid to victims of natural disasters. Environmental and climate protection is another area of importance for the bank. The bank serves more than 2 million clients with varying risk profiles in its markets. Credit Suisse's corporate governance adheres to the principles set out in the Swiss Code of Best Practice.

Credit Suisse was among the first signatories for the sustainability initiative agreements, including the UN Global Compact and the UN Environment Program (UNEP) Finance Initiative. Credit Suisse has applied the Carbon Principles to finance activities in the US power generation sector since 2008. Credit Suisse works with businesses, nongovernmental organizations (NGOs), research institutes, and rating agencies to develop sustainable products and services. Credit Suisse foundations such as Accentus,

Table 3.1 Financial Highlights 2010-2012 (Millions of CHF)

	2010	2011	2012
Net revenues	31,386	26,225	23,966
Net income	5920	2790	1685
Trading assets	324,704	279,553	256,399
Net loans	218,842	233,413	242,223
Brokerage receivables	38,769	43,446	45,768
Total assets	1,032,005	1,049,165	924,280
Customer deposits	287,564	313,401	308,312
Total shareholder equity	33,282	33,674	35,498
Basic EPS	3.93	1.37	0.82
Return on equity (%)	14.4	6.0	3.9
Cost/income ratio	78.1	88.5	91.3
Pretax income margin (%)	22.2	10.8	8

Source: Credit Suisse Reports

Empriris, and Symphasis have distributed over CHF60 million to more than1300 charitable initiatives in Switzerland and abroad. In 2012, Credit Suisse received *Euromoney*'s Award for Excellence. The Credit Suisse Green Business Initiative promotes and develops new products in the area of clean technology (cleantech), including renewable energy, water technologies, sustainable agriculture, and sustainable real estate. Credit Suisse achieved greenhouse gas neutrality for all operations globally in 2010. Table 3.1 provides the financial highlights of Credit Suisse during the 3-year period 2010-2012.

REFERENCES

1. http://www.credit-suisse.com/global/en/
2. Annual Reports Credit Suisse
3. Company Profile 2012 Credit Suisse

3.2 GOLDMAN SACHS GROUP

The Goldman Sachs Group was founded in 1869 and is headquartered in New York. The group is a major global investment banking, securities, and investment management firm that provides financial services to a diversified client base of corporations, financial institutions, national governments, and high-net-worth individuals. In 2012, Goldman Sachs was ranked first in global announced and completed M&As and in global equity and equity-related offerings.

3.2.1 MAJOR DIVISIONS

The major divisions of the Goldman Sachs Group are Investment Banking, Institutional Client Services, Investment and Lending, Investment Management, and Research.

3.2.1.1 *Investment banking*

The IBD is the leading advisor for corporations, financial institutions, financial sponsors, boards of directors, and special committees. The IBD provides a broad range of investment banking services that include strategic advisory services for M&As, divestitures, defense mechanisms, corporate restructuring, spin-offs, debt and equity underwriting of public offerings, and private placements. Services also include cross-border deals. The investment bank provides underwriting facilities for public offerings, private placements, loans, and derivatives transactions. The global structure consists of two specific segments: the IBD and the Financing Group.

3.2.1.1.1 Investment Banking division

Goldman Sachs is a market leader in providing M&As advisory services, in which they offer buy-side and sell-side advisory services, takeover defense mechanism services, cross-border M&As, and complex M&As transactions. Goldman Sachs also provides advice for transactions such as leveraged buyouts and corporate restructuring activities, including spin-offs, split-offs, and split-ups. Table 3.2 gives the details of major deals by Goldman Sachs in recent years.

Table 3.2 Recent Major Deals by Goldman Sachs

Year	Acquirer	Target	Deal Value (Billions of US Dollars)	Highlights
2011	Johnson & Johnson	Synthes	20.8	Acquisitions—Buy-side deal
2010	Schlumberger	Smith International	12	Acquisitions—Buy-side deal
2009	Pfizer	Wyeth	65	Acquisitions—Buy-side deal
2009	Sumitomo Mitsui Bank	Nikko Cordial Securities	6	Acquisitions—Buy-side deal
2010	International Power	GDF Suez Energy	25	Acquisitions—Sell-side deal
2010	PPL	E.ON sale of US businesses	8	Acquisition—Sell-side deal
2009	Berkshire Hathaway	Burlington Northern Santa Fe	36	Acquisition—Sell-side deal
2010	VimpleCom	WindTel, Orascom Tel	22	Advisory services—M&As
2009	Bharti Airtel	MTN Group	11	Advisory services—M&As
2009	Vivendi, Telecomunicações de São Paulo	GVT	7	Advisory services—M&As
2009	Saudi Telecom	Oger Telecom	3	Advisory services—M&As
2011	Ensco	Pride International	9	Advisory services for selling client—cross-border transactions
2010	Sanofi Aventis	Genzyme	21	Advisory services for selling client—cross-border transactions

(Continued)

Table 3.2   Recent Major Deals by Goldman Sachs—cont'd

Year	Acquirer	Target	Deal Value (Billions of US Dollars)	Highlights
2009	Fresenius	APP Pharma	6	Advisory services for selling client—cross-border transactions
2009	Liberty Media	Unity Media	5	Advisory services for buying client—cross-border transactions
2011	KKR	Seven Media Group	4	Private equity advisory
2011	Clayton Dubilier & Rice	Emergency Medical services	3	Private equity advisory for selling client
2010	3G	Burger King Holdings	4	Private equity advisory for selling client
2009	TPG Capital, Canadian Pension Plan Investment Board	IMS Health	5.1	Private equity advisory for buying client
2009	BlackStone	Busch Entertainment	3	Private equity advisory for buying client

Source: Collated from various sources, Goldman Sachs website

Goldman Sachs has provided advisory services for some high-profile clients who were defending against hostile takeover attempts. For example, in 2010, Goldman Sachs advised Airgas on how to fight against an unsolicited bid from Air Products, Casey's General stores against an unsolicited bid from Alimentation Couche Tard, and Potash Corp against an unsolicited bid from BHP Billiton. Goldman Sachs also advised Cadbury through an unsolicited bid from and subsequent sale to Kraft Foods in 2009.

Goldman Sachs provides advisory services for a number of corporate restructuring activities such as spin-offs and split-offs. For example, in 2011, the investment bank advised Fiat for the spin-off of its capital goods business into Fiat Industrial. Goldman Sachs also advised Motorola for its split into two companies and subsequent spin-off of Motorola Mobility for $10 billion. In 2010, Goldman Sachs provided advisory services to Brookfield Properties on restructuring of General Growth Properties for $7 billion. Goldman was the advisor for General Electric on the joint venture between NBC Universal and Comcast for $32 billion.

3.2.1.1.2 Financing Group

The Financing Group of Goldman Sachs structures and executes a number of transactions such as equity offerings, debt issuances, and derivative transactions. The Financing Group consists of various teams. The Corporate Derivatives team is involved in developing customized risk management solutions for corporations. Corporate Finance Solutions facilitates businesses to structure complex transactions. The Latin American Financing Group provides leveraged loans, structured finance, equity-linked issuances, and straight debt issuance to clients in Latin America. The Equity Capital Market team originates, structure and executes various types of equity-linked financing such as IPOs, right offerings, convertibles, and derivatives. The Investment Grade Capital Markets team is responsible for marketing, pricing, and distributing new corporate bonds, hybrid products, equity-linked products, and preference stock issues for corporations with high-credit quality ratings. The Leveraged Finance capital market team deals with leveraged buyout deals, refinancing, and restructuring deals. The team also originates, structures and executes bank loans and high-yield bond financing for corporate clients. The syndicate desk of the Leveraged Finance team also underwrites and syndicates bank loans and high-yield bonds. The Liability Management team provides advisory services for public and private debt transactions, which includes tenders and exchange offers that are executed as part of asset sales, restructuring, and refinancing. The team is involved in developing quantitative and technical solutions for investment banking clients. The Structured Finance team helps in the securitization of assets. The team provides a wide array of products such as catastrophe bonds, entertainment financing, aircraft financing, securitization of franchise royalties, intellectual property, life insurance, auto loans, and student loans.

3.2.1.1.3 Industrial sectors

The Consumer or Retail group serves industries such as apparel, hotels, supermarkets, drug stores, education, e-commerce, and food and household products. The Financial Institutions group provides financing and advisory services to banks, insurance companies, asset management firms, financial technology companies, and specialty finance companies. The Financial Sponsors group provides advisory and investment banking services to a range of institutions that includes private equity firms. The Investment Banking team provides services for healthcare sectors and related fields such as biotechnology, life sciences, and medical technology. The Industrial Group facilitates investing banking services in sectors such as aerospace and defense, automotive, building and construction, capital goods, transportation, forest products, and packaging. The Public Sector and Infrastructure (PSI) group serves the municipal and nonprofit issuers of its US market. The PSI group performs the role of underwriter for local and state governments, nonprofit healthcare systems, institutes of higher education, public power utilities, airports, and seaports. The Natural Resources group provides services for clients in the energy, power, chemicals, metals, mining, and alternative energy sectors. The Real Estate group provides financing and advisory services to real estate investment trusts (REITs), hotel and gaming companies, and retailers. The group has expertise in retail properties, hotels and golf courses, shopping centers, office buildings, and multifamily properties. The Technology, Media and Telecommunications group provides advisory and financing services to sectors in electronics, software, and Internet and cable companies.

3.2.1.2 *Institutional Client Services*

This division makes market and clear client transactions in fixed income, equity, currency, and commodity products for institutional clients such as corporations, financial institutions, investment funds, and governments. The Institutional Client Services segment also works globally to make markets and clear client transactions on major stock, options, and future exchanges. The division provides financing, securities lending, and prime brokerage services to institutional clients.

3.2.1.2.1 Securities Sales and Trading

With sophisticated electronic platforms and professionals, the Securities Sales and Trading segment strategizes, trades, and executes securities transactions in exchanges around the world. The high-touch sales and trading desk generates real-time insights to facilitate execution strategies.

3.2.1.2.2 Prime Brokerage Group

Goldman Sachs is a premier global provider of securities lending services. The Institutional Client Services segment provides 24-h access to more than 50 developed and emerging markets with trading hubs in London, New York, Hong Kong, and Tokyo. The client service experts offer long-term and short-term strategies to clients based on in-depth knowledge of financial products, with local and global market intelligence. Goldman provides global coverage with more than 100 professionals in the United States, Europe, and Asia. The Prime Brokerage Group develops financing solutions and risk models for hedge fund managers to execute a broad range of investment strategies. The Prime Brokerage services team offers global multiasset class, multicurrency reporting, and technology platforms to cover all aspects from real-time portfolio management applications to posttrade operations utilities and portfolio accounting reports. The Capital Introduction team assists hedge fund clients with targeted introductions to leading pension plans, endowments, foundations, family offices, sovereign wealth funds, insurance companies, and private banks. The Consulting Services team helps hedge fund managers to expand their businesses.

3.2.1.2.3 Securities Clearing Services

The Clearing Expertise team assists clients in executing and settling transactions in all global equities and derivatives exchanges. The back-office platform clears over 3 million trades per day. The platform enables clients to work with multiple asset classes and currencies in a single consolidated account.

3.2.1.2.4 Securities products and business groups

Institutional clients are provided with a range of securities products and services worldwide. Goldman Sachs facilitates client who trade in equities using cash accounts by bringing together buyers and sellers. The Client Services division provides services in securities commodities, such as risk management services that cover sectors in power, natural gas, crude oil, coal, refined products, and base metals. The Global Investment Research team provides commodities research. The Client Services team guides clients on investment opportunities across a wide range of exchange-traded and OTC equity-linked products. The Client Services team provides investment advice for clients in a broad range of credit products such as bank loans and investment-grade and high-yield municipal debt.

The Client Services team also provides clients with advisory services related to investment strategies in derivatives based on equity, credit, commodity, and interest rates. The services are also offered for investments in exchange-traded funds. Goldman Sachs has extensive coverage in the futures market with involvement in approximately 55 derivatives markets globally. The Sales and Trading team explores opportunities in emerging economies. Goldman Sachs is a global dealer in approximately 17 government securities, credit derivatives (e.g., interest rate derivatives and mortgage pass-throughs), and inflation-linked products. These capabilities help clients to manage global interest rate exposures and hedge macroeconomic risk. Goldman Sachs also facilitates securities mortgage services for clients through securities sales and trading, residential and commercial loan trading, agency CMO issuance, mortgage derivatives, and synthetic asset trading and restructuring of mortgage assets.

The business groups within the client services segment include Client Commission Management (CCM), Derivatives Clearing Services (DCS), GSQuartix, Pension Endowment and Foundation Solutions (PEFS) Group, Private Investor Products Group (PIPGA), and Securities Strat.

CCM serves the commission account management requirements of execution clients such as hedge funds and financial institutions. DCS provides centralized clearing for foreign exchange commodities, equities swaps, interest rate swaps, and CDS. Goldman Sachs is a market leader in OTC clearing. The GSQuartix is an investment offering that covers funds, certificates, notes, warrants, and external manager platforms within the Goldman Sachs securities division. The PEFS team focuses on strategic initiatives, asset solutions, and investment opportunities in coordination with pension funds, endowments, and foundations. PIPGA provides securities division products to retail distributors, private banks, investment managers, and private wealth management clients. Securities Strat develops quantitative and technical solutions.

3.2.1.3 Investing and lending

Goldman Sachs provides financing to clients through investments and the origination of long-term loans. This segment makes investments either directly or indirectly through funds in debt securities, loans, public and private equity securities, real estate, and power generation facilities.

Goldman Sachs Bank accepts deposits, lends to individuals and corporate clients, and deals with derivatives products that include interest rate, credit, and foreign currency products. GS Bank is the wholly owned subsidiary of the Goldman Sachs Group. The Urban Investment Group of the bank focuses on community development lending, investing, and grant making in regions of New York City, northern New Jersey, and Salt Lake City.

The Merchant Banking Division (MBD) of the group deals with direct private investing. The MBD invests in equity and credit products in corporations real estate, and infrastructure. The MBD has raised over $125 billion of capital to invest in different industries since 1986. It is one of the largest managers of private capital worldwide. Approximately $79 billion of the capital MBD raised was through investment funds focused on private equity, growth capital, infrastructure, and real estate. The division has also raised approximately $46 billion of leverage capital consisting of mezzanine financing, senior secured lending, real estate credit, and distressed debt. GS Capital Partners is a global leader in private corporate equity, which invests in a wide range of industries across the Americas, Europe, and Asia. The target investments range in size from $50 million to more than $800 million. Through the GS Direct and GS Growth platforms, the MBD invests in the capital structure of middle-market segments wherein the average target investments are in the range of $20 million. Goldman Sachs is one of the leading infrastructure fund managers globally and has raised $10 billion of capital since 2006. The GS Infrastructure Partners (GSIP) focuses on transportation infrastructure such as airports, ports, railways and roads, and utilities infrastructure (e.g., electricity, gas, water networks, and contracted power generation). Goldman Sachs established its real estate fund in 1991, and it has raised approximately $29 billion since its inception. This fund invests across multiple product types, including real estate companies and projects, loan portfolios, and debt recapitalizations.

GS Mezzanine Partners is the largest mezzanine fund in the world; it has raised more than $28 billion of leveraged capital since 1996. GS Loan Partners is one of the largest fund families that caters to the senior-secured loan asset class. GS Opportunity Partners was established to invest in stressed and distressed debts that are acquired through negotiated financing, recapitalizations, financial restructuring, and secondary market purchases. GS Real Estate Mezzanine Partners was established to invest in real estate mezzanine loans, B-notes, CMBS, preferred equity, and real estate debt.

3.2.1.4 Investment management

Goldman Sachs provides investment management services and investment products across major asset classes through managed accounts and commingled vehicles such as mutual funds and private investment funds to institutional and individual clients. The segment also provides wealth advisory services, portfolio management and financial counseling, and brokerage services to high-net-worth individuals.

Goldman Sachs Asset Management (GSAM) is one of the major leading investment managers with more than 2000 professionals in 32 offices worldwide. GSAM provides investment and advisory solutions to institutional and individual investors across asset classes and industries. The investment solutions encompass money markets, fixed income, public equity, commodities, hedge funds, private equity, and real estate. Clients have accessibility to these solutions through proprietary strategies, strategic partnerships, and open architecture programs. GSAM's clients include global pension plans, sovereign wealth funds, central banks, insurance companies, foundations, endowments, and family offices. The division manages over $800 billion in assets.

The Goldman Sachs Private Wealth Management (GSPW) team provides a range of solutions that include cash, fixed income, equities, and alternative investments. The team also offers strategic and tactical asset allocation advisory services. For brokerage service clients, GSPW offers structuring and execution services in all security and derivative products. The segment also provides select private banking services. GSPW offers in-depth insight in areas such as asset allocation, investment strategies, and wealth management in the context of changing market dynamics.

3.2.1.5 Research

The Global Investment Research division provides analysis for clients in the equity, fixed income, currency, and commodities markets. The division carries out research in trends in markets and industries, portfolio strategy, derivatives, equity, and credit securities, which comprises more than 25 stock markets and about 50 economies around the world.

3.2.2 STRATEGY

The strategy of Goldman Sachs has grown from a focused business model based on the culture of team-oriented professionals. The group focuses on controlling costs. In this direction in 2011 the group announced a $1.2 billion expense-saving initiative. The group aims to operate with a capital cushion of about 100 basis points above the regulatory requirement as stipulated under Basel III. The growth strategy focuses on emerging markets, especially BRIC countries. In 2012, the transaction volume with BRIC countries accounted for one fifth of global M&As and IPOs. Another area of focus for Goldman Sachs is technological innovation. The group facilitated the establishment of technological innovations such as Archipelago, ICE, TradeWeb, FXaII, and BrokerTec. In the equity business, a majority of shares are traded through low-touch channels. In cash fixed-income markets, about 80% of foreign exchange spot forward executions are done electronically. In derivatives approximately 50% of the liquid credit index market trades electronically. On account of the migration of low-touch equities to electronic processing, failed trades have declined by more than 95%. Goldman Sachs's goal is to market approximately 6 million positions every day.

Goldman Sachs is also emphasizing innovative financing strategies. In 2012, the company offered dollar-denominated securities known as Enhanced Equipment Trust Certificates (EETCs) for financing of Emirates' expansion of its fleet of Airbus A380s. These securities use the aircraft as collateral. The deal valued at $587.5 million was oversubscribed and attracted investors from Europe and Asia.

3.2.3 **CORPORATE SOCIAL RESPONSIBILITY ACTIVITIES**

Goldman Sachs's Community TeamWorks is the company's global volunteer initiative in association with local nonprofit organizations. In 2012, more than 25,000 Goldman Sachs employees from 48 offices partnered with more than 950 nonprofit organizations to provide a diverse array of community service projects. The group 10,000 Women is a 5-year, $100-million global initiative to serve 10,000 underserved women entrepreneurs with business and management education, access to networks, and capital funding. In 2010, Goldman Sachs launched the 10,000 Small Businesses program in the United Kingdom to serve small businesses. Goldman Sachs Gives is a donor-advised fund that provides grants to qualified nonprofit organizations. The company has contributed approximately $1.1 billion through Goldman Sachs Gives since 2010. The initiative provides 10,000 grants to various organizations in 35 countries.

3.2.4 **FUNDING SOURCES**

Balance sheet funding to manage assets and liabilities includes processes such as quarterly planning, business specific limits, monitoring of key metrics, and scenario analysis. The primary sources are secured financings, unsecured long-term and short-term borrowings, and deposits. Funding sources include collateralized financings, repurchase agreements, securities loaned, medium-term notes, savings, and demand deposits through a deposit sweep program, time deposits, and more.

The off-balance sheet arrangements of the group include stakes in special-purpose entities such as mortgage-backed and other asset-backed securitization vehicles, holding senior and subordinated debts and derivatives contracts in interest rates, foreign currency, equity, commodity, credit derivatives, and swaps. The group also enters into operating leases, provides guarantees, letters of credit, and warranties.

3.2.5 **CAPITAL MANAGEMENT**

Goldman Sachs performs an Internal Capital Adequacy Assessment Process (ICAAP) to ensure adequate capitalization in the context of various risks. ICAAP is an internal risk-based capital assessment that incorporates market risk, credit risk, and operational risk. The group evaluates capital adequacy based on an internal risk-based capital assessment supplemented with stress test results under various market conditions. The capital usage to each business is based on internal risk-based capital and regulatory frameworks. The level of usage is based on established balance sheet and risk limits.

Consolidated Capital Ratios		
	2011	2012
Tier 1 capital ratio (%)	13.8	16.7
Total capital ratio (%)	16.9	20.1
Tier 1 common ratio (%)	12.1	14.5

3.2.6 **RISK MANAGEMENT**

The group faces major risk such as market, credit, liquidity, operational, legal, and reputational risk. The risk management framework is based on core components of governance, processes, and people.

The board plays an important role in risk management policies and practices through its risk committee, which consists of independent directors. The various subcommittees involved in risk management consist of firmwide client and business standards committees, firmwide new activity committees, and firmwide suitability committees. The other subcommittees include a securities division risk committee, credit policy committee, firmwide operational committee, and firmwide finance committee.

Liquidity risk is managed through measures such as excess liquidity, asset liability management, and contingency funding plans. The liquidity policy of the group is to prefund the estimated potential cash and collateral needs in times of liquidity crisis. For this purpose, the group holds excess liquidity in the form of unencumbered highly liquid securities and cash. The group uses an internal liquidity model called modeled liquidity outflow that captures and quantifies the firm's liquidity risk. According to this model liquidity held directly in each of the subsidiaries is intended for use only by that subsidiary to meet its liquidity requirements. The modeled liquidity outflow is based on scenario analysis and includes marketwide stress and firm-specific stress tests. This model includes critical model parameters such as liquidity needs over a 30-day scenario and a two-notch downgrade of the firm's long-term senior unsecured credit ratings. The modeled liquidity outflow is calculated and reported to senior management on a daily basis. The asset liability management policies are based on conservatively managing the overall characteristics of the funding book with a focus on maintaining long-term diversified sources of funding in excess of current requirements. The contingency funding plan details the plan of action required to fund business activity in crisis situations and periods of market stress.

Market risk at Goldman Sachs encompasses interest rate risk, equity price risk, currency rate risk, and commodity price risk. The group manages market risk by diversifying exposures, controlling position sizes, and hedging in related securities or derivatives. The process consists of generating timely exposure information, which incorporates various risk metrics and a dynamic limit-setting framework. Risks for short-term periods are measured using VaR and sensitivity metrics. The long-term period risk measures are stress tests. The group has invested in technology that generates reports on different views of risk measures by desk, business, product type, or legal entity. VaR calculations employ a one-day time horizon with a 95% confidence level. The VaR calculation involves historical simulations with full valuation of approximately 70,000 market factors. Goldman Sachs uses a variety of stress-testing techniques such as sensitivity analysis, scenario analysis, and firmwide stress tests to calculate potential loss from impact of market effects on the firm's portfolios. Risk limits are set based on VaR and on a range of stress tests relevant to the firm's exposures.

Credit risk for the Goldman Sachs Group arises mostly from client transactions in OTC derivatives, loans, and lending commitments. Credit risk also arises from resale activities, repurchase agreements, securities borrowing and lending activities, receivables from brokers, dealers, and counterparties. The Credit Policy Committee and Firmwide Risk Committee establish and review credit policies and parameters. The credit risk management process includes steps such as approving transactions, setting and communicating credit risk exposure limits, and monitoring compliance with established credit exposure limits. The global credit risk management system captures credit exposure to individual counterparties and provides management with in-depth information on aggregate credit risk by product, internal credit rating, industry, country, and region. The primary measure of credit risk for derivatives and securities financing is potential exposure, which takes into consideration account netting and collateral arrangements. The basic measure of credit risk for loans and lending commitments is a function of the notional amount of the position. The group uses credit limits at various levels such as counterparty, economic group, industry, and country to control the size of the credit exposures. The group regularly uses stress tests or scenario analysis to calculate credit exposure. The stress tests include shocks to multiple risk factors during the scenario analysis involving a severe market or economic event. The company mitigates credit exposures on derivatives and securities financing transactions by entering into netting agreements with counterparties whereby receivables and payables are offset with such counterparties. Credit risk mitigation strategies also involve obtaining collaterals from counterparties on an upfront or contingent basis. The risk mitigants for loans and lending commitments include collateral provisions, guarantees, covenants, structural seniority of bank loan claims, provisions in legal documentation to adjust loan amounts, pricing, and structure. Other instruments to mitigate credit risk involve the use of credit derivatives or participation agreements.

Goldman Sachs uses top-down and bottom-up approaches to managing and measuring operational risk. In the top-down approach, the group's senior management assesses firmwide and business-level operational risks. In the bottom-up perspective, revenue-producing units, control and support functions are accountable for operational risk management on a day-to-day basis and report to senior management. The internal audit performs a review of the operational risk framework consisting of key controls, processes, and applications. The group measures operational risk exposure over a 12-month time horizon using statistical modeling and scenario analysis based on quantitative and qualitative assessment of factors. These factors include assessment of internal controls, complexity of business activities, degree of automation of the firm's processes, new product information, and legal and regulatory environment. Goldman Sachs aims to mitigate operational risk using training, supervision, and development of employees. Table 3.3 gives the highlights of the operating performance of the investment banking activities of Goldman Sachs. Table 3.4 gives the net revenues of the divisions of Goldman Sachs during the 3-year period 2010-2012. Table 3.5 provides the financial highlights of Goldman Sachs during 2008-2012.

Table 3.3   Operating Results of Investment Banking 2010-2012 (Millions of US Dollars)

	2010	2011	2012
Financial advisory	2062	1987	2062
Equity underwriting	1462	1085	987
Debt underwriting	1286	1283	1964

Source: Annual Reports

Table 3.4   Net Revenues of Divisions 2010-2012 (Millions of US Dollars)

	2010	2011	2012
Investment Banking	4810	4355	4926
Institutional Client Services	21,796	17,280	18,124
Investing and Lending	7541	2142	5891
Investment Management	5014	5034	5222

Source: Annual Reports

Table 3.5 Financial Highlights 2008-2012					
	2008	**2009**	**2010**	**2011**	**2012**
Net revenues (millions of US dollars)	22,222	45,173	39,161	28,811	34,163
Total assets (millions of US dollars)	884,547	848,942	911,332	923,225	938,555
Total shareholder equity (millions of US dollars)	64,369	70,714	77,356	70,379	75,716
Total assets under management (billions of US dollars)	798	871	840	828	854

Source: Annual Reports

REFERENCES

1. Goldman Sachs Annual Report 2012
2. http://www.goldmansachs.com

3.3 MORGAN STANLEY

Morgan Stanley is one of the largest diversified financial services companies in the world. Morgan Stanley was established in 1935, after the passage of the Glass-Steagall Act of 1933, which separated commercial banking from underwriting securities. The company is headquartered in New York City with regional offices and branches throughout the United States and principal offices in London, Tokyo, Hong Kong, and other financial centers. In 2012, the company had approximately 57,000 employees.

In 1936, Morgan Stanley handled $1.1 billion in public offerings and private placements. In 1969, Morgan Stanley acquired Brooks Harvey & Co., Brooks Harvey & Co. thereby expanding the firm's real estate business. In 1972, Morgan Stanley established its sales and trading division and became the first investment bank with an M&As group. In 1986, Morgan Stanley went public. In 1995, Morgan Stanley and China Construction Bank formed the China International Capital Corp (CICC). Morgan Stanley advised Mitsubishi Trust on its merger with Bank of Tokyo-Mitsubishi and Nippon Trust. In 2004, Morgan Stanley acquired the risk management analytics vendor Barra for $816 million and then merged with MSCI. A Morgan Stanley-led consortium acquired Canary Wharf Group in the same year. Morgan Stanley advised MTFG on its merger with UFJ to form Japan's largest bank holding company. In 2006, Morgan Stanley acquired Nan Tung Bank in China. In 2007, Morgan Stanley launched a carbon credit exchange bank. In 2008, Morgan Stanley became a bank holding company and formed a strategic alliance with the Mitsubishi UFG Group. Morgan Stanley's board of directors adopted its corporate governance policies in 1995. Table 3.6 gives the details of the major deals carried out by Morgan Stanley.

3.3.1 BUSINESS SEGMENTS

The main segments of Morgan Stanley are Institutional Securities, Global Wealth Management, and Asset Management.

Table 3.6	Major Deals by Morgan Stanley		
Year	**Highlights of Deal**	**Value of Deal**	**Role of Morgan Stanley**
1936	Bond offerings for Consumer Power	$19 million	Arranger
1953	Debt issue for General Motors	$300 million	Sole manager
1957	IBM stock offering	$231 million	Sole manager
1980	Apple IPO	$101.2 million	Lead manager
1995	Netscape IPO	$140 million	Sole manager
1998	Dupont's spin-off of Conoco	$4.4 billion	Underwriter
1999	UPS IPO	$5.47 billion	Lead underwriter
2000	China Unicom IPO	$5.65 billion	Global coordinator and book runner
2000	Deutsche Telekom bond issue	$14.6 billion	Lead manager
2001	Agere Systems IPO	$4.1 billion	Lead manager
2002	General Motors—Equity-linked securities dual tranche convertible bond	$3.3 billion	Priced the deal
2002	Weyerhaeuser bond offerings	$5.5 billion	Priced the deal
2003	144 A issue of Gazprom	$1.75 billion	Manager
2003	Debt issue for General Motors pension obligations	$17.55 billion	Lead manager
2003	Merger of Fleet Boston Financial with Bank of America	$47 billion	Sole advisor
2004	Bond offering of America Movil	$1.3 billion	Priced the deal
2004	IPO auction of Google	$1.9 billion	Comanager
2005	China Construction Bank IPO	$9.2 billion	Comanager
2006	Convertible senior note offerings for Amgen	$5 billion	Priced the deal
2006	Leveraged buyout—Sale of HCA to Bain Capital, KKR, Merrill Lynch	$33 billion	Advisor to HCA
2006	OJSC OC Rosneft IPO	$10.4 billion	Lead manager
2007	Belle International Holding IPO	$1.27 billion	Priced the deal
2007	Cosnan IPO	$1.2 billion	Lead book runner
2009	Wind power firm Longyuan IPO	$2.6 billion	Comanager
2009	Joint venture of Comcast and GE	$37.3 billion	Advisor to Comcast

Source: Collated from various sources.

3.3.1.1 Institutional Securities

Morgan Stanley provides financial advisory and capital-raising services to corporate and institutional clients through wholly owned subsidiaries such as Morgan Stanley & Co., Morgan Stanley & Co. International, and Morgan Stanley Asia Ltd. Joint venture entities such as Morgan Stanley MUSFG Securities and Mitsubishi UFJ Morgan Securities also provide advisory services to corporate and institutional clients. The Institutional Securities division is also involved in investment banking and corporate lending activities as well as sales and trading activities.

3.3.1.1.1 Investment banking and corporate lending activities

Morgan Stanley manages and participates in IPOs and private placements of debt, equity, and other securities. It is a leading underwriter of common stocks, preferred stocks, convertible securities, and American depository receipts. Morgan Stanley is also a major underwriter of fixed income securities (investment grade and noninvestment grade), mortgage- and asset-backed securities, and commercial papers.

Morgan Stanley offers financial advisory services for M&As, divestitures, joint ventures, recapitalizations, spin-offs, leveraged buyouts, and takeover defenses. Financial advisory services are also provided for rights offerings, dividend policies, valuations, financial planning, risk management, and foreign exchange exposure. Advisory services are provided to clients for project financing, sale leasing, and financing of real estate.

Morgan Stanley offers corporate lending of different types such as bridge financing and senior or subordinated loans through its subsidiaries (e.g., Morgan Stanley Bank).

3.3.1.1.2 Sales and trading activities

Morgan Stanley's sales, trading, financing, and market-making activities are done on stock and derivatives exchanges including OTC markets around the globe. The main segments of sales and trading consist of equity trading, fixed income and commodities, clients and services, research, and investments.

In equity trading Morgan Stanley acts as a principal agent and market maker in equity, equity-related products such as ADRs and GDRs, and ETFs. Equity derivatives sales, trading and market-making activities include various products including equity swaps, options, futures, and warrants that are made to institutional and individual investors.

Morgan Stanley trades, invests, and makes markets in fixed income and related securities such as corporate bonds, bank loans, distressed debt, sovereign securities, emerging market bonds and loans, convertible bonds, collateralized debt obligations, notes issued by structured investment vehicles, mortgage-backed securities, real estate loan products, municipal securities, and money market instruments. The investment bank is the primary dealer of US federal government securities and dealer or market maker of government securities in European, Asian, and other emerging regions. Morgan Stanley trades, invests, and makes markets in credit indexes, asset-backed security indexes, and property indexes. Morgan Stanley also trades, invests, and makes markets in major foreign currencies such as the British pound, Canadian dollar, euro, Japanese yen, and Swiss franc. The trading of these currencies is done on a principal basis in the spot, forward options, and futures markets. Morgan Stanley provides financing for commercial and residential real estate loan products and securitized asset classes. The financial institution also takes part in securities lending with clients, institutional lenders, and broker-dealers. The company also provides advisory services for corporations on investment strategies and corporate restructuring. The institutional securities segment also structures debt securities, derivatives, and other instruments. The segment trades, invests, and makes markets in derivatives markets (e.g., spot, forward) and futures market for commodities (e.g., metals, agricultural products, crude oil, natural gas). Morgan Stanley is also a market maker and trader in exchange-traded options and futures, swaps on commodities. Morgan Stanley has its own electricity-generating facilities in US and Europe.

Morgan Stanley provides prime brokerage services such as clearance, settlement and custody, financing, and reporting services to clients trading multiple asset classes. The client services segment oversees Morgan Stanley's institutional distribution and sales activities.

The research department provides research reports on global economy, economic trends, financial markets, portfolio strategy, technical market analysis, and specific sectors and companies. These reports are disseminated to investors through third-party distributors and through proprietary Internet sites such as Client Link and Matrix.

Morgan Stanley makes capital investments in public and private companies. The company manages investment vehicles on behalf of clients who require exposure to private equity, infrastructure, mezzanine lending, and real estate-related investments.

The operations and IT department provides the process and technology platform to support institutional securities sales and trading activity.

3.3.1.2 Global Wealth Management Group

The Global Wealth Management Group (GWMG) provides comprehensive financial services to clients globally through a network of 16,700 global representatives in 712 locations worldwide. The GWMG, which includes a 65% stake in Morgan Stanley Smith Barney Holdings, manages about $1776 billion in client assets. The clients served consist of individual high-net-worth investors and small- to medium-sized businesses. The group has offices in the United States, Australia, Hong Kong, European Union, Middle East, India, Singapore, and Switzerland.

The GWMG provides varied products and services to clients including products from Citigroup and third-party providers such as insurance companies and mutual funds.The GWMG provides brokerage and investment advisory services, which cover various investments such as equities, derivatives, foreign currencies, precious metals, fixed income securities, mutual funds, structured products, alternative investments, and unit investment trusts. The GWMG facilitates client trading in fixed income securities. The group also offers education savings programs, financial and wealth planning services, annuities, and insurance products. The group also facilitates cash management services related to deposits, debit cards, and electronic bill payment through Morgan Stanley Private Bank. The Morgan Stanley Bank National Association (MSBNA) provides securities-based lending, mortgage loans, and home equity lines of credit. The GWMG provides trust and fiduciary services and commercial credit solutions to small- and medium-size businesses in the United States. The division also provides individual and corporate retirement solutions, which include individual retirement accounts (IRAs) and 401(k) plans to corporate executives and businesses.

3.3.1.3 Asset Management

This division is engaged in merchant banking, traditional asset management, and real estate investment activities. The Asset Management business segment is one of the world's largest global investment management corporations, offering clients a wide array of equity, fixed income, alternate investments, and merchant banking strategies. The division offers these products to institutional investors and high-net-worth individuals. The division's alternative investment portfolio consists of hedge funds, funds of private equity, real estate funds, and portable alpha strategies. Morgan Stanley has minority investment stakes in alternative investment firms such as Lansdowne partners, Avenue Capital Group, and Traxis Partners. Real estate and merchant banking businesses include real estate investing segments, private equity funds, corporate mezzanine debt investing group, and infrastructure investing group. Institutional investors of Morgan Stanley include corporations, pension plans, foundations, endowments, sovereign wealth funds, and insurance companies. The Global Sales and Client Services team is focused on business development services for institutional clients. The Asset division of Morgan Stanley offers open-ended and close-ended funds to individual investors through affiliated and unaffiliated brokers and dealers. Morgan Stanley also distributes mutual funds to clients through various retirement plan platforms.

3.3.2 STRATEGY

The investment bank focuses on providing advisory services to clients on strategic transactions. Morgan Stanley also provides new opportunities for individual and institutional investors. Morgan Stanley competes with major commercial banks, brokerage firms, insurance firms, sponsors of mutual funds, hedge funds, electronic trading, and clearing platforms in critical factors such as transaction execution, capital, product and services, reputation, and price. Morgan Stanley faces intense price competition due to the fact that automated electronic trading markets have increased pressures on trading commissions or comparable fees. The investment bank also focuses on joint ventures, M&As, minority stakes, and strategic alliances in its pursuit for growth.

3.3.3 FUNDING MANAGEMENT

Morgan Stanley funds its balance sheet through diverse sources such as equity capital, long-term debt, repurchase agreement, securities lending, deposits, commercial paper, structured notes, letters of credit, and lines of credit. Morgan Stanley targets global investors and currencies through active financing programs involving structured products.

3.3.4 CAPITAL MANAGEMENT

The company aims to maintain total capital on a consolidated basis, which is at least equal to the sum of its operating subsidiaries' equity. The company initiated a repurchase program of $6 billion in 2006. By 2012, approximately $1.6 billion remained under its repurchase program. Table 3.7 highlights the different capital ratios of Morgan Stanley during the years 2011 and 2012.

3.3.5 RISK MANAGEMENT

Morgan Stanley uses an enterprise risk management (ERM) model to manage risk. The governance structure for risk comprises the board of directors, the Risk Committee of the Board, the Audit Committee of the Board, Operations and Technology Committee of the Board, the Firm Risk Committee, and senior management oversight consisting of the CEO, CRO, CFO, and risk managers. Each business segment has a risk committee that establishes limits for various risks and measures and monitors risk within the risk framework established by the firm's risk committee.

Table 3.7 Capital Ratios 2011-2012		
	2011	**2012**
Total capital ratio (%)	17.5	18.5
Tier 1 common capital ratio (%)	12.6	14.6
Tier 1 capital ratio (%)	16.2	17.7
Tier 1 leverage ratio (%)	6.6	7.1

Morgan Stanley faces market risk on account of trading, investing, and client services activities. Market risk exposures are generated in the institutional securities business segment. Trading-related market risk exists because of the activities in the GWMG segment. Nontrading market risk is accounted by the asset management segment basically due to capital investments in real estate funds and investments in private-equity vehicles. The company uses a proprietary methodology known as stress value at risk (S-VaR) to measure market and credit risk. S-VaR uses simulation to create stress scenarios based on more than 25 years of historical data to analyze market and credit risk. S-VaR also captures event and default risk in the context of credit portfolios. Market risk is monitored against limits on aggregate risk exposures, analytical measures such as VaR and scenario analysis, position sensitivity, and stress sensitivity. The summary reports made by the market risk department are submitted to firm risk committees and senior management, including the board of directors. Morgan Stanley is exposed to interest rate and credit spread from market-making activities and other trading activities in interest rate-sensitive financial instruments. Equity price and implied volatility risk arise from market-making activities in equity-related securities and derivatives. Foreign exchange risk arises due to exposure in foreign currencies and foreign currency-denominated derivatives and non-US dollar denominated financial instruments. Morgan Stanley also faces commodity price and implied volatility risk due to market-making activities and commodity positions in physical commodities such as crude and refined oil products, natural gas, electricity, base metals, and related commodity derivatives. The company measures interest rate risk by measuring the hypothetical sensitivity of net interest income to potential changes in the level of interest rates over a period of 12 months.

Morgan Stanley uses risk mitigation strategies such as diversification of risk exposures and hedging. Hedging strategies involve purchase or sale of derivatives positions in forwards, futures, swaps, and options.

Morgan Stanley faces credit risk in the Institutional Securities and GWMG business segments. Morgan Stanley's corporate lending credit exposure arises basically from loan and lending commitments used for corporate purposes, working capital, and liquidity purposes. The lending commitments include revolving lines of credit, term loans, and bridge loans. Credit risk in institutional securities arises from derivatives contracts such as swaps, lending commitments to clients, short-term and long-term funding secured by financial or physical collaterals, collaterals to clearinghouses and agencies, and investments of trading in securities and loan pools. There is credit risk in the GWMG from lending to individual investors; these loans include margin loans collateralized by securities, single-family residential prime mortgage loans, and home equity lines of credit (HELOCs). Credit risk in the Asset Management business segment results from OTC derivatives hedges used to manage market risk due to currency and interest rate fluctuations. A global credit limits framework is utilized to evaluate and manage credit risk. The Credit Risk Management department monitors credit exposures and uses stress tests to identify, analyze, and control credit risk from lending and trading activities. The stress tests incorporate market factors such as interest rates, commodity prices, equity prices, and risk parameters such as default probabilities and expected losses to identify potential credit exposure concentrations to counterparties, industries, and countries.

The Credit Risk Management department evaluates the credit ratings, strategy, market position, and industry dynamics of corporate and commercial borrowers. Margin and nonpurpose securities-based loans are evaluated based on additional factors such as the amount of the loan, degree of leverage, quality, price volatility, and liquidity of the collateral. The credit metrics used in the evaluation process are incorporated into the maintenance of the allowance for loan losses for loans held for the investment portfolio. Morgan Stanley uses collateral provisions, guarantees, and hedges to mitigate credit risk from its lending and trading activities. The company hedges its lending and derivatives exposure through portfolio and structured credit derivatives. Morgan Stanley sells or sub-participates funded loans and lending commitments to other financial institutions in the primary and secondary loan markets as additional credit risk-mitigating measures. Morgan Stanley is an active market maker in the credit derivatives markets. Morgan Stanley faces counterparty credit risk related to credit derivatives from a number of counterparties, such as banks, broker-dealers, insurance, and other financial institutions.

The company manages country risk exposure and conducts periodic stress testing to measure the impact of shocks stemming from economic or political scenarios. The stress tests include the European peripherals consisting of countries such as Greece, Ireland, Italy, Portugal, and Spain.

Morgan Stanley has implemented operational risk data and assessment systems to monitor and analyze internal and external operational risk events. The operational risk coordinator of each business segment reviews operational risk issues and reports to senior management within each business. The operational risk department is responsible for the design, ownership, and independent validation of the operational risk framework.

Morgan Stanley's liquidity risk management framework components consist of a contingency funding plan (CFP), stress tests, and global liquidity reserve. The CFP highlights the information flows, limits, targets, operating environment indicators, and mitigating strategies in the event of a liquidity crisis. Liquidity stress tests are used to model liquidity outflows across multiple scenarios over a range of time periods involving systemic stress events. Morgan Stanley has to maintain sufficient liquidity reserves (known as its global liquidity reserve) to cover daily funding needs and strategic liquidity targets stipulated by the CFP and liquidity stress tests. The factors considered in measuring the global liquidity reserve consist of unsecured debt maturity profile, balance sheet size, and funding needs in a stressed environment, including contingent cash outflows and collateral requirements. The global liquidity reserve consists of diversified cash, cash equivalents, and highly unencumbered securities such as US government securities, agency mortgage-backed securities, FDIC guaranteed corporate debt, and highly liquid investment-grade securities.

Morgan Stanley faces legal risk in the form of various legal suits. The legal and compliance division of the company has established procedures for legal and regulatory requirements. The policies are framed with respect to business ethics and practices followed globally.

3.3.6 CORPORATE SOCIAL RESPONSIBILITY ACTIVITIES

Morgan Stanley's sustainable initiatives are focused on environment, social finance, and community development. Morgan Stanley promotes clean technology initiatives by offering financial advisory services to clean technology and renewable energy companies. The global commodities group trades and structures carbon-related transactions and environmental commodities. Morgan Stanley is an active participant in the US Partnership for Renewable Energy Finance policies. The social finance activities of Morgan Stanley focus on microfinance, housing, microenergy, health care, and more. The specialized technical expertise provided by Morgan Stanley has resulted in intermediation of more than $550 million in microfinance securities, which provided capital access to more than 30 microfinance institutions thereby benefiting several million low-income entrepreneurs. Over four decades, Morgan Stanley has invested in such health sectors as pediatric care. The Morgan Stanley Global Alliance for Children's Health Foundation and Morgan Stanley International Foundation focus on health, diversity education, and encouragement

Table 3.8   Financial Highlights 2008-2012 (Millions of US Dollars)

	2008	2009	2010	2011	2012
Net revenues	22,070	23,185	31,230	32,236	26,112
Net income	1707	1346	4703	4110	68
EPS	1.45	(0.77)	2.64	1.25	(0.02)
Total assets	659,035	771,462	807,698	749,898	780,960

Source: Annual Reports

Table 3.9   Revenue Highlights by Business Segment 2010-2012 (Millions of US Dollars)

Net revenues	2010	2011	2012
Institutional Securities	16,129	17,175	10,553
Global Wealth Management Group	12,519	13,289	13,516
Asset Management	2685	1887	2219
Intersegment Eliminations	(103)	(115)	(176)
Total	31,230	32,236	26,112

Source: Annual Reports

and support of Morgan Stanley employees' community involvement. In 2012, Morgan Stanley employees did more than 176,000 h of volunteer work in more than 20 countries. Table 3.8 gives financial highlights of Morgan Stanley during the 5-year period of 2008-2012. Table 3.9 indicates the revenue highlights of Morgan Stanley by segment.

REFERENCES

1. http://www.morganstanley.com
2. Annual Report on Form 10K, December 31, 2012

3.4 UBS GROUP

UBS is a major global financial institution that serves private, institutional, and corporate clients worldwide and retail clients in Switzerland. UBS focuses on businesses such as global wealth management, client-focused investment banking, and diversified global asset management. UBS Switzerland is the largest universal bank in Switzerland. The operational structure of the group consists of the corporate center and five business divisions of wealth management, including wealth management in the Americas, investment banking, global asset management, and retail and corporate divisions. UBS is headquartered in Zürich and Basel, Switzerland, and its shares are listed on six Swiss exchanges and the New York Stock Exchange. UBS is one of the largest wealth managers and global institutional asset managers in the world. UBS has a wide presence in all major global financial centers, with a presence in more than 50 countries, and employs about 61,000 people worldwide. After a major crisis that began in mid-2007, UBS returned to profitability in the fourth quarter of 2009.

UBS predecessors have a rich tradition of 150 years. The Bank in Winterthur was founded in 1862, and in 1912, the Bank in Winterthur merged with the Toggenburger Bank to form the Union Bank of Switzerland. Basler Bankverein was founded in 1872 and, as a result of a series of mergers, eventually became the Swiss Bank of Corporation. In 1998, the Union Bank of Switzerland and the Swiss Bank of Corporation merged to form UBS. The merger was aimed to establish a global financial firm catering to the needs of corporate, institutional, and sovereign clients throughout the global markets. Ever since the foundation of the Bank of Winterthur in 1862, about 300 financial firms consisting of private banks, savings banks, wealth managers, and brokerage firms have been acquired to form the present-day UBS. In 2000, UBS acquired US brokerage firm Paine Webber and formed part of UBS Wealth Management Americas. This acquisition paved the way for UBS to establish a US foothold in pursuit of its global expansion strategy. The acquisition changed the demographic and cultural structure of UBS as the number of non-Swiss UBS employees rose to more than 40,000, accounting for 58% of the total workforce. UBS is the founding member of the Wolfsberg Group.

During the financial crisis UBS wrote off more than CHF50 billion between third-quarter 2007 and fourth-quarter 2009. To face the financial crisis, UBS raised capital through an issue of mandatory convertible notes (MCNs) of value CHF13 billion in 2007. UBS also raised CHF15 billion through public rights offerings in 2008. To derisk and reduce UBS's balance sheet, the Swiss National Bank (SNB) established a special-purpose vehicle called the SNB StabFund to acquire securities held by UBS up to an amount of $60 billion dollars. In 2009, UBS received a capital injection of CHF6 billion from the Swiss confederation in the form of MCNs. In 2011, an unauthorized trade by a trader in its investment bank resulted in a loss of $2.3 billion.

3.4.1 BUSINESS DIVISIONS

3.4.1.1 Wealth Management division

UBS's Wealth Management division provides financial services to wealthy private clients throughout the world. It provides resources such as investment management, estate planning, and advisory services for corporations and other specific wealth management products and services.

The Wealth Management division is headquartered in Switzerland with a presence in 40 countries. The division has approximately 200 wealth management and representative offices with approximately half of them outside Switzerland. In 2012, the wealth management division employed globally around 16,200 people worldwide of which 4100 were client advisors.

The integrated client service model facilitates client advisors to develop and implement systematic client-focused investment strategies that aim to identify investment opportunities in all markets to cater to the needs of clients. In the Asia Pacific regions, the division focuses on Hong Kong, Singapore, and major onshore markets such as Japan and Taiwan. The division also focuses on Brazil, Mexico, Israel, Turkey, Russia, and Saudi Arabia. The ultra-high-net-worth segment is one of the biggest growth contributors to the wealth management division. The Global Financial Intermediaries (FIM) business of the Wealth Management division supports more than 2500 financial intermediaries in major financial centers as a strategic business partner. The major global competitors for the Wealth Management division include Credit Suisse, HSBC, Deutsche Bank, JPMorgan, and Citigroup. In European markets, the main competitors are Barclays Bank in the United Kingdom, Deutsche Bank in Germany, and Unicredit in Italy. HSBC, Citigroup, and Credit Suisse banking franchises are the main competitors in the Asia Pacific region.

3.4.1.2 Wealth Management Americas

Wealth Management Americas is the leading wealth manager in the Americas region in terms of financial advisor services and invested assets. The division serves affluent clients (those with US$250,000-1 million in invested assets), high-net-worth clients (those with US$1-10 million in investable assets), and ultra-high-net-worth clients (those with $10 million in investable assets) in the United States and Canada. Currently, the division has a network of over 7000 financial advisors and $843 billion in invested assets. The division provides advisory services in wealth planning, portfolio strategies, retirement and annuities, alternative investments, managed accounts, and structured products. The division offers a broad range of equity and fixed income instruments. The main competitors are national full-service brokerage firms, domestic and global private banks, broker-dealers, and the wealth management businesses of Bank of America, Morgan Stanley, and Wells Fargo.

3.4.1.3 Investment Banking division

The IBD provides a wide range of products and services in equities, fixed income, foreign exchange, and commodities to corporate clients, institutional clients, sovereign entities, and financial intermediaries. The Investment Bank's activities in the capital market includes sales, trading, and market making across a range of securities. Investment banks provide financial solutions to clients and offers advisory and analytics services in all major capital markets.

The two segments within the division are Corporate Client Solutions and Investor Client Services. The Corporate Client Solutions unit includes client coverage, advisory, debt and equity capital market solutions, and financing solutions for corporate, financial institutions, and sponsor clients. The main business lines in this division include the Advisory Groups, Equity Capital Markets, Debt Capital Markets, and Financing Solutions. The Advisory Group provides advisory services for M&As, corporate restructuring activities for refinancing, spin-offs, exchange offers, leveraged buyouts, joint ventures, and takeover defense mechanisms. The Equity Capital Markets line offers equity capital issue services and risk management solutions. These services are offered for IPOs, rights issues, and equity-linked transactions. The Debt Capital Markets line segment facilitates raising of various debt capital such as investment grade, emerging market bonds, high-yield bonds, subordinated debt, and hybrid capital for clients. This line segment also provides capital services for leveraged buyout, bonds, and mezzanine financing. The Financing Solutions line of business provides customized solutions to clients, which includes structured financing, real estate finance, and corporate lending.

The Investor Client Services consist of the equities, foreign exchange, interest rates, and credit businesses, which serve corporate, institutional, and wealth management clients. UBS is one of the largest equities houses in the world. The division is an active player in the primary and secondary markets for cash equities and equity derivatives. The business segment structure distributes, executes, finances, and clears cash equity and equity derivatives products. The franchises provide client services for hedge funds, asset managers, and wealth management advisors. Cash equities offer full-service trade execution for single stocks and portfolios, block trading, and commission management services. The segment provides clients with a complete suite of advanced electronic

trading products and direct market access, which includes low-latency execution, innovative algorithms, and real-time analytical tools. The equity derivatives franchise provides a full range of flow
and structured products, strategic equity solutions, and convertible bonds. The franchise provides
funding requirements through a wide range of listed, OTC, securitized, and fund-wrapped products.
The equity derivatives franchise also originates and distributes structured products to institutional
and retail investors. The financing services franchise facilitates a fully integrated platform for hedge
fund clients, clearing and custody, synthetic financing, and securities lending. The financing service
executes and clears exchange-traded derivatives across equities, fixed income, and commodities in
more than 60 markets globally.

The foreign exchange, interest rates, and credit unit business consists of a foreign exchange franchise, precious metal business, rates, and credit business. The foreign exchange business line facilitates
services for G-10 and emergency currencies along with precious metals services. UBS is a leading
foreign exchange market maker in derivatives markets of spot, forwards, and options. UBS provide
world-class execution facilities of voice, electronic, and algorithmic functions. Rates and credit lines of
businesses provide sales and trading services in a number of credit and rate products such as standardized rates-driven products, interest rate swaps, medium-term notes, and corporate bonds.

3.4.1.4 Global Asset Management

The business lines of this division consist of traditional products such as equities, fixed-income, global
investment solutions, alternate assets of global real estate, infrastructure, and private equity. The
Fund Services unit provides professional services, including fund setup, accounting, and reporting
for traditional investment funds and alternative funds. This division is also involved in cross-selling of
products and services offered by asset management and investment banking businesses. Global Asset
Management is a major fund house in Europe. The division is also the largest mutual fund manager
in Switzerland and one of the leading fund of hedge funds and real estate investment managers in the
world. Global Asset Management provides services to third-party institutional and wholesale clients
and clients of UBS's Wealth Management businesses.

In the equities segment, the investment team provides a wide range of investment strategies in areas
such as core, unconstrained, long-short, small-cap, sector, indexed, and other specialized strategies.
The fixed income segment provides global, regional, and local market-based investment strategies. The
Global Investment Solutions line of business offers active asset allocation, currency, structured solutions, risk advisory, and strategic investment advisory services.

Alternative Investment Solutions (AIS) and O'Connor are two primary business lines of alternative
and quantitative investments. AIS offers a wide range of hedge fund solutions and advisory services
that include multimanager strategies. O'Connor provides single-manager hedge funds. Global Real
Estate manages real estate investments across major real estate sectors all over the world including Asia
Pacific, Europe, and the United States.

Infrastructure and private equity businesses provide direct infrastructure investment and multimanager infrastructure and private equity strategies for institutional and high-net-worth investors.

The global fund administration business provides a wide range of flexible solutions consisting of
fund setup, reporting and accounting for investment funds, managed accounts, hedge funds, and private
equity funds.

In 2012, the division sold its Canadian domestic business to Fiera Capital Corporation. In the
previous year the asset management division had acquired the ING investment management limited

business in Australia. The major competitors for the division include BlackRock, J. Morgan Asset Management, and Goldman Sachs Asset Management.

3.4.1.5 Retail and Corporate division

This division provides comprehensive financial products and services to retail, corporate, and institutional clients in Switzerland. The distributional network of the retail division has 300 branches, 1250 ATMs, and state-of-the-art electronic and mobile banking services. The Retail division serves about 85% of the 1000 largest Swiss corporations and one in three pension funds in Switzerland. The Retail division provides transaction banking services such as payment and cash management services, receivable finance, custody solutions, and trade and export finance. The division provides financing solutions to corporate clients by offering access to equity and debt capital markets, private placements, and structured credit and leasing.

3.4.1.6 Corporate Center

The Corporate Center provides control functions for business divisions in areas such as risk control, Treasury services, funding, balance sheets, and capital management. The Corporate Center provides logistics and support functions, which includes IT, human resources, regulatory relations, strategic initiatives, and administrative services. The Corporate Center also manages centrally managed positions such as the SNB StabFund option and the Legacy portfolio consisting of noncore businesses of the Investment Bank.

3.4.2 STRATEGY OF UBS GROUP

The core of UBS's strategic pursuit for growth is centered on the GWMG division and the Universal Bank in Switzerland complemented by the focus on a global asset management business and investment bank.

UBS aims to reduce the group RWA target to below CHF200 billion on a fully applied Basel III by year-end 2017. The group has targeted a total cost savings of CHF5.4 billion by 2015. UBS also plans to invest about 1.5CHF to support initiatives that promote growth and improved client services across all businesses within a 3-year period. In 2011, the UBS group announced a cost reduction program of CHF2 billion. By 2015, UBS aims to achieve additional annual cost savings of CHF3.4 billion by reducing the size of its investment bank division. By year-end 2012, UBS had improved its capital position and reduced its Basel III RWA and costs by 35%. The fully applied Basel III common equity tier ratio at year-end 2012 was 9.8%, close to the regulator's minimum requirement of 10% by 2019.

UBS has established a strong footprint in the Asia Pacific region and emerging markets since 2000. Investment bank business is being transformed with the focus on its core strength areas of advisory, research, equities, foreign exchange, and precious metals. Equities and foreign exchange business are the cornerstones of investment businesses. In 2013 the Investment Bank was reorganized into two segments: Corporate Client Solutions and Investor Client Services. UBS aims to capitalize on attractive opportunities in less capital-intensive businesses on delivery of best solutions-led advisory. UBS has plans to divest certain lines of business particularly in fixed income segments. Diversified noncore assets are managed by the Corporate Center. The UBS group aims for a return on equity of 15% and group cost-income ratio in the range of 60-70% from 2015 onward.

UBS aims to strengthen its Wealth Management division's leading position in growth markets of the Asia Pacific and emerging markets. The Wealth Management division is transforming the European model to address the changing model of client needs. The Wealth Management division aims for a growth rate of 3-5% return on equity and cost income ratio of 60-70%. The Wealth Management Americas unit focuses on high-net-worth and ultra-high-net-worth markets, which are the fastest-growing segments in terms of invested assets. In Global Asset Management, UBS focuses on strengthening its real estate and hedge fund businesses. In the real estate and corporate sectors, UBS has a leading position in Switzerland. The focus of the bank is to offer comprehensive financial products and services to retail, corporate, and institutional clients. UBS is the preeminent universal bank in Switzerland and focuses on all five business areas of retail, wealth management, corporate and institutional banking, asset management, and investment banking.

The business divisions of UBS are managed using key performance indicators (KPIs) that focus on total shareholder return, dividend yield, and capital appreciation. In its pursuit of growth in emerging markets, UBS acquired Link Investmentos, the Brazilian financial services firm, in 2010.

3.4.3 RISK MANAGEMENT

Credit risk arises from traditional banking products such as loans and loan commitments such as letters of credit and guarantees. Credit risk also arises from exchange-traded derivatives, OTC derivatives transactions, securities financing transactions such as repurchase agreements, securities borrowing, and lending transactions. Limits are established for individual counterparties and their counterparty groups covering banking and traded products. Credit risk is managed by taking collateral against exposures and using credit hedging. The majority of loans in different divisions are extended on a secured basis. A mortgage on a property is taken to secure the claim for real estate financing. UBS uses measures to evaluate collateral and determine maximum LTV ratios. Collaterals are also taken in the form of marketable securities and cash in its OTC derivatives and securities financing businesses. The OTC derivatives trading credit risk is managed by using master netting agreements under bilateral International Swaps and Derivative Association (ISDA) stipulations. Credit risk of the portfolios in divisions of investment banks and legacy portfolio are hedged through bilateral netting, collateral agreements, CDS, index CDS, and total return swaps. The model used to measure credit risk is based on three parameters: PD, exposure at default (EaD), and LGD. The PD is assessed using rating tools for various categories of counterparties, which are calibrated according to an internal credit rating scale called a master scale. EaD, which is the amount owed by a counterparty at the time of a possible default, is derived from the current exposure to the counterparty and the possible future development of that exposure. The EaD of a loan is the drawn or face value of the loan. LGD is the magnitude of likely loss in the case of default. LGD estimates include the loss of principal, interest, and cost of carrying an impaired position. LGD is determined based on the likely recovery rate of claims against defaulted counterparties, which depends on the type of counterparty and credit mitigation by way of collateral or guarantees. LTV ratios are a key factor for determining LGD for collateral such as marketable securities. Expected loss is a statistical measure that estimates average annual costs due to impairment of the current credit portfolio. The expected loss for a given credit facility is a function of PD, EaD, and LGD. UBS uses a statistical modeling approach to estimate the loss profile of the credit portfolios over a 1-year period at a certain confidence level. The group also conducts stress loss tests on a regular basis to monitor and limit the potential impact of extreme events on portfolios and to apply a limit on this basis.

UBS uses multilateral and bilateral agreements with counterparties to reduce actual settlement volumes. The significant source of settlement risk for UBS is foreign exchange transactions. UBS is a member of Continuous Linked Settlement, which is a foreign exchange clearinghouse allowing transactions to be settled on a delivery versus payment basis.

For managing country risk, the group has a well-established a risk control framework in which the risk profiles of countries of exposures are assessed based on internally developed sovereign ratings.

Market risk basically arises from the trading activities of the investment bank and includes the noncore assets transferred to the corporate center. A limit framework is used to control market risk. The two major portfolio measures of market risk used by the group are VaR and stress loss. The VaR is calculated on a daily basis on end-of-day positions. It is supplemented by a comprehensive framework of nonstatistical measures and corresponding limits. These measures include a series of stress tests and scenario analyses.

In the IBD, market risk is managed by having supplementary limits on portfolios, asset classes, and products. The back-testing procedure compares a 1-day 99% confidence level regulatory VaR calculated on positions at the close of each business day with revenues. The back-testing results are provided to senior management, the group CRO, and business division CROs.

Banking book interest rate risk exposures arise primarily from loans and deposits in wealth management, retail and corporate, and Wealth Management Americas as well as Treasury activities. The largest nontrading interest rate exposure arises from wealth management and retail divisions.

Business division CEOs and Corporate Center function heads are responsible for effectiveness of operational risk management. The Operational Risk Management Committee oversees operational risk activities. The completeness of core controls in the operational risk framework is tested using scenario analysis. The operational risk exposure and operational risk regulatory capital are measured using an advanced measurement approach (AMA) in accordance with FINMA requirements. The AMA model is a hybrid model consisting of historical and scenario component. The historical component is based on the history of operational losses incurred since 2002. Then the loss distribution approach is used to aggregate losses over one year by modeling extreme severities and frequencies separately and then combining them. The scenario component is the forward-looking view of potential operational losses based on operational risk issues faced by the bank. The Group Treasury provides the group ALCO with monthly reporting on financial resources such as the balance sheet, capital, liquidity to monitor assets, and liability management policies and processes.

For managing and measuring liquidity risks, the group employs liquidity models such as an operational cash ladder, stressed operational cash ladder, maturity gap analysis, and cash capital model. The operational cash ladder is used to monitor funding requirements on a daily basis within the limits set by the group ALCO, the group CFO, and the group treasurer. In a stressed operation cash ladder, funding requirements are analyzed in a stressed market environment. Maturity gap analysis involves analysis of assets and liabilities over a 1-year time horizon. The cash capital model measures the amount of long-term funding or stable customer deposits, long-term debt, and equity available to fund illiquid assets. The liquidity and funding limits are set by the board of directors, the group ALCO, the group CFO, the group treasurer, and the business divisions.

3.4.4 CORPORATE SOCIAL RESPONSIBILITY ACTIVITIES

UBS supports education and entrepreneurship efforts to promote sustainable business practices, which include environmental initiatives. In 2012, the group supported educational and entrepreneurship activities

Table 3.10 Financial Highlights 2010-2012 (Millions of CHF)

	2010	2011	2012
Total operating income	31,994	27,788	27,788
Net profit/loss	7556	4406	(2235)
EPS (CHF)	1.97	1.10	(0.67)
Total assets	1,314,813	1,416,962	1,259,232
Total equity	48,770	52,935	50,249

Source: Annual Reports

Table 3.11 Operating Income Highlights 2012 (Millions of CHF)

Division	Operating Income
Wealth Management	7041
Wealth Management Americas	6097
Investment Bank	8598
Global Asset Management	1884
Retail and Corporate	3728
Corporate Center	(2173)
Core functions	268
Legacy portfolio	

Source: Annual Reports

by investing CHF40 million. Investors' initiatives such as the Carbon Disclosure Project have ranked UBS as an industry leader in the banking sector and among the top 10 companies to adopt measures to combat climate change. UBS plays an active role in key international corporate responsibility initiatives such as the Wolfsberg Group (antimoney laundering), the UN Principles for Responsible Investment, the UN Global Compact, and the UNEP Finance Initiative. In 2012, UBS successfully accomplished the groupwide CO_2 emission reduction target of 40%. In Switzerland, the company launched a major education initiative consisting of six projects that centered around the UBS International Center of Economics in Society at the University of Zürich. UBS produces award-wining research on the impact of environmental, social, and governance issues on sectors and companies. Global Asset Management offers a range of sustainable investment funds with themes such as energy savings, environment, social and health care, and demographics. In 2012, the Global Asset Management division launched the UBS Clean Energy Infrastructure with the aim of offering institutional clients a wide range of Swiss infrastructural facilities in the field of renewable energies. Table 3.10 provides financial highlights of UBS during the period 2010-2012. Table 3.11 provides operating income highlights of UBS during the year 2012.

REFERENCES

1. Annual Report of UBS
2. http://www.ubs.com

CASES ON INVESTMENT MANAGEMENT COMPANIES

4.1 INTRODUCTION

There are approximately 9600 open-ended investment funds of varying sizes offered in the United States and 63,000 open-ended investment funds whose shares are offered to the public outside the United States.

One of the megatrends noted by investors is the aging of the world's population. Individuals are also living much longer in retirement without adequate preparation. Corporate and public pension plans face significant shortfalls in meeting future needs for retirement income. There has been a shift from employer-funded defined benefit (DB) plans to defined contribution (DC) plans, which transfer risk to individuals. Another major trend is the secular shift to passive investing in exchange-traded funds (ETFs) and indexing. In recent years ETF inflows have been much higher in different regions of the world. The third megatrend is the rethinking of risk in which it is known that risk-free assets such as bonds are not safe-haven assets.

4.2 THE VANGUARD GROUP

Vanguard is one of the world's largest investment management companies. Founded in 1975, Vanguard serves clients in about 80 countries. As of 2012, Vanguard mutual funds had a value of approximately $2 trillion. The mutual funds company has 170 funds in the United States in addition to additional funds in international markets. The average expense ratio was 0.19%, expressed as a percentage of average assets in 2012. In 1976, the Vanguard 500 Index, the first index mutual fund, was opened to individual investors. In the early 1980s, Vanguard introduced retirement plan investments and services with the introduction of 401(k) plans. In 1990, Vanguard introduced the first international stock index fund. By the mid-1990s Vanguard offered asset management and financial planning services. In 2004, Vanguard launched an innovative One Step autopilot program for 401(k) plans, which provides automatic enrollment, personalized advisory services, and portfolio management services.

Vanguard provides services for personal investors and institutional investors along with financial advisory services. For personal investors, Vanguard provides an array of investment alternatives such as Vanguard mutual funds, ETFs, and individual stocks and bonds. Initiatives such as Flagship and Voyager services are aimed at providing expert advice and additional personal services for investors with a higher level of assets at Vanguard. Personal investors are also offered financial planning services, retirement planning services, and college savings options that include 529 plans.

For institutional investors, Vanguard provides investment management services in an array of mutual funds, which include active and index mutual funds and commingled trusts. Vanguard provides advisory services ranging from asset allocation to portfolio construction for institutional investors such as pension plans, endowments, foundations, and more. Vanguard offers administrative and record-keeping services for defined contribution, defined benefit, or nonqualified plans. Customized plan consulting services are offered for retirement plans. Vanguard also provides proprietary research and commentary on investments, market trends, and retirement planning issues.

Vanguard also provides financial advisory services. The resources for advisory services falls into disciplines of client acquisition, client management, business management, and professional development.

4.2.1 DIFFERENT CLASSES OF MUTUAL FUNDS

Vanguard mutual funds consist of money market, bond market, balanced, stock, and international mutual funds.

4.2.1.1 Money market mutual funds

The Vanguard Admiral Treasury Money Market Fund is a conservative investment option offered by Vanguard that invests in US Treasury securities. The fund maintains a share price of $1 and the strategic objective is to provide current income to investors. The income received by shareholders depends on the current interest rate environment.

The Vanguard California Tax-Exempt Money Market Fund is designed only for California residents and seeks to provide federal and California State tax-exempt income and preserve shareholders' principal investment by maintaining a share price of $1. This fund is considered one of the most conservative investment options offered by Vanguard. Although the fund invests in short-term, high-quality securities, the amount of income that shareholders may receive is largely dependent on the current interest rate environment and the availability of eligible California municipal securities. Investors in a higher tax bracket who have a short-term savings goal and seek a competitive tax-free yield may wish to consider this option.

The Vanguard Federal Money Market Fund and Vanguard New Jersey Tax-Exempt Money Market Fund in US government securities are also conservative Vanguard investment options.

4.2.1.2 All in one funds

The All in One Fund is a diversified portfolio in a single fund. The Vanguard 529 College Savings Plan helps individuals and families save for college expenses through tax-advantaged investment plans sponsored by the state of Nevada. Vanguard manages 22 different investment options.

Vanguard Target Retirement Funds invest in more than 12,000 US and international stocks and bonds in order to diversify risks. The Lipper Vanguard Target Retirement Fund's average expense ratio was 0.17% in 2012. Vanguard Target Retirement 2045 begins with a focus on stocks and automatically shifts to more bonds. Target Retirement Funds are made up of multiple Vanguard funds with low costs. The Target Retirement Fund is based on a retirement age of approximately 65. Target Retirement Funds are subject to various risks such as interest rate, credit, and inflation risk.

Vanguard LifeStrategy Funds are a series of broadly diversified, low-cost funds with an all index fixed allocation. The four funds in this category with different allocations target various risk-based objectives. The Income Fund is the most conservative among the four bonds. The Conservative Growth Fund seeks to provide current income and low to moderate capital appreciation. Table 4.1 highlights the features of the different types of LifeStrategy Funds of Vanguard.

Table 4.1   Types of Vanguard LifeStrategy Funds

Types of Funds	Time Horizon	Risk	Target Allocation
LifeStrategy Income Funds	3-5 years	Low to moderate	20% stocks, 80% bonds
LifeStrategy Conservative Growth Fund	>5 years	Moderate	40% stocks, 60% bonds
LifeStrategy Moderate Growth Fund	>5 years	Moderate to high	60% stocks, 40% bonds
LifeStrategy Growth Fund	>5 years	High	80% stocks, 20% bonds

The LifeStrategy Funds are a series of broadly diversified, low-cost funds with an all-index, fixed-allocation approach that may provide a complete portfolio in a single fund. The four funds, each with a different allocation, target various risk-based objectives. The Income Fund is the most conservative and seeks to provide current income and some capital appreciation. The fund holds 80% of its assets in bonds, a portion of which is allocated to international bonds, and 20% in stocks, a portion of which is allocated to international stocks. Investors with a short- to medium-term time frame who can accept modest movement in share price can invest in this fund.

4.2.1.3 Bond market mutual funds

The Vanguard Total Bond Market Index Fund provides wide exposure to US investment-grade bonds. This fund invests approximately 30% in corporate bonds and 70% in US government bonds of short-term intermediate and long-term maturity. The fund tracks the performance of the Barclays US Aggregate Float Adjusted Index.

Vanguard offers intermediate-term tax-exempt funds to investors in a high tax bracket. Vanguard GNMA Fund Investor shares specialize in government mortgage-backed securities. Vanguard also offers high-yield tax-exempt and inflation-protected securities. Vanguard Long-Term Bond Index invests in investment-grade bonds with maturities of more than 10 years.

4.2.1.4 Stock funds

Vanguard offers approximately 40 stock funds that have diversified investment strategies. The Vanguard 500 Index Fund is the first fund of the industry offered to individual investors. The fund invests in 500 of the largest US companies that account for three fourths of the US stock market's value. The stock funds include categories of capital value, dividend appreciation, equity income, and others. The Vanguard Energy Fund focuses on sectors such as energy, oil, natural gas, and coal. Explorer funds invest in small companies with growth potential. Vanguard offers various categories of mid-cap and large-cap growth as well as value funds. The Morgan Growth Fund invests in the stocks of large and mid-sized US companies, which, according to the fund's advisors, are poised for faster than average growth of revenues and earnings.

4.2.1.5 Balanced funds

Vanguard Balanced Index Fund Admiral Shares (VBIAX) invest approximately 60% in stocks and 40% in bonds by means of tracking two indexes representing US equity and US taxable bond markets. Balanced funds are basically for investors who want long-term growth and income.

The Vanguard Convertible Securities Fund invests in bonds that can be converted into stocks at a predetermined price. The LifeStrategy Funds are diversified low-cost funds that provide current income and low-to-moderate capital appreciation. The fund holds about 60% of its assets in bonds including international bonds and 40% in stocks including international stocks. Vanguard also offers Managed Payout Funds, which provide supplementary income to an investor's retirement income by paying different levels of monthly distributions (or payouts). The All Managed Payout Fund invests in a number of Vanguard funds consisting of a broad range of asset classes and investments. Vanguard offers about 12 Target Retirement Funds. These funds offer a diversified portfolio within a single fund that adjusts its underlying asset mix over a period of time. The Vanguard Tax-Managed Balanced Fund invests 50% in mid and large capitalization stocks and the rest in federally tax-exempt municipal bonds.

4.2.1.6 International funds

Vanguard offers mutual funds that focus on developed, emerging, global equity, and other sector-specific assets. The Vanguard FTSE All-World Ex Index provides investors with low-cost exposure to stock markets located outside the United States. This fund seeks to track an index that consists of companies located in developed markets. The Total World Stock Index Fund provides shareholders low-cost exposure to stock markets globally, which includes developed and emerging markets. Vanguard also offers Total International Bond and stock index funds.

4.2.1.7 Index and active funds

Vanguard offers a wide range of cost-effective index and actively managed funds. The strategy of index funds is to track the S&P 500 Index. The Vanguard 500 Index Fund is an open-ended investment company or mutual fund registered under the Investment Company Act of 1940. The four classes of shares offered by the fund include Investor shares, Admiral shares, Signal shares, and ETF shares. Investors who qualify for the minimum purchase requirement can buy investor shares. Investors who meet certain administrative, service, and account size criteria can hold admiral shares and signal shares. ETF shares are listed for trading on NYSE Arca, and can be sold or purchased through a broker.

4.2.1.8 Exchange-traded funds

Vanguard offers 52 exchange-traded funds. Vanguard brokerage clients trade ETFs commission free. Vanguard ETF shares are not redeemable with the issuing fund other than in creation unit aggregations. Investors can buy or sell Vanguard ETF shares in the secondary market with the assistance of a stockbroker. The prices of mid- and small-cap ETFs often fluctuate more than that of large-cap ETFs. Bond ETFs are subject to interest rate, inflation, and credit risk. The Total International Bond ETF faces currency hedging risk. The Emerging Market Bond ETF tracks the performance of an index that measures the investment return of dollar-denominated bonds issued by governments of emerging market countries.

The Extended Duration Treasury ETF invests mainly in zero coupon long-term bonds that are price-sensitive to interest rate changes. The ETF also invests in Treasury STRIPS (Separate Trading of Registered Interest and Principal Securities) with maturities ranging from 20 to 30 years.

With a brokerage account at Vanguard, investors can invest in the stocks, ETFs, bonds, CDs, and approximately 1400 mutual funds from other companies.

4.3 **AMERICAN FUNDS**

American Funds is a family of approximately 40 mutual funds that is managed by Capital Research and Management, which is part of Capital Group Companies. Capital Research and Management serves as the investment advisor to the 33 American Funds. The American Fund was established in 1931. Each fund is divided into portions that are managed independently by investment professionals with diverse backgrounds, ages, and investment approaches. According to company reports the equity funds have beaten their Lipper peer indexes in 90% of 10-year periods and 96% of 20-year periods.[1]

4.3.1 **DIFFERENT FUNDS**

American Funds consist of growth funds, growth and income funds, equity income funds, balanced funds, bond funds, tax-exempt bond funds, state-specific tax-exempt funds, money market funds, the American Fund Portfolio Series, the American Funds Target Date Retirement Series, and the American Funds College Target Date Series.

AMCAP is registered as an open-ended diversified management investment company. The AMCAP Fund aims to provide long-term growth of capital by investing in US companies with long-term growth records. The fund has 16 share classes consisting of five retail share classes. The 529 College Savings Plan share classes can be used to save for college education. The Retirement Plan share classes are generally offered only through eligible employer-sponsored retirement plans. The healthcare sector comprises approximately 21% of the industry-sector diversification of the fund. The fund invests in about 87% in stocks and 13% in short-term securities.

American Balanced Funds invests in a broad range of securities such as common stocks, investment-grade bonds, and securities issued and guaranteed by the US government and federal agencies.

The American Funds Mortgage Fund focuses on high-quality mortgage-related securities with residential and commercial mortgage-backed securities. There are also money market and tax-exempt mutual funds under the American Funds. The Capital Income Builder Fund invests at least 90% of its assets in income-producing securities. The Capital World Bond Fund aims to provide long-term returns. The fund invests at least 80% of its assets in bonds that primarily consist of government bonds, supranational and corporate bond issuers. The EuroPacific Growth Fund invests primarily in the common stocks of issuers in Europe and the Pacific Basin.

The American Funds Portfolio Series consists of funds in categories of growth, income, balanced, and tax advantages. The American Funds Global Growth Portfolio aims to provide long-term growth of capital. The Balanced Portfolio aims to provide current income and long-term growth of capital. The tax-advantaged income portfolio aims to provide current income, a portion of which is exempt from regular federal income tax.

The American Funds College Target Date series aims to achieve objectives such as growth, income, and preservation of capital depending on the proximity to its target dates. The American Funds Target Date Retirement Series invests in bonds, equity income, and balanced funds depending on its target date. The fund attempts to achieve its investment objectives by investing in a mix of American Funds in different combinations and weights. The American Funds represent a variety of fund categories such as growth funds, growth and income funds, equity income funds, and balanced funds and bonds.

---

[1]http://thecapitalgroup.com/afsystem.html#stop_9

4.4 FIDELITY FUNDS

Established in 1946 Fidelity is one of the most diversified financial services companies in the United States. Fidelity is the leading provider of investment management, retirement planning, portfolio guidance, brokerage benefits, outsourcing, and other financial products and services. According to Investment Company Institute statistics, Fidelity is one of the largest mutual fund companies and the leading provider of workplace saving plans in the United States. Fidelity is also the United States' number-one provider of individual retirement accounts (IRAs). In 2013, Fidelity had $4.2 trillion in assets under administration, which included managed assets of $1.8 trillion. Fidelity offers services such as retirement planning, portfolio guidance, and brokerage services. Fidelity's services are offered to a client base consisting of more than 20 million individuals. Fidelity manages hundreds of mutual funds and manages one of the largest staffs of portfolio managers, analysts, and traders in the mutual fund industry. According to 2012 Pensions and Investments' annual Defined Contribution Money Manager survey results, Fidelity was ranked first in defined contribution assets under management. Fidelity offers services to more than 15 million benefit plan participants employed by 22,000 employers. Fidelity's websites handled an average of 2.9 million visits a day in the third quarter of 2013. Fidelity employs over 42,000 people with several regional centers across the United States and Canada.

4.4.1 BUSINESSES

4.4.1.1 Asset management

Fidelity is one the leading asset management companies in the world offering an array of global research and investment services for institutional investors and individuals. In 2012, the company managed $1.7 trillion in client assets. The three groups that comprise Asset Management are Fidelity Management and Research Company, Pyramis Global Advisors, and the Asset Allocation Division. Fidelity Management and Research Company provides investment advisory services to Fidelity's family of mutual funds. Pyramis Global Advisors is a multiclass asset manager that provides asset management products and services to institutional investors. Global Asset Allocation group offers investment solutions to individuals and institutions in the form of custom portfolios and managed accounts.

4.4.1.2 Personal investing

Fidelity Investments is one of the world's largest mutual fund and financial services firms, with managed assets of more than $1.6 trillion.[2] As of 2012, Fidelity serves more than 20 million individual account holders by providing retirement planning, portfolio guidance, investment products, brokerage services, and many other financial products and services to more than 13 million individual account holders.

With Fidelity accounts and $7.95 per online trades, many different types of stocks can be conducted with common stock, depository receipts, unit trust funds, real estate investment trusts (REITs), preferred securities, closed-end funds, and international stocks.

4.4.1.2.1 ETFs

Fidelity ETFs offer one of the largest selections of sector funds in the industry, which includes over 250 sector ETFs from other leading-asset managers. Fidelity's sector ETFs offer one of the lowest

---

[2]Company website.

expense ratios of 0.12% in the industry. These ETFs can be purchased commission-free online. Some of the low-cost ETF funds offered by Fidelity are the Fidelity MSCI Consumer Discretionary Index ETF (FDIS), Fidelity MSCI Consumer Staples Index ETF (FSTA), and Fidelity MSCI Energy Index ETF (FENY). Fidelity offers 65 commission-free iShares. ETFs include all 10 iShares, Core ETFs, plus a diverse selection of international, domestic, and specialized equity, fixed income, and commodities. Fidelity offers over 1400 other ETFs. Fidelity facilitates options trading with $7.95 online trading plus 75¢ per contract.

4.4.1.2.2 Fidelity trade equity index and ETF options

Fidelity offers more than 30,000 investment-grade bonds and other fixed-income securities. The Fidelity Bond Ladder helps investors invest with staggered maturity dates. Investors can choose from 4600 funds from Fidelity and other leading companies; this includes 1400 or more no-load funds.

Fidelity also promotes international investing by facilitating trade of securities in 25 countries involving exchange between 16 currencies. Fidelity offers investors investments in precious metals such as gold, silver, and palladium as a part of the diversification strategy.

4.4.1.2.3 Retirement investments

Fidelity is the leading provider of retirement saving plans in the US and the largest manager of 401(k) plan assets in the US. The retirement products offered by Fidelity can be classified on the basis of defined contribution, benefits outsourcing and payroll, investment products and consulting, and defined benefits. Table 4.2 highlights the retirement plans of Fidelity funds.

Fidelity works with more than 140,000 financial advisors and more than 5000 investment firms. 403(b) plans offered by Fidelity are suited for organizations with more than $1 million in plan assets. Nonqualified executive compensation plans are most suited for organizations with an established Fidelity 401(k) plan. Payroll services are designed for organizations with fewer than 1000 employees.

Health saving accounts (HSAs) are meant for companies with at least 500 participants. Fidelity HSAs enable employees to save tax-deferred funds for current and future qualified healthcare expenses. The balance is invested at the end of the year and helps offset qualified health-related expenses in retirement. The Fidelity HSA combines tax-advantaged savings, account management, investment flexibility, and guidance. The Fidelity Health and Welfare Benefits platform is designed for companies

Table 4.2   Fidelity Retirement Plans

Defined Contribution	Benefit Outsourcing and Payroll	Investment Products and Consulting	Defined Benefits
401(k) plans	Payroll services	Stock plan services	Defined benefits
403(b)/401(a)	Health savings account	Benefit consulting services	Total retirement outsourcing
Nonqualified executive compensation benefit plan	Total benefit outsourcing	Investment-only account	
	Health and welfare benefits	Managed accounts	
	Integrated 401(k) and payroll solutions		

Source: Collated from company website

with more than 20,000 employees, and integrates with more than 275 health insurance carriers for managing enrollment data and streamlined payment.

Fidelity's product offerings can also be segregated on the basis of size of business into small, medium, and large businesses. Fidelity's Integrated 401(k) and Payroll Solutions are targeted to organizations with up to 1000 employees. The Fidelity Stock Plan provides an integrated proprietary platform to manage equity compensation plans and employee benefits. Benefit consulting services are for organizations that require customized plan solutions. Investment-only accounts are designed for organizations that don't need Fidelity's record-keeping services. Managed accounts provide professional portfolio management services as part of the workplace savings plan.

Fidelity offers Total Retirement Outsourcing for organizations with at least 15,000 participants. This program integrates plans into one comprehensive retirement benefits program.

Total Benefit Outsourcing provides comprehensive solutions for larger organizations with at least 20,000 participants. This product enables clients to integrate and optimize all plans: 401(k)s, nonqualified, defined benefits, health and welfare, personal investing, stock plans, and HASs.

4.4.1.3 Institutional services

Fidelity is a major provider of clearing, custody, brokerage, and investment services to family offices, broker-dealers, and independent advisors. Institutional services are offered under the divisions of Fidelity Capital Markets, Fidelity Family Office Services, Fidelity Financial Advisor Solutions, Fidelity Institutional Wealth Services, and National Financial.

Fidelity Capital Markets (FCM) is the institutional trading division of Fidelity Investments, which aims to integrate institutional, retail business, and trading platforms. FCM facilitates domestic and international equity trading, which includes block and portfolio trading, listed options, and foreign exchange trading. FCM also facilitates trading in a number of taxable and tax-exempt securities. The distribution channel Fidelity Prime offers a suite of electronic brokerage trading products that includes proprietary algorithms and networks.

Fidelity Family Offices Services serves multifamily offices and ultra-wealthy investors by providing custody, brokerage, and investment services.

Fidelity Financial Advisor Solutions provides a wide range of asset management, proprietary research, retirement planning, and investment products to individual clients, institutions, and their advisors. Independent advisors are provided one-stop access to an open technology environment, specialized wealth management investment and services, and fully integrated brokerage and custody services. Fidelity offers Fidelity Advisor Funds, Variable Insurance Product (VIP) portfolios, systematic investment plans, institutional money market funds, and an array of retirement products and services.

Fidelity Institutional Wealth Services serve the needs of registered investment advisors, banks, and retirement administrators. The division provides mutual funds, ETFs, individual securities, alternative investments, managed products, insurance, retirement plans, charitable services, and Fidelity 529 Plans. The Fidelity Institutional Wealth Services also help advisors and clients in global investing opportunities. Fidelity's international trading facilitates online stock trading in 25 foreign markets and 21 US markets. Fidelity provides forex trading access in 16 currencies. The custody and reporting services include asset servicing, personal trust services, cash management and lending, and trust custody. In 2013, Fidelity Institutional Wealth services managed $660 billion in assets on behalf of 3200 clients.

Fidelity National Financial (FNF) provides broker-dealers with an array of investment products and services that include cash- and fee-based programs. FNF's investment solutions include annuities, alternate investments, cash and lending programs, fee-based programs, mutual fund solutions, and retirement products and programs. Fidelity offers brokers or dealers clearing and execution products along with integrated productivity tools. Fidelity's online brokerage platform facilitates compliance support, middle-office outsourcing, consolidated record-keeping tools, fee-based solutions, and retirement products.

4.4.2 INVESTMENT PRODUCTS

4.4.2.1 Mutual funds

Fidelity offers more than 175 funds designed to meet investor expectations. Through the Fidelity funds network investors can access 10,000 funds from hundreds of fund companies.

4.4.2.2 Types of mutual funds

Domestic funds primarily invest in stocks issued by US companies. The stock funds are categorized into large value, large blend (with value greater than $10 billion), large growth, mid-cap value, mid-cap blend, mid-cap growth, small value, small blend, and small growth. International and global stock funds invest in stocks of companies globally as well as those that are region specific or in emerging markets. The different types of bond funds include investment grade, municipal, high yield, multisector, international, and global funds. Money market funds include taxable money market, national municipal money market, and state municipal money market.

The asset allocation fund combines multiple-asset classes into a single portfolio. The different types of asset allocation funds include target date funds, target allocation funds, income and real return strategies, income replacement funds, and world allocation funds. Target date funds allocation is based on an aggressive investment strategy when the target date is far off and adopts a conservative approach when the target date nears. In target allocation funds, target allocation is made with respect to stocks, bonds, and short-term investments. Income and real return strategies combine the objective of income and total return by investments in bonds, dividend-yielding stocks, alternate investments such as commodities, and real estate. Income-replacement funds convert savings into a regular stream of monthly income. The global allocation fund provides investors global investment exposure through a single fund. Specialized funds focus on nontraditional asset classes such as real estate and alternate investments. The specialized funds include real estate, alternative funds, commodity, inverse and leveraged, and market neutral. Commodity-focused stock funds invest in companies in sectors such as energy, metals, and agriculture industries. Inverse mutual funds, also known as short funds, move in the opposite direction of their tracking index, which seeks to increase in value when the market declines and decrease in value when the market rises. Leveraged mutual funds deliver multiples of performance of the index or benchmark, which are tracked. Some funds are inverse and leveraged mutual funds. Market neutral funds, also known as long/short funds, are funds that aim to deliver consistent returns 3-6% above 3-month Treasury bill yields. In a market neutral fund, managers hold both long and short positions. The major real estate funds include core funds such as the Fidelity Real Estate Investment Portfolio, Spartan Real Estate Index, and specialized funds such as the Fidelity Real Estate Income Fund, the Fidelity International Real Estate Fund, and the Fidelity Select Construction and Housing Portfolio.

Sector funds from Fidelity represent sectors such as consumer discretionary, industrials, health care, financial, energy, consumer staples, information technology, real estate, and materials.

Index funds track the performance of a particular stock or bond index such as the S&P 500 Index or the Barclays US Index. The Fidelity index funds consist of domestic stock, international stock, bond, and asset allocation. The domestic fund aims to replicate the performance of a major US equity index such as the S&P 500 or the Russell 2000 indexes. The international stock funds track the performance of international indexes such as FTSE Emerging Index or the MSCI EAFE Index. The Bond Fund aims to mirror the performance of an index such as Barclays US Aggregate Bond Index or the Barclays US Treasury Bond Index. The Asset Allocation Index Fund consists of a diversified portfolio of index funds. The Fidelity Four-in-One Index Fund is a combination of four Fidelity stock and bond index funds (underlying Fidelity) using an asset allocation strategy aimed at high return.

4.4.2.2.1 Stock mutual funds
Fidelity offers approximately 34 domestic equity funds. The Fidelity Blue Chip Growth Fund is a diversified domestic equity fund with a major focus on large market capitalization companies. The Fidelity Capital Appreciation Fund is a diversified domestic equity fund that focuses on capital appreciation. The Fidelity Contrafund is a diversified equity fund with a major focus on large-cap growth companies. The fund's largest holding was in Google. In 2013, the Contrafund was one of the largest funds by assets with a fund value of $93.7 billion. The Fidelity Magellan Fund is a diversified domestic equity fund with large-cap growth orientation that seeks capital appreciation. The Spartan@500 Index Fund is a diversified domestic large-cap equity fund that tracks the returns and characteristics of an S&P 500 index. The fund employs a replication approach that holds the stocks in the index at approximately the same weight as the index. The Sparton 500 Index, with an asset value of $58.3 billion, occupied the fourth position among the five largest funds by asset value in 2012.

International and Global Fund normally invests in non-US equity stocks. The International and Global Fund consists of 12 funds. Among these, the Fidelity Emerging Markets Fund is a diversified emerging markets equity fund. The Fidelity Worldwide Fund is a diversified global equity fund that seeks growth of capital.

Sector Fidelity Select Portfolios consist of 11 major funds that make sector-specific investments. For example, the Fidelity Select Energy Portfolio is a sector-based fund that has an equity-focused strategy that aims to outperform the benchmark through active management. The Energy Portfolio Fund invests primarily in companies in the areas of oil, gas, electricity, and coal.

4.4.2.2.2 Index funds
Among the stock index funds offered by Fidelity are the Spartan 500 Index Fund, Spartan Extended Market Index Fund, Spartan Global ex-US Index Fund, and Spartan International Index Fund. The bond index fund is the Spartan US Bond Index Fund.

4.4.2.2.3 Asset allocation funds
Fidelity asset allocation funds consist of hybrid and life-cycle (Fidelity Freedom) funds. The hybrid funds consist of the Fidelity Balanced Fund, Fidelity Convertible Securities Fund, Fidelity Puritan Fund, Fidelity Strategic Dividend and Income Fund, Fidelity Strategic Income Fund, and Fidelity Strategic Real Return Fund. The Fidelity Balanced Fund invests across a mix of stocks and bonds to provide income and capital. This fund has a neutral allocation of 60% equities and 40% bonds. The Fidelity Convertible Securities Fund is a convertible bond fund that focuses on investing primarily in the convertible and preferred securities of speculative and investment-grade issuers. The Fidelity

Puritan Fund seeks income and capital growth and has a neutral allocation of 60% equities and 40% bonds. The Fidelity Strategic Income Fund targets a neutral strategic allocation of 40% high-yield debt, 30% U.S. government and investment-grade debt, 15% non-U.S. developed-markets debt, and 15% emerging markets debt. The Strategic Income Fund invests primarily in debt securities by allocating assets among high-yield securities, US government, and investment-grade securities, emerging market securities, and foreign-developed market securities. The Fidelity Strategic Real Return Fund targets a neutral strategic allocation of 30% Treasury inflation protected securities (TIPS), 25% floating rate debt, 25% commodities, 10% real estate income, and 10% REITs.

The Fidelity Freedom Fund invests in a combination of underlying Fidelity domestic equity funds, international equity funds, bond funds, and short-term funds using a moderate asset allocation strategy designed for investors expecting to retire within a certain period.

4.4.2.2.4 Fixed-income funds

Fixed-income funds consist of taxable bond funds, state municipal bond funds, high-yield bonds, national municipal bond funds, and international global bond funds. There are 10 taxable bond types and three state municipal bonds and high-yield bond funds. There are three national municipal bond funds and one international global fund. An example of a taxable bond fund is the Fidelity Corporate Bond Fund, which is a credit-focused bond product that seeks a high level of current income by investing at least 80% of assets in investment-grade corporate bonds, corporate debt securities, and repurchase agreements. The Fidelity California Municipal Income Fund is an example of a municipal bond fund that invests in general obligation and revenue-backed municipal securities across the yield curve. The Fidelity Capital and Income Fund is a diversified high-yield bond fund that focuses on investing primarily in the bonds of companies rated below investment grade. The fund seeks to provide a combination of income and capital growth. The Fidelity Intermediate Municipal Income Fund is a diversified national municipal bond that invests in general obligation and revenue- or tax-backed municipal securities. The Fidelity New Markets Income Fund is an emerging market bond fund that offers dedicated exposure to sovereign debt of emerging market countries.

4.4.3 **FIDELITY ADVISORY FUNDS**

Fidelity Funds is a fund of Fidelity Hastings Street Trust (the trust), which is authorized to issue an unlimited number of shares. The fund invests in Fidelity Central Funds, which are open-ended investment companies generally available to other investment companies and accounts managed by Fidelity Management and Research Company along with its affiliates. The money market central funds seek preservation of capital and current income and are managed by Fidelity Investments Money Management. Table 4.3 lists the different types of advisory funds of Fidelity.

Fidelity Advisory Asset Manager Funds seek to provide a high level of income by investing in stocks, bonds, and short-term investments. Balanced funds provide both income and capital gains. Biotechnology funds seek capital appreciation by investing at least 80% of assets in securities of companies involved in research, development, and manufacture of biotechnology products, services, and processes. The Canada Fund aims for long-term capital appreciation by investing in at least 80% of assets in securities of Canadian issuers. The Capital Fund aims at capital appreciation by investing in stocks of domestic and foreign issuers. The Communication Fund invests at least 80% of assets in securities (primarily stocks) in companies that develop, manufacture, or sell communications

Table 4.3   Highlights of Fidelity Advisory Funds

Fund Name	Number of Funds	Fund Name	Number of Funds
Asset Manager	35	Emerging Markets Income Fund	5
Balanced Fund	6	Energy Fund	5
Biotechnology Fund	5	Equity Growth Fund	6
California Municipal Income Fund	5	Equity Income Fund	6
Canada Fund	5	Equity Value Fund	5
Capital Development Fund	5	Europe Capital Appreciation Fund	5
China Region Fund	5	Financial Services fund	5
Communications Equipment Fund	5	Floating Rate High Income Fund	5
Consumer Discretionary Fund	5	Freedom Fund	59
Consumer Staples Fund	5	Global Balanced Fund	5
Convertible Securities Fund	5	Global Bond Fund	4
Corporate Bond Fund	4	Global Capital Appreciation Fund	5
Diversified International Fund	6	Global Commodity Stock Fund	5
Diversified Stock Fund	6	Global Equity Income Fund	4
Dividend Growth Fund	6	Global High Income Fund	4
Electronics Fund	5	Global Strategies Fund	5
Emerging Asia Fund	5	Gold Fund	5
Emerging Europe, Middle East, and Africa Fund	5	Government Income Fund	5
Emerging Markets Discovery Fund	4	Growth and Income Fund	5
Emerging Market Fund	6	Growth Opportunities Fund	6
Health Care Fund	5	International Discovery Fund	6
High Income Advantage Fund	5	International Growth Fund	6
High Income Fund	5	International Real Estate Fund	5
Income Replacement Fund	56	International Small-Cap funds	5
Industrial Fund	5	International Small-Cap Opportunities Fund	5
Inflation Protected Bond Fund	5	International Value Fund	5

Fund Name	Number of Funds	Fund Name	Number of Funds
Table 4.3 Highlights of Fidelity Advisory Funds—cont'd			
Intermediate Municipal Income Fund	5	Investment Grade Bond Fund	5
International Bond Fund	4	Japan Fund	5
International Capital Appreciation Fund	5	Large-Cap Fund	5
Latin America Fund	5	Leveraged Company Stock Fund	6
Limited Term Bond Fund	5	Limited Term Municipal Income Fund	5
Materials Fund	5	Mega-Cap Stock	6
Mid Cap II Fund	6	Mid-Cap Value Fund	5
Mortgage Securities Fund	5	Municipal Income Fund	15
New Insights Fund	6	New York Municipal Income Fund	5
Overseas Fund	5	Real Estate Fund	9
Series Fund	6	Short Duration High Income Fund	4
Short Fixed Income Fund	5	Small-Cap Funds	16
Stock Selector Fund	21	Strategic Dividend/Income Fund	10
Strategic Real Return Fund	5	Technology Fund	5
Telecommunications Fund	5	Total Bond Fund	5
Total Emerging Market Fund	4	Total International Equity Fund	5
Ultra-Short Bond Fund	3	Utilities Fund	5
Value Fund	15	Worldwide Fund	5

equipment. The Consumer Discretionary Fund seeks capital appreciation by investing at least 80% of assets in securities of companies engaged in manufacture and distribution of consumer discretionary products and services. The Consumer Staples Fund invests primarily in companies that are engaged in the manufacture, sale, or distribution of consumer staples. The Diversified International Fund invests primarily in non-US securities, normally in stocks. Diversified stock funds invest in growth and value stocks primarily for capital appreciation. The Electronics Fund invests in companies in the electronic sector. The Emerging Asia Fund seeks capital appreciation and invests in securities of Asian emerging market securities. The Emerging Market Discovery Fund seeks capital appreciation by investing in smaller capitalization companies in emerging markets that show secular growth trends. The Emerging Market Income Fund seeks current income and capital appreciation by investing in securities of emerging markets. The Energy Fund seeks capital appreciation by investing in securities of energy companies in oil, gas, electricity, and coal. The Equity Value Fund seeks capital appreciation by investment in undervalued securities. The Financial Services Fund seeks capital appreciation by investing in securities of financial services firms. Freedom Funds seek high total returns with the secondary objective of capital preservation by investing in a combination of underlying Fidelity domestic equity funds, international equity funds, bond funds, and short-term funds using moderate asset allocation strategy.

The Floating Rate High Income Fund aims for a high level of income by investing in floating rate debt of lower quality. The Global Strategies Fund aims to maximize total return by allocating fund assets between stocks and bonds of all types and nontraditional asset classes by investing in Fidelity funds and unaffiliated ETFs. The Gold Fund seeks capital appreciation by investing in companies involved in exploration, mining of gold, and other precious metals. The Growth Opportunities Fund aims for capital growth by investing in companies with above-average growth potential. Income Replacement Funds seek total return through a combination of current income and capital growth by investing in a combination of Fidelity equity, fixed-income, and short-term funds using an asset allocation strategy. Industrial funds seek capital appreciation by means of investing in companies engaged in research, development, manufacture, and distribution of industrial products. Inflation protected bond funds invest in at least 80% of assets in inflation protected debt securities. International Value Funds seek capital appreciation by investing in non-US securities. The Leveraged Company Stock Fund invests in common stocks of leveraged companies. The Limited Term Bond Fund aims to provide a high rate of income by investing at least 80% of assets in high-investment-grade debt securities. The New Insights Fund seeks capital appreciation by investing in either growth or value stock or both. The Stock Selector Fund aims for capital appreciation by allocating the fund's assets among Fidelity equity sector central funds. Strategic Real Return Funds aim for real return with reasonable investment risk by allocating funds using a mix of inflation-protected debt securities, floating rate loans, commodity-linked notes, and other investments. The Ultra Short Bond Fund invests in investment-grade debt securities and repurchase agreements with the aim of current income and capital appreciation.

Destiny Plans are systematic investment plans offered for investors who seek a modest sum every month and build equity over a period of years with a maximum term of 30 years. Destiny Plans are closed to new investors. The Fidelity Advisory Plan is a college savings plan and a tax-savings plan as per section 529 of the Internal Revenue Code.

Fidelity's liquidity products include international money market funds and cash management funds. Fidelity International Money Market Funds consist of various categories such as money market portfolios, government portfolios, prime money market portfolios, tax-exempt, and Treasury-only funds. The Fidelity Cash Management Fund consists of a Prime Fund, a Treasury Fund, and a tax-exempt fund. The Prime Fund and Treasury Fund focus on high income along with preservation of liquidity and capital. The principal investment strategy of the Prime Fund is to invest in US-dollar-denominated money market securities of domestic and foreign issuers that are highly rated. The Treasury Fund invests 80% of assets in US Treasury securities. The tax-exempt fund focuses on current income exempt from federal income tax. These types of funds invest in municipal money market securities. The China Region Fund seeks long-term capital appreciation. This fund invests at least 80% of assets in securities from Hong Kong, Taiwan, and Chinese issuers, and other investments that are tied economically to regions in China. Table 4.4 provides the investment fact sheet of Fidelity. Table 4.5 provides the categorization of Fidelity mutual funds by investment objectives. Table 4.6 categorizes Fidelity mutual funds by business segment. Table 4.7 gives the value of assets under management for different divisions of Fidelity.

Table 4.4   Fidelity Investments Fact Sheet (Billions of US Dollars)

	December 31, 2012	September 30, 2013
Mutual fund assets under management	1489.4	1643.3
Trust/other assets under management	201.5	209.9
Total managed assets	1690.9	1853.2
Total assets under administration	3882.0	4367.2
Total number of mutual funds	545	544

Source: http://www.fidelity.com/inside-fidelity/fidelity-facts/fidelity-corporate-fact-sheet

Table 4.5   Number of Fidelity Mutual Funds

Mutual Funds by Investment Objective	Number
Equity mutual funds	420
High-income funds	23
Fixed-income funds	61
Money market funds	38
Total	542

Source: http://www.fidelity.com/inside-fidelity/fidelity-facts/index

Table 4.6   Fidelity Mutual Funds by Business Segment

Mutual Funds by Business Segment	
Retail mutual funds	293
Institutional mutual funds	415

http://www.fidelity.com/inside-fidelity/fidelity-facts/index

Table 4.7   Division Fidelity Assets under Management (Billions of US Dollars)

	Assets under Management (June 30, 2013)
Fidelity Financial Advisor Solutions	318
Fidelity Institutional Wealth Services	660
National Financial	453.1

Source: http://www.fidelity.com/inside-fidelity/fidelity-facts/fidelity-investments-institutional-services

4.5 **T. ROWE PRICE**

T. Rowe Price is a global investment manager fund headquartered in Baltimore, Maryland, with offices in 12 countries around the world. In 2013, the fund managed $614 billion in assets. T. Rowe Price serves individuals, financial intermediaries, and institutions by offering a full range of investment strategies. The firm was established in 1937. In 1950, the firm launched its first mutual fund, the T. Rowe Price Growth Stock Fund, which is a no-load mutual fund that seeks long-term capital appreciation by investing in growth companies.

4.5.1 **BUSINESS ACTIVITIES**

4.5.1.1 Mutual funds

T. Rowe Price offers more than 75 mutual fund strategies. T. Rowe Price also provides more than 100 no-load mutual funds with low fees to address specific needs. The mutual fund categories consist of target date funds, stock funds, international funds (stocks and bonds), bond and money market funds (taxable and tax-free), and asset allocation funds. Target date funds are actively managed funds based on a diversified age-appropriate asset mix during the years up to and through retirement. Stock funds offer long-term potential by investing primarily in stocks of US or international companies.

The flagship Target Date Fund series aims to support withdrawals in retirement, which could last for 30 years or more. These retirement funds invest 55% in stocks and 45% in bonds at the target retirement date. The new Target Date Fund aims to reduce volatility by emphasizing investment in bonds near the target retirement date. Retirement 2040 has provided a maximum annual return of 10.21% since its inception in 2002, among the 23 target date funds offered by T. Rowe Price.

T. Rowe Price Domestic Stock funds consist of large-cap stock funds, mid/small-cap stock funds, and specialty stock funds. There are 28 domestic stock funds in the T. Rowe Price portfolio. The Health Sciences Fund, established in 1995, has provided a total average annual return of approximately 14% since its inception. The US Large-Cap Core Fund has provided an annual average return of 17% ever since its inception in 2009.

There are 26 domestic bond funds. The High Yield Fund was the best performing bond fund with a total annual return of 8.76% since 1984. This fund has been closed to new investors. T. Rowe Price offers 12 tax-free bonds. The Tax-Free Income Fund is the company's best-performing tax-free bond fund and has provided an average annual return of 6.17% since its inception in 1976. The Gib Growth Stock Fund was the company's best performing international stock fund (annual average return of 21.67%) with long-term capital growth invested in large established companies throughout the world. There are four international bond market funds. The Emerging Bond Market Fund has provided an annual average return of 11.47% since its inception in 1994.

T. Rowe Price offers eight money market funds. The Prime Reserve Money Market Fund has given an average annual total return of 5.35% since its inception in 1976. In 2013, the Prime Reserve Fund had a total of 344 holdings. Approximately 48% of total assets are invested in commercial papers and medium-term notes. Municipal obligations account for 27% of the securities diversification of the Prime Reserve Fund.

T. Rowe Price offers 32 allocation funds. Retirement 2040 is the most successful allocation fund, which has provided an average total return of 10.21% since its inception in 2002. The objective of the fund is to provide the highest total return with a focus on both capital growth and income. In September 2013, Retirement 2040 had a total of 18 holdings. Domestic and foreign assets constitute 60% and 30% of the total asset allocation of Retirement 2040.

4.5.1.2 Notable funds

Approximately 16 T. Rowe Price funds are most notable funds. The Mid-Cap Growth Fund has given an annual average return of 13.91% since its inception in 1992. The fund has maximum exposure in industrial and business services (21.3%), information technology (19.1%), and healthcare sectors (17.6%).

The T. Rowe Price Small-Cap Value Fund has given an annual average return of 12.28% since its inception in 1988. This small-cap fund aims for long-term capital growth by means of investing primarily in undervalued companies. This fund has maximum exposure in financials (22.2%), industrial and business services (21.8%), and consumer discretionary (13.5%).

The T. Rowe Price New Horizons Fund provides long-term growth of capital by investing in common stocks of small rapidly growing companies. This fund has given an annual average return of 11.50% since its inception in 1960. The fund's maximum investment is in sectors such as information technology (24.6%), consumer discretionary (24.5%), health care (16.7%), and industrial and business services (14%). The T. Rowe Price New Horizon and Small-Cap Value Fund is closed to new investors. The T. Rowe Price Blue Chip Growth Fund provides long-term capital growth and income. The fund has given an average annual return of 11.47% since its inception in 1986. The fund's sector diversification consists of financials, health care, industrial businesses, and consumer staples. The financials constitute 12% of the total sectoral diversification.

The Equity Income Fund offers a high level of dividend income and long-term capital growth primarily through investments in stocks. The Equity Income Fund has offered a return of 11.22% since its inception in 1985. The fund invests 19.7% of funds in sectors such as financials. The Growth Stock Fund seeks long-term capital growth through investments in stocks. The fund has given an average total return of 10.79% since its inception in 1970.

Investments in mutual funds generate only moderate market risk since investment portfolios are diversified. T. Rowe Price manages its exposure to market risk by diversifying its investments among many domestic and international funds.

4.5.1.3 Retirement investment products

T. Rowe Price is a leader in retirement investing. T. Rowe Price offers a diverse array of investment options such as traditional IRAs, Roth IRAs, and transfer or rollover IRAs. A traditional IRA offers tax-deferred growth potential with investors able to deduct all or part of their traditional IRA contributions from pretax income if certain conditions are met, thereby reducing current tax obligations. A Roth IRA is an individual retirement account for investors who target tax-free growth potential. It is an effective option for both estate and retirement planning purposes. Through the Easy Transfer IRA Service, the transfer of an IRA to T. Rowe Price is possible.

T. Rowe Price also offers small business retirement plans such as SEP-IRA, simple IRA, individual 401(K), and small business 401(K) plans for self-employed individuals and small business owners. In 2013, the SEP-IRA plan allowed self-employed individuals to make deductible contributions of up to $51,000 per participant. A simple IRA is a low-cost retirement plan for self-employed individuals or for small businesses with up to 100 employees. This plan offers most of the benefits of a 401(k) plan. The individual 401(k) retirement plan allows one-person business owners and their working spouses the opportunity to save more for retirement. Small business 401(k) plans, such as Century Retirement Solutions, are meant for employers with fewer than 500 employees. T. Rowe Price 403(b) plans provide nonprofit or tax-exempt organizations, such as churches, hospitals, and schools, an effective and low-cost way to save for retirement.

T. Rowe Price uses interactive tools to develop customized solutions for retirement needs. The Tools include FuturePath, Retirement Income Calculator, Social Security Benefits Evaluator, Distribution Calculator, Rollover Planner, and Ready-2-Retire Tool.

4.5.1.4 Planning and research

T. Rowe Price provides planning services for investing, retirement planning, college savings, and estate planning. In asset allocation, the funds are spread among different types of investments such as stocks, bonds, and short-term securities.

In the college planning category, T. Rowe Price offers college savings plans and college savings options. The most popular approach for accumulating college savings are 529 plans. The two types of 529 plans are savings plans and prepaid tuition plans. In savings plans an amount of $320,000 or more can be held in a managed account. Prepaid tuition plans enable payment of future education at discounted rates set today. College savings options consist of alternate investment options—plans and tax-savings strategies targeted at college-saving efforts. This includes select investments that limit taxes on investment earnings. The interest on redeemed US Government Series EE and Series I savings bonds is exempt from federal taxation when the proceeds are used for college tuition or for contributions to 529 plans or education savings accounts.

T. Rowe Price also facilitates tax planning and estate planning. The company provides estate planning services such as planning for tomorrow, executing wills, transferring assets, considering trust, and managing estate taxes. The research and analysis division at T. Rowe Price provides detailed analysis about global economy, market trends, mutual funds, and individual stocks. Advisory planning services are available to investors with at least $100,000 in investable assets.

In 2012, the assets under management were worth $576.8 billion. In 2012, the six price funds of growth stock, equity income, mid-cap growth, blue-chip growth, value, and new income accounted for 25% of investment advisory revenues and 21% of assets under management. Table 4.8 provides the value of assets under management of different funds of T. Rowe Price. Table 4.9 highlights the financial performance of T. Rowe Price during the period 2008-2012.

Table 4.8 T. Rowe Price Assets Under Management 2011-2012 (Billions of US Dollars)		
	2011	**2012**
Stock and blend funds	211.7	256.9
Bond and money market funds	289.4	346.9
Source: http://files.shareholder.com/downloads/TROW/2791228597x0xS1113169-13-10/1113169/filing.pdf		

Table 4.9 T. Rowe Price Financial Performance 2008-2012					
	2008	**2009**	**2010**	**2011**	**2012**
Net revenues (millions of US dollars)	2116	1867	2367	2747	3023
Net income (millions of US dollars)	491	434	672	773	884
Total assets (millions of US dollars)	2819	3210	3642	3770	4203
Stockholders equity (millions of US dollars)	2489	2882	3297	3421	3846
Assets under management (billions of US dollars)	276.3	391.3	482	489.5	576.8
Source: Annual Report T. Rowe Price					

4.6 PIMCO

PIMCO is a global investment management company, founded in 1971, that manages retirement and investment assets for investors. PIMCO products include public and private pension and retirement plans, educational institutions, foundations, endowments, corporations, and financial advice. By September 2013, PIMCO had $1.97 trillion in assets under management and $1.59 trillion in third-party client assets. The firm is headquartered in California.

4.6.1 INVESTMENT STRATEGIES

The following are the investment strategies based on asset classes.

4.6.1.1 Short duration

PIMCO focuses on investments in cash and short duration, fixed income, equity, real estate, currency, alternatives, and asset allocation by asset class. Short-term duration strategies involve investment in money market and other short-maturity fixed-income securities. Money market strategies aim to enhance short-term yields with a diversified portfolio of high-quality commercial papers and other short-term maturities. The firm's global short-term strategy aims to maximize total return along with preservation of capital by investing in money market, short-, and long-maturity global fixed-income securities on a currency hedged basis. The firm uses a diversified set of strategies that includes country, currency, sector rotation, yield curve positioning, and duration management in all major sectors of the bond market.

4.6.1.2 Fixed income

In its fixed-income asset class, PIMCO offers absolute return strategies that aim for risk-adjusted returns and capital appreciation. The long/short-fixed-income strategies are further divided into the Global Credit Opportunity Strategy (GCOS) and PIMCO Absolute Return Strategy (PARS). Based on GCOS, PIMCO invests in global credit markets consisting of US corporate credit, European corporate debt, high-yield bonds, emerging market debt, and derivatives such as asset-backed securities. PARS aims for absolute returns by means of investments in various securities and use of leverage and derivatives. The PIMCO Unconstrained Bond strategy is an absolute return-oriented fixed-income strategy that invests in a broad range of fixed-income securities without sector or instrument limitations. The unconstrained tax-managed bond strategy is an absolute return-oriented fixed-income strategy aimed at investment in an efficient tax portfolio. In a credit absolute return strategy, a portfolio consisting of investment-grade, high-yield bonds, bank loans, and other corporate securities is formed.

Emerging market strategies consist of diversified income, emerging local bond strategy, and emerging bond strategy. Global strategies invest in a broad range of fixed-income securities and global currencies. The income strategies aim to maximize current income such as retirement income using diversified income strategies, floating income strategies, and senior floating rate strategies. Inflation-linked bond strategies are used as a hedge against inflation risk and portfolio diversification by offering exposure to US TIPS.

4.6.1.3 Equity

Equity strategies aim to offer long-term returns. Active stock selection is based on different strategies such as the Pathfinder strategy, emerging markets equity strategy, dividend and income builder strategy, and long/short equity strategy. The Pathfinder strategy involves investing in stocks trading at a 30% or greater discount of their estimate of intrinsic value with a focus on quality companies. The emerging markets strategy aims to outperform the MSCI emerging markets index by investing in emerging market stocks. The PIMCO dividend strategy invests exclusively in dividend-paying equities, whereas the PIMCO dividend and income builder strategy invests in equities as well as select fixed-income securities. The PIMCO long/short-equity strategy with a 10-year record is basically a long biased equity strategy with a portfolio mix of long and short equity and cash or cash equivalent positions.

Equity market neutral strategies aim to hedge market risk by investing in a long portfolio of actively selected stocks through an equal short position in a stock index.

PIMCO's StocksPLUS strategies are based on equity market exposure through investments in equity index derivatives as well as deployment of an actively managed fixed-income portfolio through collateral backing. StocksPLUS strategies have been offered since their inception in 1986. The PIMCO Emerging Multi-Asset Strategy provides diversified exposure to broad emerging market products such as emerging market equities, emerging market corporate bonds, and currencies.

4.6.1.4 Real estate

Real estate strategies invest in inflation-linked bonds, commodities, and real estate. Inflation-linked bond strategies act as hedges against inflation risk and enhance portfolio diversification. PIMCO's All Asset strategies provide a wide range of strategies that involve investments in global stocks and bonds, commodities, real estate, and liquid alternative strategies. Other strategies involving real estate are commodities-based strategies and diversified real estate strategies.

4.6.1.5 Currency

Currency-based strategies are the emerging market currency strategy and foreign exchange strategy. The emerging markets currency strategy involves investments primarily in the currencies of and fixed-income instruments, which are denominated in the currencies of developing markets. The PIMCO foreign exchange strategy is based on a three-pronged approach that combines quantitative, qualitative, and tail risk hedging techniques in global exchange rates.

4.6.1.6 Alternatives

PIMCO offers opportunistic/distressed and hedge fund strategies that focus on global macro, credit relative, volatility arbitrage, and distressed mortgage and corporate credit opportunities. By 2013,

PIMCO had managed approximately $25.8 billion in alternative investments such as hedge funds and opportunistic funds.

4.6.1.7 Asset allocation

PIMCO asset allocation strategies create portfolios in traditional and alternative asset classes. These strategies aim for portfolio diversification by means of dynamic multi-asset and risk factor solutions. Asset allocation strategies consist of all asset strategies, diversified real asset strategies, real retirement target date strategies, tail risk strategies, and emerging multi-asset strategies.

PIMCO's tail risk strategy involves construction of asymmetric hedging over portfolios which helps clients mitigate portfolio downside risk. Tail risk hedging may involve entering into financial derivatives that are expected to increase in value during the tail events.

PIMCO's Liability Driven Investment (LDI) Solutions focus on a sophisticated liability-focused approach to benchmarking a portfolio to enhance returns.

PIMCO provides investment solutions in a variety of vehicles for individuals and institutions and advisors. PIMCO supports registered investment advisors, family offices, and investment professionals at bank trusts and brokerages and banks.

4.6.2 MUTUAL FUNDS

PIMCO offers a wide range of mutual funds across all classes of assets. The PIMCO All Asset Fund targets real returns from a portfolio of traditional and alternative asset classes. This fund invests in inflation hedging assets such as TIPS, commodities, and international stocks and bonds. PIMCO is a leading active manager of traditional and alternative strategies across asset classes, which include global bonds and stocks, real estate, and commodities.

PIMCO mutual funds are categorized into absolute return bond, alternative, asset allocation—global, asset allocation—real return, core, domestic equity, global bond, global equity, government, income, international bond, money market, municipal, real return, retirement income, retirement solutions, and short-term funds. The PIMCO Credit Absolute Fund invests in a diversified portfolio of fixed-income instruments of varying maturities. The PIMCO Mortgage Opportunities Fund aims to maximize long-term return by investing in mortgage-related assets that include agency residential and commercial-backed securities and private label residential and commercial mortgage-backed securities (MBS). This fund provides a 1-year annualized return of 7.18%.

4.6.3 FEATURED FUNDS

The PIMCO All Asset Fund consists of PIMCO funds and actively managed PIMCO ETFs. The PIMCO All Asset Fund targets real returns after adjustment for inflation in traditional assets such as stocks, bonds, cash, and alternative asset classes. The fund is suitable for long-term investors as it has the flexibility to select a range of PIMCO funds that invest in inflation-hedging assets such as TIPS, commodities, and domestic and international stocks and bonds.

The PIMCO All Asset Authority Fund shares are classified as Institutional, Class P, Administrative, Class D, A, and C. The fund invests in actively managed PIMCO mutual funds with a broad asset classification consisting of global bonds, stocks, real estate, and commodities. The primary benchmark of the fund is the S&P 500 Index. The secondary benchmark is the CPI plus 6.5%, which is relevant over a full business cycle.

The primary portfolio of diversified income fund consists of investment-grade corporate, high-yield, and emerging market fixed-income securities with 3- to 8-year average duration. This fund seeks higher income potential from multiple sectors of the global bond market. The diversified income fund offers exposure to global investment grade, high-yield corporate credit, and emerging market debt. The primary benchmark for this fund is Barclays Global Credit Hedged Index. The second benchmark is an equally weighted blend of three indexes: Barclays Global Aggregate Credit Component, BoA Merrill Lynch Global High-Yield BB-B Rated Constrained, and J Morgan EMBI Global.

The PIMCO Dividend and Income Builder Fund is a diversified portfolio of global income-producing investments in global stocks with top five-sector diversification in financials, consumer discretionary, information technology, energy, telecommunications, and services.

The Fundamental Advantage Absolute Return Strategy Fund maintains long exposure to the Enhanced Research Affiliates Fundamental Index (Enhanced RAFI 1000) and short exposure to the S&P 500 with a focus on isolating Enhanced RAFI 1000 outperformance.

The income fund consists of a portfolio of a broad range of intermediate duration bonds, which is actively managed to maximize current income.

The Municipal Bond Fund is a diversified portfolio that consists of mainly intermediate to long duration, high-quality municipal bonds that carry interest payments exempt from federal tax. The basic focus of the fund is current income and capital appreciation.

The StocksPLUS Absolute Return Fund aims for total returns that exceed that of the S&P 500. This fund was established in 1986. The StocksPLUS Strategy aims to benefit from active fixed-income and equity-derivative management. The StocksPLUS Absolute Return Fund is designed to outperform the benchmark through yield advantage and potential price appreciation in an actively managed absolute return-oriented portfolio of fixed-income securities. The fund provides exposure to the returns of the S&P 500 Index via derivatives positions.

The Total Return Fund is a diversified portfolio of high-quality bonds that are actively managed to maximize returns.

4.6.4 EXCHANGE-TRADED FUNDS

The ETFs offered by PIMCO can be classified as active/index, duration, sector, and solution. All ETFs offer access to PIMCO's portfolio management expertise, which includes trade execution and risk management. Table 4.10 lists the different types of actively managed ETFs of PIMCO. Table 4.11 shows the different types of index funds under the ETF category of PIMCO.

Table 4.10   PIMCO's Actively Managed Funds

Total Return Exchange-Traded Fund

Enhanced Short Maturity Exchange-Traded Fund

Foreign Currency Strategy Exchange-Traded Fund

Global Advantage Inflation-Linked Bond Exchange-Traded Fund

Short-term Municipal Bond Exchange-Traded Fund

Intermediate Municipal Bond Exchange-Traded Fund

Build America Bond Exchange-Traded Fund

Table 4.11   PIMCO's Index Funds

1-3 Year US Treasury Index Exchange-Traded Fund
3-7 Year US Treasury index Exchange-Traded Fund
7-15 Year US Treasury Index Exchange-Traded Fund
25+ Year Zero Coupon US Treasury Index Exchange-Traded Fund
Broad US Treasury Index Exchange-Traded Fund
1-5 Year US TIPS Index Exchange-Traded Fund
Broad US TIPS Index Exchange-Traded Fund
15+ Year US TIPS Index Exchange-Traded Fund
Investment Grade Corporate Bond Index Exchange-Traded Fund
0-5 Year High Yield Corporate Bond Index Exchange-Traded Fund
Australia Bond Index Exchange-Traded Fund
Germany Bond Index Exchange-Traded fund
Canada Bond Index Exchange-Traded Fund

On the basis of duration, PIMCO ETFs are classified as low, intermediate, ultra-long, and long funds. The PIMCO Enhanced Short Maturity Exchange-Traded Fund is an actively managed ETF that belongs in the ultra-low duration category. Long duration funds have a duration of 7-15 years and ultra-long duration funds have durations of more than 25 years. The PIMCO 25+ year Zero Coupon US Treasury Index Exchange-Traded Fund aims to capture the returns of the BoA Merrill Lynch Long US Treasury Principal STRIPS Index.

On the basis of sector, PIMCO ETFs are classified as core fixed income, US Treasury, US TIPS, municipal, corporate, global, currency, and inflation-linked funds. On the basis of solution, PIMCO ETFs are classified as core fixed income, liquidity management, alternatives, US Treasury indexes, inflation protection, tax awareness, credit, and global diversification. PIMCO Closed-End funds offer attractive income with wide exposure to a broad range of income-generating securities that include bonds in the corporate, municipal and mortgage related sectors. Closed-end income funds include the Corporate and Income Opportunity Fund, Global StocksPLUS and Income Fund, and the High Income Fund. Municipal closed-end funds include the California Municipal Income Fund and California Municipal Income Fund II and III. Table 4.12 provides the statistical highlights of PIMCO funds.

Table 4.12   PIMCO Highlights September 2013 (Trillions of US Dollars)

Assets under management	1.97
Third-party client assets	1.59
Total employees	2478
Investment professionals	736

4.6.5 MANAGED ACCOUNTS

4.6.5.1 Core products

PIMCO-managed accounts provide customized investment solutions for high-net-worth investors through financial intermediaries. Core products consist of PIMCO Total Return and PIMCO Real Return. Total Return is a core bond strategy that maximizes total return through a portfolio of superior quality intermediate term bonds. The firm manages commingled funds to enhance the diversification strategy. The strategy aims for maximum total return, which consists of income plus capital appreciation. The Total Return investment process uses top-down and bottom-up strategies that concentrate on duration, yield-curve positioning, volatility, and sector rotation. Bottom-up strategies focus on security selection process and facilitate identification and analysis of undervalued securities. PIMCO Total Return managed-account portfolios are constructed based on the core segment of individual bonds and two sector-oriented PIMCO-managed commingled vehicles.

The PIMCO Real Return strategy involves a core inflation protection strategy that focuses on maximum real return through investments in inflation-linked bonds such as TIPS. This strategy aims to maximize real returns while preserving the real capital of a portfolio. Real Return Managed Account portfolios are constructed using a core segment of individual bonds and PIMCO-managed sector-oriented commingled vehicles.

4.6.5.2 Municipal products

PIMCO is one of the largest investors in municipal bonds with $58 billion in assets under management in 2012. The PIMCO Municipal Bond Laddered Strategy aims to generate tax-efficient income and preservation of capital by investing in high-quality municipal bonds across sectors and issuers.

4.7 FRANKLIN TEMPLETON

Franklin Templeton is a global investment management company that consists of the independent multiclass investment management groups of Franklin, Templeton, and Mutual Series. The company was founded in 1947 in New York as Franklin Resources. Currently, Franklin Templeton is headquartered in California and has an extensive global presence with offices in 35 countries and clients in more than 150 countries. Franklin Templeton is the name of the global brand that is listed on the New York Stock Exchange. The company's stock is included in the Standard & Poor's 500 Index.

Franklin Templeton manages investments for individuals, institutions, pension plans, trusts, and partnerships. Franklin offers investment choices through Franklin Templeton, Mutual Series, Bissett, Fiduciary Trust, Darby, and Balanced Equity Management brand names. According to company statistics, Franklin Templeton had $749.9 billion in assets under management with 23 million billable shareholder accounts worldwide. Franklin Templeton provides services that consist of investment management, fund administration, sales, distribution, shareholder services, transfer agency, trustee, custodial, and fiduciary services as well as private banking services. The investment solutions offered include mutual funds, retirement savings vehicles, and 529 college savings plans. Sponsored investment products include a wide range of equity, hybrid, fixed-income, cash management funds and accounts, alternative investment products, and multi-asset allocation strategies. Most of the investment funds offered are open-ended mutual funds. Franklin Templeton offers taxable and tax-free fixed-income funds, hybrid funds, and growth-oriented equity funds. The wide range of Sponsored Investment Products (SIP) consists of

Table 4.13   Acquisitions by Franklin Resources

Year	Acquirer	Target
1992	Franklin	Templeton, Galbraith & Hansberger
1996	Franklin Templeton	Mutual Series Fund of Heine Securities
2000	Franklin Templeton	Ssangyong Templeton Investment Trust Management
2000	Franklin Templeton Investments	Bissett
2001	Franklin Templeton	Fiduciary Trust Company International
2002	Franklin Templeton Asset Management (India)	Pioneer ITI AMC
2003	Franklin Templeton	Darby Overseas Investments
2006	Franklin Templeton	Bradesco Templeton Asset Management, Brazil
2011	Franklin Templeton	Rensburg Fund Management Limited
2011	Franklin Templeton	Balanced Equity Management

Source: Collated from Annual Report 2012.

Table 4.14   Categories of Franklin Templeton Assets Under Management 2012 (Billions of US Dollars)

Type of Asset	Value
Equity	297.1
Hybrid (asset allocation, balanced, flexible and income mixed funds)	110.1
Fixed income	336.3
Cash management (short-term liquid assets)	6.4
Total	749.9

Source: Annual Report 2012.

products under hybrid, fixed income, cash management funds and accounts. Table 4.13 gives the acquisitions made by Franklin Templeton during the period 1992-2011. Table 4.14 lists the values of assets under management of Franklin Templeton.

The investment management fees represent a major part of the revenue. The sales and distribution fees consisting of sales charges and distribution of sponsored investment products also constitute a large source of revenue.

4.7.1 TYPES OF INVESTMENT MANAGEMENT AND RELATED SERVICES

4.7.1.1 Investment management services

The company offers investment management services for sponsored investment products, subadvised products, and managed accounts. The services include fundamental investment research and valuation analyses, company research and analyses of suppliers, customers, and competitors. Most of the investment management agreements between subsidiaries and US funds are renewed every year after an initial 2-year term. Through this agreement, the funds pay a monthly fee in arrears based on the fund's average daily net assets. The master/feeder fund of funds structure allows an investment advisor to manage a single portfolio of securities at the master fund level and have multiple feeder funds that invest in the master fund. Individual and institutional shareholders invest in the feeder funds, which offer a variety of service and distribution options. In separately managed accounts, investors and their financial advisors choose an investment manager who creates a personalized portfolio to meet investment requirements. Accounts are generally funded with securities in cash. The minimum for accounts is generally $100,000 or $250,000, depending on the equity or fixed-income investments.

4.7.1.2 Sales and distribution

Sales and distribution services also generate a significant portion of the revenue for Franklin. Fund shares are basically sold through a large network of independent intermediaries that includes broker-dealers, financial advisers, and third parties. Franklin Templeton Distributors Inc. (FTDI) acts as the principal underwriter and distributor of shares of the majority of open-ended US funds. The majority of the retail funds are distributed with multiclass share structures. Class A shares are sold without a front-end sales charge to shareholders. Class B shares have no front-end sales charges, but instead have a declining schedule of sales charges if the investor redeems within a certain number of years with respect to the original purchase date. Open US funds no longer issue Class B shares. Class C shares do not have a front-end sales charge, but have a back-end sales charge for redemptions within 12 months from the date of purchase. In the United States, Franklin Templeton offers Advisor class shares and Z shares in the Mutual Series funds. These shares are offered to qualified financial intermediaries, institutions, and high-net-worth clients. Money market funds are offered to investors without a sales charge. According to the company's annual report in 2012, around 1500 local, regional, and national banks, securities firms, and financial adviser firms offered Franklin Templeton open-ended US funds for sale. The open-ended US funds have adopted distribution plans under Rule 12b-1, under which the fund bears certain expenses related to the distribution of shares such as expenses for marketing, advertising, printing, and sales promotion.

4.7.1.3 Shareholder and transfer agency services

Franklin Templeton receives shareholder servicing fees for providing transfer agency services such as providing customer statements, transaction processing, customer service, and tax reporting. The subsidiary, Franklin Templeton Investor Services, serves as a shareholder-servicing and dividend-paying agent for the open-ended funds.

4.7.1.4 High-net-worth investment management services

Franklin Templeton provides investment management and related services to high-net-worth individuals and families, foundations, and institutional clients through the Fiduciary Trust. Fiduciary Trust Services include wealth management and estate and tax planning. The trust provides an integrated package of services known as Family Resource Management.

4.7.1.5 Institutional investment management

Franklin Templeton provides institutional investment management services to institutional clients with a focus on endowment funds, government, and corporate pension plans. Franklin Templeton Institutional offers a wide range of US and international equity, fixed-income, and alternative strategies through investment vehicles such as separate accounts, open-ended, closed-end, and unregistered funds. Franklin Templeton markets and distributes sponsored investment products through subsidiaries such as Franklin Templeton Financial Services Corp. and Templeton/Franklin Investment.

4.7.1.6 Trust and custody services

The subsidiaries of Franklin Templeton offer trust, custody, and related services that include administration, performance measurement, estate planning, tax planning, and private banking. The company also provides planned giving administration and related custody services for nonprofit organizations such as pooled income funds, charitable remainder trusts, charitable lead trusts, and gift annuities.

4.7.1.7 Management of alternate investment products

This function is performed by the subsidiary, Darby, by sponsoring and managing funds that invest in private equity and mezzanine finance transactions in emerging markets in Asia, Latin America, and Central/Eastern Europe. These investment funds are offered by Darby to institutional and high-net-worth individual investors through private placement. Franklin Templeton Institutional manages funds with exposure to global real estate opportunities. Franklin Adviser, the company's investment adviser service, manages investment partnerships that invest in derivatives products in global equity, government bond, and currency markets.

4.7.1.8 Private banking

Fiduciary Trust provides private banking services to high-net-worth clients who maintain trust, custody, and managed accounts. In 2012, Fiduciary Trust had assets worth $901.6 million and deposits of $611 million, which were secured by the Federal Deposit Insurance Corporation (FDIC). Products offered include loans secured by marketable securities, deposits accounts, and other banking services. The deposits include demand and savings deposits.

4.7.2 INVESTMENT PRODUCTS

Equity investment products focus on growth, value, or both. Income portfolios consist of taxable and tax-exempt money market instruments, tax-exempt municipal bonds, global fixed-income securities, and fixed-income debt securities of US government and mortgage institutions such as the Governmental National Mortgage Association, Federal National Mortgage Association, and Federal Home Loan Mortgage Corporation.

Franklin Templeton's five largest US funds were the Franklin Income Fund, Templeton Global Bond Fund, Mutual Global Discovery Fund, Templeton Growth Fund, and the Franklin Tax Free Income Fund. In 2012, these five funds accounted for 24% of the total assets under management. The cross-border products comprising a wide array of investment funds are registered for sale to non-US investors in 39 countries representing 11% of the total assets under management in 2012 with a value of $143.6 billion. The three largest cross-border funds are the Templeton Global Bond Fund, Templeton Global Total Return Fund, and Templeton Asian Growth Fund.

Equity funds are categorized on the basis of their investments in the Asia Pacific, Canada, Europe, the Middle East, Africa, and the United States, as well as emerging markets and global internationals. Hybrid funds invest primarily in the equities and fixed-income securities of companies located in the aforementioned regions. Fixed-income funds invest in debt securities offered by companies and government entities in different regions. Cash management funds invest primarily in money market instruments and short-term securities. Table 4.15 lists the number of funds under different types of Franklin funds.

The closed-end funds offered by Franklin Funds are the Franklin Templeton Limited Duration Income Trust, Franklin Universal Trust, Templeton Dragon Fund, Templeton Emerging Market Fund, Templeton Emerging Markets Income Fund, Templeton Global Income Fund, Templeton Russia, and the East European Fund.

Table 4.15   Franklin Templeton Funds

Type	Number of Funds
Franklin Funds	94
Templeton Funds	19
Mutual Series	8

The Franklin Short-Duration US Government Fund is an ETF that offers investors access to return and income from allocations involving a wide variety of US government securities. This ETF is designed with the flexibility to rotate allocations among multiple investment products, which include treasuries, MBS, agency adjustable rate mortgages (ARMs), and TIPS in various market cycles.

4.7.3 TYPES OF RISK

The assets under management value is affected by market risk factors that consist of changes in equity market prices, interest rates, credit spreads, and foreign exchange rates. Franklin Templeton is exposed to market risk due to investment management activities and receipt of distribution fees. The firm is exposed to interest rate risk from changes in interest rates basically due to investments in debt securities, loans receivables, deposits, and debt obligations. Franklin Templeton hedges interest rate risk due to investments in debt securities by managing the maturities of these securities and by diversification, which ensures a mix of debt at fixed and variable interest rates. The firm also monitors the interest rates and average maturities of loan and deposit portfolios. Franklin Templeton also faces foreign currency exchange risk due to international operations. Market valuation risk is mitigated through a diversified investment portfolio and derivatives agreements. Table 4.16 provides the financial highlights of Franklin Templeton during the 5-year period 2008-2012.

Table 4.16   Franklin Templeton Financial Highlights 2008-2012

	2008	2009	2010	2011	2012
Operating revenues (millions of US dollars)	6032.4	4194.1	5853	7140	7101
Operating income (millions of US dollars)	2099	1202.6	1958.7	2659.8	2515.2
Net income (millions of US dollars)	1588.2	896.8	1445.7	1923.6	1931.4
Total assets (millions of US dollars)	9176.5	9468.5	10,708.1	13,775.8	14,751.5
Debt (millions of US dollars)	269.3	121.2	979.9	998.2	1566.1
Stockholder's equity (millions of US dollars)	7074.4	7632.2	7727	8524.7	9201.3
Operating cash flows	1409.2	641.4	1651.0	1621.8	1066.2
Assets under management (billions of US dollars)	507.3	523.4	644.9	659.9	749.9

Source: Annual Report 2012

4.8 **BLACKROCK**

BlackRock is one of the largest and most diversified asset management companies in the world. The company is located in 30 countries serving the investment management needs of clients in more than 100 countries. In 2012, the company had $3.792 trillion in assets under management and revenues of $9.3 billion. BlackRock is structured around the key areas of investment strategies, client businesses, corporate operations, and business operations and technology.

4.8.1 **STRATEGY**

BlackRock focuses on five strategic areas for growth along with emerging markets. They are iShares ETFs, multi-asset solutions, retirement products, income-oriented products, and alternatives.

In 2012, the iShares Core Series consisting of 10 US ETFs was designed for buy and hold retail investors. Multi-asset solutions generated $16 billion inflows in 2012. BlackRock also focuses on new strategies for public and private pension funds and DC plan sponsors. In 2012, the LifePath target date products contributed more than $13 billion in flows. In the same year, income-oriented products such as active and index high-yield and equity dividend funds generated $18 billion in revenues. The Retail alternative mutual funds-generated assets were close to $0.8 billion. BlackRock is one of the world's largest investors in emerging markets with more than $200 billion in assets under management with a focus on index products. BlackRock has developed a specialized investment group based on the five core portfolio building blocks of alpha strategies, beta strategies, multi-asset strategies, alternatives strategies, and trading and liquidity strategies. BlackRock Solutions advisory services provide asset allocation and asset liability solutions through the proprietary risk management and trading platform Aladdin.

BlackRock has also adopted an inorganic growth strategy by means of acquisitions. The company acquired Claymore Investments, thereby expanding the offerings of ETFs in the Canadian market. The company also acquired Swiss Re Ltd.'s European private equity and infrastructure fund of funds unit for expanding alternative businesses. In 2013, BlackRock announced the acquisition of Credit Suisse's ETF business. In spring 2012, *Fortune* magazine named BlackRock the "world's most admired company in the investment industry."

4.8.1.1 Investment strategies

The major investment strategies are classified as alpha strategies, beta strategies, multi-asset strategies, alternative strategies, trading and liquidity strategies. The portfolio of investment consists of active equity and fixed income, iShares equity and fixed income, non-ETF index equity and fixed income, multi-asset, alternatives, and cash management products. BlackRock has 22 investment centers across the globe with more than 1600 investment professionals.

4.8.1.2 Alpha strategies

Alpha strategies aim for generating excess returns by managing active mutual funds, fixed-income ETFs, commingled funds, and separate accounts. Alpha strategies are Fixed Income, Fundamental Equity, Scientific Active Equity, and Private Investors. The Fixed Income team consists of 262 portfolio managers and 113 research analysts, which are organized as Americas Fixed Income and International Fixed Income. Americas Fixed Income invests in active and passive fixed-income products such as investment grade, leveraged finance, securitized products, interest rate and municipal bonds, and the iShares suite of products. International Fixed Income has exposures in regional securities in EMEA (Europe, Middle East, and Africa) and Asia Pacific. The Equity division with about 239 investment professionals is organized into two teams: Fundamental Equity and Scientific Active Equity. Fundamental Equity uses proprietary research to actively manage fundamental and quantitative equity investments. Scientific Active Equity involves a quantitative stocks selection process to manage equity investments. The Equity Dividend product is its flagship product.

4.8.1.3 Beta strategies

Beta strategies or index strategies provide market exposure through collective funds, iShares ETFs, index mutual funds, and other index-related investment vehicles. The team, consisting of 118 investment professionals in different geographical areas such as the Americas, EMEA, and Asia Pacific, manages portfolios across 600 different benchmarks. The beta strategies consist of the Index Equity Strategy and Index Asset Allocation. The Index Equity Strategy focuses on a portfolio construction process to achieve index replication or optimization. Index Equity offers products such as iShares Equity. Index Asset Allocation offers a broad range of funds of funds, target date funds, and derivatives-based funds across all asset classes. The Index Asset Allocation platform consists of approximately 1800 funds. This allocation strategy focuses on tailored rebalancing methodologies and expert beta exposure selection. LifePath Target Date and Target Risk series of funds, established in 1993, uses allocation models to balance risk and return over the investor's expected retirement horizon.

4.8.1.4 Multi-asset strategies

Multi-asset strategies focus on diversified asset allocation and personalized products for generating Alpha for retail and institutional clients. The Multi-asset strategies consist of Global Allocation, Global Market Strategies, Global Multi-Asset Strategies, and Model Portfolio Solutions. The Global Allocation Strategy focuses on absolute long-term returns. The BlackRock Global Allocation Fund is a flagship product that is broadly diversified across different asset classes in different regions, sectors, industries, currencies, and securities. The Global Market Strategy uses global macro-style strategies to generate excess returns by investing in equity, fixed income, currency, and commodity markets. Global Multi-Asset Solutions develop and manage investment solutions using multiple strategies and asset classes. Model Portfolio Solutions are designed to facilitate financial advisors and registered investment advisors to provide active and index-based investments. These models provide optimal allocations across mutual funds and iShares ETFs for institutional investors.

4.8.1.5 Alternate strategies

The alternate strategies are managed by the BlackRock Alternative Investors (BAI) division, which consists of four core teams: BlackRock Alternative Advisors (BAA), Real Estate, BlackRock Private Equity Partners (PEP), and Renewal Power. BAA is the hedge fund solution team of BAI that provides customized advice and implementation of hedge fund strategies by offering a range of products and services. The Real Estate team invests in real estate equity and debt instruments across multiple investment vehicles such as REITs, commingled funds, and separate accounts. PEP is the global provider of private market investment solutions, and offers diversified private equity portfolios consisting of primary and secondary private equity funds. Renewable Power invests in wind and solar power projects.

Trading and liquidity strategies are centered around the four main business activities of cash management, securities lending, transition management, and trading.

4.8.2 PRODUCTS AND SERVICES

4.8.2.1 Asset management for individuals

The firm offers nearly 900 investments products and solutions for individuals. BlackRock offers more than 200 open-ended mutual funds that cover the entire range of asset classes, styles, and regions. The firm offers over 80 closed-end funds globally, which are diversified across different investment styles, asset classes, and business sectors. iShares offer more than 600 products that are traded on 20 exchanges globally across a wide range of asset classes such as domestic equity, fixed-income, and emerging market instruments.

iShares is BlackRock's leading ETF platform and was launched in 2000. iShares offers more than 600 products that are traded on 20 exchanges globally. The iShares Core series, introduced in 2012, consists of 10 low-cost US ETFs that target buy-and-hold investors. Individual investors are also provided access to registered alternative funds and other vehicles.

4.8.2.2 Asset management for institutions

BlackRock offers a wide range of capabilities across investment strategies, asset classes, and global markets. The company has about $2.5 trillion institutional assets under management. The equity offerings are based on three approaches of Fundamental Active, Scientific Active, and Index. BlackRock manages active, index, absolute return, institutional fund, and ETF iShares across different benchmark styles and types. BlackRock also offers liquidity funds across currencies and customized accounts for large investors. The company has a wide spectrum of alternative instruments such as hedge funds, private equity, real estate, and infrastructure. BlackRock offers DC plan sponsors, consultants, and financial advisors a wide range of retirement solutions such as BlackRock LifePath Target Date Funds.

4.8.2.3 Global Retail

Global Retail offers open-ended and closed-end mutual funds, ETFs, alternative products, and solutions to retail and high-net-worth clients through third-party distribution partners throughout the world. US Retail and Canada serves an estimated 95,000 financial advisers across multiple distribution channels such as wirehouses, regionals, independent firms, registered investment advisors, banks, and insurance companies. The largest distributor is Merrill Lynch. International Retail provides retail funds and solutions to a broad spectrum of private investors across EMEA, Latin America, and the Asia Pacific region.

4.8.2.4 BlackRock Solutions

BlackRock Solutions is the analytical center of the firm. It has two components: the Aladdin Business and Financial Markets Advisory. Aladdin Business provides risk analytics, portfolio management, trading systems, and accounting services to approximately 150 clients. These clients include financial institutions, pension funds, asset managers, foundations, consultants, mutual fund sponsors, real estate investment trusts, and government agencies. The firm has managed $13.7 trillion in assets on the Aladdin platform. Financial Markets Advisory provides balance sheet and capital markets advisory and asset disposition services to financial institutions globally. This advisory service provides guidance in valuing and managing complex portfolios, as well as disposition of distressed assets and other services. Table 4.17 provides the financial highlights of BlackRock during the period 2008-2012. Table 4.18 gives the component wise sources of revenues for BlackRock during the year 2012. Table 4.19 lists the composition of assets under management of different types of funds of BlackRock in the year 2012.

Table 4.17   BlackRock Financial Highlights 2008-2012 (Millions of US Dollars)

	2008	2009	2010	2011	2012
Revenues	5064	4700	8612	9081	9337
Net income	856	1021	2139	2239	2438
Assets under management	1,307,151	3,346,256	3,560,968	3,512,681	3,791,588

Table 4.18   Components of BlackRock Revenue 2012

Components	Percentage
Equity-based fees	45
Fixed-income based fees	20
Multi-asset based fees	10
Others including alternatives based fees, BlackRock Solutions, performance fees, cash management fees, distribution fees	25

Source: Annual Report 2012

Table 4.19   Composition of BlackRock Assets Under Management 2012

Components	Percentage
Non-ETP Index Equity	27
Fixed-Income Active	17
Equity iShares	14
Non-ETP Index Fixed Income	11
Equity Active	8
Multi-Asset	7
Cash Management	7
Fixed Income iShares	5
Alternatives	3
Advisory	1
Total AUM (trillions of US dollars)	3.792

Source: Annual Report 2012

REFERENCES

1. http://investor.vanguard.com/corporate-portal
2. http://investor.vanguard.com/home/
3. http://retirementplans.vanguard.com/VGApp/pe/PublicHome
4. http://institutional.vanguard.com/VGApp/iip/site/institutional/home?fromPage=portal

5. http://www.americanfunds.com/
6. http://www.americanfunds.com/retirement.html
7. http://americanfunds.com/college.html
8. http://www.fidelity.com/inside-fidelity/about-fidelity/our-businesses
9. http://www.fidelity.com/mutual-funds/overview
10. http://www.fidelity.com
11. http://www.fidelity.com/mutual-funds/fundsnetwork/overview
12. http://individual.troweprice.com/public/Retail?src=CorpHome
13. http://www3.troweprice.com/fb2/mfpathways/pathways.otc?facets=notable#sthash.MsaFUvc7.dpuf
14. http://www.pimco.com/en/Pages/default.aspx
15. http://investments.pimco.com/Pages/Default.aspx
16. http://www.pimcoetfs.com/Pages/default.aspx
17. Franklin Templeton Annual Report 2012
18. http://www.franklintempleton.com
19. Annual Report, BlackRock 2012
20. http://www.blackrock.com/corporate/en-ae/home
21. http://www.blackrock.com/corporate/en-ae/products-and-services

CASES ON INSURANCE COMPANIES

5.1 TRENDS IN THE INSURANCE INDUSTRY

In mature markets, the Life and Savings (L&S) market comprising traditional savings and unit-linked products, suffers when a low-interest-rate environment and economic uncertainty prevails. The annuity segment within the L&S market is declining as industry participants reduce benefits and increase charges in the variable annuity industry.

In high-growth markets in Asian countries (e.g., Hong Kong, Singapore, Thailand) and Latin American countries (e.g., Mexico), the L&S segment is seeing double-digit growth rates due to increased accessibility of insurance products and changing individual habits. Trends such as changes in regulations have affected the L&S insurance industry in the markets of Central and Eastern European countries. In recent years, the property and casualty (P&C) insurance industry witnessed growth in both mature and high-growth markets. In Japan, the rapid aging of the population and declining birthrate and rise in the number of single-person households has been attributed to the shift in consumer needs from death insurance products to endowment insurance products that cover medical treatments.

Claims paying and credit strength ratings have become increasingly important factors in establishing the competitive position of insurance companies. Global premiums in life insurance have shown a declining trend due to the shrinking premium volume in Europe, the United States, and China. This low-interest-rate environment poses challenges for insurers due to a decline in investment returns. The interest-rate guarantees of life insurers are particularly affected in an environment of lower interest rates. The low interest also affects the margins in the liability and property segments, which would result in premium increases in long tail businesses.

The insurance business is affected by industry and economic factors such as interest rates, credit and equity market conditions, regulation, tax policy, competition, and general economic, market, and political conditions. The current low-interest-rate environment and ongoing global economic uncertainty are major challenges for the growth of insurance markets and net investment income. These challenges, along with overcapacity in the property casualty insurance industry have become compelling factors for insurance companies to divest unprofitable businesses, tighten terms and conditions, and develop advanced data analytics for improving profitability. Low interest rates affect life insurance businesses as they put pressure on long-term investment returns, thereby inversely affecting future sales of interest rate-sensitive products. Products such as payout annuities and traditional life businesses, which are not rate-adjustable, may require increases in reserves if future investment yields are insufficient to support current valuations. Equity market volatility may result in higher reserves for variable annuity guarantee features.

5.1.1 SPECIFIC RISK IN INSURANCE

Insurance risk consists of product design risk, underwriting and expense overrun risk, lapse risk, and claims risk. Product design risk refers to potential defects in the development of a particular insurance product or product group. Underwriting and expense overrun risk is the risk of product-related income being inadequate to support future obligations arising from an insurance product. Lapse risk refers to the possibility of actual lapse experience that diverges from the expected experience assumed when the products were priced. It includes the potential loss incurred due to early termination of policies or contracts in situations where acquisition costs incurred are no longer recoverable from future revenues. Claims risk arises due to the possibility that frequency or severity of claims arising from insurance products exceeds the levels assumed when the products were priced. Reputational risk is the potential risk due to negative publicity with respect to a company's business practices, which may have adverse consequences such as loss of customers, brand damage, financial loss, and litigation.

Mortality risk consists of positive and negative mortality risk. Positive mortality risk exists when more insured die than expected, which leads to higher claims than expected. Negative mortality risk arises when the insured live longer than expected, which leads to higher claims than expected. Morbidity or health-related risk comprises the risk of variability of size, frequency, and time to payment of future claims, development of outstanding claims, and allocated loss adjustment expenses for morbidity product lines over the remaining contract period. Solvency II is an insurance regulation that concerns the amount of capital that European Union insurance companies must hold for reducing the risk of insolvency.

5.2 JAPAN POST INSURANCE CO.

Japan Post Holdings Co., Ltd. is a Japanese state-owned conglomerate that operates post offices, banks, and an insurance businesses. As of 2013, Japan Post Holdings was thirteenth on the Fortune Global 500 list of the world's largest companies. The four divisions of the group are Japan Post Service, Japan Post Network, Japan Post Bank, and Japan Post Insurance. Japan Post Insurance was established in 2007. Its asset allocation consists of 77% in corporate and government bonds, 17% in loans, and 1% in foreign securities.

Japan Post Insurance provides services through agents at the post offices of Japan Post Network as well as from direct sales offices. Japan Post Insurance has an Agency Relations division for directly managing sales in 80 major cities to support sales promotion, training, and development. Japan Post Insurance also has wholesale divisions in directly managed sales offices that provide products and services to small and mid-size companies. In 2010, Japan Post rolled out "Comprehensive and Heartfelt Services" at post offices across Japan to facilitate house calls, whereby insurance needs are addressed at clients' homes. Table 5.1 lists the different types of insurance schemes offered by Japan Post Insurance.

Japan Post Insurance also provides principal riders such as accident riders, nonparticipating accident hospitalization riders, nonparticipating illness hospitalization riders, and accident hospitalization riders. These riders are concerned with provisions for death or physical disability caused by accidents, predefined hospitalization, surgery, or long-term hospitalization. The benefits for nonparticipating illness hospitalization and accident hospitalization riders is ¥15,000 daily payment for hospital stays.

During 2011-2012, Japan Post Insurance established 2.12 million new insurance policies for individuals, providing income of ¥12,538.6 billion. Insurance premiums amounted to ¥6856.4 billion. Japan Post Insurance's core profit during the fiscal year 2012 was ¥571.6 billion.

Table 5.1 Types of Insurance Offered by Japan Post Insurance

Type of Insurance	Objective	Subscription Age Group
Fixed whole life insurance	Lifetime security	20-65
Whole life insurance with twofold insurance coverage	Balance of lifetime security	20-60
Special whole life insurance	Tanoshimi with fivefold insurance coverage	20-55
Ordinary term insurance	Security with minimum burden	15-50
Ordinary endowment insurance	Security and maturity	0-75
Special endowment with twofold/fivefold/tenfold insurance coverage	Security and maturity	15-65
Designated endowment insurance	Illness	40-65
Educational endowment insurance	Education funds	18-65
Educational endowment insurance with scholarship annuity	Enhanced security in preparations for education funds	18-65
Term annuity	Retirement	45-70
Asset formation savings insurance/housing funding insurance/asset formation whole life annuity	Accumulation of assets	15-65/15-54/36-54

The solvency margin ratio is an indicator by which regulatory agencies determine whether or not a company has the sufficient financial resources to pay benefits. In 2012, Japan Post Insurance's solvency ratio was 1336.1%, which is well above the regulatory benchmark of 200%.

In 2021, Japan Post Insurance sold 2.123 million individual insurance policies with an insured amount of ¥6,215.5 billion and 210,000 individual annuity policies with an annuity amount of ¥721.9 billion. By March 2012, Japan Post Insurance had 8 million individual insurance policies and policies in force had a value of ¥23,043.2 billion. There were 887,000 individual annuity policies with an annuity amount of ¥2,781.5 billion.

Japan Post Insurance is exposed to market risk, credit risk, and other types of risk, which are unique to the provision of financial services. Each group company identifies risk that can be quantified and uses value at risk (VaR) to measure these risks. Table 5.2 gives the statistical highlights of policies offered by Japan Post Insurance during the period 2010-2012.

Table 5.2 Japan Post Insurance Policy Highlights 2010-2012

	2010		2011		2012	
	Number of Policies	Insured Amount/ Annuity Amount	Number of Policies	Insured Amount/ Annuity Amount	Number of Policies	Insured Amount/ Annuity Amount
Life insurance	40,308	¥112069.4	35,496	¥98,910	31,016	¥85854.2
Annuity	5361	¥1980.4	4886	¥1809.4	4393	¥1628.5

Source: Japan Post Group Annual Report 2012. (Policies in thousands, amount in billions of yen.)

5.3 BERKSHIRE HATHAWAY

Berkshire Hathaway is a holding company in the United States that owns a number of subsidiaries in diversified business activities. These include insurance and reinsurance, freight rail transportation, utilities and energy, finance, manufacturing, services, and retailing. The subsidiaries of Berkshire Hathaway in the business of insurance underwriting and reinsurance are GEICO, General Reinsurance, and Berkshire Hathaway Reinsurance Group (BHRG). The subsidiaries involved in underwriting P&C insurance businesses are National Indemnity Company (NICO), Berkshire Hathaway Homestate Insurance Company, Medical Protective Company, Applied Underwriters, US Liability Insurance Company (USIC), Central States Indemnity Company, Bankers Surety, Cypress Insurance Company, Boat US, and the Guard Insurance Group.

5.3.1 INSURANCE

The property casualty insurers such as Berkshire have a pay later model that receives premiums up-front and pays claims later. In the case of some workers' compensation accidents, the payments stretch over decades. The pay later model results in holding large sums of money called float. The float for Berkshire Insurance Group rose from $39 million in 1970 to 73.1 billion in 2012.

Berkshire Hathaway is involved in both primary insurance and reinsurance of property/casualty, life and health risk. The insurance business consists of underwriting and investing. The underwriting is the business responsibility of unit managers while investing decisions are the responsibility of the CEO.

A major marketing strategy of the Berkshire insurance businesses is the maintenance of extraordinary capital strength. In 2012, the statutory surplus of the insurance business was approximately $106 billion. This surplus is aimed at creating opportunities to enter into insurance and reinsurance contracts.

Business Segments and Activities	
Business Segment	**Business Activity**
GEICO	Underwriting private passenger automobile insurance by direct response methods
General Reinsurance	Underwriting excess-of-loss, quota-share, and facultative reinsurance worldwide
BHRG	Underwriting excess-of-loss and quota-share reinsurance for insurers and reinsurers
Berkshire Hathaway Primary Group (BHPG)	Underwriting multiple lines of P&C insurance policies for primarily commercial accounts

5.3.2 GOVERNMENT EMPLOYEES INSURANCE COMPANY

Better known as GEICO, this division primarily writes private passenger automobile insurance to all 50 states and the District of Columbia. The division aims to be a low-cost auto insurer and policies are marketed primarily by direct response method via Internet or telephone. GEICO has 12 million auto policies in force and insures more than 18 million vehicles. It is considered the third-largest private passenger auto insurer in United States. In 1996, GEICO became the wholly owned subsidiary of Berkshire Hathaway. The affiliate companies are GEICO Insurance company, GEICO

Indemnity Company, GEICO Casualty Company, GEICO Advantage Insurance Company, GEICO Choice Insurance Company, and GEICO Secure Insurance Company. GEICO has consistently obtained AA++ from AM Best, a leading analyst of the insurance industry, and from Standard & Poor's.

GEICO suffered its single largest loss in 2012 from Hurricane Sandy, which cost GEICO more than three times the loss incurred from Hurricane Katrina. GEICO had insured 46,906 of the vehicles that were destroyed or damaged in the storm.

5.3.2.1 Products offered by GEICO

5.3.2.1.1 Auto insurance

GEICO's auto insurance business comprises a package of several primary coverages such as bodily injury liability coverage, property damage liability coverage, medical payments, no fault or personal injury coverage, uninsured motor coverage, comprehensive physical damage coverage, and collision coverage. In bodily injury coverage, GEICO pays for bodily injury or death resulting from an accident in which the client is at fault and provides a legal defense. Property damage liability coverage provides protection if the insured vehicle accidently damages another person's property along with legal defense in most cases. In underinsured motorist coverage, property damage caused by an uninsured or a hit-and-run driver is also included. In addition to these basic coverages, GEICO offers emergency road service, rental reimbursement, and mechanical breakdown insurance. Rental reimbursement is an optional coverage that pays rental car costs when an insured vehicle is being repaired as a result of a covered claim.

5.3.2.1.2 Motorcycle insurance

GEICO insures most types of motorcycles, with different levels of coverage for accessories, bodily injury, liability, collision, comprehensive physical damage coverage, medical payments, and property damage liability coverage. ATV insurance is underwritten by GEICO Indemnity Company.

5.3.2.1.3 Umbrella insurance

GEICO provides extra liability insurance called umbrella insurance. It is designed to protect policyholders from major claims and lawsuits. Umbrella insurance also provides additional liability coverage above the limits of homeowners, auto, and boat insurance policies. It provides coverage for bodily injury liability, property damage liability, and owners of rental units against cost of liability claims.

5.3.2.1.4 Homeowner's insurance

GEICO standard homeowners' policies include broad coverage for damages to houses and permanent structures on properties. Limited coverage—a range of $200-$2000—is provided for theft of jewelry. Coverage is also provided for personal liability exposures that arise from homeownership.

5.3.2.1.5 Other insurance

Other insurance includes renter's insurance, condo insurance, co-op insurance, recreational vehicle (RV) insurance, life insurance, boat insurance, personal watercraft insurance (PWC), flood insurance, mobile home insurance, overseas insurance, commercial auto insurance, business insurance, snowmobile insurance, and pet insurance.

Renter's insurance provides protection for household articles and named events such as theft, fire, or lightning. Condominium association insurance covers the condominium building, commonly owned property, and liability insurance for the association. Most condo insurance policies cover for losses arising from fire or lightning, smoke, theft, or vandalism. Co-op insurance covers the co-op building, commonly owned property, and liability insurance for the cooperative apartment corporation but excludes losses from theft or fire. GEICO offers enhanced motorized RV and towable RV insurance. RV insurance coverage includes features such as total loss replacement and replacement cost of personal effects. In total loss replacement, coverage of a new RV is provided if the RV is totaled within the first 4 months. In replacement cost personal effects, the coverage pays for the replacement of personal items in the RV. Vacation liability coverage pays for bodily injury and property damage losses at vacation sites. Emergency expense coverage pays for hotel and transportation expenses due to a covered loss. Up to $1000 for emergency expense coverage is automatically covered at no additional cost with comprehensive and collision coverage. GEICO covers motorized RVs including Type A motor homes, Type B motor homes (van campers), Type C motor homes, and sport utility RVs. Towable RV insurance covers conventional travel trailers and truck campers. A boat insurance policy insures the holder and the boat against liability and damage in the event of an accident. PWC insurance ensures coverage for personal watercraft against accidents, vandalism, and liability.

GEICO offers three business insurance products: general liability insurance, business owners' policies (BOP), and professional liability insurance. General liability insurance covers business operations. BOP provides liability insurance and property damage coverage, which are pooled together in a package policy. Professional liability insurance, known as errors and omissions (E&O), covers businesses that offer personal and professional services. This insurance protects policyholders in the event that a client is harmed. GEICO's Military Center is dedicated to the sales and service of military policies.

5.3.3 GENERAL REINSURANCE CORPORATION

General Reinsurance Corporation (Gen Re) is a subsidiary of Berkshire Hathaway and the holding company for global reinsurance and other operations. Gen Re owns Reinsurance Corporation and General Reinsurance AG. Gen Re is one of the leading global property casualty and life health reinsurers in the world. The company has 40 offices globally, supported by approximately 1900 employees.

Gen Re conducts reinsurance business by offering property, casualty, life, and health coverage to clients globally. P&C reinsurance policies are written in North America on a direct basis through Gen Re and globally through German-based General Reinsurance AG and wholly owned affiliates. Life and health reinsurance is written in North America through General Re Life Corporation and globally through General Reinsurance AG General.

5.3.3.1 Reinsurance solutions
5.3.3.1.1 Life/health solutions
Gen Re offers life and health reinsurance protection in lines of business such as critical illness, group LTD, and Group Life/AD&D, individual disability, individual life, and Medicare supplements. Gen Re is one of the leading reinsurers of critical illness insurance globally. Critical illness provides lump sum cash payment upon diagnosis of costly conditions for diseases such as cancer, heart attack, stroke, kidney failure, and major organ transplant. Gen Re provides solutions for products such as long-term disability (traditional and voluntary), group life, and AD&D (basic, supplemental, and voluntary), long-term disability conversion, and life portability administration. Gen Re provides a variety of individual life reinsurance coverage solutions on products such as term, whole life, universal life (indexed, variable, and traditional), individual, joint, and last survivor products, supplement benefits and riders, corporate, and

bank-owned life insurance. Gen Re also provides sophisticated risk-management techniques through its worldwide network of actuaries, underwriters, marketers, and claims management specialists.

Gen Re's in-house underwriting and actuarial teams in collaboration with clients' underwriting and pricing resources aims for comprehensive underwriting and pricing strategies. Gen Re provides reliable information for assessment of risk through online life and health underwriting manuals.

5.3.3.1.2 Property/casualty insurance

Gen Re provides solutions for a wide range of auto/motor exposures and coverage that includes auto/motor liability, auto physical damage/motor home damage, accident, and transportation liability. The company also provides solutions for a broad range of property, marine, and engineering coverages.

These solutions include property exposures for boiler and machinery/machinery breakdown and commercial property in mining, oil, and petrochemicals, semiconductors, and power generation. Inland marine and ocean marine solutions are also offered. The casualty underwriters also provide such coverage as directors and officers (D&O) liability, employment practices liability (EPL), homeowners'/householders' liability, medical professional liability, personal accident, personal injury liability, and products liability. The solutions for property, marine, and engineering coverages include casualty per occurrence facultative, casualty per occurrence excess of loss treaty, casualty per risk excess of loss treaty, and quota share treaty. Gen Re offers a wide range of services and solutions for surety and bond strategies. The services and solutions are offered for contract surety/construction bonds, court bonds, federal and public officials, licenses and permits. Surety/bond reinsurance solutions include bonding per quota share, bonding per excess of loss, and crime insurance facultative.

Family of Companies	
Company	**Major Role**
Gen Re Direct Reinsurance Operations	Major global direct reinsurer in property/casualty, life/health
Gen Re Intermediaries	Reinsurance intermediary and risk advisor with specialization in delivering global reinsurance market solutions for property catastrophe, aviation, workers' compensation, catastrophe, and casualty clash exposures
GR-NEAM	Global investment advisor, basically to the insurance industry, which specializes in offering capital and investment management services. (e.g., asset management, enterprise risk and capital management, investment technology solutions, and investment accounting and reporting services)
General Star	Underwrite excess, surplus, and specialty P&C insurance on an admitted and nonadmitted basis through appointed wholesale brokers; also certain underwriting, claims, and administrative services
Genesis	Alternative insurance provider for innovative insurance solutions for municipalities, counties, special districts, public and private colleges, universities, and schools
United States Aircraft Insurance Group (USAIG)	Insurance solutions for aviation and aerospace industry, including corporate aviation, commercial aviation, pleasure and business aircraft, helicopters, airlines, airport liability, aviation products liability, and workers' compensation
Faraday	Faraday Group consists of Faraday Reinsurance and Faraday Syndicate 435. Underwriting business is carried out through teams of aviation, casualty, and property

5.3.4 **BHRG AND BHPG**

BHRG and BHPG are the two subsidiaries of Gen Re. BHRG conducts business through groups of subsidiaries that include NICO and Columbia Insurance Company. Primarily BHRG provides principally excess and quota share reinsurance to other P&C insurers and reinsurers. The underwriting activity of BHRG, which includes life reinsurance and life annuity business, is carried out by Berkshire Hathaway Life Insurance Company of Nebraska. Financial guarantee insurance is written through Berkshire Hathaway Assurance Corporation. BHRG also provides catastrophe excess of loss treaty reinsurance contracts and individual coverage for individual risks covering terrorism, natural catastrophe, and aviation risk. These catastrophe and individual risk policies provide amounts of indemnification per contract. A single loss event could produce losses under a number of contracts. BHRG also underwrites traditional noncatastrophic insurance and reinsurance coverage, usually referred to as multiline property/casualty business.

BHPG consists of a group of independently managed insurance businesses that provide a range of insurance coverage. NICO and certain affiliates underwrite motor vehicle and general liability insurance to commercial enterprises on both an admitted and excess and surplus basis. US Investment Corporation through its four subsidiaries led by USIC, underwrite specialty insurance, which covers commercial, professional, and personal lines of insurance. The policies offered by USIC are marketed in all states through wholesale and retail insurance agents. The USIC companies underwrite and market approximately 110 distinct specialty P&C insurance products. The Berkshire Hathaway Homestate Companies, a group of six insurance companies, provide commercial multiline insurance, which covers workers' compensation, commercial auto, and commercial property. Medical Protective Company (MedPro) and Princeton Insurance Company provide healthcare malpractice insurance to physicians, dentists, and other healthcare providers. Applied Underwriters provide compensation solutions for integrated workers. Boat US is a writer of insurance for owners of boats and small watercraft. Central States Indemnity provides credit and disability insurance to clients through financial institutions. Table 5.3 provides the financial highlights of the major insurance subsidiaries of Berkshire Hathway during 2011-2012. Table 5.4 provides the consolidated financial highlights of insurance subsidiaries of Berkshire during the year 2012. Table 5.5 provides the operating revenues of the insurance groups under Berkshire during the period 2010-2012.

Table 5.3   Berkshire Hathaway Financial Highlights of Major Insurance Subsidiaries 2011-2012 (Millions of US Dollars)

Insurance Operations	Underwriting Profit		Year-End Float	
	2012	2011	2012	2011
BH Reinsurance	304	(714)	34,821	33,728
Gen Re	355	144	20,128	19,714
GEICO	680	576	11,578	11,169
Other Primary	286	242	6598	5960
Total	1625	248	73,125	70,571

Source: Berkshire Annual Report 2012

Table 5.4   Berkshire Hathaway Consolidated Financial Highlights of Insurance Subsidiaries 2012 (Millions of US Dollars)

	Value
Assets	278,096
Liabilities and shareholder equity	120,024
Revenues	123,337

Source: Berkshire Annual Report 2012

Table 5.5   Berkshire Hathaway Operating Revenues of Insurance Groups 2010-2012 (Millions of US Dollars)

Insurance Group Underwriting	2010	2011	2012
GEICO	14,283	15,363	16,740
Gen Re	5693	5816	5870
Berkshire Hathaway Reinsurance Group	9076	9147	9672
Berkshire Hathaway Primary Group	1697	1749	2263
Investment Income	5186	4746	4474
Total Insurance Group	35,935	36,821	39,019

5.4 **AXA S.A.**

AXA is a major global insurance and asset management group that serves 102 million clients in 57 countries. AXA provides a range of products and services in three major business lines of P&C insurance, L&S, and asset management. As one of the world's largest insurance groups, AXA had consolidated gross revenues of €90 billion in 2012. The AXA Group was also one of the world's largest asset managers with total assets under management amounting to €1116 billion in 2012. AXA operates primarily in Europe, the Asia Pacific region, and other regions such as the Middle East, Africa, and Latin America. The five major operating business segments are L&S, P&C, International Insurance, Asset Management, and Banking.

AXA was formed by the union of several French regional mutual insurance companies called "les Mutuelles Unies." The group expanded its core operations of insurance and asset management through combinations of organic growth, direct investments, and acquisitions. The sources of funding for these expansion programs were mainly through dividends received from operating subsidiaries, debt instruments issuance through subordinated debt and borrowings, equity issue, and divestments of noncore business and assets. Table 5.6 gives the mergers and acquisitions activity of the AXA Group.

Table 5.6	AXA Corporate Restructuring 1982-2012
Year	**Merger and Acquisition Highlights**
1982	Takeover of Groupe Drouot
1986	Acquires Groupe Présence
1988	Transfer of insurance business to Compagnie du Midi
1992	Acquires controlling interest in Equitable Companies US
1995	Acquires majority interest in National Mutual Holdings Australia
1997	Merged with Compagnie UAP
2000	Acquires Sanford C. Bernstein US; Nippon Dantaï Life Insurance Company Japan
2004	Acquisition of American Insurance Group MONY
2005	FINAXA (AXA's principal shareholder) merged with AXA
2006	Acquires Winterthur Group
2008	Acquires Seguros ING (Mexico)
2010	Sale of Life and Pension businesses of AXA UK to Resolution Ltd.
2011	Sale of the Australian and New Zealand operations; sold AXA Canada to Intact Financial Corporation
2012	Launched new life insurance joint venture in China with ICBC Acquisition of HSBC's nonlife insurance operations in Hong Kong, Singapore, and Mexico

5.4.1 REGULATORY REQUIREMENTS

AXA's insurance subsidiaries' operations are subject to laws and regulations governing standards of solvency, level of reserves, permitted types and concentrations of investments, business conducts agent licensing, approval of policy forms, and more in most of the jurisdictions in which they operate. AXA has an extensive oversight authority to review the group's consolidated solvency margin. Under applicable French regulations, 100% is the minimum required consolidated solvency margin for the company. In 2012, the AXA Group had a consolidated solvency margin of 233%. The group's consolidated solvency margin ratio is sensitive to capital market conditions such as changes in the level of interest rates, level of equity markets, and foreign exchange impacts. Rating agencies consider the company's consolidated solvency margin and regulatory capital position of its insurance subsidiaries in assessing AXA's financial strength when assigning ratings.

Operational in more than 50 countries, AXA is subject to a wide variety of insurance and other laws and regulations around the world. The group faces significant compliance challenges as the regulatory environment is evolving in a rapid manner and supervisory authorities are active in enforcing regulations in their jurisdictions.

5.4.2 DIVISIONS

5.4.2.1 L&S segment

The L&S subsidiaries investment strategy is based on a design to match investment returns and estimated maturity of their investments with expected payments on their insurance contracts.

AXA offers a broad range of L&S products including individual and group savings products, as well as life and health products for both individual and commercial clients. The individual and group life insurance policies consist of savings and retirement products, health, and personal protection products. In some countries, AXA offers a range of banking services and products that supplements insurance offerings. The L&S segment accounts for 61% of the group's revenues. In the L&S segment, AXA operates basically in Western Europe, the United States, and Japan. L&S products offered by AXA include term life, whole life, endowment, deferred annuities, immediate annuities, and other investment-based products. The health products offered consist of critical illness and permanent health insurance products, though specific products offered vary from market to market. AXA products are distributed through exclusive and nonexclusive channels that vary from country to country. The proprietary channels include exclusive agents, salaried sales forces, and direct sales. The nonproprietary channels include brokers, independent financial advisors, aligned distributors, wholesale distributors, and partnerships.

The fees and revenues for most of the L&S products accrue over time while the costs for the issuing company in the initial year are higher than the costs in subsequent years on account of first-year commissions and the costs of underwriting and issuing contracts. As a result, the rate of policies remaining in force and not lapsing, termed the persistency rate, plays a vital role in profitability. In 2012, the total surrenders and lapses amounted to €25,056 million. A majority of individual L&S products issued by AXA have front-end charges (subscription fees) or surrender charges aimed at offsetting a portion of the acquisition costs.

5.4.2.2 P&C insurance

AXA's P&C segment provides a broad range of products that includes motor, household property, and general liability insurance for both personal and commercial customers, basically targeting small to medium companies. AXA also offers engineering services to support prevention policies in companies. The property casualty insurance segment accounts for approximately 35% of the group's revenues. It includes the insurance of personal property such as cars, homes, and liability (personal or professional). The P&C insurance products are distributed through exclusive agents, brokers, salaried sales forces, direct sales, and banks. AXA Global P&C has managed the P&C global business line of the group since 2010.

5.4.2.3 International insurance segment

This segment focuses on large risks, reinsurance, and assistance. The AXA Group subsidiary AXA Corporate Solutions Assurance provides global insurance programs to large national and multinational corporations. The two intragroup insurance companies, AXA Global Life and AXA Global P&C, are responsible for analysis, structure, and placement of reinsurance treaties for AXA Group insurance companies. AXA Global P&C activity is mainly driven by its property pool, which provides coverage for natural catastrophes. AXA Corporate Solutions Assurance is one of the top five major players in Europe. It underwrites large insurance risks such as property damage, liability, construction risks, fleets of motor vehicles, marine, and aviation. The company also provides loss prevention and risk management services. The products of AXA Corporate Solutions are distributed through domestic and international brokers. Specialized brokers distribute marine and aviation business products.

AXA Assistance offers emergency and daily services as well as health management through a new range of products and claims management. This division provides various assistance services such as medical aid for travelers, automobile-related road assistance, home assistance and health services to companies in the sectors of banking, insurance, utilities, telecommunication, and automobiles. AXA Assistance has expertise in the home services market. It operates as a business-to-business company along with direct sales and marketing to sell its products.

AXA Liabilities Managers is the group's specialized unit that manages the AXA Group's P&C run-off portfolios. This unit primarily manages the internal run-off portfolios of AXA UK, AXA Germany, and AXA Belgium along with health run-off portfolios in the United States.

AXA Corporate Solutions Life Reinsurance Company is a reinsurance company that manages a book of reinsurance contracts of variable annuities with guaranteed minimum death (GMDB) and income benefits (GMIB).

5.4.2.4 Asset management

AllianceBernstein and AXA Investment Managers are the principal investment management companies of AXA. AllianceBernstein provides diversified investment management and related services to individual clients and to private and institutional clients that include AXA and its insurance subsidiaries. Diversified asset management services are provided through separately managed accounts, hedge funds, mutual funds, and other investment vehicles. AllianceBernstein also provides research portfolio analysis and brokerage-related services for institutional investors. AXA Investment Managers provide global products to individual and institutional investors through mutual funds and dedicated portfolios. AXA Investment Managers deal with a variety of products such as fixed income, real estate, structured finance, multi-asset client solutions, and private equity.

5.4.2.5 Banking segments

Banking segment operations are primarily conducted in Belgium, France, Germany, and Central and Eastern Europe. The bank products and services in Belgium are distributed by a network of 864 exclusive independent bank agents. AXA France, with more than 750,000 registered customers, offers retail banking products in direct linkage with the group's insurance business. AXA Bank in Germany maintains a pension and asset management business and focuses on private customers in retail banking. AXA Bank in Hungary focuses on retail deposit business.

5.4.3 RISK MANAGEMENT

Group Risk Management (GRM) is the central department that is responsible for the coordination of risk management within the AXA Group. The local risk management departments headed by local chief risk officers (CROs) implement the risk management standards and guidelines stipulated by GRM at the operational level. The short-term economic capital model is a powerful metric used to control and measure exposure to most risks in line with the Solvency II framework.

Asset loss management aims at matching assets with the liabilities assumed by selling insurance policies. Products that involve hedging programs based on derivatives instruments are designed with the support of dedicated teams at AXA Bank Europe, AXA IM, and AllianceBernstein.

Exposure to financial market risk arises in the AXA Group due to its core business of financial protection in insurance and asset management. Financial market risk arises also from financing activities by means of equity and debt. Asset liability management (ALM) is used as optimal strategic allocation with respect to liability structure. AXA's exposure to market risk is mitigated through its high level of diversified operations in different geographical regions and natural hedging between products and jurisdictions. The market risk in its L&S and long-tail P&C portfolios arises from a decline in returns on assets that could reduce investment margins or fees on unit-linked contracts. A rise in yields on fixed-income investments could adversely impact the solvency margin leading to increasing policyholder surrenders due to competitive pressures. A decline in asset market value of equity, such as in real estate, could also adversely impact the solvency margin. The cost of hedging guarantees for certain products such as unit-linked, variable annuities also rises due to financial market volatility. P&C activities are also subject to foreign exchange rates and inflation. Inflation may increase the compensation payable to policyholders so that the actual payments could exceed the reserves set aside.

The main financial risk for the AXA Group consists of interest rate risk, spread risk, equity risk, credit risk, and liquidity risk. The AXA Group analyzes interest-rate sensitivity and equity market fluctuations by measuring European embedded value (EEV) in L&S businesses. The sensitivities of nonlife businesses are measured using the adjusted net asset value method. Embedded value (EV) is a valuation methodology used for valuation of long-term insurance business. EV measures the present value of cash available to shareholders, net of taxes and minority interests. EEV is a refined method based on EV, which was adopted by the CFO Forum of European Insurers. The AXA Group also calculates a group EVA.

Each of the major operating subsidiaries is responsible for managing its liquidity position in coordination with the company. The principal sources of liquidity are insurance premiums, annuity considerations, deposit funds, asset management fees, and cash flows from investments. A portion of the cash flow from property, casualty, and international insurance is invested in liquid, short-term bonds and other listed securities for managing liquidity risk. AXA has a well-established liquidity risk management framework whose assessment is performed through quarterly monitoring of liquidity and solvency requirements in stressed environments. In 2012, the group's companies held more than €80 billion in government bonds issued by eurozone countries. In 2012, the group held €12.1 billion in committed undrawn credit lines. The group has also strengthened its liquidity position by having broad access to various markets through standardized debt programs. For example, in 2012, the group had a maximum envelope of €6 billion in French commercial paper, $1.5 billion in US commercial paper, and €14 billion under an euro medium-term note program.

AXA faces credit risk due to its transactions with counterparties, which includes brokers and dealers, commercial and investment banks, hedge funds, clearing agents, market exchanges, and clearinghouses. In reinsurance arrangements, reinsurers assume a portion of the losses and related expenses. The group remains liable as the direct insurer on all risks insured. AXA is subject to reinsurers' credit risk with respect to the ability to recover the amount due from such reinsurers.

The group credit risk committee handles the issuer exposure that breaches the group's limit tolerances on a monthly basis and provides actions for excessive credit concentrations. Credit risk diversification and analysis policies on the basis of credit ratings are implemented by investment departments and monitored by risk management teams. AXA uses credit default swaps to manage credit risk management activities.

Exposure to interest rate risk arises as does market price and cash flow variability on account of changes in interest rates. During a period of declining interest rates, the demand for life insurance and annuity products goes up due to minimum guarantees. As a result, premium payments on products with flexible premium features increase leading to a higher percentage of insurance policies and annuity contracts. These creates asset liability duration mismatches. The group would increase provisions for guarantees, which are included in life insurance and annuity contracts during a period of rising interest rates. In periods of increasing interest rates, the trend observed is that policyholders forego insurance protection by surrendering life insurance policies and fixed annuity contracts and seek alternate higher investment return avenues. Interest rate risk is mitigated by maintaining an investment portfolio with diversified maturities that has a weighted average duration approximately equal to the duration of the estimated liability cash flow profile. AXA manages its exposure to foreign currency fluctuations through hedging of currencies.

The group also faces operational, financial, and reputational risk in the event of default by counterparty service providers. These third-party service providers support a range of services that includes policy administration, claims-related services, security pricing for insurance, and asset management businesses.

Regulatory and other legal restrictions prevent the group from transferring funds freely either to or from all the subsidiaries. The subsidiaries are also subject to restrictions on the amount of dividends and debt repayments.

Derivatives such as equity futures, Treasury bond futures, interest rates swaps and swaptions, equity options, and variance swaps are used to hedge risks under guarantees. The Accumulator product guarantees a series of variable annuity products such as GMDBs, guaranteed minimum accumulation benefits (GMABs), GMIBs, and withdrawal for life benefits (GMWB) are in place for the purpose of hedging. These hedging instruments along with volatility risk mitigation techniques such as capped volatility funds or asset transfer programs within unit-linked funds are aimed at reducing policyholders' investment in higher risk assets in times of increased interest rate volatility. On the basis of various assumptions, AXA determines the appropriate level of insurance reserves, deferred acquisition costs, employee benefits reserves, and measures of values such as L&S new business value and EEV.

As a global company, AXA is subject to various tax regimes and regulations. The insurance risk for L&S and P&C is addressed through four major processes that are performed jointly by central and local committees. Profitability analysis is carried out for launching new products based on well-established underwriting rules. The optimization of reinsurance strategies is used to mitigate the group's exposure to reduce the volatility of financial indicators and protection of solvency. Technical reserves are reviewed periodically. The emerging risk initiatives are discussed within underwriting and risk communities.

Reinsurance purchasing is an important part of the AXA Group's insurance activities and risk management. In-depth actuarial analyses and modeling are conducted on each portfolio by AXA Global P&C, AXA Global Life, and GRM to optimize the quality and cost of reinsurance coverage. Frequency risk as well as specific severity risk in P&C and life insurance are estimated using catastrophe modeling software. Operational groups monitor their risk reserves periodically. Claims reserves are estimated and booked on a file-by-file basis by claim handlers. AXA has established processes to qualify and quantify emerging risk that could become significant over a period of time. AXA has a defined operational framework to identify and measure the operational risk that would arise from failure of its systems and resources. Table 5.7 provides the revenue highlights of different segments of AXA during the period 2007-2012. Table 5.8 gives the value of assets under management and the consolidated shareholder equity holdings of AXA during the period 2007-2012. Table 5.9 gives the values of gross written premiums in terms of main product lines for AXA in the year 2012.

Table 5.7 AXA Revenue Highlights 2007-2012 (Millions of Euro)						
	2007	**2008**	**2009**	**2010**	**2011**	**2012**
Life and savings	59,845	57,977	57,620	56,792	52,431	55,016
Property and casualty	25,016	26,039	26,174	25,986	27,046	28,315
International insurance	3568	2841	2860	2847	2876	2987
Asset management	4863	3947	3047	3328	3269	3343
Banks	339	412	395	459	485	466
Total	93,631	91,216	90,123	89,412	86,107	90,126

Source: Annual Reports

Table 5.8 Other AXA Financial Highlights 2007-2012 (Billions of Euro)						
	2007	**2008**	**2009**	**2010**	**2011**	**2012**
Assets under management	1281	981	1014	1097	1065	1116
Consolidated shareholder equity	45.6	37.4	46.2	49.7	46.4	53.7

Source: Annual Reports

Table 5.9 AXA Gross Written Premiums by Main Product Lines 2012 (Millions of Euro)	
	Value
Investment and savings:	
Individual	18,491
Group	2848
Life contracts (including endowments)	22,442
Health contracts	7639
Other	2152
Total	53,572

Source: Annual Reports

5.5 **ALLIANZ**

Allianz Group is a global financial service provider. Its parent company, Allianz SE, is headquartered in Munich, Germany; it is the leading P&C insurer globally. Allianz is among the top five life insurance companies in the world and a worldwide leader in credit insurance Allianz Group serves approximately 78 million retail and corporate clients in more than 70 countries with around 144,000 employees worldwide. Allianz is also one of the largest asset managers with third-party assets of €1438 billion under management in 2012. In 2012, the Property/Casualty segment contributed approximately 44% of revenues while the Life/Health segment contributed 49% of total revenues. Asset Management and Corporate contributed approximately 6% and 1% in 2012.

The company was rated AA by Standard & Poor's, Aa3 by Moody's, and A+ AM Best in 2012. The solvency ratio was 197% in 2012.

Alliance is one of the most valued financial services firm in the world as reflected by the weighting of Allianz shares in major German, European, and global indexes. In the STOXX Europe 600 Insurance index, Allianz weightage constituted 14.4% in 2012.

Allianz focuses on expanding its brand presence in digital and social media by expanding its multi-channel approach and has established Facebook as an additional platform for sales. Allianz is expanding its business-to-business to customers in automotive and roadside assistance and international health and corporate assistance areas.

Allianz offers a wide range of property/casualty and life health insurance products to both corporate and private clients. The key markets based on premiums are in Germany, France, Italy, and the United States. Most of the insurance markets are served by local Allianz companies.

5.5.1 PRODUCTS AND SOLUTIONS

Along with Allianz Global Investors and the Allianz Bank, Allianz offers a complete range of solutions that include insurance, provision, asset management, and banking services. Allianz is the leading property, casualty, life insurer, and the number-three health insurer in Germany. The main sales channels of Allianz are agents, brokers, and special intermediaries in industrial client business.

5.5.1.1 Private insurance

The insurance solutions for individuals include personal, mobility, home and building, leisure insurance, and financing solutions. Car insurance solutions are offered for direct purchase. Allianz also provides a wide range of international healthcare plans for individuals. Allianz also provides asset management products for all major asset classes, which include equities, fixed-income, alternative investment, and other funds.

5.5.1.2 Business insurance

Allianz provides insurance solutions for business and corporate customers. The company provides building and infrastructure insurance, liability, employee and health insurance, transport insurance, and financing solutions. Allianz offers customized property, casualty, marine, aviation, and specialty insurance solutions as well as risk consulting through international insurance programs. Allianz provides solutions for managing credit risk, which include credit insurance, bonding, and fidelity insurance. The company also provides cross-border employee benefit solutions for multinational companies. International medical coverage and asset management solutions are provided for institutional clients.

Business insurance covers large corporations small and medium companies, and credit insurance. The Alliance Risk Transfer division provides tailored insurance, reinsurance, and other nontraditional risk management solutions for corporate and financial clients throughout the world. The reinsurance product range covers structured quota shares, structured whole account covers, structured per risk covers, as well as retroactive products such as loss portfolio transfers. The Insurance Linked Markets (LIM) division focuses on structuring of event-driven insurance risk such as earthquakes and hurricanes into forms that are accessible to capital market investors.

The Allianz Global Corporate and Specialty (AGCS) division provides insurance programs to various industrial sectors. Allianz provides insurance programs for aerospace and defense-industry businesses, which cover specialist products in general aerospace and aviation products, space, property, liability, marine hull, marine liabilities such as ports, marine cargo, financial lines, and risk-consulting areas.

The company provides services to all major original equipment manufacturers throughout the world. The company provides a wide range of automotive industry risk coverage such as customized property and business interruption coverage, general and public liability coverage, product recall coverage, cargo coverage for goods in transit or in storage, and freight liability for logistics specialists.

The specialized insurance service covers all areas of the aviation industry such as airline insurance and general aviation insurance. Aerospace insurance involves manufacturers and supplier liability, airports, airfield and ground handlers, and air traffic control. Treaty insurance involves specialist reinsurance of worldwide aviation insurance risks and portfolios. AGCS provides insurance programs for construction industry insurance for global clients. Clients include construction industry financiers and investors, banks, architects, designers, contractors, material suppliers, engineers, and construction professionals.

AGCS provides a range of chemical and petrochemical-sector insurance products. Allianz Financial Services Global Practice Group provides a comprehensive product range and network across 150 countries. Financial services clients include large retail and investment banks, asset managers, venture capital, and private equity funds. The global insurance coverage for financial services industry covers all risk property damage coverage, prospectus, and IPO coverage, mergers and acquisitions coverage, international insurance programs, risk consulting, and claims management. AGSC provides tailored services for the food and beverage manufacturing insurance industry such as product recall, environmental liability, product tampering/contamination coverage, D&O liability, cargo and goods in transit, professional indemnity, risk consulting, and business continuity support. AGCS is among the few insurers that provides a complete range of healthcare risk portfolios. In the heavy industry sector, AGCS provides clients with solutions such as all risk property damage coverage, all risk business interruption coverage, public and general liability, and engineering and machinery breakdown coverage. Insurance products are also designed to cover manufacturing, marine, oil and gas, pharmaceuticals, power and utilities, real estate, textiles, transport, and logistics.

The Allianz Risk Consulting team provides a flexible range of risk management services that ranges from basic hazard and human element reporting to analysis of industrial operations and financial exposures in sectors that range from aviation, energy, engineering, marine, and property. Euler Hermes is one of the major leading providers of trade-related insurance solutions. Credit insurance protects clients' businesses from nonpayment of commercial debt.

5.5.1.3 Asset management

Allianz Global Investors offer a broad range of funds for major asset classes and investment styles. The absolute return strategies are aimed at minimizing systematic exposure to the stock or bond market with a focus on diversification. The credit solutions offered include investment-grade bonds, high-yield bonds, convertible bonds, and bank loans. The division also focuses on emerging market strategies that focus on developing economies. Municipal bond strategies invest in securities issued by state and local governments and related institutions.

5.5.1.4 Global division lines

Global Reinsurance represents all reinsurance business conducted at Allianz Group through subsidiaries such as Allianz SE Reinsurance (Allianz Re) and Allianz Risk Transfer AG and its subsidiaries. Allianz Global Reinsurance serves about 400 clients in 90 countries. Credit and Bond Reinsurance and Agricultural Reinsurance provide new tailored products to clients. Allianz Worldwide Care provides health insurance for employees, individuals, and their dependents. Allianz's Global Direct provides insurance coverage online or over the telephone. In 2011, Allianz Direct had more than 3 million policies with over €1 billion in gross written premiums. Allianz Global Life is a specialized provider of retirement and group life solutions. Allianz Global Life provides international group plans for accident, death, and dismemberment of corporate and governmental clients.

Allianz Real Estate is a major leading property investment and asset manager. Allianz Managed Operations and Services provides Allianz companies worldwide with in-house services in the fields of information technology (IT), operations, and services.

5.5.1.5 Global assistance and services

Allianz Global Assistance is a world leader in travel insurance, assistance, and personal services. Roadside assistance products are provided to clients in sectors such as the automotive industry, banks, insurance, financial institutions, and the travel industry.

5.5.2 RISK MANAGEMENT

Allianz is exposed to a variety of risk through its insurance and asset management activities. These include financial market, credit, insurance, operational, business, and strategic risk. Financial risk such as interest rate risk arises due to the duration mismatch between assets and liabilities for long-term savings products. Credit and credit spread risk are driven by assets backing long-term savings products. P&C premium or underwriting risk are driven by human-made catastrophes as well as accident-year claims uncertainty. The internal risk capital model is based on a VaR approach using Monte Carlo simulation. The Monte Carlo simulation uses 50,000 scenarios based on market, credit, insurance, and other sources of risk based on the net fair value of assets and liabilities under potentially adverse conditions. Market risk is managed through strategic asset allocation benchmarks, equity, and interest rate sensitivity limits. Credit risk is managed through country limits and single counterparty concentration limits. Underwriting risk is managed through minimum underwriting standards, natural catastrophe limits, and reinsurance programs. Business and operational risk are managed through appropriate internal controls and adequate product design.

Changes in profitability are measured on the basis of loss ratios. The volatility of the underwriting profitability measured over 1 year is the premium risk for the group. There are clear underwriting limits and restrictions for the group. The other risk faced by Allianz include strategic risk, liquidity risk, and reputational risk. The Group Risk Committee (GRC) defines the risk standards and forms the major limit-setting authority supervised by the board of management.

5.5.3 CORPORATE SOCIAL RESPONSIBILITY ACTIVITIES

Allianz has a groupwide strategy of offering green products and services focused on mitigating the negative physical or economic effects of climate change. About 130 green products covering business segments such as reinsurance, assistance, and asset management are offered to customers. Green products include tailor-made insurance products for large-scale renewable energy projects and green-building insurance to cover facilities and offices that are energy efficient. Allianz also provides a safety net to more than 17 million people in Asia, Africa, and Latin America through its micro-insurance offerings. The products offered include life insurance products, savings plans, and crop index insurance. The Allianz Group is a signatory to the United Nations Principles for Responsible Investment.

Table 5.10 Allianz Financial Highlights 2010-2012 (Millions of Euros)

	2010	2011	2012
Revenues	106,451	103,560	106,383
Premiums earned	63,337	63,688	66,045
Operating profit	8243	7866	9501
Net income	5209	2804	5491
Total assets		641,472	694,621

Source: Annual Report

Table 5.11 Allianz Total Premiums Written by Property Casualty Insurance 2010-2012 (Millions of Euros)

	2010	2011	2012
Property casualty insurance (gross premiums)	43,895	44,772	46,889
Life health insurance (statutory premiums)	57,098	52,863	52,347

Source: Annual Report

Table 5.10 provides the financial highlights of Allianz during 2010-2012. Table 5.11 provides the total premiums written by the property/casualty and life health insurance divisions of Allianz during the period 2010-2012.

5.6 GENERALI GROUP

The Generali Group is a major player in the global insurance and financial products market. The group's parent and principal operating company is Assicurazioni Generali, which was founded in 1831. The group is a market leader in Italy. It has a presence in over 60 countries with leading insurance operations in the Western European markets of Germany, France, Austria, Spain, Switzerland, and Eastern Europe.

The Generali Group is the biggest life insurer in the European market and offers products such as savings and family protection policies, unit-linked policies, and complex plans for multinational clients. The portfolio in the nonlife segment includes mass-coverage products such as car, home, accident, and health, and commercial and industrial coverages. Generali is also a major leader in the retail segment and is a major global player in the field of assistance coverage, which includes worldwide services in the motor, travel, and health lines of business. In the insurance sector, the group has a multichannel distribution strategy consisting of a global proprietary sales network of agents, financial advisors, and brokers that are supplemented by bancassurance and direct channels. The group has approximately 65 million clients worldwide and a strong distribution network of 82,000 professionals with more than €400 billion in assets. In 2012, Generali's insurance turnover was approximately €70 billion. In 2012, the group had a sales network consisting of 1349 agents, 2379 underwriters and subagents, and 3334 agency collaborators. The company is consistently ranked high among the prestigious ethical indexes such as FTSE4Good, Advanced Sustainable Performance Indexes (ASPI), and STOXX ESG Leaders Indexes.

5.6.1 STRATEGY FOR GROWTH

Generali is among the world's largest 50 companies according to Fortune Global 500. The five major markets of the company's operations are in Italy, Germany, France, Spain, and Eastern Europe. Generali Group's major strength lies in its strong brand position in Italy and other regions in Europe. The group is focusing on a diversified international presence in emerging markets and other mature markets. Currently, it has expanded its business from insurance to encompass a wide range of asset management, property and financial services. Banca Generali Group is a market leader in financial services in Italy. BSI Swiss Group provides a range of private banking services.

In 2012, Generali Group undertook a major organizational restructuring. An international group management committee was established to monitor the strategic priorities and business performance of the group. Generali aims to achieve a strong capital position by improving its Solvency I, economic capital, and capital adequacy rating. The target aim of the group is to achieve a solvency ratio of 160%. The capital adequacy and leverage ratios are adequate for AA ratings. The group is focused on initiatives such as selling off noncore and nonstrategic assets along with having an increased focus on insurance as a means for achieving these objectives. The group is also focusing on matching assets and insurance liabilities as part of harmonization of duration and risk profiles. The group also focuses on maintenance of an optimal debt structure and an evaluation of its refinancing needs. There is now a greater degree of centralization in the decision-making process. New central functions are group reinsurance, group Treasury capital, value management with key responsibilities of optimization of capital. The group also has plans for cost-saving initiatives with target savings of €600 million by 2015. The Generali Group has identified saving opportunities in areas of procurements, ICT expenses, and real estate facility management. The group also focuses on P&C business to improve business performance. Table 5.12 discusses the restructuring activities undertaken by Generali Group during 2006-2013.

Table 5.12 Generali Group Restructuring by Group 2006-2013	
Year	**Activities**
2006	Acquires Banca Unione di Credito in Switzerland
	Acquires Croatian insurance company Libertas Osiguranie
	Acquires majority stake in Serbian insurance company Delta
	Purchases majority stake in Ukrainian insurance company Garant Auto e Garant Life, Orel G
	Purchases 65.5% stake in Italian insurance company Toro Assicurazioni
2007	BSI acquires Swiss Bank Banca del Gotardo
	Joint venture with Czech Group PPF, which is related to the insurance activities of Generali and PPF in Central European countries

Table 5.12	Generali Group Restructuring by Group 2006-2013—cont'd
Year	**Activities**
2008	Closure of joint venture with Czech Group PPF and incorporation of Generali PPF Holdings with 51% stake in General PPF Holdings
	Generali PPF Holdings purchases majority stakes in Romanian insurance company Ardaf e Rai
2009	Merger of Alleanza Assicurazioni and Toro into Generali
	Purchase of 30% stake in Guotai AMC
2011	Selling of stake in Afore Banorte Generali (Mexican-based pension business)
	Selling of 51% stake in B-Source Swiss bank service provider
2012	Selling of 69% stake in Migdal Insurance and Financial Holdings, Israel-based insurance and financial company
2013	Agreement for the sale of Generali Group US life reinsurance business
	Agreement for the sale of minority stakes held by Generali in Seguros Banorte-Generali and in Pensiones Banorte Generali

Country	Group Subsidiaries	Country	Group Subsidiaries
Italy	22	United Kingdom	2
Austria	6	Africa	2
Belgium	2	United States	3
Bulgaria	4	Argentina	3
Croatia	1	Brazil	1
Czech Republic	3	Columbia	2
France	7	**Ecuador**	1
Germany	19	Guatemala	1
Greece	1	Martinique	1
Guernsey	2	Panama	1
Hungary	3	China	14
Ireland	1	Hong Kong	2
Liechtenstein	2	India	2
Netherlands	3	Indonesia	1
Poland	4	Thailand	2
Portugal	3	Japan	1
Republic of Montenegro	2	Philippines	1
Republic of Siberia	1	United Arab Emirates	1
Romania	1	Vietnam	1
Slovakia	1		
Slovenia	1		
Spain	4		
Switzerland	7		
Turkey	1		

Table 5.13   Generali Group Financial Highlights 2010-2012 (Millions of Euros)

	2010	2011	2012
Gross written premiums	73,188	69,159	69,613
Total investments	372,155	369,126	392,658
Solvency ratio (%)	132	117	150

5.6.2 PRODUCTS AND SERVICES

The Generali Group operates in all classes of insurance. Lines of business include coverage for mass risks such as third-party liability and personal injuries, highly complex industrial plants, policies for family protection, and extensive contracts targeted at multinationals. The group also offers life insurance products and individual and group pension schemes.

5.6.2.1 Major groups

Alliance Toro was formed by the merger of two market leaders, Alliance Life Insurance and Taurus in the nonlife sector. The major brands include Alliance, Toro, Lloyd Italico, Augusta, and subsidiaries. Banca Generali offers a complete range of financial planning, banking, and insurance services. BSI is a major growing bank in Switzerland. In 1998, BSI became part of the Generali Group. Table 5.13 provides the financial highlights of Generali Group during the period 2010-2012.

5.7 NIPPON LIFE INSURANCE

Nippon Life Insurance is the second largest insurance company in Japan, after Japan Post. Nippon focuses on insurance, asset management, and research. The company was founded as the Nippon Life Assurance Company in July 1889; after World War II, the company was renamed Nippon Life Insurance Company in 1947.

Nippon Life Insurance invested ¥150 billion during the 6-year period starting in 2006 to implement the New Integration Plan. The New Integration Plan is the central strategy of the Future Creation Project. Nippon is using a new wireless device called REVO that uses state-of-the-art technology. This technology helps sales representatives supply customers with information that matches particular requirements based on family composition, age, and other parameters. Nippon is focusing on a multichannel service framework by strengthening the Nissay Life Plaza customer service center, corporate sales, agencies, and other financial institutions. Nippon is counted among the top 10 shareholders of around 20% of all publicly listed Japanese companies. During the Great East Japan Earthquake, Nippon Life made full payments of all accidental death benefits and other relevant claims. The company also implemented various other measures such as simplifying the process for claiming insurance payments and benefits. In 2012, the number of policies in force was 14.48 million units. The total amount of policies was ¥181432.5 billion. The equity replacement ratio is the ratio of foundation funds (kikin) and reserves to optimum equity. In 2012, the company's equity replacement ratio was 63%. The dividend payout ratio, which is the ratio of the reserve for policyholder dividends to available financial resources, was 96% in 2012.

5.7.1 **BUSINESS STRUCTURE**

5.7.1.1 *Insurance and related business*

Nine Nippon companies are involved in insurance and insurance-related businesses. Underwriting insurance is based on life insurance business licenses. Company subsidiaries and affiliates handle insurance-related operations and are in involved in corporate pension system management, life insurance policy confirmation work, life insurance policy solicitation, and nonlife insurance and life insurance brokerage agency work.

5.7.1.2 *Asset management*

There are 30 Nippon subsidiary companies involved in asset management and related businesses. These subsidiaries engage in different activities such as investment management, investment advisory, trust and custody services, credit guarantee services, leasing, venture capital, real estate investments, mortgage loans, and finance agency services.

5.7.1.3 *General affairs and related operations*

Nine subsidiary companies engage in temporary staffing services, printing and book binding services, software development, information processing services, system administration, survey and research services.

5.7.2 **PRODUCTS AND SERVICES**

Nippon offers Mirai no Katachi, a product that offers the flexibility for customers to choose from 11 types of insurance coverage. Mirai no Kata offers coverage in four categories: death coverage, serious diseases and nursing coverage, medical coverage, and asset formation and retirement coverage. Death coverage can include whole life insurance, term life insurance, and term life insurance with survival benefits. Serious diseases and nursing coverage can include dread disease insurance, physical disability insurance, and nursing care insurance. Medical coverage includes general medical insurance, which covers hospitalization and surgery, cancer medical insurance, and limited injury insurance. Asset formation and retirement coverage consists of annuities and endowment insurance. Annuities enable systematic planning of living expenses after retirement. Endowment insurance enables asset formation over a set period while providing death protection.

Nissay juvenile insurance (Genki) provides insurance protection for children. There are two types of protection in this category. Juvenile insurance provides for children's education, expenses, and wedding costs. Children's medical insurance covers children's hospitalization and surgery. In asset formation and retirement coverage, three single payment products are offered. Nissay single payment whole life insurance (My Stage) provides death coverage for life while enabling asset formation with a single premium payment. Nissay single-payment annuities supplement post-retirement living expenses with a single premium payment. Nissay single-payment endowment insurance provides death protection for a set period while facilitating asset formation with a single premium payment. Nippon deals with the Tough brand of nonlife insurance products. In 2011, Nippon Life launched sales of Long, which is long-term automobile insurance with special pay-outs such as accident-free payouts to policyholders who have no accidents during a coverage period of 3 years.

Nippon Life provides insurance products for corporations in the category of provisions for executives and employees, provisions for owners and asset formation. In self-reliant products, insurance premiums

Table 5.14   Nippon Financial Highlights 2012 (Millions of US Dollars)

	Amount
Assets	622,544
Revenues from insurance and reinsurance	65,563
Profit	5936

Source: Annual Report

Table 5.15   Number of Nippon Policies in Force 2010-2012

	2010	2011	2012
Individual insurance	11,775,230	11,510,549	11,339,098
Individual annuities	2,939,764	3,024,773	3,149,513

Source: Annual Report

are carried by employees rather than the corporation. General welfare group term life insurance provides survivor coverage. New group disability income plans provide disability coverage. General medical life insurance provides medical coverage plans. Pension plans include defined benefit corporate pension plans, employees' pension fund insurance, new insured pension plans, and defined contribution pension plan for retirement coverage. Nissay key man insurance and Nissay long-term insurance provides for survivor coverage. Workers' asset formation housing funding insurance is an asset formation promotion plan for buying a home. Other asset formation plans consist of different types of savings plans.

5.7.2.1 Major strategic investments

In 2011, Nippon Life purchased 30-year convertible subordinated notes for €500 million issued by the finance subsidiary of the integrated financial service provider Allianz.

Nippon is focusing on a strategy for expansion. The company has expanded its network into seven countries in Europe, North America, and Asia where it has established 17 subsidiary companies and four representative offices. Nippon holds a 26% stake in Reliance Life Insurance, a life insurance subsidiary of Reliance Group, one of the largest business houses of India. Nippon also acquired a stake in Bangkok Life Assurance Public Company Ltd. Nippon Life Insurance has established a network in the Chinese life insurance market through a joint venture with Nissay-SVA Life Insurance. In 2012, Nippon Life signed an MOU on a business alliance with AIA Group Ltd., one of the largest insurers in the Asia Pacific region. Table 5.14 gives the financial highlights of Nippon Life Insurance in 2012. Table 5.15 provides the statistics on the number of policies in force by Nippon Life during 2010-2012.

5.8 MUNICH REINSURANCE

Munich Reinsurance was established in April 1880. The company is one of the world's major players in the reinsurance industry. Munich Reinsurance serves approximately 40 million clients in more than 30 countries. The three main businesses of the company are primary insurance, reinsurance, and Munich

Health. Munich Re provides primary insurers with coverage against peak risks such as large natural catastrophes. Munich Re operates in the life and P&C segment of the reinsurance industry. The primary insurance business of industrial clients, public private partnerships, and business in specialist segments are carried out by Risk Solutions. Credit, aviation and space, agriculture, enterprise and contingency risk are dealt by the Special and Financial Risks unit.

5.8.1 BUSINESS DIVISIONS

5.8.1.1 Reinsurance
Munich Re operates in all classes of reinsurance. The products offered include traditional reinsurance products, extensive services, and consultancy services. Munich Re also provides the services of transfer of risk to the capital markets. Munich Re does business directly with primary insurers and via brokers.

5.8.1.1.1 Nonlife reinsurance
Nonlife reinsurance solutions are provided to casualty and property, marine, and aviation segments. Munich Re provides capital market solutions. In addition to traditional reinsurance and financial reinsurance, Munich Re provides alternative risk transfer products. Risk trading involves transferring risk to the capital market through securitization by means of insurance-linked securities (ILS) and subsequent trading of such securities on the secondary market. Munich Re is a service provider of ILS in different categories of risk. In the catastrophe category, the products offered include cat bonds, cat swaps, and risk swaps. In the life risk category, the products offered include extreme mortality bonds and value in force securitization.

Munich Re provides an intelligent crop insurance system through an innovative solution called SystemAgro. Through this sustainable solution, Munich Re brings together farmers, governments, international donor organizations, and NGOs. The system is based on public private partnerships. Munich Re offers cyber-risk products including reinsurance for accumulation perils such as worm and virus-related losses.

Munich Re provides support for clients by covering financial risk and using the capital markets for reinsurance needs. Munich Re devises individual coverage for protection of clients' whole risk position through a combination of capital market/alternative risk transfer and reinsurance coverage. Capital, balance sheet, and result management solutions cover reinsurance solutions such as financial reinsurance and Solvency II concepts. Credit insurance solutions cover political and commercial risks. Insurance of contingency events includes event cancellation, film and residual value insurance, prize indemnity, and productivity risk insurance.

NatCatSERVICE is one of the most comprehensive natural catastrophic loss databases provided by Munich Re where approximately 1000 events are recorded and analyzed every year. The information collated is used to perform risk and trend analyses on the extent and intensity of individual natural hazard events in various parts of the world.

Munich Re's NATHAN (Natural Hazards Assessment Network) Risk Suite aims to optimize the assessment of natural hazard risks. Munich Re's retakaful unit is a fully fledged retakaful operator that conducts worldwide general (nonlife) and family (life) retakaful business. In the area of retroactive reinsurance, Munich Re provides Customized Portfolio Solutions. In the area of workers' compensation insurance, Munich Re provides advice to employers, insurers, and governments for designing national solutions.

5.8.1.1.2 Life reinsurance

The products and services in this line of business include automated underwriting, capital management, product development, Retakaful, risk management, and solvency. Individual automated solutions facilitate bancassurance and online sales. Munich Re provides tailor-made solutions for occupational disability products. For risk management, Munich Re offers risk transfer, risk assessment, and claims handling solutions. Munich Re Internet Assessor (MIRA) is an Internet-based underwriting integrated solution tool. MIRA generates clearly structured digital risk profile documentation that delivers clear structured rating suggestions. Munich Re also provides range of Solvency II services.

5.8.1.1.3 Health reinsurance

The products and services offered cover services such as automated claims handling, medical underwriting, Solvency II, statistical solutions, and predictive modeling. Automated claims handling is an intelligent and consistent claims handling business tool offered by Munich Re. The Rule Engine is a computer-based service that supports the automated processing of 50,000 claims per day. In the domain of medical underwriting insurance, the company offers NORMRISK, which is a state-of-the-art tool for assessing individual health insurance risks. The solution has more than 100,000 users. Munich Re offers predictive modeling to create sophisticated data capture and analysis methods. The predictive modeling uses advance technologies to turn data into business intelligence.

5.8.1.1.4 Risk solutions

Corporate Insurance Partner offers insurance solutions for industrial firms and corporate clients in different lines of business. Munich Re, the leading provider of engineering insurance, has developed customized risk transfer solutions. Corporate Insurance Partner provides services such as assessing and insuring property risks. The company also provides optimum insurance coverage for energy companies. The company also offers project operators, contractors, and power plant owners insurance coverage. Corporate Insurance Partner develops targeted coverage for individual liability risk scenarios.

Risk transfer solutions are also designed for individual liability risk scenarios. Under executive liability coverage, Corporate Insurance Partner offers products such as D&O, public offering of securities insurance, EPL, and pension trustee liability. For financial institutions, products offered include crime policies that cover first-party losses, which include infidelity of employees, premises, transit, forgery, or alteration. Professional indemnity policies are third-party coverage with a focus on negligence of employees. The company also provides customized professional liability solutions to clients and brokers and solutions for special enterprise risk that consist of 1-year full-transfer terms to structured solutions with multiyear and multiline elements. Green Tech Solutions provide unique expert resources and know-how in the area of renewable energies.

5.8.1.1.5 Claims

Munich Re's claim team consists of more than 20 business units around the world that cover the full spectrum of claims management across all classes of business.

5.8.1.2 Primary insurance

The primary insurance operations of Munich Re are carried out by the ERGO Insurance Group. The group is one of the leading insurance providers in Germany and Europe, where the focus is on bancassurance activities. ERGO offers a wide range of insurance, provisions, and services for private, commercial, and industrial clients. ERGO has sales partnerships with banks in many European countries. The brands offered by ERGO are complemented by specialist groups in health, legal expenses, and travel insurance sectors. Life insurance and property casualty insurance is provided under the ERGO brand. DAS is the legal insurer brand of ERGO, which is Europe's number one in the market. DKV is ERGO's health insurance specialist, which provides comprehensive health and nursing care insurance. ERGO Direkt is the group's expert in direct marketing, which focuses on easy-to-understand insurance products such as supplementary dental insurance, long-term-care daily benefits, term life cover, and death benefits insurance. ERV is ERGO's travel insurer, which is the market leader among Germany's travel insurers. The brand has a presence in more than 20 countries.

5.8.1.3 Munich Re Health

The basic aim of this division is to pool global health expertise in reinsurance, primary insurance, and risk management. Munich Health serves clients and partners in more than 40 countries. The division offers solutions covering the healthcare chain through different affiliated companies. The services include medical underwriting under NORMRISK HEALTH, automated claims-handling Rule Engine, statistical solutions for predictive modeling, and Solvency II consulting services. Munich Health provides tools for standardized medical risk assessment for its reinsurance clients. Munich Re also offers new automation options and test algorithms for transmission of claims notification and claims processing data.

5.8.1.4 Asset management

MEAG MUNICH ERGO AssetManagement GmbH (MEAG) handles the investment activities of Munich Re and ERGO. MEAG manages asset classes such as fixed interest securities, equities, and real estate.

5.8.2 STRATEGY

Munich Re follows active capital management. The company pursues a policy of stable dividends. Excess capital is returned to shareholders in the form of dividends and buybacks. The company has a total of 143,000 shareholders. The majority of shares are held by institutional investors such as banks, insurers, and investment companies. Warren Buffett is the largest shareholder of Munich Re. Berkshire Hathaway holds a stake of 11.2% in Munich Reinsurance Company.

The fundamental investment strategy of Munch Re is ALM. Investment risk is measured in relation to changes of values in liabilities. Through ALM, the company aims to minimize the effect of capital market fluctuations. Features such as maturity patterns, currency structures, and inflation sensitivities are analyzed for liabilities. Investments with similar characteristics are considered for assets. The company uses derivatives financial instruments to hedge fluctuations in interest rate, equity, and currency markets. Recently, the organic growth in motor business due to strategic relations and expansion of the worldwide agricultural portfolio have led to an increase in premium income. Fire insurance also witnessed an increase in rates particularly in the markets of loss-affected regions of Australia, Asia, and Japan. In the financial risk segment, credit and bond reinsurance are important classes of business.

The innovation platforms of Munich Re are its Special Enterprise Risk unit and product development divisions of American Modern and Hartford Steam Boiler (HSB), which develop new coverage in strategic partnerships with industrial and primary insurance clients.

Munich Re has products in the fields of climate change and energy. In its wind power plants sector, Munich Re insures manufacturers against serial losses due to guarantee and maintenance contracts. Munich Re offers insurance solutions for unexpected deviations in the weather compared to long-term averages.

Another trend is the use of reinsurance solutions for capital optimization. The Financial Solutions unit devises special life reinsurance solutions for capital relief in connection with guaranteed products. Munich Re has developed solutions for risk coverage in public infrastructure projects through public private partnerships.

New products released in 2012 include insurance products that protect against the risk of manufacturer's insolvency. HSB introduced contractor E&O coverage, which targets artisan type contractors. In 2012 ERGO established a joint venture with a local partner in China. ERGO also signed a joint venture with the Avantha Group in India to offer insurance products for private clients. The company focuses on property insurance in India through its joint venture partner HDFC. In the United States, the insurance product SystemAgro combines the interests of governments, farmers, and the insurance industry within the framework of a public-private partnerships. In 2012, Munich Re transferred US hurricane and European windstorm risk with total volume of €100m to the capital market.

Munich Re has occupied a place in the FTSE4Good and Dow Jones Sustainability Index since 2001. Munich Re signed the Principles for Sustainable Insurance of the United Nations Environmental Programme Finance Initiative.

5.8.3 RISK MANAGEMENT

The Integrated Risk Management (IRM) division is responsible for supervising risk with the support of decentralized structures in all units of the group. The division is headed by the CRO. The CRO reports to the central committee, which is responsible for groupwide issues related to strategy, financial control, and risk management. The Global Underwriting and Risk Committee is the special risk committee for reinsurance. ERGO IRM manages risk for primary insurance. The Munich Health segment is in charge of risk matters related to that segment. Munich Re uses economic earnings at risk as its criteria to protect capital and limit the likelihood of a loss year. In 2012, economic earnings at risk were €4.8 billion.

The company compares the internal risk model with the current status of Solvency II and also participates in quantitative impact studies and stress tests such as the European Insurance Stress Test. The internal control system is the worldwide system that manages operational risk.

Underwriting risk arises due to activities in property and casualty insurance and life and health insurance businesses. It is the risk of insured losses in the property casualty business exceeding expectations. Underwriting risk in P&C consists of premium and reserve risk. Premium risk is the risk of future claim payments related to insured losses that have not yet occurred being higher than expected. Reserve risk is the risk of technical provisions that are established to cover losses that have already been incurred being insufficient. Line managers have the responsibility of managing premium risk. The underwriting power granted to the operating units is based on the mandatory groupwide instructions or limited capacity budgets. The reserves for losses and claim settlement costs are carried out in accordance with actuarial practices. Underwriting risk in life and health insurance consists of biometric and lapse risk. Random fluctuations in insurance benefits or lapse behavior can lead to a short-term fall in the value of the portfolio. Changes in client biometrics or lapse behavior has a long-term effect on the value of a portfolio. Morbidity risk is important in health insurance. The most significant risks in life insurance is mortality, longevity, and disability risk. Limits are set for short-term pandemic scenarios and longer-term longevity scenarios.

Market risk, which is the risk of economic losses that result from price changes in capital markets, consists of equity risk, general and specific interest rate risk, property risk, and currency risk. General interest rate risk relates to changes in risk-free interest rate curves while specific interest rate risk arises owing to changes in credit risk spreads on government bonds or credit default spreads. Fluctuations in market prices affect underwriting liabilities. Market risk is managed by setting suitable limits, early warning systems, and ALM. The company hedges market risk through use of derivatives financial instruments. Strategies are devised based on simulation of market fluctuations by applying stress tests, sensitivity, and duration analyses.

Munich Re uses a cross-balance sheet counterparty limit system to monitor and control groupwide credit risk. The limits for each counterparty consisting of a group of companies or country are based on its financial situation as determined by internal fundamental analyses, ratings, and market data along with the risk appetite as stipulated by the board of management. Operational risk is the risk of losses that results from inadequate or failed internal processes, accidents caused by the actions of personnel, or system malfunctions. The Security and Continuity Risk Framework of Munich Re defines the rules for a standard groupwide procedure for identifying and assessing security risk for people, information, and property. Liquidity risk is managed by defining limits for minimum liquidity requirements. The management of liquidity risk includes setting known and expected payment obligations through regular detailed liquidity planning at an individual entity level, central cash flow reporting systems, margin calls, and collateral requirements for derivatives transactions. Strategic risk issues are focused on by the Strategic Committee, while cases involving reputational risk are managed by the Reputational Risk Committee.

The internal risk model determines the capital required to ensure Munich Re's ability to meet its commitments even after extreme losses. The internal risk model analyzes the profit and loss distribution of available financial resources over a 1-year time period. These internal risk models are based on specially modeled distributions for risk categories of property and casualty, life, and health, market, and credit and operational risk. Every risk is depicted in both reinsurance and primary insurance. The economic risk capital (ERC) is the amount of capital required by the company with a given risk appetite to cover unexpected losses in the coming year. ERC is based on the economic profit-loss distribution across all risk segments and corresponds to 1.75 times the VaR of this distribution over a 1-year time period with a confidence level of 99.5%. Country risk is analyzed based on ratings and independent analyses of the political, economic, and fiscal situation in the countries in which investments are made. The company also faces tax risk, supervisory risk, and legal risk. Table 5.16 provides the consolidated financial highlights of Munich Reinsurance during the period 2008-2012. Table 5.17 gives Munich Re's financial highlights of the gross premiums written during 2008-2012. Table 5.18 provides the combined ratio highlights of Munich Re during the period 2008-2012.

Table 5.16   Munich Re Consolidated Financial Highlights 2008-2012 (Billions of Euros)

	2008	2009	2010	2011	2012
Gross premiums	37.8	41.4	45.5	49.5	52
Net earned premiums	35.7	39.5	43.1	47.3	50.5
Market capitalization	22.9	21.5	21.4	17.0	24.4
Return on equity (in %)	7	11.8	10.4	3.3	12.6
Assets	215.4	223.4	236.4	247.6	258.4

Table 5.17   Munich Re Financial Highlights Gross Premiums 2008-2012 (Billions of Euros)

	2008	2009	2010	2011	2012
Reinsurance	21.9	21.8	23.6	26	28.2
Primary insurance	17.0	16.6	17.5	17.4	17.1
Health insurance		4.0	5.1	6.0	6.7

Table 5.18   Munich Re Combined Ratio Highlights (in Percentages)

	2008	2009	2010	2011	2012
Reinsurance	99.4	95.3	100.5	113.8	91
Primary insurance	90.9	93.2	96.8	99.1	98.7
Health insurance		99.4	99.7	99.5	100.2

5.9 AMERICAN INTERNATIONAL GROUP

American International Group, better known as AIG, is a major international insurance organization that serves customers in more than 130 countries. It has one of the world's most extensive worldwide property casualty networks. AIG is listed on the New York Stock Exchange and the Tokyo Stock Exchange. The company serves commercial, institutional, and individual customers throughout the world. It has been in operations for about 90 years. AIG serves approximately 98% of Fortune 500 companies. In 2012, AIG's revenue amounted to $65.7 billion. The total net premium written by AIG property casualty amounted to $34.4 billion in 2012. The average claims paid each business day by the property casualty business amounted to $34.4 billion in 2012. AIG facilitates about 18 million Americans in retirement planning. AIG employs around 63,000 employees. AIG Property Casualty is the top US-based commercial insurer in the United States and Canada, the largest US-based property casualty insurer in Europe, and a major foreign property casualty insurer in Japan and China.

AIG earns revenues basically from insurance premiums, policy fees from universal life insurance, and investment products. Operating expenses consist of policyholder benefits, claims incurred, and interest credited to policyholders.

5.9.1 **AIG PROPERTY CASUALTY**

AIG Property Casualty is a leading provider of insurance products for commercial, institutional, and individual customers. AIG Property Casualty offers an extensive range of products and services through its various multichannel distribution network. AIG Property Casualty operations are segregated into commercial insurance and consumer insurance. In 2012 commercial insurance constituted 59% of net premiums while consumer insurance accounted for 41% of net premiums.

5.9.1.1 Commercial products

The commercial products AIG Property Casualty offers consist of casualty, property, specialty, financial, distribution, and others. The casualty products offered include general liability, commercial automobile liability, workers' compensation, excess casualty, and crisis management insurance. Casualty products also include risk management and customized structured programs designed for large corporate customers and multinationals. Property products offered include industrial energy sector and commercial property insurance products that cover exposures to human-made and natural disasters. Specialty products under commercial products consists of aerospace, environmental, political risk, trade credit, surety, and marine insurance. Specialty product offerings are also made for small and medium-sized enterprises. Financial products offered include various forms of professional liability insurance such as D&O, fidelity, employment practices, fiduciary liability, network security, kidnap and ransom, and E&O insurance. The commercial insurance products are distributed through a network of retail and wholesale brokers and branches.

5.9.1.2 Consumer products

The consumer products AIG Property Casualty offers include accident, health, and personal. Accidental and health products consist of voluntary and sponsor-paid personal accidental and supplemental health products for individuals, employees, and associations. Products also include a broad range of travel insurance products and services for leisure and business travelers. Personal products offered include automobile, homeowners', and extended warranty insurance. Personal products for high-net-worth individuals are offered through the Private Client Group. These products include umbrella, yacht, and fine art insurance and specialty products such as identity theft and credit card protection. The consumer insurance products are distributed through agents and brokers.

AIG Property Casualty operates through major companies such as the National Union Fire Insurance of Pittsburgh, New Hampshire Insurance Company, American Home Assurance Company, Lexington Insurance Company, AIU Insurance Company, Chartis Overseas Ltd, Fuji, Chartis Singapore Insurance, and AIG Europe Ltd. AIG Property Casualty has a significant presence in the three major geographic regions of the Americas, Asia Pacific, and EMEA (Europe, Middle East, and Africa).

5.9.2 **AIG LIFE AND RETIREMENT**

AIG Life and Retirement is the premier provider of life insurance and retirement services in the United States. This division has two operating systems: Life Insurance and Retirement Services. The Life Insurance segment offers life insurance and related protection products. Retirement Services offers investment, retirement savings, and income solution products. AIG's newer operating segments are retail and institutional products. Retail product lines include life insurance, accident and health (A&H), fixed and variable annuities, and income solutions. Institutional product lines include group retirement, group benefit, and institutional markets. The institutional market products consist of stable value wrap products, structured settlements, terminal funding annuities, private placement variable life, and annuities and guaranteed investment contracts. In 2012, life insurance and A&H products comprised 66% of the life insurance segment. Institutional products and group benefits constituted 15% and 13% of the life insurance business in 2012. The Retirement Services segment's of retirement products constituted 44% of the retirement services premium. Brokerage services and retail mutual funds and fixed annuities accounted for 17% and 10%, respectively. The rest was accounted for by the variable annuities.

AIG Life and Retirement has one of the largest broker-dealer networks in the United States and offers a range of retail mutual fund offerings. AIG Life and Retirement is the leading retirement plan provider in K-12 schools, higher education, health care, government, and other nonprofit organizations. The AIG Life and Retirement division operates through three major companies: American General Life Insurance Company, the Variable Annuity Life Insurance Company (VALIC), and the United States Life Insurance Company. The AIG Life and Retirement division serves over 18 million customers.

5.9.2.1 Life insurance products

The Life Insurance segment provides a wide range of protection and mortality-based products. These products are generally marketed through the four major brands of American General, AGLA, AIG Direct, and AIG Benefit Solutions. These products are classified as life insurance and A&H, institutional and group benefits. The primary products are term life insurance, universal life insurance, and A&H products. Life insurance and A&H products are marketed through independent insurance agents under the American General brand. AIG Direct is the proprietary direct-to-consumer distributor of term life insurance and A&H products.

Products offered under the institutional category of life insurance include structured settlement and terminal funding annuities, fixed payout annuities, private placement variable annuities, variable life insurance, corporate-owned life insurance, bank-owned life insurance, and stable value wrap products.[1] American General brand markets these products through independent marketing organizations and structured settlement brokers.

Group benefits is another major segment of life insurance. In 2012, the Property Casualty and Life Retirement divisions combined their US group benefits businesses and renamed it AIG Benefits Solutions.

5.9.2.2 Retirement Services

The Retirement Services segment offers investment, retirement, and income solutions, products, and services. The products offered include group retirement, fixed annuities, and variable annuities. The group retirement products are marketed under the VALIC brand. The products in group retirement include fixed and variable group annuities, group mutual funds, group administrative and compliance

---

[1]A structured settlement is an insurance arrangement whereby a claimant for a personal injury claim receives periodic payments on an agreed schedule rather than as a lump-sum amount. Private placement life insurance is a form of variable universal life insurance that is offered privately through a public offering. Corporate-owned life insurance is life insurance for employees' lives that is owned by the employer, with benefits payable either to the employer or directly to the employees' families. Bank-owned life insurance is a form of life insurance that is purchased by banks whereby the bank is the beneficiary and/or the owner. Stable value wrap contracts are financial instruments that provide limited guarantees for stable value fund portfolios, preserving the principal while providing steady, positive returns for participants.

services. Fixed annuities include single and flexible premium-deferred fixed annuities marketed by the Western National brand. Variable annuities offer stock and fixed-income portfolios, guaranteed death benefits, and guaranteed retirement income solutions. Variable annuities are marketed through SunAmerica Retirement Markets. Brokerage services include operations of the Advisor Group, which is one of the largest networks of independent financial advisors in the United States.

5.9.2.3 Distribution network

AIG distribution consists of affiliated and nonaffiliated networks. The affiliated distribution network consists of VALIC career financial advisors, AGLA career agents, the Advisor Group, and AIG Direct. VALIC consists of more than 1200 financial advisors, whereas the Advisor Group has 6000 independent financial advisors. The nonaffiliated distribution network consists of banks, independent marketing organizations, broker-dealers, and benefit brokers. There are approximately 600 banks and 69,000 financial institution agents. AIG is associated with 1700 independent marketing organizations and more than 150,000 licensed independent agents. There are also more than 120,000 licensed financial professionals.

5.9.3 OTHER OPERATIONS

Mortgage Guaranty or United Guaranty Corporation (UGC) is a leading provider of private residential mortgage guaranty insurance. Through its products, UGC protects mortgage lenders and investors from loss due to borrower default and loan foreclosure. UGC insures over 1 million US mortgage loans and has operations in nine other countries. The primary product offered by UGC is mortgage insurance (MI). MI protects mortgage lenders from loss from mortgage defaults on high loan-to-value conventional first-lien mortgages. UGC also provides homeowner support. The other operations include Global Capital Markets (GCM), Direct Investment Book (DIB), and Retained interests. GCM includes the operation of AIG Markets, a derivative portfolio of AIG Financial Products and AIG Trading Group. DIB consists of a portfolio of assets and liabilities held by the AIG parent company in the Matched Investment Program.

5.9.4 STRATEGY

AIG has rebranded its core insurance operations under the AIG name with a new AIG logo. AIG has a strategic partnership with People's Insurance Company (Group) of China Ltd. AIG has also acquired Woodbury Financial Services and Fuji Fire and Marine Insurance Co.

Since 2009, AIG has divested businesses with a strategic view on a renewed focus on core businesses, to repay government support the company received during the economic crisis, and to improve its financial flexibility and risk management.

AIG aims to divest its largest noncore asset, International Lease Finance Corporation (ILFC), which was the leading aircraft leasing business. In 2012, AIG entered into an agreement to sell 80.1% of ILFC for approximately $4.2 billion in cash with an option for the purchaser to buy an additional 9.9% stake.

Other noncore divestitures include AIG Star, AIG Edison, Nam Shan, and MetLife Securities in 2011. In 2011, AIG completed recapitalization. The Department of Treasury exited ownership of AIG through six offerings of AIG common stock in 2011 and 2012. The total amount stood at $51.6 billion. The group is focusing on growth in high-value lines of business and geographies. Underwriting excellence is aimed at enhancing pricing and risk selection tools through investment in data mining, science, and technology underwriting. The main strength of the casualty and property division is based on diversification and global franchises. The division operates in more than 90 countries and jurisdictions. Another strategic focus is on bringing cost efficiency to its businesses. AIG has strategic plans to reduce loss costs by bringing efficiency in servicing customer claims and introducing fraud detection tools. Other highlights of strategic plans are mitigation of reserve development and legal costs and establishing effective pricing strategies.

In 2012, AIG undertook major organizational restructuring in which distinct product divisions, shared annuities, and life operations were created along with a unified all-channel distribution system for all AIG life and retirement products. The group consolidated European operations into a single European insurance company, AIG Europe Ltd. Restructuring of activities in the Asia and Pacific regions are also underway.

AIG aims to expand its distribution networks to capitalize on growing demand for income solutions and life and retirement products. The company also focuses on developing innovative life offerings through consumer-focused research. AIG recently adopted a new reinsurance framework to improve the efficiency of legal entity capital management and support global product lines. The reinsurance markets include local and global reinsurance markets in the United States, Bermuda, London, and Europe, which can be directly accessed through reinsurance intermediaries. The emphasis of AIG's worldwide insurance policy on investments is in fixed-term securities issued by corporations, municipalities, and governmental agencies along with a secondary focus on common stocks, private equity, hedge funds, and other alternative investments.

The AIG Life and Retirement segment aims to increase sales of products by fully leveraging its unified all-channel distribution. The strategic focus of the Life Insurance and Retirement segment also includes disciplined underwriting, active expense management, product innovation, and improvement of operational efficiencies through investments in technology.

5.9.5 RISK MANAGEMENT

AIG has an IRM process for managing risk throughout the organization. The enterprise risk management (ERM) framework provides senior management a holistic and consolidated view of risk positions. The company conducts enterprisewide stress tests under different scenarios to understand exposure to risk. The GRC is the senior management group that assesses all risk on a global basis. The board of directors oversees the management of risk through the finance and risk management committee. All major insurance businesses have a risk and capital committee that is responsible for identification, assessment, and monitoring of all sources of risk within their respective portfolio. ERM develops a companywide risk appetite statement that articulates the risk-taking capacity by setting consolidated capital and liquidity tolerances as observed under expected and stressed economic and business conditions.

Credit exposures for the group arise from fixed-income investments, equity securities, deposits, repos, reverse repos, commercial paper, leases, and reinsurance recoverables. Counterparty risk arises from derivatives activities, collateral extended to counterparties, insurance risk cessions to third parties, financial guarantees, and letters of credit.

The chief credit officer and credit executives are responsible for development and maintenance of credit risk policies and procedures such as managing the approval process for credit limits, program limits, and credit transactions. Other responsibilities involve administering regular port-folio credit reviews of investment, derivatives, and credit-incurring business units. The group also conducts credit research to find risk concentrations in countries, sectors, and asset classes. The single largest credit exposure is the US government, which constituted 25% of total equity in 2012. The other largest credit concentrations are Canada and Japan. The largest industry credit exposure was to global financial institutions, which consist of banks and finance companies, securities firms, insurance and reinsurance companies.

AIG is exposed to market risk due to the insurance and capital market businesses. Market risk arises in insurance operations from potential mismatches in asset liability exposures. For example, the life insurance and retirement businesses collect premiums or deposits from policyholders and invest the proceeds in long-term fixed maturity securities. The margin spread for the company is based on the difference between the asset yield and costs payable to policyholders.

Market exposures can be categorized as benchmark interest rates, credit spread or risk premiums, equity and alternate investment prices, and foreign currency exchange rates. The market value of fixed maturity securities portfolios changes as the benchmark interest rates such as treasury yield curve or swap curve change. The market risk exposures are measured and quantified by a number of measures such as duration/key rate duration, scenario analysis, stress testing, and VaR.

Liquidity risk arises from financial interest rate changes, potential reputational events or credit downgrade, and catastrophic events that increase policyholder claims. Each business unit is respon-sible for managing liquidity. Current cash and liquidity positions are reviewed for changes and mea-sured against minimum liquidity levels. Cash flow forecasting is used to track future cash inflows and outflows. AIG Parent liquidity risk tolerance levels are established for base and stress scenarios for a 2-year time period to maintain a minimum liquidity buffer.

Each business unit is responsible for managing its operational risks. AIG uses a risk and control self-assessment (RCSA) to identify key operational risks and evaluate the effectiveness of existing controls to mitigate risk. This standard RCSA process is followed for certain key processes such as Sarbanese-Oxley, business continuity management, IT security risk, and compliance and vendor management.

Insurance operation risk is managed through prelaunch approval of product design, development and distribution, underwriting, and maintenance of exposure limits. AIG also uses reinsurance to man-age insurance operations risk.

AIG manages risk in the General Insurance segment through aggregations and limitations of con-centrations at multiple levels of policy, lines of business, geography, industry, and legal entities. In Life Insurance, the risk includes mortality and morbidity in insurance-oriented products. In Retirement Services, risk is attributed to inadequate cash flows to cover contract liabilities in retirement savings-oriented products. Risk in life insurance and retirement services is managed through product design, medical underwriting, external traditional, and external catastrophe reinsurance programs. The risk in the MI business is managed through the geographic location of insured properties, economic conditions in the local housing markets, credit quality of borrowers, and more.

5.9.6 CORPORATE SOCIAL RESPONSIBILITY ACTIVITIES

Tata AIG has developed an innovative microinsurance program to help farmers in rural India track 350,000 heads of cattle and protect their livelihood. After Hurricane Sandy the company paid

Table 5.19   AIG Financial Highlights 2008-2012 (Millions of US Dollars)

	2008	2009	2010	2011	2012
Premiums	60,147	48,583	45,319	38,990	38,011
Total revenues	(11,777)	70,173	72,829	59,812	65,656
Total benefits, claims, and expenses	92,519	86,200	52,582	59,696	56,334
Net income (loss)	(102,882)	(9726)	12,285	21,330	3700
Total investments	636,912	601,165	410,412	410,438	375,824
Total assets	848,552	838,346	675,573	553,054	548,633
Total equity	48,939	88,837	106,776	102,393	98,669
Property casualty combined ratio (in %)	102.1	108.4	116.8	108.8	108.6

Source: Annual Reports

Table 5.20   AIG Segment Revenues 2012 (Millions of US Dollars)

Segment	Revenues
AIG Property Casualty	39,781
AIG Life and Retirement	16,767
Other Operations	9974

Source: Annual Reports

out $175 million to clients. In 2012, the company launched a matching grant program that included a 2:1 match ratio for employee donations up to $5000 to qualifying nonprofit organizations. Table 5.19 gives the financial highlights of AIG during the period 2008-2012. Table 5.20 provides revenues of AIG in the year 2012 by segment.

5.10 METLIFE

MetLife was established in 1864. MetLife companies offer insurance, retirement, and savings products. MetLife serves more than 90 million customers in more than 50 countries. MetLife, its subsidiaries and affiliates, offers life insurance, annuities, P&C insurance, and financial services to individuals. MetLife offers group insurance, retirement, and savings products and services to corporations and other institutions. The company also provides services to more than 90 of the top 100 Fortune 500 companies. For individuals, the company offers life insurance, accident and health insurance, disability income insurance, credit insurance, auto and home insurance. The retirement products offered include retirement planning and savings products. The company offers first-class benefits packages for employees and customized pension administration and benefits funding solutions for employers. MetLife operates in Latin America, Europe, Asia, and the Middle East in addition to the United States. Products and services are marketed through various distribution channels. Retail life, disability, and annuity products for individuals are sold through sales forces and third-party organizations. MetLife Investments has about 750 professionals and staff to support its global operations. In 2013, the diversified portfolio consisted of $454 billion in assets under management. Corporate and foreign government bond portfolios and structured finance portfolios constituted approximately 52% and 15% of the managed assets, respectively. MetLife's P&C business gross losses from Hurricane Sandy were approximately $150 million.

MetLife is organized into segments reflecting three different geographical regions. These segments include Retail Group, Voluntary and Worksite Benefits, Corporate Benefit Funding, Latin America (Americas), and Asia, EMEA.

Retail Life provides products such as traditional life, universal life, annuities, and retained asset accounts. The life insurance policies offered include term life insurance, whole life insurance, universal life insurance, variable universal life insurance, and survivorship life insurance. MetLife's individual disability income insurance includes monthly benefit payments and noncancelable and guaranteed renewable coverage.

Corporate Benefit Funding products consist of capital market products, pension closeouts, structured settlements, and other benefit funding products. Corporate and others contain the surplus portfolios for the enterprise as well as the portfolios used to fund the capital needs of the company.

From 2008, through its affiliate bank, MetLife Bank has been engaged in the origination, sale, and servicing of forward and reverse residential mortgage loans.

5.10.1 STRATEGY

One of the priorities of MetLife is to shift its business mix from market-sensitive, capital-intensive products toward protection-oriented and lower-risk products. The company has introduced a new voluntary and worksite benefits solution to focus on low capital-intensive products. The company is also focusing on cross-selling protection-oriented accident and healthcare product offerings for mid-sized employers. The company aims to generate at least 20% of operating earnings from the emerging markets by 2016. The emerging markets business contributed to an overall operating earnings growth of 18% in Asia and 13% in Latin America.

MetLife has grown both organically and through worldwide acquisitions. MetLife expanded its presence in Eastern Europe regions such as Hungary, Romania, and Czech Republic through the acquisition of Aiva's life businesses. MetLife was able to add a large diversified distribution network through this acquisition. MetLife's partnership with Punjab National Bank (PNB) gave it access to over 70 million PNB customers in India. MetLife is the leading insurer in Chile, having acquired AFP Provida for approximately $2 billion in cash. In 2010, MetLife acquired American Life Insurance company (Alico) from American International Group for $16.4 billion. The acquisition facilitated MetLife to expand its global presence in life insurance with an additional 90 million customers in more than 60 countries.

MetLife derives approximately one third of its operating earnings from outside the United States. In 2012, the company designed a new organizational structure composed of the Americas, EMEA, Asia and global employee benefits. MetLife has aimed at 1 billion in cost savings by 2016. The company also has invested $400 million in technology and process improvements.

The company has designed investment strategies, product designs, and interest crediting rate strategies to mitigate risks from low interest rate environments. The company uses ALM strategies that include the use of derivatives such as interest rate swaps, floors, and swaptions to mitigate risk of sustained low interest rates. The company also uses business actions such as shifting its sales focus to less interest rate-sensitive products. The company manages investment risk through in-house fundamental credit analysis of underlying obligors, issuers, transaction structures, and real estate

Table 5.21   MetLife Revenue Highlights 2012 (Millions of US Dollars)

Segment	
Retail	19,939
Group Voluntary and Worksite Benefits	17,436
Corporate Benefit Funding	9436
Latin America	4845
Asia	12,793
EMEA	4279
Corporate and others	(578)
Total	68,150

Source: Annual Reports.

Table 5.22   MetLife Operating Revenues 2010-2012 (Millions of US Dollars)

	2010	2011	2012
Premiums	27,071	36,269	37,911
Universal life and investment products	5817	7528	8212
Net investment income	16,855	19,638	20,472
Other revenues	1393	1652	1756
Total	51,136	65,087	68,351

Source: Annual Reports.

properties. The company manage credit risk, market risk, and liquidity risk through industry and issuer diversification and asset allocation. Table 5.21 gives the revenue highlights of MetLife based on segments and regions in the year 2012. Table 5.22 provides the operating revenues of MetLife during the period 2010-2012.

5.11 CHINA LIFE INSURANCE GROUP

China Life Insurance and its subsidiaries is the largest commercial insurance group in China. The group is also one of the largest institutional investors in the capital market of China. In 2011, its insurance premiums amounted to ¥357.8 billion. The total assets of the company stood at ¥1956.2 billion in 2011. It is the first insurance company to be triple listed in the New York, Hong Kong, and Shanghai stock exchanges. China Life's development strategy is based on three phases. In Phase I, the company aims to strengthen its leading edge of core business in life insurance and asset management. In Phase II, the growth stage, the company intends to focus on property, casualty, and pension business to transform China Life into a comprehensive insurance provider. In Phase III, the banking, funds, securities, and trust businesses will be integrated into the core business of China Life through various channels.

5.12 **AIA GROUP**

AIA Group along with its subsidiaries is the largest independent publicly listed Pan Asian life insurance group. AIA was founded in 1919. AIA is a market leader in the Asia Pacific region except in Japan on the basis of life insurance premiums. AIA offers products for individuals and corporations. The company offers a range of products and services such as life insurance, savings plan, accident and health insurance. AIA Group also offers employee benefit plans, credit life, and pension services to corporate clients. AIA Group serves more than 27 million individual customers and more than 16 million participating members of group insurance schemes. AIA Group is listed on the main board of the Hong Kong Stock Exchange.

AIA Group uses an inorganic growth strategy for expansion. AIA Group acquired a 92% shareholding in one of the leading insurance companies in Sri Lanka. AIA also acquired ING Malaysia, the third-largest life insurer in Malaysia, for $1.73 billion. The acquisition gave AIA a distribution force of more than 9000 agents and a long-term bancassurance partnership with a leading Malaysian banking group. In May 2013, AIA had total assets of US$147 billion. The operating profit after tax in 2012 was $2159 million. In 2012, the solvency ratio was 353%. In 2012, the total regulatory capital for AIA amounted to US$4811 million as measured under the Hong Kong Office of Commissioner basis.

AIA's partnership team is responsible for value creation through bancassurance, direct marketing, and intermediated distribution channels. AIA is the leading provider of group insurance in the Asia Pacific region with more than 100,000 corporate clients and more than 13 million group insurance scheme members. In 2012, AIA introduced an internal enterprise social network called Wave, which uses the Jive software platform to facilitate more efficient connectivity. The company focuses on group insurance in Thailand and Singapore.

5.13 **ING**

ING is a global financial institution headquartered in the Netherlands that offers banking, investments, life insurance, and retirement services to a wide range of customers. The company serves more than 48 million private, corporate, and institutional customers. ING has operations in more than 40 countries in Europe, North America, Latin America, Asia, and Australia. According to Bloomberg data from 2013, ING ranks among the top 20 European financial institutions by market capitalization. ING Insurance had a solvency ratio of 212% in the third quarter of 2013. ING Insurance (INGV) is the company that holds ING's insurance and investment management businesses in Europe and Japan. In a major corporate restructuring exercise as stipulated by the European Commission, the banking and insurance/investment management businesses became separate standalone businesses within the ING Group. These restructuring exercises were aimed at getting state aid from the Dutch government in 2008 and 2009. NN is the new name for ING Insurance, which includes National Nederlanden, ING Insurance International, ING Life Japan, and ING Investment Management International. ING is the number-one life insurer in the Netherlands. Insurance products are offered through a broad group of financial intermediaries, independent producers, affiliated advisers, and sales specialists.

The ING banking business line is divided into three main groups: Retail Banking Benelux, Retail Banking International, and Commercial Banking. The insurance/investment management (IM) activities are structured by region. The insurance activities are carried out by Insurance Benelux, Insurance

Table 5.23 ING Income Highlights: Insurance Operations 2009-2012 (Millions of Euros)				
2008	**2009**	**2010**	**2011**	**2012**
39,142	26,664	28,035	29,133	26,689

Central and Rest of Europe, Insurance US, US Closed Block VA, and Insurance Asia/Pacific. ING Investment Management is part of the insurance activities. Insurance Benelux consists of ING's life and nonlife insurance, investment, and pension businesses in the Netherlands, Belgium, and Luxembourg. ING's retirement services, life insurance, and investment management operations in the United States are managed by Insurance US.

Insurance US includes ING's retirement services, life insurance, and investment management operations in the United States. US Closed Block VA consists of ING's closed-block variable annuity business in the United States, which has been closed to new businesses since early 2010. Insurance Asia/Pacific is a leading foreign life insurance company in the region with a presence in Japan, Malaysia, South Korea, Thailand, China, Hong Kong, and India. ING US is one of the largest providers of life insurance in the United States. It is one among the top-five providers of term insurance and one of the top providers of universal life insurance based on premiums sold. ING US is one of the top-five largest providers of medical stop-loss insurance in the United States based on in-force premiums.

In 2012, ING Insurance refined its sales process for the development of new products. A five-point gauge was developed to make process improvements, which consist of Net Promoter Score, customer complaints, welcome call analysis, policy persistency rate, and agent turnover rate. The Solvency I ratio for the insurance group was 245% in 2012. Table 5.23 provides the income highlights of the ING Insurance group during the period 2008-2012.

5.14 ZURICH INSURANCE GROUP

Zurich Insurance Group is the leading Swiss multiline insurance provider with a global network of subsidiaries. The company provides a broad range of general insurance and life insurance products and services for individuals, small businesses, mid-sized and large companies. The company employs around 60,000 employees. In 2012, Zurich completed 100 years of operation in the United States. The company has major operations in Germany, Italy, Spain, Switzerland, and the United Kingdom.

The business segment consists of General Insurance, Global Life, and Farmers Exchanges. In General Insurance, the businesses are P&C insurance and services to individuals, commercial, and corporate customers. General Insurance provides a variety of motor, home, and commercial products and services for individuals, small and large businesses. Global Life provides life insurance, savings, investment, and pension solutions to individual, commercial, and corporate customers. Farmers Exchanges provide management services related to P&C insurance to individual and commercial customers. Farmers Exchanges include all reinsurance assumed from the Farmers Exchanges by the group. Farmers Exchanges are major writers of personal and small commercial lines of business in the United States.

Table 5.24   Zurich Financial Highlights 2011-2012 (Millions of US Dollars)

	2011	2012
Gross written premiums	47,748	51,285
Policy fees	2452	2692
Total revenues	52,983	70,414
Net income after taxes	3775	3967
Total investments	311,953	333,934
Total assets	386,971	409,267

Source: Annual Report 2012

Zurich manages insurance risk by establishing limits for underlying authority. The group also requires specific approvals for transactions, which involve new products and use of a variety of reserving and modeling methods. The group also uses specific risk reinsurance treaties. The group's underwriting strategy involves diversification of general insurance risks across industries and geographic regions. The business operating profit amounted to US$4.1 billion in 2012. Table 5.24 gives the financial highlights of the Zurich Insurance Group during the period 2011-2012.

REFERENCES

1. Japan Post Annual Report 2012
2. http://www.geico.com/information/aboutinsurance/
3. http://www.genre.com/aboutus/meet-genre/?c=n
4. http://www.genre.com/reinsurance-solutions/?c=n
5. http://www.berkshirehathaway.com/2012ar/linksannual12.html, Berkshire Annual Report 2012
6. http://www.berkshirehathaway
7. http://www.reuters.com/finance/stocks/companyProfile?symbol=BRKa
8. http://www.axa.com/en/investor/resultsreports/reports/
9. http://www.axa.com/en/
10. AXA Registration Financial Annual Report 2012
11. http://www.allianz.com/en/products_solutions/index.html
12. Allianz Group Annual Report 2012
13. http://www.generali.com/
14. http://www.generali.com/Generali-Group/Worldwide-Group/Europe/
15. Generali Annual Report 2012
16. http://www.nissay.co.jp/english/annual/pdf/ar2012.pdf
17. http://www.nissay.co.jp/english
18. http://www.munichre.com/publications/302-07805_en.pdf
19. http://www.munichre.com/en/munichhealth/competencies/default.aspx
20. http://www.munichre.com/en/primary_insurance/default.aspx
21. http://www.munichre.com/en/reinsurance/default.aspx
22. http://www.aig.com/Chartis/internet/US/en/2012%20AIG%20Annual%20Report%20(lower)_tcm3171-484181.pdf

23. 2012 AIG Annual Report
24. https://www.metlife.com
25. MetLife Annual Report 2012
26. http://www.chinalife.com.cn/publish/yw/596/index.html
27. AIA Annual Report 2012
28. http://investors.aia.com/phoenix.zhtml?c=238804&p=irol-reports
29. http://www.ing.com/Our-Company/About-us/Profile-Fast-facts.htm#insurance:investment_management__im_
30. ING Annual Report 2012
31. http://www.ing.com/Our-Company/About-us.htm
32. http://www.zurich.com/internet/main/sitecollectiondocuments/about-zurich/fact-sheet-en.pdf

CASES ON PENSION FUNDS

6.1 PENSION FUND TRENDS

According to the 2012 P&I/Towers Watson Global 300 pension funds ranking report, the assets under management (AUM) of pension funds amounted to US$14.0 trillion in 2012. According to the report, North America was the largest region in terms of AUM, accounting for 40.5% of total worldwide assets. Europe was the second-largest region, followed by the Asia Pacific region. The Defined Benefit Fund accounted for 68.5% of total assets.

6.2 SOVEREIGN PENSION FUNDS

6.2.1 GOVERNMENT PENSION INVESTMENT FUND JAPAN

The Government Pension Investment Fund (GPIF) was established to manage and invest the reserve funds of the Employees' Pension Insurance and the National Pension of Japan. The investment return was 10.23% in 2012. The investment income amounted to ¥11222.2 billion in 2012. The value of investment assets amounted to ¥120.5 trillion. The investments included domestic bonds, FILP bonds, domestic and international stocks, and short-term assets. The three significant characteristics of Japan's pension schemes are universal pension coverage, social insurance-type format, and intergenerational dependency. In the intergenerational dependency method (pay-as-you-go) method, the working-class generations support the older generations with their contributions. Falling birth rates and an aging population have put more burden on working-class people. To encourage growth of social security pension schemes, the government has adopted a fixed schedule of the contribution rate for employee pension insurance. Pension benefits are basically increased in line with increases in per capita disposable income of active workers for new beneficiaries. With the introduction of an automatic balancing mechanism, the pension index is modified to lower the pension benefit level in tune with rates such as the decrease in the number of covered pensions by the social security pension schemes and the projected average annual increase rate of life expectancy.

The GPIF is responsible for the management and investment of reserve funds according to the provisions of the GPIF law. The fund contributes to the stability of Employees' Pension Insurance and National Pension by portfolio-based investments to generate returns and ensuring liquidity for pension benefit payment. Portfolio-based investment is based on principles of diversification in which a policy asset mix is made based on target allocation. The target allocation for domestic bonds and international bonds is 67%, while the target allocation for domestic and international stocks is 11% and 9%, respectively. The target allocation for short-term assets is 5%.

The governance structure of the GPIF is supervised by the Ministry of Health, Labor, and Welfare. The ministry established medium-term objectives of 3-5 years for each agency under its jurisdiction. The heads of the agency formulate medium-term plans to achieve the objectives. An evaluation committee consisting of external experts evaluates the performance of each agency with respect to targets. The Investment Committee consists of experts from finance, the economy, and other related experts appointed by the Ministry of Health, Labor, and Welfare. The committee monitors the implementation of the investment policy of the GPIF. The basic investment strategies used are active and passive investment management strategies. In March 2013, investments in domestic bonds amounted to ¥63.8 trillion in which passive investment accounted for ¥57.7 trillion consisting of nine funds. Domestic stocks and international stocks accounted for ¥17.6 trillion and ¥14.9 trillion. International bonds and FLIP bond investments amounted to ¥11.8 trillion and ¥10.7 trillion.

Risk management techniques involve monitoring the deviations of actual portfolio from the policy asset mix. Market risk, price risk, liquidity risk, and credit risk are also managed. Derivatives such as stock futures, bond futures, and currency forwards are also used for hedging risk. GPIF also has an established internal control system to ensure proper operations.

6.2.2 GOVERNMENT PENSION FUND NORWAY

The Government Pension Fund Norway is part of the Government Pension Fund. Folketrygdfondet is commissioned to manage the Government Pension Fund Norway and the Government Bond Fund on behalf of the Norwegian Ministry of Finance. The strategic benchmark portfolio consists of 40% interest-bearing instruments and 60% equity instruments. The strategic benchmark index consists of two asset class indexes: an equity index and a fixed-income index. Each asset class index contains two strategic regional indexes: the Norway and the Nordic region. The strategic fixed-income index has 85% of the financial instruments included in the Barclays Capital Global Aggregate Norway. This strategic fixed-income index consists of loans issued in Norwegian kroner, euros, pound sterling, Swiss francs, Swedish kroner, and Danish kroner. Approximately 15% of the fixed-income index consists of Barclays Capital Global Aggregate Scandinavia. The strategic equity index have 85% of the Oslo Stock Exchange Main Index and 15% of the VINX benchmark. The Management Mandate for the Government Pension Fund requires Folketrygdfondet to have a strategic plan for its management activities. The benchmark index comprising the equity index and fixed-income index is split into two regional indexes of Norway (85%) and Denmark, Finland, and Sweden (15%). The mandate requires Folketrygdfondet to establish principles for valuation, performance measurement, and the management and control of risk. The GPFN and asset management organization Folketrygdfondet are owned by the state. Folketrygdfondet is the largest individual institutional investor in the Norwegian financial market. The invested capital comprises approximately 5% of the stock market and 3% of the bond market. In 2012, the company made profits of NOK 15,639 million.

6.2.3 ABP NETHERLANDS

The Stichting Pensionenfonds ABP is one of the largest pension funds in the world. It is the pension fund for employees in the government, public, and education sectors. The fund provides assurance of income security for old-age retirement, in the event of death, or occupational disability to approximately 2.8 million beneficiaries. By March 2013, the fund had an invested capital of €292 billion. The Stichting Pensionenfonds ABP is an independent body with its own board of trustees. Social partners represented by employers and employees manage the ABP.

ABP's Participants' Council and Employers' Council offer advisory services to the board. De Nederlandsche Bank is the external institution that supervises the ABP's board. The ABP board of trustees defines the risk frameworks within which ABP Investments operate. The ABP offers products that actively support aging along with actively publicizing the flexibility of the pension scheme. The ABP creates a strategic investment plan every 3 years. The ABP's long-term strategy is to achieve an average return of 7% annually. Every investment made in all asset classes is assessed based on environmental, social, and governance criteria. ABP has deployed new tools in social media as part of its marketing strategy. In 2012, the ABP created a YouTube channel that primarily shows informative videos. The fund also started promotions through Twitter and Facebook. In April 2013, the ABP launched an app with a pension quiz and information about funds and pensions. The strategic mix of investments consists of a maximum investment of 20% in an equity market of developed countries, 16% in credits, 12% in index-linked bonds, 10% in treasuries, and 9% in real estate. Other investments are made in emerging market equities, private equity, commodities, opportunities funds, and hedge funds. In 2012, the cost of pension fund management was €88 per participant. The investment portfolio is made up of 13 asset classes.

6.2.3.1 Products
6.2.3.1.1 ABP Flexible Early Retirement Pension
The ABP Flexible Early Retirement Pension offers the option of early retirement. The pension is available only to people who were born before January 1950 and who have accrued pension rights with ABP since April 1997.

6.2.3.1.2 ABP Retirement Pension
The ABP Retirement Pension scheme is initiated by a retiree at the age of 65 years. It also applies to people who were born before 1950 and who have accrued pension rights with ABP since 1997 in an uninterrupted manner.

6.2.3.1.3 ABP Multi-Option Pension
The ABP Multi-Option Pension helps clients decide their own retirement date between the 60th and 70th birthdays. The pension entilement depends on years of services as well as the number of years of accrued pension.

6.2.3.1.4 ABP Incapacity Pension
In the ABP Incapacity Pension, the claimant receives part of his or her salary from the employer during the first 2 years of a serious illness, After the 2-year period, Social Security may grant a state benefit. The ABP Incapacity Pension supplements this stream of income. This pension is available to people who accrue pension rights on their first sick day and who receive a WIA benefit from Social Security and who were laid off or have changed jobs.

6.2.3.1.5 ABP Surviving Dependents Pension
In the case of a retiring person's death, the partner may be entitled to the ABP Surviving Dependents Pension. Ex-partners and children under the age of 21 years are also eligible.

6.2.3.2 Asset liability management
Asset liability management is one of the main tools for evaluating financial risk and for periodic testing and preparation of financial policies. The financial policy of ABP consists of risk determination,

contribution rates,[1] indexation, investment policies, and determination of provisions for pension liabilities. The financial management of a fund basically focuses on long-term perspective. The short-term financial management policy is based on indexation or adjustment to investment policy. A recovery plan stipulates the imposition of a recovery surcharge on the contribution rate that is evaluated on a periodic basis. Decision on indexation is based on four classifications.

The pension fund's governance structure consists of the board of trustees and several council committees. The Fund Policy Committee advises the board of trustees on financial policy, pension policy administration policy, and policy implementation.

The ABP manages risk through the various committees to which risks are allocated. ABP risk management is based on the enterprise risk management standard of the committee of the sponsoring organization of the Treadway Commission. Strategic financial risk faced by the ABP includes interest rate risk, investment risk, underwriting risk, and wage inflation risk. Asset liability management is one of the main tools for evaluating financial risk. Outsourcing and reputational risk are important nonstrategic financial risks faced by the organization. The ABP outsources the administration of a pension scheme, asset management, and fund support services with third parties. Outsourcing risk arises from noncompliance of ABP mandates by third-party outsourcing agents.

Interest rate risk is the risk to the funding ratio of movements in the market interest rates. Pension liabilities are sensitive to market rate interest movements. The duration of pension liabilities is longer than pension investments. Hence, in an environment of lower interest rates, financial position is affected severely. In terms of investment, the ABP is exposed to credit risk, liquidity risk, commodity risk, equity, and alternative investment risk. Underwriting risk reflects the negative results on the actuarial assumptions that are used to determine the provisions for pension liabilities. An example of underwriting risk is rising life expectancy. The ABP aims to index pensions every year in line with wages in the public sector and education to minimize wage inflation risk. Operational risk, financial reporting, and compliance are other risks faced by the ABP. The ABP uses a diversification strategy across business sectors, asset classes, and markets to minimize risk. Strict limits apply to ABP investments. Limits are set for credit and interest rate risk. Credit risk is managed on the basis of ratings and by applying counterparty limits. Derivatives are also used to hedge risk. Table 6.1 lists the financial highlights of ABP Netherlands during the period 2007-2011.

6.2.4 NATIONAL PENSION SERVICE OF KOREA

The National Pension Service (NPS) of Korea was established in 1987 through the National Pension Act of Korea. The NPS has more than 20 million contributors, 3.3 million beneficiaries, and 400 trillion (won) in assets. The NPS has reserves of more than $280 billion. The National Pension Fund was established to pay pension benefits to the insured, including old-age, survivor, and disability pensions. The committees for investment for the NPS consists of the National Pension Fund Management Committee headed by the Ministry of Health and Welfare, the National Pension Fund Evaluation Committee, and the Risk Management and Investment Committee. NPS investment plans are based on strategic asset allocation, which determines an asset mix based on long-term target rate of return, risk tolerance, and capital market expectations. The National Pension Fund Committee develops a 5-year asset allocation

---

[1]Contribution rate is expressed as a percentage of salary for people starting to save for a pension in a defined contribution (DC) plan or personal retirement savings plan.

Table 6.1 ABP Netherlands Financial Highlights 2007-2011 (Millions of Euros)					
	2007	**2008**	**2009**	**2010**	**2011**
Total assets (A)	216,513	172,878	208,064	237,182	246,109
Retirement and Surviving Dependents pensions	150,844	189,400	197,745	221,975	259,976
Disability/Incapacity pension	2188	1993	1908	1705	1637
Flexible pension	1512	1402	1198	995	757
ABP extra pension	131	133	182	222	277
Provision for pension liabilities (B)	154,675	192,928	201,033	224,897	262,647
Gen reserve (A–B)	61,838	−20,050	7031	12,285	−16,538
Funding ratio of pension fund (A/B)	140	89.6	103.5	105.5	93.7
Contribution rate for surviving dependents pension in %	19.6%	20%	20.4%	20.6%	20.9%

Source: Annual report 2011

plan on an annual basis. Tactical asset allocation refers to modifications of asset allocation based on sudden changes in the market environment. Asset classes include domestic and overseas fixed-income, domestic and overseas equity, and alternate investments. In 2011, the market value of equity accounted for 24% of the portfolio. The fixed-income sector accounted for 68% of the portfolio.

6.2.5 CENTRAL PROVIDENT FUND SINGAPORE

The Central Provident Fund (CPF) is a government-sponsored comprehensive social security plan that provides benefits related to retirement, health care, home ownership, family protection, and asset enhancement. Singaporean employees and employers make monthly contributions to the CPF, which are processed for ordinary, special, medisave, and retirement accounts (RAs). The savings in ordinary accounts (OAs) are meant for buying houses, payments for CPF insurance, investment, and education. The special accounts (SAs) are meant for old age and investment in retirement-related financial products. The Medisave accounts provide for hospitalization expenses and approved medical insurance. CPF savings earn a minimum risk-free interest of 2.5%, which is guaranteed by the government of Singapore.

In 2012, the CPF had 3.4 million members. In 2012, total CPF member balances were $230 trillion. In 2012, 3.5 million members were insured under the MediShield scheme and 616,000 members under the Home Protection Scheme (HPS). The HPS fund paid out $89.8 million in claims to 1100 members. In 2009, CPF introduced CPF LIFE, which provides members with a monthly payout for as long as they live. CPF LIFE has in fact doubled the total number of annuities in force in Singapore. The standard and alternative basic plans are the two choices of CPF LIFE plans. The standard plan is the default plan and offers higher monthly payouts, while the alternative basic plan offers lower payouts with a higher bequest. In 2012, the CPF home page received over 22.6 million hits. The 2012 statistics reveal that of the 52.2 million transactions performed on the electronic service platforms of the CPF board, approximately 48.7 million were online transactions. The CPF portal integrated with the customer relationship management system supports personalized services and enables the company to send targeted messages to CPF members. Employers can submit their employees' CPF contribution details using the e-submission service on "my cpf portal." The Club 55 service at the CPF board's five service centers is aimed at providing services for senior citizens. The availability of self-service kiosks islandwide have made it easier for CPF members to carry out transactions.

6.2.5.1 *Operations*
6.2.5.1.1 Retirement schemes
CPF members have the option to withdraw their CPF in OAs and SAs after setting aside the CPF minimum sum once they reach the age of 55. In addition, CPF members who are able to meet the CPF minimum sum have to set aside the Medisave required amount in their Medisave account when they make CPF withdrawals. The Minimum Sum Topping Up (MSTU) scheme was introduced to encourage CPF members to make cash top-ups or transfers from their CPF accounts to their own or dependents' SAs and retirement accounts so the recipients can set aside more for their retirement. A number of top-up schemes such as the Voluntary Contributions to Retirement Account (VC-RA) scheme and Ordinary Account to Special Account Transfer scheme were merged into a single MSTU scheme. On account of high life expectancies in Singapore, CPF members at the age of 55 are automatically included in CPF LIFE if they have at least $40,000 in their RAs. CPF members who are not automatically included can apply to join CPF LIFE anytime before age 80. CPF members under 55 who prefer to set aside more cash for retirement can transfer their CPF savings from an OA to Savings to SA up to the prevailing minimum sum. Under the CPF investment scheme, after setting a side $20,000 and $40,000 in OAs and SAs CPF members can invest in fixed deposits, Singapore government bonds, and Treasury bills, statutory board bonds, annuities, endowment insurance policies, investment-linked insurance policies and unit trusts, and exchange-traded funds. Upon a CPF member's death, his or her savings will be paid to his nominated beneficiaries. The CPF Education scheme is the loan scheme that helps CPF members use CPF savings from OAs to pay for a spouse or a child's subsidized government tertiary education.

6.2.5.1.2 Health care
CPF members who withdraw their CPF savings at or after age 55 need to set aside the Medisave sum of $38,500 or the actual Medisave balance, whichever is lower, in their MAs to meet their healthcare needs during retirement. Under the Medisave400 scheme, a CPF member can withdraw up to $400 a year from the Medisave account to pay for one's own or a dependent's approved chronic illness treatments, vaccinations, and health screenings. Self-employed persons are required to contribute to Medisave based on their annual net trade income. MediShield is a basic medical insurance scheme that provides CPF members and their dependents with financial protection against high medical expenses arising from prolonged or serious illness. The annual premiums for MediShield range from $33 to $1123, depending on the insured's age. The annual claim limit and lifetime claim limit are $50,000 and $200,000, respectively. Private insurers have integrated their enhancement plans with MediShield as integrated plans, and act as a single point of contact to collect premiums and process claims.

6.2.5.1.3 Homeownership
The Public Housing scheme allows CPF members to use their CPF savings to buy flats financed with HDB housing loans or bank loans and to pay their housing loans. The CFP withdrawal limit for CPF members availing CPF to service their bank loans is 120% of the Valuation Limit. The Valuation Limit

refers to the market value of the flat at the time of purchase or the purchase price, whichever is lower. Under the Private Properties scheme CPF members can use their CPF savings to buy private properties and to pay their housing loans. Members can buy multiple properties using the CPF. If a member owning a property wishes to buy another property with CPF, then the member has to set aside half of the prevailing minimum sum in their ordinary and/or SAs. CPF members are required to refund the amount of CPF savings they have withdrawn plus the accrued interest when they sell their properties. The Dependents Protection scheme is an opt-out term insurance scheme that provides CPF members and their families with financial help should the insured CPF member become permanently disabled or die before the age of 60.

6.2.5.1.4 Workfare

The Workfare Income Supplement (WIS) scheme was introduced in 2007 to help Singaporeans improve their retirement adequacy. Workers aged 35 and above who earn an average gross monthly income of not more than $1700 and live in properties with an annual value of $13,000 or below are eligible for WIS of up to $2800 for work done. The Workfare Training Support (WTS) scheme was introduced to complement WIS by facilitating workers to upgrade their skills through training. Under the WTS scheme, eligible WIS participants can receive a Training Commitment Award up to $400 a year when they complete the requisite training. Table 6.2 gives the financial highlights of CPF Singapore during the period 2007-2013.

Table 6.2   CPF Statistics 2008-2013

	2008	2009	2010	2011	2012	September 2013
Total number of CPF members (millions)	3.23	3.29	3.34	3.38	3.42	3.48
Total number of active employers	108,279	114,837	118,940	123,263	128,373	133,454
Total members balance (millions of dollars)	151307.1	166,804	185,888	207545.50	230157.7	248110.2
Ordinary account (OA) (millions of dollars)	65,341.1	70593.8	77939.5	85084.8	91,862	97142.8
Special account (SA) (millions of dollars)	30,547.3	35,389.2	40,392.7	46,533.7	53,191.9	58,775.4
Medisave account (MA) (millions of dollars)	42,928.2	46,238.0	50,671.2	55,329.3	60,024.4	64,221.2
Retirement account and others (RA) (millions of dollars)	12,490.5	14,583.0	16,884.6	20,597.7	25,079.3	27,970.7

Source: http://mycpf.cpf.gov.sg/CPF/About-Us/CPF-Stats/CPF_Stats.htm

6.2.6 CANADA PENSION PLAN

The Canada Pension Plan (CPP) is a contributory earnings-related social insurance program. The two major components of the CPP are the Canada Public Retirement Income System and Old Age Security. The CPP Investment Board manages the CPP assets. The CPP retirement pension provides monthly benefits to eligible Canadians. Eligible members must have made at least one valid contribution (payment) to the CPP to qualify for a CPP retirement pension. The standard age to receive a pension is 65. There is also a provision to take a permanently reduced CPP retirement pension as early as age 60 or take a permanently increased pension after age 65. In post-retirement benefits, the employee receiving a CPP retirement pension may increase the retirement income with a lifetime benefit. CPP disability benefits consist of CPP disability benefits, children's benefits, and other disability resources. The CPP disability benefit is a taxable monthly payment available to people who have contributed to the CPP and who are not able to work regularly due to disability. The CPP children's benefits provide monthly payments to the dependent children of disabled or deceased CPP contributors. The CPP also provides survivor benefits. In this scheme CPP survivor benefits may be paid to the estate, a surviving spouse or common-law partner, and/or to children. In pension-sharing schemes, married or common-law couples in an ongoing relationship may voluntarily share their CPP retirement pensions.

In 2012, the prescribed contribution rate was 4.95% of a salaried worker's gross employment income between $3500 and $50,100, up to a maximum contribution of $2,306.70. The employer matches the employee contribution, effectively doubling the contributions of the employee. If a worker is self-employed, he or she must pay both halves of the contribution. The CPP Investment Board was established in 1997 as an independent organization to monitor and invest the funds held by the CPP. The CPP Investment Board created the CPP Reserve Fund. The CPP Investment Board invests in public equities, private equities, bonds, private debt, and real estate infrastructure.

6.2.7 EMPLOYEES PROVIDENT FUND MALAYSIA

The Employees Provident Fund (EPF) is the social security institution that was established by the Laws of Malaysia Employees Provident Fund Act of 1991. The EPF provides retirement benefits for members through management of their savings. Members of the EPF consist of private and nonpensionable public-sector employees. By September 2013, the EPF had 13.81 million members, and the total number of active employers was 515,165. The mandatory contributions are calculated on the basis of the monthly wages of an employee. The portion of an employee's contribution is 11% of the monthly a salary if the employee earns wages or a salary of MYR5000, and the employer contribution is 13%. For employees who earn above MYR5000, the contribution remains at 11%, but the employer contribution is 12%. The EPF makes investments in Malaysian government securities, money market instruments, loans and bonds, equity, and property. The EPF guarantees a minimum of a 2.5% dividend annually.

In 2004, the EPF implemented the Balanced Score Card management system to transform the organization into a world-class social security organization. In 2010, the EPF launched the Malaysia Retirement Savings scheme for self-employed people and later for housewives. In 2011, the EPF extended its list of critical illnesses under the Health Withdrawal Plan from 39 illnesses to 55. In 2012, the EPF managed an annual return on investment of 6.87%. The gross investment income in 2012 was MYR31.02 billion. The investment strategy is predominantly focused on fixed-income instruments while maintaining exposure in equities. In 2012, the EPF invested US$4.73 billion in new capital for global equity mandates and US$1.45 billion in global bonds and sukuks.

The EPF board is reponsible for overall risk management. The investment panel manages risk related to investment decisions. The Board Risk Management Committee assists the board in managing operational risk management activities. The EPF adopts tools such as value at risk, duration tracking error, beta measurement, simulation, and stress testing to manage market risk. The EPF uses a statistically based internal risk rating known as the corporate rating template to assess credit exposures. Credit risk systems were installed to compute credit value at risk for the EPF's credit-related assets and provide creditworthiness or probability of default for both public and private companies. The investment panel, through risk appetite statements, defines the level of risk the EPF is able to tolerate. This forms the basis of investment funds allocation. The EPF has adopted the MS ISO 31000:2010 as the main practice guide for managing operational risk. The Corporate Risk Scorecard has been adopted for the implementation of operational risk management in the EPF.

6.2.8 NATIONAL SOCIAL SECURITY FUND CHINA

In 2000, the Chinese government established the National Social Security Fund (NSSF) and the National Council for Social Security Fund to manage and operate the assets of the NSSF. The NSSF acts as a social security reserve to meet the retirement needs of the future aging population. The funding sources of the NSSF include fiscal allocation from the central government, allocation from the lottery public welfare proceeds, or equity assets that are derived from reduction or transfer of state-owned shares or capital raised by other methods. The Social Security Fund (SSF) manages the individual account funds and investment proceeds from provinces, autonomous regions, and municipalities that run pilot projects for individual accounts. SSF, the government agency, is the independent legal institution responsible for the management and operation of the NSSF. SSF manages the individual account funds and investment proceeds for the provinces, autonomous regions, and municipalities that run pilot projects for individual accounts. The Investment Committee examines and approves the strategic assets allocation plan and annual investment plan. The Risk Management Committee examines and discusses the risk policies and risk reports of the NSSF. The total AUM in 2011 were RMB868.820 billion. Domestic investments include bank deposits, bonds, trust investments, securitized products, stocks, and securities. Overseas investments include monetary market products such as bank deposits, bank bills, bonds, stocks and security investments, and derivatives. The investment portfolio of the NSSF has limits of stock assets less than or equal to 40%, while bank deposits, Treasury bonds, and policy bonds must be greater than or equal to 40%. In investments, the fixed-income assets accounted for 50.67% of assets in 2011. Domestic stocks accounted for 26.22%, overseas stocks accounted for 6.17%, and industrial investments accounted for 16.30%.

6.2.9 FEDERAL RETIREMENT THRIFT US

The Thrift Savings Plan (TSP) is a retirement savings and investment plan for federal employees and members of the uniformed services, which was established by the Federal Employees' Retirement System Act of 1986. The TSP offers savings and tax benefits similar to the benefits of 401(k) plans offered by private companies to their employees. The TSP is a defined contribution plan wherein the retirement income received is based on how much the participant and agency contribute to the account during a working year and the earnings accumulated over that time.

The Federal Retirement Thrift Investment Board (FRTIB) is responsible for the administration of the TSP. The FRTIB is an independent government agency that is managed by five presidentially appointed board members and an executive director. The TSP encourages employees to participate in a long-term retirement savings and investment plan. The TSP offers many advantages such as automatic payroll deductions, diversified choice of investment options, traditional pretax contributions, and tax-deferred investment earnings. TSP contributions are payroll deductions. The two types of employee contributions are regular and catch-up. Regular employee contributions are payroll deductions from basic pay before taxes are withheld (traditional contributions) or after taxes have been withheld (Roth contributions). Participants have to contribute the maximum regular contributions to be eligible to make catch-up contributions. Catch-up contributions are payroll deductions that participants who are 50 or older are eligible to make in addition to regular employee contributions. Catch-up contributions are voluntary and can be either traditional pretax or Roth after-tax. The IRC elective deferral limit is the maximum amount of employee contributions that can be contributed in a calendar year. The IRC elective deferral limit for 2013 was $17,500. The catch-up contribution limit for participants was $5500 under the IRC section. The TSP offers two kinds of tax treatment for employee contributions when a participant makes a contribution election. In a traditional TSP, the participant defers paying taxes on contributions and earnings until the amount is withdrawn. In Roth contributions, the participant pays taxes on the contributions that are made and gets earnings tax-free at withdrawal.

The TSP offers two investment avenues. In the first category, participants can invest in Lifecycle (L) funds, which are a professionally designed mix of stocks, bonds, and government securities. In individual accounts, participants can choose any or all of the individual TSP investment funds such as G, F, C, S, and I Funds. The L Funds are designed to help participants manage their TSP retirement savings. There are five L Funds based on time periods. For example, L 2050 is meant for participants who require their money in 2045 or later. Each L Fund invests in a mix of the five individual TSP funds.

The L Income Fund is designed to preserve the account balance, while protecting against inflation. The Government Securities Investment (G) Fund invests in short-term US Treasury securities. The principal and interest are guaranteed by the US government. The interest paid by the G Fund securities is calculated monthly based on the market yields of all US Treasury securities. The Fixed-Income Index Investment Fund (F) is invested in a separate account that is managed to track the Barclays Capital US Aggregate Bond Index. This broad index represents the US government, mortgage-backed, corporate, and foreign government bonds. The Common Stock Index Investment (C) Fund invests in a separate account that is managed by BlackRock and tracks the Standard and Poor's (S&P 500) Stock Index. The Small Capitalization Stock Index (S) Fund invests in a stock index fund that tracks the Dow Jones US Completion Total Stock Market Index. This index represents small and medium companies that are not included in the S&P 500 Index. The International Stock Index Investment (I) Fund invests in a stock index fund that tracks the Morgan Stanley Capital International EAFE (Europe, Australasia, Far East) Index. This index is made up of primarily large companies in 22 advanced countries.

TSP funds face risk such as currency risk, inflation risk, market risk, and prepayment risk. The two types of loans provided by TSP funds are a general-purpose loan and a loan for the purchase or construction of a primary residence. The lower limit of the loan is $1000 while the upper limit is $50,000. The TSP provides two types of withdrawals: a financial hardship service withdrawal and an age-based in service withdrawal. In the event of the death of a participant, the account amount is distributed to the beneficiary. The TSP Fund expense ratio was 0.027% in 2012. Table 6.3 provides the value of thrift saving fund balances for different types of funds of the Federal Retirement Thrift. Table 6.4 provides the thrift fund savings statistics of the Federal Retirement Thrift in the year 2012.

Table 6.3 TSP Thrift Savings Fund Balances in January 2012 (Millions of US Dollars)	
Fund	**Fund Balances**
G Fund	132,095
F Fund	21,269
S Fund	23,748
I Fund	15,845
L Income Fund	5170
L 2020 Fund	14,408
L2030 Fund	10,710
L 2040 Fund	7754
L 2050 Fund	845
Total	302,142

Source: http://www.frtib.gov

Table 6.4 TSP Thrift Savings Fund Statistics 2012 (Millions of US Dollars)	
Total plan participants	4,538,000
Loan outstanding	7956
Contributions	1961
Withdrawals and loan disbursements	1330

Source: http://www.frtib.gov

6.2.10 CALIFORNIA PUBLIC EMPLOYEES RETIREMENT SYSTEM

The California Public Employees' Retirement System (CalPERS) is the United States' largest public pension fund in terms of total net assets as of June 30, 2012. The CalPERS administers health and retirement benefits to more than 3000 public school, local agency, and state employers. There are approximately 1.6 million members in the retirement system and 1.3 million members in the health plans. By June 2013, the CalPERS had $3.9 billion in employee contributions and $8.1 billion in employer contributions. CalPERS membership consists of 1,102,440 active and inactive members and 551,627 retirees, beneficiaries, and survivors from state, school, and public agencies.

The PERF is the main pension trust fund in which CalPERS retirement benefits are paid. As of June 30, 2012, the PERF was expected to be near 74% funded on an average basis. The CalPERS provides administration of long-term-care benefits and the post-employment benefit fund for retiree health and supplemental savings plans.

The CalPERS comprises a total of 12 funds. Funds can be classified as fiduciary funds and proprietary funds. In fiduciary funds, the CalPERS acts as an agent or trustee for others and is responsible for handling the assets placed under its control. Proprietary funds provide services such as administration of a health care and long-term care program for external users for which fees are charged. The costs of providing services are recovered with fees and charges.

Fiduciary funds consist of pension trust funds, post-employment defined benefit funds, and two agency funds. The defined benefit plans, which are administered by the CalPERS, include the PERF,

Legislator Retirement Fund, Judges Retirement Fund, Judges Retirement Fund II, and the California Employers' Retiree Benefit Trust Fund. The defined contribution plans include the State Peace Officers' and Firefighters Defined Contribution Plan Fund, the Public Agency Deferred Compensation Program, and Supplemental Contribution Program Fund. The major proprietary funds include enterprise funds such as Public Employee Health Care Fund, Public Employees Contingency Reserve Fund, and the Public Employees Long-Term Care Fund.

6.2.10.1 Programs and services

The CalPERS provides a variety of retirement and health benefit programs and services and a defined benefit retirement plan. Retirement benefits are based on a member's years of service credit, age at retirement, and final compensation. A number of retirement formulas are determined on the basis of member's employer, occupation, safety, and industrial aspects. The three types of retirement options offered include service retirement or normal retirement, disability retirement, and industrial disability retirement. Disability retirement is offered for members who are unable to perform their jobs because of illness or injury. Industrial disability retirement is for injured members whose disability is due to a job-related injury or illness. In the disability retirement scheme, the cause of disability need not be job related. The CalPERS also provides death benefits to eligible beneficiaries or survivors. The CalPERS provides retirement benefits for the Legislators' Retirement System, Judges Retirement System, and Judges Retirement System II. The California Employers' Retiree Benefit Trust Fund was established by the CalPERS in March 2007 to provide California public agencies with a professionally managed investment vehicle for prefunding other post-employment benefits such as retiree health benefits.

The CalPERS Supplemental Income 457 Plan is a deferred compensation retirement savings plan public agency and school employers may offer their employees for retirement income.

The CalPERS provides health benefits to approximately 1.3 million public employees, retirees, and their families. It is the third-largest purchaser of health care in the nation. The fund spent more than $7.02 billion in 2012 to purchase health benefits. The program covers state employees by law and local public agencies. The CalPERS offers three types of health plans: Preferred Provider Organizations, Health Maintenance Organizations (HMOs), and Exclusive Provider Organizations. These health plans offer Medicare supplemental plans for members who are eligible for Medicare. The CalPERS Board reviews health plan contracts annually. The CalPERS Long-Term Care Program facilitates members to plan for high-cost, long-term care services. The program is designed for California public employees, retirees, and their family members aged 18 to 79. By June 2013, more than $1.2 billion in benefits had been paid since the program's inception.

6.2.10.2 Investments

The strategic initiatives of the fund are aimed at actively managing and assessing funding risk through an asset liability management framework to guide investment strategy and actuarial policy. CalPERS's average investment return for the past 25 years is 8.5%. The funded status, which reflected the percentage of assets that have to pay long-term benefits, was 73.6% in 2011.

The CalPERS is one of the largest public pension funds with assets amounting to $260.9 billion in 2013. Investments are made across domestic and international markets. The market value of the investment portfolio was $271.5 billion in 2013. The asset allocation mix is made on the basis of factors such as liabilities, benefit payments, operating expenses, and employer and member contributions. The CalPERS follows a strategic asset allocation policy that identifies the percentage of funds to be invested in each class. In 2013, the fund had invested approximately 54% in public equity and 12% in private equity. The growth funds accounted for 65% of the investments. Income funds accounted for 15% of investments. In 2013, the total public equity fund market value was $150.2 billion.

The CalPERS is one of the largest institutional investors in both US and international stock markets. Stock investments are basically passive investments. The Private Equity Program established in 1990 has generated $24 billion in profits. The program invests through investment components of Partnership, Direct, and Fund of Funds. In 2013, the PE program had a total exposure of $42.5 billion. During that period the PE Program contributed $57.8 billion and obtained distributions of $48.6 billion.

The CalPERS manages US public equity investments both actively and passively through external managers and internally managed portfolios. Nearly 40% of the plan's total investments are held in US public equities. The CalPERS manages all passive strategies in-house across a variety of portfolios covering both domestic and international markets. The CalPERS has an internally managed enhanced index fund. The CalPERS has also invested in hedge funds since April 2002. The CalPERS invests approximately 17% of its portfolio in fixed-income securities. Other fixed-income securities consist of commercial real estate mortgages, corporations, residential mortgages, treasuries, and agencies. The investments made by the CalPERS in inflation assets consist of programs of inflation-linked bonds and commodities. The liquidity program consists of subprograms of the US Treasury of durations of 2 to 10 years and short-term portfolios. The CalPERS also has a securities lending portfolio that generates income by lending securities to qualified borrowers through low-risk collateral investment strategies. The CalPERS Real Assets program consists of real estate, infrastructure, and forestland.

The final cost a retirement system incurs is equal to benefits paid plus the expenses that result from administration and financing. These costs are paid through contributions to the plan and investment earnings on the system's assets. The actuarial valuations rely upon data that are extracted from central databases. The databases are created from data supplied by individual employers. Under the Entry Age Normal Cost Method, projected benefits are determined for all members. For active members, liabilities are spread out in a manner that produces level annual costs as a percentage of pay in each year from the entry age to the assumed retirement age. Under the Term Insurance Cost Method, no actuarial accrued liability is given for active members, while all liability is due to current beneficiaries. The normal cost is calculated as the amount needed to provide benefits to survivors of death, which are expected in the next 1-year period. The funding objective of a retirement system is to be able to pay long-term benefit promises through member contributions as a percent of salary that is approximately level from year to year. In this process, members and employers pay their fair share for retirement services that were accrued in the particular year by the retirement system's members. A short-term solvency test aims at checking the retirement system's funding progress. In the process of the short-term solvency test, the plan's present assets, consisting of investments and cash, are compared with three parameters. These parameters are based on member contributions on deposit, the liabilities for future benefits to persons who have retired or been terminated, and the liabilities for projected benefits for already rendered service by active members. Table 6.5 gives the income highlights of the CalPERS during the period 2007-2011.

Table 6.5 CalPERS Income Highlights 2007-2011 (Millions of US Dollars)			
Year	Member Contributions	Employer Contributions	Investment and other Income
2007	3512.074	7242.802	−12492.908
2008	3882.355	6912.376	−57363.897
2009	3378.866	6955.049	25577.529
2010	3600.089	7465.397	43907.435
2011	3598.437	7772.913	196.014
Source: http://www.calpers.ca.gov			

6.3 CORPORATE PENSION FUNDS

The main types of retirement plans can be categorized as government-sponsored plans, personal plans, annuities, and employer-sponsored plans. The largest government-sponsored retirement plan is the Social Security plan. The individual retirement account (IRA), which can be categorized based on tax treatment, is one of the most popular personal plans. Annuities are contracts that are established with an insurance company. There are fixed and variable annuities. Employer-sponsored plans consist of qualified and nonqualified plans. Qualified plans consist of defined benefit plans and defined contribution plans. Nonqualified plans do not meet IRC or ERISA requirements; they consist of plans such as 457 plans. Defined benefit plans consist of pensions and annuities. Defined contribution plans consist of profit-sharing plans, stock bonus plans, money purchase pension plans, combination plans, thrift or saving plans, ESOPs, 401(k)s, 403(b)s, target benefit plans, and cash benefit plans.

6.3.1 GENERAL MOTORS PENSION PLAN

The General Motors corporate pension plan is the largest corporate pension plan with total liabilities of $100 billion. GM was the first US automaker to establish a pension plan in 1950 as part of the Treaty of Detroit. Ford and Chrysler later established their own pension plans. GM's pension obligation to the United Auto Workers was $71 billion in 2011.[2]

The GM deferred pension plan is payable from the first day of the month if the employee is age of 65 or at age 62 if the employee has 10 years of pensionable service. The pension is also payable at an appropriately reduced rate at any time after age 55 if the employee has at least 10 years of pensionable service. The reduced pension must not be any less than the guaranteed minimum pension (GMP) at state pension age. The GMP is the part of the pension that relates to contracting out of the State Earnings Related Pension Scheme (SERPS). Any amount of pension that is reduced owing to early retirement must not be less than the GMP at GMP age. The part of the deferred pension that represents the GMP is increased annually in the period to age 65 for men and age 60 for women before it comes into payment by a rate set by the government. After the date of retirement, the employee can choose to take part of the pension in the form of a lump sum that is currently tax-free. There is an option to exchange part of the pension for a dependent's additional pension. After receiving a pension, it may

---

[2]Ben Klayman, GM won't tackle pension talks with UAW until 2015: http://www.reuters.com/article/2013/09/27/us-autos-gm-pensions-idUSBRE98Q16520130927.

increase on April 1 each year to help offset the effects of inflation, which is left at the discretion of the company. An employee who is totally and permanently disabled prior to attaining age 65 and has at least 10 years of credited service is eligible for total and permanent disability retirement.

An alternative to a deferred pension is the transfer of accrued benefits, which include additional voluntary contributions (AVCs), to another tax-approved or tax-qualified pension scheme.

In 2012, General Motors Co. decided to provide select US salaried retirees a lump-sum payment offer and other retirees with a continued monthly pension payment securely administered and paid by the Prudential Insurance Company of America. The retirement plan was expected to result in a $26 billion reduction of GM's US-salaried pension obligation. It was stated that approximately 42,000 salaried retirees and surviving beneficiaries would be eligible to receive a voluntary single lump-sum payment option. GM also has plans to purchase a group annuity contract from Prudential under which Prudential will pay and administer future benefits to the remaining US salaried retirees. Approximately 118,000 salaried retirees will benefit from these changed schemes. According to the new advocated plan, those who retired between 1997 and 2011 can make three choices with respect to retirement receipts: they can receive a one-time single lump-sum payment or continue with current monthly benefits payable by Prudential, or receive a new form of monthly benefit based on marital status, which involves a single-life annuity or a joint and survivor monthly benefit payable by Prudential. Those who retired before 1997 will continue with the current monthly benefit payable by Prudential. The active salaried employees and retirees who have received pension benefits on or after December 2011 will be moved into the new GM pension plan offering a lump-sum payment or monthly pension benefit.

6.3.2 IBM PENSION

The IBM Pension is one of the largest corporate pension funds in the world. The IBM Personal Pension Plan consists of a tax-qualified plan and a nontax qualified plan. Since 2008, the nontax qualified plan was renamed the IBM Excess Personal Pension Plan. The Qualified Plan was designed to provide tax-qualified pension benefits to US regular employees. From 2008 onward, all eligible employees including executive officers became eligible for company contributions under a new defined contribution plan called the IBM 401(k) Plus Plan. A participant's years of credited service are based on the years the employee participates in the plan. Under the plan, participants are eligible for company contributions up to 10% of eligible pay, which depends on their pension plan formula participation and the amount contributed to the plan. Benefits under the qualified plan are determined under the pension credit formula. The pension credit formula is based on a participant's total point value divided by an annuity conversion factor. The total point value is based on total base points times final average pay plus total excess points times final average pay in excess of Social Security-covered compensation. The IBM Excess Personal Pension Plan (nonqualified plan) provides plan participants with benefits that may not be provided under the qualified plan owing to tax limits on eligible compensation. The benefit provided to a participant is payable only as an annuity that begins on the first day of the month following a separation from service from IBM.

The IBM Pension Plan is responsible for the payment of the GMP from age 60. All employees employed by IBM after April 6, 1978 are "contracted out" of the additional state pension (SERPS to 2002 and State Second Pension [S2] from 2002). In such cases, both the employee and IBM have paid a lower rate of national insurance (NI) and the IBM Pension Plan is responsible for paying a replacement pension benefit from age 60 for that period of contracted-out service.

C, N, I, and DSL plans are the defined benefit pension plans of IBM. Defined benefit pension plans are also known as final salaries. They provide a benefit based on salary and service. Employees who have left IBM have two options with the defined benefit pension. In the first option they can leave the pension within the IBM Pension Plan. Any pension in excess of the GMP will increase for each complete year from the date the employee leaves IBM until the date he or she retires. The amount of revaluation applied to the deferred pension is set by the government each year. In the second option, the participant can transfer the pension to another registered pension scheme, which could be a new employer or a personal pension arrangement.

M Plans are money purchase pension plans that are defined pension contribution plans. When a participant joins an M Plan, a notional RA is set up on behalf of the employee. IBM operates Smart* Pensions as a part of the You* Flexible Reward scheme. Smart* Pensions provide the opportunity for employees and IBM to pay lower NI contributions and employees also benefit from tax savings. Under the Smart Pensions scheme, the gross salary of an employee is reduced by an amount equal to 3% of the pensionable salary and IBM will credit the RA with the same amount. This is known as an M Plan Smart* contribution. IBM will also credit the RA with an additional 8% of the pensionable salary, which is known as a Basic M Plan contribution. The M Plan is closed to new employees except those joining IBM as a result of a qualifying outsource or acquisition.

The IBM Retirement Fund is the corporate pension fund with approximately $40 billion in AUM. The fund invests in the public equity, fixed-income, private equity, venture capital, mezzanine, and real estate segments. The firm also acts as a limited partner for various investment vehicles. It typically commits a minimum of $25 million per partnership. The fund allocates a maximum of 10% to alternative investments.

6.3.3 BOEING COMPANY EMPLOYEEMENT RETIREMENT PLAN

The Boeing Employee Retirement Plan was initiated in 1955, and Boeing Company makes all contributions to the plan. Pension benefits are calculated based on two formulas. In the standard benefit formula, benefits are based on years of credited service. The alternate benefit formula is based on years of credited service, final average earnings, and Social Security-covered compensation. The plan pays employees the benefit, whichever is greater. Employees can receive the vested plan benefit at age 65 or as early as age 55 when if the employee retires with 10 years of vesting service. In such case, the participant receives a reduced benefit. In the Boeing plan several payment options are available. Generally all options pay benefits monthly during the lifetime. Pension benefits are insured up to certain limits by the Pension Benefit Guaranty Corporation of US.

Employees are eligible to participate in the plan on completion of a 12-month eligibility waiting period in which the employee completes at least 1000 h of service. Another condition is that the employee must be a union-represented employee covered under the applicable collective-bargaining agreement between Boeing and the unions. The employee must also be on the active payroll and paid through the company payroll department. The employee must be credited with 45 h of service for each week for which he or she is eligible for pay. Different payment methods are available under this plan. Under a single life annuity, the retiree receives a monthly benefit payment that will continue for the rest of life. No benefit payments are made after death to dependents or a spouse. Married people must produce spousal written consent to elect this option. In 50%, 75%, or 100% surviving spouse options (joint and survivor annuity), a monthly benefit payment is ensured. But in the case of the death of the retired employee, the surviving spouse receives payments. The life annuity with a 10-year certain option guarantees monthly pension benefits for the entire life. If the employee dies within 10 years after the benefit payments begin, the beneficiary will receive the same monthly benefit amount for the rest of the 10-year period. If an employee decides to retire before age 62, then the accelerated income option can be used. The accelerated income option allows an employee to collect a larger than normal portion of the pension benefit up to age 62 and 2 months and then a smaller benefit afterward. The single life annuity is reduced to pay for this option. In the deferred benefit payment, payments must begin no later than the first day of the month after reaching age 65.

Employees and their dependents can also enroll in company-sponsored healthcare coverage such as traditional medical plans. The major plans are the Boeing Company Employee Health and Welfare Benefit Plan, Boeing Company Employee Health Benefit Plan, Boeing Company Retiree Health, and Welfare Benefit Boeing Company Voluntary Investment Plan. The Boeing Company Voluntary Investment Plan is a qualified defined contribution profit-sharing plan in which an employee can contribute up to 20% of base pay or 15% if the concerned union has not bargained for a 20% maximum.

Catch-up contributions are designed to help employees exceed the maximum contribution limits that are imposed by law on retirement savings plans. In an employer profit-sharing contribution plans, the company may make a profit-sharing contribution to the savings account based on a percentage of the base pay. In roll-over contribution plans, employees have the facility to directly roll over to the plan all or a portion of pretax contributions that are held in a conduit or traditional individual IRA. The plan also accepts direct rollovers from simplified employee pension IRAs.

Investment options for the fund fall into four categories: life-cycle funds, indexed funds, actively managed funds, and the Boeing Stock Fund. A life-cycle fund is a diversified investment portfolio that includes a mix of broad asset classes aimed at maximizing long-term growth. The life-cycle funds consist of the Lifecycle Retirement Fund, Lifecycle 2010 Fund, Lifecycle 2020 Fund, Lifecycle 2030 Fund, and Lifecycle 2040 Fund. The indexed funds consist of the Bond Market Index Fund, Balanced Index Fund, S&P 500 Index Fund, Russell 2000 Index Fund, and International Index Fund. The actively managed funds consist of the VIP Stable Fund, Large Companies Value Fund, Large Companies Growth Fund, Large Companies International Fund, Small/Mid Companies Value Fund, and Science and Technologies Fund. The Boeing Stock Fund invests almost entirely in the common stock of the Boeing Company. While working for the Boeing Controlled Group, the funds in this account can be accessed by taking out a loan, taking an in-service withdrawal, or a hardship withdrawal.

In 2011, Boeing had an underfunded pension liability of $16.5 billion.[3] According to the Employee Benefit Research Institute 7% of US corporate employees have only defined-benefit pension plans and 69% have defined-contribution plans such as 401(k)s.

6.3.4 AT&T PENSION PLANS

Eligible employees can enroll in the AT&T Retirement Savings Plan, which is the company's 401(k) savings plan. The plan allows employees to save for retirement through payroll deductions. If an employee does not initiate actions to enroll in the AT&T Retirement Savings Plan, then he or she will be automatically enrolled in the plan and a 3% before-tax basic contribution will be deducted from pay the first full pay period after the 60th day of employment. Employees can choose from a wide range of investment

---

[3] http://www.bizjournals.com/seattle/news/2013/01/10/boeing-union-showdown-looms-on.html?page=all

options and have the choice of contributing on a before- or after-tax basis. Employees can save up to 50% of their salary, which could include 6% as a basic contribution and 44% as a supplementary contribution. The company will match 80% of basic contributions.

In 2012, AT&T had $58.9 billion in pension obligations, while the fair value of its plan assets was $45.1 billion.[4] The company's pension plan covers 600,000 current and former employees.

The different pension schemes of AT&T are AT&T Pension Scheme 2001, M Plan, C Plan, N Plan, I Plan, and M Plan. The AT&T Benefit Plan 401(k) plan had $45.8 billion in net assets by 2012. This plan has been in effect since 1984 and is a single employer plan. The AT&T Pension Benefit 401(k) plan has more than 225,916 active participants.

The company offers a non-HMO medical option, which includes medical, surgical, prescription drug, and mental health/substance abuse benefits.

The AT&T Pension Plan is noncontributory. An employee can retire with a service pension anytime after the minimum age and service requirements are met. The net credited service for any age category is 30 years of service. The minimum age for service pension for 25 years of net credited service is 50. pensions may be reduced for individuals before age 55. The plan pays lifetime pension benefits in addition to the income received from Social Security.

Sickness disability benefits are available to employees after six months of employment. Disability benefits begin on the eighth calendar day of an employee's absence for disability due to sickness or off-the-job injury. Employees are eligible for long-term disability plans after six months of employment service. The plan allows payment in combination with other sources of disability income equal to 50% of base pay. Employees have sickness or death benefits from the first day of their employment. The plan provides a year's pay to a qualified beneficiary such as a spouse or dependent children.

6.3.5 BT PENSION SCHEME

The BT Pension Scheme is one of the largest pension plans in the United Kingdom. The BT Pension Scheme Section A is for members who joined the pension plan before 1971. The BT Pension Scheme (BTPS) has been set up under a trust deed and is governed by rules and provisions of the Principal Civil Service Pension Scheme. The BTPS is closed to new members. Existing members can opt out of the BTPS without leaving service by giving one month's notice. Employee contributions of 6% of the pensionable salary are deducted from the pay before the tax is applied. Smart Pension schemes provide the opportunity for employees and BT to save NI contributions. In Smart Pension schemes, employees do not pay pension contributions directly. Instead, the contractual gross pay is reduced by the contributions the employee pays and BT pays this amount to the BTPS. In addition, BT also pays its own contributions. Employees can also pay AVCs into a defined contribution fund to increase retirement benefits. The normal pension age (NPA) under the BTPS is 60 years of age. On retirement, the employee will receive a pension payable for life plus a lump sum of three times the pension based on pensionable service expressed in years and days and final pensionable salary. The pension is calculated using the formula[5]

$$\frac{\text{Pensionable service}}{80} \times (\text{Final pensionable salary} \times 94\%) = \text{Annual pension}$$

[4]http://online.wsj.com/news/articles/SB10001424127887324577304579059422759453750
[5]http://www.btps.co.uk/147/section-a

The lump sum will be three times the annual pension and is currently tax free, provided it does not exceed one quarter of the standard Lifetime Allowance.

Early retirement pension from age 50 onward is also possible. The reduction in pension depends on the age at the time the pension started.

Under the BTPS if an employee is unable to continue work due to serious ill health the employee will receive a health retirement pension consisting of an ill health pension and lump sum. In the case of death within 5 years of retirement, the trustee will pay a lump sum equal to the difference (if any) between five times of the annual pension on the date the employee died and the total pension and lump-sum payments already received. In addition, if the employee has a nominated dependent or spouse, he or she will receive one half of the pension. In the case of death after 5 years of retirement, the spouse or nominated dependent would receive the full pension for the first 91 days and then the pension would be reduced to half. In the case of death after retirement, the child pension is also applicable.

If an employee leave the BTPS before the NPA, he or she will be entitled to a deferred pension and lump sum payable at the NPA.

BT Pension Scheme Section B is applicable to members who joined the company during the period between December 1, 1971 and March 31, 1986. Contributions by members are based on the contribution earnings threshold (CET). The CET for 2013-2014 is £45,305, and is reviewed annually. If pensionable salary earnings are below the CET, the contribution rate is 7% and, if earnings are above the CET, the contribution rate is 8.5%. The value of the pension savings in a tax year depends on whether the savings are defined benefits or defined contributions. Each component is valued and then added together to see if the value exceeds the annual allowance.

BT Pension Scheme Section C is applicable for members who joined section C in the period April 1986 to March 2001. The pensionable salary is compared to the CET. If the pensionable salary is below the CET, the contribution rate is 6% and above the CET the contribution rate is 7%.

6.3.6 GENERAL ELECTRIC PENSION PLANS

General Electric has one of the largest corporate pension plans in the world. General Electric offers its employees a number of benefits including health, retirement, and pension plans. In 2010, GE's retirement benefits covered approximately 250,000 retirees and dependents in the United States. Upon hiring a new employee, GE offers a 3% company retirement contribution that vests after 3 years. In addition, GE also offers a 401(k) with a 50% company match on up to 8% of pay, which is immediately vested. GE retirees who take part in the GE Principal Pension Plan and have completed 10 or more years of service are eligible to access GE's health and life insurance benefits upon retirement. GE employees contribute 3% of their annual pay to the retirement benefit fund. Retirement benefits are available to qualifying employees at an unreduced level at the age of 60 or 62 with Social Security benefits.

GE sponsors a number of pension plans. The Principal Pension plans along with affiliates and other pension plans represent 99% of total pension assets. The Principal Pension plans are the GE Pension Plan and the GE Supplementary Pension Plan. The GE Pension Plan is a funded and tax-qualified retirement program. The GE Pension Plan gives benefits to US employees based on the greater of a formula recognizing career earnings or a formula that considers length of service and final average earnings. Salaried employees who commenced service on or after January 1, 2011, and employees who commenced service on or after January 1, 2012, are not eligible to participate in the GE Pension

Plan but could participate in a defined contribution retirement program. The normal retirement age as defined in this plan is 65. The accumulated benefit an employee earns over his or her career with the company is payable after retirement on a monthly basis for life with a guaranteed minimum term of 5 years. The employees vest in the GE Pension Plan after 5 years of qualifying service. The plan also provides for Social Security supplements, spousal joint, and survivor annuity options and requires employee contributions. The GE Pension Plan was underfunded by $13.3 billion at the end of 2012 as compared to $13.2 billion at December 2011.

The GE Supplementary Pension Plan is an unfunded plan that provides supplementary retirement benefits to high-level employees. This plan is offered to employees at the executive level to provide for retirement benefits above amounts available under the company's tax-qualified and other pension programs. The Supplementary Pension Plan is not qualified for tax purposes. Employees are generally not eligible for benefits under the Supplementary Pension Plan if they leave the company prior to reaching age 60. The normal retirement age as defined in this plan is 65. The GE Supplementary Pension Plan had projected benefit obligations of $5.2 billion and $5.5 billion in 2011 and 2012.

The GE Excess Benefit Plan is unfunded and nonqualified for tax purposes. The benefits under the Excess Benefits Plan are payable at the same time and manner as the GE Pension Plan. The GE Pension Plan 401(k) has 107,016 active participants and 184,906 retired or separated participants.[6]

In the other pension plans category, GE offers 40 US and non-US pension plans with pension assets or obligations greater than $50 million. The cost of pension plans in 2012 was $4.37 billion.[7] Table 6.6 gives the statistics of GE pension plans.

Table 6.6   GE Pension Plan Participants

	Principal Pension Plans	Other Pension Plans	Total
Active employees	101,000	35,000	136,000
Vested former employees	192,000	44,000	236,000
Retirees and beneficiaries	226,000	31,000	257,000
Total	519,000	110,000	629,000

Source: Form 10-K 2012, http://www.ge.com/ar2012/pdf/10K-2012

REFERENCES

1. P&I/TW 300 Analysis, August 2013
2. http://www.gpif.go.jp/en/
3. http://www.gpif.go.jp/en/fund/pdf/Review_of_Operations_in_Fiscal2012.pdf
4. http://www.ftf.no/en/t-213-About-Folketrygdfondet.aspx
5. http://www.ftf.no/en/c-305-The-Government-Pension-Fund.aspx
6. http://www.abp.nl/en/about-abp/about-us/
7. http://www.abp.nl/images/ABP-Annual-Report-2011_tcm160-148430.pdf
8. http://www.nps.or.kr/jsppage/english/about/about_01.jsp

[6]http://401k-plans.findthebest.com/l/180394/Ge-Pension-Plan
[7]http://www.ge.com/ar2012/pdf/10K-2012.pdf

9. http://mycpf.cpf.gov.sg/NR/rdonlyres/7B172485-F47E-4535-A9C8-343D31A2A042/0/Retirement.pdf
10. http://mycpf.cpf.gov.sg/NR/rdonlyres/70F9CA8A-F9A0-48AE-9960-81CC218AB760/0/Health care.pdf
11. http://www.hrsdc.gc.ca/en/isp/common/hrsdc/ris/rismain.shtml
12. http://www.kwsp.gov.my/portal/documents/10180/741076/Akauntabiliti_-_Accountability.pdf
13. http://www.ssf.gov.cn/Eng_Introduction/201206/t20120620_5603.html
14. http://www.tsp.gov/PDF/formspubs/tspbk08.pdf
15. http://www.frtib.gov/search.html?q=Search+Agency+Regulations+%26+Reports& scb_Reports=Reports&scb_FOIA_Reports=FOIA_Reports
16. http://www.tsp.gov/investmentfunds/fundsoverview/comparisonMatrix.shtml
17. http://www.tsp.gov/planparticipation/about/purposeAndHistory.shtml
18. http://www.calpers.ca.gov
19. CalPERS Annual Report 2012
20. The Boeing Company Employee Retirement Plan, Summary Plan Description 2007 Edition www.boeing.com/companyoffices/empinfo/benefits/pension/spd
21. http://www.boeing.com/assets/pdf/companyoffices/empinfo/benefits/pension/Resources.pdf
22. http://www.thepensiondepartment.co.uk/pdfs/retirees/retirees_member_booklet.pdf#view=Fit
23. http://media.gm.com/media/us/en/gm/news.detail.html/content/Pages/news/us/en/2012/Jun/0601_pension.html
24. http://www.smartpensionsuk.co.uk/index.php/28/m-plan
25. http://www.smartpensionsuk.co.uk/reports/2012/DB/
26. http://www.hartlinkonline.co.uk/attpensionscheme/ssp/ATT/ATT_User_Guide.pdf
27. http://www.cwa1120.org/att/att%20benefits%20guide%20for%20dobson%20employees.pdf
28. http://www.indiana.edu/~busx420/HRMWebsite/hrm/articles/benefits/att_ben.pdf
29. 1BTPS Section A Booklet June 2013
30. BTPS Section B Booklet June 2013
31. BTPS Section C Booklet June 2013

CASES ON PRIVATE EQUITY FIRMS

7.1 KOHLBERG KRAVIS ROBERTS

Kohlberg Kravis Roberts (KKR) is a leading global investment firm that has executed many large and complex global private equity transactions. Founded in 1976, KKR's success was built around the single core concept of partnership. In 1977, the firm made its first acquisition, valued at $26 million. In 1979, KKR made the significant buyout of Houdaille Industries, a mid-sized publicly traded company for $380 million. In the 1980s, many of the well-known retail and consumer brands, such as the Safeway Stores (largest food retailer), Duracell (manufacturer of alkaline batteries), and RJR Nabisco (a global leader in consumer products) became part of the KKR portfolio. In 1989, KKR bought out RJR Nabisco for $24.88 billion, which was labeled as one of the largest buyouts. In the 1990s, the partnership was diversified into new and highly regulated industries such as banking, insurance, power generation, and transmission. Later, KKR established business platforms in the fast-growing global markets of Europe and Asia. KKR established the publicly traded specialty finance company KKR Financial Holdings to focus on debt investments as a separate asset class. KKR also established KKR Asset Management (KAM) to diversify debt operations. The capital market business was established in 2007 to provide expertise in a range of capital market solutions. The private market business emphasizes developing the Energy and Infrastructure and Natural Resources platform. Since 2010, KKR and Co is traded on the New York Stock Exchange.

In December 2012, KKR had $75.5 billion in assets under management (AUM). KKR has completed more than 200 private equity investments with a total transaction value of $470 billion.

7.1.1 BUSINESS REVIEW

KKR businesses encompass growing areas of energy and infrastructure, real estate, growth equity, and debt investing. The three main segments of businesses are private markets, public markets, and capital markets and principal activities.

7.1.1.1 Private markets

KKR has a global private equity portfolio of more than 80 companies that comprise sectors such as retail, consumer products, health care, industrial, energy, media and communications, financial services, and technology. KKR aims to invest in industry-leading franchises and companies that have significant growth potential. The KKR strategy consists of associating with portfolio companies as strategic partners and providing assistance in the operations of businesses. KKR is involved in the expansion strategy of these companies and operational improvements. Generally, KKR invests capital in companies that have achieved certain developmental transition points. KKR has taken publicly listed companies private and acquired divisional assets through corporate divestiture. KKR also has strategic partnerships with family-owned businesses. In 2013, KKR made private investments in 10 companies. The role of KKR's Portfolio Management Committee (PMC) is to provide expertise, support, and oversight of the private equity portfolio. The PMC consists of professionals who are members of KKR's private equity industry teams, KKR Capstone and KKR Senior Advisors. KKR Capstone consists of a global team of approximately 60 operating executives who provide portfolio companies with a differentiated set of cross-portfolio services that include indirect sourcing, corporate insurance, and risk management, metrics management, centralized IT contracting, and environmental sustainability. KKR Capstone provides functional expertise in areas such as pricing, organizational design, sales force effectiveness, and operational efficiency.

KKR has invested in energy and infrastructure for many years based on the principles of value-added investment strategy. KKR's real estate investment business focuses on investing across the capital structure and makes investments in real estate and real estate transactions. In 2011, KKR committed $700 million of equity to 13 real estate transactions in the United States and Europe. In 2012, the private market segment had $49.1 billion in AUM. KKR is a world leader in private equity. It raised 17 funds with $66.7 billion of capital commitments in 2012. In 2010, KKR launched the KKR Natural Resources Fund, which acquires and operates oil and gas properties in mature basins in the United States. Table 7.1 gives the investment statistics of KKR during different time periods.

7.1.1.2 Public markets

KAM provides a wide range of investment products across equity and debt instruments. KAM adopts various strategies such as leveraged credit strategies, liquid long/short equity strategies, and alternative credit strategies. Leveraged credit strategies include leveraged loans and high-yield bonds. Alternative credit strategies include mezzanine investments, special situation investments, and direct senior lending. KAM also manages investment funds, structured finance vehicles, and separately managed accounts. From 2005 onward, KKR managed credit vehicles in the form of collateralized loan obligations. Prisma Capital Partners offers commingled and separate account portfolios of hedge funds. KKR Financial Holdings is the publicly traded specialty finance company. KKR Financial Advisors is the wholly owned subsidiary of KAM, which invests in investment-grade corporate debt, marketable equity securities, and private equity. In 2012, the segment had $26.4 billion in AUM.

Table 7.1 KKR Investment Statistics 1977-2013	
Period	**Private Market Investment—Number of Companies**
1977-1979	6
1980-1989	30
1990-1999	48
2000-2010	100
2011-2013	38

7.1.1.3 *Capital markets and principal activities*

The KKR Capital Markets (KCM) business provides a full range of capital market solutions to clients' specific needs. KCM originates, structures, and executes full capital structures, which include asset-based lending, high-yield debt-revolving credit facilities, mezzanine capital, leveraged loans, unit ranche loans, private equity, bridge loans, and public equity. KCM provides advisory and execution services for a broad range of complex financial transactions such as acquisition financing, pre-IPO capital issues, private-equity syndications, IPOs, exchange offers, and restructurings such as spin-offs/split-offs, dividend recapitalizations, and buybacks. KCM provides a distribution platform for global mutual funds, pension funds, and sovereign wealth funds. In 2012, the segment had $4.8 billion in investments at fair value.

The principal activities business involves investments in KKR's own private equity funds and portfolio companies. In 2012, the principal activities segment generated over $1 billion in investment income.

7.1.2 **CLIENT AND PARTNER GROUP**

KKR has a Client and Partner Group that raises capital across all products, asset classes, and types of fund investors.

7.1.2.1 *Partners*

KKR's partners can be categorized as investment partners and portfolio partners. Large public and corporate pension plans, financial institutions, family offices, insurance companies, endowments, and foundations are the major investment limited partners. KKR also partners with limited partners to invest in private equity funds, credit funds, and new sectors such as energy and infrastructure. KKR's portfolio partnership spans about 14 industry segments located in the markets of the United States, Europe, and Asia. Portfolio partnerships aim to provide operational improvements in functional areas.

7.1.2.2 *KKR mutual funds*

KKR mutual funds consist of the KKR Alternative High Yield Fund, KKR Alternative Opportunities Fund, and KKR Investment Opportunities Fund. The KKR Alternative High Yield Fund seeks to generate a high level of income and capital appreciation. The fund allocates capital across a portfolio consisting of below-investment-grade fixed-income investments, high-yield bonds, notes, debentures, convertible securities, and loans. The AUM amounts to $115.4 million. The KKR Alternative Opportunities Fund, also known as the Master Fund, primarily invests in corporate opportunities where balance sheet distress or broader market dislocation have created mispricing of securities. The AUM in this category amounts to $38.7 million. The KKR Income Opportunities Fund is a nondiversified, closed-end management investment company that seeks a high level of current income with a secondary objective of capital appreciation. The fund invests in a targeted portfolio of loans and fixed-income instruments of US and non-US issuers and implement hedging strategies.

7.1.3 **STRATEGY**

KKR focuses on private equity investments consisting of multiples of invested capital and attractive risk-adjusted IRRs by means of high-quality investments that are made at attractive prices.

KKR doesn't participate in hostile transactions that are not supported by the target company's board of directors. The global network of experienced managers and operating executives provides support for sourcing and selecting investments. PMCs, along with investment professionals, are entrusted with the responsibility of achieving strategic and operational objectives. Operational guidance is obtained from operating consultants at KKR Capstone, senior advisors, and "100 Day Plans." During its three decades the company has generated approximately $79.2 billion in cash proceeds from the sale of private equity portfolios in IPOs and secondary offerings, dividends, and sales to strategic buyers. Each private equity fund is organized as a single partnership or a combination of separate domestic and overseas partnerships, and each partnership is controlled by a general partner. Each private equity fund's general partner is generally entitled to a carried interest that allocates to it 20% of the net profits realized by the limited partners from the fund's investments.

KKR competes with investment managers for both fund investors and investment opportunities. Competitors include investment funds, investment banks, and finance companies. The competition for investor capital has increased as the number of private equity funds focusing on natural resources, infrastructure, credit, equity, and hedge funds is on the upward trend. The company aims to renew its focus on capital markets business primarily in North America, Europe, Asia Pacific, and the Middle East.

7.1.4 RISK IN BUSINESS

Risk to KKR business depends on difficult market conditions that adversely affect the value or performance of the investments managed, thereby affecting cash flows of KKR businesses. The volatility in debt financing markets affects the ability of investment funds and portfolio companies to obtain attractive financing for their investments, and hence increase the cost of financing and potentially decrease the net income of KKR. Investors in funds such as separately managed accounts may pay lower management fees, which could also result in lower cash flows for the firm. Investments in assets such as real estate, infrastructure, and natural resources expose the firm to increased risk and liability. The investment opportunities of the firm also involve business, regulatory, and other complexities. KKR private equity funds make investments in large capitalization companies. Hence, financing large transactions becomes more difficult and exiting larger deals presents additional challenges. KKR also faces market risk, credit risk, and exchange rate risk. Table 7.2 gives the financial highlights of KKR during the period 2008-2012.

Table 7.2 KKR Financial Highlights 2008-2012 (Millions of US Dollars)					
	2008	**2009**	**2010**	**2011**	**2012**
Fees income	235.1	331.2	435.4	723.6	823.9
Investment income	(12865.2)	7753.8	9179.10	1456.1	9101.9
Net income	(13048.4)	6889.3	8082.2	876.5	7776.4
Total assets	22441.0	30221.1	38391.2	40377.6	44426.30

7.2 **BLACKSTONE GROUP**

Blackstone Group is a major global investment and advisory firm with a global business platform consisting of private equity, real estate funds, hedge fund solutions, credit funds, and advisory and restructuring activities. Blackstone was established in 1986. In 2012, Blackstone launched its first dedicated energy fund, Blackstone Energy Partners, at $2.5 billion. The company also launched the Tactical Opportunities platform. In 2011, Blackstone launched its social media platform. In the same year Blackstone completed the first close of its Renminbi denominated fund for equity growth investments in China. Blackstone purchased a 40% stake in Patria, Brazil's leading alternative asset manager. In 2008, Blackstone emerged as one of the largest credit-oriented alternative asset managers by acquiring GSO Capital Partners. In 2007, Blackstone completed its IPO listing in the NYSE.

7.2.1 **BUSINESSES OF BLACKSTONE**

7.2.1.1 *Asset management*

7.2.1.1.1 Private equity

Blackstone is one of the world's largest independent asset managers, and serves major financial institutions such as pension funds. Blackstone offers private equity funds, real estate funds, hedge solution funds, credit-oriented funds, and closed-end mutual funds. In 2012, the total AUM amounted to $210 billion. The senior staff committed $6 billion to the investment funds at Blackstone. Approximately 84% of its investor base has reinvested in successive Blackstone funds. The company has invested in fast-growing markets and regions in North America, Europe, and Asia. Blackstone's investments span a broad range of industries and continents covering a wide range of industries. The company provides private equity to portfolio companies to launch new business initiatives, acquire companies, and upgrade technologies and systems. The revenues at portfolio companies amount to over $90 billion. The total employees at the portfolio companies is approximately 700,000.

The private equity portfolio of Blackstone can be categorized on the basis of industry, geography, and investment type. Blackstone has made equity investment in portfolio companies that are located in America, Asia, Australasia, Europe, and the Middle East. The company has made substantial investments in Indian companies and has invested in all major industrial groups. The major debt-based investment types are based on bridge financing, convertible preferred debt, minority debt portfolios, and distressed debt securities. Equity-based investment types are based on equity—control, joint control, equity minority, and growth equity for startups. Industrial type investments are based on joint ventures with majority interest, preferred equity with minority interest, secured loans, and senior debts. In 2000, Blackstone made investments in 19 equity portfolio companies. In 2011, Blackstone made investments in 17 companies. Some of the equity portfolio companies are Transtar, US Radio, UCAR International, NYSE LIFFE, iPCS, Aspen, Columbia House, Alliant, Caesars, Maldivian Air, and others. Table 7.3 gives the investment statistics of Blackstone during different time periods.

The Portfolio Operations Group provides strategic advice on six core areas of revenue realization, operations, services and infrastructure, purchasing and cross-selling, leadership development, and health care. The Portfolio Operations Group established CoreTrust and Equity Healthcare.

CoreTrust is a joint procurement program for enhancing the purchasing power of about 60 portfolio companies. Approximately $2 billion in annual spending is managed through group purchasing programs in more than 70 categories that include IT hardware and software, office supplies, hotels, insurance, energy, and telecommunications.

Table 7.3 Blackstone Group Equity Portfolio Client Statistics 1988-2013	
Period	**Number of Companies in Which Investments Were Made**
1988-1999	2
1990-1999	34
2000-2009	101
2010-2013	38

Equity Healthcare is a proprietary healthcare purchasing group that facilitates portfolio companies to deliver cost-effective care to employees and families. Equity Healthcare covers a total of 320,000 members. As of September 2013, the company had $63 billion total AUM in private equity portfolios.

7.2.1.1.2 Real estate

Blackstone is one the largest real estate global private equity firms with $69 billion in AUM. The real estate portfolios include premier properties in the United States, Europe, and Asia, which consist of a diverse mix of hotels, offices, retail, industrial, residential, and healthcare investments. During the last 5 years, Blackstone real estate funds have invested over $25.3 billion in equity through active debt and equity funds. The investment strategy is based on acquiring high-quality income-producing assets at discounts to replacement costs and undertaking portfolio or financial restructuring and later selling the investments. The holding period for the assets is generally more than 3 years. During the period 2005-2007, the company sold more than $60 billion in assets. The Investment Committee approves real estate investments globally.

Blackstone acquired Centro's US portfolio consisting of 600 community shopping centers in 2011. In 2009, Blackstone acquired a 50% stake in the Broadgate Estate in London, which consisted of a 4.4 million-square-foot portfolio of Class A office buildings. In 2007, Blackstone acquired Waldorf-Astoria as a part of its acquisition of Hilton Hotels. In 2011, BREP acquired Valad, the Australian company consisting of real estate in Australia and New Zealand. In 2004, Blackstone acquired the real estate division of WCM Group consisting of 31,000 apartments in Germany. In 2011, Blackstone acquired a 37% interest in Manyata Business Park, a 12.9 million-square-foot Class A office park in Bangalore, India. In 2011, Blackstone acquired a 60% stake in Hotel del Coronado, a 757-room luxury beachfront resort located in California.

Blackstone Real Estate Debt Strategies (BREDS) was established in 2008 to provide debt investment opportunities. This segment has approximately $9 billion in AUM. The segment's investment strategy consists of mezzanine debt, recapitalizations, and legacy debt investments aimed at debt instruments on a discounted basis, listed equity, and debt securities with a focus on value and preferred equity in real estate. BREDS has emerged as one of the most active real estate lenders and debt investors with over 185 separate loan originations and purchases in the United States and Europe.

Blackstone Mortgage Trust is Blackstone's real estate finance arm, which focuses on originating mortgage loans backed by commercial real estate assets.

7.2.1.1.3 Hedge fund solutions

Blackstone Alternative Asset Management (BAAM) is one of the largest global discretionary allocators to hedge funds. BAAM had about $53 billion in AUM as of September 2013. Approximately 70%

of the AUM is in specialized or customized solutions. BAAM investor clients include leading global institutional investors such as pension funds, sovereign wealth funds, and central banks. The Blackstone Alternative Alpha Fund (BAAF I AND II) are equity-focused registered funds of hedge funds that aim to earn long-term risk-adjusted returns by adopting equity investment strategies. The BAAF focuses on diversifying allocation to global macro, multi-strategy, and credit strategies.

The Blackstone Alternative Multi Manager Fund (BXMMX) aims for capital appreciation through investments in nontraditional or alternative investment assets. Principal investment strategies of the fund are fundamental strategies, global macro strategies, opportunistic trading strategies, quantitative strategies, managed future strategies, and multi-strategy strategies.

7.2.1.1.4 Credit solutions

GSO is one of the major credit-oriented alternative asset managers, and aims for superior risk-adjusted returns and capital preservation of global clients. GSO offers a broad range of public and private corporate credit instruments across multiple strategies. GSO's financing solutions include leveraged loans, high-yield bonds, distressed debt, mezzanine lending, and rescue financing. GSO has provided $16.2 billion capital in privately originated transactions with $63 billion in total AUM.

GSO closed-end funds consist of the GSO Strategic Credit Fund, GSO Long-Short Credit Income Fund, and GSO Senior Floating Rate Term Fund. The GSO Strategic Fund invests in a diversified portfolio of loans and other fixed-income instruments of predominantly US issuers, which includes senior-secured loans and high-yield corporate bonds of different maturities. The GSO Long Short Credit Income Fund is a closed-end fund that aims for current income and capital appreciation through long-short strategy of investments in secured loans, high-yield loans, and fixed-income instruments. The GSO Senior Floating-Rate Term Fund invests in senior-secured floating-rate loans.

7.2.1.1.5 Tactical Opportunities

Blackstone has established a proprietary investment strategy called Tactical Opportunities, which focuses on a global multi-asset class approach to investing in illiquid assets.

7.2.1.1.6 Strategic Partners

The Strategic Partners Fund Solutions is a major investor in the secondary market for institutional and private interests in private equity, real estate, and venture capital. Strategic Partners has raised over $11 billion in capital commitments, made more than 700 transactions for investors, and acquired more than 1500 underlying limited partnerships, representing 700 different fund sponsors.

7.2.1.2 Financial advisory services

7.2.1.2.1 Blackstone Advisory Partners

Blackstone is a leading independent global advisor with expertise in a wide range of transactions. Established in 1985, Blackstone Advisory Partners has expertise in a wide range of financial and strategic services such as mergers and acquisitions (M&As) activity, spin-offs, joint ventures, minority investments, asset swaps, divestitures, takeover defenses, distressed sales, private placements, and structured products. Blackstone Advisory Partners has provided advisory services for M&As deals worth $525 billion.

Select Advisory Transactions by Blackstone 2005-2010	
Year	**Advisory Transaction services**
2010	Blackstone served as the independent advisor to AIG for the sale of Alico to MetLife Inc. Blackstone helped AIG pursue a dual-path IPO process for Alico
2008	Blackstone advised Aquila on the $2.8 billion sale of its stock to Great Plains Energy
2007	Blackstone was the sole advisor to China Development Bank's for £6.6 billion strategic minority interest in Barclays
2005	Blackstone advised Comcast Corporation on its $17.6 billion joint acquisition of Adelphia Communications
2007	Blackstone advised Kinder Morgan (major pipeline transportation and energy storage company) on a $22 billion buyout management by its CEO
2008	Blackstone provided advisory services for Kraft for the separation of its Post Cereals business through a tax-free split-off and merger with Ralcorp, valued at $2.6 billion in value
2008	Blackstone advised Nestlè on its $3.7 billion acquisition of Kraft Food's frozen pizza business
2008	Blackstone advised Procter & Gamble for the separation of its Folgers coffee business through a tax-free split-off and merger with Smuckers
2009	Blackstone advised Publicis (major advertising firm) on its cross-border carve out of Razorfish from Microsoft
2008	Blackstone advised Reuters Group on its merger with Thomson Corporation, valued at £10 billion
2009	Blackstone advised Stiefel, a major dermatology company, on its sale to Glaxosmithkline, valued at $3.6 billion
2008	Blackstone advised GdfSuez (second-largest utility company in the world) for the merger of Gaz de France, valued at €93 billion and subsequent spin-off of 65% of the Suez environment
2010	Blackstone advised Xerox on its acquisition of Affiliated Computer Services (major BPO company), valued at $6.4 billion

7.2.1.2.2 Restructuring and Reorganization

Blackstone Restructuring and Reorganization is a major advisor to restructuring companies and creditors. Blackstone provides a wide range of advisory services related to restructuring, specifically in regard to debtor advisory, creditor advisory, out-of-court solutions, and distressed mergers and acquisitions.

The restructuring has involved $1.4 trillion in total liabilities. The restructuring team consists of 50 dedicated restructuring professionals based in both New York and London. Blackstone advised Allied Capital on its out-of-court restructuring of $1.01 billion in liabilities. Blackstone advised Delta on its successful reorganization under Chapter 11, restructuring more than $9 billion of net debt and lease obligations. Blackstone also dealt with one of the world's biggest bankruptcies involving Enron. Blackstone was the global restructuring adviser for various deleveraging transactions undertaken by Ford. Blackstone was also the restructuring advisor for Xerox. Blackstone advised Winn Dixie in its Chapter 11 proceedings. Blackstone advised Northern Rock on a range of strategic options and developed its restructuring plan. Blackstone was retained as MBIA's financial advisor and was involved in all aspects of MBIA's strategy with respect to the Eurotunnel restructuring.

7.2.1.2.3 Park Hill Group

Park Hill Group, established in 2005, provides fund placement services for alternative investment managers. Park Hill has served as a placement agent to more than 145 funds and has raised more

Table 7.4   Blackstone AUM 2008-2012 (Billions of US Dollars)

Year	Value
2008	95
2009	98
2010	128
2011	166
2012	210

Source: Blackstone Form 10-k Annual Report 2013.

Table 7.5   Blackstone Financial Highlights 2008-2012 (Billions of US Dollars)

	2008	2009	2010	2011	2012
Revenues	(0.35)	1.77	3.12	3.25	4.019
Assets	9.5	9.4	18.8	21.9	28.9

Source: Blackstone Annual Reports.

Table 7.6   Segment Revenue Highlights 2010-2012 (Billions of US Dollars)

	2010	2011	2012
Private equity	0.83	0.58	0.83
Real estate	1.04	1.58	1.63
Hedge fund solutions	0.37	0.34	0.46
Credit	0.48	0.39	0.78
Financial advisory	0.43	0.39	0.37

Source: Blackstone Annual reports.

than $210 billion for a diverse range of investment strategies. The group also assists Blackstone in raising capital for its own investment funds. Table 7.4 gives the value of Blackstone's assets under management during the period 2008-2012. Table 7.5 provides the financial highlights of Blackstone during the period 2008-2012. Table 7.6 provides the revenues for Blackstone during 2010-2012 by segment.

7.3 BAIN CAPITAL

Bain Capital is one of the leading private alternate asset management firms with $70 billion in AUM. Bain Capital's affiliated advisors make private equity, public equity, fixed-income, credit, venture capital, and absolute return investments across multiple industries.

7.3.1 BAIN CAPITAL PRIVATE EQUITY

Bain Capital was founded in 1984 in Boston. The company has raised 15 private equity funds that consist of 10 global private equity funds, three European funds, and two Asian funds. Bain Capital Private Equity has eight offices in three continents. It provides capital and experience to companies in all development phases. The company has been involved in a number of successful startups, turnarounds, and carve-outs from large corporate partners. In the early phases of an investment, Bain Capital focuses on development of a strong partnership with management that leverages the industry, operational, financial, and global expertise to create a strategic plan for the business. Bain Capital has nearly 800 private equity limited partners (LPs), which include endowments, public and corporate pensions, financial institutions, funds of funds, family offices, and sovereign wealth funds. Approximately 8-10% of private equity fund commitments come from professionals.

Private equity investments are basically made in sectors comprising consumer, retail, and dining, financial and business services, health care, industrial and energy, technology media, and telecom. In 2002, Bain Capital, in partnership with TPG and Goldman Sachs, acquired Burger King and revived its health. Burger King undertook a comprehensive multiyear workout program to stabilize franchise financial health. Nearly new 100 international stores were opened up. In 2006, the company was successfully taken public. Bain Capital acquired Dollarama, the largest dollar store chain in Canada, in 2004.

In 2003, Bain Capital invested in Samsonite, the world's largest branded manufacturer and distributor of luggage, casual bags, business cases, and travel-related products.

In the financial and business services sector, Bain Capital has invested in Bright Horizons, Cerved Group, Datek/Ameritrade, and Team System. Bain Capital was a founding investor in Bright Horizons, which is a leading operator of on-site, employer-sponsored child care, early education centers, and work/life solutions. In 2009, Bain Capital acquired Cerved, Italy's leading provider of credit and business information. In 2000, Bain Capital acquired Datek, one of the largest online brokerage firms in the United States. In 2002, Bain Capital facilitated the merger of Datek with publicly traded Ameritrade to create the largest online brokerage firm in terms of trading volume. After Bain Capital exited its investment, the company was acquired by TD Waterhouse to form TD Ameritrade. In 2010, Bain Capital acquired Team System, the Italy-based developer and distributor of ERP software applications for automating processes.

Bain Capital is a major investor in the healthcare sector. In 1994, Bain Capital managed the successful turnaround of Physio Control, a subsidiary of Eli Lilly. After turning around the company, Bain Capital led it to a successful IPO in 1995. In 1994, Bain Capital acquired Waters, a manufacturer of liquid chromatography instruments for the pharmaceutical and life science industries. In 1995, Bain Capital acquired Wesley, a struggling division of Schering Plough, which had losses of $12 million a year. After a series of strategic initiatives, the company had a successful IPO and doubled its sales. In the industrial and energy sector, Bain's investments are primarily in the areas of chemical, distribution, transportation, and mining services.

In the technology media and telecom sector, Bain Capital invested in DoubleClick, Gartner Group, and ProSieben Group. Its current portfolio includes Applied Systems, Atento, BMC Software, Clear Channel Communications, NXP, and Skillsoft.

Bain Capital has completed more than 250 investments, which can be classified on the basis of investment type, business life cycle, industry, and geography.

Bain Capital Industrial and Energy Investments 2003-2007	
	Investments
1994	Bain Capital invested in Steel Dynamics to build a greenfield production facility. After a successful IPO, Bain Capital exited the business in 1996.
2003	Bain Capital acquired SigmaKalon, a major provider of decorative and industrial coatings in Europe. In 2008, Bain Capital sold the company to PPG Industries.
2004	Bain Capital acquired Brenntag, a global distributor of specialty and industrial chemicals. After realizing significant returns, Bain Capital sold the company in 2006.
2005	Bain Capital and Advent International acquired Boart Longyear, which was the largest provider of contract drilling services and consumables for mineral exploration. The company undertook a series of acquisitions and divestitures. In 2006, Bain Capital investors exited their investments and the company completed an IPO.
2007	Bain Capital acquired a minority stake in China-based specialty chemical manufacturer Feixiang. Bain exited its investment in 2011.

7.3.2 BROOKSIDE CAPITAL

Brookside Capital is one of the leading global long/short hedge funds. The company follows a bottom-up approach to identifying the research process.

7.3.3 SANKATY ADVISORS

Sankaty Advisors is the credit affiliate arm of Bain Capital. It is the leading private manager of fixed-income and credit instruments. The division had about $20.3 billion in AUM as of September 2013. The investments of Sankaty consist of leveraged loans, high-yield bonds, mezzanine debt, structured products, and distressed debt. The Middle Market Group of Sankaty manages approximately $2 billion in funded assets. The Middle Market Group invests in companies that have EBITDA of greater than $10 million. The group aims to invest in funds in the range of $20-$75 million.

7.3.4 BAIN CAPITAL VENTURES

Bain Capital Ventures (BCV) is the venture arm of Bain Capital with approximately $70 billion in AUM. BCV manages over $2 billion in committed capital with more than 65 active portfolio companies. BCV makes investments across all different growth stages, which range from seed capital through late-stage growth equity and growth buyouts. BCV investments range from a few thousand dollars up to $60 million in growth equity capital. BCV invests in enterprise and consumer industries. The enterprise industry sector consists of Enterprise SaaS, Commerce Technology, Financial Services, Data and Info Services, Marketing Technology, Infrastructure and Cloud, Health IT and Services.

7.3.5 ABSOLUTE RETURN CAPITAL

Absolute Return Capital (ARC) is the absolute return affiliate of Bain Capital. The aim of ARC is to produce attractive risk-adjusted returns by managing assets in fixed-income, equity, commodity, and currency markets.

7.4 CARLYLE GROUP

Carlyle Group was founded in 1987 in Washington, DC. The group is a global alternative asset manager with AUM amounting to $185 billion across 122 funds and 81 fund of funds vehicles. The Carlyle Group has 1450 professionals operating in 34 offices in North America, South America, Europe, the Middle East, North Africa, Asia, and Australia. The four major business segments of Carlyle are Corporate Private Equity, Global Market Strategies (GMS), and Real Assets and Solutions. Carlyle has expertise in the industrial sectors of aerospace, defense, and government services, consumer and retail, energy, financial services, health care, industrial, technology, and business services.

7.4.1 BUSINESS SEGMENTS

7.4.1.1 Corporate Private Equity

The Carlyle Corporate Private Equity segment was established in 1990 with AUM of more than $58 billion. This segment has 30 private equity funds classified on the basis of industry or geography. Buyout funds and growth capital funds are the major primary areas of focus for private equity teams of the Carlyle Group. There are 21 buyout funds that focus on a particular geographic area such as Asia, Europe, MENA, South America, the United States, or a particular industry sector. There are nine growth capital funds that focus on middle-market and growth companies.

Carlyle's Asia team focuses on buyouts, privatizations, and strategic minority investments in partnerships with management teams in Asia. The Carlyle Asia Buyout Group has made investments in Asian companies in a range of sectors including financial services, media and telecommunications, manufacturing, and consumer.

Carlyle Asia Partners I, which was established in 1999 with $750 million in capital commitments from international investors, has conducted leveraged buyout transactions in Asian companies such as Boto International, Caribbean Investment Holdings, China Pacific Insurance, KorAm Bank, Willcom, and exited. The second Asian buyout fund, Carlyle Asia Partners II (CAP II), was raised in 2006 with capital commitments of $1.8 billion. Carlyle Asia Partners III, with capital commitments of $2.55 billion, was founded in 2007 to make leveraged buyout transactions in Asia.

The Asia Growth team invests in country-specific high-growth companies with leading market positions in China, India, Japan, and Korea. The Asia Growth funds consist of the Carlyle Asia Venture Partners II, LP (CAVP II), Carlyle Asia Growth Partners III, LP (CAGP III), and Carlyle Asia Growth Partners IV, LP (CAGP VI). These funds have capital commitments of $1.04 billion, $164 million, and $680 million, respectively.

Other buyout funds are based in Africa, Europe, Japan, MENA, Mexico, South America, and the United States. Carlyle Europe Technology Partners is a sector-focused Pan European growth capital and buyout fund that focuses on businesses with enterprise value between €25 million and €150 million. The Global Financial Services Buyout team focuses on management buyouts, growth, capital opportunities, and strategic minority investments in financial services.

7.4.1.2 Real estate

Carlyle Group focuses on real estate markets in primary cities in China, Japan, Europe, and the United States. The Real Assets and Solutions segment of Carlyle Group, with $40 billion investments, was established in 1997. The focus of the funds are on real estate, infrastructure, energy, and renewable resources.

Asia Real Estate consists of Carlyle Real Estate Partners and Carlyle Real Estate Partners II, with equity capital of $410 million and $486 million. These funds make value-oriented real estate investments and development projects with a focus on China and Japan. Europe Real Estate consists of three funds with capital investments of €3.39 billion. The US Real Estate team makes investments primarily in residential, hotel, industrial, office, and retail sectors of major markets in North America. This segment has six funds with capital commitments of approximately $7.58 billion.

The Carlyle/Riverstone Holding team makes private equity capital investments for management buyouts and strategic joint ventures in the energy and power industry. There are six Carlyle energy funds with $15.2 billion in capital commitments. Carlyle Power Partners invests in power generation and related assets in North America. In 2012, Carlyle acquired Cogentrix Energy from Goldman Sachs. Carlyle Infrastructure Partners has target equity investments in the range of $75-$150 million with a preference for majority control or significant minority rights.

7.4.1.3 Global Market Strategies

GMS, which consists of 63 funds, was established in 1999 to pursue investment opportunities across credit, equities, derivatives, and interest rate products. These funds have AUM worth more than $35 billion. GMS funds consist of carry funds and hedge funds. There are six carry funds that focus on different strategies such as distressed and corporate opportunities, corporate mezzanine targeting middle-market companies, and energy mezzanine opportunities in energy and power companies. GMS has a 55% stake in Claren Road Asset Management and Emerging Sovereign Group. Claren Road Asset Management deals with two long/short credit hedge funds that focus on global high-grade and yield markets. Emerging Sovereign Group has seven emerging market equities and macroeconomic hedge funds. Through its 55% stake in Vermillion Asset Management, GMS has four funds that focus on commodities investment. GMS also has 43 structured credit funds that invest in senior secured bank loans through structured vehicles and investment products.

7.4.1.4 Global Solutions segment

The Global Solutions segment had its origin in 2011 with the acquisition of a 60% equity stake in AlpInvest, a leading private equity asset manager that manages a global private equity fund of funds program. The primary areas of focus for AlpInvest are fund investments, coinvestments, and secondary investments. Funds of funds make capital investments in buyout, growth capital, venture, and other alternative asset funds. AlpInvest makes coinvestments in specific deals along with other private equity and mezzanine funds. AlpInvest also has funds that acquire interests in portfolio funds in secondary market transactions. AlpInvest Partners had AUM of $48 billion as of June 2013. Table 7.7 gives the details of funds

Table 7.7 GMS Funds Raised 2007-2013 (Billions of US Dollars)							
	2007	2008	2009	2010	2011	2012	2013
Corporate Private Equity	18.8	5.5	0.3	2.6	1.6	7.8	9.2
Real Assets	7.6	8.3	0.8	1.5	2.1	0.3	1.6
Global Market Strategies	4.7	6.3	0.1	0.3	2.4	5.2	5.2
Funds of Fund Solutions					0.5	0.6	2.2
Total	31.2	20.1	1.2	4.4	6.6	14.0	18.3

Source: http://ir.carlyle.com/keyMetrics.cfm

Table 7.8   GMS AUM 2007-2013 (Billions of US Dollars)

	2007	2008	2009	2010	2011	2012	2013
Corporate Private Equity	48.5	45.2	48.8	56.3	51.1	53.3	62.2
Real Assets	21.7	27.3	27.7	30.6	30.7	40.2	39
Global Market Strategies	10.4	13.8	13.3	20.6	24.5	32.5	35.4
Fund of Funds Solution					40.7	44.1	48.4
Total	80.6	86.3	89.8	107.5	147	170.1	185

Source: http://ir.carlyle.com/keyMetrics.cfm

raised by different segments of Carlyle Group during the period 2007-2013. Table 7.8 provides the value of AUM in different segments of Carlyle Group during the period 2007-2013.

7.5 TPG CAPITAL

TPG Capital is a global private investment company with $55.7 billion in capital under management. TPG has been involved in major deals such as the bankruptcy turnaround of Continental Airlines and Oxford Health Plans. In 2000, TPG acquired a 51% stake in South Korea's oldest and largest bank, Korea First Bank, and revitalized it by repositioning it as a retail bank with better financial controls and risk-assessment tools. TPG also used proprietary models to generate significant returns to MEMC Electronic Materials. In 2007, TPG Growth and TPG Biotech jointly founded Elevance Renewable Sciences to build the world's largest renewable specialty chemical business. In the energy sector, TPG has invested in MI Energy (E&P oil company in China) and the Kazakhstan oilfield Emir. TPG has made investments in a wide range of industries such as financial services, travel and entertainment, technology, industrials, retail, consumer products, media and communications, health care, and more. TPG specializes in traditional buyouts, turnarounds, and proprietary opportunities. TPG has made buyouts in growth firms with major brands and market shares that include, for example, Beringer Wine Estates, Findexa, Neiman Marcus, PetCo, and SunGard. TPG's turnaround deals include J. Crew, Graphic Packaging, Burger King, Grohe, and Myer. Minority investments and partnership deals by TPG in the proprietary framework include Endurance, Lenovo, Eutelsat, and Mobilecom. TPG has a major international presence with 17 offices in 10 countries.

7.5.1 INVESTMENT PLATFORMS

TPG Capital is a principal investment platform, with a presence in Asia, the United States, Europe, Australia, and Latin America. TPG Capital makes investments in companies through restructuring and acquisitions in a wide range of industries such as financial services, travel and entertainment, technology, health care, media, and communications. Equity investments range between $10 million and $1 billion. The TPG Growth platform focuses on smaller buyouts and growth equity investments in middle-market segments representing a wide range of industries. The investment structures utilized by TPG Growth include leveraged buyouts, growth equity, and private investments in public equities. TPG Biotech is the life science venture capital platform that aims to support physicians, scientists, and entrepreneurs to build innovation-based businesses. TPG Biotech's investment focus is on drug discovery development, personalized medicine, medical technologies, industrial biotechnology, and pharmaceutical services. TPG Alternative and Renewable Technologies partners with companies to develop and deploy alternative and renewable technologies. The TPG Opportunities Partners platform pursues actively managed credit-related investment opportunities by purchasing or originating special situation or distressed investments across credit cycles. TPG Specialty Lending (TSL) is a specialty finance investment company that focuses on middle-market lending. TSL offers fully underwritten and creative financing solutions across different capital structures in a wide variety of industries. The investment types offered by TSL include senior-secured loans (first lien, second lien, unitranche), mezzanine debt, noncontrol structured equity, and common equity. The transaction size ranges from $10 to $250 million.

REFERENCES

1. http://www.kkr.com/businesses/private-markets
2. http://www.kkr.com/businesses/public-markets
3. KKR & Co. LP Annual Report 2012
4. http://www.blackstone.com/businesses/aam/private-equity/portfolio/show/all/?type=all&value=
5. http://www.blackstone.com/businesses/aam/private-equity/portfolio-operations-group
6. http://www.blackstone.com/businesses/financial-advisory/restructuring-reorganization
7. http://www.blackstone.com/businesses/aam/real-estate
8. http://www.blackstone.com/businesses/aam
9. http://www.baincapitalprivateequity.com/about/history#sthash.SFQxGuhc.dpuf
10. http://www.baincapitalprivateequity.com/about#sthash.8vw3GlDP.dpuf
11. http://www.baincapitalprivateequity.com/about/strategy#sthash.AELQ5rfl.dpuf
12. http://www.baincapitalprivateequity.com/industries
13. http://www.baincapitalprivateequity.com/industries/financial-business-services/case-studies/bright-horizons#sthash.K1xnpX6w.dpuf
14. http://www.sankatymmg.com/Approach/Default.aspx
15. http://www.baincapitalventures.com/why-us/what-we-do/#sthash.ge5EPWRI.dpuf
16. http://www.carlyle.com
17. http://www.carlyle.com/our-business
18. http://www.carlyle.com/our-business/corporate-private-equity/asia-buyout
19. http://www.carlyle.com/our-business/real-assets/asia-real-estate
20. http://tpg.com/platforms
21. http://www.tpggrowth.com/
22. http://www.tpgspecialtylending.com
23. http://investing.businessweek.com/research/stocks/private/snapshot.asp

CASES ON HEDGE FUNDS

8.1 BRIDGEWATER ASSOCIATES

Bridgewater Associates is a global investment management firm established in 1975. The firm manages approximately $150 billion in global investments for a wide range of institutional clients, which includes foreign governments, central banks, corporate and public pension funds, university endowments, and charitable foundations. Bridgewater is the largest hedge fund manager in the world. Bridgewater Associates is credited with the "All Weather" strategy, which is based on the concept that return on assets is a function of the variables of cash, beta, and alpha. The All Weather strategy is based on the idea that asset classes react in ways based on the relationship of cash flows to the economic environment. Bridgewater Associates has been the leading absolute return manager since its inception, according to a study by LCH Investments. In 2012, Bridgewater Associates received the top commendation in the first IPE Pension Fund Perception Programme (PFPP) Awards for asset managers.

8.2 ADAGE CAPITAL MANAGEMENT

Adage Capital Management is a Boston-based hedge fund sponsor that manages S&P 500 assets that are predominantly for the endowments and foundations of institutions such as Harvard University, Northwestern University, Dartmouth College, the American Red Cross, and Getty Foundation. Adage Capital Management also provides services to pooled investment vehicles and invests in equity markets. The fund uses fundamental analysis with a focus on intra-industry valuation methodologies to make investments. The fund manages assets worth $8.9 billion. In 2013, Adage Capital invested in Calithera Biosciences and PTC Therapeutics.

8.3 YORK CAPITAL MANAGEMENT

York Capital is a hedge fund manager established in 1991. The firm is headquartered in New York with offices in Washington, London, and Hong Kong. The fund provides services for foundations, endowments, and high-net-worth individuals. The firm manages a series of hedge funds that include York Enhanced Strategies, York Select, York Global Value, York Total Return, and York European Opportunities, York Credit Opportunities, and the 1974 Commodore Select Funds. In 2010, Credit Suisse's Asset Management division acquired a minority interest in York Capital for $425 million.

The firm invests in companies undergoing restructuring, mergers and acquisitions, spin-offs, and split-ups. The company employs fundamental analysis with an event-driven strategy and a bottom-up stock-picking approach to make its investments. The firm's AUM is in the range of $3-5 billion.

8.4 GRAHAM CAPITAL MANAGEMENT

Graham Capital Management (GCM), established in 1994, is a leading alternative investment management company. GCM's focus is on macro-oriented quantitative and discretionary investment strategies in the global fixed-income, currency, commodity, and equity markets. GCM is an employee-owned hedge fund sponsor. GCM manages separate client-focused equity, fixed-income, and balanced portfolios. GCM employs such investment strategies as multistrategy, discretionary, quantitative, global macro, relative value, equity long/short, and arbitrage strategies as hedging techniques.

8.5 PERSHING SQUARE CAPITAL MANAGEMENT

Pershing Square Capital Management is an activist hedge fund located in New York. In 2005, Pershing bought a significant share in the fast-food chain, Wendy's International. In 2007, the fund owned a 10% stake in Target Corporation, which was valued at $4.2 billion through the purchase of stock and derivatives. The firm invests in equity and fixed-income markets around the world. The investments are also made in derivatives instruments. The company invests in value stocks by employing fundamental analysis.

8.6 MAN GROUP

Man Group is one the leading independent alternative asset managers. The British company manages $52.5 billion in assets under management. The group is a leader in liquid high alpha investment strategies. AHL/MSS is the systematic investment platform of Man, which focuses on delivering a range of absolute return, long-only, and momentum-based quantitative funds. GLG is the major discretionary multistrategy global investment management business that offers a range of absolute return and long-only strategies across different asset classes, sectors, and geographies. GLG investment professionals cover equity, macro, emerging markets, credit, fixed-income, convertible bond, and thematic strategies.

In 2012, Man Group acquired FRM, which is among the top 10 global industry allocators to hedge funds by assets under management. It is one of the largest independent European-based funds of hedge funds, which manages commingled funds and advises institutional clients. FRM specializes in open architecture hedge funds and alpha strategy solutions for institutional investors. FRM has the most extensive buyside managed account platform in the world. By 2013, the AUM for FMS amounted to $8.2 billion. FRM provides services across multiple functions such as investment portfolio management, research, and risk management. FRM's seeding platform aims to identify new and early stage hedge fund managers and support their development through significant public and committed investments of seed capital and guidance. FRM's managed account platform is the core component of the product offering, which provides access and control in more than 70 hedge fund managers. FRM, with the support of a managed account platform, provides a set of liquid investment solutions in thematic strategies that range from diversified portfolios to concentrated portfolios that emphasize managed futures, commodities, equity market neutral, and equity long short.

8.7 BREVAN HOWARD ASSET MANAGEMENT

Brevan Howard is a global alternative asset manager that manages institutional assets across a number of diversified strategies. The firm's primary business activity is to act as investment manager for certain investment funds for which Brevan Howard Capital Management acts as manager. Brevan Asset Management manages $40 billion in assets. The Brevan Howard Master Fund was launched in 2003. The emerging markets hedge fund has $2.8 billion in AUM.

8.8 OCH-ZIFF CAPITAL MANAGEMENT GROUP

Och-Ziff Capital Management is one of the largest institutional alternative asset managers, with $39.2 billion in AUM as of December 2013. The firm was founded in 1994. Och-Ziff manages multistrategy funds, credit funds, collateralized loan obligations (CLOs), real estate funds, and other alternative investment vehicles. Institutional clients include pension funds, funds of funds, foundations and endowments, corporations, private banks, and family offices. Och-Ziff funds invest across multiple strategies and geographies with a focus on positive absolute returns across market cycles. The funds do not rely on extensive leverage to generate investment returns. Pension funds constitute the maximum of 32% of the fund investor base. The primary strategies employed by Och-Ziff include convertible and derivatives arbitrage, corporate credit, long/short special equity special situations, merger arbitrage, private investments, and structured credit.[1]

REFERENCES

1. http://www.bwater.com
2. http://www.adagecapital.com
3. http://www.grahamcapital.com
4. http://www.man.com/2/investment-management
5. http://www.frmhedge.com/thematic-portfolios
6. http://www.frmhedge.com/portfolio-workouts
7. http://www.ozcap.com

---

[1]Price discrepancies that exist between convertible and derivatives securities and the underlying equity lead to convertible and derivatives arbitrage. Corporate credit includes credit-based strategies such as high-yield debt investments in distressed businesses, investments in bank loans, senior secured debt, and mezzanine financing. Long/short equity special situations involve fundamental long/short and event-driven investing. The events include corporate events such as spin-offs, recapitalizations, and restructurings. Merger arbitrage is basically an event-driven strategy that involves multiple investments in firms that are focusing on merger activity. Structured credit strategy involves investment in mortgage-backed securities, collateralized loan obligations, and collateralized debt obligations.

CASES ON ISLAMIC BANKS

According to the Global Finance Report 2013, sharia-compliant finance is the fastest-growing area of finance worldwide, with more than 500 financial institutions (FIs) providing Islamic financial products. According to Beirut-based Union of Arab banks, Saudi Arabia's Al Rajhi Group was the world's largest Islamic bank in 2011.[1] According to the E&Y World Islamic Banking Competitiveness Report 2013, global Islamic banking assets with commercial banks will amount to $1.72 trillion in 2013 compared to $1.54 trillion in 2012. The report states that the six rapid growth markets of Qatar, Indonesia, Saudi Arabia, Malaysia, United Arab Emirates (UAE), and Turkey constitute approximately 78% of international Islamic banking assets. Islamic banks in this region account for 17 of the top 20 Islamic banks. Islamic banks serve 38 million customers globally.

9.1 SAUDI AL RAJHI BANK

The Al Rajhi Bank, founded in 1957, is one of the largest Islamic banks in the world with total assets of US$71.2 billion. In 1978 the various entities under Al Rajhi were merged into Al Rajhi Trading and Exchange Corporation. In 1988, the bank was established as a Saudi share-holding company. Headquartered in Riyadh, the bank has a wide network of more than 500 branches, 100 dedicated ladies' branches, and 3300 ATMs. The bank also has 25,000 point-of-sale terminals and 130 remittance centers in Saudi Arabia.

Al Rajhi focuses on diversification through expansion in investment, corporate, and retail banking sectors. The bank has an emphasis on innovative banking and investment services through the concept of e-banking. Al Rajhi has an international presence in Malaysia, Kuwait, and Jordan. It was the first foreign bank to be awarded a full banking license by Bank Negara in Malaysia. The bank has a paid-up capital of SR15 billion and is listed on the Saudi Stock Exchange. Al Rajhi is the largest commercial bank in terms of market capitalization in Saudi Arabia. In 2012, the bank had 4.57 million customers and occupied the top position in terms of loans, advances, and profitability. The bank focuses on maintaining its strong retail position in the Kingdom of Saudi Arabia. Retail financing accounts for 65% of the bank's financing assets and approximately 70% of net income. The growth in current accounts can be attributed to factors such as strong branding and wide distribution channels. The bank expects new opportunities in retail accounts because of the government's initiatives on local job creation including Saudization in the private sector. The bank has also introduced more than 100 ladies' branches as the trend of females joining the workforce is increasing. The bank also focuses on mortgage financing.

---

[1] http://www.emirates247.com/business/economy-finance/saudi-al-rajhi-remains-biggest-islamic-bank-2011-10-29-1.425770

All of the products and services offered by the bank are sharia-compliant products. The four main business segments of the group are Retail, Corporate, Treasury and Investment services, and Brokerage. The financing needs of the retail and corporate sectors are met through five sharia-compliant product groups, namely Corporate mutajara, installment sale, murabaha, credit cards, and Istisnaa. In 2012, net financing accounted for approximately 64% of the consolidated total assets of the group. In 2012, investment sale was the largest financing product, which accounted for three fourths of net financing followed by Corporate Mutajara. Personal financing was the largest contributing sector to the growth in the bank's net financing portfolio. The Corporate segment offers a wide range of sharia-compliant products such as working capital finance, trade finance, cash management, and term financing for the corporate sector including small and medium enterprises (SMEs). The three major areas of corporate banking business are FIs, cash collections, and trade. The Treasury segment operates in both local and international foreign exchanges and money markets to source funding and make investments. Al Rajhi deals in more than 40 currencies. Al Rajhi Bank has partnerships with approximately 180 corresponding banks. These partnerships facilitate correspondent banking businesses, remittance needs, or funding of short-term needs. Cash collections are basically in terms of fees. The bank has 162 remittance or Tahweel Al Rajhi centers, which have a wide network of correspondent banks.

Investment banking, advisory services, brokerage, and asset management are provided through Al Rajhi Capital Company (ARC), a wholly owned subsidiary of Al Rajhi Bank. ARC is one of the top-five asset managers in Saudi Arabia offering mutual funds. In 2012, the Al Rajhi MENA Dividend Growth Fund was established. ARC is a major player in the brokerage market of Saudi Arabia. It offers trading in major GCC and international stock markets and sukuk by means of a number of channels such as telephone, Internet services, automated phone trading, and specialized central trading units. ARC's Investment Banking division offers strategic advisory services for fund raising and debt/corporate restructuring. In 2012, ARC carried out deals worth $4 billion. Al Rajhi was the first bank in Saudi Arabia to offer mobile share trading in Saudi Arabia. The bank also launched the Web 2.0-based online banking (Al Mubasher) as a strategic initiative to attract young customers. The group offers takaful services in automobile, health, home, personal services, and travel.

A major portion of retail financing is funded through current accounts, which are long-term deposits. The major sources of revenue are obtained through retail banking, corporate banking, and other sources. Retail banking generates retail processing fees, which are driven by retail financing. Corporate banking generates fee-based income on account of corporate restructuring, arranging deals, and granting loans. Other sources include remittance businesses, trade, and credit cards.

The bank's cost-to-income ratio has averaged in the range of 26-28% during the last few years. The nonperforming loan ratio was 2% in 2012.

As a strategy for the future, Al Rajhi Bank plans to focus on SMEs. The plans involve rolling out payroll cards, a lockbox system for cash deposits, and the introduction of social cards such as Haj/Umrah cards for visiting pilgrims. The bank has innovated sharia-compliant refinancing models for both retail and corporate customers. Table 9.1 provides the financial highlights of Al Rajhi Bank during 2008-2012. Table 9.2 provides the financial highlights of Al Rajhi Bank segment wise in the year 2012.

Table 9.1   Al Rajhi Bank Financial Highlights 2008-2012 (Millions of SR)[a]

	2008	2009	2010	2011	2012
Operating income	10,575	11,505	11,661	12,502	13,983
Operating expenses	4050	4738	4890	5124	6098
Net income	6525	6767	6771	7378	7885
ROA (in %)	4.51	4.05	3.81	3.64	3.23
Net financing	109,293	112,148	120,065	140,313	171,941
Customer deposits	118,741	122,862	143,064	177,733	221,343
Total assets	163,373	170,731	184,841	220,731	267,383
CAR Tier 1 ratio	14.6	13.82	15.23	14.71	14.68
CAR total capital ratio	21.39	19.30	20.63	20.03	19.83

[a]*Saudi Riyal; 1 USD = 3.75 SR*
Source: Annual Report 2012

Table 9.2   Al Rajhi Bank Segment Financials 2012 (Millions of SR)

	Retail	Corporate	Treasury	Investment and Others	Total
Total assets	128,452	54,592	81,304	3035	267,383
Total liabilities	173,998	54,325	2517	14	230,914
Total income from operations	9557	1926	1250	1250	13,983
Total operating expenses	4423	1355	49	271	6098
Net income	5134	571	1202	978	7885

Source: Annual Report 2012

9.2 KUWAIT FINANCE HOUSE

Kuwait Finance House (KFH) is a pioneer Islamic bank established in Kuwait in 1977. KFH offers a wide range of sharia-complaint products and services that cover banking, real estate, trade finance, investment portfolios, corporate, commercial, and retail markets. Banking services include accounts and deposits, customer segment, cards, and other services. Accounts and deposits consist of current accounts, savings accounts, electron accounts, Baitii accounts for minors, investment deposits, and Jameati accounts. KFH also offers the Al Rubban Program for men, Al Sundus for women, along with ATM cards. The various investment deposits consist of Al-Khumasiya Investment deposits, Al Kawthar Investment deposits, and Continuous Investment deposits. An Al Khumasiya investment deposit lasts for 5 years with 100% of the deposited amount invested and automatically renewed for a similar period. In an Al-Kawthar investment deposit, returns are credited to the account on a monthly basis. In continuous investment deposits, the substantial profits are distributed on an annual basis. In Thulathiya Investment deposits, the profit is distributed every 3 months. Al-Sedra investment deposits last for 1 year and are renewed automatically for a similar period. The cards offered include promotion cards, credit cards, and prepaid cards.

Corporate credit services include murabaha, ijarah, istisna, and cooperative marketing. The products in cooperative marketing aim to finance local trade and encourage national products. KFH buys high-demand goods from an original source factory supplier and sells them to cooperatives. KFH offers local and international real estate services. The Investment segment offers investment wakala contracts. The wakala contract authorizes KFH to manage the investor's investments according to agreed conditions. KFH also offers private banking services. The strategic focus is on development of retail banking services, which includes development of wealth management services and corporate banking services. The focus is also on greater coordination among KFH international banking subsidiaries. KFH has acquired approximately 40% of the local market share. The banking cards department offers a KFH Dollar Card in the US dollar, MasterCard Al Kheir, and Al Tayseer cards. More than 50,000 privilege discount cards were distributed with prepaid cards.

In its pursuit of international expansion strategy, KFH has established branches in Turkey, Bahrain, Malaysia, and Kuwait. KFH is one of the most important players and makers of a sukuk market at the global level. KFH has 15 subsidiaries and direct investments in four subsidiaries.

9.2.1 RISK MANAGEMENT

Risk management is implemented through a governance process that emphasizes independent risk assessment, control, and monitoring, which are overseen directly by the board and senior management. The three lines of defense for managing risk consist of the business unit, risk management, and financial control and assurance functional units such as regulatory compliance, auditing, and more. KFH has an independent chief risk officer and chief financial officer, who have direct access to the Board Risk and Assets Committee and the Board Audit Committee, respectively. KFH is exposed to credit risk in its financing, leasing, and investment activities when customers fail to perform in accordance with murabaha, istisnaa, and ijara contracts. Credit risk also arises when there is default by counterparties in sukuk transactions. The objective of credit risk governance is to establish and maintain a performing financing portfolio that minimizes the occurrence of customer default. Credit decisions are based on an assessment of the customer's ability to service and repay the debt. Collateral is taken as security to mitigate loss in the event of default by the customer. KFH aims to ensure diversification of exposures according to standard portfolios, business sectors, and geographical distribution borders. The bank complies with credit concentration limits per customer at 15% and maintains adequate ratios of liquid assets at 18%.

Exposure to market risk arises from fluctuations in exchange rates, share prices, real estate prices, and values of inventories and commodities. Foreign exchange and commodity risk arising from KFH's Treasury activities are managed within the Treasury. Equity price risk is managed within the investment department. Liquidity risk management in KFH is governed by the bank's liquidity risk management framework. In this framework, the bank's funding requirement in the short and medium terms are measured under normal operating and stressed conditions. The bank maintains a portfolio of highly marketable and diverse assets that can be easily liquidated in the event of an unforeseen interruption of cash flow. KFH is also exposed to reputational risk arising from nonadherence to sharia. KFH acts as an investment agent in restricted deposits. The hedging instruments used are currency swaps, profit rate swaps, and forward contracts. Table 9.3 provides the financial highlights of KFH during the years 2011 and 2012.

Table 9.3 KFH Financial Highlights 2011-2012 (Millions of US Dollars)		
	2011	**2012**
Assets	47,857	52,278
Profit	131.930	438.477
Depositor accounts	31,579.9	33,396.18
Total equity	5,536.043	5,829.034
Source: Annual Report 2012.		

9.3 **DUBAI ISLAMIC BANK**

The Dubai Islamic Bank (DIB), established in 1975, is the largest Islamic bank in UAE. DIB provides a range of innovative banking products, including credit cards, financing products, e-accounts, Internet accounts, and banking solutions. DIB provides services to retail, commercial, corporate, and institutional clients. Other significant divisions of DIB are Johara Ladies Banking, Wajaha Wealth Management, Business Banking, Corporate Banking, and Treasury. The bank provides specialized services for women and high-net-worth individuals.

Personal Banking Products and Services of Dubai Islamic Bank			
Accounts	**Credit Cards**	**Finance**	**Takaful**
Al Islami Current Account	Al Islami Classic credit cards	Al Islami Personal Finance	Al Islami Takaful Saving and Investment Program
Al Islami Current Account Plus	Al Islami Gold credit card	Al Islami Auto Finance	Al Islami Riayati
Al Islami 2 in 1 Account	Al Islami Gold premium credit card	Al Islami Home Finance	Al Islami Auto Insurance
Al Islami Savings Account	Al Islami Platinum credit card		Al Islami Namaa
Al Islami E-Savings Account	Al Islami Platinum Plus credit card		
Al Islami Investment Deposit Account	Al Islami Infinite card		
Shaatir Savings Account	Al Islami Internet card Wala'a Dirhams		
	Al Islami Business credit card		
	Johara credit cards		
	Al Islami Classic charge card		
	Al Islami Gold charge card		
	Al Islami Platinum charge card		
	Al Islami debit cards		

Islami Salary in Advance is a temporary salary advance of up to one month's net salary for cash needs. The wealth management services offered include wajaha, private banking, and financial planning services. The financial planning services are related to Islamic structured products such as 5-year capital protected notes, 5-year sharia-protected notes, 10-year sharia-compliant notes, income funds, mutual funds, and investment plans. The Business division is involved in providing short-term loans for working capital purposes, financing property, import and export shipping, and mergers and acquisitions services. DIB provides merchant banking, corporate banking, and Treasury products to corporations. The Corporate division provides sharia-compliant innovative financial solutions that include corporate finance, investment banking, project finance, trade and commodity finance, and capital and debt market products. DIB is involved in funding of commercial aircrafts, infrastructural projects, commodity trading, and real estate development. Public, corporate, and high-net-worth customers are offered Treasury products such as money market instruments and investment products including sukuk, foreign exchange hedging solutions, profit-enhanced products, profit rate swaps, and derivatives.

The bank has 82 branches in UAE. DIB has a majority shareholding in Tamweel, the UAE-based Islamic home finance provider. DIB established Emirates REIT, which was Dubai's first real estate investment trust. DIB was the arranger for the first fully UAE Islamic bank aircraft financing deal for the purchase of an A 340-500 by Emirates Airlines.

In 2012, DIB introduced a new service named Al Islami Business Online, which is a portal enabling companies to access more than 75 services at the click of a button. In 2012, the bank also unveiled Shaatir with innovative features, which was developed specifically for children. DIB's Express Banking Terminals were developed to give customers 24-h access to a wide range of banking services.

DIB has established subsidiary banks in Pakistan and Jordan. DIB holds interest directly or indirectly in 24 subsidiaries. DIB also has holdings in 28 special-purpose vehicles.

In 2012, the bank repaid in full a US$750 million 5-year sukuk from its own sources. DIB was also involved in many significant sukuk transactions such as a $650 million 7-year Islamic bond issued for Jebel Ali Free Zone, the government of Dubai's $1.25 billion dual tranche 5-year and 10-year sukuk. The significant corporate sukuk deals carried out by DIB include Majid Al Futtaim's $400 million 5-year debut sukuk issuance and Emaar's $500 million 7-year sukuk.

DIB has won a number of awards across diversified sectors, which include retail, corporate, investment banking, corporate social responsibility, and consultancy services.

9.3.1 RISK MANAGEMENT

The board of directors supported by the Risk Management Committee and the risk management department is responsible for overseeing the risk management system in the bank. The Asset and Liability Management Committee is responsible for managing the bank's assets and liabilities. DIB manages credit risk exposure through diversification of financing and investing activities to avoid undue concentration of risk with few customer groups. The probability of default of individual counterparties is determined using internal tools for categories such as real estate projects. Moody's rating models are calibrated to the bank's internal rating scale for corporate, contracting, and SME businesses. For mitigating credit risk, the principal collateral types for Islamic financing and investing are mortgages over residential and commercial properties, corporate guarantees, charges over business assets, and financial instruments. Concentration of risk is managed by client/counterparty and by geographical region and industry sector. To mitigate liquidity risk, DIB has diversified funding sources in addition to its

Table 9.4   DIB Financial Highlights (Millions of AED)[a]

	2011	2012
Total assets	90588.46	95364.70
Customer deposits	64929.84	66800.85
Sukuk financing instrument	4173.98	4673.96
Total income	5004.86	5026.32
Net profit	1056.415	1192.154
CAR (in %)	18.2	17.4
Tier 1 (in %)	13.6	13.9

[a] $1 = 3.67 AED
Source: Annual Report 2012

core deposit base. The primary tool for monitoring liquidity is maturity mismatch analysis, which is monitored over successive time bands and across functional currencies. The bank's Islamic derivatives are settled on the basis of a unilateral promise to buy or sell currencies and profit rate swaps under murabaha sales agreements. Sharia allows use of derivatives only for hedging requirements of clients. DIB faces market risk due to its exposure to diverse financial instruments, which includes securities, foreign currencies, equities, and commodities. Trading market risk is mitigated by establishing limits, independent mark-to-market valuation, reconciliation of positions, and tracking of stop losses for trading positions on a timely basis. The bank is exposed to profit rate risk due to mismatches or gaps in the amounts of assets and liabilities and off-balance sheet instruments that mature or reprice in a given period of time. DIB uses an operational risk-tracking system to track operational risk events across the bank. For regulatory capital requirements, the bank follows a standardized approach for credit, market, and operational risk as stipulated by the UAE central bank and Basel II requirements.

In 2012, DIB had a capital adequacy ratio of 17.4% and Tier I capital ratio of 13.9%. Table 9.4 provides the financial highlights of DIB during the year 2011-2012.

9.4 ABU DHABI ISLAMIC BANK

Abu Dhabi Islamic Bank (ADIB) was established in 1997. ADIB has a network of 70 branches and 460 ATMs. The major strategic initiatives undertaken by the bank are based on the objectives of achieving a market leadership position, creating an integrated financial services group, and, at the same time, pursuing international growth opportunities. Major service sectors of the ADIB are private banking, personal banking, business banking, and wholesale banking. These service sectors are further supported by cards, transaction banking, Treasury, corporate finance, investment banking, and wealth management. ADIB has an international presence in Egypt, Iraq, the United Kingdom, Saudi Arabia, Qatar, and Sudan.

The ADIB group structure consists of financial services and nonfinancial services. The financial services group consists of banking (ADIB, Saudi Installment house), subsidiaries (Abu Dhabi Islamic Securities Company, ADIB UK), associates and joint ventures (National Bank for Development, Abu Dhabi National Takaful Company, and Bosna Bank International), and international branches based in

Qatar, Sudan, and Iraq. Nonfinancial services consist of real estate (Burooj Properties and MPM Properties) and manpower (Kawader Services Company).

Retail banking deals with small and medium businesses and individual customer deposits that provide consumer and commercial murabahat, ijara, Islamic covered cards, fund transfer, and trade facilities. Wholesale banking handles financing and other credit facilities, deposits, and current accounts for corporate and institutional customers. Private banking handles finances, credit facilities, deposits, and current accounts for corporate and institutional clients. The Capital Markets division handles money market brokerage, trading and Treasury services, and management of the bank's funding operations by use of investment deposits. The Real Estate division handles the acquisition, selling, development, and leasing of land and buildings, management, and resale of properties.

Retail banking is a major segment of growth for ADIB. In 2012 the bank's network consisted of 75 branches and 535 ATMs, and the personal banking sector had 500,000 customers. The different accounts provided by ADIB are GHINA savings accounts, current accounts, electron accounts, Banoon children's saving accounts, time deposit accounts, and UAE Egypt accounts. The financing solutions offered include car financing, car ijarah, Tamweel financing, travel financing, instant financing, shares financing, boat financing, and education financing. ADIB also provides a range of life and takaful products. The takaful products offered include motor takaful, covered card takaful, cash cover takaful, and Al Khair tadawul takaful.

ADIB banking business offers a wide range of financing solutions such as business finance, business vehicle finance, business asset finance, business working capital finance, and trade finance. The wholesale banking services of ADIB are classified as corporate banking, global transaction services (GTS), government and public sector services, community banking, and FIs. Corporate banking offers a wide range of sharia-compliant Islamic banking solutions, which include murabaha, istisnaa, ijara, and Islamic-covered drawings. GTS is a unit of a wholesale banking arm that provides cash and trade management solutions across all industry segments.

In business banking ADIB offers a world-class platform for SMEs, which covers a free dedicated call center, online banking, and a centralized customer complaint management. In partnership with zawya, ADIB launched an SME portal. In wholesale banking, the bank launched the emerging corporate business targeted at clients with annual turnovers in the range of AED100-500 million. The Transaction Banking division launched the ADIB 360, which integrates retail and corporate product and services. The division also introduced three trade finance products, namely open account murabaha, availization, and export finance. ADIB is one of the top Islamic loan and sukuk book runners in the UAE market. ADIB was involved in notable deals such as a US$1.75 billion multi-tranche syndicated deal for Dubai duty-free, a US$1.2 billion deal for Jafza, and US $175 million Islamic syndicated deal for Srilankan Airlines. Other major activities of ADIB are private banking and Treasury services.

ADIB entered the Saudi Arabian market through the acquisition of a majority stake in the Saudi Installment House (SIH) along with management control. ADIB also has a presence in Qatar and the UK market.

In 2012, the bank raised US$1 billion hybrid Tier 1 capital issue. The Tier 1 sukuk was the world's first sharia-compliant hybrid Tier 1 sukuk. ADIB is one of the most liquid banks in the UAE with central bank placements of AED4.9 billion.

ADIB has partnered with Etihad Airways to introduce a sharia-compliant airline card in the UAE. ADIB also introduced a *161# mobile banking service that enables customers to perform all banking

Table 9.5   ADIB Financial Highlights 2008-2012

	2008	2009	2010	2011	2012
Total revenues (millions of AED)	2198.6	2520.3	3074	3425.8	3565.6
Net profit (millions of AED)	851.1	78	1023.6	1155.1	1201.2
Total assets (billions of AED)	51.2	64.1	75.3	74.3	85.7
Customer financing (billions of AED)	34.2	40.5	48	48.8	51.2
Customer deposits (billions of AED)	37.5	48.2	56.5	55.2	61.3
Customer financing to deposit ratio (in %)	91.18	83.94	84.85	88.51	83.48
Total CAR (in %) Basel II	11.64	16.96	16.03	17.39	21.42
Cost efficiency ratio (in %)	40.4	39.40	42.30	42.30	43.81

Source: Annual Report 2013

transactions. Dana Women's Banking offers a new suite of products, services, and special lifestyle benefits. ADIB partnered with Visa and Etisalat to launch the UAE's first Islamic telecom cards. ADIB was also among the first to introduce ADIB Instant Finance, which provides finance facilities to ADIB chip-enabled debit and covered cards.

The board of directors is responsible for the establishment and oversight of the bank's risk management framework. The Group Risk Policy Committee assists the board in risk management responsibilities. Treasury is responsible for managing the funding and liquidity risk of banks. The bank manages credit risk exposure through diversification of financing activities, limiting transactions with specific counterparties. Credit exposure related to trading activities is managed through master netting agreements and collateral agreements with counterparties. Commercial credit risk exposures are risk-rated using Moody's Risk Analyst rating system. In 2012, the bank established a new credit risk reserve via an apportionment of AED400 million from the retained earnings, which serves as an additional buffer to capital. Stress testing is an important part of the risk management function in the bank. Table 9.5 provides the financial highlights of ADIB during the period 2008-2012.

9.5 AL BARAKA ISLAMIC BANK

Al Baraka Islamic Bank (AIB) was established in 1984. The bank is licensed by Central Bank of Bahrain as an Islamic retail bank with an authorized capital of $600 million. AIB Bahrain is one of the banking units of Al Baraka Banking Group, which is a Bahrain-based joint stock company listed on the Bahrain and Dubai stock exchanges. The group has a wide geographical presence in the form of subsidiary units in 14 countries. AIB is a leading provider of Islamic investment banking products and services. AIB offers current account and saving accounts to individuals, companies, establishments, and social organizations. The Mudaraba investment account is a high-yield account that enables customers to deposit specific sums of money for specific periods. The bank invests these funds, and profits are shared between the bank and customer in accordance with the agreement signed between two parties and the provisions of Islamic sharia. AIB has introduced a wide range of banking instruments for international companies. AIB offers its corporate clients services in three categories of international asset management, international trade finance services, and corporate banking services. The Investment division provides a full range of investment banking and corporate banking products and services that include advisory services on strategy, raising of equity, and the like. The Commercial and Corporate segment offers services related to murabaha, istisna, and musharaka.

9.6 QATAR ISLAMIC BANK

Qatar Islamic Bank (QIB), the largest Islamic bank in Qatar, was founded in 1982. QIB has 31 branches in Qatar with more than 170 multifunction ATMs. QIB has an international presence in the United Kingdom, Lebanon, Malaysia, and Sudan. QIB has stakes in Qatar-based sharia-compliant companies such as Oinvest, Al Jazeera Finance, Aqar Real Estate, and Damaan Inslamic Insurance Company (Beema).

As a part of its strategic priorities, the bank is involved in financing in the trade sector, national infrastructure projects, and major industrial SMEs. QIB focuses on improving its wholesale, private banking, and wealth management operations. It operates under the supervision of a sharia board, which comprises eminent sharia scholars. The bank has more than a 35% and a 9% share in the Islamic banking market and banking sector in Qatar, respectively. QIB international is accountable for international banking activities of the QIB group.

QIB's personal banking unit provides accounts, individual finance, and credit cards. QIB offers all types of accounts that include current, savings, or term deposits. Individual finance includes personal, real estate, car finance, and salary transfer. Credit cards offered include debit cards, Visa electron card, credit cards including classic, gold, or platinum as well as the QIB Qatar Airways cobranded card, Visa Infinity, a prepaid travel card, MasterCard, and an Internet card.

QIB has a dedicated program called Tamayuz, which allows wealthy customers to benefit from unique banking services through follow-up and processing of financial transactions. QIB also focuses on private banking. QIB provides a wide range of electronic services to customers around-the-clock through mobile banking, telephone banking, e-banking, ATMs (withdrawal/deposit), and SMS service. QIB offers a series of takaful service in cooperation with Damaan Islamic Insurance Company. The services provided include saving plans, car takaful, family insurance, travel takaful, and more.

Wholesale banking include services such as corporate financing, trade services, contracting and real estate financing, SME financing, corporate Internet banking, and an operations service sector. The Wholesale Banking segment provides corporate financing solutions to finance major companies in the public and private sector with a focus on infrastructure projects and the oil and gas industry. Trade services include finances for trading activities involving cars, building materials, clothes and fabrics, medical equipment, and tools. In contracting and real estate financing, QIB provides companies with bank guarantees to enter public tenders, financing real estate projects, and real estate traders. In SME financing, QIB's Aamaly program is aimed at serving small and medium-sized companies. Corporate Internet banking provides control of accounts, cash management services, fund transfers, bill payment, and report generation. The operations sector services include issuance of documentary credits, issuance of current account credits, local trade operations, speculation contracts, and Istisna operations. Table 9.6 provides the financial highlights of Qatar Islamic Bank during the period 2008-2012.

Table 9.6   QIB Financial Highlights 2008-2012 (Millions of QAR)

	2008	2009	2010	2011	2012
Total assets	33,543	39,877	51,877	58,275	73,192
Operating income	2555	2402	2280	2682	3105
Deposits	16,592	20,361	30,370	27,853	43,147
Net profit	1643	1365	1262	1322	1241

Source: QIB Profile 2013

REFERENCES

1. http://www.gfmag.com/tools/best-banks/12474-worlds-best-islamic-financial-institutions-2013.html#ixzz2oq5z0svS
2. Global Islamic banking assets set to top $ 1.7 trillion, http://www.tradearabia.com/news/BANK_247645.html
3. Al Rajhi Bank Annual Report 2012
4. http://www.kfh.com/en/about/investor-relations/annual-report/pdf/KFH-EN-2012.pdf
5. http://www.dib.ae/docs/investor-relation/2012_annualreport_en.pdf
6. http://www.dib.ae/treasury/derivatives
7. http://www.adib.ae/sites/default/files/Annual_Report_2012.pdf
8. http://www.adib.ae
9. QIB-Profile 2013.pdf
10. http://www.qib.com.qa/ar/index.aspx

CASES ON SOVEREIGN WEALTH FUNDS

10.1 SOVEREIGN WEALTH FUNDS

According to the Generally Agreed Practices and Principles (GAPP) known as the Santiago Principles, sovereign wealth funds (SWFs) are special-purpose investment funds that are owned by the general government but which exclude state-owned enterprises in a traditional sense. In other words, a sovereign wealth fund is a state-owned investment fund that invests in real and financial assets such as stocks, bonds, real estate, precious metals, and alternative investments. The sources of funding for SWFs are basically the revenues realized from commodity exports or foreign exchange reserves, which are held by the central bank. Some of the sovereign funds that are held by the central bank accumulate foreign currency deposits, gold, special drawing rights, and IMF reserve positions that are held by central banks. Most of the SWFs are located in the Middle East, the Americas, and Asia. Most of the SWFs have been created by resource-rich and export-oriented nations with the aim to diversify their total revenue base and hedge export revenues due to energy and price volatility. There are approximately 71 sovereign wealth funds in different regions of the world. The regions of the Americas and the Middle East have 18 and 17 sovereign funds, respectively. Asia, Europe, Africa, and Australian regions account for 15, 6, 9, and 6 funds, respectively.

Sovereign wealth funds vary in diversity with respect to size, investment strategy, investment management, and operational structure. The trend observed is that SWFs are pursuing direct investment strategies, which also includes coinvestment. SWFs also invest in private equity and managed accounts. Investments are also made in a range of debt funds that target financing of private equity buyouts.

According to Sovereign Wealth Fund Institute data, approximately 59% of funding sources for SWFs was accounted for by the total oil, gas, and related sectors. Regionwise, Asia accounts for 40% of SWFs, while the Middle East accounts for 35% of sovereign wealth funds. The global SWFs control an aggregate of approximately US$6.105 trillion.[1] During the 2008 global economic recession, global SWFs including those in the Middle East curbed their investment activity.

10.1.1 GOVERNMENT PENSION FUND GLOBAL — NORWAY

The Government Pension Fund Global (GPFG) is Norway's sovereign wealth fund, which is the world's largest sovereign wealth fund with an estimated value of $716 billion in 2013. The fund was established in 1990 as a fiscal policy tool to support long-term management of Norway's petroleum revenue. The fund on an average holds around 1% of the world's shares and approximately 2% of all listed companies

---

[1]http://www.swfinstitute.org/fund-rankings/Dec2013

in Europe. The GPFG's sources of funding are from the revenues produced by Norway's oil and gas assets located basically in the North Sea. The sovereign wealth fund is administered by Norges Bank Investment Management (NBIM). NBIM manages the fund on behalf of the Norwegian people. The ministry determines the fund's investment strategy based on the advice from NBIM and parliamentary forums. The ministry transfers petroleum revenue to the fund. The fund invests in international equity and fixed-income markets and real estate. The fund was called the Petroleum Fund until 2006 and was then renamed the Government Pension Fund Global. Despite its name, the fund has no formal pension liabilities. In 2013, NBIM established a corporate governance advisory board to strengthen long-term active ownership. Some of the sovereign wealth enterprises of the GPFG are NBIM s.a.r.l, Burlington Number 1 (Limited Partner), and Prologis European Logistics Partners s.a.r.l. NBIM s.a.r.l is a Luxembourg-based entity that overseas real estate investments in Europe for the GPFG. Burlington Number 1 manages rental income from Regent Street Investment. Prologis European Logistics Partners Sarl is a 50:50 euro-denominated joint venture with Prologis, which has distribution facilities in 11 target European global markets.

10.1.2 SAMA FOREIGN HOLDINGS — SAUDI ARABIA

SAMA Foreign Holdings (SAMA FH) is managed by the Saudi Arabia Monetary Agency (SAMA), the central bank of Saudi Arabia. SAMA Foreign Holdings was established in 1952 in Saudi Arabia, which is the largest crude oil exporter in the world. The strategic objective of the fund is to invest surplus oil revenues in low-risk assets such as sovereign debt instruments, fixed-income securities, and equities. According to SWF Institute data, the assets under management of SAMA Holdings amounted to $675.9 billion in 2013. Sanabil Al Saudia Fund is a sovereign wealth fund managed by the Public Investment Fund. SAMA FH operates as an independently managed fund within the central bank. According to the SWF Institute, the fund deposits in cash deposits, fixed income, and equities.

10.1.3 ABU DHABI INVESTMENT AUTHORITY — UNITED ARAB EMIRATES

The Abu Dhabi Investment Authority (ADIA) was established in 1976 and is owned by the emirate of Abu Dhabi in the UAE. The fund manages the excess oil reserves of the emirate of Abu Dhabi.

The ADIA generated returns of 6.9% in the year 2012. The fund's returns averaged 8.1% over a 30-year period.[2] According to SWF Institute data, the fund had assets under management worth $627 billion in 2013. The ADIA cochaired the International Working Group of 26 sovereign wealth funds, which produced the "generally accepted principles and practices of sovereign wealth funds" (Santiago Principles) in 2008. The Santiago Principles were aimed at developing internal frameworks and governance practices for sovereign wealth funds. The ADIA invests in various financial markets such as equities, fixed-income, Treasury, infrastructure, real estate, private equity, and hedge funds. The global portfolio of the ADIA is segmented into subfunds, which cover specific asset classes. Each asset class has its own fund managers and in-house analysts. The ADIA purchases US institutional real estate through various subentities. The ADIA buys partial-interest ownership with leading real estate managers. The ADIA has a sizable stake in Citigroup. The ADIA is also one of the biggest investors

---

[2]http://www.thenational.ae/business/economy/global-volatility-lowers-abu-dhabi-investment-authority-s-returns#ixzz2q4ek5uHG

in the emerging markets. The fund lowered its target exposure to developed market stocks in 2012 to a range of 32–42% from 35–45% in 2011.[3] Approximately 80% of its assets are administered by external managers. About 60% of its fund is passively managed through tracked indexed funds. The funding sources for the ADIA are from the Abu Dhabi National Oil Company (ADNOC) and its subsidiaries. Some of the wealth enterprises under the ADIA include Procific, Tamweelview European Holdings SA, and Tawreed Investments. Tamweelview is the European real estate investment arm of the ADIA. Tawreed Investments focuses on infrastructure.

10.1.4 CHINA INVESTMENT CORPORATION — CHINA

China Investment Corporation (CIC), established in 2007, manages the foreign exchange reserves of China. CIC makes direct investments in institutional real estate and infrastructure. CIC capital is raised through the issue of special Treasury bonds. China Investment Corporation International and Central Huijin Investment are two subsidiaries of CIC. CIC International was established in 2011 with a mandate to invest and manage overseas assets. Central Huijin, the wholly owned subsidiary of CIC, holds a controlling stake in key state-owned financial institutions in China.

The mission of CIC is to make long-term investments to maximize the risk-adjusted financial returns to shareholders. CIC was established with the issuance of special bonds worth RMB1.55 trillion by the Ministry of Finance, which was used to acquire approximately US$200 billion of China's foreign exchange reserves. CIC has a three-tiered governance structure that includes a board of directors, a board of supervisors, and an executive committee. CIC has a well-established risk management system and manages risks through an internal set of positions, departments, and committees. CIC also appoints external fund managers to assist with the management of its international investment portfolio. In 2013, the assets of CIC amounted to $575.2 billion. According to the CIC Annual Report 2013, in 2012 the fund had an annualized return of 10.60% for overseas investments and a cumulative annualized return of 5.02% since its establishment.

CIC has a three-layer asset allocation framework that comprises strategic asset allocation, policy portfolio, and tactical asset allocation. Strategic asset allocation is based on long-term investment guidance. Policy portfolio is the asset allocation plan for a 3-year period, based on mid-term economic projections and asset valuation analysis. CIC has a diversified portfolio mix comprising cash, equities, fixed income, absolute return, and long-term investments. Absolute return investments are investments in hedge funds. Long-term investments include private equity investments and investments in energy, mining, and real estate infrastructures. The fund maintains a large proportion of index and enhanced index investment in public markets to capture benchmark returns. CIC aims for alpha returns by focusing on active strategies. In 2012, CIC invested £450 million for a 10% stake in Heathrow Airport Holdings.

10.1.5 STATE ADMINISTRATION OF FOREIGN EXCHANGE — HONG KONG

The State Administration of Foreign Exchange (SAFE) is the Hong Kong branch of the Chinese sovereign wealth fund. The fund is set primarily as a foreign currency reserve. The SAFE Investment Fund is responsible for managing China's foreign exchange reserves. This Hong Kong

---

[3]http://gulfbusiness.com/2013/05/abu-dhabi-fund-adia-turning-to-emerging-markets/#.UtEB_2xfqkY

subsidiary was established in 1997 with capital of US$20 billion. According to SWF Institute data, the SAFE managed assets worth $567.9 billion in 2013. The SAFE invests in low-risk bonds, listed stocks, and private equity. In 2013, the UK-registered Gingko Tree Investment, which is the wholly owned unit of the SAFE, invested more than $1.6 billion in at least four deals in London and Manchester. The SAFE is focusing on the diversification of its foreign exchange holdings into higher yielding assets such as $500 million investments in real estate equity fund managed by Blackstone Group.

10.1.6 KUWAIT INVESTMENT AUTHORITY — KUWAIT

The Kuwait Investment Authority (KIA) was established in 1953. The KIA aims for the diversification of the Kuwaiti economy by investing surplus oil revenues across local and international asset classes. By December 2013, the KIA had $386 billion in assets under management. The KIA investment strategy consists of direct investments and special-purpose portfolios. The fund aims to strengthen the financial services sector in Kuwait. During the economic crisis of 2008, the KIA injected approximately US$5.4 billion into the Kuwait Stock Exchange. The KIA has equity stakes in several private-sector companies in Kuwait, which span sectors such as financial services, telecommunications, building materials, food and beverages. The KIA established the National Technology Enterprises Company (NTEC) with capital of US$360 million to focus on investments in life sciences, energy, water, information, and communication. The fund is also focusing on the healthcare sector with plans to establish the Kuwait Health Assurance Company (KHAC) with an estimated capital of US$1.1 billion to privatize expatriate health care. In 1996, the KIA established the Kuwait Small Projects Development Company (KSPDC) with capital of US$358 million for the development of SMEs in Kuwait. The KIA also established the National Investment Fund Portfolio with capital of $350 million to provide financial assistance to young Kuwaiti nationals to establish their businesses.

10.1.7 HONG KONG MONETARY AUTHORITY — HONG KONG

The Hong Kong Monetary Authority (HKMA) was established in 1935. The exchange fund is managed by the HKMA. The exchange fund acts as a stabilizer of the Hong Kong currency and banking system and invests primarily in its local exchange. Approximately one third of assets are managed by global external managers. The exchange fund consists of three portfolios. The backing portfolio primarily holds liquid US-denominated assets that provide backing for the monetary base of Hong Kong as under the currency board arrangements. The investment portfolio invests in the equity and bond markets of member countries of the Organization for Economic Cooperation and Development. The strategic portfolio established in 2007 holds shares in Hong Kong Exchanges and Clearing Ltd. acquired by the government. Real Gate Investment Company is the wholly owned company of the HKMA, which makes investment in real estate joint venture companies. The HKMA regularly reviews its investment strategy and operations. In 2013, the fund managed assets worth $326.7 billion dollars. In the post-economic crisis of 2008, the fund invests in emerging markets bonds and stocks, private equity, and real estate.

10.1.8 GIC PRIVATE LIMITED — SINGAPORE

GIC Private Limited, formerly known as the Government of Singapore Investment Corporation, was established in 1981 under the Singapore Companies Act and is wholly owned by the government of

Singapore. The basic aim of the sovereign wealth fund is to provide a reasonable risk-adjusted rate above global inflation over a 20-year investment horizon. The investment framework of GIC is classified into a reference portfolio, policy portfolio, and active portfolio. The reference portfolio, which comprises 65% global equities and 35% global bonds, follows a passive investment strategy for long-term objectives. The reference portfolio is not a short-term benchmark for GIC. The policy portfolio focuses on six core asset classes comprising developed market and emerging equities, nominal bonds, cash, inflation-linked bonds, private equity, and real estate. The policy portfolio aims to enhance long-term returns through portfolio construction and diversification. The active portfolio focuses on active skill-based strategies.

The geographical distribution of assets are 44% in Americas, 25% in Europe, and 28% in Asia. The asset mix consists of public equities, fixed-income securities consisting of nominal bonds and inflation-linked bonds, alternatives that include real estate, private equity and infrastructure, and natural resources. The real estate assets span multiple-property sectors, including office, retail, residential, industrial, and hospitality. GIC also invests in index and hedge funds. The GIC Private portfolio's 20-year annualized real rate of return for the year ending March 31, 2013 was 4.0%, compared to 3.9% in the previous year.[4] GIC evaluates its investment performance against relevant benchmarks such as MSCI and Barclays Global indexes. In 2013, according to SWF Institute data, GIC had assets worth $285 billion.

10.1.9 TEMASEK HOLDINGS — SINGAPORE

Temasek Holdings is an investment company established by the government of Singapore in 1974. Temasek is supported by 10 affiliates and offices in Asia and Latin America. Temasek owns a $215 billion portfolio as of March 2013. The portfolio covers the broad spectrum of industries consisting of financial services, telecommunications, media and technology, transportation, industrials, life sciences, consumer, and real estate. The fund invested approximately 31% in financial services, 24% in telecommunications, media, and technology, and 20% in transportation and industrials. In 2013, 65% of investments were in Singapore dollars, 11% in Hong Kong dollars, and 6% in US dollars. Total shareholder return for Temasek since its inception is 16% compounded annually.[5] In 2013, the fund had a profit margin of 12.3% and average return on assets of 6.1%. In the financial services sector, Temasek has investments in companies such as AIA, Bank of China, Industrial and Commercial Bank of China, and Standard Chartered. In the telecom, media, and technology sector, portfolio companies include Bharti Airtel, MediaCorp, and Singapore Telecommunications. In the transportation and industrial sector, the portfolio companies of Temasek Holdings include Singapore Airlines, Singapore Power, Keppel Corporation, and Evonik Industries. Temasek's investment strategy focuses on tapping the potential of transforming economies such as China, India, and Southeast Asia through investments in sectors such as financial services, infrastructure, and logistics. The sovereign fund also aims for leveraging growing middle-class consumer demands through investments in sectors such as telecommunications, media, and technology, consumer, and real estate.

---

[4]http://www.gic.com.sg/images/pdf/GIC_Report_2013.pdf
[5]http://www.temasek.com.sg/portfolio/portfolio_highlights

10.1.10 **QATAR INVESTMENT AUTHORITY — QATAR**

Qatar had the world's highest GDP per capita ratio of US$102 in 2012. Qatar had one of the world's highest industrial growth rates of 27% in 2012. The country also has one of the world's largest reserves of natural gas. The Qatar Investment Authority (QIA) is the country's sovereign wealth fund, established in 2005 to manage the oil and gas surpluses of Qatar. The basic objective of the QIA is to generate revenues through diversification. According to SWF Institute data, the QIA managed assets worth $170 billion as of December 2013; it is one of the top 10 largest SWFs in the world.

The QIA follows a multidimensional investment strategy consisting of investments in multinational corporations, opportunistic investment strategy, branding focused asset investments, and other long-term investments.[6] Qatar Holding is the investment arm of the QIA and Qatari Diar is the property investment company. The QIA has significant stakes in assets representing industrial sectors such as hospitality, real estate, financial services, commodities, and retail. The QIA has investments in financial services firms Credit Suisse, Barclays, Agricultural Bank of China, and the London Stock Exchange. The QIA also has stakes in Volkswagen, Porsche, Tiffany, LVMH, Sainsbury, and Harrods and investments in Royal Dutch Shell, Total Alf, and BAA (which owns London Heathrow Airport). QIA's real estate investments include the Le Lido at the Champs-Élysées in Paris, the CityCenter in Washington, and the London Olympic Village. During the European Union economic crisis, the QIA invested in assets in regions of Greece, Spain, France, and Germany. QIA invested US$150 million in the UK venture capital fund for clean energy. The QIA has plans to expand Harrods brands into the hotel business and has also provided domestic banks with funds worth $2.8 billion for capital requirements. The fund is focusing on investments in mineral exploration and extraction in Africa and South America.

REFERENCES

1. http://www.swfinstitute.org/sovereign-wealth-fund/
2. Emerging trends in the Sovereign Wealth Fund landscape, Middle East May 2013, http://www.kpmg.com/AE/en/Documents/2013/Emerging_trends_in_the_regional_SWF_landscape.pdf
3. http://www.sama.gov.sa/SITES/SAMAEN/REPORTSSTATISTICS/Pages/AnnualReport.aspx
4. http://www.swfinstitute.org/swf-article/the-abu-dhabi-investment-authority-is-a-buyer-of-hotels-47998/, Sovereign Wealth Fund Institute Retrieved 21 August 2013
5. http://www.china-inv.cn/cicen/investment/investment_asset.html
6. http://www.china-inv.cn/cicen/include/resources/CIC_2012_annualreport_en.pdf
7. http://online.wsj.com/news/articles/SB10001424127887323699704578323670119279066
8. http://www.swfinstitute.org/swfs/hong-kong-monetary-authority-investment-portfolio
9. http://www.gic.com.sg/en/our-business/overview
10. http://www.temasek.com.sg/abouttemasek/corporateprofile

---

[6] http://www.kpmg.com/AE/en/Documents/2013/Emerging_trends_in_the_regional_SWF_landscape.pdf

Index

Note: Page numbers followed by *b* indicate boxes, *f* indicate figures and *t* indicate tables.

Printed in the United States
By Bookmasters